Houston

The Unknown City, 1836–1946

Marguerite Johnston

Texas A&M University Press

College Station

Dedicated to Charles Wynn Barnes

The paper meets the requirements of
ANSI/NISO Z39.48-H-1992
(Permanence of Paper).
Binding materials have been chosen for durability.

LIBRARY OF CONGRESS CATALOGING-IN-PUBLICATION
DATA

Johnston, Marguerite, 1917–2005
    Houston, the unknown city, 1836–1946 /
Marguerite Johnston. — 1st ed.
        p. cm.
    Includes bibliographical references and index.
    ISBN 0-89096-476-9
    ISBN-13:978-1-60344-523-8 (pbk.)
    ISBN-10: 1-60344-523-4 (pbk.)
    1. Houston (Tex.)—History.   I. Title.
F394.H857J64   1991
976.4'1411–dc29   91-8102
                                            CIP

Houston⌣

Publication of this book was made possible by a gift from
Sara and John Lindsey of Houston, Texas.

Table of Contents

List of Illustrations

Acknowledgments

I EXPRESS MY DEEP APPRECIATION to the following:

To the Elkins Foundation, the Brown Foundation, the Hobby Foundation, and S. I. Morris for the substantial funding that made this work possible.

To the George Butler Foundation for financial support of the research and the McAshan Foundation for its contribution.

This book has grown over some forty years on conversations and interviews with many people, some no longer living. Because of their love for their city, Houstonians old and new were generous with their time, their memories, their family papers, pictures, privately printed books, and encouragement. My gratitude goes to them all, though some of the material they provided will not appear until publication of the second volume of this history of Houston, now in preparation.

This book owes much to Agnese Carter Nelms, Ima Hogg, Mamie Culpepper Wren, Dr. Andrew Forest Muir, John Dreaper, Howard Barnstone, Hugo Neuhaus, Jr., David Bintliff, Dudley Sharp, Marion Law, George Bruce, and William Kirkland, who in their lifetimes shaped my understanding of Old Houston, and to the Rt. Rev. J. Milton Richardson, who first set me on the search for Houston's history.

I wish to thank Dr. Harold Hyman, Rice University professor of history, for launching this project by placing it under the aegis of the Rice Center for the History of Leadership Institutions.

Special thanks must go to Dr. John Boles, editor of the *Journal of Southern History,* my mentor at C.H.L.I., who offered encouragement and the invaluable judgment of a professional historian whose specialty is the South.

Nancy Booth, director of the Woodson Research Center of Fondren Library not only made research easy and pleasant, but provided security for rare photographs lent to me.

For their great help in illustrating this volume, my thanks to Edward Bourdon, who has spent a lifetime photographing Houston and Houstonians: Dr. Louis J. Marchiafava and Dr. Tom Kreneck of the Houston Public Library Metropolitan Research Center; Stephen Bonario of the University of Houston M. D. Anderson Library Special Collections; and Kathleen Hartt of the Museum of Fine Arts Archives.

For other help of many kinds my thanks to Oveta Culp Hobby, Patricia Toomey, Susan Clayton McAshan, Diana Hobby, David Henington, Chris Coleman, Frances Heyck, Mary Elizabeth Merrem, Ellen Robbins Red, Kate Patton O'Neill, Virginia Kirkland Innis, Sarah Emmott, Mary Cullinan Cravens, Stephen Fox, Ferne Koch, Barbara Dillingham, Ellen Wilkerson, Chaille Thompson, Dr. Michael E. DeBakey, Dr. R. Lee Clark, Dr. William Spencer, Sarah Meredith Peterson, Nancy Wren Harris, Barbara Sheffert, Ellen Garwood, Gervais Bell, Dr. Kenneth Lipartito, Peggy Buchanan, George Fuermann, Camilla Blaffer Trammell, Vesta Eidman, Mimi Crossley, Carl Cunningham, Roger Powers, James Mousner, Randon Dillingham, Numai Blevins, Lorene Pouncey, Gene Richardson, Dr. Patrick Nicholson, Velma Sanford, Helen Seymour, Kenneth DeVille, Aline Wilson, Terry Diehl and Margaret Walker of the *Houston Post* library staff, Margaret Jamieson of the *Houston Chronicle* library staff, Maxine Alcorn and the staff of the Clayton Library, and Ealise Fontenette.

My thanks also to these Houstonians for granting me recorded interviews and use of their family papers and photographs:

Dr. Samuel C. Adams, April, 1986; Ben Anderson, Mary Anderson, May 21, 1986; Essemena Anderson, Leland Anderson, April 12, 1989; Ralph Anderson, August 4, 1987; Mark Edwin Andrews, Bonner Means Baker, Burke Baker, Jr., James A. Baker III, David Bintliff, Edward Bourdon, Mary Martha Boyd, Dr. Jack Brannon, July 10, 1985; Mary Catherine and Edwin Rice Brown, George S. Bruce, Jr., Laura Bruce, Lou Breedlove, Allen H. Carruth, Elizabeth Carter, Victor Carter, Stephen Cook, Dr. Elizabeth Stripling Crawford, Dr. R. Lee Clark, Dr. Denton A. Cooley, Dr. E. L. Crain, Jr., Phyllis Crain, Mary Cullinan Cravens, Charlotte Darby, Charles W. Duncan, Jr., Dorothy Dunn Davis, Tom Martin Davis, March 25, 1985; Dr. Michael E. DeBakey, Barbara Dillingham, Charles Dillingham, James A. Elkins, Jr., December 27, 1984; Margaret Elkins, Carolyn Fay, Kenneth Franzheim, Preston Frazier, Eleanor Freed, Jack Harris, Elizabeth Haynsworth, Terry Hershey, Frances Heyck, Nancy Heyl, Fred Hofheinz, Eugenia Hunt, Lennie Hunt, Ed Hunter, Juliana Itz, Jeanette Jaworski, Tom Johnson, Annette Jones, John T. Jones, Jr., Barbara Jordan, Dr. Blair Justice, Rose Keeper, Dr. Peter Kellaway, Allie May Kelley, William A. Kirkland, Arthur Koch, Ferne Koch, Francita Koelsch, Caroline Wiess Law, Moses Leroy, Max Levine, Malcolm Lovett, Martha Lovett, Judge Myron Love, Dr. Fred Rice Lummis, Jr., Peter C. Maffit, Carroll Masterson, Harris Masterson III, Edward Mayo, Nancy Nelms Maxwell, Mary Elizabeth Merrem, Dominique de Menil, John de Menil, S. I. Morris, Jr., S. M. McAshan, Jr., Susan Clayton McAshan, Virginia Drane McCallon, Glen McCarthy, Dr. Mary Ann McKinney, Clark Nealon, Hugo Neuhaus, Jr., Tom Needham, Frank Oltorf, Jane Blaffer Owen, Estelle Perlitz, J. R. Parten, Mary Kempner Reed, Wilhelmina Cullen Robertson, February 10, 1986; Mildred Hutcheson Rouse, Dewey Roussel, Gladys Russell, Georgia Safford, Ann Sakowitz, Louisa Sarofim, Henrietta Hutcheson Schwartz, Judge Woodrow Seals, Dudley C. Sharp, Tina Sharp, A. Frank Smith, Jr., C. Cabanne Smith, Dr. William Spencer, Clare Sprunt, Louise Stevenson, Henry J. N. Taub, Judge Geraldine Tennant, Chaille Thompson, Camilla Blaffer Trammell, Ann Trammell, W. Bryan Trammell, Jr., McClelland Wallace, Mark Westheimer, Kathryn Wilcox, Ellen Wilkerson, Isabel Brown Wilson, Jane Zivley.

And finally, my deepest appreciation goes to Sara and John Lindsey, who have supported this project from the beginning and have in fact made this book possible.

By Way of Introduction

HOUSTON is probably the most overpublicized yet least accurately known city in the United States. Precocious from its birth in 1836, it has doubled its population every decade since then. But when World War II ended, it was still a comfortable southern town where good manners and good humor prevailed, where wealth was understated, where everybody seemed to know everybody else. Though old Houston society warmly accepted and absorbed like-minded newcomers, the city was dominated by second- and third-generation families. Their children and grandchildren are still at the heart of the city.

To the amusement of old-timers, many newcomers arrive expecting Houston to be as western as the El Paso shown on the television screen. Those moving here from bigger cities often arrive with missionary zeal – ready to bring culture and enlightenment to this remote outpost of civilization. It has always been like this. Mrs. William Fairfax Gray, who came from Virginia in January, 1839, wrote in her diary, "better than I had expected." As Mrs. Gray did, the cultural missionaries gradually realize that there is more to Houston than they had expected.

Old Houstonians have never tended to speak of themselves as Texans. They are Houstonians. This stems from an instinctive awareness that Houston has its own character. Just as a baby is born with its adult potential, Houston today is an older, bigger outgrowth of its earliest self. Its characteristics are clearly defined: When Houston was born, its people came from all parts of the

world. They still do. By 1980, the Houston public schools had children enrolled from seventy-two different language backgrounds. Early Houstonians and their descendants have always traveled everywhere. They have always thought that anything was possible. It therefore seems appropriate that Mission Control should guide NASA's space shots from Houston and that the first word spoken from the moon was *Houston*.

Early Houstonians showed great concern for the sick and the poor, risking their lives in yellow fever epidemics to tend the dying, looking after the hungry and homeless. It seems a logical twentieth-century development for the Texas Medical Center to have been started by private Houston philanthropy and for it to be recognized as a world center created by the continuing gifts of Houston money, ideas, and volunteer time.

Miss Ima Hogg, patron of the arts and one of the great philanthropists of the mid-twentieth century, once said, "Houston was lucky. The first people who got rich here, in the days long before oil, were *nice* people. They gave their money to schools, hospitals, charities, parks, the library, the arts. They set the pattern. This is what Houstonians do once they get a little money."

And finally, Houstonians have always taken it for granted that they would serve their government at the highest national and international levels. In the days of the Republic of Texas, President Sam Houston's cabinet was composed of new Houstonians like Albert Sidney Johnston and Memucan Hunt. Before the Civil War, James Reily of

Houston was President Buchanan's ambassador to the court of the czar in St. Petersburg. They were the first of a legion who have held cabinet and subcabinet posts, or who have represented the president of the United States in foreign capitals. President George Bush and Secretary of State James Baker will not be the last.

Neither the massive philanthropy that has improved the lives of millions of people—through science or the arts—nor the impressive record of national leadership has been fully recognized.

This will not be a definitive history of the city of Houston; such a book would run to many volumes. This book says little of politics, little of battles. Rather, it will be a reminder, a spotlight on those Houstonians who have shaped this city, and who have helped shape the modern world.

Houston

Chapter One

Born of Revolution

HOUSTON was a city from the hour of its birth. It was born on the audacity of three young New Yorkers who believed that anything was possible and imparted that belief to the city they founded. It was laid out to be the capital of a republic, just as Washington had been not long before, just as Brasilia and Canberra would be in the twentieth century. The first settlers came by sailing vessel from the big cities of the United States and Europe, bringing with them their city ways and expectations. Houston had a newspaper in its first month, a theater in its first year. And it was born of revolution.

Spain had claimed Texas for three hundred years when the first Anglo-American colonists arrived. Texas had a Spanish governor in 1691. San Antonio and Laredo dated from the eighteenth century. But the Texas Gulf Coast region was uncharted, unknown, and unsettled. Though French traders had spread out from New Orleans early in the eighteenth century, though Spanish missionaries had crisscrossed southern Texas, the site that would one day nurture Houston seems to have been let alone.

When Napoleon sold the vast territory of Louisiana to the United States in 1803, Americans began to look across the boundary at the tempting lands beyond the Sabine River. Though not keenly interested in its remote territory, Spain had laws governing colonization. In 1820, New Englander Moses Austin journeyed to San Antonio de Bexar seeking permission from the Spanish governor to settle three hundred families in Texas; he was granted the contract in 1821. Within

fifteen years, Austin's Old Three Hundred were claiming their independence from Mexico and fighting a revolutionary war to secure it.

After obtaining his contract to colonize, Moses Austin died from the hardships of the journey.[1] His son Stephen F. Austin took over the role of colonizer or empresario.[2] At twenty-seven, Stephen explored prairies and forests that had no settlements except for Indian camps. He chose the region between the Colorado and Brazos rivers for his first colony before making the twelve-hundred-mile trip to Mexico City to claim his father's grant. There, he was caught up in the revolution that broke Spain's hold. The end of Spanish rule nullified all Spanish contracts. Austin had to re-apply to the new government of Mexico.

Stephen Austin was discriminating. He would accept "no frontiersman who has no other occupation than that of hunter . . . no drunkard, no gambler, no profane swearer, no idler." Of the original "Old Three Hundred," most were substantial farmers from the southern United States, and their numbers grew. They built cotton gins, steam sawmills, and gristmills. They produced cotton, sugar, grains, and vegetables. They raised cattle and tanned hides. Austin acquired contracts for additional colonies. Within little more than a decade, some forty thousand Anglo-Americans were productive citizens of Mexico.

Their success attracted new waves of Americans across the Sabine River. Many of them headed for the lands along Buffalo

Bayou and the San Jacinto River. From South Carolina, young Ezekiel Thomas obtained a league of land on the north side of Buffalo Bayou.[3] The grant was signed by Estevan Austin on August 16, 1824. Thomas died at the age of thirty-seven, two years before the founding of Houston, but through his daughter Rebecca Jane he founded one of the city's first families.[4]

A descendant of the founders of Harrisburg, Pennsylvania, John Richard Harris sailed his own vessel, *The Rights of Man,* up the bayou in 1823. Granted one *sitio* of land, he set up a trading post and mill at the junction of Buffalo and Brays bayous. In 1826, he laid out Harrisburg, but in 1829, while in New Orleans buying supplies for the town, Harris caught yellow fever and died in five days. But his daughter Mary Jane started the family line in Houston.[5]

Ultimately, Stephen F. Austin had permission to settle twelve hundred families in Texas. He allotted John Austin, a distant cousin, two leagues (about 8,856 acres) in the form of a square on the Buffalo Bayou. This was the future site of Houston.

In 1826, the state government of Coahuila-Texas gave David G. Burnet and Joseph Vehlein permission as empresarios to settle six hundred families northeast of what is now Houston. A few months later, it authorized Lorenzo de Zavala to settle five hundred families in the vicinity.[6] Having been ignored for three hundred years of Spanish rule, the region in which Houston would rise suddenly became hot real estate —a quality it has never seemed to lose.

Instead of completing their contracts, Burnet, Vehlein, and de Zavala transferred their titles to the Galveston Bay and Texas Land Company on October 16, 1830. Its board was composed of substantial businessmen from Boston and New York.

They began what some historians consider one of the greatest real estate promotion schemes in the history of the country. The company issued stock and offered to sell scrip that authorized the holder to settle in Texas after meeting all colonization require-

ments. The scrip sold for five or ten cents an acre. It conveyed no land, but many people thought it did. Advertised in the United States and Europe, the scrip sold at a fast clip.

Many New Yorkers were among the buyers, including Augustus C., Charlotte, and John K. Allen. The Allens were as precocious as the city they were to found. At seventeen, Augustus had graduated from the Polytechnic School at Chittenango, New York, and was teaching mathematics there. He quit at nineteen to become the bookkeeper and part owner of the H. and H. Canfield Company in New York City. In May, 1831, Augustus married Charlotte Baldwin, daughter of Dr. Jonas Baldwin, founder and mayor of Baldwinsville, New York.

If Augustus was a prodigy, so was John. At ten he became a clerk in a shop; at sixteen he went into partnership with a young friend in a hat store. He sold his share of the store to follow Augustus to New York City and become a stockholder in the Canfield company.

Lured by the promotional advertising— an art they were later to emulate with success—the Allens left New York for Texas in 1832. Augustus was twenty-six, Charlotte twenty-seven, and John twenty. With scrip in hand authorizing them to settle in Texas, they went first to San Augustine, then to Nacogdoches. Possibly it was here that they first met the famous Sam Houston—soon to be their good friend and mentor.

Six feet four inches tall, Houston at thirty-nine had already been a general, a congressman, and the governor of Tennessee. He had scandalized East Coast society and achieved nationwide notoriety three years before by abruptly separating from his wife, resigning as governor, and going to live with his boyhood friends, the Cherokee Indians. By 1832, he had apparently put this personal tragedy behind him and was crossing Texas on some kind of unofficial mission for U.S. President Andrew Jackson. Houston wrote President Jackson that Texas was the "finest country upon the globe," and that he would probably make Texas his "abiding place."

Mexico had organized the state of Coahuila-Texas with the promise that when the Austin colonies had enough people, they could form their own state government. With a population nearing forty-six thousand, the colonists met in San Felipe and voted to ask for separation from Coahuila and for statehood in Mexico. The government in Mexico was still in revolutionary turmoil but it was aware of the Americans' surging interest in Mexico's Texas territory. When Stephen Austin went to Mexico City to present the colonists' petition for statehood, he was imprisoned for eleven months. In 1834, General Santa Anna abolished constitutional freedoms, claimed dictatorial powers over the country, and set out to stop all American immigration.

Never far below the surface, the desire for Texas to be free of Mexico began to flare. Texans met again at San Felipe in November, 1835, to form a provisional government. The Texas revolution had begun.

While still a colony of uncertain future, Texas exerted an extraordinary pull. It drew settlers from all states and many European countries. Though some were adventurers or roughnecks or outlaws, an incredible number were citizens of property, established in their own communities, willing to give up everything to strike out for Texas.

The Texans' move to break with Mexico and form a new nation made news throughout the United States and western Europe. Long before they declared their independence, they were joined by a fresh wave of settlers. Travel was slow and expensive, but the newcomers were eager to share in the birth of a nation.

Young Sidney Sherman of Massachusetts and Kentucky threw himself and all he owned into the Texans' cause before he ever saw Texas. He came prepared to stay. Col. William Fairfax Gray of Virginia landed by chance in the thick of it while on a business trip. He responded with the enthusiasm of an adventurous schoolboy. He would spend the next two years planning and carrying out the removal of his large family to Texas.

This portrait of Col. William Fairfax Gray hangs in the San Jacinto Historical Museum. *Courtesy Houston Metropolitan Research Center, Houston Public Library*

Memucan Hunt, a North Carolina planter and businessman, came with a thousand volunteers for the war of independence and, at twenty-nine, was commissioned brigadier general by President Burnet. Georges Capron had come from France with his brothers, expecting to settle in New Orleans. A trip to Texas so captivated him that he rushed back to New Orleans to recruit forty other young men to join in the coming war for Texas freedom. All these men would become first settlers in the as-yet-unborn Houston. They would found family lines in Houston extending into the sixth generation and beyond. Capron's great-great-granddaughter would one day marry Sherman's great-grandson.

At middle age, Colonel and Mrs. Gray were among the oldest of the immigrants. Despite their years, they typified the men and women who would shape early Houston. Their diaries describe what it was like to uproot and move to the new country in 1835 to 1838.

In Virginia, Gray had been a publisher and had captained a company of Virginia Militia in the War of 1812. His wife was the daughter of the mayor of Fredericksburg. They attended the century-old St. George's Episcopal Church, and moved in a graceful society. They had entertained the aging Marquis de Lafayette when he returned to the United States to review his youthful adventures.

"Gray was a cultured man," Dr. Andrew Forest Muir wrote in a biographical sketch on Colonel Gray. "Besides playing the flute, he was a reader and accumulated a library of some 250 volumes. . . ." Gray was admitted to the Virginia bar at the age of forty-seven—too late in life to build a practice that would support his large family in the quiet elegance to which they were accustomed. He therefore took on the commission of two Washington speculators to inspect lands in Mississippi, Louisiana, and Texas.

Starting out in October, 1835, he traveled by stagecoach from Fredericksburg over the Blue Ridge and across Virginia to the Mississippi River. He kept a detailed diary of the trip. All along the way the stagecoach dropped off some passengers and picked up others. When one passenger got sick, they called the doctor and stood by solicitously while the patient was cupped and bled. A great camaraderie of the road sprang up.

Steamboat travel was faster and smoother. Colonel Gray saw a world on the move. "At Portsmouth, at the termination of the Ohio and Erie Canal," he wrote in his diary, "emigrants from all over the civilized world . . . a number of Germans, from Saxony, coming on our boat as deck passengers. . . . We passed a great number of emigrating parties in Virginia. . . . Where they had slaves, they were uniformly for Missouri; those that were without were for . . . some other State north of the Ohio. . . . It is a melancholy sight to see so many wealthy, intelligent and useful citizens leaving old Virginia, and

many poor families, women and children, going to unknown parts to encounter untried difficulties and hardships."

Copying maps and gathering data for his employers, Gray moved from Cincinnati down the river to Memphis and plantation country. He liked Vicksburg and admired the new theater in New Orleans. But nowhere in his diary does he seem to be seeking a new place to live. When he met his first Texans in New Orleans, he was unimpressed.

Riding west across Louisiana, Colonel Gray met Capt. Sidney Sherman of Kentucky, who was to become a friend, a hero at San Jacinto, and the founder of one of Houston's first families.[7]

From Massachusetts, Sherman was a successful businessman when he married Isabel Cox in Frankfort in April, 1835. Interest in the Texas fight for freedom was keen in Frankfort and Cincinnati. News traveled up the Ohio River, carrying the contagion, but it is hard to understand the fever that the Texans' cause stirred in so many young men so far away.

Not nine months after their April wedding, and with the approval of his bride, Sherman sold his business, his factory, and other property. Thirty years old, he armed and uniformed fifty-two volunteers wanting to go fight Santa Anna. On New Year's Eve, 1835, in a violent snowstorm, Captain Sherman and his splendidly equipped company boarded a steamer at Cincinnati, bound for Texas. Mrs. Sherman went with them as far as Natchez before returning to her parents' home. There she would wait a long year before Texas was freed and she could join him.

Captain Sherman had given his fortune to Texas and was ready to risk his life and his wife's happiness on the strength of his convictions. With his youthful idealism and zeal, he must have had a strong influence on the older Colonel Gray.

Leaving the United States, Colonel Gray crossed the Sabine River into Texas on January 28, 1836. He traveled over the icy roads of this foreign territory with Sherman and his men. They were at once caught up in the Texas Revolution. In Nacogdoches, four days after entering Texas, the lifelong Virginian cast his vote for delegates to the convention that would meet in Washington-on-the-Brazos and then hurried on to attend the convention. He wrote in his diary, "I was desirous of becoming A CITIZEN as soon as possible." He apparently had no further worry about women and children going to unknown parts to encounter untried difficulties.

The Texans met in Washington on March 2, 1836. Under Pres. David Burnet, the interim government issued its declaration of independence and adopted a constitution for the Republic. It then fled before the approaching Mexican forces.

Like the younger, less encumbered Sidney Sherman, Colonel Gray seems to have fallen totally under the spell of this new nation.[8] While Sherman and his men followed Sam Houston to battle, Colonel Gray rode with President Burnet and Vice-President de Zavala from Washington to Harrisburg. Going on to New Orleans, Gray wrote President Burnet, "I shall return to Texas with as much speed as my affairs in the U.S. will admit, to make my future home among you."[9]

He was on his way home to tell his wife and children that they were about to leave the United States to live in a nation not yet established, in some town he had yet to choose. He seemed to have no doubts that the Texans would establish their freedom during his absence and that he would return to settle in a safe and stable country.

The Allens were equally free of doubt. Throughout 1835 and early 1836 they seemed to have a superb confidence that Texas would soon be an independent nation. While the Texas revolution raged across the countryside—Gonzales, Goliad, Concepcion, San Antonio—the Allens went about their business of finding and buying a site for a city.

For the next two months, the Texas armies met disaster and defeat—in Agua Dulce, at the Alamo, at Refugio, at Goliad. Santa Anna set fire to San Felipe and burned Harrisburg to the ground. Then came the final battle.

The story is carved on the eight walls of the San Jacinto Monument:

On this field on April 21, 1836, the army of Texas commanded by General Sam Houston, accompanied by the secretary of war, Thomas J. Rusk, attacked the larger invading army of Mexico under General Santa Anna. The battle line from left to right was formed by Sidney Sherman's regiment, the artillery commanded by George W. Hockley, the infantry by Henry Millard, and the cavalry under Mirabeau B. Lamar. Sam Houston led the charge.
. . . in the army of Texas at San Jacinto were natives of Alabama, Arkansas, Connecticut, Georgia, Illinois, Indiana, Kentucky, Louisiana, Maine, Maryland, Massachusetts, Michigan, Mississippi, Missouri, New Hampshire, South Carolina, Tennessee, Texas, Vermont, Virginia, Austria, Canada, England, France, Germany, Ireland, Italy, Mexico, Poland, Portugal, and Scotland.

The Texans were outnumbered. They were tired, hungry, and angry. They had only rifles, tomahawks, and bowie knives. To Sidney Sherman's battlecry "Remember the Alamo!" they charged. It was midafternoon. The Mexicans were resting, expecting an attack the next morning. Roused abruptly, scrambling to form disciplined ranks, they fell before the onslaught. The battle lasted perhaps twenty minutes. General Houston had his horse shot from under him and mounted another. Two Texans were killed in action. Houston's ankle was shattered.[10] Capt. Moseley Baker took a bullet. Vice-President de Zavala turned his home across the bayou into a hospital. Of the thirty Texans wounded, seven more would die.

The Texans killed hundreds of the enemy, took hundreds more prisoner—including General Santa Anna.

No man who fought that day quite realized what the battle would mean. The monument inscription concludes, "San Jacinto was one of the decisive battles of the world.

The freedom of Texas from Mexico won here led to annexation and to the Mexican war, resulting in the acquisition by the United States of the states of Texas, New Mexico, Arizona, Nevada, California, Utah, and parts of Colorado, Wyoming, Kansas and Oklahoma. Almost one-third of the present area of the American nation, nearly a million square miles of territory changed sovereignty."

Chapter Two

The Capital

WITHIN WEEKS of the historic Battle of San Jacinto and some fifteen miles away, the Allens bought a site, drew a city map "almost without instruments," and planned to sell it to the new Republic of Texas as a capital. The land Augustus thought suitable, at the junction of Buffalo and White Oak bayous, had been granted to John Austin by the Mexican government. When he died in a cholera epidemic in 1833, it had gone to his widow, who later married Dr. T. F. L. Parrott, and to his father, John P. Austin of New York.

In Columbia, the Allens bought half a league from the agent for John's father, "in consideration of the price of one dollar per acre, one half of which has been paid in hand, . . . and the other half is secured by promissory note. . . ." The remainder was due in eighteen months. They then saddled up for the trip to Brazoria.

Two days later in the residence of Dr. and Mrs. Parrott, they bought from Mrs. Parrott the other half of the league "granted to her late husband John Austin, which is the lower league of the two lying near the head of tide on Buffalo Bayou, which said land she acquired by inheritance." They paid five thousand dollars—one thousand in cash and the balance secured by notes. For a little over three thousand dollars they had gained clear title to some 8,850 acres and were ready to do business.

No twentieth-century marketing expert could have promoted a city more shrewdly. The Battle of San Jacinto had stirred excitement in the United States and the capitals of Europe. The Allens named their new city after the hero of the hour, the victor at that battle. And they did so gracefully. They invited their famous friend to a formal dinner at their home in Nacogdoches, and in the course of the evening, young Mrs. Allen said, "General, will you do us the honor of naming our city?" General Houston, always gallant, bowed and said, "But Madame, that privilege must be yours." (As indeed it should, her money having done much to finance the purchase of the land on which Houston was to rise.) "Then," said Mrs. Allen, "we ask your permission to name it after you."[1]

Although John and Augustus have always been named the founders of Houston, there is no doubt that Charlotte Allen was an unacknowledged partner in the enterprise. This was an era when women were not credited with being city founders.

Houston was never a crossroads community. It was a city from the start, as the Allens had intended it to be. They hired Gail Borden, Jr., and his brother Thomas to survey the property and lay out the town.[2] The Bordens were engineers who had surveyed land for the Austin colony. Gail Borden was an inventor and visionary whose name endures on the process he invented for condensing milk. The Bordens mapped wide streets suitable for a big city, although none would be paved for decades. They set aside Court House Square, Congress Square, a Church Reserve, and a School Reserve.

The Allens advertised Houston in the newspapers of Europe and the United States:

The town of Houston, situated at the head of navigation, on the west bank of Buffalo Bayou, is now for the first time brought to public notice because until now, the proprietors were not ready to offer it to the public with the advantages of capital and investment. By reference to the map, it will be seen that the trade of San Jacinto, Spring Creek, New Kentucky and the Brazos, above and below Fort Bend, must necessarily come to this place, and will at this time warrant the employment of at least ONE MILLION DOLLARS of capital, and when the rich lands of this country shall be settled, a trade will flow to it, making it, beyond all doubt, the great interior commercial emporium of Texas.

Although it was still a town only on paper, the Allens set out to induce the government of the new Republic of Texas to choose Houston as its first capital.

Usually, when one army defeats another, it takes over a government as well as a territory. But the Texas declaration of independence from Mexico and the victory at San Jacinto on April 21 left a diverse group of men with the task of building a capital, shaping a government, and getting a constitution ratified by the people. As interim president of the new nation, David G. Burnet called an election for September 5, and a first meeting of Congress on October 3 at Columbia. With Sam Houston elected president of Texas and Mirabeau B. Lamar vice-president, the newly formed Congress began its unaccustomed work.[3]

When Congress met to choose a site for its capital, several cities were competing. Galveston was not in the running because it was an unpeopled island. Houston was the dark horse. Very dark. So far there was not a house in Houston.

John K. Allen nominated the newly named but unbuilt city. He said: "I consider that the seat of government ought to be on the coast, because it combines the advantage of a safe and speedy communication with the United States and with the interior of the country at the same time." Houston, he said, would be the best choice in terms of national defense against "the enemy on

the sea." Allen stressed the city's healthful climate and inexhaustible quantity of pine timber. The bayou, he said, "is navigable at all times for boats drawing six feet of water and is within 10 hours' sail of Galveston Island."[4]

Finally, he assured the members of Congress, "Houses and comfortable accommodations will be furnished at Houston in a very short time, and if the seat of government is there located, no pains will be spared to render the various officers of the government as comfortable as they could expect to be in any other place in Texas." Young John Allen must have been persuasive. Francis Lubbock saw him as "a very bright, quick man, with much magic about him, and well calculated to enthuse the young." Or perhaps it was the promise of all those creature comforts. On the fourth roll call, Congress chose Houston over Matagorda and Washington-on-the-Brazos by a margin of twenty-one votes. But it was only to be the seat of government until 1840, when a permanent location would be agreed upon.

Congress voted that the "president be and is hereby authorized, to cause to be erected a building, suitable for the accommodation of the congress of the republic, and such other buildings as may be necessary. . . . Provided, the sum or sums so expended shall not exceed $15,000."[5] Congress then adjourned on December 22, 1836, with plans to reconvene on May 1, 1837, in the new capitol.

The choice of Houston by Congress was a coup. It meant that Houston would be the seat of government for the important three years in which the Republic of Texas would be established, would be recognized as an independent nation by France and England, and would become known throughout the Western world as a place where a man could get free land—thousands of acres of it. By this stroke, the Allens ensured Houston's survival when many other speculative towns of the time died in the bud.

The Republic had chosen its capital. The

Allens had only to build it. Augustus Allen was newly turned thirty, Charlotte was thirty-one, and John K. Allen was twenty-six years old. They persuaded their young friend Francis Lubbock, who was twenty-one, to ship a stock of goods to Houston. They came with him on the steamship *Laura* to the town they had staked out. Lubbock wrote his account of that trip in *Six Decades in Texas.*[6]

After passing Harrisburg: "No boat had ever been above this place, and we were three days making the distance to Houston, only six miles by the dirt road, but twelve by the bayou." The boat moved slowly because they had to rig Spanish windlasses to clear the channel of logs and snags. Lubbock's account belies John Allen's estimate of a ten-hour trip to Galveston.

"Capitalist, dignified judge, military heroes, young merchants in fine clothes from the dressiest cities in the United States, all lent a hand," Lubbock wrote. He was describing the people who would become Houstonians. Chafing at the slow progress, Lubbock and others took a yawl and set out upstream to find the city. They passed it by entirely and realized their mistake only when they ran into White Oak Bayou and struck brush: "We then backed down the Bayou, and by close observation discovered a road or a street laid off from the water's edge. Upon landing, we found stakes and footprints, indicating that we were in the town tract. This was the first of January, 1837, when I discovered Houston."

The *Laura* was the first steamer to reach Houston's landing. But the "capitalist, dignified judge, military heroes and young merchants" were not the first arrivals. Walking up the freshly cleared dirt street, Lubbock found a few small tents, a large one used as a saloon, several houses being built, and logs being hauled in to build the first hotel. He promptly contracted with J. S. Holman "to put up for me a small clapboard house . . . paying $250." For that he got one room twelve feet square with an adjoining shed.

Sam Houston, first president of the Republic of Texas, in his prime, circa 1837. *Courtesy Houston Metropolitan Research Center, Houston Public Library*

Made of hand-sawed lumber, it had no windows, and "the bedstead put up in the corner was made by driving forked sticks into the ground and laying poles across with clapboards for slats to support the moss mattress." The first Houstonians had to be made of stern stuff.

Capt. Robert Boyce, recently of the Army of the Republic, walked to Houston from Columbia, reaching the capital on January 18 in the midafternoon. "It then consisted of clapboard camps and tents; not even a log house was finished," he wrote. "After breakfast the next morning we discovered a new white tent in which a New Orleans merchant had opened a clothing store. Here, for $4, I purchased an outfit and dressed up like a gentleman."

Mrs. Allen was the first woman to arrive. Almost sixty years later, on her eighty-ninth birthday, she recalled that when she landed at the foot of Main Street, only one log cabin had been completed and the men who had occupied it moved out to let her move in. On the day after her arrival, President Houston escorted her on a ride out to the Lamar encampment—three miles from the bayou.[7] But so new and unmarked was the trail between camp and town that they lost their way on their return and barely made it back by dark.

Chapter Three

In Context

THE WORLD that Houston was about to enter would have seemed familiar to Thomas Jefferson. Kings ruled the major nations of the earth. Louis Philippe was on the throne of France. The unknown Princess Victoria had not yet come to the throne of Great Britain. Garibaldi had not yet united the kingdoms of Italy.

No steamship had crossed an ocean. The Clipper Ships were at their peak. No passenger train had yet run. People traveled by waterways, stagecoach, horseback, carriage, wagon and mule. No baseball game had been played. No photograph had been taken, no telegraph sent, no postage stamp stuck with its own glue. Documents, letters, and diaries were written with quill pen. Formal balls and cotillions depended upon string ensembles to provide music for the minuet and the square dance. And no bride had walked down the aisle to the strains of Wagner or Mendelssohn.

The United States had perhaps fifteen million people. It extended no farther west than the Mississippi River. It had only recently bought Florida, where the Seminole wars were grinding on.

San Francisco, San Diego, and Santa Fe were old established cities in Mexico. San Antonio and Laredo were still Spanish in language, custom, and religion. Washington, D.C., was a new, raw young capital springing up beside the old and more refined Georgetown. Ottawa, Dallas, and Galveston were yet unborn. Atlanta was nothing more than a spot on a railroad map labeled "Terminus." Birmingham's valley cradled a virgin forest. Sophisticated and French in its culture, New Orleans was suffering from its unsettling shift of rule from Spain to France to the United States.

Why did so many people want to be in on the founding of Houston? The obvious attraction was the offer of free land. Spain and Mexico between them had granted some twenty-six million acres by 1835. But there was still plenty of land in Texas. The new Republic was prepared to give it away generously. And the sooner you came, the more you were likely to be granted.

The new Constitution of the Republic of Texas allowed all heads of families living in Texas on March 4, 1836, "except Africans and Indians," to have first-class headrights of one league and one labor. A league was 4,428 acres, a labor was 177. Single men over seventeen years old could have a third of a league −1,476 acres. Over the next five years, the giveaway continued and so did the influx of people to accept it. Congress gradually cut the number of acres until the vote of 1841. This gave 640 acres to family heads and 320 to single men who came between January 1, 1840, and January 1, 1842.

Even so, how tempting is 4,000 acres of land in some far-off, unknown, undeveloped country called Texas? Apparently very tempting. There were plenty of takers. All in all, in its short life the Republic of Texas granted 36,876,492 acres of land in headright certificates—and in a far more orderly fashion than the great Oklahoma land rush that was yet to come.

There must be an excitement to starting

a new nation that is impossible to grasp from our highly organized present. In Sam Houston's first term, Congress had to institute a court system, divide the country into counties, establish a post office department and mail routes, order the public lands to be surveyed into sections of 640 acres each, reorganize the Ranger force, and plan for the borrowing of $5 million.

While the president and Congress were attending to the nation's business, Houston was busy growing.

Most of the people who came were young and enterprising. When they bought their site and drew their town map, the Allens were under thirty and in many ways typical of the settlers arriving on every steamer coming up the bayou. All were willing to take chances to gain a new and more rewarding life.

Many were inspired by the idea of building a new nation dedicated to the freedoms so gloriously sounded in the Texas declaration of independence and the still-new Constitution of the United States. The battles of Lexington and Concord were scarcely more than sixty years into history. Many Houstonians had fathers or grandfathers who had fought in the American Revolution. Quite a few remembered the excitement of the War of 1812.

Not all who came to Houston would stay. Many would pick up their land grants and move on to other parts of the Republic. Those named to posts in the cabinet or the State Department would travel to other world capitals to represent their new country. Few would give up and go back to the United States.

Silas Dinsmore of Matagorda wrote: "Among the population of Texas are found natives of nearly every state of the Federal Union, and of every nation in Europe. The intercourse which they have had with the world and with each other has had the tendency to vanish [*sic*] bigotry and obliterate prejudices and most of them are able to estimate with little partiality, the pretensions of all, according to their merits.

"AS A PEOPLE," Mr. Dinsmore wrote, "they possess superior intelligence." He added with conviction, "It is the enlightened who look abroad to ascertain in what region may be found the greatest advantages combined to contribute to a happy worldly abode. It is the strong and the courageous who exert their energies, and who hold in contempt the obstacles and dangers which they feel may be overcome by an effort. And thus it is the exposed frontiers that are found to be inhabited by the brave and the enterprising—while the feeble, the timid and the ignorant cling to the land of their nativity."

However amusing his vehemence in praising a group of which he was a member, Silas Dinsmore had a valid point. While a sense of adventure is to be expected of healthy young men, not all Texans were young, not all bachelors. Many had much to lose. A number of women came with their husbands. Many men came to arrange housing before bringing their families to Texas. And all were coming to a great unknown.

When they left Virginia or Saxony or Connecticut or England, these people knew less about Houston than any astronaut knew about the moon before landing there. They would soon be far more cut off from their families and friends than an astronaut in orbit, who is in constant conversation with Mission Control–Houston. When thirty-eight-year-old Millie Stone Gray left her home in Virginia to set sail for the Gulf Coast, it must have been with the acceptance that she might never again see her family or her lifelong friends.

On the other hand, so long as they were prepared to help build the city, settlers should not find Houston less convenient or more dangerous than most other cities of the era. At the time, no big city had much to offer in the way of public utilities. Most fire departments were composed of volunteers with buckets and hand pumps. People drank well or cistern or river water everywhere. In New York, as in Houston, they lighted their own homes with candles or whale oil lamps.

They heated them with log fires or with coal burned in grates or iron stoves.

With the arrival of the first doctor, bringing with him his powders, his leeches, and his cupping instruments, Houston could provide much the same medical care as any city in the world. The unknown town was probably as healthy a place to live as any other. New York City had been plagued by yellow fever epidemics since the seventeenth century, and the land that would one day become Central Park was a filthy slum inhabited by lowlifes and mongrel dogs. Houston's temporary tent city could be no worse and it did not stand long. The building boom was on, and soon—as John Allen had promised—new Houstonians would be as comfortably housed as they could be anywhere else in Texas.

Chapter Four

Fiesta

HOUSTON was chosen as the capital of the Republic of Texas on November 30, 1836. On January 1, 1837, it was a city of tents, but exploding in growth. The sound of hammer and saw, the smell of sawdust, paint, horses, and whiskey, and the shouts of carpenters and workmen filled the early spring air. By April 1, Thomas K. Ward, a contractor, managed to persuade enough carpenters to leave other jobs and the Round Tent bar to begin work on the capitol building. It had not begun sooner because the lumber had not arrived from Maine. On April 15, the national archives arrived from Columbia.

By April, 1837, Houston was a town of five hundred people—four hundred of them male. First mapped by Gail Borden with sixty-two blocks, the townsite had to be enlarged by adding a row of blocks on each of three sides. Houston had already begun to annex.[1]

On April 21, the new Houstonians celebrated the first anniversary of the Battle of San Jacinto with a parade, a flag raising, and speeches. Excitement grew on the arrival of the schooner *Rolla,* the first oceangoing vessel to come up the bayou under its own sails. It had taken four days to make twelve miles from Harrisburg.

In the evening, everyone went to the ball. Because the shortage of women in the city was so acute, urgent invitations, printed on white satin, had gone out to neighboring plantations.

"Ladies and gentlemen came on horseback distances fifty and sixty miles, accompanied by men servants and ladies' maids, who had charge of the elegant ball costumes for the important occasion," Adele Looscan wrote. "From Harrisburg they came in large row boats, that . . . being preferable to a horseback ride through the thick undergrowth."[2]

Last year's heroes were this year's gallant escorts. Col. Sidney Sherman—whose battle-cry of "Remember the Alamo!" reverberated through history—and Capt. Mosely Baker were both there with their ladies.

President Houston donned a black velvet suit trimmed with gold cording, a ruffled shirt, and a scarlet cassimere waistcoat. He wore boots, Francis Lubbock recalled, "with short red tops . . . laced and folded down in such a way as to reach but little above the ankles, and were finished at the heels with silver spurs. . . . The weakness of General Houston's ankle, resulting from the wound [he sustained in the Battle of San Jacinto], was his reason for substituting boots for the slippers universally worn by gentlemen for dancing."

Sam Houston could carry off with flair any costume he fancied. Judge Jo C. Guild, who had known him as a Tennessee congressman, wrote: "Houston stood six feet six inches in his socks, was of fine contour, a remarkably well proportioned man, and of commanding and gallant bearing. . . . His fine features were lit up by large, eagle-looking eyes . . . [he was] possessed of a fine address and courtly manners and a magnetism approaching that of General Andrew

Jackson. He enjoyed unbounded popularity among men and was a great favorite with the ladies."

Houston's biographer, Marquis James, noted that the war department, "by no means incapable of error, undertakes to whittle Sam Houston's stature down to six feet and two inches. . . . But no escaping it, there was something about this man that made light of yardsticks."

President Houston's party included British consular officer Joseph Tucker Crawford, the Mosely Bakers, the Francis Lubbocks, Miss Mary Jane Harris, and John Birdsall.[3] They met at Captain Baker's house, a one-room clapboard with a fine carpet laid to cover the bare dirt floor. Just after sundown, they went together to the ball.[4]

Dancing had already begun to the music of violin, bass viol, and fife. The room, some twenty by fifty feet, "could easily accommodate several cotillions," Adele Looscan wrote, "and although the citizens of Houston were very few, all the space was required for the large numbers who came from Brazoria, Columbia, San Felipe, Harrisburg and adjacent country."

When the presidential party arrived, the musicians struck up *Hail to the Chief.* "The dancers withdrew to each side of the hall, and the whole party, General Houston and Mrs. Baker leading, and maids bringing up the rear, marched to the upper end of the room."

When they had laid aside their wraps and changed to slippers, they formed a new cotillion. General Houston led it with Mrs. Baker, who was gowned in white satin with a black lace overdress. Mrs. Sherman wore a white velvet ball gown that she had brought from Kentucky. Other ladies wore white mulls or colored satin, all cut low at the neck, and with spreading skirts that cleared the ankle. They had feathers or exquisite Mexican flowers in their hair. The gowns were as elegant as those worn in major cities of the world, but styles varied depending on the date when the wearer migrated to the new country.

Colonel Sherman is thought to have worn the blue broadcloth uniform lined with gold satin and trimmed in gold braid that he had worn in battle.[5] Other gentlemen were in formal evening dress reflecting the influence of England's Beau Brummel. Their cravats of white muslin or silk were tied high, just below the points of their very high collars. Evening coats were cut away to reveal a ruffled shirt and handsome waistcoat. The tight pantaloons ended above the ankle.

All this handsome display was brought together in an unfinished, two-story room with no ceiling to conceal the bare beams. Although sperm candles in wooden chandeliers lighted the ballroom, there was still no roof to the building. Fortunately, it did not rain.

At midnight they all adjourned to the hotel of Ben Fort Smith—a two-room log building. "Under this shed, quite innocent of floor or carpet," Adele Looscan wrote, "the supper was spread: tempting turkeys, venison, cakes and other viands in rich profusion; the excellent coffee and sparkling wines invited all to partake freely, and soon the witty toast and hearty laughter went round." They returned to the ball, shifted from the sedate cotillions to the livelier Virginia reels, and danced until dawn. It was noted by one observer that President Houston remained sober throughout the ball.[6]

On May 1, when Congress met for the first time in its new capital city, the capitol still lacked a roof. The *Telegraph and Texas Register* granted that "Houston is merely a city in embryo." But the embryo city had a newspaper. Leaving their printing presses in the bayou where Santa Anna had dumped them, the Bordens had bought new presses and ink in Cincinnati. Thomas Borden then sold his interest in the paper to Dr. Francis Moore. In mid-April Gail Borden and Dr. Moore put their presses aboard the *Yellow Stone,* moved from Columbia to

Houston, and set up shop in a rented shanty. It was described by Moore:

Without a roof, and without a floor,
Without windows and without a door.

The *Telegraph* appeared in Houston on May 2, 1837. It would continue to be the dominant paper in Houston and an influence on the state until after the Civil War. Gail Borden had secured freedom of the press in Texas by dauntlessly publishing throughout the revolution in Harrisburg, Columbia, and Houston. But now he sold out to Jacob W. Cruger and was off to become the Republic's first collector of customs, stationed at Galveston.[7]

By May 16, the *Telegraph* reported that "the rapidity of building the town is completely astonishing." The reporter wrote that he had "commenced boarding a few days since in the upper part of town, then a retired place." Presumably he was referring to the outer reaches of Texas Avenue. But with houses springing up, his quiet neighborhood was giving way to progress. On his way to breakfast downtown, he would see lumber in a heap, and on his return in the evening, a house would be there already framed, boarded up, and perhaps roofed.

This gentleman "pitied the poor Indian who strolls about the streets amazed to see white men gathering, thick as the leaves of the forest, and rearing a mighty city where so recently they hunted the prairie deer and the buffaloe [*sic*]. The Capitol but yesterday was merely framed, now lifts its towering form above the puny buildings round, like a gigantic oak amid the prairie bushes."

John James Audubon found the towering form still roofless when he arrived on May 15. The great naturalist had reached Galveston Bay three weeks before. There his ship was boarded by Texas Navy officers who told him that the U.S. sloop of war *Natchez* had attacked a Mexican squadron off shore at Velasco and had captured a brig and run two other vessels ashore. The U.S. Navy considered them pirates because they were plundering American vessels to stock their galleys with provisions.

Audubon had come to Texas to add to his portfolio of American wildlife. The Galveston he saw in April, 1837, was "a rough village. . . . A heavy gale blew all night, and this morning . . . thousands of birds, arrested by the storm in their migration northward, are seen hovering around our vessels. . . ." Audubon and his friends went on a deer hunt on the island and killed four.

Unfazed by pirates and naval skirmishes, would-be Houstonians were arriving on the island daily, eager to take a steamer up the bayou. The less well-heeled rowed the entire distance. Audubon and his party set out for Houston by sailing vessel and small boat. "About noon we entered Buffalo Bayou at the mouth of the San Jacinto River, and opposite the famous battle-ground of the same name. Proceeding smoothly up the bayou, we saw abundance of game."

The Gulf Coast was being battered by rainstorms; the bayou was swollen. The trip under sail took them even longer than it had the *Rolla,* and they had to resort to the rowboat. It took eight hours to row twelve miles.

"May 15. We landed at Houston, the capital of Texas, drenched to the skin, and were kindly received on board the steamer *Yellow Stone,* Captain West, who gave us his stateroom to change our clothes, and furnished us refreshments and dinner." By several accounts, the bayou steamers were much more comfortable and roomy than the oceangoing sailing vessels.

With the bayou flooding, "there was a wild and desolate look cast on the surrounding scenery," Audubon wrote. "Shanties, cargoes of hogsheads, barrels, etc. were spread about the landing; and Indians drunk and halooing were stumbling about in the mud. . . . These poor beings had come here to enter into a treaty proposed by the whites."

Audubon walked up Main Street to call at "the President's house," a two-room dog-trot with dirt floors. He met several members of the cabinet, "some of whom bore the stamp of men of intellectual ability." He met "Mr. Crawford, an agent of the British Minister to Mexico, who has come here on some secret mission." And while "President Houston was engaged on national business . . . we amused ourselves by walking to the capitol, which was yet without a roof. The floors, benches, and tables of both houses of Congress were as well saturated with water as our clothes had been in the morning."

When at last Audubon saw Sam Houston, the president was striding out of a grog shop where—as a longtime friend to the Indians—he had gone to put a stop to selling them spirits. "He is upwards of six feet high and strong in proportion. . . . Our talk was short; but the impression which was made on my mind at the time by himself, his officers, and his place of abode, can never be forgotten." Though his stay was brief, John James Audubon was made a citizen of the Republic of Texas by act of Congress—after his departure.

Responding to the advertisement and newspaper accounts, people began to come to Houston from Europe, the United States, and Mexico. They came largely by sailing vessel, down the East Coast to Galveston Island, then by paddlewheel steamer up the bayou. Some would come overland by river, stagecoach, and horse. But there were few covered-wagon pioneers.

Although Houston attracted its share of con men, ruffians, and scoundrels, the diaries and newspapers of the day suggest that a surprising number of those who came to settle were well-dressed, well-behaved, well-educated.

They brought with them the clothes they would have worn in New York or Paris. The ladies wore full skirts that cleared the ankle. Exaggerated crinoline and hoops were another twenty years in the future.

Gentlemen, when not in military uniform, wore cutaway coats, vests, ascots, and the new long, tapered pants that buttoned at each side with a strap under the foot. There were, of course, dashing men who plunged into buckskins and bright-colored blanket coats, just as many modern newcomers adopt cowboy boots and hats without ever having roped a cow. Working men wore whatever seemed best suited to the job. And Sam Houston apparently donned whatever garment he thought socially or politically effective, whether buckskin or velvet.

Chapter Five

Modern City

HOUSTON was being planted on virgin soil—a town where none had ever been before, in a republic still in the process of taking shape. At times the land seemed to be fighting off occupation. The lashing flood of April, 1837, was followed in October by a hurricane that caused the bayou to rise four feet at the foot of Main Street. February of 1838 was the coldest in the history of Anglo-American Texas. Temperatures dropped to sixteen degrees below freezing on February 2 and to twenty-two degrees below on the sixteenth. Galveston Bay was frozen. Snow and ice lay on the ground in Houston. But nothing slowed the flow of newcomers.

The first Houstonians brought with them their musical instruments, their libraries, their servants, their furniture, and in some cases the lumber with which to build their houses. This was wise. The advertisements had described "Pine, Ash, Cedar and Oak in inexhaustible quantities. . . . In the vicinity are five quarries of stone." Twentieth-century geologists put no faith in those quarries in this coastal region of sand, gravel, clay, and black gumbo, and however inexhaustible the quantity of trees, there was no sawmill.

An unnamed traveler noted: "Laboring hands were exceedingly scarce, so that a house carpenter, even if he was not more than an ordinary hand, would readily command, after being boarded, the sum of three dollars a day." He wrote, "When I arrived, Houston was not only the center of most of the spirit and enterprise of Texas, but it seemed to be the focus of immigration . . .

as it continued to be during the summer. . . . Houses could not be built near as fast as required, so that quite a large number of linen tents were pitched in every direction over the prairie, which gave to the city the appearance of a Methodist camp-ground. Some of these tents . . . measured more than a hundred feet in circumference, with conical tops, thirty or forty feet in height supported by . . . a pole in the center."

Optimistically, Louis de France came to teach fencing, but he found that duels were more often fought with guns. The first duel occurred before Houston was a month old. On May 14, before the roof had been put on the Capitol but after Congress had moved in, a group of young men gathered in the Senate chamber "to discuss some grave and heavy matters connected with the science of government; which they thought it was important to the world that they should decide."

The contractor, who had lost a leg at the siege of Bexar, rushed to protect his Capitol building. Ward blew out the candles and cursed the debaters. One young man slapped Ward on the cheek. Prevented from shooting him on the spot, Ward sent a challenge the next day. The two met on the dueling grounds just outside the city limits (marked by Texas Avenue) and at ten paces both fired and missed. Ward demanded a second round. This time the young man managed to shoot Ward in his wooden leg, which apparently satisfied the honor of both men.

Dr. Francis Moore used the Ward fight

to start an editorial campaign in the *Telegraph* against dueling: "We had an affair of honor settled here yesterday, no blood shed however, all was amicably adjusted by merely shooting into WOOD. If all duels were settled by merely shooting at blocks, instead of BLOCKHEADS, the practice would be far more consonant with the dictates of wisdom and justice."

The first criminal code of the Republic had banned dueling in 1836, but it had curious loopholes. Though several utterly irrational duels in that first year were barefaced murder, neither peace officers nor the courts interfered. Continuing his editorial crusade against dueling, Dr. Moore ran for the Senate in 1839 determined to push through a law that would abolish the practice. This he did. The measure passed both houses, and despite fairly casual prosecutions, dueling had disappeared from Houston by 1840, and from Texas by 1841.

However indifferent to killings in duels, courts in Houston often applied the Republic's harshest laws for other crimes. In January, 1838, John Houston, found guilty of having stolen $780, was sentenced to thirty-nine lashes on his bare back and was branded on his right hand with the letter *T*. The notorious but popular Pamela Mann, owner and operator of the hospitable Mansion House, was sentenced to death on being convicted of forgery. Her sentence was later commuted.

Gambling, though illegal, stirred less ire. First Chief Justice Andrew Briscoe was fined five hundred dollars for playing cards. Peter Gray was fined twenty dollars for smoking in court, and another twenty for sitting on a table in court. Slightly more than a year later, Peter Gray was named district attorney.

The first laws of the Republic called for such harsh punishments that they simply failed to work. The *Telegraph and Texas Register* reflected general opinion when it said that the Republic needed a penitentiary to end "the terrible and disgraceful punishments of hanging, branding or whipping. . . ."

In the summer of 1837, Houston was in-corporated as a city, James S. Holman, the Allens' agent and district clerk of Harrisburg County, was first mayor. By the end of the year, Houston was a town of fifteen hundred people. The ratio was still four men to one woman. Though some of the women were play actresses and some servants, a large number were gentlewomen who had had the courage to come with their husbands to this remote outpost.

Mary Austin Holley wrote, "The main street of this city of a year extends from the landing into the prairie—a beautiful plain of some six miles wide, and extending with points and islands of timber quite to the Brazos. . . . The Capitol [is] 70 feet front— 140 rear—painted peach blossom about ¼ mile from the landing. We kept our lodge in the boat. . . . The President . . . dined with us 2 days, one of which was Sunday, and gallanted us to the Capitol, in . . . which is a gallery of portraits of distinguished characters of the last campaign."

Although the government of Texas was giving away free land by the hundreds of thousands of acres, the Allens were selling their Houston property, lot by lot, and prospering. They had risked much and earned their prosperity. The brothers brought their father, mother, four brothers, and a sister from New York to Texas. One by one, Charlotte's brothers came down from Baldwinville.

Mrs. Holley found the Allens "a very genteel people and live well. Have a good house and elegant furniture (mahogany—hair sofas —red velvet rocking chair and all nice and new and in modern style.)"[1]

The Allens were pioneer philanthropists as well as Houston's first developers. They had helped finance the Texas Navy and were generous in giving lots to institutions or persons they wished to honor. Although Congress had voted to spend as much as fifteen thousand dollars for a Capitol building, the Allens paid for its construction and rented other buildings to the government at a nominal sum of seventy-five dollars a month.[2] They also gave the land on which the Methodists and Presbyterians built churches.

The Allens opened their house without charge to many honest wayfarers. Their bookkeeper, William R. Baker, later estimated that their hospitality cost them some three thousand dollars a year, but the Allens considered it a further investment in the development of their city.

The city was building up. Eugenia Price was reared on a Virginia plantation between Richmond and Norfolk. Widowed after the birth of her daughter, Bettie Tighlman, she scandalized plantation society by marrying the overseer, John Andrews. They sailed for Texas through such storms that she vowed never to set foot on a boat again. They had planned to live in Harrisburg but thought the cost of land there too high. In 1837, they bought a block on Austin Street in Houston from the Allens. They had their house shipped down from Baltimore, each cypress plank and beam numbered. Built at 411 Austin, it had five bedrooms upstairs, a parlor, a library, a small sitting room, and a big dining room. Mr. Andrews became Houston's fifth mayor, and in its lifetime, 411 Austin housed five generations of their descendants.[3]

Andrew Briscoe, who had come to Texas in 1833, was a signer of the Texas declaration of independence, a captain in the Battle of San Jacinto, and first chief justice of Harris County, appointed by President Houston. When he and Mary Jane Harris were married in August, 1837, they bought a two-story house that Thomas Ward had built on speculation. It faced Main Street at Prairie. There they lived through the births of their children, including Andrew Birdsall, Adele, and Jessie.[4] When they moved to New Orleans, they sold the house to Judge John Birdsall. Harvey Allen, youngest of the Allen brothers, succeeded Briscoe as chief justice of Harris County.[5]

In 1838, it was still hard for travelers to find lodgings. Gustav Dresel, a young German businessman, wrote cheerfully that in his boarding house fourteen men slept in the same room "on loose boards in the attic, which we reached by means of a ladder. . . . a rope, stretched from one side to the other, served for hanging up our clothes. In a German inn, where I met naturalists, doctors and other educated people, the guests lay on and under the tables at night. It occurred to no one to complain."

When the first northers of fall blew in, Dresel found that "there were only three stoves in the whole of Houston. We used to light fires in front of the saloon in the evening and stand around them and enjoy —not excepting the President—hot drinks with merry speeches. The City Hotel was then the chief gathering place. In that spacious wooden shack we were often 100 and 150 at the table. All the nations were represented."

Sophisticated shops and services began to fill the rapidly rising one-story buildings. Hart & Donaldson offered bread, biscuits, cakes, and superfine flour in 1837. And in 1838, Thomas W. House, a young Englishman, came to town from New Orleans. By year's end, Loveridge & House had a bakery on Main Street. They advertised, "Ornamental, pound and sponge cakes; fancy sweet biscuits of all kinds, and pies of every description; candies and confectionaries of all kinds, equal to any made in the United States; cordials of every description constantly on hand; pies, cakes, custards and sweet-meats made to order; orders for ball and marriage suppers thankfully received and promptly answered."

Within another two years, Shearn & House would be offering "ice cream, fresh frozen, 11 forenoon, 3 and 6 in the afternoon," as well as iced lemonade for parties.[6] Charles Shearn was another young Englishman. The two would grow in wealth and service to the young city.

M. J. Matossy, "wishing to devote all of his time to the business of distilling, offers for sale his confectionary establishment." J. Wilson was distilling whiskey and other liquors. But most spirits, from wine to hard liquor, were imported from Europe.

Houston was rife with barbers. Henry Tucker, a free black man, had a large following. Many barbers ran newspaper ads: "T. C. Lecompte, haircutter from Paris. Dressing room. 1st barber of Houston and republic. Price, shave 25 cents haircutting 75 cents." Several offered Indian restorative to promote growth of hair. And Henry Dobelman advertised "tooth drawing, cupping, bleeding, and other surgical operations."[7]

Houston was also rife with dentists. In newspaper ads, T. Carraway, self-styled surgeon-dentist, offered to attend ladies in their residences. H. Marks, also a dental surgeon, offered to "replace from a single tooth to a full set of incorruptible teeth; will plug, file, extract, cleanse, and perform every requisite operation, in a skillful and easy manner." And Dr. T. Evans "inserts natural or porcelain teeth 1-entire set. Correct irregularities incidental to children. Diseased teeth extracted with least possible pain with Mr. E.'s improved instrument."

Every steamboat up the river brought in new shipments to merchants. Some sold their wares out of warehouses, others from shops in Long Row. Byer & Cobb dealt in dry goods and groceries at Number 6 Long Row.[8] Charles DeRall sold fabrics at Number 7, whereas Samuel Maas announced that he had "French goods received . . . from Havre and Marseilles opposite Long Row."

But the merchant who came early, stayed to make a fortune, and founded a major university was William Marsh Rice. Born in Massachusetts in 1816, he landed in Texas in 1838, penniless, stripped of all his possessions by a shipwreck off Galveston. But he got to the Republic in time to be issued a headright certificate to 320 acres of land by the Harrisburg County board of commissioners in the town of Houston.

He went into the wine and spirits business briefly. Though he never drank anything stronger than water, he contracted "to furnish with Liquors the Bar of the Milam

House." In addition to the cost of the liquors, he was to receive three dollars a day and board.

Soon he was buying and selling land. Then he went into storekeeping. He and his partner, Ebenezer B. Nichols, became commission and forwarding merchants. They brought goods from New Orleans and New York by boat up the bayou and delivered them by ox wagon to settlers and plantation owners inland. They soon had customers and clients all over the Gulf Coast. Within a year the small, slim young New Englander was on his way to wealth.

To enable Houstonians to get away from the rat race of city life, Beauchamp Springs opened in July, 1838, starting as a park for picnics and parties, but with expectations of selling lots. The *Telegraph and Texas Register* reported that with its "inexhaustible supply of pure, cold and wholesome water," it was "one of the most pleasant and fashionable resorts in the vicinity." It was a mile and a half out of town. Spring water hauled into Houston by cart cost seventy-five cents for a thirty-gallon barrel.

John Kirby Allen, cofounder of Houston, died of congestive fever on August 15, 1838, at the age of twenty-eight. He was buried in Founders' Cemetery. At that age, he had made no will. Ultimately, differences over sharing of the estate with the many other Allen brothers led to an estrangement that in 1850 led to the quiet separation of Charlotte and Augustus Allen, a pair who had adventured so well together.

From the outset, Houstonians began to plant trees.[9] Though lush magnolias and oaks shaded the bayou, the city lay on open prairie. Merchants imported garden supplies, and the more enterprising opened nurseries on the edge of town. Phineas Jenks Mahan, who had arrived in time to take part in the revolution, was soon advertising in the *Telegraph and Texas Register:* "Practical Gardener, 1½ miles above Houston, Being in correspondence with several nurserymen in the U.S. shall be happy to receive orders for fruit, shade and ornamental trees, grape vines and farming and gardening tools, etc. The trees to be paid for on delivery at Houston in the proper season for setting out."

This was the Houston that Millie Gray found on her arrival at the beginning of 1839.

Chapter Six

Magnet

TEXAS continued to have an incredible hold on the imagination of people in Europe and America. Aristocratic young Germans like Prince Solms-Braunfels set up the Adelsverein through which they hoped to send colonists in great numbers to the new country. Devout Bavarians left behind home and fortunes to seek greater religious freedom in this promised land. Successful men in the United States from New York to Florida gave up medical practices, military careers, and federal judgeships to come to Texas. On their travels, gentlewomen from England and the United States stopped off to see Houston and to write about it.

Once infected with Texas fever, a man did not easily recover. After his first journey from Virginia to Texas, William Fairfax Gray had been welcomed home to Fredericksburg by a band and the Rifle Grays in uniform. He was an important figure in one of the most cultivated societies in the United States, but he saw a future for his family in Texas that Fredericksburg did not offer. Whatever the costs, he was determined to emigrate.

It had taken him nine months to make his first trip from Virginia to Texas and back. He prepared to make the round trip twice more—first to establish himself in the new Republic, then to bring his family down.

Returning to the Gulf Coast in February, 1837, he found that a new capital city was being built. Always drawn to the heady centers of government, he promptly settled upon Houston, opened a law office on Travis Street, and became clerk of the House of Representatives during the second session of

Congress. His law practice took him to Columbia, Marion, Brazoria, or Washington in all kinds of weather. He wrote long letters to Mrs. Gray in Fredericksburg, sending them as he could by a journeying friend. It was seven weeks before he got his first letter from home.

Twenty-two months after immigrating, Colonel Gray went back to Virginia to fetch his family. Millie Gray, thirty-eight years old, was leaving her birthplace, her family, her life-time friends, the comforts of home, all that was familiar.

Her diary gives a clear picture of the experience, and of a Houston that was barely two years old: "Nov. 20th, 1838, at 10 o'clock at night I went on board the *St. Boat Rappahannock* at Fredericksburg with a heavy heart," she wrote. "Left Mr. Barton's house where were assembled all my beloved Sisters & Brothers. . . . Passed a restless, disturbed night. Arrived at Baltimore about 8 o'clk on Thursday morn. 22d." After four days in Baltimore, they boarded "the *Brig. Delia*. Capt. Walker, for Galveston in Texas. . . . There was with me Peter, Edwin & Allan, Kate & Alice, Margaret Stone & our servants, Dinah, Lucy & John, Jane & her child & Armistead. We found the cabin of the Brig very neat, tho' small."[1]

They lay becalmed off Baltimore through Tuesday, but at last the breeze sprang up and they were on their way to a new world, a new country, a new city, a new life. Travel was slow. They weathered gale and seasickness, enjoyed a passage through blue waters off the Bahama Banks, and arrived off Galveston on December 21. The Gray party of fifteen people had been at sea a month.

Born as the naval base for the Texas Navy, Galveston was growing rapidly as a port city and the way station for immigrants bound for Houston. The place that Colonel Gray had seen without a house in April, 1836, and John James Audubon had found "a rough village" in April, 1837, had improved greatly by Christmas, 1838.

"There are some large houses & all better looking than we had been taught to expect —We are struck however with the singularity of houses without chimneys. They are all heated by stoves." In the warm, balmy days just before Christmas, the Grays went ashore for a trip to the beach to collect shells. They spent Christmas week on the brig, and when a norther blew in, Mrs. Gray and her daughters were confined to their cabins, sewing, writing, and reading *The Life of Sir Walter Scott*.

At last, on the morning of December 29, "we heard the joyful tidings of 'a Steamboat coming in'—she proved to be the *Putnam*. Mr. Gray went on board of her immediately & secured a passage for ourselves & our furniture, etc. but the Capt. will not take the Lumber—which we regret—it will add to our expense and we shall have to pay $25 per day every day after tomorrow that we keep it on board the Brig."

They boarded the *Putnam* next day. Mrs. Gray found it "a very elegant boat. . . . We found one Lady with 3 children on Board. Capt. Sterett very polite & gentlemanly. We had quite a party to dinner and a very handsome entertainment. This Boat seems almost like a palace, compared to our Brig—and *my* appetite is really enormous." The *Putnam* must have been palatial if its dining salon could provide both dinner and entertainment for the Gray family of nine, their four guests from Galveston, and the Lady with three children.

Already the Grays were seeing acquaintances from Richmond or New York whom they had met in Fredericksburg or whose friends or relatives they knew. As other

passengers came aboard, Mrs. Gray was cheered to see how many of the present or future Houstonians were pleasant, educated people.

The Grays had expected to start for Houston early New Year's Day and arrive by nightfall. But Mrs. Gray later wrote: "We arrived at the landing of this precocious city on Wednesday, Jan. 2nd between 10 & 11 o'clock in the morning, after a rather agreeable trip up the Bayou.[2] We were introduced to several persons on board, amongst them the Revd. Mr. Chapman and Mr. Gray's friend Judge Birdsall (late Atty. Genl.)."[3]

Though the Allens had laid out their town at the head of navigation, navigation was not yet easy. Mrs. Gray noted: "The Bayou became so narrow at last that I thought it would be no difficult matter to jump ashore. . . . Once we were in an ugly situation, a snag having got entangled in one of the wheels. . . . After seeing the number of floating logs, etc., in the Bayou I ceased to wonder at the one wheeled Boats I had seen." And, accustomed to the clear streams of Virginia, Mrs. Gray commented, "The water is pleasant, BUT MUDDY. . . . Every body tries to get rain water—to drink at least."

A steamboat docking in Houston was a sociable event: "On our arrival here, we were joined on board the Boat by Mr. Doswell and Mr. John Morris—who I felt rejoiced to see. He appeared like an old friend. . . . Young Mr. Harris procured a carriage to bring his Grandmother Mrs. Birdsall up to his Sister's Mrs. Judge Briscoe, and very politely insisted on our all coming up in it to our house."[4]

This was a one-story house with a wide central hall on Fannin Street across from Court House Square. The folding doors at front and back were flanked by windows with venetian blinds. Stairs led up from the hall to an attic room, measuring sixteen by eighteen feet, with dormer windows. The walls were of tabby, a concrete made of seashells, and the woodwork was neatly painted. As a precaution against fire, the kitchen was in a separate building behind the house. With the main hall as dining room and the attic room as a dormitory, that house was to see a constant flow of guests, coming and going. Some stayed as boarders while house hunting. Several were officials of the new government or distinguished visitors to it.

"We were agreeably surprised with its appearance," Mrs. Gray wrote. "Eve [Evelina] was delighted to see a nice walk from the gate to the front door, covered with shells. It did not look clean & white very long, for I never saw anything like the mud here. It is tenacious black clay, which cannot be got off of anything without washing—and is about a foot or so deep. Although everything looks better than I had expected,[5] my heart feels oppressed & it requires an effort to wear the appearance of cheerfulness. I could (if I were a weeping character) sit down & fairly weep —and if asked for what I could not tell. . . ."

Mrs. Gray must have been speaking for hundreds of newcomers like herself. But she had no time to be homesick. She was immediately caught up in a round of visits, calls, new arrivals and was soon shuttling back and forth to Galveston by steamboat as casually as a later generation would catch the Interurban.

Houstonians were constantly on the move, going to Galveston or Brazoria on business, or to other countries on the business of the Republic. Clergymen, seeking foreign mission funds from their denominations in the United States, traveled thousands of miles by sailing vessel, horse, riverboat, and stagecoach. Newspapers advertised: "For New Orleans, in Forty Hours, splendid low pressure steampacket Columbia, Capt. Wade, will leave Galveston Bay the 8th and 22nd of each month."

Thomas J. Rusk and James Reily, attorneys and counselors at law, announced the opening of their office: "Gen. Rusk is now in the East but will be in this city so soon as the Indian difficulties in that part of the Republic are settled." Although Peter Gray, now twenty, was sent to East Texas on a mis-

sion to the Indians by Secretary of War Albert Sidney Johnston, few Houstonians traveled east or north in their country for fear of those Indians.

Memucan Hunt made a number of trips to Washington, first to assist William H. Wharton in winning U.S. recognition of the Republic, then as President Houston's first minister to the United States. Though his plea for the prompt annexation of Texas was rejected, he managed to negotiate a boundary in 1838 before coming back to Houston to serve newly elected President Lamar as secretary of the navy. By sailing vessel and horseback, Bernard Bee made many trips to Mexico City, on similar and potentially more hazardous missions.[6]

Most women stayed in Houston and let the world come to them, except for taking a jaunt to Galveston by boat or to Matagorda on horseback. Perhaps typical, Mrs. Gray's life was in constant flux. Her diary from January, 1839, to February, 1840, sounds like a perpetual houseparty. Had she kept a diary, Mrs. Augustus Allen's would have sounded the same.

The Grays entertained the French admiral, commander of the French fleet "now off the coast." Judge Birdsall and Dr. Ashbel Smith came to call. Mrs. Gray regretted the loss of Bernard Bee and his wife to Washington because of his appointment as minister to the United States. The Grays had as boarders Albert Sidney Johnston, secretary of war; Memucan Hunt, secretary of the navy; and Pres. Mirabeau B. Lamar.

In addition to presidents, cabinet members, and diplomats of the Republic who regularly took their meals with the Grays, Mrs. Gray had as her houseguests Episcopal Bishop Leonidas Polk and his party for three or four days when he came on his first visitation. Vast and impressive, whether as West Point cadet or bishop or—in days to come—Confederate general, Bishop Polk had traveled thousands of miles by horse, stagecoach, gig and wagon, riverboat, and steamer to visit this foreign mission field. Given such renowned company, such traveled company, it is unlikely that Houstonians found conversation dull.

Meanwhile, the Consular Service of the Republic of Texas, begun by the government in 1835, proliferated. By 1837, consuls from Texas were scattered in cities of the neighboring United States from New Orleans to New York. The Republic opened a legation in London in Pickering Place with Gen. James Pinckney Henderson as chief.[7] During the last two years of the Republic, Texas would have consuls in Marseille. Bordeaux, Cette, Rouen, Bayonne, and Paris in France; in London, Liverpool, Falmouth, Plymouth, Kingston-upon-Hull, and Newcastle-upon-Tyne in England; in Dublin, Ireland; in Glasgow and Greenock in Scotland; and in Amsterdam, Rotterdam, Antwerp, and Bremen.

The organization of the foreign service was nebulous, communications slow. But those new Houstonians were representing their country abroad with a vigor that inspired British and European immigration in a strong, steady flow.

Chapter Seven

Lively City—1839

BY THE START of 1839, Houston was a city of 2,073 people—1,620 male, 453 female. It had two theaters and three newspapers. Social life was brisk with regularly announced balls, quadrilles, and cotillions. One such party was a benefit to raise funds to pull the snags out of Buffalo Bayou—a forerunner of twentieth-century museum and charity balls.

Houstonians celebrated the Fourth of July with cannon fire, a parade of the Milam Guards and Sunday school children, and a patriotic oration. They seemed unaware that they were celebrating the independence of a foreign country. Houston used gunfire on any excuse: to announce the arrival or departure of a steamboat or to welcome any passing dignitary. Newspapers reported casually that "Sam Houston arrived Wednesday from Washington. Customary salute from arsenal." Or, "The Fannin Artillery fired 13 guns at 2 p.m. Sunday, during the visit of M. Dumanoir, commander of the fleet on the Gulf Station." On a Fourth of July, the *Morning Star* could rightfully headline the "Thundering of Cannon." These must have been live shells, because in 1841, the city passed an ordinance whereby "no guns shall be fired on vessels or banks of the bayou at the foot of Main Street unless the guns are directed to the northwest side of the bayou, $20 to $100 fine."

J. R. Codet of New York opened the Dancing and Waltz Academy in April, 1839. He was almost immediately rivaled by M. Grignon, "accomplished dancing master," who "engaged a saloon at Exchange Hotel to give lessons in dancing, teaching waltzing and fashionable dance in vogue in Europe. If encouraged," he promised, "will open school. . . . Also cotillion party every Friday night, good orchestra, private lessons for ladies in their own dwellings."

An attractive plantation society was growing up in the surrounding countryside. Cotton grew white in the fields. Neighborhood balls were given at one plantation house or another. Houstonians went out for visits by barouche, horseback, or pirogue. On such a visit, Mary Austin Holley wrote of dining off rabbit soup, yankee pickled pork, venison steaks, with snap beans, fine Irish potatoes, lettuce, and strawberries from the garden. Houston and Galveston were the cities to which plantation society turned.

Houston's first two years were kaleidoscopic. While many Houstonians were eager for U.S. annexation and statehood, several leading citizens opposed it vehemently— Mirabeau B. Lamar, Albert Sidney Johnston, Bernard Bee, and James Reily among them. Further, because the city was to be the capital only until 1840, there was constant debate and uncertainty over Houston's future as the seat of government. And because the first president was not eligible for reelection after his short two-year term, the city was enlivened by the political battles between Sam Houston and Mirabeau B. Lamar: Houston was president from 1836 to 1838, Lamar from 1838 to 1841, Houston again from 1841 to 1844.

They had opposing views on almost every issue. Sam Houston naturally preferred to see the capital in his namesake city; Lamar wanted one on Texas' western frontier. Houston wanted to keep the promises made to Indian tribes for their help in the revolt against Mexico; Lamar wanted to drive them out of the country—and did. Houston favored annexation; Lamar wanted to stretch the boundaries of the Republic of Texas westward across New Mexico and, presumably, to govern that enlarged nation. Texans then and historians now have tended to line up behind one or the other of these two strong statesmen.

Although scarcely brilliant, the city's intellectual climate was perhaps above average for a town of two thousand. It was lent stimulus by several remarkable men. The U.S. chargé d'affaires, Alcée Louis La-Branche, had received a liberal education at the Université de Sorreze, France. Young, handsome, and spirited, he lent charm to Houston society for several years until he resigned to take over a sugar plantation in his native Louisiana.

Lorenzo Zavala de Carrea, son of Gen. Lorenzo de Zavala, was often in Houston from the family plantation on Buffalo Bayou opposite the San Jacinto battleground. General de Zavala had been governor of the state of Mexico and minister of the Republic of Mexico to France. He had served as vice-president of Texas in Burnet's interim government. All this made his son a well-traveled man. After his father's death, the young Zavala joined the Texas cavalry, taking with him his French valet. Colonel Gray's diary refers to him as "a fine sprightly youth, small stature, black eyes, good teeth . . . a light, active person speaks Spanish, French and English, a native of Yucatan."

Dr. Ashbel Smith, who had both a baccalaureate and a medical degree from Yale, had gone to France for further study. In Paris he enjoyed the society of the Marquis de Lafayette, S. F. B. Morse, who was studying art, and James Fenimore Cooper, who was living there. Smith, who came to Houston as early as 1837, was a member of Phi

Beta Kappa.[1] So was Andrew Janeway Yates, a merchant in Houston until he moved his business to Galveston.

Regularly, in the city's first years, visitors were surprised by the contrast between the fairly primitive houses and the quality of life inside. Ferdinand Roemer found Dr. Smith's plantation house "a common, two-roomed log cabin, built of partly-hewn logs." It had a bed, a table, and a few chairs with rawhide seats. But the tall cabinet against the wall "contained chiefly books which formed a small but carefully selected library. Not only were the Greek and Roman classics represented, but also the best and choisest [sic] selection of English and French literature."

Ashbel Smith had as medical colleagues Dr. Alexander Ewing, who was chief surgeon of the Texas army and considered "a profound student," and Dr. Phillip Anderson, chief surgeon of the Texas navy, who was "with the exception of Dr. Ashbel Smith, the most learned man in Texas at that time." These were the opinions of Dr. B. H. Carroll, an early twentieth-century historian.

Ezekiel W. Cullen, St. Augustine County's representative, was a handsome man with blue-gray eyes, and black curly hair, sideburns, and moustache. He was in Houston for the Third Session of Congress to present the report of the Educational Committee. A native of Georgia and a lawyer, he cited "the necessity for the Republic and the duty of Congress" to provide public education. He introduced a bill that would grant three leagues of land out of the public domain to each county of the Republic for public education. The bill also authorized a survey of fifty leagues of vacant land for the establishment of two colleges, or universities. This was the first such law and it laid the basis for Texas public school and university systems.[2]

Ezekiel Cullen did not linger in Houston. To him it was "a mudhole, a graveyard, an *abominable* place."

Joining his sister, Charlotte Allen, Horace Baldwin came down from New York and so distinguished himself with the community that within five years he was elected mayor of Houston.[3]

In 1839, Capt. Justin Latham, a native of Mystic, Connecticut, who had sailed to China, the East Indies, and Europe as a merchant mariner, brought a cargo into Houston from Boston. He was so pleased by what he found that, at age twenty-five, he brought his wife and daughter Justina down and started a mercantile business.[4]

The most interesting writing of the time was largely in diaries and memoirs. But Massachusetts-born Dr. Francis Moore, Jr., physician, surgeon, lawyer, and Houston's second mayor, set a lively standard for wit and invective as editor of the *Telegraph and Texas Register.*

Gail Borden, known throughout Texas as an engineer and surveyor, had started the *Telegraph* in 1835 in San Felipe, with his brother Thomas and Joseph Baker as partners.[5] In April, 1836, as Santa Anna's army neared, the Bordens moved the paper to Harrisburg. There the Mexicans seized the presses and threw them in Buffalo Bayou—an effective method of censorship. Undaunted, and in a historic defense of press freedom, the Bordens bought new presses and printing supplies in Cincinnati.[6]

When they resumed publication in Columbia, Moore bought part interest. He and Gail Borden moved the paper to Houston in May, 1837, and Dr. Moore became its new editor.

Interested in natural history, he wrote articles on Texas geography that were later published in books in Philadelphia and New York. Moore's editorials were couched in strong, often caustic language. In an accident in his youth, Moore had lost one arm. Sam Houston once said that Moore could write more lies with one hand than most men could with two. But then Moore was pro-Lamar, anti-Houston. Years later, as governor of the state of Texas, Sam Houston forgave Moore his sins and appointed him state geologist. Scientists might consider this an overreaction, though Moore had a lifelong interest in geology and had once briefly studied paleontology. Most scientific interest in the Houston of 1839 was concentrated on phrenology—the "science" of analyzing bumps on the head.

Although most private libraries were devoted to law books, William Longthorp owned works of Shakespeare, Byron, Coleridge, and Benjamin Franklin. John Faber, Jr., had eighteen volumes of Schiller, two of Victor Hugo, and Goethe's *Faust*. And Julia Neil, who was declared *non compos mentis* in the early 1840s, owned a volume of Aristotle.

A group of young professional and businessmen founded the Houston Franklin Debating Society. They discussed the worth of annexation to "the States of the North," whether Texas should wage offensive or defensive war against Mexico, and "the Influence of the Fair Sex." This last lecture was such a success that it was reprinted in the *Telegraph* at the request of the members.

They later regrouped, first as the Philosophical Society of Texas, and then as the Houston Young Men's Society. Debaters asked the questions "Have the Crusades been beneficial to mankind?" and, much more to the point, "Ought duelling to be punished as a capital crime?" Ahead of their time, they wondered, "Can the treatment of the Indians by our ancestors be justified?"

This society may have prompted the start of the Houston Circulating Library.[7] The library opened in the Henry F. Byrne and Company's book, stationery, and fancy store at Number 7, Long Row. The *Morning Star* praised it as "a large and well selected assortment of miscellaneous works." Among the nine hundred or more books were works of Boswell, Byron, Fielding, Irving, Johnson, and Shakespeare, as well as those of popular writers of the time. The library was open every day, but only to subscribers, who paid twenty dollars for a year, twelve dollars for six months, or eight dollars for three months. Inasmuch as the project folded after

As the capital of the Republic of Texas, Houston caught the imagination of Europeans. From the 1840s through the 1860s, English and European publications carried scenes like this one, show-ing Houston built on rolling hills. *Courtesy George Fuermann City of Houston Collection, Special Collections, University of Houston Libraries*

six months, only short-term subscribers got their money's worth.

The Freemasons had established Texas' first fraternal lodge in Brazoria in late 1835, only to lose their property to Santa Anna's invading soldiers. Anson Jones, its master, received its charter from Louisiana on his way to San Jacinto; he took it with him to the battle in his saddlebags. In October, 1837, so many of the charter members were in Houston that they could reconstitute the lodge, which became Holland Lodge Number 1. In December, 1837, the Texas Grand Lodge was organized at a meeting in the Senate chamber, with President Houston presiding. Anson Jones was elected grand master. Continuously thereafter, the Masons played an influential role in the religious and civic life of the city.

Painters drifted through doing portraits,

and some sent sketches and watercolors to Europe, where Texas was still a novelty. Many of these pictures showed more imagination than accuracy.

Music was the universal entertainment. Houstonians played trios and duets after private dinner parties. Professionals and amateurs alike were at first limited to instruments easily brought along in a trunk, but pianos began to arrive by 1838. The distinguished Viennese musician Emil Heerbrugger gave concerts, and Houston children could take voice, pianoforte, violin, guitar, flute, and clarinet lessons under Johannes Hennings.

As to theater, the great dramas came more frequently from off stage than on, as Sue Dauphin has related in her *Houston by Stages.* Before Houston was a year old, John Carlos, a businessman, announced plans to build a theater. In the *Telegraph and Texas Register,* editor Moore "rejoiced" that Carlos had acquired a building at Main and Franklin and was "fitting it up in a neat and handsome style." Carlos said that he was awaiting the arrival "of a respectable theatrical corps" on the steamboat *Columbia* out of New Orleans. When it arrived, it was headed by Henri Corri, a ballet dancer and bit player at the Camp and St. Charles theaters in New Orleans. Corri's troupe included players from London, Boston, and New York, and because he had brought them to Houston at his own expense, he had no intention of forking them over to Carlos to manage. He said, "It will be the greatest pleasure of my life to say in after years that I have been the founder of the legitimate drama in the Glorious Republic of Texas."

Because Carlos had the only suitable building and Corri the only respectable theatrical corps, they had to make do with each other temporarily. The first production was Sheridan Knowles's *The Hunchback,* double billed with a farce, *The Dumb Belle, or I'm Perfection.* The *Telegraph* crowed that "the actors have exceeded the expectations of even their most sanguine friends." But the battles between Carlos and Corri were fought in open competition, with the result that Houston soon had two theaters instead of one.

The newspapers regularly reviewed the productions and reported on the arrival and departure by steamboat of various actors and actresses, much as Hollywood gossip columnists of the 1930s and 1940s reported on the arrival in town of Tallulah Bankhead, Greta Garbo, or Clark Gable.

Fairly early on, Mr. Lewellen came to Houston as the republic's first Shakespearean actor. He played *Richard III* to a standing-room-only audience, and followed that triumph with performances of *Othello* and *Damon and Pythias.* The critics approved, although they were disappointed in the supporting female cast. In New York and Saint Louis, Mr. Lewellen had starred chiefly in equestrian melodramas "with a magnificent horse named, variously, Mazeppa, Timour, Conancheotah, etc. depending on the current production. Commentators with an unkind bent have even suggested that the horse was the star of the plays." A year later Lewellen gave Houston the cultural benefits of the horse's talents.

But early enthusiasm for live theater did not cloud critical judgment. The theatergoing public thought *The Dumb Girl of Genoa* so badly performed that they hanged Carlos in effigy from a pine tree in front of the theater. And when it was rumored that one actor had been bitten by a mad dog, the *Morning Star* said that the report was too good to be true, but that the company might stage *Hamlet, Lear,* or *Othello* to let the actor make the most of his newly acquired madness.

On the other hand, the *Star* published a press agent's announcement that might have given pointers to Cecil B. DeMille's:

Engagement of April 29, 1839. Unprecedented! Unparalleled! Unheard of Attractions!!!! First night of the 'Ensanguined Shirt.' First appearance of High P. Ranter [*sic*], who is engaged for six nights only and cannot possibly be re-engaged on account of sickness in the family. First appearance of Miss F. Ranter since her recovery from the whooping cough. First night of the real earthquake. . . . This piece has been got up without regard to expense, weather or anything else. . . . Among other things which have been secured especially for this piece are 400 streaks of lightning with thunder to match and 300 alligator skin shields with brass knuckles and knobs.

Somehow, after four hundred streaks of lightning with matching thunder, the alligator-skin shields seem anticlimactic.

Chapter Eight

Melting Pot

STEPHEN F. AUSTIN, Sam Houston, Mirabeau B. Lamar, the Allens, Shermans, Bakers, Hunts, Birdsalls, Briscoes, and Grays. . . . A roll call of the founders and leaders of Houston would leave the impression that the early city was an exclusive enclave of Anglo-Americans. In fact, they were outnumbered, if all the other ethnic groups were totaled together—blacks, Germans, Mexicans, Indians, Swiss, French, and English among them.

The Texan army alone had drawn men from across the world. At San Jacinto on that April afternoon, Sam Houston led into battle men from twenty-four American states, from Austria, Canada, England, France, Germany, Ireland, Italy, Mexico, Poland, Portugal, and Scotland.

The Galveston Bay and Texas Land Company had advertised in Europe, with a particular eye to Switzerland and Germany, and the ads had borne fruit. Well-to-do Europeans thought of profitable colonization, and those seeking political and religious freedom were lured by the promise Texas seemed to offer.

John Hermann, a Swiss who had fought in Napoleon's army and received a sabre wound at the Battle of Waterloo, came to Houston in 1838. He and his wife landed in Houston "with $5 and three children," his son George Hermann said. "My mother pawned her jewelry, and my father bought a little flour and sugar and established a bakery on Main Street."

Like Harrisburg, Frost Town existed before Houston was conceived, only to be absorbed by it at a later date. It was a small community on the south bank of Buffalo Bayou below the horseshoe curve. In 1835, the Allens—Augustus, Charlotte, and John—had moved there from Nacogdoches to scout out the Gulf Coast. But Frost Town rapidly became Germantown with the waves of new immigrants. F. H. Heitmann, H. P. Fisher, John F. Usener, and Ignaz Veith built houses there with beautifully plotted flower and vegetable gardens. Other Germans came on up to Houston.

Gustav Dresel, a well-educated young businessman from Mainz, arrived in August, 1838. He landed at the foot of Main Street at about nine o'clock in the evening and immediately spied a friend, "my colleague of the office of Klendgen and Levenhagen in New York, little Robert Levenhagen of Rostock."

He found lodging with the Gerlachs and adapted cheerfully to sleeping on their attic floor in company with thirteen other men. At nineteen, Dresel was an ideal frontier townsman—able to take the discomforts without souring on the adventure.

The front porch of the house "served the neighborhood as a happy gathering place in the evening. As seen from here, the gay-colored, wild, and interesting city of Houston looked very picturesque. The few cabins, the numerous tents, the Capitol, the President's Mansion, and the many camps of recently arrived immigrants offered a novel and peculiar sight."

Henry Kesler, a Silesian, was proprietor of the famous Round Tent, a bar where soldiers spent their scrip certificates for brandy, cocktails, gin toddies, and claret punches. At his more elegant Kesler's Arcade, he provided German newspapers and music for his customers. The City Council sometimes met there because Kesler was a councilman, as well as a member of the board of health. In his garden ten miles out of town, he raised corn and mulberry trees for sale.

Dresel noticed a wide variety among the fifteen hundred new Houstonians: "The President, the whole personnel of the government, many lawyers . . . a larger number of gamblers, tradesmen, artisans, former soldiers, adventurers, curious travelers from the United States, about a hundred Mexican prisoners, daily new troops of Indians—all associated like chums on an equal footing."[1]

But where the older, more sedate John James Audubon had seen drunken Indians and blackguards, the young German businessman took a more tolerant view: "Indians of several tribes were camping in and about Houston to sell furs and venison for lead, powder, cottons and rugs. . . . Every Indian considered himself fortunate to see and shake hands with General Houston . . . for during Houston's eight years' stay among the savage inhabitants of the woods, they had learned to revere this venerable general and wise counselor."[2] (In fact, Houston lived only three and a half years with the Indians on the Arkansas River, and in that period he had made four trips back to Washington and Tennessee.)

Dresel found work with George Fischer as bookkeeper and salesman, replacing "a nice young man from Bremen," who had died after three days of "the fever." Fischer, a Hungarian, spoke fluent German, English, Spanish, Slavonic, and French. Dresel was to have one hundred and fifty dollars a month and free quarters in Fischer's wooden cabin. "We sold wholesale corn and corn meal, sides of bacon, ham, potatoes, onions, flour, butter, lard, hardtack, sugar, coffee, powder and lead, in short everything that was necessary in the way of foodstuffs and drinks. We also had a supply of porcelain, ready-made clothes, rugs, pearls and cottons for the Indians." William Marsh Rice, arriving a few months later, plunged into a similar trade.

Dresel enjoyed the Indians who thronged about the porch offering to barter their furs and such herbs as sarsaparilla and sassafrass. He was captivated by the Indian maidens, admiring their quiet dignity as well as "a small, dainty foot and daintily formed arms." He had the foresight to worry about the future of the Indians in white-dominated Texas and the United States.[3]

Laboring-class Germans also came. The *Houston Morning Star* of December 17, 1839, was "delighted to see the florid-complexioned and blue-eyed sons and daughters of Germany. . . . A large number of these hardy and industrious persons are now in our place, seeking for employment and an honest livelihood." The editorial was a job-placement ad: "Whoever wants assistance to cultivate his soil, servants for his house, artisans to work in the shop, day-laborers, shoemakers and so forth, can find in the honest Germans, who now have possession of the Capitol, the very persons to suit him."[4]

By 1840, of Houston's fifteen hundred to two thousand people, some four hundred were German. Prince Solms-Braunfels was commissioner of the Adelsverein, founded by German aristocrats to encourage German colonization in Texas. Ultimately it resulted in one of the largest migrations from Europe in American history. Though many Germans went on to Fayette County and west to the Hill Country, Houston drew a share.

The death of their oxen stopped Conrad and August Bering in their tracks on the way to a land grant in Fredericksburg. Emigrating from Kassel, Germany, in 1842, the brothers had got as far as Houston when their team died, and so they simply stopped and went to work. Cabinetmakers by trade, they went into making cabinets and dealing in lumber. August Bering IV would be carrying on the enlarged family business some one hundred and forty years later.

The names of city streets and in twentieth-century city directories reflect the staying power and contribution of German families: Bering, Binz, Boettcher, Heitmann, Henke, Hermann, Hofheinz, Holtkamp, Keller, Koehler, Kuhlmann, Meyer, Neuhaus, Priester, Sauter, Schweikart, Settegast, Stude, Rudersdorf, and Usener among them.

Of the first Europeans who came, several were Jewish. Michael Seeligson had a store near the steamboat landing until he moved to Galveston, where he ultimately became mayor. Lewis Levy, Henry Wiener, Isaac Coleman, and Maurice Levy were early settlers.

Lewis Levy wrote to a Jewish newspaper advising Europeans to come to Texas, where "thousands of acres of land can be bought . . . for the small sum of from 25 cents to $1 per acre; good arable, fertile land, where a man can make his living to his liking, and more independent than the Autocrat of Russia or the Emperor of Austria themselves. Indeed, I would not exchange my fifteen acre lot, with the house on it, and the garden around it . . . near the city of Houston, for all the thrones and hereditary dominions of both those noted persons."

Jacob de Cordova was the most prominent of the early Jewish settlers. A Sephardic Jew who came to Philadelphia from Jamaica as a young boy, he lived in Galveston briefly in 1837 before coming to Houston. He was a charter member of the Houston Chamber of Commerce in 1840 and helped draft its constitution. He was elected an alderman and later became a Harris County representative to the Texas Legislature. He introduced the Order of Odd Fellows into Texas and founded the first Houston chapter.

By 1843, Houston had seventeen Jewish adults from Germany, Jamaica, Holland, England, France, Louisiana, and Ohio. But as yet there was no rabbi. In the ecumenism of early Houston, Hannah Levy and Henry B. Wiener and Rachel Caroline Levy and Samuel L. Isaacs were married at Christ Church by the Episcopal rector.

British immigration began with such early arrivals as T. W. House in 1837 and the Paynes in 1841. It swelled in the late 1850s on the lure of cotton and railroading. In 1841, Hannah Payne, an Englishwoman and teacher, came up from Galveston with her thirteen-year-old stepdaughter, Keziah. They had left others of the family in Funchal, Madeira. Hannah taught Keziah German, French, and Latin, in addition to the "three Rs," and before they owned a piano taught her to play one on a marked piece of paper laid on the table. Still in her teens, Keziah joined her mother in teaching and in nursing the sick, and over the years she was at times the organist for Christ Church and for the Methodist Church.

Although not common, Spanish was spoken in the capital city—certainly by the Zavalas, who also knew English and French. And Col. Juan N. Seguin, who had led the company of Mexican Liberals in the Texas army at San Jacinto, was San Antonio's representative to Congress. George Fischer was his official interpreter.

Aside from the Anglo-Americans, the largest and most enduring body of Houstonians were the blacks—some slaves, some free, some indentured by their own choice. The first blacks in Texas and in Houston were free men and women. Mexico had banned slavery, and the colonial society was open and equal to all. Sam McCullough was a member of the Goliad garrison. Hedrick Arnold, one of Erastus (Deaf) Smith's spy company, was credited by some historians with guiding Ben Milam into San Antonio when the Texians stormed the stronghold in December, 1835.

Most of the free blacks had valuable skills and prospered. But the Anglo-Americans from the South brought slaves and slavery with them, so that by 1820, slaves outnumbered the free blacks. By 1850, they made up 22 percent of Houston's population. In the thirty years in between, Houston and Galveston were centers of the slave trade in Texas. Only one person devoted his business exclusively to the slave trade, but many merchants sold slaves as a routine part of business.[5]

Although slavery was considered essential to the plantation economy, although many city founders had brought their servants with them, Houston had mixed attitudes toward the system. The City Council passed laws to regulate the black population, and others to protect blacks, with the result that the courts were filled with cases involving black Houstonians. The offender in each case was usually a white man who had violated one of these city ordinances.

While Houston had its share of cruel and brutal slaveowners, there were a number of solid citizens willing to go to great lengths to help out a black Houstonian they knew. When, for example, the Houston City Council passed an ordinance on April 10, 1839, calling for the departure within thirty days of all persons of African descent—meaning free persons, not slaves—it evoked a spate of signed petitions from white men pleading that exceptions be made.

The petitions ran to a pattern: "We the undersigned, citizens of the City of Houston and Republic of Texas, would respectfully represent unto your honorable body. . . ." The petition would explain that Henry Tucker, "a man of color, free born, came to this country July A.D. 1838, is of the most respectable character . . . and has been acting in the Capacity of a Barber and as such gives entire satisfaction to a respectable and numerous patronage." In language so elaborately respectful as to sound like irony, they would plead that Tucker be allowed to continue to live in Houston. Tucker's petition was signed by more than thirty men, including such notables as Albert Sidney Johnston, Ashbel Smith, and A. C. Allen.

In 1841, when Congress passed a similar law requiring that all free persons of color leave the Republic by January, 1842, it stirred an even larger whirlwind. Zylpha Husk inspired several petitions, explaining that she was a free-born native of Georgia who had moved to Texas in 1835, that she earned her living as a washerwoman, and that if she

and her thirteen-year-old daughter Emily were forced to move, they had no place to go. One petition carried fifty signatures, another sixty-two.

In February, 1840, during President Lamar's first term, Congress passed a bill that set fines of twenty to two hundred dollars for selling "ardent spirits or intoxicating liquors" to a slave without written permission from his owner or overseer, and for buying from a slave any cotton, meat, or other produce without written permission. Slaves were forbidden to carry guns without the owner-overseer permission. These provisions stemmed from the fact that most slaves in Houston had time off work from Saturday noon to Monday morning. Many were allowed by their owners to hire themselves out for pay or to grow and make things to sell on their own. Some slaves lived out in town in quarters that they rented.

This same legislation provided that anyone convicted of unreasonably or cruelly treating a slave should be fined "not less than $250 nor more than $2,000." And it concluded, "If any person shall murder any slave, or so cruelly treat same as to cause death, the same shall be felony and punished as in other cases of murder."

In her book *Travelers in Texas,* Marilyn Sibley has shown what visitors thought of this new country. Many from the Northeast arrived prepared for the worst horrors of slavery as portrayed by abolitionists, but after a fair look concluded that, with all its flaws, the actual practice in Houston could have been worse. Because slaves and the white owners lived and worked together all day, every day, black children playing with white, there was a sense of family in the relationship.

Just as William Fairfax Gray wrote, "I have nine whites and nine blacks in my own family," so did Dr. Ashbel Smith refer to his servants. A neighbor asked him, "Well, Mr. Smith, you have no white family?"

Rutherford Hayes, as a young man, visited a large plantation in the Brazos bottom. Writing home to Ohio that he had not changed his principles on slavery, young Hayes added, "We have seen none of 'the horrors' so often described." He reflected the local attitude when he wrote, "Guy, Uncle and myself complete the white portion of the family."

Despite various legal attempts in parts of the South to limit the education given to slaves, many slaveowners had all children on the plantation taught their ABCs. Edwin Rice Brown of Deer Park and Houston said that on his grandfather's Mississippi plantation, white and black boys played together, as was the custom throughout the South.

In the hot summer time, my grandfather would not let them go swimming until the shadow of the trees reached a line that he drew in the dirt. They'd all be lying there in the shade watching the shadow, and when it hit, they all raced for the pond and the last one in got dunked. My father had more buttons to undo than the Negro boys had and he was always the one that got dunked.

My grandfather insisted that the black children be taught because he thought they were smarter than white children up to the teens at least. He said they lived much closer to their families and closer to nature and were more observant."

The visiting strangers, Sibley found, tended to support "the popular thesis that the worst masters were usually born elsewhere than in the South. After talking to a northern woman who owned slaves, [Frederick Law] Olmstead wrote that she 'entirely sustained the assertion that Northern people, when they come to the South, have less feeling for the Negroes than Southerners usually have.'"

Young Hayes also saw the obligations of slaveownership. "It is often thought that Southern ladies have an easy time of it with their 'help,'" he wrote home, "but it is not so. A good manager has quite as much 'vexation of spirit' as you ever have who are changing 'girls' once a fortnight. Mrs. Perry, for example, . . . is the nurse, physician and spiritual adviser of a whole settlement of slaves."

Some Germans seemed unable to deal easily with blacks. Count von Boos Waldeck had nineteen slaves on a plantation near Rutersville. His blacksmith, who was worth some two thousand dollars, had always conducted himself properly and been well treated. But the count's inexperienced German overseer whipped the blacksmith for a fancied slight. The man left and refused to return until after much talk and an agreement made with the master. The slave had the law on his side, but in addition he knew his own skills and his own value.

When a Houston owner tried to send one of his men to help out on a plantation, the slave simply ran away and came home to his owner. He did not like plantation work and had no intention of putting up with it.

Nonetheless, to be a slave – however benign the owner – meant lack of freedom in this land of the free. No slave could change jobs or change bosses, could travel without special passes, could move to another town at will. No slave could testify in court against a white person. The slave was completely dependent upon the good will and character of his or her owner. Though many slaveowners tried to keep families together, there was no guarantee that they would. Under the law, slave families could be separated by sale. A slave was defined by law as property, not a person.

Lay My Burden Down, Ben Botkin's recorded interviews of former slaves, gives some insight on what it must have been like.[6] Botkin found that slaveholders ranged from the brutal to the benign. In between were owners who treated their slaves as they did their cattle, aware of their commercial value but with no thought to their feelings, dignity or souls.

One account is of a master who marched his slaves over icy roads from Georgia to Texas. When one woman could not keep up, he shot her and kicked her as she lay dying. The next account tells of an owner who brought his slaves from Georgia to Texas by sailing vessel and stagecoach, making the whole trip a treat and an adventure. And there was Miss Sallie, "the best mistress anybody ever had. She wouldn't let one of her slaves hit a tap on Sunday. They must rest and go to church." Withal, what comes through is the total vulnerability of slave life.

Nothing can paper over the fact that human beings were advertised and sold to the highest bidder from the slave blocks in downtown Houston. But the records of the Republic show instances in which a free person of color would indenture a son or daughter for two or three years, with the understanding that the child would be well cared for and taught a trade.

Zylpha Husk, the "free woman of color" who had inspired petitions asking Congress to let her live in the Republic, had apparently come to Houston from Alabama. In an elaborate legal document filed in Montgomery in 1827, her daughter Emily "voluntarily and with approbation of the said Zylpha Husk her mother," indentured herself to the age of sixteen as an apprentice to George B. McLesky. The court document bound McLesky to teach Emily to read and write and, "to the power, wit and ability of the said Emily," instruct her in the arts of carding, spinning, weaving, and sewing, using "all due diligence to make the said Emily as perfect in the said acts as possible." McLesky was also bound to provide her "good and sufficient meat, drink and apparel, washing, lodging and all other things for an apprentice during said term." Emily, in turn, agreed to conduct herself "honestly and obediently towards the said Geo. B. McLeskey and also honestly and orderly towards the family of the said George B. McLeskey."

The McLeskeys and the Husks must have moved to Houston in tandem, because the contract was legally ended in Houston. Harris County records of 1839 show that McLeskey did "hereby renounce make acquittance and release to the said Zylpha Husk all my right, title and interest to an indentured apprentice in indenture to me by the said Zylpha." Emily was free.

Under a similar agreement in July, 1840, Nelly Norris, a "free woman of color," apprenticed her son Thomas to Benjamin F. Tankersley of Harris County to have him taught "some trade or business." There are also records where a woman, having gained her freedom, petitioned to be bonded to a master of her own choosing.

And the will of William Smallwood of August 24, 1844, is not unique. In it he willed everything he owned to "my Negro Girl June, now in my possession," and declared that "her and her heirs shall forever be free."

Free blacks operated restaurants and shops patronized by both free and unfree black Houstonians. One black couple, noted for appearing always in the latest Paris fashions, taught white Houstonians how to dance the cotillions and reels of the day. Black servants were often allowed to drive the owner's horse and carriage on a Saturday or Sunday outing. Black balls were frequent.

Even so, the Houston newspapers regularly carried from various parts of the Republic the notices of runaway slaves, with rewards offered for their return. Court dockets were loaded with cases stemming from slavery: harboring runaway slaves, buying from slaves, assault and battery on slaves, intent to murder slaves, selling spirits to slaves, selling liquor to slaves, stealing slaves, cruel treatment of slaves, murder of slaves. The charges of attempted murder and murder were both aimed at men who were, themselves, slaves.

Chapter Nine

A Foreign Mission Field

HOUSTON was a sophisticated small city in its last months as capital of the Republic. By 1839, it had well-furnished houses, interesting people, a round of balls and cotillions, places to dine, hotels, shops, books, theaters, a number of saloons, stables, horse racing, daily steamboats to Galveston and easy access to the rest of the world in travel.

But a number of people felt keenly the lack of any church. From its first days, ministers and missionaries had come to the new country. Newspapers often announced services to be held by one such visitor after another. Episcopalians were among the first to come. In 1835, the Rev. Richard Salmon of Connecticut and New York set out with fifty-four people to found an Episcopal colony. Although he seems to have left his colonists in Natchez, he got to Columbia in time for the First Congress and, with a Presbyterian minister, was elected Senate chaplain. On December 28, 1836, he read the burial service for Stephen F. Austin at the Bryan-Perry graveyard at Gulf Prairie.[1] On reaching Houston, he opened the Houston City School. Supported by the city, it was housed in a new schoolroom near the capitol. Salmon also became secretary of the Houston City Council. But he did not stay long enough to assemble a congregation.

The second Episcopal priest to come was R. M. Chapman. He was a twenty-nine-year-old Virginian who had been made deacon in Pittsfield, Massachusetts. The Foreign Committee of the Episcopal Board of Missions appointed him a missionary to Texas, but without station or salary. On his own, he arrived in November, 1838, and in December was called upon to open the Senate with prayer. For the next six months, as he wrote to *The Spirit of Missions,* "I preached once a day and sometimes twice in the capitol, one of the large halls having been kindly afforded for religious meetings by the Secretary of State."

The first Methodist missionary was the Rev. Littleton Fowler. He had entered the itinerancy in Kentucky, but he came to Texas from his post at LaGrange College, Tuscumbia, Alabama. He arrived in Houston on a Sunday morning in November, 1837, and that afternoon preached to a large assembly. The next day he was elected chaplain of the Senate. Throughout his stay, he held services in the Capitol. As an itinerant, Mr. Fowler went to other parts of Texas when Congress adjourned and came back for the next session. During his stay in Houston, as he later wrote, he "obtained from A. C. Allen a deed to half a block of land for a church . . . fronting on Texas Avenue between Milam and Travis Streets."[2] The Allens gave the half-block to the circuit rider for Methodist use. The Methodists thereby became the first to own land on which to build a church.

Dr. W. W. Hall, the first Presbyterian minister to come, served as chaplain of the Second Congress of the Republic, the first held in Houston. He lived in a tent for the few months of his stay, supporting himself by preaching.

In March, 1838, the young William Y.

Allen arrived.[3] Still studying for the Presbyterian ministry, he was warmly received. Years later he wrote:

Soon after my arrival in March, 1838, A. C. Allen made me a present of a town lot. . . . I had a small room built upon it, where I studied, and slept on a sack of prairie hay. Several months in 1839, I shared my room and bed with Mr. Chapman, the Episcopal Deacon, who was the first Episcopal preacher in Houston.
He had the Grays and the Bees and the Rileys as his followers, while I had the Burkes and Baileys and Cones and Robinsons.

This beguiling sentence reflects the ecumenical spirit that pervaded Houston or at least Houston's would-be churchgoers. Nonetheless, through Mr. Allen, the Presbyterians too received a lot by gift from the Allens.

In September, 1838, Mr. Allen returned to the United States, to be ordained as an evangelist to the Republic of Texas. Back in Houston by the spring of 1839, he took part in founding the Texas National Bible Society and the first Temperance Society in Texas "with the countenance (but not active cooperation) of President Sam Houston." Apparently, Sam Houston was not yet ready to pledge abstinence.

Despite all this religious ferment, Houston arrived at mid-March, 1839, with no formal church organization. Then, abruptly, it acquired two in two weeks.

On March 16, 1839, Col. William Fairfax Gray circulated a paper to organize Houston's first church: "The undersigned agree to unite together as a Christian Congregation in the City of Houston – to observe the forms of worship, and be governed by the Constitution of the Protestant Episcopal Church in the United States of North America." Twenty-eight men signed their names to the parchment that now rests in the Christ Church Cathedral archives in the Houston Public Library.

The signers in alphabetical order were: George Allen, Harvey H. Allen, Ambrose Andrews, John D. Andrews, Bernard E. Bee, George D. Biggar, John Birdsall, Henry H. Godfry, Peter Gray, William Fairfax Gray, John D. Groesbeeck, Paget Halpen, DeWitt Clinton Harris, H. E. Hartridge, M.D., Charles Hedenberg, Memucan Hunt, A. Kasson, Charles Kesler, W. Doswell Lee, Thomas Viscount Mortimer, George Moffitt Patrick, Erastus S. Perkins, Tod Robinson, Henry Thompson, James Webb, Arthur F. Woodward, Corodon C. Woodward, and Andrew Janeway Yates.

Next, the Rev. Mr. Chapman and Colonel Gray called a meeting of "the members of the Episcopal Congregation of the City of Houston" for four o'clock in the afternoon of Monday, April 1, in the office of John Birdsall. Bernard Bee would soon be off, first to Washington, then to Mexico City; Memucan Hunt would soon be on a similar shuttle. James Webb, a Virginian who had resigned a U.S. district judgeship in Florida to come to Texas, would move to Austin as President Lamar's secretary of state. But on this first meeting of the new congregation, they all managed to be there. They elected a vestry, and on the motion of Ambrose Andrews, portrait painter, they voted to call their association the Protestant Episcopal Church of Houston. Sometime in the next few months, the name Christ Church was adopted.

Meanwhile, on March 31, the Rev. Mr. Allen called a meeting of his people to organize the First Presbyterian Church of Houston. The charter he presented said, "For the purpose of promoting Divine Worship, and our mutual edification in the knowledge and practice of piety, we whose names are hereunto subscribed, do agree to associate ourselves together as a Presbyterian Church. . . ." This document was signed by A. B. Shelby, Marian Shelby, J. Wilson Copes, James Bailey, James Burke, Sarah Woodward, Isabella R. Parker, Edwin Belden, Harris G. Avery, Sophia B. Hodge, Jannett Scott. It is interesting on two counts: unlike the Episcopalians, the Presbyterians included women among the church's charter members, but Charlotte B. Allen, whose Presbyterian devotion had inspired her husband to give the church lot, was not one of them.

Houston now had two chartered but homeless congregations. By this time, Augustus and John Allen had brought their parents and the whole Allen family to Houston from New York.[4] Houston's development had become the family business. One of the Allens, without the knowledge of the others, had promised the Rev. Mr. Allen that in addition to his own lot on which his tent stood, the Presbyterians could have Lots 1 and 2 in Block 68 as a church site. In 1839, unaware of the promise, Henry R. Allen sold those lots to Dr. Niles F. Smith.

Quite a bit of cross-purpose selling and deeding was going on at the time. But in July, 1840, before this particular discrepancy was noticed, the Presbyterians started building their church on what they thought of as their property on Main Street at Capital Avenue. The upshot was that in 1841, H. R. Allen bought back the promised lots from Dr. Smith and for the consideration of one dollar he deeded Lots 1 and 2 in Block 68 to the Trustees of the Presbyterian Church. The deed was recorded January 16, 1843, a year after the church had been dedicated. It reads "on which the Presbyterian Church NOW stands." Despite the confusion, the Presbyterians fared far better than the Episcopalians in the matter of the Allen generosity.

Though Houston's Methodists could claim the lot given to the Rev. Littleton Fowler, they still had not chartered a congregation. In her *History of Shearn Church,* Mrs. I. M. E. Blandin listed ministers as having been "regularly appointed to Houston, without having stayed long or formed a church. In accordance with the Methodist custom of circuit riding, these men tended to spend as much time in Galveston, Austin and other Texas counties as they did in Houston."

In 1840, however, a Methodist minister, the Rev. T. O. Summers arrived. He preached in a room over a store on Capitol Avenue. "The first permanent organization was made in 1841, by Mr. Summers," Mrs. Blandin wrote. She cited Thrall's *History of Methodism in Texas* for a partial list of the charter members. Among them were Charles Shearn, John H. Walton, Mosely Baker, Dr. and Mrs. John L. Bryan, Mr. and Mrs. Andrew McGowen, and Dr. Francis Moore.

On the lot given them by the Allens, the Presbyterian congregation first built a simple meeting house and later a small church. The Methodists had their lot by 1837 but no church organization for another four years. The Episcopalians, who had organized the first church on March 16, 1839, had neither lot nor meeting house.

Until the 1960s, the legend flourished that the Allen brothers had given the Episcopalians the lot upon which Christ Church stands. The legend may have grown from the church's first list of subscribers. Though Colonel Gray had only twenty-eight signatures on the March 16 charter that founded the church, in the next two weeks he managed to round up forty-five contributors who signed pledges.

Capt. Mosely Baker, who would later be a charter member of the Methodist church, pledged one hundred dollars. Secretary of War Albert Sidney Johnston pledged fifty dollars—probably because he liked the Grays and was a frequent boarder at their house. Dr. Ashbel Smith, soon to represent the Republic as minister to France, also pledged fifty dollars. All of this was in the spirit of philanthropy that has been a lifelong characteristic of Houston.

It was perhaps in this spirit that Augustus Allen wrote on the famous subscription list: "A. C. Allen Four Hundred Dollars in Lumber ($400). Also half of Block 55 for church and school—so long as it is used for that purpose." He underlined his signature with a double looped flourish. This block had been shown on Gail Borden's map as Schoolhouse Preserve. Gradually it appeared that Augustus Allen had attached strings to his pledge. The Episcopalians learned that to gain ownership of the lot, they must build "a substantial building 60 feet by 40," and complete it by May 28, 1843. Such a building would cost six thousand dollars. In the meantime the capital had moved to Austin; many members and subscribers had moved away. The Christ Church members could not meet the deadline.

Instead, they bought the lot in an effort that took three years and ultimately cost them four hundred hard-earned dollars. For this sum they gained clear title to half a block on Texas Avenue between Fannin and San Jacinto—the site of their first church, the site of Christ Church Cathedral ever after. Colonel Gray, its founder, did not live to see the first little brick church built in 1843. But his legacy remains. His son Peter was a founder of Baker and Botts. His grandson would later become one of the city's most beloved ministers. And of the three pioneering first churches, only Christ Church still stands on its historic site from the days of the Republic.

The Rev. John Mary Odin, a missionary priest, organized the first Roman Catholic church in Houston, beginning in January, 1841.[5] In August, the Catholics broke ground for their first church on the corner of Caroline and Franklin overlooking a deep ravine. They named it St. Vincent de Paul.[6] Bishop Odin said the first mass in the new church in July, 1842. A few days later, the *Morning Star* reported that "the pews of the Catholic Church will be sold Saturday the 23rd at public auction to raise money for finishing the interior." Houston members subscribed $150; eleven pews were sold for $143, but the bishop had to pay the balance of $800.

The First Baptist Church, destined to become Houston's largest, was organized as the Missionary Baptist Church of Christ on April 10, 1841. It was founded with thirteen charter members, including Obedience and Gardner Smith. Obedience Smith owned all of southwestern Houston of that period; her grant stretched west from Main Street and south from Buffalo Bayou. Though the Rev. James Huckins was their first pastor, they also heard sermons by two notable preachers, Judge Robert E. B. Baylor and Dr. Rufus C. Burleson. Judge Baylor was a member of the Texas Congress, despite a law barring preachers. Dr. Burleson became pastor of the church in 1848. He and Judge Baylor later founded Baylor University.

All of Houston's first ministers came as missionaries to a foreign field. They felt their responsibility to black Houstonians. The Rev. Charles Gillette, first rector of Christ Church, held Sunday afternoon classes and services for the servants of the congregation. The first wedding he recorded in the Parish Record was that of "Thomas, a servt. of Mrs. A. C. Allen, to Melinda, a servt. of E. S. Perkins." Before the Civil War, slave couples were customarily married in Christ Church, their children baptized there. The bishop of the Episcopal Diocese of Texas, the Rt. Rev. Alexander Gregg, was the son of a South Carolina plantation owner. He believed that whites and blacks should worship under the same roof. Consequently, Christ Church continued to have black members after the Civil War, and their children attended Sunday school with the white children, a custom taken for granted well into the twentieth century.

In its first years, the Methodist pastor held regular Sunday afternoon services for blacks in the building used by whites. As the white membership grew, the Methodists in 1851 built an adjacent church for blacks facing Milam Street. "This was the only church for Negroes anywhere between the Trinity and the Brazos," Mrs. Blandin says in her history of the Shearn Methodist Church. As a result, black Baptists as well as black Methodists attended. Blacks were licensed as local preachers and exhorters, and they performed baptisms in the bayou.

By the end of 1843, the first four congregations had each built a church, most of them measuring forty by sixty feet, and all were soon outgrown.

The Lutherans, who organized in 1851, and the first Jewish congregation in Texas, chartered by the state legislature in 1859, belong to another decade and another chapter. But in their early struggles, all congregations worked together. They shared the Capitol when it was available. They provided a minister for services in the Presbyterian meeting house when it was without a minister. They ministered to people of other faiths than their own. Each offered its building to members of other faiths who were seeking to organize. Houstonians were too close in their hopes and shared dangers to be divided by denominational lines.

Chapter Ten

Woeful Times

THE YEAR 1839, which had begun so brightly, lapsed into months of grim tragedy. By midsummer yellow fever was epidemic. Before cold weather came, it would decimate the city, killing 240 of Houston's 2,000 people.

"We have suffered much in sickness and death," Colonel Gray wrote in October, 1839. "Some of our best citizens have fallen . . . John Birdsall . . . the Hon. Henry Humphreys, presiding judge of the county court, a man of worth . . . Dr. Edmund R. Anderson, my family physician, who died in my house, having removed hither two days before his death. He was a martyr to his professional zeal; having been exposed two nights in succession to long rides in the country, and by losing the road having had to sleep overnight on the open prairies. He was a fine physician and a gentleman. These three were all of my immediate circle and I feel their loss heavily."

Though Houston attracted its share of quacks and charlatans, it was fortunate in the character of its leading physicians, such as Dr. Anderson and Dr. Ashbel Smith. They were honorable in providing the best medical knowledge of the time for their patients. The tragedy lay in the lack of knowledge.

"I am not accurately informed of the whole number of deaths, but think, for the last month, they will have averaged four or five a day," Gray wrote. All these deaths were occurring in a small city that spread only from Buffalo Bayou to Texas Avenue. The decimation was all-too-evident to the survivers.

Millie Gray's diary was as poignant:

"Sickness – Sickness – Sickness – all around and many deaths. Summoned early in the morning to see Judge Humphreys who is dying. Over there nearly all day. . . . Much occupied with Dr. Anderson who we had brought over here this evening. He is exceedingly ill. . . . Poor Dr. Anderson breathed his last about ½ past 2 o'clock. We carried him to the grave this evening. . . . There are a fearful number of new graves. This was the 6th today. This is an awful disease and does not seem to be understood by the physicians."

Despite the organization in March of two church congregations, Houston was without the solace of the church by midsummer, when the epidemic was at its worst. "During the gloomy period just past," Colonel Gray wrote in October, "we have been without the aid of any clergyman. The Presbyterian, who had been preaching here for eighteen months, has . . . gone to the new metropolis, the city of Austin, to reside. Many of the dead have been buried without christian rites. Over several I have read our funeral service, and the same has been done by other laymen."

Houstonians responded in character. Lacking hospitals, they opened their homes to dying friends. Lacking undertakers and clergy, they gave what final care they could to the dead. When the burial ground was filled, they bought more land.

"This has been a much more fatal summer throughout the South than the last," Colonel Gray added. "The sickness has not been confined to Houston nor to Texas. I have cause of much thankfulness that my large family remains entire. . . . I have nine whites and nine blacks, large and small, of my own family, and have had an average of ten or twelve boarders during the summer. . . . Myself, my wife and elder children have had excellent health. Indeed, my wife's health, which was delicate in Virginia, has decidedly improved here." With the coming of cool weather, the epidemic subsided. But yellow fever was only the most flagrant cause of death.

By August, 1841, Houston had six thousand graves in its cemeteries. The living population would not reach six thousand until after the Civil War. Yet Houston offered no greater threat to life than other cities of the time. As they did around the world, Houston women died in childbirth and of childbed fever. Babies and children died of diphtheria and whooping cough, and men were killed by heart attack or by accident. Appendicitis was usually fatal; malaria and tuberculosis took somewhat longer in killing their victims.

A further source of Houston's general malaise was "the new metropolis"—the city of Austin. Though Houston had been promised the status of capital only until 1840. Houstonians had hoped to hold on to it. By January, 1839, East Texas, West Texas, and South Texas factions were competing for the capital. By joining forces in Congress, the east and the west knocked Houston out of the running. Then the central part of the Republic joined with the west to choose a location on the frontier.

On a motion proposed by Ezekiel W. Cullen of San Augustine, Congress passed a law appointing a five-man commission to locate land, lay out a town, and build the necessary buildings. It called for the site to be between the Colorado and the Brazos rivers and north of Old San Antonio Road. The Republic therefore paid twenty-one thousand dollars for 7,135 acres on the west bank of the Colorado River and the work began—as it had in Houston three years before—to build a new capital city of Texas. President Lamar had played only a quiet part in all this, but he had never cared for the city named after his chief political opponent. He also had the vain hope of gaining sovereignty over New Mexico. For that purpose, he supported a site on the western frontier —and he got it.

By the fall of 1839, senators and representatives from all over the Republic had left Houston for Austin. So had everyone who had any dealing with the government—or who hoped to. The first capitol of the Republic stood empty on the corner of Main Street and Texas Avenue.

Stores lost customers. Churches lost paying members. A number of doctors, lawyers, and businessmen moved west to the city of greater opportunity. New Orleans wholesalers began to refuse credit to Houston merchants. In temporary financial embarrassment, some men sent their wives and children back to their families in the United States.

Passing through Houston somewhat later, Prince Solms-Braunfels, agent of the Adelsverein, wrote: "Houston . . . has more houses than citizens. . . . Farmers bring their cotton here and sell it to the native businessmen, who in turn transport it by water to Galveston. This alone affords the town some life. Otherwise it would be only a gathering place for loafers of the surrounding bottom lands, who go there mainly to gamble and to trade horses with the hope of defrauding someone."

Although harsh, the prince's comment may have been fairly accurate. Houston had lost many of its best citizens to yellow fever in the epidemic, or to Austin with the removal of government.

Houston was having its first depression.

Chapter Eleven

Up from Depression

HOUSTON'S DEPRESSION of 1839–40 was sharpened by the depleted state of the Texas national treasury and the falling value of Texas money. In 1840, treasury notes of the Republic fell first to fifty cents on the dollar, ultimately to ten cents. The first flour imported to Houston in 1837 had sold for thirty dollars a barrel in gold. Prices on all staples grew steadily more reasonable as supplies flowed in throughout 1838 and 1839. But with the weakened currency of 1840, a barrel of flour cost eighty dollars; corn meal eight dollars a bushel; corn four dollars per hundred ears; sugar forty-two cents a pound. Beef from the roaming herds of Spanish cattle was still cheap and good at two cents a pound.

Mirabeau B. Lamar had shown courage at the Battle of San Jacinto. He believed in educating all children—a policy that most Americans and Texans of the time considered expensive and foolish. His vision of a nation of homeowners led the Texas Congress to pass a homestead law, the first of its kind on the continent. He won recognition of the Republic from France and Britain. But Mirabeau Bonaparte Lamar had been well named. He was an expansionist who hoped to gain control of a territory stretching to the Pacific. This dream, combined with his real hatred of Indians, prompted him to throw the resources of the Republic into killing them off. His wars not only killed tremendous numbers of Indians, but cost the Republic $2.5 million in three years.[1]

In the sagging economy, there was worried talk of bankruptcy, even of famine. But it was not in the city's character to worry long. Before 1839 had ended, merchants began to lay brick sidewalks along Main Street, a boon to women whose long skirts made walking dusty in dry weather and almost impossible in wet. In early 1840, the newspapers were heralding the start of stagecoach lines between Houston and Austin. And with the coming of spring, Houston organized its first Chamber of Commerce.

The *Morning Star* pointed out that stocks were low in most stores not because of credit troubles but because of the brisk trade to the interior.

Yellow fever did not return with hot weather in 1840, and after a lethargic summer, Houston doctors published a fee schedule of five dollars a visit. Further, payable in advance and doubled on night trips, there were charges of two dollars for mileage, two dollars for bleeding and for each tooth extracted, and five dollars for cupping.

Cotton was beginning to leave Texas through Houston. In 1839, eight bales were sent down to the coast, the first of a widening flow that would enrich planters, buyers, exporters, and shippers. Between June 1, 1841, and May 5, 1842, 2,460 bales of cotton were exported, along with 72,816 feet of lumber and 1,803 hides. Four commercial steamers plied the bayou.

By city ordinance of June 8, 1841, the city became officially the Port of Houston, with a wharfmaster and rates of wharfage. The most unusual shipment sent down the bayou was that of William P. Smith, who had been commissioned by the Earl of Derby to collect botanical, geological, and ornithological specimens in Texas. The cargo put aboard the steamboat *Mustang* bound for Galveston included bears, deer, antelope, panthers, leopards, lynxes, squirrels, foxes, wild hogs, wolves, coyotes, crows, prairie hens, and fourteen hundred plants. Smith was handed a $9.60 bill for wharfage. He later complained on grounds that Galveston had charged only half as much.

Matilda Charlotte Houstoun saw the high banks on a bright, frosty winter day. An Englishwoman who had come to America with her husband on his yacht, she wrote: "Such magnolias–eighty feet in height and with a girth like huge forest trees–what must they be when in full blossom!"

During the last week of 1840, all mail contracts in Texas expired. Because the act creating new contracts had been suspended by Congress, Houston was cut off from news of the nation's capital–an irksome reminder that it was no longer the seat of national power.

Rumors of an advancing Mexican army prompted an editorial from the *Morning Star* of December 31, 1840, headed "WAR." Not long after, President Lamar directed his foray into territory that is now New Mexico, but which Mexicans had good reason to consider their own. Houstonians had no great liking for Lamar, aware that he had preferred a western site over Houston for his capital. But a company of Houston Pioneers under Capt. Radcliffe Hudson and Lt. Thomas S. Lubbock marched off to join the ill-fated Santa Fe expedition.

With Sam Houston's reelection to the presidency in late 1841, the city's spirits rebounded. This was a new, rejuvenated Sam Houston. His wedding to the pure and beautiful Margaret Lea in Marion, Alabama, had dismayed his old friend Bernard Bee: "I have never met an individual more totally disqualified for domestic happiness," he wrote a friend. "He will not live with her six months." But the marriage transformed Houston from a hard-drinking, often unhappy man, into a teetotaler and a devoted husband. (It also started a family line that would reach the sixth generation in Houston by the 1980s.)[2]

Houstonians welcomed the newlyweds joyously in the greatest celebration since the first anniversary of the Battle of San Jacinto: cannons roaring, military parades, a reception at the home of Mayor J. D. Andrews on Austin Street. The ball in the Houstons' honor that evening at the City Hotel held a note of triumph. Now, many Houstonians believed, their city would again become capital of the Republic.

When the chronic threat of invasion by Mexico flared again, Houston hummed with rumors that Austin was a hotbed of spies and, by its far-western location, due to fall to the Mexican armies at any moment. President Houston called a state of emergency and did indeed move the government back to Houston for the spring and summer of 1842. But when the Mexican army took San Antonio in the fall, he moved it on to Washington-on-the-Brazos. This ended Houston's hope of regaining the seat of government.

In March, 1843, the Gulf Coast enjoyed a rare sight. The young Charles Gillette, newly of Houston from Connecticut, was on a trip to hunt bear and shoot geese with his brother Henry in Independence. On the road between Washington and Independence, he saw "something resembling a roll of bright cloud." By the second night on the prairie, as he wrote in his diary, he realized that it was a comet: "The tail was long, spanning nearly a third of the heavens."

Houston newspapers of March, 1843, reported the sight and printed learned dissertations on comets, but in seeing a comet spread its tail over a third of the sky, while alone on an open prairie, Charles Gillette had an experience not granted to many.

Despite its second loss of the capital, Houston did not falter in its stride back to prosperity. In 1841, Cornelius Ennis had made the first shipment of cotton direct to Boston from the port of Galveston. That year, William Marsh Rice and like-minded merchants began to offer a gold cup to the planter who brought in the first twenty bales, and a silver one for the first five. Over primitive, often muddy, deeply rutted roads, the great ox teams pulled the cotton drays into town. Houston got its first cotton compress in 1844, and by 1845 the city was ready to ship out almost fifteen thousand bales.

Rice and his partner Ebenezer B. Nichols were flourishing as commission and forwarding merchants. They brought goods from New Orleans or New York up the bayou by boat and took them by ox wagon to inland settlers and plantation owners. In September, 1844, William Marsh Rice wrote the secretary of the treasury in Austin that at the first opportunity he would send to New Orleans for the articles that had been ordered: paperweights, quills, sealing wax, sand, red ink, inkstands, and red tape. By the twenty-fifth of October these had been sent forward to Austin "in great haste."

A month later, the United States agreed to annex Texas.

Chapter Twelve

Americans Again

FROM THE FIRST DAYS of the Republic, the proposal to make Texas a state of the union was controversial on both sides of the border. In Texas, Houstonians like James Reily and Bernard Bee strongly believed that Texas should remain a nation. In the United States, a Bostonian charged that "One who would befriend Texas would dethrone God." John Quincy Adams raged that "the admission of Texas would be identical with the dissolution of the Union."

The issue, of course, was slavery. Moral outrage against the institution was growing stronger by the day. The anti-slave forces in Congress could not brook the idea of adding senators and representatives who would represent slaveholders. Southern congressmen could not accept a future in which the abolitionist North would be able to expand to the Pacific, while the slaveholding South would be blocked at the Sabine River by the Republic of Texas. They threatened to secede and form a new union with Texas.

But on March 1, 1845, the United States Congress voted to annex Texas. In convention on July 4, Texans ratified the treaty. Houstonians, who had voted 241 to 44 for annexation, celebrated. And on February 16, 1846, Anson Jones, the last president of the Texas Republic, lowered the Lone Star flag and raised the Stars and Stripes in its place. But on April 21, Houston celebrated San Jacinto Day just the same, with a picnic at Market Square honoring veterans of the revolutionary army, and a grand ball in the Capitol Hotel that night.

Houston rode to statehood on a boom.

The *Telegraph* cited records of the Galveston Customhouse to prove the claim of two Houston merchants that they had imported and sold more goods in 1845 than had all the merchants of Galveston combined. Houston was not so big a city as Galveston, but had all the interior as its market.

The new wharves had been outgrown. Steamboats from Galveston often bypassed them to moor along a mudbank where free black men waited with two-wheel, horse-drawn carts to haul passengers' luggage to the hotels. The brick sidewalks had been replaced with high banks, rather like levees. To cross from one side of Main Street to the other meant walking down the slope on one side and back up the bank on the other.

Ferdinand Roemer, a German scientist who came in 1846, found a motley clientele at the Capitol Hotel. He noted "a number of men clad mostly in coarse woolen blanket-coats of the brightest colors—red, white and green," but he preferred "the elegantly dressed gentlemen who stuffed their trouser legs into their boots." These superior creatures wore "the black frock coat . . . the universal mark of the American gentleman."

Unimpressed by the hotel, which he found "rather pretentious," Roemer was quite taken by Houston's saloons. In a backhanded compliment, he wrote: "Some of them (considering the size of the City) were really magnificent when compared to their surroundings. After passing through large folding doors, one slipped immediately from the streets into a spacious room in which stood long rows of crystal bottles on a beautifully decorated bar. . . . Here stood an experienced barkeeper, in white shirt sleeves, alert to serve the patrons the various plain as well as mixed drinks (of which latter the American concocts many)."

The United States declared war on Mexico in May, 1846. When the call went out from Gov. J. Pinckney Henderson for four regiments of volunteer riflemen from Harris, Galveston, and Jefferson counties, Harris County filled the entire Texas quota. Albert Sidney Johnston, Mirabeau B. Lamar, and James Reily were among those answering the call. In characteristic Houston fashion, more than a hundred of the volunteers were leading professional and businessmen; the response would be the same on December 8, 1941.

The Mexican War lasted two years. With the treaty of Hidalgo, signed on February 2, 1848, Mexico at last renounced all claims to Texas. For $15 million, Mexico ceded to the United States the vast territory that President Lamar had hoped to claim for the Republic of Texas. From it were carved the states of California, Nevada, Utah, and Arizona and part of New Mexico, Colorado, and Wyoming.

The war did not slow the flow of newcomers to Houston. There were now no vacant houses. Business was brisk. One builder had the contract to build twelve brick buildings. Shops along Main Street and Congress Avenue advertised castor oil for sale by the barrel or the gallon, brandy fruits and West India preserves, Java and Rio coffee. They also offered "table diapers, Looking-plates and Looking-escapes, Swedish and American Iron, cast steel, English blister steel, American can steel, and Balsam of Wild Cherry."[1] In 1847, moving to the outskirts beyond the Long Row stores, Nathaniel Kellum built a substantial two-story house and had a sawmill, a brick yard, a tannery, and a blacksmith shop.

Benjamin Armistead Shepherd, a Virginian who had come to Houston in 1844, opened a private banking operation in 1847.[2] His Commercial and Agricultural Bank was

When the government moved to Austin, the Allens added attic windows to the former capitol and turned it into a hotel. This photograph dates from the late 1850s, when a coach carried travelers from the depot to the Capitol Hotel. *Courtesy George Fuermann City of Houston Collection, Special Collections, University of Houston Libraries*

the first chartered bank in Texas and Shepherd the state's first banker. Three years later, he bought Kellum's property, only to sell it in 1851 to Zerviah Noble. Mrs. Noble opened a school "at the large, airy and commodious house . . . universally known as the late residence of N. K. Kellum." She offered instruction to "Misses generally, and Masters under the age of twelve in the various branches of an English education, with Drawing, Painting, Worsted Embroidery, and Music if required."[3]

Francis Lubbock's mercantile business was doing so well that he felt able to buy four hundred acres on Sims Bayou, six miles from Houston, for seventy-five cents an acre.

The marriage of Augustus and Charlotte Allen was no longer happy. Though they were not divorced, Augustus left for Brazos Santiago in August, 1849, on being appointed inspector of customs by President Zachary Taylor. He was never to come back to the city he had cofounded.[4]

Houston merchants profited from the Gold Rush, which brought forty-niners through town to buy supplies on their way to riches in the West. In the decade of the

1850s, Houston enjoyed the strength of the U.S. dollar.

The invention of Daguerre had swept into town. Allen and Whitfield's Daguerrian Gallery, above Lockhart & Company's Main Street Store, urged that passersby "Secure the Shadow, ere the Substance fade." Ad men in late twentieth-century Houston used the same theme in advertising portraits done in color photography.

William Marsh Rice, after eleven years in Texas, was a substantial businessman of thirty-four. In 1850, his brother Frederick, four

William Marsh Rice, 1850, when he was thirty-four. *Courtesy Woodson Research Center, Fondren Library, Rice University*

years younger, came down from Massachusetts and joined him in business. Methodists back home, both became Episcopalians in Houston, perhaps influenced by William's partner, Ebenezer Nichols. William Marsh Rice contributed regularly to Christ Church, and there, on June 19, 1850, he married eighteen-year-old Margaret Bremond, Paul Bremond's daughter. The reception at the

Capitol Hotel was described as "the most splendid affair ever given in the city."

Because Galveston had outstripped Houston in population, Rice and Nichols decided that their firm should have a Galveston office. Nichols sold the house he had begun to build to Rice and moved to Galveston, where he built one of the great antebellum mansions of that city. Rice moved the half-finished building to the north side of Court House Square, where it was finished elegantly with rosewood paneling. This was not only one of the best residential sections of Houston but just a step away from business.[5]

Mr. and Mrs. Cornelius Ennis and the Gray family lived on the Fannin Street side. The courthouse was a small red brick building with a white cupola and a board fence surrounding it.

Houston was still a small town of some four thousand people. Yet there was, perhaps, something unusual in the distances they traveled.[6] Dr. Ashbel Smith had retired to Evergreen Plantation on Galveston Bay on his return from the Mexican War, but in 1848 was appointed to the board of visitors of the U.S. Military Academy at West Point. In 1849, he delivered the annual oration before the Phi Beta Kappa Society of Yale University. And in 1851, he went as a commissioner from the United States to the London Industrial Exposition.

This could be expected of a cosmopolitan man of unusual intellect. Travel was more unusual for a child. Frances Blake was a little girl who lived on the corner of Texas Avenue and Caroline. She went to Sunday school at Christ Church, taught by the invigorating young minister from Connecticut, Charles Gillette. At his prompting, at age twelve she entered the Hartford Female Seminary in Hartford, Connecticut. It was run by the Beecher family of which Harriet Beecher Stowe and Henry Ward Beecher were members. To get there the child had to go by sailing vessel, riverboat, and stagecoach. She stayed in Hartford until she graduated.[7]

Young Charlotte Baldwin, daughter of former Mayor Horace Baldwin and niece of Mrs. Augustus Allen, for whom she was named, had married John Randon at Christ Church in 1848, only to be widowed after the birth of her daughter Libbie. But when she married Frederick Allyn Rice in August, 1854, he had to go to Syracuse, New York, to claim his bride. Presumably she had returned to the family fold there after John Randon's death. It was Charlotte and Frederick who had the ten children who perpetuated the Rice name in Houston; although he was twice married, William Marsh Rice remained childless.

James Reily, lawyer and friend of the Rices and Bremonds, was off to Russia, again traveling in the service of his country. Under President Lamar he had been commissioned to negotiate the sale of $1 million worth of Texas government bonds. In Sam Houston's second presidential term, Reily had gone to Washington as chargé d'affaires for the Republic. There he had dealt with Daniel Webster in drafting the Treaty of Amity and Commerce and Navigation between the United States and Texas and had made a name for himself in Washington for his diplomatic skill. Pres. James Buchanan appointed him U.S. minister to the court of the tsar in St. Petersburg, where he served with such distinction that he was commended by Buchanan and by congressmen of both parties.

In the comparatively peaceful 1850s, Houston could modernize. A Brown and Tarbox stagecoach broke records by running from Austin to Houston in thirty-six hours and from Washington-on-the-Brazos to Houston in ten. The company manufactured its own coaches. Of the new coach, the *General Taylor*, the *Texas State Gazette* wrote: "Its running gear is strong ash, the body and panels are magnolia; its leather springs and its axles were forged in their own shop; the boxes were cast and polished at McGowen's furnace. Thus from the tire to the top railing . . . it is nothing but Texan and Texan workmanship. . . . The body is long, narrow and trim, giving ample room for three rows of passengers."

Thomas W. House, who had gone from baker to wholesaler in a decade, paid forty thousand dollars to buy out James H. Stevens and Company, dealer in dry goods and groceries. This was the biggest sum of money to change hands in Houston up to that point, and with it, House became the biggest wholesaler in the state. He was on his way to becoming the richest man and biggest landowner in Texas.

A commission merchant, wholesale grocer, cotton and wool factor, hardware and dry goods dealer, he handled hides, whiskey, syrup, guns, axes, chains, and blacksmiths' supplies. He once said that a keg of his nails could be found in every church in Texas. He began a private banking operation that proved tremendously helpful in loans to churches struggling to pay for new buildings. Despite his warm friendship with his partner, Charles Shearn, and his marriage to Shearn's daughter, Mary Elizabeth, House never joined the Methodist Church that was so dear to the Shearn family heart. But he gave it a support and leadership greater than that of many members. Both English-born, Mr. and Mrs. House had seven children. The oldest was named for her mother, the seventh and youngest would become famous as Woodrow Wilson's Colonel House.[8]

In 1851, House helped organize the Houston and Galveston Navigation Company "to navigate steamboats between Houston and Galveston and on other streams tributary of Galveston Bay." It carried passengers, freight, and the United States mail.

Harvey Baldwin, a New Yorker who had built the world's first plank road, came to Houston to visit his sister, Mrs. Augustus Allen. Dazzled by Baldwin's success in New York, Houston flirted with the idea of a plank road, but soon gave it up to concentrate on railroads as the coming thing. Among the pioneer railroad builders were Paul Bremond, Sidney Sherman, William R. Baker, William Marsh Rice, Cornelius Ennis, William J. Hutchins, A. S. Ruthven,

B. A. Shepherd, T. W. House, W. A. Van Alstyne, James H. Stevens, Dr. Francis Moore, and Frederick Rice.

There was a steady traffic of saddle horses, horse-drawn carriages, mule-drawn wagons, teams of oxen, and stagecoaches on the roads to Richmond and Huntsville. Traffic was heavy on the Austin Turnpike. And from the 1840s on, Houston businessmen were bent on building railroads. In 1848, Paul Bremond became president of the Galveston, Houston and Red River Railroad to link Houston and Galveston with North Texas—the first railroad incorporated in the state.

Bremond's early career paralleled that of his son-in-law and friend, William Marsh Rice. Born in New York state, the son of a French doctor, Bremond at sixteen went into business for himself in Philadelphia and within six years had built up a nice fortune. Ruined in the panic of 1837, he migrated to Galveston with his wife and two children. He shipped his furniture and merchandise ahead, and, like Rice, lost everything when the brig carrying his cargo sank within sight of Galveston Island. In 1842, he moved to Houston, where he soon prospered as a merchant.

He was an interesting man, a visionary. He believed in spiritualism and founded a society for its study in Houston. He believed that spirit advisors guided his railroad projects, spurring him to overcome setbacks. "Seemingly he was being advised by the best railroad talent in purgatory," Dr. Andrew Forest Muir wrote, "for not only did he actually build a railroad but indeed he built on a shoestring one of the most valuable railroad properties in the United States."

On January 1, 1853, Bremond broke ground for his thirty-million-dollar project and renamed it the Houston and Texas Central Railway. Though his stockholders were Houston merchants and businessmen who would ultimately become wealthy, none of them had yet amassed the kind of fortune to underwrite such ventures. Bremond therefore began with very little money, was often unable to pay his workers, and fin-

ished in a triumph of persuasion and determination over financial reality. He ultimately paid off every contractor and worker who had trusted him.

Meanwhile, Gen. Sidney Sherman formed the Buffalo Bayou, Brazos and Colorado Railway Company in 1851 to build a line from Harrisburg to the Brazos River. The railroad line was the first to be completed in Texas. Pulled by the wood-burning *General Sherman,* the first train arrived at Stafford's Point from Harrisburg in August, 1853. This was the start of an era that would see Houston become a major American rail center by 1900.

While rail companies and their rails proliferated, teams of oxen were hauling the cotton bales from plantations to Houston. During 1854, thirty-eight thousand bales were brought to town. In May, 1855, the *Houston Telegraph* reported that "not less than four thousand bales of cotton had arrived in this city in the last two weeks on ox-wagons, giving employment to 4,690 yoke of oxen and 670 wagons and drivers."

The streets were congested. In addition to the routine traffic of saddle horses, carriages, gigs, mule wagons, and stagecoaches, there were these 9,380 oxen—seven yoke hitched to each long dray—plodding through a town that lay largely between Texas Avenue and the bayou, though the boundary had been moved out to Lamar Avenue. In fact, Houston had twice as many oxen as people using its streets.

Still unpaved, the wide streets became impassable in heavy rains or bayou floods. Cotton, hides, corn, and farm produce coming in from the north had to cross Buffalo Bayou on the low bridge that led to Louisiana Street. To get their freight up to Market Square, the ox teams had to pull the heavy drays up a steep, sandy bank. It was such a hard pull that teamsters often had to hitch two teams to one dray.

Then, of course, there were the camels. In 1853, U.S. Secretary of War Jefferson Davis proposed trying out camels as beasts of burden in desert warfare. It took him two years to persuade Congress to spend thirty thousand dollars to finance the tests. But in due course, a joint army-navy commission brought seventy-five camels to Indianola by a sailing vessel with a specially rigged camel deck. Over a period of months, the camels were put to the test. Six camels, it was found, could carry as much as twelve horses could haul in wagons and in almost half the time. They could travel muddy roads on which no wagon would move. And they could climb mountain trails where no wagon could go. In his report to Washington, Lieutenant Colonel Robert E. Lee, commandant of the Department of Texas, officially commended "the endurance, docility and sagacity of the camel."

The project stirred the imagination of an Englishwoman—although the "endurance, docility and sagacity" of the camel may have had little to do with it. In 1858, to the puzzle of everyone, and prompting the suspicions of quite a few, she brought into Galveston a shipload of camels. She then asked about a place to pasture them until they could be sold. Francis Lubbock agreed to take care of her herd on his Sims Bayou plantation (the four-hundred-acre spread six miles from Houston that he had bought for seventy-five cents an acre). A chartered steamboat landed some forty camels at the mouth of the bayou. Long after, Lubbock wrote: "On finding themselves once more on solid ground, they showed their high spirits by jumping, rearing and frisking about like sheep."

Governor Lubbock's brother-in-law, Jules Baron, and Sam W. Allen, whose ranch adjoined Lubbock's, watched the unloading. Baron, a newcomer from Louisiana, said that surely nobody could lasso one of those huge beasts. Sam Allen bet ten dollars that *he* could. Mounting his horse, he swung a loop over a large camel and brought it to the ground. Lubbock commented that "Baron had not learned that Texans generally accomplish what they undertake."

The slave trade had been outlawed in 1808, but the illegal importation of Africans continued for another fifty years. Lubbock suspected that the Englishwoman was a "blackbirder," using camels as a cover for bootlegging slaves into Texas. This was the gossip all along the Gulf Coast from Galveston to Indianola. However, Lubbock could find no evidence to support his suspicions.

Arab drivers tended to the camels. Adele Looscan and others of Lubbock's friends sometimes came out to ride one especially docile beast. From time to time, the Arabs rode their camels into downtown Houston. There they towered over the horses, carriages, gigs, mule wagons, stagecoaches, and the thousands of oxen and their drays. Houston was having its first traffic jam.

This was due more to the smallness of the town plan than to the largeness of the population. Galveston was the new state's biggest city with slightly more than five thousand people, followed by San Antonio and Houston with more than four thousand each. Austin still numbered its people in the hundreds. And in 1856, Dallas was founded.

Chapter Thirteen

Antebellum

THOUGH THE NORTH and the South were tensing for war, Houston strode through the 1850s with vigor. Its men and its products were going to the far corners of the earth on adventure or business.

As a midshipman at the U.S. Naval Academy, Edwin Fairfax Gray had cruised to the East Indies and Montevideo, as well as along the West Coast of Mexico and California. On graduation at twenty-three, he was ordered to report to Macao or Hong Kong to join the East India Squadron in China and was given five hundred dollars on which to get there. On the way, he stopped in London, visited a cotton-spinning mill in Manchester, and attended services at the Chester Cathedral; in April, 1853, he reported for duty in Shanghai.

His letters home to Houston refer to Nankin, Shanghai, and Hong Kong, and to the civil war in China. The blond, blue-eyed Houstonian was about to take part in one of the historic events of the century. He was attached to Commodore Matthew C. Perry, commander in chief of the Naval Forces of the United States in the East India, China, and Japan seas.

On July 2, 1853, Gray wrote home: "We got underway this morning for Japan. The TREMENDOUS expedition to JAPAN HAS STARTED!" He then added wryly, "Consisting, however,—instead of an overwhelming force—of simply two steamers and two sloops of war." The two steamers towed the two sloops to Japan.

Commodore Perry anchored his squadron of four ships in lower Tokyo Bay. On July 4, Gray wrote: "The commander amused himself and the squadron. . . . At noon we fired a salute of 17 guns, in commemoration of the day. This squadron has been engaged all day in exercising the crews with small guns, and the incessant reports of pistols, muskets and carbines have, I find, given me a severe headache."

Every day, to the annoyance of Passed Midshipman Gray, the commodore put his crew through a great show of gun drills and firing, as though flexing the squadron muscles for a foray. After making his point, Perry negotiated a treaty with the Tokugawa shogunate that permitted American ships to use two Japanese ports. This was the expedition that opened Japan to the trade of the western world after two centuries of isolation.[1]

Meanwhile, the Houston and Galveston Navigation Company plied steamboats up and down the bayou. The brig *William Marsh Rice,* named for its owner, sailed regularly to Boston. Among other things, it fetched ice from New England for the lemonade, chilled wines, juleps, and ice cream that were so delightful in Houston summers. With his brother Frederick as full partner, Rice had offices in a three-story building. He dealt in land and had become a developer. In 1859, Rice, Cornelius Ennis, Abraham Groesbeeck, and other businessmen incorporated the Houston Cotton Compress Company. This move gave them control of cotton from the plantations to the cotton exchanges abroad.

Harris County was the leading exporter

of Texas cattle because of its closeness to the trade routes and markets of the United States.[2] In addition to cattle raised in Harris County, West Texas herds were often driven to Houston for shipment to New Orleans by steamboat. The *Times Picayune* of September 29, 1851, reported that "the business of sending live stock, in the shape of beeves, from Texas to this city has become an item of importance. . . . Every steamer brings its cargo of the article. . . ."

Samuel W. Allen was king of the cattle trade.[3] His wife had inherited the 350 acres of the Ezekiel Thomas ranch on the north side of the bayou. Mr. Allen added to it tremendous tracts of land on the south side, including 1,300 acres that he bought from his friend Francis Lubbock. Some years later, with his son, Samuel E. Allen, he would add another 10,000 acres in Brazoria County. At one time his ranch holdings were the largest in the state.[4]

Allen shipped his cattle by shallow-draft, side-wheel steamer to Galveston for transfer to larger ships. He deplored this system because in rough weather the cattle often arrived in New Orleans bruised and scuffed. But Houston was fulfilling the promise of John Kirby Allen that it would become the gateway for all of Texas to the markets and trade routes of the world.

The Turnverein, Houston's first German society, was organized on January 14, 1854. Ten men met "in Gable's house" to form a society "where each feels as a brother to the other and lives for him and with him as a brother." The charter members were T. Heitmann, F. Reimann, a Mr. Marschall, Louis Pless, John F. Thorade, Robert Voight, E. B. H. Schneider, August Sabath, E. Scheurer, and L. Scheihagen.

The great wave of German immigration that had begun in 1844 was tapering off, but the stream of Europeans continued. Large numbers of Irish came in the late 1840s and early 1850s. In June, 1855, a shipload of Polish, Bohemian, and Swiss immigrants arrived, and in November, the *Semi-Weekly Telegraph* reported the arrival of seven hun-dred Poles, "men, women and children, all dressed in their national costumes." Among them they added Polish, French, German, and Czech to the city's conversation.

Despite frequent lapses into inactivity, the Houston Lyceum could trace its ancestry back to the Houston Franklin Debating Society of 1837. For men only, it reorganized for a fresh start in May, 1854, to present debates, lectures, and even musicales. Beginning in 1855, its weekly public debates were on such subjects as: *Are women capable of the same mental improvement as men?* And, *Is the light literature of the present day beneficial to the mind?* And, *Was the conspiracy of Brutus against Caesar justifiable?* There must have been a prankster on the program committee for the group debated the question *Ought bachelors over thirty years of age be taxed for the support of old maids?*

Along the way, the Houston Lyceum amassed and managed to keep together a library for use of members only. This was the nucleus of the Houston Public Library.

In 1855, Peter Gray was elected district judge, becoming, in the words of Chief Justice Oran Roberts, "the very best district judge upon the Texas bench." And B. A. Shepherd became the first man in Texas to engage exclusively in the banking business.

Houston continued to attract men of outstanding qualities. John T. Brady was a native of Maryland with a college and legal education that was above average for the times. He was President Buchanan's district attorney for the Territory of Kansas when he became interested in Texas and moved to Houston, arriving in 1856. He made his home on the bayou near Harrisburg and married Gen. Sidney Sherman's daughter, Lennie.[5] From the start he was interested in deepening the channel and bringing big ships to the port of Houston.

In 1856, Postmaster O. L. Cochran opened his insurance agency, the first in Texas. It celebrated its centennial in 1956 as the oldest firm in Houston. T. W. House, Cornelius Ennis, and W. J. Hutchins were operating banks of their own in connection with their cotton and mercantile transactions. S. M. McAshan went to work for the House Bank, thereby becoming the first of a long line of bankers in the family.[6]

With Houston now twenty years old, streets were still unpaved, but covered sidewalks sheltered shoppers from rain or summer sun.

Newspapers references show that from the start the city tried to maintain a hospital. In 1839, the *Morning Star* printed a notice that the City Hospital could accept no patient who had not lived in Houston at least six months. The *Weekly Telegraph* of July 30, 1856, carried the report of Henry Vanderlinden, chief clerk of the Charity Hospital. Between 1847 and 1856, he had recorded 136,985 admissions – of which 121,138 were foreigners – and 21,080 deaths. The hospital income for the period was sixty-six thousand dollars. That amounts to less than fifty cents per patient.

On March 11, 1857 physicians formed the Houston Medical Association. The founders were Dr. William H. Howard, Dr. Greenville Dowell, Dr. R. H. Boxley, Dr. H. W. Waters, and Dr. J. S. Duval, who was elected first president.

A year later the city paid twenty-five hundred dollars for fifteen acres and "good buildings" for use as a municipal hospital. In 1861, the Houston Medical College offered to maintain a charity hospital with only moderate cost to the city, if the property were given to the college. The contract was signed, but with the coming of the Civil War, the hospital would be used chiefly for soldiers.

With all its progress, Houston continued to be short on schools. Despite the historic legislation by which the Republic had established the principle of state aid to public schools, Houston still had only private schools and not enough of them. Academies and seminaries opened, often with highly educated professors who were graduates of East Coast and European universities. Few lasted more than a term or two, none was

housed in a building designed for the purpose.

In 1844, Professor Henry F. Gillette had opened his Houston Academy in the Telegraph Building at Main and Preston. He offered reading, writing, orthography, arithmetic, grammar, geography, Latin, Greek, mathematics, science, and the higher branches of English education, at fees ranging from two to four dollars a course. He promised to teach all branches necessary to enter any college in the United States. But this quite remarkable institution closed two years later when Gillette moved to Independence.

Several Houston leaders, even men who were young and childless, met often and worked hard to provide public education in Houston – Peter W. Gray, William Marsh Rice, the Rev. Charles Gillette, and the Rev. C. Richardson among them. They made little headway.

A second Houston Academy was chartered on August 29, 1852. Among its incorporators were Rice, Gray, Cornelius Ennis, and T. W. House, who was in on every project likely to benefit the city. It opened in 1853. The Turnverein started a gymnastic school for girls and boys on the Verein tenet that "only in a healthy body dwells a healthy soul."

At the end of 1858, the Houston Academy moved into a new two-story brick building that cost twenty thousand dollars and accommodated four hundred students. It had separate classrooms for boys and girls, thereby housing the Houston Male Academy and the Houston Female Academy. Dr. Ashbel Smith was superintendent. In addition to the usual academic subjects, the faculty of five teachers taught fencing, painting, gymnastics, and dancing. With the Civil War, the building would become a military hospital for the duration, and the school's six-hundred-volume library would be used by wounded soldiers.

The iron horse, however primitive, was replacing the oxteams. It could pull nineteen wagons carrying an average of thirty-two bales each; the seven yoke of oxen did well to haul from three to ten bales on one long dray. The *Tri-Weekly Telegraph* reported in October, 1858, that "the largest train that ever came into Houston with cotton was on Friday. There were nineteen cars with 522 bales."

Anson Jones, last president of the Republic of Texas, committed suicide in the Capitol Hotel on January 11, 1858, and in December, Mirabeau B. Lamar died of apoplexy at his home near Houston. But Sam Houston, having served his term as senator, left Washington and made a successful run for governor. He hoped to throw his influence against the rising threat of secession. He brought as a present to his beloved Margaret a set of hoops, which were increasingly fashionable as skirts grew more and more voluminous.

Houstonians voted overwhelmingly for their old hero, but the city was increasingly split on the issue of secession. Harriet Beecher Stowe's *Uncle Tom's Cabin,* first printed in 1852, had become a nationwide best seller. A Lyceum debate on secession stirred such interest that it had to be repeated for five nights. In 1860, more than half the people of Houston were foreign born. Many others were from New York and New England. This was not the solid Anglo-Southern society of Charleston or Montgomery or Richmond. Debates and public meetings grew stormy.

The Episcopalians' first small brick church, which faced Fannin Street, had been outgrown before it was completed. In 1859, with Benjamin Botts as chairman of the building committee and Edwin Fairfax Gray as architect, they laid the cornerstone of a new building to face Texas Avenue. As contractors were surveying the lot, Joe Young from near Liberty was driving a herd of cattle down Texas Avenue.

"What are you doing?" he asked. "Building a church," they replied. Young roped a steer and handed the surveyor the rope, saying, "Let me make the first contribution." The incident left its mark in the steer's head on the seal of the Episcopal Diocese of Texas. Almost a century later, the Rt. Rev. James DeWolfe, bishop of Long Island, had that steer's head engraved on his episcopal ring, a reminder of his years as rector of Christ Church, Houston.

In 1859, William Escrage Kendall, a lawyer in Houston and Richmond, closed his practice and left for a year of travel in Europe, the Holy Land, Egypt, and Turkey. He would return to serve the Confederacy, marry General Sherman's daughter Belle, and found a family line in Houston.

Texas travelers had already made a reputation. Dr. William Tucker Dickinson Dalzell, a medical doctor and Episcopal priest, was a popular Houstonian in the 1850s. On his way east to raise money to build the new Christ Church, he wrote to the Houston *Tri-Weekly Telegraph:* "At the St. Charles, New Orleans, I found that self-interest, if nothing more, secured me every attention and comfort. Less than two years ago I had spent a few days of the greatest discomfort at this same hotel. But then I was registered as a Philadelphian, where now I was a Texian. . . . Texas travel, as it is now called, having become of such consequence and so remunerative . . . the proprietors are anxious to attract it to their house."

The year 1860 was the richest year commercially that Houston had ever had. Cotton was flowing in so massively on new railroad lines that it overflowed the warehouses and had to be stacked up on the sidewalks. Part of Main Street had been covered with shell. Although it, too, raised dust in dry weather and grew mushy in rains, the pale gray oyster shells weren't quite so sticky as the basic black gumbo on which Houston stands.

The Houston and Central Texas Railway shops opened. In early January, 1860, the Texas Telegraph Company began service to Galveston. With a Galveston dateline, its first formal news dispatch announced "BY

TELEGRAPH! Special Dispatch to the *Houston Telegraph*. . . . The first train over the Galveston and Houston road is expected to leave this city next Monday morning."

Coming from Liverpool, Rabbi Samuel Raphael, his wife, and their six children reached Houston in April, 1860, after a ten-week voyage on a full-rigged ship.[7] He took over Congregation Beth Israel, which was still without a temple.

The San Jacinto Yacht Club held its first regatta on April 12, 1860, on a forty-mile course between Lynchburg and Clopper's Point. A year later, as though oblivious to the storm of secession, the Houston Base Ball Club was organized at a meeting held over J. H. Evans's store. Its president was Frederick Allyn Rice.

In 1860, a young Irishman named Dick Dowling announced that he had chartered a bank at the corner of Main Street and Congress Avenue "for the purpose of dealing in the exchange of liquors for gold, silver and bank notes." The bank served meals and became a center for Houston's large numbers of Irish Catholics.[8]

A newspaperman climbed four stories up to the roof of the unfinished Hutchins House at Travis Street and Franklin Avenue to report: "In every direction new houses appear. Away out on the prairie to the south and west . . . the city is spreading street by street, until it is impossible to find the landmarks as they were even three or four years ago, while nearby stately brick stores are rising on every block."

In 1860, Houston's city limit on the southwest was Lamar Avenue.

Chapter Fourteen

War

IN MARCH, 1861, Texas voted to secede. The swift swing to the new Confederacy, the fall of Fort Sumter, and the start of the Civil War came in a rush that surprised Houston. Despite Gov. Sam Houston's staunch opposition to secession, Texas had been caught up in the rapids that carried it with the South and out of the union it had joined only fifteen years before.

It was an agonizing time. Lt. Col. Robert E. Lee of the U.S. Second Cavalry was in San Antonio when he made his fateful decision to join the armies of Virginia. Jefferson Davis, his former chief, so recently Secretary of War of the United States, was on his way to the presidency of the new Confederate States of America. In Houston, David Rice, brother of William Marsh Rice, set forth as an officer in Hood's Brigade. But his son William, who had been sent by his Uncle William to the best New England prep schools, enlisted in the Thirty-Seventh Massachusetts Volunteers.

As governor-elect, Francis Lubbock traveled to Richmond to offer his support to President Davis. He believed that only by quick, concerted action could the Confederacy prevail. Returning to Texas, he issued a proclamation calling on every able-bodied Texan to enlist. The Richmond government asked for twenty companies of infantry. Thirty-two companies answered the call. Richmond asked for eight thousand men from Texas; it got thousands more—Albert Sidney Johnston among them. An honor graduate of West Point, Johnston had left the United States upon the death of his young wife. He had fought in the battle of San Jacinto, was given command of the Texas army, and was made secretary of war by President Houston. Now, three decades later, and again answering the call of a new nation, he was named Confederate commander in the West.

"Texas supplied 135 general officers and colonels to the South, including two professionals of superior talent, John B. Hood and Albert Sidney Johnston," T. R. Fehrenbach wrote in his history *Lone Star.* "Hood became a temporary full general in 1864, while Johnston's tragic death at Shiloh is believed by some historians to have markedly affected the outcome of the war."

When the war began, more than half of the people of Houston were foreign born.[1] But Houstonians of all races and backgrounds were united by the call to arms—as they would be again in 1917 and 1941. Houston men drained out into the Confederate army on a swift and compelling tide.

Capt. Benjamin A. Bott's Bayou City Guards were posted for service in Virginia. More than one hundred strong, they joined Hood's Brigade and moved immediately into frontline warfare.

Capt. William Gentry's Volunteers, Capt. Ashbel Smith's Bayland Guards, Capt. Hal Runnell's Van Dorn Infantry, Capt. Edwin Fairfax Gray's Sumter Guards, Capt. J. H. Manley's Houston Artillery, Capt. F. Odlum's Home Guard, Capt. Peter W. Gray's Texas Grays, Capt. D. McGregor's Home Guards, and Capt. A. T. Morse's Houston Cavalry were quickly ready for duty. By

April, five hundred Houston men—or one Houstonian in every ten—were ready for immediate campaign service.

German Texans of the Hill Country bitterly opposed secession and ultimately faced a fratricidal war with angry Confederate forces, but Houstonians born in the Northeast, or in Europe, including the Germans, were as committed to their new nation as any Southerner. In the seven years since its founding, the Turnverein had enlisted some one hundred members, and almost to a man they volunteered to do battle for their adopted country.

Meanwhile, units from other parts of Texas were passing through Houston. Six companies from Camp Van Dorn, near Harrisburg, camped at the Houston depot of the Texas and New Orleans Railroad on the night of August 20. Early next morning, bands played and crowds cheered, as two trains pulled out carrying the Texans to the Neches River. There they would go by riverboat to Niblett's Bluff on the Sabine.

One soldier, N. A. Davis, described the trip: "The road being new, it was exceedingly rough. Sometimes we made about 20 miles to the hour and again we went a little minus nothing. For we would have to back down and take a new start. We were several times swamped in the grass, and one time, the boys said, we were bogged down in the cockleburrs."

Despite their single-minded response, Houstonians soon found themselves answering a variety of calls to duty. Peter Gray, for example, formed and captained the Texas Grays, was elected to the House of the Confederate Congress and served for as long as it endured, volunteered as an aide to Gen. John B. Magruder for the New Year's battle of 1863 in Galveston, and was appointed fiscal agent of the Trans-Mississippi Department in 1864 by President Davis. On both sides, armies of the Civil War were more casually organized than those of the twentieth century. Several of Houston's medical doctors served as company commanders first, as physicians second.[2]

Frank Terry and Tom Lubbock, who had fought at Manassas, came home to recruit a regiment of rangers for service in Virginia. Response was swift. When Terry's Texas Rangers arrived in Houston, each of the 104 men was armed with a double-barreled shotgun, a six-shooter, and a two-edged knife, twenty-four inches long and weighing three pounds. It was called a Texas toothpick. The Rangers lent new excitement to Houston's sedate traffic, riding their cow ponies like Cossacks, mounting and dismounting on the run, picking articles off the ground at full gallop. It was reported that Capt. J. C. Walker, commander of the regiment's Harris County company, was riding up Main Street in orderly fashion when, spurring his horse into a gallop, he jumped over an ox team. All of these shenanigans were in the first heady days of answering the challenge.

The oddest recruit of the period volunteered to the Union army in 1861. Dressed as a man, Sarah Emma Seelye walked from her home in La Porte to Houston to make her way to the Union lines. As Frank Thompson, she served in the Second Michigan Infantry for two years as soldier, scout, and spy. Stricken with malaria, denied a furlough, she so feared detection that she deserted. Later, as a woman, she served as a nurse.[3]

Black Houstonians, free and slave, shouldered the responsibilities of keeping the city afloat. Until this time, the fire department had been an elite organization of influential young men—a social club with a serious purpose. At the company's last meeting in May, 1861, E. B. Bremond was foreman, David K. Rice treasurer, and J. C. Baldwin president.

"Captain David Rice . . . was one of the handsomest men to be found anywhere," Dr. S. O. Young wrote in *True Stories of Old Houston*. "He had the complexion of a girl . . . but he was one of the most gallant soldiers in Lee's Army." Houston's firemen went off to war, many never to return. Houston blacks took over the fire fighting. They, too, felt the camaraderie of an elite club.

Houston had a hook and ladder outfit and two fire machines. It took ten to fifteen men on each side of the machines to pump water. "The Negroes made splendid firemen and it was a pleasure to watch them at a fire," Dr. Young wrote. "They threw their whole souls into the work and seemed never to grow weary, although it was the hardest kind of work and frequently lasted for two or three hours without stop or rest." At one fire where four or five houses were ablaze, he remembered "the Negroes fighting the fire like demons, and singing like angels. . . . John Cook, better known to everyone as Big John because of his great size, was choir leader. He would sing a verse alone and then the others would take up the refrain. . . ."

Life throughout the city changed abruptly. Houston was far from the major battles east of the Mississippi and was protected by long expanses of desert on the west and forest on the north and east, but it was vulnerable from the coast. In July, 1861, the Gulf Coast came under blockade. Railroad building stopped and exports thinned to a trickle. The flow through Houston of the imported goods on which Texas had always depended was stringently cut. Dr. W. H. Eliot, druggist, fitted up machinery to make printer's ink, which was no longer available from the States. Houstonians experimented with ground dried okra or crisp-baked sweet potatoes for coffee. They made their own candles out of tallow. They used castor oil in their lamps and wrapping paper for stationery.

In December, 1861, a partial evacuation of Galveston began. Confederate batteries were removed from the beach and patients from the Galveston Hospital were brought up to rented buildings in Houston. The December 11 issue of the *Galveston News* was printed on brown wrapping paper on the *Telegraph's* press.

The Confederacy leased John Kennedy's Trading Post for use as an ordnance department.[4] In a singularly courteous tone, the ordnance officer ordered the people of Harris County to send him "all arms of every kind and description which can be conve-

niently spared." The building became an arsenal, filled with cannons, small arms, bombs, and ammunition, and was kept under heavy guard day and night.

In May, with the occupation of New Orleans, the fall of Galveston became imminent. The islanders began to flee to the mainland, coming "in boats loaded to the gunwales, in wagons filled with household goods . . . and in trains with passengers riding on top of the coaches." Houston, already crowded with soldiers, opened its doors. On October 9, William B. Renshawm, commander of the Union forces, demanded the surrender of Galveston and took the island. He had captured an almost empty city. Only the nuns of the Ursuline Convent stayed on, preparing their quarters to serve as a hospital for sick and wounded soldiers of either side.

Because Galveston was a bigger city than Houston, the evacuation came close to doubling Houston's population. The great influx of refugees strained the city's fabric. Homes, boarding houses, and hotels were filled to capacity, empty stores and warehouses were used for housing and hospital beds, and the churches overflowed.

The First Presbyterian Church, which had been dedicated in 1842 and completed in 1847, was built of brick and elegantly paneled. Its communion service had been a gift of Charlotte Baldwin Allen, the congregation's continuing benefactor. But on October 25, 1862, when the neighboring bakery caught fire, so did the church and not all the efforts of the volunteer firemen could save it.

Houston's first brick church, the First Methodist Church, had stood on Texas Avenue between Travis and Milam for almost twenty years. But one Sunday morning not long after the worshipers had filed out, the church fell down—to lie in ruins until after the war. The congregation was granted use of the African Methodist Church on the same lot.

Keziah Payne, who was the Florence Nightingale of Houston in her willingness to nurse the sick and the dying, was quietly married in 1862 to Adolphe de Pelchin. Their wedding was at Christ Church, where she served as organist. De Pelchin was a charming young Belgian musician, a widower with a child whom Keziah loved. The marriage brought her brief happiness, much unhappiness, and soon ended in separation. But her husband's name would endure in the children's home she founded years later.

With imports blockaded, prices rose: flour ten dollars a sack, tea five to six dollars a pound, molasses twenty dollars a barrel. But homegrown bacon and butter were twenty cents a pound, eggs twenty-five cents a dozen, prairie beef still cheap. Episcopal Bishop Alexander Gregg spoke out sternly against profiteering, against charging such extortionate prices for hard-to-get essentials that only the rich could afford shoes. He had good reason: some merchants asked one hundred dollars for a pair of boots, thirty dollars for a pair of garters. At midsummer, William and John T. Brady sailed two ships through the blockade, bringing munitions and clothing to Houston. But for the greater part of four years, Houston homes, hotels, and restaurants were lighted at night by homemade candles.

The enemy was literally at Houston's gate. Christmas of 1862 was darkened by grim forebodings.

Having taken New Orleans and Galveston, Union forces were driving to capture all the ports along the Gulf. In Houston, Lt. Gen. Bankhead Magruder decided to retake Galveston. The *Neptune* and the *Bayou City*, which had given so many peacetime trips to Houstonians, were converted into gunboats with cotton bales around their gunwales and decks. Marching down Main Street to the steamboat landing, three hundred Confederate soldiers filed aboard behind the bales. Among them were Captain Peter Gray and Lieutenant Dick Dowling.

The "cottonclads" headed down the bayou, supported by two tenders loaded with riflemen. Magruder concentrated a land force at Virginia Point, just opposite Galves-

ton Island. In the hours of darkness on December 31, his troops waded across into the city and set up their artillery in the marketplace. At dawn on New Year's Day, Magruder launched a joint assault by land and by sea. His soldiers attacked and drove the Union garrison to the north end of the island. Meanwhile, Confederate troops advanced against the wharf under cover of artillery from the marketplace. The cottonclads faced the flotilla of four Union ships in the harbor—a steamer, a brig, a gunboat, and a transport.

Union gunfire sank the *Neptune*, but the *Bayou City* ran in close, while the soldiers aboard riddled the Union vessels with rifle fire. When all her officers were killed, the U.S.S. *Harriet Lane* surrendered. The Union brig ran aground and was scuttled by her crew. The gunboat and transport escaped to the Gulf. The Union garrison on the island surrendered. It had lost 50 soldiers. Magruder had 26 dead, 117 wounded. In command of guns on the waterfront, nineteen-year-old Lt. Sidney Sherman, Jr., was wounded by grapeshot from a gunboat and died in the Ursuline Convent a few hours later.

The *Bayou City* steamed back to Houston flying a bat of cotton above the *Harriet Lane*'s ensign at her masthead, and was greeted by the whistles of the "Magruder Fleet," a flotilla of cottonclad bayou boats. General Magruder brought more than 350 prisoners of war back to Houston and earned a commendation from Pres. Jefferson Davis in Montgomery. Houston celebrated New Year's Day of 1863 with the elation of victory and soon after gave a Main Street parade and a ball at Perkins' Hall in honor of the general and his staff.

One encounter in the Battle of Galveston epitomized the tragedy of the War Between the States: When the *Harriet Lane* surrendered, Magruder sent Maj. A. M. Lea of the Engineers Corps to take charge of the ship. On board, he found his son, fatally wounded. Lieutenant Lea was the ship's executive officer. Lieutenant Lea was buried in the Galveston cemetery with military and Masonic honors—the Confederate father reading the Episcopal funeral service over his Union son's grave.

Like women throughout the Confederacy, Houston women were knitting socks, tearing up linen sheets to make bandages, and cutting up carpets to make blankets for soldiers. Margaret Bremond Rice and her friends arranged a benefit concert for Hood's Brigade. William M. Rice and Company gave two hundred dollars toward the purchase of a home for the family of Albert Sidney Johnston, Rice's longtime Houston friend who was killed at Shiloh, and began to give fifty dollars monthly for the relief of soldiers' families.

Slaves were doing all that was possible to keep the plantations, the farms, and the granaries going, but the loss of white manpower to the army was taking its toll on the economy. Wives and children of soldiers were becoming destitute. People gave what they had. "Citizens surrendered their specie, and women donated jewelry to provide foreign exchange for blockade runners," T. H. Fehrenbach wrote in *Lone Star.* "Years of accumulated wealth, of all kinds, was willingly given up to the needs of war. Relief committees were active, collecting food, clothing and money. In Houston alone, $3,000 per week was raised by private subscription by the start of 1863."

The *Tri-Weekly News* on March 14 wrote: "The Taxable Patriotism of our citizens seems to be inexhaustible. Their contributions to every new Concert, Fair or Festival . . . seems to exceed those given at the preceding entertainment."

An air of gaiety pervaded the town. Even during the blockade years, Houston ladies managed to keep up with fashions. Silks rarely slipped through the blockade. But hoop skirts were so popular that Martha Kirk, wife of William Oxsheer, used at least twenty-five yards of hard-earned homespun on one dress with a skirt measuring four and one-half yards around the hem.

Although serious in their fund raising, Houstonians were exhilarated by their sense of war service. They gave some of their most cherished possessions to be sold by lottery. A March 21 sale included two sewing machines, a five-octave melodeon, a guitar, an "elegant white crape shawl," two acres of land near town, a gold watch and chain, a fine table cover, a model of the *Harriet Lane,* and an oil painting. Houston was still a small town of no more than five thousand. These people were drawing from the same pockets and purses with each lottery and sale. They had no outside philanthropists or foundations to call upon. But they were making a game of stripping themselves of their worldly goods and assets for the cause of the Confederacy.

Prices continued to rise as commodities grew more scarce: flour cost fifty dollars for a hundred-pound sack; milk was one dollar a quart, and beef, normally cheap and plentiful, climbed to twenty-five cents a pound. Even at seventy-five cents a pound, salt was scarce. Tea and coffee had disappeared. Rents soared and hotel rooms shot up to five dollars a day.

In February, Houston became the military headquarters for the Confederate District of Texas, New Mexico, and Arizona. To ward off invasion from the bayou, dirt breastworks were thrown up on its north side near the Galveston Railroad depot. They proved too hard to man, and soon became known as Fort Humbug.

Though James Reily had never wanted Texas to join the Union, he had served the United States in shining good faith, first as commander of a Texas regiment during the Mexican War, and later as President Buchanan's ambassador to the tsar in St. Petersburg. But his first loyalty was to his adopted country—Texas. When Texas seceded, he became the colonel in an Arizona brigade. It was sent to Louisiana, where at Bayou Teche on April 14, 1863, "James Reily met his death while at the head of his brigade leading them into battle."

Margaret Bremond Rice, gentle and generous, died in August. She had served her neighbors in epidemics, cared for sick and disabled soldiers from the war, and led the community in relief to women widowed by war.

And, on the evening of August 11, after a long illness, Sam Houston died at his home in Huntsville, murmuring, "Margaret! Texas!" His young wife and Texas had been the enduring loves of his long and colorful life. The city bearing his name mourned him, for as the *Huntsville Item* commented, "With all his faults, they loved him still."

Having lost Galveston at New Year's, the Union forces plotted a new strategy: to land at Sabine Pass, capture Beaumont and Houston, and sweep on to retake Galveston Island. All of this was part of a grander plan whereby Union forces would invade the Texas heartland.

The Davis Guards from Houston, stationed at Fort Griffin, guarded the Texas side of the pass. The company of forty-two men was armed with two old twenty-four pound smoothbores, two thirty-two pounders, and two howitzers. They were under the command of their junior lieutenant, Richard Dowling—who had left his wife and two children, as well as his Bank of Bacchus Saloon in Houston, to serve with his fellow Irishmen of the Davis Guards.

On September 8, 1863, while a landing force of five thousand Union troops waited offshore with escort warships, four Union gunboats bombarded Fort Griffin for an hour and a half. The gunboats then withdrew, apparently expecting surrender from a little garrison that was so clearly outgunned and outmanned. But Dowling held his fire. He let the returning Union warships come within twelve hundred yards, and then under heavy barrage himself directed the fire of his old guns with precision into each Union ship as it came within range. With a hole in its steam drum, the U.S.S. *Sachem* fell out. Shells clipped the tiller rope of the *Clifton,* leaving the gunboat adrift under the continuing barrage. The *Clifton* ran up a white flag. Battered, the rest of the flotilla headed out to sea and back to New Orleans.

Facing an armada and five thousand troops, twenty-five-year-old Dick Dowling and his Houston Irishmen repulsed the attack without losing a man. The United States had lost two ships, one hundred men killed and injured and three hundred and fifty taken as prisoners. After this small, brilliantly fought battle the Union forces made no further major effort to gain control of the Gulf Coast of Texas.

In the diverse fortunes of war, Lawrence Sullivan Ross entered the Confederate army as a private, his brother Peter as a captain. Both were in their twenties. Serving with the Sixth Texas Cavalry, Peter had risen to the rank of lieutenant colonel. When not yet thirty, he was so badly wounded that he was not expected to live. When a telegram came from Confederate States Army headquarters making him a brigadier general, he asked as his dying wish that the commission be given to his younger brother Sullivan.

Sul, meanwhile, had risen in the ranks, earned his commission, and distinguished himself with the Texas Brigade.[5] He was therefore promoted to brigadier general. He served all four years of the war, and later became the first governor to occupy the great capitol building in Austin. Ultimately he became president of Texas A&M University. It is for him that Houston's Sul Ross Street is named.

"And that," said Hugo Neuhaus, "is how Sul Ross became a brigadier general. But Peter lived, after all, and finished out the war as a lieutenant colonel."[6]

The September 3, 1863, issue of the *Weekly Telegraph* was printed on green wrapping paper. Eventually newsprint became so scarce that the publishers resorted to wallpaper.

By December, 1863, Houston had become the nerve center of the Trans-Mississippi Department, with gray-uniformed officers galloping through town on the way to the arsenal or the quartermaster's depot. In January, 1864, Houston began to tear down old warehouses and shacks to get firewood.

For a decade, Augustus C. Allen had served as U.S. consul in Minatitlan, the

Isthmus of Tehuantepec. But when his health began to fail, he went to Washington, D.C., for treatment. Learning of his illness, and despite their long estrangement, his wife Charlotte tried to go to him but was unable to gain passage through the lines. On January 11, 1864, Houston's chief founder died in the Willard Hotel in Washington; he was buried in Greenwood Cemetery, Brooklyn, New York.

Although the war brought tragedy, it also brought adventure and excitement. The blockade that stopped the flow of cloth, shoes, needles, pins, newsprint, and candles into Texas also stopped the flow of cotton to the mills of England and New England. Blockade runners soon found that a fleet of foreign vessels was waiting for them in the Mexican waters off Matamoros. Further, French and British warships patrolled the Gulf of Mexico to challenge any U.S. infringement on freedom of the seas.

Blockade running was a very personal kind of business—not an investment left to hired hands. To be on the scene, T. W. House kept a second house in Galveston. Edward Mandell House, who would become known as Woodrow Wilson's Colonel House, was about six years old at the time, and long after he wrote of going with his father to the beach in the late afternoon to scan the horizon for Union gunboats. If few were visible, or if the weather was right, House would start his ship on her voyage that night.

Though T. W. House served the Confederacy loyally and well, he never had much hope that the Confederate armies could defeat the far larger, better-equipped forces of the Union. He therefore avoided accumulating Confederate currency and added to his gold reserves in England whenever possible. At war's end, he had $300,000 in gold laid away in England.

Frederick Heitmann and his partner H. S. Fox were less fortunate. Born in Germany, Heitmann had come to Houston in 1855 and was in the cotton-forwarding business. Blockade running looked risky but reward-ing. The partners decided to sell all their holdings, buy all the cotton they could, and gamble for the big win. Unfortunately, they saw their fortune sink under fire from Union gunboats.[7]

With the death of his wife at forty-two, William Marsh Rice left his house on Court House Square to be used as a military hospital and went off to Matamoros and Havana. There he was part of the chain of the blockade run, feeding supplies to Houston and the Confederacy when possible, while seeing to his own business interests. Frederick Allyn Rice was stationed in Houston as captain with the local defense forces and thereby able to handle the firm's business.

While blockade runners could smuggle into Houston supplies needed by the Confederate army, there was no way to move them on across the Mississippi to the troops at the front. Confederate soldiers were going hungry in Virginia while five million head of cattle ranged across Texas. Though Texas produced quantities of shoes, uniforms, and rations, Hood's brigade marched without shoes in the Tennessee winter of 1863.

Houston's Bayou City Guards, representing more than a hundred of Houston's families, fought with Hood's Brigade. The Guards took part in twenty-four major engagements, including those at Manassas, Gettysburg, and Chickamauga. Casualty lists show that they paid the price: A. Angel and John Bell were killed at Manassas. Curtis Noble fought at Shiloh, was wounded at Nashville. Sam Bailey, wounded at Manassas and Gettysburg, was killed at Spotsylvania. Robert Campbell was wounded at Manassas, at Chickamauga, and at Darby Town. Thomas P. Bryan was killed at the Battle of the Wilderness. S. Cohn was killed at Gettysburg. The list goes on.

Hood's Brigade was in thirty-eight general engagements and one hundred and sixty skirmishes. Of its 1,027 officers and men, 377 were killed in battle—more than a third.

Terry's Texas Rangers had become one of the most noted cavalry regiments in the

Confederate Army. Mustered in June, 1861, it was out of actual service only twenty-one days in four years of war. "Terry's Rangers were never excelled, in Union eyes, for reckless mobility and heroic dash," Fehrenbach wrote. "Two-thirds of Terry's men were killed, their bones scattered in a hundred sites. Ross's Brigade fought valiantly on both sides of the Mississippi. The graves of the Texan educated elite lay scattered in a grim procession across six states." Of Houston men who fought for the Confederacy, eighty-five are buried in Glenwood Cemetery.

"The one great contribution of Texas to the Southern cause was men," Fehrenbach concluded. "Southerners sacrificed more to a general war than any body of Americans before or since. The losses were enormous: 200,000 soldiers died [total Confederate losses], and a quarter of Texas's most vigorous manpower was killed or incapacitated."

Texas had sent between sixty thousand and seventy thousand men to fight for the Confederacy. But the industrial might of the North was the enemy that gallantry alone could not conquer.

Chapter Fifteen

Les Belles Parisiennes de Houston

Throughout the war, Houston travel abroad continued to an astonishing degree. Well-to-do Houstonians had always tended to send their teen-age children abroad to school. Will Palmer was among the Houston youngsters who were caught in Paris by the war.[1] Instead of yanking these young people home, other Houston men decided to get their wives and daughters out of the current unpleasantness by sending them to Paris, too.

Lt. Col. William J. Hutchins was chief of the Confederate State Cotton Bureau; his task was to ship cotton out by wagons through Mexico and bring in arms and supplies. From Matamoros, he sailed to Liverpool on the brig *St. George*. Mrs. Hutchins and their daughter Ella went with him to London and then on to Paris.

In June, 1864, Frederick Allyn Rice seized the chance to let his beloved stepdaughter, Libbie Randon, go to school in Paris. She traveled with Cornelius Ennis, who was escorting Mrs. Ennis and their six daughters to Europe before returning to the business at hand. It took the Ennis party thirty-two days to get from Houston to Matamoros.

William R. Baker, who had come to Houston from Baldwinsville, New York, in 1837 was a director of the Houston and Texas Central Railway in the prosperous years before the war. Capt. Ludowick Latham owned the biggest furniture store in town. In early 1864, these gentlemen arranged for Mrs. Baker to take her daughter Lucy and young Justina Lathem, both sixteen, to Paris by way of Matamoros and Havana.

They must have left Houston in the pleasant weather of March and reached London in the cold gray days of a late London spring. Tina's first letter, dated only 1864, was sent home from London by a Dr. Davis, "who is now on his way to Texas."[2] Her letters reflect the life enjoyed by the other Houston girls who spent the war years abroad.

"After a very delightful passage across the ocean, we are at last in Europe," she wrote. The voyage had been uncomfortably cold, "caused by our not having any fire on board. We are staying at the Grosvenor Hotel in a very quiet part of the city. I am very much pleased with it, although it has the appearance of a very gloomy city, there is so much fog and smoke in the atmosphere." Mrs. Baker took her charges to see Westminster Abbey, the House of Parliament, the Tower of London, and to the opera and theater.

By May, they were in Paris. "You do not know what a beautiful place it is," Tina wrote her sister Abbie. "I should like you and Lucy to take a peep into the toy stores of Paris and see the exquisite toys of all kinds they have."

For the first year, however, Justina was often homesick. "Tell Ma I do not think she will ever send another child to France, if I am spared to tell my story," she wrote darkly. "We are speaking nothing but French —everything I learn, music and all, is in French. . . . I am studying very hard this year, my dear Father, as it is my last year, for I should never survive to stay here one minute after the session is finished. Deliver me from boarding school of any kind, but particularly *French boarding schools.*" Her day, which ran from 6 A.M. to 9 P.M., was punctuated with prayers, piano practice, literature lessons, brisk walks in the garden however cold the weather, study sessions, and recitation. Tuition was five hundred dollars for ten months.

It is not clear how Captain Latham got hard currency through the blockade to his daughter or for her to Mrs. Baker, but as an experienced seafarer, he undoubtedly had agents around the world. Further, as William Marsh Rice's letters from Matamoros show, there was a steady, if difficult, flow of Houstonians along the route used by blockade runners.

Though many of Tina's letters never reached Houston, those which survived reveal a brisk traffic between Houston and Paris. By 1865 her letters were peppered with names of Houstonians in Europe: "Laura Shepherd is with Mrs. Sellers. . . . Mrs. Hutchins and Ella are still in Paris but expect to leave for Geneva very soon. Mr. Souter is a Baron over here. He wishes to be remembered to his friends in Houston, and expects to return in September."[3] Mrs. Ennis was there with her six daughters and "dear, darling little Libbie. We naturally sympathize with each other, being the only two of the party without our mamas." They were all going to Brighton for a holiday.

At this stage, Tina was still aware of the problems of money in the Confederacy. When smart Parisians went to Dieppe for August in 1865, Mrs. Baker and Mrs. Ennis took the girls to the much less fashionable St. Valery because "we poor Confederates had to seek an economical place." Tina had just turned eighteen.

Though enjoying travel with her friends, Mrs. Baker was worried about Lucy's health and began to insist that her husband come to Paris to escort them home. She had no intention, she said, of undertaking another ocean voyage without his support. His answers were not saved, but nothing suggests that he planned to come. Month after

month, year by year, this debate shuttled across the Atlantic.

Justina and the other Houston girls were enjoying Edinburgh, London, and Paris. She and the Bakers, Mrs. McCravens and Emma, were invited to Sir William Nichols's castle in Scotland, but Mrs. Van Alstyne and Maria were not. The reason: Sir William's son had courted Maria, only to be snubbed, and Sir William was unforgiving. Mrs. Van Alstyne shared his regrets, but Maria was adamant.[4]

"A few days before we left the castle we were invited by one of Sir William's friends, the Earl of Kinnoule, to spend the day at his Castle in Perthshire. . . . The Castle and grounds are lovely though I do not think there is anything that can surpass Murthly. We were elegantly entertained by the Lords and Ladies, though I was particularly pleased with the eldest son, Lord Dupplin, a charming young gentleman."

As Tina turned eighteen, she began reminding her father that he had always promised her a proper wardrobe when she was old enough "to dress." In January, 1866, Tina wrote him firmly: "It is impossible for me to remain here any longer than next August . . . for if I have to come without another change of clothes to my back, except the ones I have on, I am *coming*. It is utterly out of the question to think of keeping me another year. You do not realize, Pa, that you have a daughter in her 19th year, and that is old enough to stop school."

She needed the money no later than July, she explained. "I am now nearly old enough to dress. I think I can manage to get a wardrobe that would answer for a small place like Houston with $1,000.00 but I can make use of as much more as you seem disposed to send me, my dear Father."[5]

In June, 1866, Tina wrote, "Lucy has been very very ill with inflammatory rheumatism, not able to move. It commenced in one foot and two days after appeared in the other, from that it went up her side to her heart. The Doctor ordered a fly blister immediately to be put on her left side, and that was all that succeeded in relieving her. She is much better now."

This strengthened Mrs. Baker's determination not to embark without her husband's company. "Mrs. B. says you must repeat to Mr. B. when you see him, for fear her letter may not reach its destination, and she wants him to hurry up and come. We are looking for him certainly in August."

In July the plaint continued: "When does Mr. Baker expect to leave for Europe? Very soon, I hope, as Mrs. B. says she will never return without him. She says . . . if he expects her to return by not keeping her well supplied with money, he is very much mistaken, as there are plenty of poor houses in Europe." So far as these letters reveal, Mr. Baker never did go to Europe, Mrs. Baker did come home, and Lucy lived to become – for a short few years – a happy wife and mother.

In January, 1867, the Houston girls watched the throngs of ice skaters in the Bois de Boulogne, including Napoleon III and the Empress Eugenie. "A more beautiful sight a person need not want to see than the Bois de Boulogne in snow. . . . The Emperor skates very well, but the Empress was obliged to have assistance. She looked very prettily dressed in a walking dress of black velvet, and elegant furs."

They were looking forward to a ball at the Tuileries, given by the Emperor and Empress, and they went to "a grand party at General Dix's – the United States minister. Not *mine,* however," wrote Tina, still an unreconstructed Confederate. "The majority there were Yankees – the General, his wife and daughter were exceedingly agreeable and polite to us, knowing that we were Southerners."

And then, as daughters feel free to do, she added, "Now Ma, you must not think this vanity, when I assure you that the three little Texas girls Lucy, Emma and Tina, carried the evening at General Dix's. . . . We took our leave about one o'clock after many cordial invitations to attend the Reception *every* Saturday evening." But the stay in Paris was beginning to wind down. In January,

1867, Tina wrote, "Mrs. Hutchins and Ella left for Texas last Tuesday."

On April 1, Tina wrote to her sister Abbey about the opening of the Universal Exhibition. The Houston girls saw the grand entrance of the Emperor and Empress in their four carriages and four. "The Empress was dressed in a purple satin robe with a long train and velvet bonnet to match. She wore a black satin cloak with velvet trimming. Nothing could have been a greater success." But – "Tell Pa I am waiting patiently to hear from him about money matters."

Finally, on April 2, 1867, "Give thousands of love to Ma and Pa, Lucy and little brother. I am so happy at the thought of being with you all once more *so soon,* that I can hardly contain myself. We leave the 18th of May on the *Scotia.* Good-bye. Affectionately, your Sister, Tina." Justina Lathem was sailing home to Houston after more than three years in Paris.

With the war over, T. W. House and his wife decided to go home to England for a visit, chiefly to her family in Bath. They sailed on the *Laura,* which crossed the Atlantic using both steam and sail, and took with them George, James, and young Edward. The boys spent six months in school in Bath. They returned by Halifax and Boston, and the boys drove their mother to distraction by swarming over the ship and into the riggings.

At the war's end, Mrs. John Dickinson also decided to go abroad. She had never met her husband's family in Dundee, Scotland. Taking their several children with her, including Ella, Nannie, and small John, she went off for a year of touring Europe and England, having French and dancing lessons for the children, and visiting her in-laws in Scotland. Her Houston friends and relations were disapproving. Not because she was leaving her husband for a year – he was beautifully tended to by her mother, Mrs. John D. Andrews, who lived across the street at 411 Austin. Rather, they were shocked because to make the extended tour, she had "dipped into her principal."

Chapter Sixteen

Defeat

THE War Between the States, which ended so decisively on April 9 at Appomattox, petered out in disappointment and bitterness west of the Mississippi. In May, 1865, General Magruder and Gov. Pendleton Murrah sent Col. Ashbel Smith and W. P. Ballinger to New Orleans in a futile attempt to negotiate "an honorable peace" between Texas and the United States. Gen. Edmund Kirby-Smith arrived in Houston, stormed at all available soldiers for not joining him in a continued war minus the rest of the Confederacy, and angrily notified the Federal authorities that the Trans-Mississippi Department was open for occupation. On June 2, aboard the U.S.S. *Fort Jackson,* he and General Magruder met Brig. Gen. E. J. Davis and formally surrendered Texas to the Union. Under Reconstruction, Davis would become governor of the state.

Meanwhile, Confederate soldiers were coming home, their uniforms ragged, their hair unkempt. Many of them went to the quartermaster and commissary stores and simply took what they needed. The government they had served was no more.

In Galveston on June 19, 1865, in the name of President Johnson, Gen. Gordon Granger of the Union Army proclaimed that the authority of the United States was restored over Texas, that all acts of the Confederacy were null and void, and that the slaves were free.[1] The historic Juneteenth has been celebrated ever since by Texas blacks and, often over the years, by their white friends.

Houston was taken over by federal troops with the arrival on June 20 of the 34th Iowa Regiment and five companies of the 114th Ohio Regiment. They marched from the depot to occupy the courthouse. As a small boy, E. N. Gray saw them come. "Somehow these soldiers did not look right to me. Their uniforms were not ragged enough, were of a much darker color than any I had seen before, and their guns were too shiny. They had a flag, too, that was different. . . ."[2]

By June 23, U.S. troops had taken formal possession of the state. Military authorities at Houston notified the mayor that they would not interfere with municipal government. They promised to protect the rights and property of citizens, to establish peace and good order. When the Amnesty Office of the provost marshal opened on June 25, Mayor William Anders and many other leading Houstonians swore allegiance to the United States and were readmitted to citizenship.

Perhaps because they were the first Yankees to come when every Houston soul rebelled at the thought, perhaps because of a difference in customs, the Illinois and Ohio regiments were often in conflict with the citizenry. They were later replaced by a western regiment who were, Gray thought, "good men and most of them were gentlemen." Some fared so well that they ultimately settled in Houston.

But military occupation had its foibles. The federal troops placed a cannon in front of the courthouse. Every morning at dawn and every evening at sundown for the raising and lowering of the flag, they fired their cannon. On the first morning, the concussion shattered the windowpanes of the houses around Court House Square. The Gray home faced the square. "Glass was scarce and expensive," Dr. E. N. Gray wrote in his memoirs, "and the citizens protested vigorously." Military red tape, however, could not be cut. Day after day, therefore, the cannon roared. "Nothing remained for the citizens but to take the window sashes out before sunrise and put them back in again after the sunset gun was fired. I remember seeing my father do that many times."

Unreconstructed Confederates in Houston were stiffnecked toward the Stars and Stripes. They and the occupation troops were locked in a silent battle. Noticing that some Houstonians detoured to keep from walking under the U.S. flag, federal officials stretched a rope across Congress Avenue and hung a large flag from it—directly over the sidewalk. But however muddy the street, Houstonians would step out into the mire. Dr. Gray wrote, "I have seen the most refined ladies raise their skirts and go through mud over their shoe tops rather than walk under that hated flag."

In 1866, Horace Taylor became Houston's first postwar mayor, elected before Reconstruction had tightened its grip on the city. Born in Massachusetts and reared in Charleston, he moved to Houston in 1848. He and his wife Emily had a gracious home at the end of Preston Street overlooking Buffalo Bayou. He had succeeded in the cotton business, was active in the Presbyterian Church, and for a time had been an alderman on the City Council. He set out to refresh a city that showed the neglect of wartime.

His administration laid new shell on the streets, installed a culvert in the gully at Caroline and Congress so that it could be filled and leveled, and for the first time posted street names at each corner. The bigger task was to restore an economy depleted by four years of war. As a start, Taylor decided to take none of the three-thousand-dollar mayoral salary.

Mayor Taylor, his brother-in-law banker T. M. Bagby, and the City Council pushed the formation of the Houston Direct Navigation Company, with Capt. John Sterret as general agent. Its aim was to bypass the port of Galveston by sending barges to Boliver Roads to meet incoming ships. By unloading their oceangoing vessels onto barges in midchannel, ship captains could avoid the high Galveston wharfage fee and move their freight directly to railroad docks in Houston. The company prospered and, on its profits, Captain Sterret ordered a luxury steamboat built in Louisville for the bayou. He named it the *T. M. Bagby;* Houstonians, well versed in steamboats, pronounced it "a floating palace."

In the first relief of peacetime, white Houstonians thought that they could go back to the normal freedoms of antebellum life. Four days before his death, President Lincoln had spoken to a crowd celebrating the collapse of the Confederacy. He showed an attitude of understanding and reconciliation toward the South.

But Houstonians soon found that Texas had not been readmitted to the Union, nor had Texans regained the right of self-government. Houston had to deal with a Congress that had no Texas members. In many ways Reconstruction proved to be a greater hardship on the city than war.

Houston now witnessed a new flow of emigration. While many Confederates emigrated to Brazil and stayed there, others came through Houston on their way to Mexico—among them Generals Edmund Kirby-Smith and John Magruder, two former Louisiana governors, ex-governor Edward Clark of Texas, and Governor Murrah. But former governor Francis Lubbock was in prison, having been captured with President Davis in May, 1865, and imprisoned at Fort Delaware.

With his wife Rosalie and three children, Col. Edwin Fairfax Gray made his way slowly on a fifteen-hundred-mile journey ending in Mexico City, perhaps with the thought of making a career in the army of the Emperor Maximilian.[3] As graduates of U.S. military academies, Gray and other officers felt more vulnerable to charges of treason than Confederate soldiers who had come into service from civilian life.

The Grays stopped off at Monterrey and other cities along the way, putting the children in school at each stop, and Fairfax Gray studied Spanish every day of the journey. Reaching Mexico City in early 1866, they became part of the small English-speaking colony. Fairfax Gray was immediately commissioned by the Emperor Maximilian to beautify Mexico City. Gray designed parks and boulevards and supervised the landscaping. Fairfax and Rosalie went often to balls and soirees held at Chapultepec Palace. Their children went to a French school.

Small William Fairfax Gray II was charmed by the fine French band that gave concerts in the Alameda Park across from their house. "All the fashion and wealth of the city assembled at these concerts," he wrote many years later, "coming in carriages, on horseback, and on foot, attired in Parisian fashions, the occasion being deeply tinged with the air of Vienna. . . . Maximilian and Carlotta were at the zenith of their glory and power in that year of 1866–67."

The power vanished when—under the strongly invoked Monroe Doctrine—Napoleon III withdrew the French forces. The glory was shortlived. Maximilian was captured and executed. As amnesty became possible, the Grays gave up the ex-patriate life and started home.

Maj. Benjamin F. Weems was a Virginian who had volunteered to Terry's Texas Rangers because he happened to be in Brazoria County when the word of war came through. He had studied engineering and at nineteen was chief of a crew engaged to lay a road across the Isthmus of Tehuantepec. At twenty-one he came to Houston on a railroad project and apparently liked what he saw. At war's end, he came back to stay, becoming an influential civic leader.[4]

Meanwhile, the city had experienced a brief, hectic flush of prosperity. The mills of New England, England, and France were hungry for cotton. Despite the best efforts of blockade runners to ship it out during the war, Houston had stored a tremendous amount in its warehouses. Cotton sales in 1866–67 brought in welcome gold and silver, enabling Houstonians to make up for the deprivations of the long blockade years.

Perhaps it was this prosperity, however temporary, that eased for Houstonians the federal intrusion on their civic affairs and the presence of Yankees among them.

Houston did not suffer in the Reconstruction period many of the hardships common across the South. Instead, it received a great influx of attractive southerners from states east of the Mississippi. For the first time, Houston's prevailing accent became southern. It continued to be southern for the next eighty years.

On the first anniversary of Juneteenth, 1866, Houston freedmen and women gave a banquet and invited all their former owners as guests of honor. Houston blacks and Houston whites knew each other well and had gone through the Civil War together. Many black Houstonians went easily into business with skills that had made them valuable as slaves. They drove their own hacks, did blacksmithing, and ran barber, shoe repair, and tailoring shops.

Black Houstonians lived in the same streets as white Houstonians and rode in the same train cars and stagecoaches. Official segregation was still a quarter of a century down the road. For now, free to call their time their own, black Houstonians set about organizing their own lives. They founded a debating society and the Thespian Club. Although the Episcopal Church in Texas had always had black members in church and Sunday school and although some stayed with Christ Church throughout their lives, most black parishioners chose to form their own congregations.

When the Methodists were able to replace the church that had collapsed, the black members moved the building they had shared with the whites to a lot at the corner of Bell and Travis. Frank Vance bought it for the congregation for twelve hundred dollars. In August, 1866, twelve black Houstonians founded the Antioch Baptist Missionary Church, Houston's first black Baptist church. It held services in a one-room meeting house near the bayou. The Rev. John Henry Yates was its first pastor.

At the war's end, there was also an influx of blacks from plantation country. Their need for housing and employment, combined with the government that the military dictatorship in Austin imposed upon Houston, made for uncertainty and resentment.

Even so, the *Houston City Directory* of 1866 (the city's first) is filled with advertisements that imply a brisk business and social life. The Houston Club, organized in 1865, had its club room "over William Clark's Store."

The firm of Gray and Botts, attorneys at law, had an office on Fannin between Congress and Preston, opposite the courthouse. Like Gray a native of Fredericksburg, Virginia, Walter Browne Botts had come to Houston in 1857 and been elected to the legislature. During the Civil War, he served as a colonel in Hood's Brigade. This partnership of Gray and Botts was the start of the firm that was ultimately to become Baker Botts.

Fresh from his Civil War adventures, Decimus et Ultimus Barziza came to Houston to open a law practice. Son of a Venetian count and French-Canadian mother, Barziza was, as his name implies, the tenth and last child born of the marriage in Williamsburg, Virginia. Like so many Texans, he served with Hood's Brigade. Twice taken prisoner of war, Captain Barziza had once escaped by jumping out of a moving train, and lived to return to his unit.[5]

W. D. Cleveland, who had come to Houston from Tennessee before the war, reopened his business as a cotton factor. S. M. McAshan became cashier of the T. W. House private banking business. Robert Elgin—pronounced with a hard *g* rather than a soft

one—came to Houston as commissioner of the Houston and Texas Central Railroad.[6] A. Sessums was a general commission merchant at the corner of Main and Franklin; H. Wiener was an auctioneer and commission merchant.

Westheimer and Billig had a livery stable on the corner of Milam and Congress. A native German, M. L. Westheimer had come to Houston in 1859. He had a farm and stables out in the country west of town. After the war, as his brother's children grew old enough, he brought five nephews and three nieces over from Germany. He had a number of employees and started a little school for their children. Other neighborhood children came as well. The shell lane that led to the schoolhouse came to be known as Westheimer Road.[7]

Except for the Houston Academy, what schools there were had stayed open during the war, but only one child in four attended. School funds were so low that in 1865, Mayor William D. Andrews donated his salary for the year toward tuition for poor children, and teachers halved their fees. Musician and teacher, French-born Gustave Duvernoy had come to Houston in midwar. The son of an artillery captain in Napoleon's army, he was educated in Germany, took part in the German revolution of 1848, and after three months in prison emigrated to America. In Galveston he married Dorothea Sellner, a native of Prussia. He joined the faculty of Houston's first high school and became choir director and organist for both the Church of the Annunciation and Congregation Beth Israel.

After the war, Mary Brown, a convent-bred Irish woman, who had first taught conduct and deportment to young girls at St. Vincent de Paul, opened her own academy. The Freedman's Bureau opened three schools for Negro children.

Houston and Galveston had lost hundreds of men in the Civil War, many of them fathers of families. In September, 1866, former Confederate officers chartered a home for the orphaned children. Commonly called the Confederate Orphans' Home, it was supported by both cities. Within two years it was being called the Orphan's Home at Bayland and housed as many as two hundred and fifty boys and girls.

Houstonians could subscribe to British periodicals for four dollars a year. The local *Weekly Telegraph* and the *Tri-Weekly Telegraph* carried tempting ads. Bremond & Company on Main Street offered "Staple and Fancy Family Groceries! Coffees, teas, chocolates, sugars, tobaccos, choice liquors by barrel and case. Fruits, vegetables, fish, oysters, lobsters, pickles, ketchups, sauces. Dried fruits, candles, soap, starch, etc. etc. etc. In fact, we keep at the lowest market rates, all articles kept by grocers."

A "Patent Baby Tender or Magic Spring Cradle" was offered for sale by G. A. Forsgard. This remarkable invention could be "instantly converted into A Reclining Couch, a High Chair, A Baby Walker, A Nursery Chair, A Baby Jumper, A Hobby Horse, A Spring Chair, or an Ottoman."

The Old Capitol Hotel advertised: "This famous old hotel, after having been thoroughly repaired, refitted and refurnished, is now open for the accommodation of the public. The table will always be furnished with the best of the market. Attentive servants will provide for the comfort of guests." And Perkins Hall, again under the original auspices of Brother Perkins, stocked "the choicest foreign wine, liquors and cigars. Free lunch every day at half past 10 o'clock."

The Houston and Texas Central Railway Company had as its officers William J. Hutchins, president; James F. London, secretary; W. R. Baker, A. J. Burke, T. W. House, William M. Rice, Cornelius Ennis, and Charles Burton, directors; and H. W. Benchley, conductor. Benchley was the grandfather of Robert Benchley, the twentieth-century humorist. Hutchins had bought the railroad in 1861 at a sheriff's sale, but could add little to its network of tracks until after the war.

In 1866, Mr. Hutchins's daughter, Ella, became the first vice-regent from Texas of the Mount Vernon Ladies Association, the young organization chartered to save George Washington's home for future generations.[8]

The Houston Gas Company was organized in 1866. It was not an immediate success. "While it did not meet with actual opposition, it did meet with . . . an almost fatal indifference on the part of the public," B. H. Carroll wrote in his history of Houston. The company built a plant to manufacture gas out of coal and oyster shells, laid mains, and then had to persuade Houstonians to use this new, piped-in source of light. At the start, commercial places like hotels, restaurants, and saloons were the only subscribers. But once the city contracted with the company to light the streets, gas became first acceptable, then popular. Each evening at dusk, the lamplighters moved from post to post, lighting the street lamps.

As a company director, Dick Dowling was the first to light his home with gas. The heroic commander at the Battle of Sabine Pass had ended the war with the rank of major. In the lilting humor of the Irish, he reopened his Bank of Bacchus at Main and Congress, listing himself as president and cashier, and offered a wide variety of spirits "with liberal discounts on deposits." But at twenty-eight, he was a sound businessman. he became a member of Hook and Ladder Company Number 1, the city's first fire department. He sold and bought real estate. Soon he owned some three thousand acres of land in surrounding counties, and half-interest in a steamboat plying the Trinity River. He helped found the first oil company in Houston, and one of his associates actually brought in a small well near Beaumont. He contributed generously to the relief of women and men left destitute by war.

The first attempt to found a national bank in Houston originated with a Galvestonian. Benjamin McDonough of Galveston was Pres. Andrew Johnson's kinsman. He went to Washington to obtain a presidential pardon for having been a rebel. He then applied to the comptroller of the currency "in behalf of myself and associates, residents of Houston, Texas," for permission to organize "a national bank . . . with a capital of $100,000." Oddly: he had never been a banker and had no associates lined up, but apparently thought it a good idea. It was. With Dr. Ingham Roberts of Houston he made many trips to Washington and New York, wrote scores of letters, and at last gained the important national charter.[9] Forty-four Houstonians "of diverse business and professional activities" subscribed the capital. Ninety years later, this would become the First City National Bank.

Neither W. J. Hutchins, Houston's richest man, nor B. A. Shepherd, Houston's first banker, was a part of the first subscription. But within a year, Bill Kirkland wrote in his history of the bank, Shepherd was added to the board, "too able a businessman and banker not to be added . . . dominating and running the bank for twenty-five years."

By the end of 1866, twenty-five brick buildings were rising downtown. The *Daily Telegraph* reported on brick houses going up, describing "the large, portly, roomy, suburban residences . . . of the merchant princes. Others are neat box-houses or cottages, built in the Gothic style, painted in different colors, white predominating." This suburb lay out beyond Texas Avenue, and soon would extend to Rusk.

In 1867, William Marsh Rice married his brother's sister-in-law, Elizabeth Baldwin Brown. (It is for her that the Elizabeth Baldwin Park on Elgin and the Elizabeth Baldwin Literary Society at Rice University are named.) Libbie was the niece of Charlotte Allen and the daughter of former mayor Horace Baldwin. After marrying John Brown in Houston, she had lived in San Francisco and New York, but upon his death she returned to Houston. With their marriage, Mr. and Mrs. Rice began to spend the winter months in Houston, the summer months in New York, keeping hotel or apartment suites in both places, going often to spas and health resorts. Thirty years on, this wedding of 1867 would pose a threat to Mr.

Rice's plans to endow an educational institution.

The Houston Base Ball Club, founded six weeks after secession, apparently died at birth. But after the war, baseball began in earnest. With teams playing all across the state, the Galveston Robert E. Lees held the state championship. Abner Doubleday, who has often been credited with originating the game, was living in Galveston. A former Union Army officer, he was commissioner of the Freedman's Bureau. Possibly, he prompted and coached the team.

To celebrate San Jacinto Day in 1868, the Houston Stonewalls met the Galveston Lees on the battleground. The Houston *Daily Telegraph* reported that "from the first innings it was apparent to the most disinterested that the Lees (although the vaunted champions of the state) had at last met more than their match." The Lees gave up after eight innings when they had five runs to the Stonewalls' thirty-four. The umpire pronounced the Stonewalls the new champions of the state of Texas.

Military rule was beginning to chafe. Alexander McGowan, who had been mayor in 1858–59, was again elected in 1867. But on December 5, the commanding general of Houston's military district took control of the city and left the mayor with little authority.

Things grew worse when the heartily disliked E. J. Davis was named governor by way of an election in which no former Confederate soldier was allowed to vote. In August, Davis turned McGowan out of office and appointed J. R. Morris mayor and T. H. Scanlan Third Ward alderman. A month later, Davis fired the city recorder and marshal. Finally, in 1870, he turned out everybody who had been elected and appointed Scanlan mayor. This stirred such indignation that former governor Francis Lubbock was drafted to lead a protest.[10]

Apparently during the war, Houston lost its camels. The camels, which Colonel Robert E. Lee had considered superior to the army mules, served both sides during the conflict. Union forces used them near the Texas–New Mexico line. Confederate forces used them to pack salt from the flats above Brownsville and to carry cotton into Matamoros. But the success of railroads dimmed the future of camel freight trains. Bethel Coopwood, however, kept a remnant of the Texas Camel Corps on his ranch near Austin well into the 1880s. Coopwood maintained law offices in Austin, San Antonio, and Mexico City. On trips to Mexico City he rode one camel and loaded the other with luggage.[11]

Texas did not give up easily on camels. From the day in the 1850s when he had roped a camel on Governor Lubbock's Sims Bayou ranch, Samuel W. Allen had thought of ways in which the family could make a camel herd profitable. He and his wife still had large holdings of ranchland in Harris and Fort Bend counties.[12] Their son, Samuel E. Allen, had been raised as a cattleman. They had links with the Morgan shipping lines. So father and son imported camels with the idea of carrying mail and freight across the Arizona desert. They organized the Oriental Textile Mills and began to manufacture camel's hair cloth and other products.

The summer of 1867 brought yellow fever, and by September it had become the worst epidemic ever to strike the city. Keziah Payne de Pelchin, immunized by her childhood bout of yellow fever in Galveston, moved from case to case, tending, soothing, doing what could be done—which was little.

A strapping young man, six feet tall, with blue eyes and russet hair, Dick Dowling came down with what seemed to be a light case just before the birth of his only daughter. He went back to work, but after four days had a relapse and died in his sleep on September 23, 1867. He was twenty-nine. The *Houston Telegraph* considered him "Houston's most important citizen." The Houston Hook and Ladder Company Number 1 bore his body to St. Vincent's Church and after a short service, he was buried in the church cemetery.[13]

At war's end, Hugh Rice, who had come from Ireland by way of Virginia, became engineer in chief of a survey of Buffalo Bayou, San Jacinto River, and Galveston Bay. He had the vision to see the need of a turning basin. His report of August, 1867, urged "widening the channel at the city of Houston, for the purpose of affording seagoing and other ships, ample room to turn around without delay or inconvenience." It would cost seven hundred thousand dollars. "What a paltry sum," he wrote, "in comparison with the proposed profitable purposes to be accomplished." Shortly after presenting his report, he too died of yellow fever and was buried at St. Vincent's.[14]

Ten people died one day, twenty-nine the next. Yellow fever claimed all nine members of one family, seven members of another, and killed eight doctors—including the city health officer. Before the epidemic ended, 492 men, women, and children had died in the town of fewer than five thousand people. Again, Houston had been decimated, but Galveston was hit even harder.

In addition, many northern soldiers died, so many that the town sexton could not keep abreast of the daily burials. This unreconstructed gentleman, H. G. Pannell, was hauled before the federal commandant who said to him, "Mr. Pannell, they tell me you dislike to bury my soldiers."

"General," said Pannell, "whoever told you that told a damned lie. It's the pleasantest thing I've had to do in years. I would like to bury every damned one of you." The general clapped Pannell in the brig but had to let him out almost immediately because his services were urgently needed.

Chapter Seventeen

Recovery

DESPITE personal losses to war and epidemic, Houston remained characteristically intent on the future. At war's end, the Star State telegraph line, which linked Houston with Galveston and Orange, was absorbed by the Southwestern Telegraph Company. It, in turn, was absorbed by Western Union, so that by 1867 Houston was connected to every telegraph line in the United States.

The *New Orleans Times* wrote, "Houston is an interesting little city of ten or twelve thousand inhabitants . . . having four railroads . . . two considerable foundries, two cotton factories, several saw and planing mills and two beef packeries. . . . She is now proposing and actually at work to cut a ship canal down the channel of her tortuous and narrow bayou to the Bay."[1] Though still under the cloud of the recent rebellion, the city of Houston had the audacity to ask Congress to designate it a port of entry.

The interesting little city attracted newcomers. Mr. and Mrs. William H. Kirkland moved to Houston from Bay City and rented the Christ Church rectory until they could find a permanent home. Their daughter Rosa was seventeen and their son William Hines was a year old. James Roane Masterson joined his younger brother Archibald — the first Masterson to come to Houston. Both were lawyers. They and all their brothers would become judges.[2]

After his grand tour of 1859, William Escrage Kendall had served the Confederacy as a guide and scout in the Virginia mountains he knew so well. With the war ended, he married Belle Sherman, Gen. Sidney

Sherman's daughter. They took a leisurely six months of travel by way of a honeymoon before he went into raising cotton near Richmond. After a few years of plantation life, they settled again in Houston to give their children a better education.[3]

In March, 1868, a horsecar began to run every forty-five minutes on the Tap Railroad. The fare was ten cents. But by early April, the Houston City Railroad had laid enough wooden rails on McKinney to run its first mule car. The *Brownsville Ranchero* predicted admiringly that "within two months . . . street cars will traverse the entire city."

The railroad age, which had begun in Houston during the 1850s, was in full swing. By 1861 there were 357 miles of railroad centered on the city, and by 1876 there were to be 1,503 miles. Attracted by railroading, many English, Scots, and Cornish men came to Houston.

With all this high-powered activity, few Houstonians gave much thought to the fact that young George Hermann had come home from the war and settled into his family place between McKinney and Walker. He first worked as a stock keeper on Gov. Francis Lubbock's Sims Bayou ranch, but before long he began to buy and drive cattle on his own. He was a quiet fellow, warm to his friends but of a saving disposition. They liked to say that he still held the first dollar he ever made. The day would come when all those savings would be left to enhance Houston, the city of his birth.

Houstonians celebrated San Jacinto Day of 1868 with a free barbecue at the battlefield, and three days later they held a ball at Hutchins House in honor of the 17th U.S. Infantry, on the eve of its departure for "the frontier." This suggests that Yankee soldiers had made some pleasant friendships as an army of occupation.

Trotting horses had become so popular that by 1869 the city had to reprint an old antispeeding ordinance. Several leading citizens were arrested and charged with driving their carriages at a gait faster than a walk.

Houstonians liked noise. Every wedding was marked by a charivari. Men armed with cowbells, horns, tin pans, and bull fiddles would serenade the bridal pair until invited in for refreshments. But for several years after the Civil War, nobody had the heart to celebrate the Fourth of July: Vicksburg and Gettysburg had each fallen that day. Instead, they turned their enthusiasm to Christmas. For weeks before, boys gathered wood for bonfires. Come the day, they gathered around it with firecrackers, fireworks, and "dollar pistols." These were cap pistols that made a satisfying bang. Even grown-ups took part in Roman candle battles on Main Street.

Because of heavy German immigration, the Catholics had long since outgrown their first church, St. Vincent de Paul at Franklin and Caroline. In 1866, Fr. Joseph Querat, the first full-time parish priest, set out to build a new one and commissioned the distinguished Galveston architect, Nicholas J. Clayton. On April 25, 1869, Houston turned out en masse for the laying of the cornerstone. From the old church to the new site on Texas Avenue at Crawford, Father Querat led a procession that included city, county, and federal officials in black frock coats, prelates in bright robes of office, the parish members, and the fire department in full dress uniform. Not quite two years later, the towering spire of the Church of the Annunciation took its enduring place on the Houston skyline.

The Rev. Zacharias Emmich was the first rabbi to serve Congregation Beth Israel. From Frankfort-on-the-Main, he was an early leader in the Reform movement and apparently served the congregation intermittently; he both preceded and followed Rabbi Samuel Raphael. After the war, the congregation paid the city of Houston two thousand dollars for three lots on the south side of Buffalo Bayou. The building committee consisted of Sol. Rosenfield, Sam Sterne, Henry Fox, M. H. Levy, A. Cramer, and I. Colman, with Mannheim Jacobs presiding. On June 16, 1870, a procession of more than one thousand Houstonians formed on Main Street near the Masonic Temple and marched behind Schmidt's Band to the site on Franklin. The chief rabbi of the New Orleans Portuguese Synagogue asked a blessing, and the cornerstone was laid with Masonic honors.[4]

Justina Latham, who had come home from Paris in 1867, was a cosmopolitan young woman who spoke fluent French, played the piano, and carried about her an ineffable French chic. She was the pride of her father, Capt. L. J. Latham. He was in no hurry to marry her off to anybody, certainly not a "newcomer" to Houston like young W. D. Cleveland.

Cleveland had come to Houston from Tennessee before the war. Until he was wounded, he had served as a captain with Hood's Brigade in Virginia. He later joined Terry's Texas Rangers in Tennessee until the war's end. Houston society welcomed him back to the extent that he was elected to the vestry of Christ Church even before he was baptized, and he was soon well established as a cotton factor.[5]

Captain Latham had all the self-confidence of the seafarer and successful businessman. By this time he had made his fortune, lost it, and made another. He liked to sit out in front of his furniture store—the biggest in town. He was Houston's weatherman, and picnics were likely to be postponed if Captain Latham said it was going to rain.

This strong-minded gentleman apparently would brook no discussion of a romance or marriage between his Tina and W. D. Cleveland. But finally one May day in 1869, Captain Latham received a note from young Mr. Cleveland. It said, in effect, "I will be at your gate tomorrow morning at seven o'clock, and with me will be a minister. If Miss Justina comes out, and I think she will, we shall go to Christ Church and be married. We should like to have your permission and blessings." The minister was the Rt. Rev. Alexander Gregg, Miss Justina did come out, and in the early morning of May 26 the three of them walked over to Christ Church where the young couple were married by the bishop.

Not all young women had the advantage of the European education that Justina had had. But well-bred mothers taught their daughters nice manners, whether in Houston or on surrounding plantations. In her memoirs of her childhood on a plantation between Houston and Galveston, Lucie Campbell Lee wrote of how her mother's determination that girls be properly trained for polite society led Mrs. Campbell to start a school.

"I like to think about that school," Mrs. Lee wrote, "not the hum-drum drone of us little folks with the B-A-bay, and B-E-be of our daily lessons, but of the classes in Composition and Rhetoric, Polite Conversation and Drawing Room Manners, French, the Foundations of Music, etc. This last was a triumph of ingenuity for there was not a piano in the community. An ironing board with pasteboard keys, white and black, seemed to inspire four girls who yearned to play. My mother's guitar was auxiliary to this silent instrument. . . .

"Our simple little parlor took on the drawing room atmosphere when the class withdrew there for Polite Conversation and Drawing Room manners. Even the number of steps to take before pausing was taught, and 'Never, never let your heels touch the floor. A lady's step should be *gliding* and not heard.' A low and deep bow on presentation was urged. One would think they were to be presented at Court, these country girls."

So many people of quality had come from

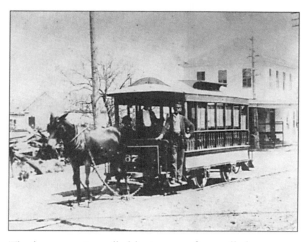

The horsecars (so called but more often pulled by a mule) began to run in 1868 and by 1874 had a citywide system requiring four turntables. *Courtesy George Fuermann City of Houston Collection, Special Collections, University of Houston Libraries*

Virginia, Kentucky, the Carolinas, Tennessee, and Alabama that Houston's society became markedly Southern. In that burst of high spirits and extravagance which often seems to follow a war, the social whirl became lavish to the point of absurdity—but great fun. Plantation parties were the rage. On sidesaddle, ladies came wearing plumed hats and riding habits with sweeping trains that almost touched the ground. The lady had to catch her train up over her arm to walk. Gentlemen on horseback, wearing velvet doublets, hose, and plumed hats, jousted, riding at full gallop with fixed lances aimed at small hanging rings. He who picked off the most rings could crown his lady queen for the day. After the all-day picnic the guests went to the ballet at the newly completed Hutchins House and wound up with a ball where the Virginia reel and minuet were danced in colonial costume.

With the first availability of imports, Houston women could spread their hoopskirts to the full fifteen-foot diameter *Godey's Lady Book* prescribed, using twenty-five yards of silk and as many more in braid, laces, and other ornamentation. By their great size, the skirts made waists look tiny. Houston ladies wore their hems touching the floor all around, even trailing a train—just as women did in Boston, New York, or London. Presumably they glided, not letting their heels touch the ground, as a lady should.[6]

When fashion shortened walking skirts almost up to the top of the boots, it became much easier to cross Houston's still unpaved streets. Though little girls were allowed skirts halfway to the knee, many wore pantalettes, white and ruffled, to cover their well-stockinged legs.

Rather like the Easter Parade in New York or the Sunday afternoon stream of open carriages in the Bois de Boulogne, Houstonians staged brilliant spring and autumn dress parades. Just after midafternoon on the appointed day, the best-dressed men and women of the city rode their thoroughbred horses, or drove their phaetons, barouches, landaus, or sulkies, to join the procession on Main Street. From horseback, bachelors doffed their hats and bowed to lovely young ladies riding in carriages with papa and mama.

But Dr. Mary Walker, a pioneer woman suffragist, showed her independence by wearing well-tailored trousers.

In such a society, Ella Hutchins—one of the Houston girls who had spent the war years in Europe with her mama—married Lord Stewart of Scotland. He brought to his bride silver plate and fabulous jewels, including the "black diamond" once owned by Mary, Queen of Scots. Libbie Randon, another of the Paris contingent, married George Porter. Rosa Kirkland married L. T. Noyes.

In summer, gentlemen played billiards at the hall of Messrs. Prindle & Holmes, sculled on the bayou in the new paired-oar boat of the Andax Rowing Club, or drilled with the Light Guards. Boys learned to swim in the bayou; the favorite swimming holes were in Buffalo Bayou at the foot of Austin and White Oak Bayou where Beauchamp Spring still bubbled. Houston women

joined the Dramatic Club, or read and discussed Mark Twain's new novel, *The Gilded Age.*

Hoping to set medical standards and curtail rampant quackery, Houston physicians called a meeting of Texas physicians in April, 1869. Twenty-eight doctors met at the Hutchins House to organize the Texas State Medical Association.[7] The Houston Bar Association was founded in 1870, and Peter Gray was elected its first president.

On March 30, 1870, Texas was readmitted to the Union. Though still under state-appointed government, Houston was flourishing. It rode through the 1870s on a surge of enterprise and prosperity. Col. John Brady organized the Harris County Fair Association and was its first president. He promoted the first Texas State Fair and invited Horace Greeley to open it.

Colonel Brady had come home from war with a new interest in deepening the ship channel. At his own expense, he dredged the bayou along the stretch that became the turning basin. In so doing, he created Brady's Island, a remnant of his own property on the bayou. Partly in response to his efforts the Houston Ship Channel Company was organized to dredge the bayou to a minimum of nine feet.[8]

The city invested in the Buffalo Bayou Ship Channel Company. In July, 1870, after three years of consideration, Congress designated Houston a port of delivery and called for a surveyor of customs to be posted in the city.

The *T. M. Bagby* and other steamboats were like those plying the Mississippi. The *Diana,* built at a Pennsylvania shipyard for use on Buffalo Bayou, was a handsome 170-foot side-wheeler with a thirty-two-foot beam. Businessmen liked to go aboard in the late afternoon, have a nice dinner, listen to the band, dance or play cards, have a good night's sleep, and finish breakfast the next morning in ample time to attend to business before catching the next boat back up the bayou to Houston. When trains overtook

By no means the largest of the steamboats that plied the bayou, the *Sinclair* carried cotton and passengers to Galveston. Shown here in 1868, it was docked upstream from Allen's landing. Samuel L. Allen's cotton warehouse stood on the site of the latterday M. & M. Building, which became the University of Houston's downtown campus. *Courtesy Houston Metropolitan Research Center, Houston Public Library*

the steamboats, Pullman, club, and dining cars adopted similar overnight schedules between cities.

The first Chinese to land in Houston were laborers hired to build the railroads. In 1870, three hundred of them arrived in their native dress, each carrying a bed mat, a rice bowl, and chopsticks. Soon after, the Scandinavian Club of Houston brought five hundred immigrants to Texas.

Indians still came into town to trade at Kennedy's Trading Post. Dr. E. N. Gray wrote in his memoirs that "they were a mixed tribe of Coushattas, Alabamas, Seminoles and perhaps others. Their village was on Green's Bayou. Every Saturday they brought in buckskins, venison, wild turkeys and other game to trade for powder, lead, calico and whiskey. Sometimes they would give a war dance or play a game of ball very much like the Canadian game of lacrosse."

John Kennedy had leased his store at 813 Congress to the Confederacy for an armory, but he kept his mill over on the gully that later became Caroline Street. The mill ground meal for the army and the city throughout the Civil War. When he regained the use of his trading post on Congress, Kennedy was often seen walking from mill to store wearing a fine layer of corn meal dust.

Charity was still very personal. Houston's poor and needy were being cared for largely by the ladies' societies of the Episcopal, Presbyterian, Methodist, and Catholic churches. Often in pairs, the churchwomen visited their assigned families on a fairly regular basis. While delivering food baskets or clothes for a new baby, they could remind children or parents to come to Sunday school and church.

Waves of newcomers continued to come. Despite the steady growth, Houston managed to keep the quality of a small Southern town, taking care of its own.

Chapter Eighteen

Prosperous Peace

IN THE BOOMING 1870s, Main Street was lined with fancy restaurants serving imported delicacies as well as oysters, shrimp, and fresh fish from the bay.[1] It was also lined with saloons, many with a gambling parlor upstairs. One day, one gambler shot another in an argument over cards. The slain man's friends wanted him to have a Christian burial; his opponents did not.

At the time and a block away, the Rev. Julyan Clemens was sitting in his study at Christ Church, working on a sermon. Bill Mead, one of the gambler's friends, appeared at the study door to ask if Mr. Clemens would come to the saloon to read the funeral service. Mead explained that there was some opposition to the plan and promised that he and a friend would guard the rector and the proceedings with pistols drawn.

Mr. Clemens was a slender, dark-haired young man from Cornwall. Like so many others, he had arrived in Houston by way of Fredericksburg, Virginia. There he had married Sue Scott, a cousin of Ben and Browne Botts, and through them had been called to Christ Church.

Mr. Clemens responded immediately to Mr. Mead's request, pausing only long enough to put on his vestments. In the parlor over the saloon, he read the Episcopal service for the dead over the defunct gambler and then delivered a little sermon on the evils of gambling. This so impressed Mr. Mead that he became a devoted parishioner. One Sunday when the church roof was set on fire by sparks from the big wood stove, Mr. Mead was first man up on the roof to douse the flames.

All major churches were downtown and within an easy walk from home for most of their members. Court House Square still had private homes on all sides. E. L. Coombs, the jeweler, lived with his family in a large white house facing Prairie; the Frank Cargills lived on Congress, Dr. and Mrs. Perl on Travis. Dr. David Stuart's big house with the art glass windows was on Texas Avenue. The R. M. Elgins lived on Texas at Austin. The Charles J. Graingers lived on Texas with their daughters, Eliza, Alice, Georgia, Fannie, Sue, and Lily. The Christ Church rectory on Texas had a lovely rose garden and one of Houston's first bathrooms. The tub and wash basin drained out through a pipe and down a little brick gutter.

In 1870, a "fellowship of disciples" began to meet on Sunday morning "for the breaking of bread and prayers." The five disciples met in the office of Dr. J. A. Throckmorton, an English immigrant. This was the birth of what would become the First Christian Church.

Professor and Mrs. Horace Clark moved to Houston in 1871 to open a school for girls. For the next eight years, their academy was one of the best in the city. The Clarks were a remarkable pair of educators. Horace Clark had been chairman of the faculty and principal of the female department at Baylor University in Independence until 1866, becoming president in 1868.

The Clarks were both musical. As they

had at Baylor, they required music study at their academy. Professor Clark was also the minister of the First Baptist Church. Through his ministry and his music, a friendship grew between him and the Rev. Mr. Clemens of Christ Church. All Houston was startled when Clark was confirmed in the Episcopal church in 1877 and shortly after that, ordained an Episcopal minister. In his private journal and in his tiny, meticulous hand, the Reverend Mr. Clemens wrote impishly, "One in the eye for the Baptists!" Mr. Clark became rector of the Episcopal church in Corpus Christi. But Mrs. Clark, throughout her life, held fast to her Baptist faith.

The Samuel Allens, father and son, prospered in ranching. Before the war, they had chartered Morgan Steamship Company freighters to deliver cattle from their docks on Sims Bayou to New Orleans—sometimes at the rate of five thousand head a week. When Charles Morgan fell out with the Galveston port authorities, he shifted his interest to Houston. He laid a double-track railway from Houston to the mouth of Sims Bayou. By dredging the Morgan's Point pass, he could send oceangoing vessels to meet the train. The first was the *Clinton* from New York.[2] Thereafter, railroads delivered cattle from other parts of Texas to Houston and by rail to the Morgan steamers. They could bypass Galveston. With their own docks and cattle pens on Sims Bayou, the Allens were at the profitable hub of the cattle business.

Early in 1874, Preston Avenue east of Main Street was given a topping of shell— an advantage of the older, more settled neighborhood. Texas Avenue was not yet paved, but was shaded by trees. Houston was still a city of cisterns, one by each house. They not only provided drinking water, but had shelves down the sides where butter and milk could be kept cool.

In 1874, Mrs. Andrew Briscoe moved back to Houston and into a house at 620 Crawford. Judge Briscoe had died in New Orleans in 1849, leaving her to fifty-four years of widowhood and a career of civic leadership.

The town was building up. Mr. and Mrs. Cornelius Ennis had moved out on Congress to Jackson and Crawford. This was the rapidly growing Quality Hill section overlooking the bayou. The big mansion of Col. and Mrs. W. J. Hutchins stood on Franklin at LaBranch, the pride of Quality Hill. In the mid-1870s, the whole family lived there: Mrs. Hutchins's mother, Mrs. Ruth Harris; W. J. Hutchins, Jr., Rushmore, Leigh, Miss Eva, small Spencer and Arthur, and—interestingly —Mrs. Ella Hutchins Stewart.

Lord Stewart had apparently left the scene, whether by death or divorce. But this remarkable woman, who was fluent in French, thanks to her Civil War years abroad, translated books and plays for publishers. She later married Seabrook Sydnor, for whom Seabrook, Texas, is named, and remained a leader in society, outshone only by her brother Spencer. The Sydnors lived out their lives in the family mansion—as did all the other Hutchins children.

These big Victorian houses, built on Quality Hill and along Main Street, were designed for large families. Young married couples, widowed aunts, unmarried sons and daughters, young relatives coming to Houston from plantation or small town— all could be comfortably accommodated. In an era when many well-bred children were left orphans, when husbands died of scarlet fever or wives of childbirth, it was a warm and practical family solution. The custom continued well into the twentieth century, although by the 1930s, many of the older mansions had become hospitable boarding houses. For decades Houston had as wide an array of Victorian mansions as Galveston, until they were swept away by city growth.

Houstonians were also moving out from the heart of town toward the southwest. Rusk Avenue on each side of Main was becoming one of the loveliest residential streets. The W. D. Clevelands moved out to

Rusk, as did the Peter Grays, the Frederick Allyn Rices, the T. M. Shirleys, the William Fultons, and the S. L. Hohenthals.

Keen on all things west of New York, newspaperman Horace Greeley found Houston a "smart, young, growing community." Like most, he granted that the city was too flat. If it had only "rejoiced in a few hills and ledges," he would have liked it even better. But he concluded: "As she is, Houston is one of the loveliest cities that ever rose from a level plain, and stands so high above the Bayou that she may cleanse and keep sweet if she only will." No Chamber of Commerce committee could have asked for more.

A tower had been built in 1860 to house a city clock and a three-thousand-pound fire alarm bell, but Houston felt the need of a new market and municipal building. In 1872, the city officials called in an architect and construction began. Things soon went awry. It was noticed that there was no stairway between the first and second floors. Many rooms had no floors, others had no windows. As an afterthought, a theater was added upstairs; it was grand, with fluted columns and crystal chandeliers.

Houstonians had mixed feelings about this development. They were proud of the imposing new building in Market Square, but were appalled at the cost: $470,000. (This was one hundred times as much as either of two new churches would cost ten years later. In the 1870s, a Victorian mansion could be built for $5,000.) They also resented the fact that the huge indebtedness had been added to the city by a Reconstruction government. Mayor Thomas Scanlan bore the onus of what was considered the Market Place scandal.

Apparently ill-fated from the start, the Market House had a leaky roof. It was not easy to rent either the market space or the theater. The building was soon known as "Our White Elephant." When it caught fire in 1876, the first man to notice the blaze found that the rope of the big fire alarm bell had been cut. The Market House,

once greeted as magnificent, burned to the ground.

The street railway system had turntables at the Fairgrounds near Main and Mc-Gowen, on Main Street, at the Market House, and at the Union and Central depots. The *Houston Telegraph* reported that "there were twenty-three persons on the car which was drawn by one mule with perfect ease at the rate of fully ten miles an hour."

Streets continued to be a municipal problem. Now that cotton no longer arrived on the long drays pulled by seven span of oxen, now that camels no longer wandered up Main Street, traffic had thinned out. The *Telegraph* complained: "One of the mistakes made in laying off the city of Houston was in putting it ten miles too far up the bayou. But the mistake has gone into history . . . the error cannot be remedied. . . . But a greater mistake was made in . . . laying off the streets. . . . Our streets are far wider than are or ever will be needed for business. . . . What should be done is to narrow them by at least fifteen to twenty feet."

Banks were growing in number and wealth. B. A. Shepherd was president of the First National Bank, A. P. Root cashier, and L. J. Latham vice-president. F. A. Rice was president of the Houston Savings Bank, with Benjamin A. Botts vice-president. To encourage savings, this bank announced that it would accept deposits "of one dollar and upward, and allow six percent interest on all deposits of ten dollars or over remaining sixty days or longer." The private bank of T. W. House stood next door to the First National Bank; S. M. McAshan was treasurer.

Judge James A. Baker who had succeeded Peter Gray on the bench of the 11th District Court, moved to Houston from Huntsville in 1872 to join Gray & Botts in their law practice.[3] They had their offices on the west side of Court House Square in a pair of rooms in Gray's Opera House, which Gray owned.[4]

Lacking other cures, doctors of the 1870s prescribed travel and a change of climate for most pulmonary ailments. In 1873, when Peter Gray was found to have tuberculosis, he and his wife went abroad, traveling across Europe for his health. When he came home in 1874, he was appointed to the Texas supreme court. But after two months, failing health forced his resignation. He died on October 3, 1874, at the age of fifty-four.[5] Houston honored him by naming Gray Avenue after him; at the next session of the Texas legislature a county was named for him. As Chief Justice Oran Roberts said, Peter Gray was "a man who ought to be remembered." Like William Marsh Rice, Peter Gray had no children, but the family lines of both were perpetuated in Houston by nephews and nieces.[6]

The old Episcopal-Masonic burial ground near Buffalo Bayou was gradually being abandoned. In 1872, when Glenwood Cemetery on Washington Street was opened, many bodies were moved from the old burying ground to the new. The naturally beautiful site of Glenwood was enhanced by the best available landscape artists.

"Wealth, moved by grief, has uttered its sorrow in many costly marbles and towering shafts, and many a marble angel with drooping wings broods over the resting places of the dead." Who could improve on the words of B. H. Carroll in his 1912 *History of Houston?*

Dr. T. J. Broyles and Dr. D. F. Stuart opened the Houston Infirmary in "the old Brashear home" across from Glenwood in 1874. Dr. Stuart was a West Virginian who had studied at the Jefferson Medical College in Philadelphia and the Medical College of Louisiana before serving as surgeon in the Confederate Army. He settled in Houston in 1867 as chairman of the City Board of Health and was a founder of the Texas Medical Association.

The Rev. John Henry Yates had been brought to Houston as a slave from the Chesapeake Bay area of Virginia. When he became first minister of the Antioch Mission in 1868, he immediately bought the site on Clay Street for the church he intended

to build. This was some of the first real estate to be owned by black Houstonians. In 1875, Jack Yates laid the cornerstone for the Antioch Baptist Church, which would take four years to build. Pastor of Antioch from 1868 to 1891, Yates was the mentor not only of his congregation but of the entire neighborhood of Freedmen's Town in Fourth Ward. He urged freedmen to buy land and to buy their own homes, and he helped them do it—to the lasting benefit of Houston.[7]

The Houston Lyceum had lost out to the ravages of war and yellow fever. But in the mid-1870s, young men who enjoyed a good debate set out to revive it. When the public schools opened in 1876, the privately owned Houston Academy folded, leaving its considerable library in the hands of Owen L. Cochran, a civic and business leader. Cochran gave the library of more than nine hundred books to the Houston Lyceum. This lent it fresh impetus and prompted other Houstonians to add to the collection. The Lyceum began to buy books regularly from local bookstores and opened a reading room for its members—all of them male. It subscribed to *Appleton's Journal, Harper's Magazine, Scribner's Magazine,* and *Scientific American.*

The Houston Cotton Exchange and Board of Trade was organized in the parlor of the Hutchins House. Colonel C. S. Longcope was its first president, to be succeeded by W. D. Cleveland and George L. Porter. S. M. McAshan was president of the Young Men's Real Estate and Building Associates. Young Owen L. Cochran was carrying on his father's insurance business at 30 Main Street, and lived around the corner from the Hutchinses with his widowed mother.

Weddings continued to link old families. Owen Cochran and Alice Shepherd were married at the home of her father, B. A. Shepherd. George W. Cleveland married Eva H. Richardson at the home of Mrs. A. S. Richardson. And R. H. Culpepper married Mamie Kate Clark at the home of Professor Horace Clark.

A memorable wedding was that of Georgia Grainger to Alfred Ryland Howard in October, 1875. The Grainger house stood facing Christ Church; the Graingers had seven daughters. Starting with the wedding of the first, Charles Grainger established the custom of laying a red carpet across Texas Avenue from his front door to the church. By 1875, Mr. Grainger had died and the bride was given away by a family friend, Col. John T. Brady. But true to the tradition, she walked across Texas Avenue to her wedding on the red carpet.

In 1882, Minnie Rice, the daughter of the Frederick Allyn Rices, married Henry Holt Lummis from Anderson. On graduation from the University of the South at Sewanee in 1879 with a bachelor of law degree, he had come to Houston to join the firm of Hutchinson and Carrington. After his marriage, he entered the lumber business with his father-in-law and ultimately took over management of the Rice estate.[8]

In the 1870s, New Orleans gave Houston two outstanding music teachers. Emma J. Lott, who had studied piano, theory, and harmony under outstanding musicians of the country, moved to Houston in 1873. She was a composer as well as a teacher and was organist for the First Presbyterian Church and later the Shearn Methodist Church. After marrying C. A. Bujac in 1875, she pursued her career for another forty years.[9]

Lucie Palmer, born on the Louisiana plantation of her doctor father, had a French education at Sacred Heart Convent in New Orleans and at fifteen played a Beethoven concerto with the orchestra of the French Opera. This was allowed because it was a *charity* concert; her parents would never have let her play professionally. While married to George Loening of Bremen, Germany, she often played for music-loving Ludwig I of Bavaria. Though King Ludwig had abdicated, he spent much time in the Bavarian capital. After her husband's death, when she was twenty-two and had two children to support, she began giving piano lessons. Her marriage to Lorenzo Grunwald brought her to Houston. Professor Clark entrusted

to her the instruction of his son, Horace, Jr., and with her founded the Philharmonic Society.

Rich in music teachers, Houston was still poor in public education. Though the Congress of the Republic of Texas had laid the basis for a statewide system of schools and universities, no money had ever been appropriated. Like other communities, Houston had struggled for forty years with a variety of private and parochial schools, some highly thought of, many short-lived. Public schools were sketchy.

What public schools there were closed entirely in late 1874. The Houston *Daily Telegraph* of January 30, 1875, announced: "German-English School—The Free Schools having closed, the German-English School, corner Milam and McKinney streets, will be opened again as a private school on Monday, the First Day Of February . . . Teachers —W. J. R. Thoenssen, Mrs. K. DePelchin."[10]

Wealthy Houstonians sent their children to private academies and to boarding schools in the East or in England, France, or Switzerland. Quite a few taxpayers disapproved of the whole idea of public schools as an unnecessary "charity," and frowned upon the mixture of rich and poor children that might ensue.

But from the start, Houston's most respected leaders shared Thomas Jefferson's belief that public education is essential to democracy, and worked to provide it in their city for all children. The three Negro schools that had been opened in 1866 by the Freedmen's Bureau were replaced in 1870 by the Gregory Institute, housed in a new eight-thousand-dollar building at Jefferson and Louisiana.

Bombarded by telegrams of invitation, Jefferson Davis came to Houston in May, 1875 as honor guest of the State Fair. He was met at the station by his old friend, former Governor Francis Lubbock, by Mayor J. C. Lord, and by a throng of cheering Houstonians. The Houston Light Guard escorted him to the home of Major T. R. Franklin, a rich, naturalized Englishman. During his stay, Mr. Davis was offered the presidency of the proposed Texas A&M College and of a railroad to the Pacific. A special train was put at his command for his travel in Texas. The mayor and City Council gave him a gala dinner before he entrained for Dallas. It was a heart-warming welcome for the one-time leader of the Lost Cause.

Davis wrote home to his wife Varina, "The country is beautiful, abounding in flowers. There is a refined society, a goodly number of old Mississippians and their descendants. The people have a robust, healthy look, and are cheerful and confident of their future."

The Houston Light Guard had been chartered in April, 1873, with Col. Edwin Fairfax Gray as company commander, Henry Johnson as first lieutenant, and Decimus et Ultimus Barziza as second lieutenant. It was rapidly winning favor. Smartly uniformed in Confederate gray, composed of popular men, the guard drilled and practiced to achieve perfection. In its first public appearance, it marched in the Mardi Gras parade of King Comus in February, 1874. A year later, under Capt. Jo Rice, it competed in Austin, winning a sword valued at five hundred dollars. The guard claimed "the distinction of being the first guard of honor Mr. Davis had after the war."

Free public schools at last opened in Houston in 1876. As a result of state and local legislation, the city assumed control. The mayor appointed the board of trustees and a board of examiners. Tuition was abolished, and attendance was compulsory for four months a year for all children aged eight to fourteen. Pupils older or younger were charged four dollars or less a month.

In 1877, Edward Mandell House went off to Cornell University, where his studies ranged from botany to Anglo-Saxon literature, from ancient history to modern language. But after two years, he came home to care for his beloved father, now widowed, who had suffered a stroke.

When Thomas William House died in January, 1880, he left a tremendous estate—

including a quarter of a million acres of land in sixty-three counties. His will provided that all his properties and businesses be kept intact for five years and thereafter be equally divided among the children: T. W. House, Jr., John, Charles, George, Edward, and Mary Caldwell. Although T. W. House had freed his slaves before the famous Juneteenth declaration, most of them stayed on the Arcola Plantation where cotton and sugarcane grew, and which had the largest sugar refinery in Texas. At his brothers' request, Edward stayed on to help manage the businesses and the plantation. But his Cornell years had stirred his interest in politics and government.

Texas still had no state universities. Houstonians like Dr. Ashbel Smith had been prodding the Texas legislature to remedy the lack. Formerly chief justice, Gov. Oran M. Roberts (1879–83) was determined to give Texas youth the benefits of higher education. The creation of Texas Agricultural & Mechanical College in 1876 started a spate of legislation. The Sam Houston Normal Institution at Huntsville and the Agricultural and Mechanical College for Colored Youths were created in 1879. The governor asked Dr. Smith to find a site for what would become Prairie View University.

Rep. Joseph Chappel Hutcheson of Houston introduced the bill that established the University of Texas. Hutcheson, who had served in a Virginia regiment during the war, was a graduate in law of the University of Virginia. With his wife Mildred, he had come to Houston by way of Grimes County in 1874.

Dr. Smith was off to Paris again, this time as Texas commissioner to the World Exposition of 1878. Because of his medical studies in 1832 and his service as chargé d'affaires for the Texas Republic in 1842–44, he spoke excellent French. He remained a bachelor, but as a physician and scholar he was a leader in every movement to support education. As president of the new University of Texas board of regents, he spent the last eight years of his life seeking professors of the highest quality for the faculty. He knew that the university must begin with a reputation for excellence.[11]

In the winter of 1879–80, Houston confirmed its reputation as the muddiest town in Texas. It rained every day for three months. Signs along Main Street warned: "Keep out. No bottom here." As the mud deepened, the streets became impassable. Haulers laid planks across the mud to tote freight into the stores by hand. When someone died, the pallbearers had to carry the coffin to the streetcar line, load it onto a streetcar, unload it at the gate of Glenwood Cemetery, and, with it, slog through the mud to the grave.

Ulysses S. Grant came to Houston in 1880, on the first train to arrive at the new Union Station. March 29 newspapers reported that five thousand Houstonians shouted themselves hoarse crying, "Grant! Grant! Grant!" So many followed him to the Hutchins House and crowded around him on the balcony that it was in danger of collapsing. Grant had been general of the Union armies, and president during some of the worst days of Reconstruction. But he had also approved the election that ousted the scalawag governor from office in Austin.

The Women's Christian Temperance Union, founded in 1874, was becoming a national force. In 1880, its president, Frances E. Willard, came to Houston on her first tour through the South, and in consequence Houston women met at Shearn Methodist Church to form a Houston chapter. They had a good case to argue. The annual average consumption of hard liquor in the United States was massive. Drunks staggering out of saloon doors at all hours of the day were a common sight in downtown Houston and other cities. And the woman with a hopelessly alcoholic husband had no way of supporting herself and her children.

The WCTU women, ahead of their day, set out to educate the public on the dangers not only of alcohol but of tobacco and narcotic drugs as well. This was a period of widespread morphine addiction, especially among well-to-do women. The Houston chapter had a broad interest in the welfare of women. It persuaded the city to employ a police matron at the jail. It helped to establish a girls' industrial school at Denton and the Crittenden home "for unfortunate girls." It opened a boarding house for working women and girls that paved the way for the YWCA in Houston.

People die, inevitably. But the causes of death change from decade to decade. Yellow fever, so deadly in 1839 and 1867, was rare in the late 1870s. In his ten years as rector of Christ Church, the Rev. Mr. Clemens faithfully listed the causes of death with each funeral he conducted. "Inflammation, Fever, Consumption and Congestion" were rife in the community. Of five persons dying of congestion within a few days of each other, three were under thirty. Abbie Latham Tryon, the little sister whom Tina Latham had often written from Paris, died of childbirth, one week after the death of her day-old son. She was twenty-nine.

But some of the causes as inscribed by Mr. Clemens were more remarkable: "Erysipelas, Spinal Infection, Asthma, Drunkenness [this man died at thirty], Dysentery, Shot [the victim was forty—the gambler perhaps?], Worms [age forty-five], Meningitis, Heart Disease, Apoplexy [a Lutheran minister], Paralysis, Pneumonia, Accident."

And at the bottom of the finely written page: "L. W. Daly, buried Glenwood Cemetery, Dec. 13, 1876. Cause of death— Spiritualism."

Chapter Nineteen

On with the New

HOUSTON always welcomed the newest inventions and discoveries. Connecticut had the nation's first telephone system in 1878. Houston had the second in 1880. By 1884, Houston had two hundred telephones in use, with a long-distance line to Galveston. As one advantage to the party line, shut-ins could listen to the service and sermon at Christ Church by telephone.

In March, 1880, Houston got its first electric arc streetlight.[1] In 1882, New York City and Houston were the first two cities in the country to build electric power plants. Houston scheduled its first train to New Orleans in 1880, but by 1890, Houston was a rail center of the region, with 234 trains arriving and departing each day.

In 1882 and only two years old, the Houston Electric Light and Power Company had one hundred lights "distributed through every ward," requiring ten miles of copper wire and six hundred poles and crossarms. It contracted with the City Council to furnish thirty-two lights to burn all night: "The company will light the city by placing the electric lights on 30-foot poles at the various intersections . . . so that in a short time Houston will be brilliantly illuminated at night." The lights were like those used on Brooklyn Bridge.

Houston embraced electric lighting more quickly than it had gas only sixteen years before, but still thought electricity experimental. In December, 1882, a *Houston Post* article headed "Edison's New Engine" carried the subhead ". . . relative to the success or failure of the electric light of Professor Edison." For another several years, prudent builders would install elaborate chandeliers with electric lights hanging down and gas lights flaring up from fluted glass shades. If one source failed, the other could take over.

But the *Post* was enthusiastic. Citing the $168 gas bill that the Kendall & Jones bar and billiard saloon paid in November, the *Post* predicted that "the two electric lights they will use . . . giving a more brilliant light, will cost them $45 per month."

This was the Christmas season. "Last night," the *Post* continued, "there were fifty electric lights burning in the city, and a beautiful light they made. The streets at night are crowded with strangers and citizens going from place to place admiring the wonderful electric light and holiday goods displayed in the various stores."[2]

Then with a final note of pride: "The electric light in the *Houston Daily Post* office was turned on at dusk and flooded the office with a perfect burst of white light. The light is soft, steady and diffusive." Thus did a thirty- or forty-watt bulb outshine the gaslight that had seemed so brilliant in contrast to the kerosene lamp. It would be a while before other cities caught up with Houston and New York with home use of electric lights.

Despite its enthusiasm for electricity, the *Post* was floundering in the early 1880s. Gail Borden Johnson had started it on February 19, 1880, and then combined it with the Houston *Telegraph,* formerly the *Telegraph and Texas Register.* By this tenuous line, the *Post* could claim the Republic's first newspaper as an ancestor. But with disagreements and financial troubles the paper changed hands more than once and then folded. Not, however, for long.

Rienzi M. Johnston, the paper's political correspondent in Austin, moved his family to Houston in 1885. A Georgian, he had worked at the Savannah *Morning News* and the Austin *Statesman* before joining the *Post*. With Julius Watson as business manager, Johnston created a new *Houston Post*.[3]

Newspaper type was still set by hand throughout the world. The Linotype machine had been invented in 1884 by Ottmar Mergenthaler, but only the New Orleans *Times-Democrat* and the Louisville *Courier-Journal* had put the new invention to use. Threatened with a strike in 1890, Watson looked for an alternative to typesetters. Learning that the eight existing Linotype machines were in storage in Chicago, he bought them all and the *Post* became the first modern newspaper west of the Mississippi, one of three in the country. The paper was to match this feat when it became a pioneer in computer-set type in the 1970s.

Not yet thirty, Watson obtained the franchise for all territory west of the Mississippi, and went on to make a fortune selling the Linotypes. With part of his profit, he bought out other stockholders to gain control of the *Post*. But at thirty-eight, Julius Watson died of tuberculosis, leaving his paper and fortune in trust for his six-year-old son. Colonel Johnston, G. J. Palmer, and H. F. MacGregor managed that trust so well that they turned an enlarged estate over to Roy Watson after his graduation from Princeton in 1918.[4]

The decade of the 1880s brought a number of newcomers who would make lasting contributions to Houston. Martin Tilford Jones, a Tennesseean who came to Texas in 1873, established a lumber business in Terrell, near Dallas. In 1883, with his wife Louise, he moved to Houston and organized the M. T. Jones Lumber Company with two sawmills and lumber yards scattered across the state.

Young Presley Ewing, after two years in the law office of Judge E. P. Hamblen, went home to Ariel, the family plantation on Bayou Lafourche, to marry his childhood sweetheart. The two adjoining Louisiana plantations produced two remarkable young people. The son of a Confederate surgeon, Ewing was a law graduate of the University of Mississippi. For seven years, he had been engaged to Mary Ellen Williams of neighboring Sunnyside. In their waiting years, he had been the mainstay of his widowed mother; he put himself and his brothers through college. Nell Ewing, who had read all of Dickens by the age of nine, would become as influential in Houston as her successful husband. She was a crusader, who introduced six o'clock closing in Houston stores, organized the first Parent-Teacher Association, and pushed to place women on the school board.[5]

James A. Baker, Jr., brought his bride, Alice Graham, to Houston. Strikingly beautiful, she became a leader in settlement work in the Second Ward and in the promotion of a tuberculosis hospital.

Col. James H. Tennant, who had fought for the North in the Civil War, came down to Houston, attracted by the flourishing railroad industry. He would build the Houston, Galveston and La Porte Railroad and develop the town of La Porte.

"We move anything. We ship to all parts of the world." The promise was painted on the side of the horse-drawn moving vans of Sid Westheimer who founded Westheimer Transfer Company in 1883. He had a big, two-story brick livery stable with a resident veterinarian.[6]

The Houston Light Guard, meanwhile, was ready for nationwide competition on the drill field. The guardsmen won fourth prize in New Orleans in 1881, fourth prize in Nashville in 1882, beating a crack Boston unit. By this time, Houston was supporting the Light Guard with an enthusiasm that pro football and baseball teams might envy a century later. Houston businessmen voted to stage an interstate drill in Houstin in 1884—fairly sure that the Light Guard would triumph. They raised the money to give a five-thousand-dollar first prize and to entertain visiting companies. H. Baldwin Rice was manager of the drill. Invitations went out to all the finest drill teams in the country. The War Department sent three army officers to judge and make an official report to Washington.

The drill was held on the old fairgrounds, where later Fannin School would be built. In a week of marching in quick time, double time, and whatever time the judges specified, the Houston Light Guard lived up to all local expectations. The judges declared their performance "nearly perfect." Having won, the guard offered the prize money to cover their visitors' traveling expenses but were politely refused. The next year the guard won twelve thousand dollars in first prizes in drills at Mobile, New Orleans, and Philadelphia. Thereafter they were lavishly entertained at the armories of two famous regiments in New York. They were on their way to greater fame.

After forty-five years of mud, after dabbing at the problem with wagonloads of shell, after many failed attempts to plank the streets, Houston got its first pavement in the summer of 1882. Property owners gave ten thousand dollars to pave two blocks of Main Street with limestone squares laid on gravel. Merchants paid five hundred dollars each to have gravel spread on fifteen blocks of Congress and Franklin. But by the next winter, the relentless mud was oozing up over the limestone squares. In 1885, Main Street was paved with cobblestones all the way out to Texas Avenue—one-quarter of a mile.

In the mid-1880s, the ship channel was busy. Seven tugs, two steamboats, eighteen barges, ten steamships, and twenty-two schooners plied the channel on regular schedules.

The Houston Cotton Exchange operated out of one room of a house owned by Judge E. P. Hill. The 125 members had to chalk up on a blackboard all local, domestic, and foreign quotations. With a clear need for more room, they bought a lot on the west corner of Travis and Franklin for fifty-two hundred dollars. Architect Eugene Heiner designed a four-story building with a basement, to be built of red pressed brick with white sandstone trim. Vice-President H. W. Garrow assured the members that it would be "an ornament to our city." It cost some forty-five thousand dollars, but as it brought in revenues, there was no need to raise fees. A seat on the cotton exchange cost five dollars. The twelve-dollar annual dues could be paid in installments.

In the 1880s, John L. Sullivan gave a sparring exhibition at Pillot's Opera House, and Edwin Booth packed Pillot's Opera House with his performance in *Hamlet*. Crowds thronged to the fairgrounds to see the mule races. When vagrant cows became a problem downtown, the marshall brought in "a real live cowboy . . . entrusted exclusively with the enforcement of the stock ordinance."

Houston's fashionable young ladies were beginning to play tennis. An etiquette book of the 1880s commented, "The exercise is not of an exhausting character, and affords ladies a training in easy and graceful movements." The ladies pictured in the book wear hats with veils tied back, dresses with small waistlines, bustles, and short trains. Presumably all this concealed tightly laced corsets. The bustle revival of the mid-1880s took that fashion to a new extreme so that a lady might look normal from the front, but at the back, she wore a protrusion, as horizontal as a shelf, jutting out just below the waist.[7]

Schools were growing more and more crowded. The Houston public schools had been subsidized by the Peabody Educational Fund until 1882, and the school board had opened a Normal Institute for Negro teachers in the Gregory Institute. Because the system seemed so well established, the Peabody Fund withdrew. Nobody foresaw that Houston's rapid growth would bring in far more children than the classrooms could house.

Throughout the 1880s, Miss Mary B.

Brown's Young Ladies' School was the prestigious private school for girls. It had been founded before the Civil War; Adele Briscoe Looscan was an 1866 graduate. In 1886, the *Houston Post* considered it "the Vassar of the South." Its excellent faculty taught French, German, English, and mathematics to young girls from Houston's best families. Among its graduates were the daughters of W. D. Cleveland; Sally Brashear, who became Mrs. Sam McAshan; Martha Kosse, who married Dan Japhet; Annie Cabiniss who married C. G. Pillot; Annie Hume, Adele Looscan's niece; and Sophie Reichardt, who became Mrs. Fred Boettcher. Elizabeth Bell Bates, daughter of a respected Fort Bend County family, was a student there in 1881. She ultimately became the wife of Brazil's ambassador to the United States, although between Miss Brown's and Washington lay a colorful life and two other marriages.

Meanwhile, Mr. Cleveland sent his sons off to school. Alexander Sessums Cleveland and W. D. Cleveland, Jr., went to Sewanee Military Academy at an early age and, after two years at the University of the South, entered Yale.[8] Billy Cleveland was an outstanding athlete and went with the Yale football team to Europe in the early 1890s.

Calling a mass meeting at Pillot's Opera House, a group of Houston leaders founded the Young Men's Christian Association in 1885. William D. Cleveland was elected president, and Rufus Cage recording secretary.

As a port city, Houston maintained a lively interest in the rest of the world. In the 1880s the *Houston Post* carried daily accounts of what had happened in the Parliament in London. It also reported that Russia was "sounding Japan regarding a joint occupation of Corea." Its biggest ads shouted, "Europe! Through Tickets. From or to any point in Great Britain or the Continent of Europe via the Houston and Texas Cent'l Railway."

George Hermann responded. In 1885, he went by train to New Orleans, Washington, and New York, keeping a diary of his observations. He went from New York by steamer to travel through England, France, Germany, Austria, Italy, and his parents' homeland, Switzerland. This was the one big indulgence he ever allowed himself in his long and frugal life.

In contrast, his contemporary, Eugene Pillot, went regularly back to his native France. Born in Haute Saone, he had come came to Texas in 1837. In 1866, he was one of the founders of the Houston Direct Navigation Company, and in 1875 was one of the three men who chartered the Houston East & West Texas Narrow Gauge Railroad. In the last twenty years of his life, he made seven trips across the Atlantic.

Young Herman Eberhard Detering liked to move about the town and had a knack for spotting opportunities. The son of a furniture manufacturer in Germany, he came to Houston in 1881 at the age of nineteen. He started out as a clerk in Henry Henke's grocery on Market Square, but soon he bought a tiny neighborhood grocery on Washington Avenue. He moved in over the shop and went to work to build his fortune.

On his first trip down the ship channel for a picnic, he saw the value of the channel and began to buy land along its banks—sometimes a hundred acres or more, sometimes simply a slim easement along the way. Later he would buy land on the fringes of this city that was sure to grow. In 1885 he went back home to see his mother, his last trip to Germany. Thereafter, Houston would be home to him, his children and grandchildren.[9]

A fourteen-year-old South Carolina boy, with fifty dollars in borrowed money in his pocket, stepped off the train in Houston in August, 1886. His name was Robert Alonzo Welch. He was met by his cousin Chris, who in another ten years would found the respected Welch Academy for boys. Robert went to work for the Bute Company, a paint firm, working up to become a salesman and bookkeeper. This was the start of a quiet, hard-working bachelor life that would lead to the formation of the Robert A. Welch Foundation—a major benefactor of the Texas

Medical Center and of universities through-out Houston and Texas.[10]

In the late 1880s, the telephone company had 265 subscribers. Houston had "immediate delivery" postal service. The Houston Gas Company had twenty miles of mains. The six streetcar lines had replaced the old wooden rails with fourteen miles of steel track. Their stables had fifty mules to pull twenty cars. A new Louisiana Street bridge was opened across Buffalo Bayou.

The Houston Water Works was a some-time thing. For the city's first forty years, Houstonians drank rainwater collected in cis-terns and used bayou water for industry and to put out fires. Because the fire companies had to pump their own water, a fire alarm brought out every able-bodied man and boy.

In 1878, the city contracted with a New York firm to build a waterworks supplied by Buffalo Bayou. The twenty-five-year contract promised the city fifty fire hydrants, three million gallons of water a day from a 150,000-gallon reservoir, free water for three public fountains, and, for fires, enough pressure to throw six streams one hundred feet high.

In 1881, Houston businessmen, headed by former Mayor T. H. Scanlan, bought the sys-tem. Ten years later it failed when a fire swept through twenty acres of the city. Despite a messenger on horseback sent to urge greater effort at the pump house, it was forty min-utes before enough water flowed to put up a feeble twelve-foot stream.

Meanwhile, in 1887, Henry Thompson had drilled a well 180 feet deep in his yard at Franklin and LaBranch. It released a pure artesian well that gushed up in a two-foot fountain and flowed at the rate of fourteen hundred gallons an hour. This started a rush to drill. By 1891, the Water Works Company had fourteen artesian wells supplying seven square miles through forty miles of pipe. Houston, it seems, was standing upon the nation's third-greatest artesian reservoir. However great, the reservoir would not be able to keep up with Houston's growth and its demand for water.

Newly graduated from Jefferson Medical

College in Philadelphia, Dr. S. C. Red came to Houston in 1887 to establish his practice. Born at Gay Hill in Washington County, he had attended Washington and Lee Univer-sity and had been the first student to receive a B.A. from the University of Texas. He joined his uncle, Dr. David F. Stuart, founder of the Houston Infirmary. Dr. Red supervised the first nurses' training school in Houston and introduced ambulance ser-vice. He pioneered in the treatment of hip fractures and in the use of diphtheria anti-toxin.

The Sisters of Charity of the Incarnate Word opened St. Joseph Hospital in 1887 in the pleasant residential section around La-Branch and Crawford and between Elgin and downtown. Of all the hospitals of the pe-riod, this one would survive and grow into a major medical center.

And in 1888, Jacob Nathan Taub, a native of Hungary who had come to the United States six years earlier, brought his wife and children to Houston. He and three of his sons started selling tobacco and knicknacks from a pushcart in downtown Houston to gain a start in their own tobacco business. A year after their arrival, the last child of the family was born. This was Benjamin, who would become a financial and charitable power in the city, and for whom the Ben Taub Hospital would be named.

A Houston newspaper reported that "this season all dresses are made wide at the top. A lady wearing this dress with a Warner cor-set and three or four underdresses would have the appearance of having a very slender waist and wide hips." A Houston lady could also buy a pair of web silk stockings, hand-somely embroidered, for fifty dollars. The fashion reporter, almost surely male, edito-rialized that the purchase would require that the lady learn to kick. "She can—if she has the kick down fine—find many opportuni-ties for showing off her stockings."

The city's southern accent gained British overtones. Though most of the young En-glishmen were in the cotton business, Al-fred Lawrence-Toombes was a leather merchant. Two other young Englishmen came as church organists. But Houston was still polyglot.

Harper's Magazine in 1890 described the city marketplace: "The German farmers come in from distances of 20 miles and more, hauling their produce in wagons. . . . Nearby on the side walk a Chinese peddler displays his wares. . . . This thin-faced Italian had a wagon laden with game, all killed close by. . . . The respectable looking colored man and woman sell cold food – fried catfish to tender chicken, hard-boiled eggs and heaps of golden cornbread and roasted potatoes. . . . The butchers are nearly all Germans, with a Frenchman and an American or two.

"In and out of the building they surge, for all of Houston is here . . . black, white, brown and yellow – Negroes, Americans, Mongolian, Irish, Dutch, French, Germans, Italians, and Spanish – they are all there, laughing, teasing, talking, quarreling, gesticulating, bargaining, staring, keeping appointments and making new ones, being proper or improper, polite or rude as the case may be."

These were all Houstonians. It is not quite clear just which among them were "Americans" by *Harper's* definition.

Chapter Twenty

Fin de Siècle

THE PARIS EXPOSITION and the opening of the Eiffel Tower in 1889 began the modern era for the Western world. With Houston as the chief rail center of Texas and Texas ranking third in railroad development among the nation's states, Houston was fulfilling the expectations of John and Augustus Allen.

It tended to double its population every ten years. The census of 1890 gave the city a total of 27,557—three times that of 1870. By 1893, Houston had an estimated population of 50,000. The southerners who had come after the Civil War were followed a decade later by farsighted northerners, attracted by agricultural, railroad, and port development. And, like iron filings to a magnet, enterprising young men were moving to Houston from the plantations, timberlands, and small towns of Louisiana and East Texas—often bringing substantial business with them.

Houston began the last decade of the nineteenth century optimistically. Nice people were getting rich off cotton, lumber, railroads, and land. Business took on an elegant tone. Businessmen who lived on Quality Hill wore tall silk hats when they drove to town in their carriages with velvet upholstery.[1] Their offices were often handsome with red plush chairs. Most were equipped with brass spittoons, as were hotel lobbies and saloons. The great houses with turrets, balconies, circular rooms, ballrooms, and indoor tennis courts were warm in hospitality. Euchre was the popular game, and at balls Houstonians in full evening dress danced the lancers and the waltz.

In June, 1891, Houston got its first electric streetcar. Until that moment, nobody in Houston had ever seen a vehicle moving down the street under its own power. Running on an exclusive right of way, pulled by a loudly puffing engine, a train was, somehow, different. This new car seemed uncanny. The town turned out to stare. In the courthouse, a jury was hearing a case. With the word that the new electric car was coming, the judge called a recess. Spectators, judge, jury, and court officials ran out to see.

The judge said, "I felt that no person over whose actions I had immediate control should miss this strange and novel sight." Some Houstonians viewed the contraption with distrust, if not alarm, and said that a horse, a mule, or their own two feet were quite good enough, thank you.

But within a short time, the City Council had to regulate the speed of trolleys. It set a limit of six miles per hour in town, eight miles an hour in residential and industrial sections. It is not clear what prompted this caution. In 1874, Houston newspapers had bragged that one mule could draw a car holding twenty-three people "at fully 10 mph." Rosario Bonanno (later Bonario) had been driving a horse car since 1875, but with the arrival of the trolleys he retired—accepting a gold watch from the company for his years of service.

Houston had become very aware of the state's young attorney general, James Stephen Hogg. Still in his mid-thirties, he was a vast man, six foot three, weighing two hundred and fifty pounds. He was fighting the growing power of out-of-state corporations

—railroads, insurance companies, and manufacturers—charging that they were taking all possible profit out of Texas and giving little in return.[2]

Houston's prosperity rested on lumber, cotton, and cattle. Thirty-year-old John Henry Kirby, head of the two biggest timber companies in East Texas, moved to Houston to expand his interests. Edward Andrew Peden founded the Peden Iron and Steel Company. Edward Mandell House and his brothers had inherited a ranch stocked with Longhorns. Every year they shipped four-year-old steers and old cows to Saint Louis, Kansas City, and San Antonio. Fair freight rates were essential to all of these operations, as they were to farms and businesses throughout the South.

By 1889, Jim Hogg realized that his enforcement of existing laws was not enough—he needed more and stronger ones. He decided to run for governor. Edward House, who until then had concentrated on family business, became so interested in Hogg's ideas and his election campaign that he moved to Austin. Unwittingly, he had taken the first step toward Washington, the Woodrow Wilson presidency, and the Versailles Peace conference that lay twenty-seven years ahead. Meanwhile, his brother, T. W. House, Jr., bought out his brothers to take over the House Bank.

Jim Hogg was elected as the state's first Texas-born governor.

Pursuing his dream of a deep-water ship channel, Col. John Brady bought two thousand acres of land along the bayou. He planned a park where 3,750 magnolia trees would bloom and was an organizer of the Houston Belt & Magnolia Park Railway. It linked town and park, but his ultimate goal was for it to connect all other railroads coming into Houston with deep-water unloading docks at Long Reach and at Brays Bayou. However, he died on June 21, 1891. For years after, Houstonians picnicked and played in the eden of magnolia trees he had created.

William Marsh Rice had never returned to his house on Court House Square after the death of his wife Margaret. In 1867, he moved to New York City and bought a farm in New Jersey, which he developed into a lovely country place. But he and his second wife, Libbie, liked to come to Houston in midwinter. Sometimes they visited Frederick and Charlotte Baldwin Rice—his brother and her sister. Sometimes they put up at the Capitol Hotel, so that Mr. Rice could mosey around town, dropping in on his friends.

On one such visit, in 1891, Rice gave the first endowment of two hundred thousand dollars "for the foundation of an institute for the advancement of literature, science and art." The idea had been simmering for years.

In the late 1880s, Cesar Maurice Lombardi was president of the Houston School Board. Born in Switzerland and educated at Jesuit College in New Orleans, he knew that Houston needed a high school building, but the Houston City Council considered his proposal "highfalutin' nonsense." Therefore, in 1886 or 1887, he nabbed Rice and urged him to build a high school for the city. "I reminded him that he had made his fortune in Houston," Lombardi wrote long after, "and that . . . Houston should become the beneficiary of his surplus wealth."

Rice said he would think about it.

Perhaps a year later, Emmanuel Raphael approached Rice. English-born Raphael was the son of Rabbi Raphael. As a banker, he had handled a number of Rice's business transactions, and by 1880, he was president of the Houston Electric Light and Power Company. He asked his old friend to support a library fund drive.

Rice said he would think about it.

Finally in April or May, 1891, Rice gave his answer. He said it was up to Houston to provide a high school and a public library. Instead, he would endow an institution of learning, similar to the Cooper's Institute in New York, but not to be built until after his death.

With Raphael, Rice drew up an outline of his ideas and formed the first board to carry them out. He appointed his brother,

Frederick Allyn Rice; his attorney, James A. Baker; Alfred S. Richardson; James Everett McAshan, a native Texan, a banker, and a man with an unusual interest in education; Lombardi; and Raphael.

Under a deed of indenture dated May 13, 1891, the trustees agreed to hold Rice's note for two hundred thousand dollars, together with the "interest, issue, income and profits thereof," as an endowment for the school William Marsh Rice envisioned. This gift was historic, the largest sum ever given in philanthropy by a Houstonian.

It was only the start. In 1892, Rice gave ten thousand acres of farmland in Jones County, and the next year fifty thousand acres of pine timber lands in Louisiana.[3] Next he added almost seven acres fronting on Louisiana Street. The deed listed it as the "Site of the Institute." His last gift in 1894 was the Capitol Hotel property, but its revenues were to go to the Rices so long as they lived. To please his wife, he made her a cosigner on these gifts.

When Dr. Edgar Odell Lovett was inaugurated as first president of the institute, he said of Mr. Rice: "He made a fortune in Texas. . . . He gave his fortune—the whole of it—to Texas, for the benefit of the youth of the land in all the years to come." William Marsh Rice had not only founded an institution, but he had set an example that future Houstonians would respect and emulate. None of this should leave the impression that William Marsh Rice was a sweet, sentimental old man. Quite small in stature, he was peppery and sharp-tongued almost as a matter of policy. When one of his nephews protested Uncle William's harsh remarks to a butcher, Rice replied with a chuckle, "That's the way to get the best cuts of meat."

The Bayland Home had moved to Houston, with Keziah Payne DePelchin as its matron. She was paid sixty-five dollars a month, from which sum she was to "hire such assistance as needed." From her lifetime of nursing the sick, she knew how many children were left with a single parent or none.

In the spring of 1892, when she came across two homeless little ones, she simply founded a home for children and announced it in the next day's *Houston Post*. With the help of Mrs. W. C. Crane, she rented a small cottage and began.

In January, 1893, Faith Home was chartered. Mrs. DePelchin charged ten cents a day or seventy-five cents a week, if the parent could pay. She was trying to support the charity on her Bayland salary and was known to walk across town from Bayland to Faith Home to save the five-cent streetcar fare. Houston women surged to help her. Mrs. Charles Dillingham and Mrs. B. F. Weems were named to the first Faith Home Board, and for years, only women were elected to it. It was not an orphan asylum, Mrs. E. N. Gray later wrote, "but a comfortable home where the father who has lost his wife may place his little ones . . . a home where the mother may shelter her helpless children while she earns a living."

In 1890 to 1900, "Old Houston" meant those families that had come during the days of the Republic or before the Civil War. But in each decade, the best of the newcomers were accepted warmly. Money was never important to acceptance. Those who had nice manners, good taste, and a great willingness to serve the community soon blended into the old Houston society, becoming a part of it and emerging as civic and social leaders. New blood, new energies, new ideas for the city have regularly revitalized Houston's civic and corporate body.

H. W. Garrow, for instance, became president of the Houston Cotton Exchange in 1892—a post he was to hold for ten years. A native of Mobile, Alabama, and a graduate of the Virginia Military Institute who had served the Confederacy, he had come to Houston in 1877 and been a leader in the cotton business ever since.

A colonel in the Union Army, Charles Dillingham had settled in New Orleans after the Civil War. But in 1885, when appointed receiver for the Houston and Texas Central Railway, he moved his family to Houston.

By 1893, he was vice-president of the South Texas National Bank and on the building committee for the Presbyterian church—though not a church member. He would later serve with Ross Sterling and Camille G. Pillot on the first ship channel navigation commission.

The decade of the 1890s brought a number of such men to Houston. In 1891, Samuel Fain Carter, a rising young lumberman, came from Beaumont. The son of J. Q. A. and Mildred Richards Carter of Alabama, he was brought in infancy by his parents to Sherman, Texas.[4] In East Texas, he built up a successful lumber business with M. T. Jones, but in his mid-thirties, he sold his Beaumont interests for twenty-five thousand dollars. With this capital he founded the Emporia Lumber Company—his start toward making his fortune in Houston.

In 1892, Theodore F. Heyck, born in Port Lavaca and reared in Galveston and Abilene, left a promising career with a bank in Big Springs to enter the cotton business in Houston. A few months later he became general manager of the Consumers Cotton Oil Company in Texas, Arkansas, and Louisiana.[5]

In 1892, Robert Scott Lovett came to Houston and joined the firm of Baker, Botts, Baker & Lovett. Born in San Jacinto County, Lovett had gone to high school in Houston, read law at home, and been admitted to the bar at Cold Springs in 1884. His first client was the Houston East and West Texas Railway Company, and he soon became general attorney for the Texas and Pacific Railway Company. The Lovetts built a mansion—one of Houston's handsomest—on the corner of Main and Gray.

Edwin B. Parker, a native of Missouri, had earned his law degree at the University of Texas in 1889. After four years with the Missouri, Kansas and Texas Railroad, he came to Houston in 1893 to practice law with Baker, Botts, Baker & Lovett. He married Katherine Putnam, a gifted pianist, and by 1897 was a partner in the firm.

Judge Edwin Hobby moved with his family from Livingston to Houston to become John Henry Kirby's attorney. A native of Florida, he had come to Texas in 1860, fought for the Confederacy with the rank of captain, married Eudora Pettus in Richmond, served three terms in the Texas Senate, and had been elected district judge. Withal, he had become the leading authority on land law in Texas and author of the definitive book on the subject.[6]

The twenty thousand black Houstonians shared in the general prosperity. A survey of November, 1893, found that Houston had more black homeowners than any other two cities in Texas, with most of the houses valued at from two thousand to five thousand dollars. This was a time when two thousand dollars could build a comfortable bungalow and five thousand a large Victorian house. One black Houstonian owned fifty rental houses. The black community maintained an orphanage and shelter for the blind and for the aged. The older Houston neighborhoods were not segregated by race.

For more than twenty years, the Rev. Jack Yates had encouraged black Houstonians to buy property. As pastor of Antioch Baptist Church in Freedmen's Town from 1868 to 1891, he urged members of his congregation to invest in Fourth Ward real estate and became a notable property owner himself. He helped the newly freed men to negotiate land deals, and if they could not read or write—and many could not—he handled their taxes and secured their deeds. From home ownership, increasing numbers of black Houstonians followed the Yates example to invest in real estate. The tendency has continued ever since.

The city seemed to lay railroad tracks more easily than it paved streets. In 1893, pavement was still limited to the quarter-mile of stones put down on Main in 1885. The *Houston City Directory* of 1893 also listed four miles of cypress and bois d'arc blocks, "perhaps the most durable wooden pavement known," and three-quarters of a mile of cypress planks. The city contracted for six and a quarter miles of vitrified bricks.

Meanwhile, the city of Houston Heights was being planned. A forest covered the high land rising sixty-two feet above the bayou a mile and a half from the Grand Central depot. Oscar Martin Carter, who owned Houston's two mule car railway lines, was president of the Omaha and South Texas Land Company. D. D. Cooley, the company treasurer, moved to Houston to plan and manage the new town. They bought 1,765 acres and subdivided it with separate residential and factory sections. In May, 1892, they began work. They cut eighty miles of streets and alleys, macadamized Heights Boulevard, and built an electric street railway system to connect the new suburb to Houston. They also built a steam freight line to link with the Houston and Texas Central Railroad to haul factory raw materials and products. They spent $750,000 on improvements before the first lot was offered. S. D. Wilkins

Designed by George E. Dickey, the new First Presbyterian Church, completed in 1896, was considered one of the finest west of the Mississippi. *Courtesy Houston Metropolitan Research Center, Houston Public Library*

bought it and became the new town's first postmaster.

Daniel Denton Cooley was originally from Ashland and Lincoln, Nebraska. When he moved to Houston, he brought with him his wife Helen and three sons: Denton, Arthur, and Ralph. "My father was Ralph," said Dr. Denton Cooley, "and he was three years old. Even before coming, my grandfather had plans for the new city he envisioned. It was to be elegant, with broad boulevards and gracious houses. To do justice to Heights Boulevard, he insisted that they build two bridges across White Oak Bayou. He built the big Victorian mansion with turrets and cupolas to set an example of the kind of house he wanted to see on Heights Boulevard.

"It was a great house for a little boy to play in. They grew mushrooms in the basement because it was dark and damp. The attic had all sorts of things in it, like my grandmother's sidesaddle. And you could look out from the cupola and see for miles. Grandfather used to tell me that he could look down from there and see wolves coming into the yard in the dark. And the barn was made to hold hay and the carriage for the horses."[7] The panic of 1893 slowed growth of the Heights for several years, but gradually it became one of Houston's loveliest neighborhoods.

Both the Episcopalians and the Presbyterians had outgrown the churches they had built after the Civil War. In 1893—just before the panic—both began to raise money and deal with architects. The Rev. William Hayne Leavell, an impressive man, six foot three inches tall with white hair and mustache, made building his first order of business when called to the First Presbyterian Church. The Presbyterians decided to give up their first site on Main at Capitol Avenue—the historic gift of the Allens. They bought from T. W. House a half-block on Main at McKinney for twenty-one thousand dollars and sold the Capitol site for forty-five thousand.[8] Even so, the new church left the congregation owing thirty thousand dollars. After eight years and many of Dr. Leavell's most persuasive sermons, the debt was cleared and the church dedicated.

The Episcopalians had paid the Allens a hard-earned four hundred dollars for their half-block on Texas Avenue between Fannin and San Jacinto. So they simply tore down the lovely little church designed by Edwin Fairfax Gray and began to build a new one. The congregation had to borrow twenty thousand dollars in gold coins to finish the church and spent years paying it off. The 1893 building, now Christ Church Cathedral, still stands on the first site dating from the days of the Republic of Texas—the only one of the early churches to do so. It cost $36,691 to build.

Rosa Allen, engaged to Robert Cummins Stuart III, had planned for her wedding to be the first in the new building. This was appropriate: Rosa was descended from Ezekial Thomas, an Austin colonist. Rosa's grandmother was said to be the first Anglo child born in the county. Her fiance was a descendant of Frances Blake Stuart, who had gone to Christ Church as a child in the days of the Republic. The church choir rehearsed "To Thee O God Enthroned on High" to sing as a processional to the music of *Lohengrin*.

Sallie Ashe, however, decided to be the new church's first bride and staged her wedding to Charlie Fitch the evening before Rosa Allen's. For two successive nights Houston society in formal white tie and evening dress heard the choir sing "To Thee O God Enthroned on High" as it led the bride to the altar. Apparently the two brides remained friends.

Along with the rest of the country, Houston endured the panic of 1893. It hit some investors and developers hard. It left church congregations with heavy debts, halted the development of new subdivisions, and caused some businesses to fail. It brought hard times but in Houston, at least, it was short lived.

In 1894, Emma Richardson Cherry, a professional artist who had studied in New York and Paris, saved a part of Houston's heritage. Until the Civil War, the house begun by E. B. Nichols and finished by William Marsh Rice on Court House Square had been one of Houston's finest. Its sills of heart-pine measured eighteen by twenty-four inches. It was paneled with rosewood. Vacated by Rice, the house was used as a hospital during the yellow fever epidemic of 1867, then as a hotel. John D. Finnigan, a hide and leather merchant, bought the property for twenty-five hundred dollars, and a few years later put the house up for sale.

Mrs. Cherry asked her husband, Dillin, to buy the front door for her. He offered twenty-five dollars. Because no other bids were made, he received the whole building for his twenty-five dollars. The Cherrys moved the worn but splendid old house to Fargo Street—then in open country. It took forty-six nights and cost four hundred and fifty dollars to move, but the house lost not a single brick. Mrs. Cherry set up her studio and the school that would polish the talents of art students for the next thirty years.[9]

Valentine's Day of 1895 found Houston blanketed in white, with icicles hanging from the eaves.[10] Snow had begun to fall the evening before, and fell all night and all day. By Valentine's night, it measured two feet deep, with drifts shoulder high. Trains and streetcars halted. Lacking transportation to school or work, the whole town went on holiday. The ingenious improvised sleds. But John E. Patrick, manager of the Houston Transfer Company, had a sleigh. Hitching it to a handsome pair of bay horses, he went to the rescue of those trying to walk to town, including County Commissioner Baldwin Rice. The *Houston Post* reported that the rescue missions were interrupted by raging snowball battles. Stores sold out of rubber boots before the snow melted.

Charlotte Baldwin Allen, the last of the three founders of the city, died on August 3, 1895, at the age of ninety. She left an estate of $51,867 to be administered by her nephew, A. C. Allen. She left bequests to two churches, her grandson, and to "three

Main Street residences were blanketed with a rare   cover of snow in 1895. *Photograph* © *Houston Post*

well-loved friends–Mrs. D. F. Stuart, Mrs. A. A. Szabo and Mrs. Sinclair Taliaferro."[11] Her grandson Pierce Allen Converse was Charlotte's only living descendant when she died.

In 1896, the Ladies Parish Association of Christ Church opened Sheltering Arms at 1517 Hutchins Street as a refuge "for homeless and friendless old women." Mary Jane Harris Briscoe (Mrs. Andrew Briscoe) was a founder and the first president.[12] The Florence Crittendon Rescue Home for Girls was organized in 1896. The board bought two and a half lots at the corner of Elgin and Caroline for seven hundred dollars and built a home. Girls came from all parts of Texas. In its first fifteen years, the home cared for more than one thousand unwed mothers.

George Hermann–whose name was pronounced *Harmon*–had grown up with Houston since his birth in 1843. In 1872, he formed a partnership with W. J. and J. J. Settegast to sell land and cattle. From 1884 on, he devoted his time to real estate. By the 1890s, he was a very rich man. Oil wealth was yet to come. He was unmarried. His parents

and his two bachelor brothers were all dead and buried in Glenwood Cemetery. He lived frugally. Penuriously. Though kind to a poor person in trouble, he never gave money to popular civic causes. Yet for years, he wanted to give to his city both a charity hospital and a park. It proved to be not easy. In 1898 he offered Harris County a block of land bounded by Texas and Capitol, Hutchins and Broadway (later Dowling Street), as site for a hospital. The county was to build on it within five years, or it would revert to him. The five years passed, the land reverted, and he sold it to railroad interests for $125,000. He would not see the hospital or the park in his lifetime.

At the century's end, Houston business thrived. The Barden-Sheets Electrical Construction Company advertised that it led in fine residence work and offered bells, fans, elevators, electric lights, and burglar alarms. James Bute sold "fine wall papers, picture frames, window shades and art goods" at Main Street and Franklin.

President of the Continental Lumber Company at twenty-three, Lynch Davidson opened a lumberyard in Houston in 1897. He was on his way to building one of the South's largest retail lumber companies with yards in fifteen cities and close to a hundred thousand acres of ranch and timberland.[13] Japhet & Company were wholesale dealers in liquors and cigars. Isidore Japhet, who had founded the company in 1869, was president of the American Brewing Association; his son Daniel entered the firm in 1893. Sweeney, Coombs, and Fredericks had joined forces to become the city's leading jewelers, occupying the turreted building designed by George E. Dickey at 301 Main Street. George Heyer's drugstore was growing in elegance and the range of services. F. Gieseke & Son dealt in fine boots. Milby & Dow were dealers in coal and makers of hammered fire and building bricks.

Dr. Minnie C. Archer announced a practice limited to diseases of the eye, ear, nose and throat. But Drs. Boxell and Spann were specialists in chronic diseases of the eye, ear, nose, throat, lungs, heart, stomach, liver, bowels, kidneys, bladder, skin, blood, nervous system, and diseases of women. They further promised: "The Alcohol, Morphine and Tobacco Habits positively and quickly cured by a new method absolutely without injury or danger." This suggests that both medicine and society had at last discovered that morphine was not a harmless panacea.

The Houston Business League, organized in 1895, elected Rienzi M. Johnston chairman and W. W. Dexter secretary. The Houston Baseball Association was chartered in December of that same year with a capital stock of three thousand dollars. John Henry Kirby was president, Si Packard vice-president and Sam Taub secretary and treasurer.

In March, 1895, to the dismay of Judge and Mrs. Hobby, sixteen-year-old Will Hobby quit high school to take a job at the *Post*. It was in the circulation department and paid eight dollars a week. It let Will Hobby into the newspaper world that enchanted him. There he got to see and speak to Gov. Jim Hogg and meet Gentleman Jim Corbett, world heavyweight boxing champion. One reporter took him along to interview Geronimo, the Apache war chief.

A few months later, William Sydney Porter went to work as a reporter on the *Post* at a salary of fifteen dollars a week. A man in his middle thirties, he had been a ranch hand, a clerk in the state land office in Austin, a bank teller, and a magazine editor. His column, "Some Postscripts," became one of the paper's most popular features. He was already shaping the style that would make him famous as a writer of short stories.

Will Hobby admired Porter, seeing in him not only a good newspaperman but a kind one. Will would fetch sandwiches and, over lunch, the sixteen-year-old boy would listen to the newspaperman spin tales. One day, when an important looking visitor came into the business office asking for Porter, young Will Hobby proudly pointed to his friend's desk. The man was an officer from Austin bringing a summons for Porter on charges of embezzlement. Porter left the *Post* and Houston forever. But after serving a prison sentence, he went on to write the short stories signed O. Henry. His young friend went on to become governor of the state and publisher of the paper for which both had worked.

Chapter Twenty-One

Houston's Builders

CLUBS were important at the century's end. They were not only a source of amusement for their members, but they were a part of Houston's social and civic structure. Choral and musical societies provided music for the community. Church societies looked out for the sick and poor. Drama societies provided the local theater—Houstonians have always loved acting, both as amateurs and professionals. Reading societies furthered the library. Bicycle clubs and the Turnverein encouraged exercise. Social clubs determined the elite and set the pace for society. And the Houston Light Guards pervaded the entire fabric of the city.

From the city's earliest days, Houstonians had relished the theater, both as patrons and actors. An occasional young person of good family would take to the professional stage as a last fling before settling down to serious business. Amateur theatricals were seasonal. Richard Mansfield played Houston in *Beau Brummel* in 1893, and in *Prince KARL* in 1894 with predictable results.

"The Mansfield Club is named for Mr. Richard Mansfield the actor," the *Houston Blue Book—1896* reported. "The Club . . . has rendered with much credit some difficult plays and the several members have in some instances acquitted themselves in manner equal, almost, to the most talented professionals."

The Ladies Reading Club was founded by Adele Looscan, who became its first president. Its members felt the need of a public library. The Houston Lyceum had been exclusively for men for fifty years until 1887 when, short on revenue, it voted to admit women. It hired Margaret Hadley Foster as its first librarian at a salary of twenty-five dollars a month, but it continued to be for members only. Once it let down the bars to women, however, the Lyceum gained new impetus.

In 1899, the Ladies Reading Club persuaded the City Council to allot two hundred dollars a month for the Lyceum, thereby making it a public institution. Working with the Reading Club, the Women's Club wrote Andrew Carnegie, the Scottish industrialist who was helping cities across the country to build libraries. Mrs. W. E. Kendall, the president, received an answer from "Skibo Castle, Ardgay, N.S., 28 Oct. 1899."

Carnegie offered fifty thousand dollars for a building if Houston would provide a site and four thousand dollars a year for maintenance. With the endorsement of Mayor Sam Brashear, the Ladies Reading Club called together five clubs to form the City Federation of Women's Clubs. It was chartered in August, 1900, for the sole purpose of buying a site to take up the Carnegie offer. When the new federation had raised $7,880, the city bought the corner lot at McKinney Avenue and Travis Street from the First Presbyterian Church. With fifty thousand dollars from Andrew Carnegie and ten thousand from the city, the library could be built. On May 2, 1902, Mrs. Kendall laid the cornerstone. The stone building in Italian Renaissance style was to be lighted by gas and electricity.

Many contributed. In memory of their

daughter, Mr. and Mrs. Norman S. Meldrum set up the Norma Meldrum Children's Library Fund to buy books for children. Later, John E. T. Milsaps, a Salvation Army officer who had traveled widely, gave his collection of four thousand volumes, some of them rare and valuable, as well as curios and photographs from remote countries.

The Houston Lyceum, with its debates, musicales, and lectures, was no more. The Houston Public Library was its legacy. Miss Julia Ideson, a graduate in the first class of library science at the University of Texas, came to Houston as head librarian. Within ten years, she would make the library a center of Houston's intellectual life.

The Philharmonic was Houston's first serious musical club. Paul Bremond was first president, and Lucie Palmer Grunewald and Horace Clark its chief instigators. Mrs. J. O. Carr, Mrs. Annie Giraud, and Mrs. M. C. Culpepper were active members. The Philharmonic acted as a nucleus from which several other musical clubs grew.

Organized in the home of Mrs. E. A. Peden, known for her beautiful singing voice, the Woman's Choral Club set high standards. To become a member, an applicant had to perform in concert to prove her command over a wide classical repertoire. The first president was Mrs. Willie Hutcheson, *Houston Post* music critic.[1] She was followed by Mrs. E. B. Parker, an accomplished pianist, who was in turn succeeded by Mrs. W. H. Kirkland, who had a lovely voice. Not only did the fifty members perform well, but they brought concert artists to Houston.

In this period, young Lucie Hickenlooper of San Antonio spent much of her time in Houston studying music under Mrs. Grunewald, her grandmother. In 1896, at the urging of the composer Edward MacDowell, Mrs. Grunewald took Lucie off to Paris where—at eighteen—she became the first American pianist to win a scholarship to the Paris Conservatoire de Musique.

When Lucie Hickenlooper returned to New York for her debut at Carnegie Hall, her manager balked: It was hard enough to

The Houston Carnegie Library opened in 1904 at Travis and McKinney. *Postcard photograph*

book a woman on the concert circuit, much less one named Hickenlooper. Reaching back up the family tree, Lucy renamed herself Olga Samaroff—a name that was to win distinction in musical circles across Europe and America. She did, however, refuse to be palmed off as a Russian, claiming her American heritage and her Texas birth proudly throughout her life. It amused her to tell the story of her re-baptism to new acquaintances, as she did when she first met Leopold Stokowski, whom she later married.[2]

German-born Houstonians founded first the Houston Saengerbund and then the State Saengerfest. In singing, the Germans so dominated the stage that when the Houston Quartette Society (founded by Anton Diehl) decided to go statewide, it seemed necessary to specify the "*English* Singing Societies of Texas."

In 1887, the Third Ward Euchre Club was organized in the home of Mrs. Peter N. Gray. Writing twenty years later in *Key to the City of Houston*, Margaret Hadley Foster had to admit that "this alone would vouch for the club's respectability and freedom from low aims." The Wednesday Morning Whist Club, founded in 1894, elected Mrs. B. F. Weems president at its first meeting and kept her in office for the rest of the club's life. But to Mrs. Foster's distress, bridge was gaining over whist in popularity. She seemed to feel that bridge was more open to low aims than whist.

Hally Bryan (Mrs. Emmet Perry) and her cousin, Betty Ballinger, two of Moses Austin's great-granddaughters, founded the Daughters of the Republic of Texas one summer day in 1891 when they were reading Yoakum's *History of Texas*.[3] Before the year was out, a large San Jacinto Chapter of the DRT was founded in Mary Jane Briscoe's home on Crawford Street. Chapters of the Colonial Dames, Daughters of the American Revolution, and the United Daughters of the Confederacy were all established by 1900.

The new sport of cycling led to the Star Wheel Club for Men and the Ladies Cycle Club. A sketch in the 1896 Blue Book shows a lady cyclist wearing a hat, a fitted jacket to well below the hip, and knickers or bloomers fastened snugly below the knee. The jacket had huge leg-o-mutton sleeves.

State bicycle matches were held in Houston on July 4, 1892, when one hundred and fifty men raced. In October, a Houston team made the first run to Galveston, starting at five o'clock in the morning and arriving at three in the afternoon. After pedaling over the rutted, unpaved roads, they were so tired that they caught the train home.

The Benevolent and Protective Order of Elks met at Elk's Hall on the sixth floor of the Binz Building. The Houston Club had "commodious and handsomely appointed apartments in the Mason Building."

The Blue Book describes the Z. Z. Club as "the oldest and strongest social organization in the state and its membership is composed of the *elite* of the city." It was founded in 1858, when a group of young men met by candlelight in Henry Sampson's store. They wanted to form a dancing club, but only Rufus Cage and Henry Sampson, Jr., knew the new "round dances."

Round dances like the waltz and polka were as vigorous as the older square dances. Etiquette books took this into consideration, advising that "the refreshment room should, if possible, be on the same floor as the ballroom, because it is . . . dangerous, for ladies, heated by the dance, to encounter the draught of the staircase." But from her view in 1908, Mrs. Foster regretted that the round dances "were fated to entirely put out of countenance the old square dances which the good people of Houston had before found so enjoyable."

By the 1896 season, the Z. Z. Club was giving a cotillion a month, and it began to introduce the season's debutantes. In the early 1900s, the Z. Z. Club gave the annual debutantes' German, a "society ball" during the Christmas holidays, and a German just before and just after Lent.[4] But there was also a touch of *noblesse oblige*. In 1902, the club asked the Bayland Orphans Home, the Faith Home, and the Free Kindergarten for the names of all children in their care and, at a Christmas dinner in the ballroom, gave every child an especially chosen present.

The arbiter of the Z. Z. Club and of all Houston society was Spencer Hutchins, the son of W. H. Hutchins. He was a brother of the cosmopolitan Ella Hutchins Stewart Sydnor, who had studied in Paris and who was herself a leader in charitable as well as social life in Houston. Handsome, polished, a beautiful dancer, Spencer Hutchins was an officer in the Light Guards. In the Z. Z. Club roster of officers, his title was quite simply "Leader." Regardless of who became president, he held his unique office from the mid-1880s until he died twenty years later. He had no successor.

"He ruled the social life of Houston and South Texas," Bruce A. Olson wrote in the *Houston Review*. "His chosen coterie, with their wives, daughters, sisters and sweethearts, constituted Houston's 'four hundred.'" Known as "The Indispensable Spencer," he presented the debutantes not only of Houston but of Galveston, Austin, and San Antonio as well. First families of Houston and other Texas towns, as the *Houston Press* once commented, "followed his footsteps with a curious reverence."

With presentation by the Z. Z. Club, parents of debutante daughters were spared the expense – if they chose to be – of giving elaborate balls. A girl could be pleasantly and respectably brought out at an afternoon tea. Mrs. Clark C. Wren, née Mamie Culpepper, said, "In my day, all a girl needed was a few really nice skirts and a great many pretty little blouses." It was, after all, the era of the Gibson Girl. With her red-gold hair and delicate profile, Miss Mamie Culpepper was a Houston incarnation of Charles Dana Gibson's ideal.

Debutantes enjoyed a merry whirl. The Concordia Club, Houston's leading Jewish club with 110 members, gave twelve parties a year, including two lavish balls. The first of the season in November was always in honor of the debutantes; the second was on New Year's Eve. "For these two grand occasions, no expense nor trouble is spared to make them brilliant successes," Mrs. Foster wrote in the *Key to the City of Houston*, "and it would be hard to find a ball where richer jewels or handsomer gowns can be seen."

With its historic win in 1884 against the best militia of the country, the Houston Light Guards began to ride a triumphant wave. At Galveston in 1885, they took first prize of forty-five hundred dollars in what historian B. F. Carroll called "the most perfect drill ever witnessed in the United States." In 1888 in Austin they again took first place. Thereafter, the Houston guardsmen were asked not to compete again – the ultimate accolade. Instead, the people of Galveston had them as guests and gave them five hundred dollars for an exhibition drill.

The company was not merely for show, as Bruce Olsen points out in his excellent study for the *Houston Review*. Under the state charter, it was a volunteer militia. It was mobilized at least sixteen times between 1873 and 1903 to deal with strikes, racial conflicts, and political feuds; to protect a black prisoner from a lynch mob; and to keep civil order in Galveston after the 1900 hurricane. Many Houstonians won their military rank in the Light Guards, and in 1898 the company marched off for a year of war in Havana, where its remarkable discipline proved itself.

The commanders in order of service were Fairfax Gray, John Coffin, Jonas Rice, George Price, James A. Baker, Jr., Thomas Scurry, F. A. Reichardt, George McCormick, R. A. Scurry, C. Hutchinson, Milby Porter, and Dallas J. Matthews.

To the end of her life, Charlotte Allen always sat on her front porch to watch the annual parade. Captain Jo Rice was her great-nephew.[5] Once, as he led his company down Main Street, she stopped the parade and said, "Jody, I just want you to remember that the blood of William Wallace flows in your veins."

Jody's grandson, Hugo Neuhaus, Jr., said, "My grandfather thought that William Wallace must be some kind of fantastic hero. Years later when he took my mother and her sisters to Scotland, my grandfather said to them, 'You know, I am descended from William Wallace.' A man who overheard him turned and said 'There never was a greater scoundrel in the world!' That cooled my grandfather's ardor for his forebears."

The bystander must have been an Englishman. Sir William Wallace (1272?–1305) is identified by at least one encyclopedia as "a Scottish patriot who led a revolt against King Edward I of England. The story of his life has stirred the national pride of Scots for more than 600 years."

In all the rosters, regardless of who was captain or lieutenant or private, one listing was always the same: "Perpetual drummer, John Sessums (colored)." Sessums worked as chief porter at the First National Bank and was always given time off to travel with the guard. But after a new bank president came in, when Sessums asked for his usual days off, he was turned down. As was their custom, the Light Guards marched in full parade to the railroad station.

As a small boy, Bill Kirkland heard the story of what happened: "They marched up Main Street, turned on Franklin, headed for the railroad station. John was on the curb and he couldn't stand it. He quit his job and went with them."

The success of the Houston Light Guards

prompted the forming of fifteen other militia companies in Houston between 1873 and 1900—many of them started by former Light Guardsmen. John Sessums founded and captained the Davis Rifles and the Sheridan Guard, two of the three black companies of the period.

Military organizations were intensely popular across the country. Gentlemen found in them a fraternity for civic duty, self-discipline, recreation, and society. Military schools for teenage boys were thought to build character. Churches and schools had junior drill teams. Small children were clad in coats and hats of military cut.

Using thirty thousand dollars of accumulated prize money and floating a thirty-thousand-dollar bond issue, the Light Guards called on the prominent architect George F. Dickey to build an armory at the corner of Texas and Fannin. It was as much clubhouse as armory, with a dining room, game rooms, billiard tables, and a reading room with easy chairs and twenty-five magazine subscriptions. It was open from eight in the morning until midnight, and every Thursday was ladies' day. The guard gave parties and balls, presided over, of course, by the autocrat of Houston society, Lt. Spencer Hutchins.

Olson argues that the Houston Light Guards held the real power of the city. Generation by generation, sons entered the guard as their fathers retired. Older members kept their bond through annual reunions or through the Houston Light Guard Club. They all lived within a short walk of each other. They "worked together, married one another's sisters and formed social bonds that lasted a lifetime," Olson writes. "The Light Guards mustered the cream of Houston's young men. . . . Light Guardsmen owned, managed and worked in the businesses that formed the basis of Houston's economy in the last quarter of the nineteenth century."

Between 1874 and 1908, a member of the guard served as president of the Houston Cotton Exchange every year except between 1879 and 1881. Seven of Houston's mayors were Light Guards. At least fifty-eight guardsmen were elected or appointed to political offices in the city or county. Olson concludes that the Houston Light Guards "served with courage, honor and good sense during a number of racial and civil disturbances and in the Spanish-American War; and, both as a company and as individuals, accepted a responsible role in the community."

Good Old Days

DESPITE periods of depression and a war with Spain, the years from 1890 to World War I were the good old days for Houston. It was a time of explosive growth: It would mark the dramatic birth of Rice Institute, the oil boom, the migration to Houston of the oil pioneers, the revolution caused by the automobile, and, as always, the steady arrival of young, enterprising men and women from many parts of the world. Yet, the town continued to be Southern and serene.

Texas Avenue was a wide, gentle, unpaved street of big Victorian houses and churches. Gaslights hung over the street from tall stands shaped like shepherd's crooks. Each evening at dusk, the lamp lighter moved from lamp to lamp.[1] Shearn Methodist Church, lovely with its graceful spire, stood at 809 Texas. Christ Church was between Fannin and San Jacinto, the First German Evangelical Lutheran Church at Texas and Caroline, and the towering Church of the Annunciation stood at Texas and Crawford. The Houston skyline was defined by steeples. Main Street had the First Presbyterian Church on the corner of McKinney, the Central Christian Church at Bell, the Second Church of Christ (Scientist) and the Second Presbyterian Church at Dennis. The First Baptist Church was at Fannin and Walker.[2]

Houston prospered in the mid to late 1890s. Jacob Binz started the skyscraper era in 1894 with his six-story Binz Building at Main and Texas Avenue. It was the first to be built of concrete, stone, and steel. He built a foundation to support twenty stories, though skeptics considered this impossible. The hydraulic elevators drew people from as far away as Oklahoma City to see the lifts "operated by water." The Binz Building, which cost sixty thousand dollars, survived six fires over the years without serious damage. Amazingly, in this city of vast spaces, the reason for the skyscraper in Houston was the same as in New York: the high cost of land.

The *Houston Blue Book, 1896* reflects a leisured life in which a lady had an "at-home" day on which she would receive callers. It also reflects a hospitable life in which big Victorian households included maiden aunts, orphaned nieces and nephews, and young persons new to Houston and not yet ready for a home of their own.

The Blue Book listed the homeowner, the telephone number, the address, and all who lived there. It gave several pages of advice under the title "Social Code," explaining the fine points of when to call, how long to stay, and when to leave cards. It listed the at-home days of those ladies who kept this custom. Mrs. Rufus Cage, Mrs. E. W. Hutchinson, Mrs. R. E. Bering, and Mrs. J. M. Bering all chose to be at home on Wednesdays. Mrs. Charles Dillingham was at home on Thursday.

Mr. and Mrs. Denton Cooley had moved into their mansion on the Boulevard and Sixteenth Avenue, Houston Heights, with their sons Denton, Arthur, and Ralph Clarkson. The Levys, with Miss Harriet Levy as mainstay of the family, were living in their big

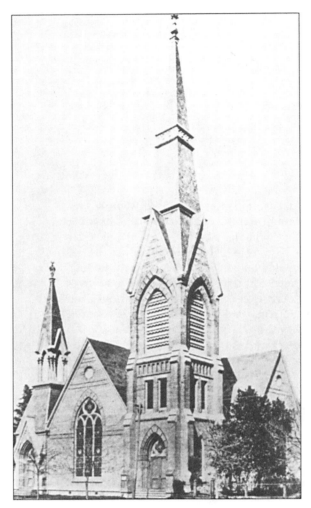

With its 130-foot spire, the Charles Shearn Memorial Church was greatly admired for its architecture. *Courtesy Houston Metropolitan Research Center, Houston Public Library*

white house at 2016 Main—Abe M., Joe, Haskell, and Hyman Levy and Mr. and Mrs. Joe Goldman. The Honorable and Mrs. J. C. Hutcheson lived at "1417 McKinney and Washington" (this was Congressman Hutcheson) and listed their family as Miss Mildred Hutcheson, Rosalie, Joseph, Allen, and Palmer Hutcheson.

Some of the big houses, like that later built by the W. T. Carters at 2310 Main, had ballrooms.[3] Others had indoor tennis courts.

Few had more than one bathroom. They had fireplaces in every room, sliding doors between dining room and parlor, high ceilings, and tall windows. Few had central heat. None, before 1900, had ceiling fans. Most had sleeping porches, designed to catch the gulf breeze, where the children or the whole family slept in rows of single beds. Most of the houses had lovely lawns and gardens for summertime garden parties.

The drought of 1896–97 provided a cliff-hanging drama in the long efforts to bring a deep-water channel to Houston. Just before retiring from Congress in 1896, Joseph C. Hutcheson had introduced a bill asking for a survey for a twenty-five-foot channel. It passed both houses, but so quietly that newly elected representative Thomas Henry Ball was unaware of it. A thirty-seven-year-old attorney from Huntsville, he had no idea that the ship channel was the most important thing in life to those Houstonians who had fought for it, year after year, in countless trips to Washington.[4] But he soon learned. Before it was over, Tom Ball would give almost forty years of legislative effort to developing the Port of Houston.

At the insistence of Captain Hutcheson and successive delegations from Houston, the congressional River and Harbors Committee was coming down to see Buffalo Bayou. All of Houston was ready to explain how easily the bayou could be transformed into a deep-water ship channel. But the dry summer of 1896 grew drier. The fall rains did not come. Neither did the winter rains. By the end of the year, Buffalo Bayou had become a muddy trickle. In despair, two weeks before the congressional group was due to arrive, the local committee wired the congressmen not to come.

Too late. They were on their way. Fortunately, they had other projects to inspect before reaching Houston. Just before their arrival, a blue norther swept Texas, drenching the watershed of the Buffalo Bayou with a gullywasher. The bayou rose and overflowed.

"This little bayou of ours that was usually only a few feet deep in the city was, at that time by the grace of God, five feet above every bank from here to Galveston!" Joseph Hutcheson crowed on his eightieth birthday. They got their survey, but to persuade Congress to adopt the project would be the main burden of Tom Ball's career in Congress and compel him to run for one term more than he wanted to.

Houston saw its first automobile on March 16, 1897—an electric car, brought in by Montgomery Ward & Company of Chicago. Given a ride, the *Houston Daily Post* reporter wrote, "This horseless carriage was built especially for the company at a cost of $3,000 . . . as an advertising novelty. It is run by a set of storage batteries, 28 cells. . . . The tires are solid rubber. . . . It weighs 2,000 pounds." It was viewed more as an oddity than as a sign of the future.

Irish-born William L. Foley was the dean of the mercantile industry of Houston. He reached Houston in 1872 by way of New York. After four years of clerking in various stores, he opened Foley's in 1876. When his brother died in Ireland, he sent for his nephews, James and Pat, and in 1900, both entered the business. Kiam's was a popular department store at 320 Main Street, Krupp and Tuffly's was a fine bootery and Levy Bros. Dry Goods Co. was the place for ladies to shop.

Though the family was originally from New York, Abe Levy was born in Houston and in 1886 made ten dollars a week clerking at Foley's. But he was determined to become Houston's greatest dry goods merchant. In 1887, he and his brothers bought a small store on the corner of Main and Congress. Their business philosophy, often expressed, was "Treat employees fairly and they will do the same for you." Within five years they had to move to larger quarters, and in 1897 they were ready to build the store they had always envisioned. Houston was startled when the Levy brothers paid a thousand dollars a front foot for their site, but their store immediately earned a reputation for quality that it was to keep for the next half-century.

Jules Settegast, Jr., was the son of a cattleman associated with George Hermann. Because of his father's poor health, the younger Settegast gave up college and came home to take over his father's business.[5] Keenly proud of his native city, Settegast worked vigorously in civic affairs through the Chamber of Commerce and later the Texas and Southwestern Cattle Raisers' Association. Born in Galicia, Poland, Joseph Weingarten had come to Houston as a small child with his parents. He attended the public schools and in the 1890s went to Massey Business College. In 1901 he and his father opened their first grocery store.

In August, 1898, M. T. Jones died. His will called for his nephew Jesse to come to Houston from the Dallas office to manage the Jones lumberyards, sawmills, and timberland.[6] Jesse Jones, twenty-four years old, moved down and took over a new office in the six-story Binz Building. This was the start of his career in Houston, which would last fifty-four years and during which he would build more than fifty major buildings. By his will, M. T. Jones changed Houston's future.[7]

By this time, the very young Jones had a solid business reputation. At nineteen, while working for his uncle in Dallas, he had obtained a loan of five hundred dollars from a Dallas bank. He put the money in a lock box and, when payment was due, repaid the loan with interest. A few months later, he borrowed two thousand dollars and followed the same procedure. Not only did he establish a credit rating, but he learned how to borrow and use money as capital for profitable ventures.

Gradually, in the last years of the century, Ludwig Edvard Neuhaus and his grown children moved to Houston from the family plantation near Schulenberg. Born in Germany, he had come through Houston in 1846 as a young man of twenty-four, stopping only to buy a horse that would take him to Fayette County. After buying a large tract of land at a dollar an acre and starting to build on it, he went home to Germany, where he married. His children were all born at his Hackberry Planatation: Franz Carl Ludwig (to be known in Houston as Charley or C. L.), Wilhelm Oscar, Agnes, and Julius Victor. By 1900, all four of them and their own children were living in Houston.[8]

Until 1900, Court House Square was Houston's only park. It was an easy walk from most houses in town and, for those who preferred to drive, there was always a small boy eager to earn a nickel by tending the horses. The square had benches shaded by big trees. Ladies from nearby churches used it for bazaars and Easter egg rolls because it was fenced and they could charge ten cents admission at each of the four gates. Lighted by gas lamps, it was open until midnight. Young couples and families with children gathered there on pleasant evenings to stroll and see friends.

Christ Church started its annual May fete in 1899 with a May pole in the church lawn on Texas Avenue and a pageant climaxed by the crowning of a king and queen. Other churches were represented at the court by a duke and duchess. The city grew, but the annual Christ Church May fete continues to take place in the grassy quadrangle, shadowed by Texas Avenue skyscrapers.

In his two years in office from 1898 to 1900, Mayor Sam Brashear launched Houston on a drive for more parkland. The city bought the Noble house and some land around it to start Sam Houston Park.[9] This was farsighted in a time when open prairie and woodland surrounded the city. As the century began, there was such an abundance of quail in Houston Heights that hunters were charged with flagrant violations of the game laws. Young men shot squirrels in what would some day become Montrose and River Oaks. And only a mile south of town, they could find deer, turkey, prairie chickens, ducks, quail, jacksnipe, plover, cranes, and curlew.

In 1899, Jesse Andrews joined Baker & Botts. The son of Dr. Mark Edwin Andrews of Waterproof, Mississippi, he had attended the University of Texas, where he played on the university's first football team, earned a baccalaureate and a law degree, and passed his bar examinations. In November, 1900, Andrews married Celeste Bujac. "They married at seven o'clock in the morning at Christ Church," their son Edwin said, "because they wanted to go to New Orleans on their honeymoon. The train left at eight and they could go on passes from the firm." Quite a few Houston weddings were timed for that morning train to New Orleans.

The 1900 census gave Houston a population of 58,203, but the *Houston City Directory* claimed 87,783 in May, when Pres. William McKinley came to visit. Bill and Laura Kirkland were taken by their nurse to watch the president's parade. "I saw him sitting in an open carriage," Mr. Kirkland said eighty-four years later. "People were throwing bouquets." Small Bill's grandparents, the Alexander Port Roots, lived in a big house on the block that became Root Square. They had horses and a cow, turkeys and guineas. Because the Kirkland children – Bill, Laura, and Mary Porter – lost both their parents in childhood, they grew up in the care of the Roots.

President McKinley, so warmly welcomed by Houston in May, 1900, was shot in Buffalo, New York, on September 6, 1901, and died eight days later. Houstonians felt the tragedy keenly. Marching in uniform without side arms, all of the city's military units marched to Christ Church for the memorial services. Rabbi Henry Barnstein of Congregation Beth Israel joined the Rev. Henry Aves in paying tribute to the slain president.

After a stormy falling out with Rienzi Johnston, publisher of the *Houston Post,* Marcellus E. Foster resigned as managing editor and started a paper of his own. The first edition of the *Houston Chronicle* appeared on October 14, 1901, at two cents a copy. With his by-line of "Mefo," Foster continued as a major influence in the city. He refused to speak to Johnston for years, but his daughter Medora married Johnston's grandson, Neill T. Masterson, Jr.

After practicing law for more than twenty years in Brenham and LaGrange, Lewis Randolph Bryan moved with his wife and children to Houston, thereby giving the city another line of direct descendants of Moses Austin.[10] He was Austin's great-grandson, and grandson of the Moses Austin Bryan who had acted as Sam Houston's interpreter in his meeting with Santa Anna. In 1902 Bryan was elected president of the state bar association.

John Coalter Means moved his family to Houston and a house on Crawford Street in 1902, when his daughter Bonner was a child of eight.[11] "He took me to Longfellow School the first morning and told me how to get home," Bonner Means Baker (Mrs. James A. Baker, Jr.) remembered at ninety-one. "But when school let out, I went in the wrong direction and got lost. I saw two swinging doors and some men's feet and I went in. I didn't know what a saloon was. I had never even heard the word. And one of those men took me by the hand and took me within two blocks of my house. Houston is an awfully nice city."

After seventeen years of practicing law in Bastrop and LaGrange, Judge Hiram Garwood moved his practice to Houston in 1902. Born in Bastrop and a graduate of the University of the South, he had served in both houses of the Texas Legislature and as a Bastrop County judge.

In 1902, Mrs. M. T. Jones and her daughters, Augusta and Jeanette, were in Europe. They had inherited a fortune from the millionaire lumberman, including the lumber business being managed by Jesse Jones. While in New York on business, he received a cable from his Aunt Louisa, asking him to join them in France. As a man of twenty-six, he was captivated by Paris.[12] He and his cousin Augusta toured the Continent. Riding in an open landau in Rome, Jesse passed King Victor Emmanuel in his carriage. The young king lifted his hat and bowed. In a park in The Hague, the Houstonian saw Queen Wilhelmina of the Netherlands out for a drive. He bowed, and she

replied with a regal nod. Europe, he decided, was a friendly place. On the way home, he stopped in London for the coronation of Edward VII.

Now versed in the ways of royalty, he returned to Houston and in November was crowned King Nottoc IV. This suggests that Mr. Jones was a rising star socially as well as in business. The No-Tsu-Oh crown was quite an honor for so young a man who had lived in Houston only four years.

For those coming from New York in 1900, Gulf Coast living was sometimes a shock. Despite Houston's efforts at developing a water system, many houses still depended on cisterns for drinking water. Copper screens for windows and doors were not yet common. Rose Keeper's parents, Mr. and Mrs. Phillip Bumar, brought their five children from Buffalo to Houston in 1902, when she was seven years old. Friends had found for them a house on Nance Street in Fifth Ward. "It was just a big square building: no screens on the windows, no indoor plumbing, a cistern to catch rain water for our water supply," Mrs. Keeper recalled eighty-four years later.[13] "Sometimes during the summer the cistern would go dry. When you turned on your faucet at the bottom of the cistern you got a pan full of wiggle tails. Can you imagine why people had all those fevers? There were ants, there were ditches in front of the house where mosquitoes bred and crawfish grew. The streets were dirt with a little gravel mixed in. The dust was terrible. Can you imagine us coming from a big modern city to something like this?"

But the Bumars opened a grocery store and soon found pleasantness in small-town Houston. The business district was along Main Street at Congress, Preston, and Prairie. One treat was to drive the horse and buggy to Bergheim's Drugstore on Main. "They would bring ice cream out to us served on a tray, in tall glasses with a tall spoon that had a twisted handle, a sort of silver wire handle twisted. I can still taste that ice cream." When the early movies were made, they were shown on the wall of the

United Cigar Store catercornered across from Bergheim's. "While we sat in our buggy and ate our ice cream, we would watch those movies on the outside of the building." Rose Keeper also recalled the Chinese restaurant on Congress Avenue where they could get a good meal for twenty-five cents and the deluxe meal for thirty-five cents.

"In those days, people had a washer woman who used to come and carry the clothes home to launder, with a big basket on her head," Mrs. Keeper said. "Or if you had enough space, as we did, she would wash them in the yard. No equipment of any kind. You built a fire and heated the water in a big galvanized tub. Ours was oblong with a handle on each end. All the white clothes were boiled—bedding and everything. It was a two-day job. And another day for ironing. Everything had to be starched and ironed, shirts, dresses, sheets, towels, everything."[14]

This was also a day before beauty parlors. Most ladies had a woman come once a week to shampoo, fluff, and wave the the long hair of every woman and girl in the house. Many men had a barber come to the house for a weekly trim.

Houstonians began to suspect the qual-

ity of water coming from their faucets. In theory, the artesian wells, first drilled in 1887, provided drinking water, and the bayou water was used only for industry and the fire hoses. With good reason, rumors grew that the dirty bayou water was being tapped for human consumption. The privately owned Houstonian Water Works company firmly denied this.

But in 1906, the scandal broke—thanks to the impish initiative of young Mary Emily Cunningham Donaldson (Mrs. William John Donaldson).[15] Walking down the street one day, she saw a broken water main gushing. She saw *fish* jumping about in the flooded street. Fetching a Mason jar from home, she filled it with fish. She then took her evidence to City Hall and left it with a note of explanation on the desk of the city attorney. Tipped off, he arranged for witnesses to catch water company employees removing fish from supposedly artesian water pipes. This was the proof needed to bring action. The city bought the water company, and in the next three years drilled sixty-six new wells from three hundred to thirteen hundred feet deep. Thereafter, the water mains carried pure well water to all households.

Chapter Twenty-Three

Murder

THE DEATH of Mrs. William Marsh Rice in Waukesha, Illinois, July 24, 1896, started the sequence of lawsuits that in a strange way ultimately led to the murder of her husband. Elizabeth Baldwin Rice, who had spent most of her adult years in and out of Houston, and Orren T. Holt, her Houston lawyer, acted on the premise that half of all the vast Rice estate belonged to her under Texas community property law. On June 1, 1896, in her suite at the Capitol Hotel – unbeknownst to her husband – she signed a new will with bequests amounting to $1,250,000. Mrs. Holt witnessed it; Mr. Holt was named executor. The ailing Mrs. Rice then left for Waukesha to get out of the Houston heat. There she died on July 24.

Capt. James A. Baker, Mr. Rice's lawyer, was to comment drily, "She was very, very liberal." The largesse Baker noted included $25,000 to her doctor, $5,000 to her nurse, bequests to several Houston churches, $50,000 to each of two sisters, $200,000 to a niece, $100,000 to that niece's daughter, $50,000 to her father, $25,000 to each of two cousins, and to the city a park to bear her name. The will further provided that should the Rice estate prove larger than expected, these bequests would be doubled. Holt promptly filed the will for probate in Texas.

All this was legal by the premise upon which it was drawn. But it was a poser for William Marsh Rice, who had planned for his money to build a great educational institute. Coming to Houston, and on advice of Captain Baker, he filed suit against Holt in the U.S. Circuit Court at Galveston, "in

which he claimed to be, and always since his second marriage to have been, a resident of the state of New York. As such, his property was not subject to disposal by his wife under the laws of Texas, and he prayed the court to remove the cloud on his title to his real property in that state."[1]

Understandably, all those in Houston and New York who had been so generously remembered were determined that Mrs. Rice's last wishes should be respected. The Rice Institute board and Captain Baker's law firm were equally determined that Mr. Rice's wishes should be carried out.

The suit would be decided on the answer to one question: Where was the legal residence of William Marsh Rice? Now eighty, Mr. Rice had lived in New York City and on his New Jersey farm ever since June, 1867. But Mrs. Rice's heirs could argue that he owned the Capitol Hotel in Houston and kept an apartment there for his own use. On the one hand, Mr. and Mrs. Rice were listed in the *New York Social Register.* On the other, Mrs. Rice made the society page of the Galveston *Daily News* in May, 1895, with her reception for Winnie Davis, the "Daughter of the Confederacy," who was in Houston for the United Confederate Veterans' thirtieth reunion. All these points were made, supported, and added to by scores of witnesses and depositions on both sides.

Preparations for the suit moved tediously from 1896 through to 1899, and in the process, two figures entered the stage of what was to become Houston's most famous murder: Charles Jones and Albert Patrick. While in Houston to plead his case, Mr. Rice hired Charles Jones as general factotum – to be valet, secretary, cook, companion, friend. And Orren Holt employed Albert Patrick to help him gather depositions in New York to support the claim of a Houston residency.

Patrick, in essence, was part of the legal opposition to William Marsh Rice in this court case that was vital to the future of Rice Institute. A graduate of the University of Texas Law School, Patrick had moved to New York from Houston in 1892 after falling into disfavor with the Houston Bar Association on several grounds. First there was the matter of the Arthur Volck divorce.

Born in Huntsville, Elizabeth Bell Bates Volck was from a well-established Fort Bend County family and a graduate of Miss Brown's School. Her husband was a well-respected dentist in Houston. They lived with their two small children at the Capitol Hotel. But they were not compatible. Young, impetuous, volatile, Mrs. Volck was apparently undismayed when Dr. Volck sued for divorce on the charge that she had embarrassed him by undressing without drawing the shades, and by using unseemly language to him at his office. (She called him a "horrid thing!") The divorce was granted.

Mrs. Volck then sued her former husband, charging that he had received a sum of money from a railroad executive in an out-of-court settlement for an alienation of affections suit. She wanted her half of the settlement under Texas community property laws. She got it.

Taking one of her sons with her, she went to New York where she married Arthur Hearn, the heir of a major department-store fortune. When he died, he left her his entire estate with expressions of love and admiration for his beloved wife. She later married Domicio da Gama, Brazil's ambassador extraordinary and plenipotentiary to the United States. Moving to Washington, she established her credentials for membership in the Daughters of the American Revolution and took her place in international society. When her husband became ambassa-

dor to the Court of St. James, they lived in London. When Senhor da Gama died, he willed her his fortune with expressions of love and admiration, making Senhora da Gama one of the wealthy women of the time. Miss Brown's School proudly claimed her as an alumna.[2]

All this would be irrelevant but for one thing: Albert Patrick managed to have a hand in both the original divorce suit and in the divorced wife's suit against her husband.[3] This did not sit well with the Houston Bar Association. Further, he was so unwise as to move for the impeachment of a federal judge in Galveston. The judge instructed the district attorney to start disbarment proceedings against Patrick. At that point, as Sylvia Morris wrote, "Patrick prudently decided that New York City offered a wider scope for his talents."

He used those talents to plan and achieve the murder of William Marsh Rice. Through his work for Holt in support of Mrs. Rice's will, Albert Patrick had interviewed everyone in New York with any knowledge of William Marsh Rice. It was easy to make friends with and gain dominance over Charlie Jones. Through Jones, he introduced a doctor of his own choosing into Mr. Rice's confidence. Through Jones, who typed all Mr. Rice's letters, he learned every detail of Mr. Rice's business, exactly how much money was deposited in each bank account, exactly when and how Mr. Rice signed official papers. He also began to practice signing Mr. Rice's name. He often signed it to affectionate letters addressed to himself and typed by Charlie Jones. These he filed for future proof of Mr. Rice's devotion to his dear friend Patrick. In pure murder-mystery style, he had Jones address and mail empty envelopes to him with dates corresponding to the affectionate letters on file.

In all fairness, his first goal was one of simple fraud: to forge a will that would bring to him the entire Rice estate. He created this masterpiece in the summer of 1900, a document that seemed to have been drawn up, witnessed, and signed with the name of

William M. Rice over the date of June 30. It would later become famous in the New York newspapers as "the Patrick will." This was a fair attribution of authorship.

He may have been willing then to let Mr. Rice die of old age. Mr. Rice was eighty-four and, aided by prescriptions from the inept and unqualified Dr. Curry, was growing frailer. Nonetheless, in August, Patrick had Jones ask his brother in Galveston to buy chloroform for him. William Jones posted four ounces of chloroform to Charlie Jones at the Rice apartment at 500 Madison Avenue and soon after sent two more, as well as two ounces of laudanum.

Still the conspirators might not have acted. But the Galveston Hurricane of September 9, 1900, heavily damaged much of Rice's Houston property. A week later his Merchants and Planters Oil Company was almost totally destroyed by fire. Informed by telegraph, Mr. Rice planned to rebuild. He authorized his Houston manager, Henry Oliver, to draw up to $150,000 from the Rice account with S. M. Swenson and Sons in New York. His nephew, Benjamin Botts Rice, sent the first draft for $25,000 by House's Bank. Meanwhile, Capt. James Baker estimated that rebuilding would cost $200,000 or more.

Patrick could see hundreds of thousands of dollars draining out of the bank accounts he had so carefully inventoried. It was time to stop the drain. Sunday night, September 23, Patrick spent an evening at his boarding house, playing hymns on the piano to accompany two ladies who were his fellow lodgers. While Patrick played hymns, and on careful instructions from Patrick, Charlie Jones poured two ounces of chloroform into a sponge, placed it in a towel folded into a cone, and placed the cone over the face of the sleeping William Marsh Rice. Within thirty minutes, he was dead.

When the doctor who signed the death certificate blamed old age, Patrick came to the apartment and took over. He called the undertaker to Madison Avenue and told him that Mr. Rice had always wanted to be cre-

mated. But the undertaker explained that the crematory furnaces could not be brought to proper heat in less than twenty-four hours. Patrick had researched everything but that.

Monday morning James Baker in Houston received a telegram from Charlie Jones announcing the death. "Death certificate old age, weak heart, diarrahue [*sic*]. Left instructions to be interred at Milwaukee with wife. Funeral ten a.m. tomorrow at 500 Madison Avenue. When will you come?" Captain Baker informed Frederick Rice. Though the news saddened them, a death in bed at eighty-four is rarely suspect. Baker wired Jones to give the keys to the apartment and Rice's papers to Norman Meldrum, a Houston banker and friend who was staying at the Waldorf-Astoria at the time.

But that same morning, Albert Patrick sent a $25,000 check signed "William Marsh Rice" to be cashed by Swenson and Sons. The cashier, who knew that Rice rarely wrote so large a check, didn't trust the signature. He took it to his superior. Then they noticed that the check had been made out to "Abert Patrick" but endorsed "Albert Patrick." After months of practice, Patrick had painstakingly forged and endorsed a check, but misspelled his own name. This brilliant murderer, who had plotted the perfect crime, had made a disastrous slip.

While the messenger went to fetch another check, Eric Swenson went to look at the William Marsh Rice signatures on other documents in the vault. Increasingly suspicious, he telephoned the apartment and insisted on having Mr. Rice's personal confirmation of the check. Jones could only say that Mr. Rice was dead. Eric Swenson refused to honor the check, consulted an attorney, and telegraphed Captain Baker: "Mr. Rice died last night under very suspicious circumstances. His body will be cremated tomorrow morning at nine o'clock. Interment at Waukesha."

Baker and Frederick Rice ordered a stop to the cremation and set out for New York on the next train. Meanwhile, Swenson's lawyer had consulted the New York district attorney. The countermove had begun. Directly after the funeral service, the body was taken to the morgue for an autopsy. The vital organs were removed for analysis.

When Captain Baker and Frederick Rice reached New York, they went to the apartment and were astonished to be greeted warmly by Albert Patrick as though he were acting host in residence. Captain Baker and Patrick had been on opposite sides of the prolonged litigation over Mrs. Rice's will. Baker knew that in all that time, at least, Rice and Patrick had never met. How had they become acquainted?

Patrick assured them that he had become Mr. Rice's cherished friend and heir. The story he spun was this: The suit had dragged on so long that he had gone to Mr. Rice personally to seek an out-of-court settlement for a fraction of the $1,250,000 Mrs. Rice's heirs were seeking. From that time, a friendship had blossomed. Patrick displayed the letters that he had had Charlie Jones type expressing this new-found affection.

Patrick showed the two Houstonians a will of June 30, 1900, naming Patrick residuary legatee and also a general assignment dated September 21, 1900. This remarkable document purported to show that before his death, William Marsh Rice had turned all his cash and securities over to Patrick. In return, Patrick was to pay Rice $10,000 a year so long as he lived. "The old man had tired of life and had tired of business," this heir-presumptive explained. Patrick had already cleaned out every one of the Rice accounts in New York to the total of $250,000.

For every question Captain Baker posed, Patrick had an answer. For every doubt, new evidence—newly manufactured evidence. And Captain Baker believed not a word of it. Oddly, Albert Patrick was quite willing to give to Captain Baker the original will of 1896 by which the Rice estate would finance an educational institute in Houston. He let Baker take notes on the "new will" of June 30.

"During the next few weeks," Sylvia Morris wrote in *William Marsh Rice and His Institute,* "James Baker can almost be said to have saved the Rice Institute single-handed. . . . Baker, working with the cooperation of the district attorney's office, accumulated sufficient evidence that on October 4, 1900, a fortnight after William Marsh Rice's death, Albert Patrick and Charles Jones were arrested for forgery and sent to the Tombs."

That was the start.

While the press romped from headline to headline with the story, New York investigators continued their investigation, scanning autopsy reports, questioning both Patrick and Jones. Patrick vowed innocence. Early on, Charlie Jones broke, beginning a series of confessions, often contradictory, once attempting suicide with a pen knife thoughtfully slipped to him through the bars by Albert Patrick.

Released on bail through the efforts of a rich brother-in-law in St. Louis, Patrick was immediately rearrested and charged with first-degree murder on the basis of affidavits supplied by Jones and the coroner's office. At last on April 23, 1901, Albert Patrick was indicted for murder as well as for forgery in the longest indictment ever drawn up by the New York district attorney's office.

With that began a trial that fascinated New York for months. With appeals, it ran to more than three thousand pages of court records. The defense fought back, trying by every ploy to make Captain Baker the villain of the piece. Patrick's attorney charged that Captain Baker had invented Jones's confession in order to gain control of the Rice fortune. "We've seen it amply proved that every one of the Texas contingent had his price."

But Captain Baker emerged as the hero of the New York press and public. Patrick was found guilty and sentenced to be executed. Agile as always, Patrick filed an appeal and announced his engagement to the lady who, on that fateful Sunday evening, had sung hymns to his accompaniment on the boarding house piano. The appeals court upheld the verdict. Patrick then went on into years of appeals, aided by his brother-in-law, and ultimately won a pardon from the governor.

Rice Institute was secure. Holt gave up on the suit for Mrs. Rice's legatees, and settled out of court for $200,000. The Elizabeth Baldwin Park was bought and given to the city. When various bequests had been honored and legal fees paid, on April 29, 1904, Captain Baker and the Rice Institute board took control of assets totaling $4,631,259.08. Three and a half years after the death of William Marsh Rice, they could begin to build the school he had founded.

Chapter Twenty-Four

Oil

PETROLEUM had been discovered in Pennsylvania in 1859 with a well that came in at seventy feet. Texas newspapers stirred excitement in 1865 by reporting oil discoveries in many parts of the state. But at the start of the twentieth century, petroleum was still chiefly used to make kerosene for lamps and stoves. Gasoline was a troublesome by-product that had to be thrown away. Natural gas would continue to be burned off in flares for decades. Nonetheless, the oil industry was the fastest-growing industry in the country. In 1900, John D. Rockefeller and Standard Oil handled eighty percent of the nation's oil business and an even larger share of business overseas. Everybody in the industry was looking for more ways to use this abundant resource.

Born in 1860 in Sharon, Pennsylvania, Joseph S. Cullinan at the age of twenty-one started working for Standard Oil in the Pennsylvania fields. When he left thirteen years later, he knew how to drill a well, put up a tank farm, lay a pipe line, or run a refinery. In 1897 he moved with his wife Lucie to Corsicana in East Texas, where a small field had been discovered. There Cullinan started his own company and soon became the biggest operator in the Corsicana field. For $150,000 he built the first refinery worthy of the name west of the Mississippi.

Meanwhile, Pattillo Higgins, a brickmaker, noticed the oil seepages and gas smells around Beaumont. He began to buy land and hunt oil. In 1893 he hired Walter B. Sharp, a young drilling contractor from Dallas, to make test wells on his property at Spindletop, a scarcely noticeable mound in the otherwise flat Gulf Coast. Sharp's drill bogged down in Spindletop's shifting sands at about four hundred feet. Higgins had to give up for lack of money.

And for lack of money, Walter Sharp walked back home to Dallas, though he could easily have asked his brother to send him the fare. Sharp was a rangy, handsome, six-foot three-inch redhead who believed in the power of the drill to wrest oil from the earth. In 1895 he started again at Sour Lake, a mineral spa about fifty miles from Beaumont. There he ran his own small refinery and continued to drill water wells. He mastered cable tools and rotary-rig drilling and originated the method of using mud to drill through caving sands. By 1897 he had successfully drilled a twelve hundred–foot water well in Alabama. That year he met Joseph Cullinan in Corsicana. Threads were coming together that would gradually weave a strong network of oil business relationships – a network that would ultimately find its center in Houston.

Cullinan had magnetism. He was a leader, not a driver. Always hunting new uses for oil, he tried spreading it on the streets of Corsicana and Dallas to keep down the dust, and on Christmas Day, 1898, he lighted the fire of the first oil-burning locomotive in Texas. It made a run from Corsicana to Hillsboro.

In October, 1900, Anthony Lucas, a Dalmatian mining engineer who had made a name in saltdome prospecting, came for a try in Beaumont. He contracted with the

Hamill brothers of Corsicana, to bring in heavier machinery than any yet used at Spindletop. In October, 1900, Jim, Al, and Curt Hamill spudded in and began to drill on land leased from Pattillo Higgins. The drill pushed through the quicksands to more than eleven hundred feet. On the morning of January 10, 1901, the crew had paused to change the bit when the well broke loose, shooting oil high into the sky. From 70,000 to 100,000 barrels of oil a day poured out over the gentle slope of Spindletop. Oil was bringing eighty or ninety cents a barrel. The Hamills brought the well under control using a valve rushed to Spindletop from St. Louis, but it took ten days. Oil worth from $56 million to $90 million had been lost. Still, there seemed to be no end to the underground supply.

When Walter Sharp came to see the geyser, he found his own drill pipe only a few yards away. It had been jutting up from the ground ever since the sands defeated him in 1893. Within the week, however, he had five rigs working on Spindletop, using his fluid mud technique to cope with quicksands. Telegraphing his friend Ed Prather in Dallas to come at once with all the cash he had or could borrow, Sharp began trading in leases.

From boyhood, Howard Robard Hughes was an adventurer. Born in Missouri in 1869, he went to three different schools before entering Harvard in 1893. After two years there, he left to study law at the University of Iowa. Without finishing that, he went into law practice with his father at Keokuk, Iowa, before going into lead and zinc mining at Joplin, Missouri. Inevitably, such a spirit would be drawn to the adventure of Spindletop. He arrived in 1901, and immediately entered the drilling and contracting business. Walter Sharp, his brother J. R. Sharp, Ed Prather, and Howard Hughes formed the Moonshine Company. Hughes and Sharp followed the oil industry from one field to another. They were on their way to enormous wealth.

The rush to Spindletop outdid the Gold Rush. Word came that more than four thousand railroad tickets to Beaumont had been sold in New York and Ohio. On the day the first well was capped, a special train brought twenty-five hundred people from Houston alone. Beaumont was awash in sightseers and speculators. Its population of eight thousand doubled within a fortnight, only to double again. Just as Houston merchants had profited from the trade of the Gold Rush in 1849, so did Beaumont businessmen – from grocers to gamblers – profit in those months of the Spindletop boom. Spindletop in 1901 attracted to Beaumont and drew together young men who would become giants in the oil industry. They came from Corsicana, from Austin, from Houston, from New Orleans and Mississippi. Friendships and partnerships that would endure were formed in that first booming year. Within two to four years, most of the Beaumont pioneers would move to Houston, bringing the core of the oil industry with them.

Joseph Cullinan reached Beaumont while the Lucas well still gushed. Former Gov. James Hogg and his associates, who had formed the Hogg-Swayne Syndicate, were not far behind. Cullinan formed the Texas Fuel Company, planning to buy oil cheaply in Texas and sell it to Standard and other northern refiners for a profit. The company was chartered in January, 1902. Cullinan's attorney, James Lockhart Autry, came down from Corsicana to draw up the charter.[1]

The company's first backing came from the Hogg-Swayne Syndicate; its general manager was William T. Campbell. Born in London in 1859, Campbell attended Rugby before sailing for America in 1875. He had been a successful newspaper publisher and banker before coming to Beaumont in 1901.[2] They were joined by New Yorkers John J. and Lewis H. Lapham, leather merchants who had oil wells in Kansas and Pennsylvania. Arnold Schlact, a brilliant financier, handled all the Lapham oil affairs.

Cullinan believed that however cheap the price per barrel might be, they should produce oil as well as buy it. His wealthy Eastern partners thought it too soon for so young a company to go into the risky business of oil exploration. On his own, therefore, Cullinan formed an affiliate of Texas Fuel—the Producers Oil Company, with Walter B. Sharp as its president.

Meanwhile, Governor Hogg and William Campbell went to England seeking capital. Governor Hogg was just past fifty; Campbell, whom the governor liked to call "Little Willie," was forty-two.[3] Both were big men. Sailing on the Cunard liner *Saxonia,* Governor Hogg read up on Oliver Cromwell and William Pitt. They had expected to make a quick business trip. But Mr. Campbell had boyhood friends and relatives in England, and Governor Hogg had friends whom he had entertained in the United States. One of these Englishmen swept the Texans off to stay in his London town house. The business trip became a festive sojourn. They were invited for weekends at country houses where they enjoyed seeing the farms and cattle. In London they were honored at a sixteen-course dinner by Lord and Lady Deerhurst attended by U.S. Ambassador and Mrs. Joseph Choate, German Ambassador Metternich, Lord Cecil, and other peers. When invited to speak, Governor Hogg expressed his admiration for British contributions to international law, justice, and democratic government.

Over six feet tall, weighing almost three hundred pounds each, blue eyed and tawny haired, the vast men from Texas were a success. But the offer of a presentation to King Edward at the Court of St. James gave them pause. They thought of their great bulk in the prescribed court costume—black velvet knee breeches and coat, silk stockings, low-quartered shoes, full-shirt front, low-cut vest. They expressed their regrets. They later met King Edward informally at a garden party.[4]

Meanwhile, Anthony Lucas, whose well had started the boom, joined forces with J. N. Guffey to form the Guffey Petroleum Company, the predecessor of Gulf Oil Cor-

poration. They built the first refinery in Port Arthur.

On April 7, 1902, the Texas Company was chartered as a $3 million corporation under the laws of Texas. Joseph Cullinan was president. R. E. Brooks represented Hogg-Swayne. W. T. Campbell, John W. Gates, J. C. Hutchins, and Lewis H. Lapham were all members of that first board. Thomas J. Donoghue, who had come down from Pennsylvania to join his friend Cullinan, was elected to the board in November.[5] T. P. Lee, from the West Virginia fields, joined the company and soon became general superintendent of productions. As Cullinan's lawyer, James Autry directed its legal affairs from its birth until November, 1913.

The Texas Company had offices in Beaumont and New York, but because the Cullinans lived in Corsicana, it was declared the home office. It sold oil to northern refineries and to Louisiana sugar planters as fuel for grinding sugar cane.

In its first full year, the Spindletop field brought in eighteen million barrels of crude oil, amounting to twenty percent of the national production. Wells were clustered together on the dome as densely as trees in an East Texas pine forest. With oil so plentiful and uses for oil still few, the price dropped to an all-time low of three to five cents a barrel. Ed Prather, an independent oilman, sold one million barrels of oil for five cents each. The average for the year was twenty-one cents a barrel.

The Texas Company had contracted to supply one million barrels at twenty-five cents a barrel through Producers, its affiliate. To be sure of meeting the contract, Producers bought fifteen additional acres with big producing wells. But in the fall of 1902, the wells stopped flowing. First the Producers Company tried pumping, then blowing with compressed air. Still confident, it ordered blowing equipment and contracted for six new wells at six thousand dollars apiece. But salt water had invaded the Spindletop wells. Production dropped from sixty-two thousand barrels a day to twenty thousand, then to five thousand. Spindletop was to take a rest for twenty years or more before new equipment would drill to deeper formations.

All this had happened in less than a year from the day that the Lucas well blew in.

Before the Spindletop strike, Joseph Cullinan had been watching Sour Lake, the old spa where Sam Houston once took mud baths. The Texas Company took an option to buy a large tract for $1 million. Sharp drilled first one well on the tract, then another. Each showed some oil. As disaster loomed at Spindletop, a well at Sour Lake blew in as a gusher on January 8, 1903— almost exactly two years after the Lucas gusher of 1901. The Texas Company produced 3,813,000 barrels of petroleum that year. The company started paying dividends shortly after its first birthday.

In 1901, Governor Hogg had bought forty-one hundred acres of Varner Plantation land at seven dollars an acre in Brazoria County. Will, Ima, Mike, and Tom found it a delightful place for school vacations of riding horseback, going coon hunting, and fishing. Governor Hogg soon noticed that fumes rising from artesian wells would catch fire briefly from a lighted match. In the summer of 1902, when activity at Spindletop was sagging, he went home to Varner Plantation and set out to create a model farm. He had a Swedish vegetable gardener deploying twenty-five workers to cultivate one thousand of the plantation acres. Varner began shipping winter vegetables, English peas, and strawberries to northern markets. Governor Hogg spent what oil money he received on Varner. But he was sure that the day would come when Varner would produce oil for his children. Long after, it became the Varner-Hogg State Park, a gift to the state of Miss Ima Hogg.

The Humble Oil and Refining Company, a combination of several independent companies, was not formed until 1917. But of the nine men who were its founders, seven were in Beaumont in the Spindletop days. Orphaned at an early age, Walter W. Fondren had come to Texas at seventeen to work as a farmer. He moved to Corsicana in 1897 as a roughneck.[6] When oil was found at Spindletop, he moved to Beaumont as a skilled driller. He was rapidly becoming known as an expert in the field.

William S. Farish, born in Mississippi and a great-nephew of Jefferson Davis, was newly graduated from the University of Mississippi with a law degree. He came to Beaumont in 1901 to inspect Spindletop for an uncle in England. Robert Lee Blaffer, who had gone to Tulane and was the son of a well-established New Orleans businessman, started out in the coal business in New Orleans. But he was quick to see oil as coal's successor. He came to Beaumont to buy oil for Southern Pacific Railroad locomotives. Early in 1902, Farish and Blaffer met in a rooming house in the overcrowded boomtown. Blaffer, twenty-seven, and Farish, twenty, formed a partnership in 1904. In the first years, they were often so short of money that they had to live in a shack in the field. Blaffer once offered his gold watch as security for a drilling crew's wages. But by 1908, they were well established.

Ross Sterling in 1903 had a feed store at Sour Lake. Born in Anahuac in 1875, he was the son of a Confederate officer, who was a self-educated doctor. Sterling had quit school to operate his father's market boat.[7] Tall and handsome, he was said to be "the hardest working white man anybody ever saw." He would become the founder and president of the first Humble Oil Company.

At the time, Harry Wiess, the youngest founder of that future company, was growing up in Beaumont. His grandfather had come to Texas in 1835. His father and grandfather were in the lumber business. He was a sixteen-year-old schoolboy when the Spindletop excitement exploded around him. For him, prep school at Lawrenceville and four years of Princeton lay ahead before he entered the oil business.

His father, however, saw the potential for investment. William Wiess had been a steamboat captain in his youth and a Confederate officer in the Civil War.[8] When Spindletop blew in, Captain Wiess, nearing sixty, was a substantial lumberman, property owner, and banker. With friends, he formed two small oil companies – Paraffine and Reliance.

In 1904 and 1905, Houston's era as center of the oil industry began to take shape. In 1904, Joseph Cullinan moved his family from Corsicana to Houston, and the James Autrys moved from Beaumont to Houston. Howard Hughes brought his wife to Houston in time for the birth of their son, Howard, Jr., on Christmas Eve, 1904.[9] In 1904 Walter Sharp brought his family from Dallas to Houston in time for the birth of his son Dudley.[10] The children of Cullinan, Sharp, Hughes, Autry, and Donoghue would grow up playing together.

In 1904, R. L. Blaffer and Will Farish moved their base to Houston to concentrate on the nearby Humble Field, as did Walter Fondren and his wife. By this time, Fondren was a highly respected driller and producer.

John Crotty had left his native Albany, New York, to learn all he could about the oil business in West Virginia. In 1904 he moved to Houston and formed his own company to supply equipment for the oil industry.[11] H. T. Staiti, a native of Marshall, had an early interest in geology; in 1896 the Associated Press reported his prediction that oil would be found at Spindletop. He drilled the first well at Humble, and in 1903, he moved to Houston from Beaumont. The Staitis built the great house at 400 Westmoreland, surrounding it with gardens and arbors.[12]

After graduation from the University of Texas, Joseph Allen Tennant, son of Col. James H. Tennant, earned an M.S. degree at Massachusetts Institute of Technology. He became a consulting engineer in Houston, helping develop the oilfield tools needed for such major South Texas fields as Goose Creek and Old Ocean. He designed and built one of the first gas recycling fa-cilities in the world at the Old Ocean field.

Spindletop captivated Robert Welch, who lived in Houston and worked for the James Bute Paint Company as bookkeeper and salesman. The least flamboyant of men, Robert Welch was so keenly interested in petroleum that his friends nicknamed him "Pete." In 1901 he bought an acre in the middle of the Spindletop field and sold it for a profit of fifteen thousand dollars – only to see it resold a few weeks later for one million dollars. This did not dampen his interest. He used his fifteen thousand dollars to invest in the Goose Creek field, made a profit on that, and in 1905 began buying more Goose Creek acreage. His first well in 1907 was a dry hole, but he founded the Ashbel Smith Land Company with himself as president and continued to buy. This company's profits were the start of an estate that would be worth $42 million when he died in 1952.[13] However, he did not quit his job as bookkeeper and secretary-treasurer of the James Bute Paint Company for another twenty years.

Niels Esperson, a native of Bornholm, Denmark, had been in the oil business in the Oklahoma Territory and Kansas before joining exploration of the Humble field. With his wife Mellie, he moved to Houston in 1904.[14] Though Niels Esperson became one of Houston's most successful men, it was his wife who built the skyscraper in his name.

From 1904 on, most of the Texas Company board meetings were held in Houston or Beaumont. Because Varner was too far away for commuting, Governor Hogg took a suite at the Rice Hotel. He moved his Austin office to Houston. Though he died two years later, his move brought to the city his most important legacy: his son, Will, and his daughter, Ima. From 1904 on, the Hogg family considered Houston home.

The Thomas Donoghues moved to Houston in 1907, when the Texas Company headquarters were moved over from Beaumont. Thomas J. Spencer, a Virginian who had joined the company in 1906 and spent a year in the New York office, left the Texas Company to move to Houston and go with Producers Oil Company.[15] Meanwhile, Harry Wiess, a schoolboy when Spindletop blew in, had become a second-generation oil man. After graduation from Princeton in 1909 as a civil engineer, he entered his father's oil companies, the Paraffine and the Reliance. Ross S. Sterling chartered the first Humble Oil Company of the name in 1911 and moved its headquarters to Houston in 1912. It was named for the Humble field where he and his associates had been drilling.[16]

In seven years of partnership drilling, Walter Sharp and Howard Hughes had become a significant team in the oil industry. Both men were inventive, a trait they would pass on to their sons, Dudley and Howard. They met problems by inventing the equipment to solve them. Back in Corsicana in 1897, Sharp had originated the method of drilling with mud that is still in use. When a gusher caught fire in Shreveport, Walter Sharp devised a way to drill at a slant, tapping the flow from the side and drawing oil out by the new well. This was a device that proved useful ever after. But oil men were still stymied by rock. The existing bits wore down before they could penetrate the hard strata. After a setback in completing wells at Pierce Junction and Goose Creek, Howard Hughes—with Sharp's approval—took time out in 1907 to concentrate on inventing a bit that could cut through hard rock. They formed the Sharp-Hughes Tool Company and filed for patents in 1908.

Sharp's son Dudley said: "My father and Mr. Hughes would take the bit all wrapped up in a burlap bag out to the rig, and send the crew away. Then they would put the bit on the end of the pipe and lower it into the hole where the crew could not see it. Then they would call the crew back to do the drilling." Within a year they had tested and begun to manufacture the rock bit. The rock bit transformed the industry because it could grind through hard rock strata that no earlier bit could pierce.

When Walter Sharp died in 1912, at the age of forty-two, Houston and the oil industry felt a sense of calamity. Few men had been so respected and so beloved. One of his last thoughts was for an employee who had been hurt in a drilling accident: "Take care of Ran Hewitt!" All who had known him rushed to pay tribute.[17] Howard Hughes bought the Sharp share and continued the firm as the Hughes Tool Company. Made independently wealthy by the sale, Walter Sharp's widow became a quiet philanthropist and a stimulating civic leader who broadened the interests of younger Houston women.

In his lifelong distrust of absentee ownership, Governor Hogg had exacted a promise that the Texas Company would never be moved out of Texas. But the understanding was not put in writing. The New York office grew, but the headquarters remained in Texas wherever the company president might be. Preferring the field, Joseph Cullinan was rarely in either New York or Houston. Arnold Schlaet, whose talents in the early years had complemented those of Cullinan, began to complain. The death of Governor Hogg and other original stockholders robbed Cullinan of his control of the executive committee. In November, 1913, the executive committee moved the Texas Company headquarters to New York City. The company that Cullinan had started with a $3 million incorporation had grown in the eleven years to more than $36 million.

Joseph Cullinan, Judge Autry, Will Hogg, E. F. Woodward, and T. P. Lee withdrew to form the Farmers Oil Company of Houston. They acquired an abandoned field, drilled down deeper to a new, untapped stratum, and soon were producing oil at the rate of sixty dollars' return on each dollar invested.

Ross Sterling's small Humble Oil Company was flourishing, with his older brother Frank a director and his sister Florence M. Sterling as treasurer. Controlling half a dozen small banks and his feed stores, Ross Sterling was a remarkable businessman, known for his acute judgment of properties and the swiftness with which he invested. He also had the expertise of Walter W. Fondren to draw upon. Considered the leading driller on the Gulf Coast, serving as a combined production superintendent and petroleum engineer, Fondren was often called "the *real* oil man of the company."

As president of the Gulf Coast Oil Producers Association, W. S. Farish saw that the small independent companies should combine to gain strength against the giants. All the old ties of the Spindletop days had endured, linking Farish and Blaffer in business and friendship with the Sterlings and Fondren. In 1917, the Humble Oil and Refining Company was chartered. It combined small companies, all tracing their start back to Spindletop, all successful. In a complex rearrangement of the stock and oil properties, nine men became the company founders: R. L. Blaffer, L. A. Carlton, W. S. Farish, W. W. Fondren, C. B. Goddard, Jesse Jones, F. P. Sterling, R. S. Sterling, and H. C. Wiess.[18]

In the fourteen years before World War I, diverse men, who had grasped the opportunity of Spindletop, came to Houston and made it their home, bringing the oil industry with them and giving the city a vital injection of fresh leadership.

The Beaumont Crowd and the New Suburbs

"HOUSTON has grown so big in the last eight years that it has lost much of its sweetness and homelikeness that once so characterized it. . . . One constantly hears the old Houstonian saying: 'There are so many new people that I can't keep up with them. And such nice people, too. It seems a pity not to know them all.'"[1]

This was written in 1908. The eight years had spanned the mass migration from Beaumont to Houston. The migration began because as an oil boomtown, Beaumont could not build city services to keep pace with the hordes moving in. Houston offered social and cultural advantages. It had enough hotels, office buildings, and apartment houses. It had streetcars, a waterworks, telephones and telegraphs for businessmen. It had theaters, a library, and a great many business, civic, and social organizations. It even had an embryo country club.

In 1903, one hundred Houstonians organized the Houston Golf Club with memberships costing twenty-five dollars each. Through William Marsh Rice II, a charter member, the Rice Institute let them lease for one dollar a year forty-five acres on old San Felipe Road across Buffalo Bayou from Glenwood Cemetery.[2] They built a simple clubhouse and laid out a nine-hole golf links. This was "country." Houston homes still closely encircled the downtown business district.

Houston felt the social and cultural impact of the Beaumont migration. In each generation Old Houston has welcomed newcomers who are ready to serve and improve the city. Through successive waves of newcomers, Houston has kept its youthful vitality. The Houston of lumber, cotton, cattle, rice, and land fortunes opened its doors hospitably to the social set that the oil industry brought to the city.

Those who came to be known as "the Beaumont crowd" were young, dynamic, and attractive. They were wealthy and, in most cases, growing wealthier. Yet they seemed charmingly unaware of it. They enhanced any institution or cause they liked, as well as any social circle.

Within a year of coming to Houston, Walter Sharp bought a lovely place out in the country. It had belonged to Gus Sauter, the owner of Sauter's Restaurant and apparently a man of excellent taste. It had tall trees, a lake, a rose garden, and a large house with big log fireplaces. It lay out on Main Street, past the city limits at Eagle and near the fork of old Richmond Road.[3] Dudley Sharp, who would become President Eisenhower's secretary of the air force, was born and reared there. One of the first Houstonians to call on Mrs. Sharp was Mrs. A. S. Cleveland. Mrs. Sharp's son Dudley would one day marry Mrs. Cleveland's daughter Tina.

Walter Fondren, busy drilling for oil, gave his wife Ella ten thousand dollars and asked her to move and settle the family. Mrs. Fondren bought a house in Westmoreland, furnished it, and had enough money to buy a thousand shares of stock in a friend's company. The company became Texaco, and her investment grew into the millions.[4] Then

Walter Sharp, whose inventions benefited the oil industry, is seen here with his two sons, Bedford (*left*) and Dudley. *Courtesy Woodson Research Center, Fondren Library, Rice University*

and throughout their later years as philanthropists, Mrs. Fondren was a keen and intelligent partner to her husband.

Many of Beaumont crowd rented quarters in older sections, around Crawford and Hadley, until they could build the big houses of Courtlandt Place, Montrose Boulevard, and Shadyside where they would ultimately live. The Joseph Cullinans rented a house on Rusk and Crawford. "It was a wonderful house," as Mary Cullinan Cravens remembered from her early childhood.

Victorian. Built by a German. Maurice Hirsch lived next door to us. His sister was a violinist. They were a Jewish family, and they would get together with groups of their friends at night and play symphony music. We would be on the sleeping porch that faced their house. And that was my first taste of symphony music. It was a private serenade. They were wonderful.
Because I was a child, you know, I went all over the neighborhood, went in every house.

Everybody had lived there long before we moved here; they were the old South. Cater-cornered across was a family in a very old house, a beautiful two-story house. They were cultured people who had apparently been hurt by the war. The Civil War. That was just forty years before. And here we are forty years from World War II and are still talking about it.

Except for Harry and Olga Wiess, Beaumont had not so much bred the Beaumont crowd as channeled it to Houston from other points of origin—from Corsicana, Dallas, New Orleans, and New York, from Tennessee, Mississippi, Pennsylvania, and Kansas.

The Hogg family, for instance, reached Houston by way of Beaumont from their law office in Austin and their homeplace at Varner Plantation. With their growing oil interests, former governor James Hogg and his son Will made Houston the base of family operations. R. Lee Blaffer, originally of New Orleans, and Will Farish, originally of Meyersville, Mississippi, formed their partnership in Beaumont before bringing it to Houston. The Cullinans, the Autrys, and the Donaghues, leaders in the Beaumont crowd, still thought of Corsicana as home when they came to Houston.

In early 1909, the *Houston Post* commented that "next to W. S. Farish, R. Lee Blaffer is the best catch in town." In April, 1909, he went out to Lampasas, there to be married to the beautiful Sarah Campbell, daughter of the late W. T. Campbell. One of the founders of the Humble Company was marrying the daughter of one of the founders of the Texas Company, with Ima Hogg as her maid of honor. The young couple went off to Europe on a three-month honeymoon. There Mrs. Blaffer plunged into the art museums she had so long wanted to see and began her lifelong career as a collector.

As the first decade of the century ended, many Houstonians were fleeing the noise and congestion of city life. As newcomers, the Beaumont crowd gravitated to the newer neighborhoods. The new suburbs banned business, while welcoming corner groceries outside their gates. All supplied water, sewerage, gas, electricity, and telephone lines. All were served by streetcars running into town. Some used the word "paved" to mean that their streets were covered by shell or gravel. All laid wide concrete sidewalks.

The *Key to the City of Houston* described each neighborhood: "Westmoreland, a South End suburb, has been a boon to homeseekers desiring to be rid of the noise, dust and heat of the city," the *Key* said. Until 1902, the land had been occupied by florists' gardens. Six years later and pointedly pastoral, Westmorland was proud that it had "no noisy streetcars within her gates. It has no clubs or schools, but it has a great many club women and many school children who go into the city to club and school . . . as many think the true suburbanite should." This was the 1908 bedroom community. Westmoreland claimed to have all its streets paved—Emerson, Flora, and Garrott. Most of Houston remained in shell, and shell was, indeed, dusty.

By this time, Houston Heights, sixteen years old and a vaunted sixty-two feet above sea level, had six thousand residents and handsome mansions along its boulevards. The new Hyde Park challenged the Heights by claiming to be "the highest around the city . . . about 12 feet above Main Street at McGowen Avenue." Capt. J. C. Hutcheson was president of the Hyde Park Improvement Company; W. I. Williamson, vice-president; and J. C. Hooper, secretary. Each lot measured a quarter of a block. The company paid a bonus to the electric company to extend the Louisiana car line into the addition.

Planned an an exclusive residential section between Westmoreland and Avondale, Courtlandt Place was laid out in 1907 with twenty-six large lots and was one block from the South End Car. An established Houston businessman of fifty-three, C. L. Neuhaus built the first house at Number 6 Courtlandt in 1910, but first he built a structural model of it with every stud and joist

in place.[5] In 1910, Sterling Myer called on Sanguinet and Staats and A. E. Barnes of Fort Worth to design his Jacobean-style house at Number 4. He was chief stockholder in the Courtlandt Improvement Company. The same architects designed Number 8 for A. S. Cleveland in 1911.

Over the preceding thirty-five years, W. T. Carter had built up the family lumber business in East Texas. He had large holdings in the virgin forests and built the first all-steel sawmill at the Carter mill town, Camden. The forty-room Carter house was a landmark in Polk County. But in 1908, he moved his office and his family to Houston.[6] After graduation from the University of Chicago, W. T. Carter, Jr., entered the Carter Lumber Company business and married the beautiful Lillie Neuhaus.

The young Carters formed a family enclave in Courtlandt. In 1912, W. T. Carter, Jr. built at Number 18. His brother-in-law James J. Carroll planned the house at Number 16 but called upon Birdsall Briscoe for the interiors. Briscoe designed Number 20 for Dr. and Mrs. Judson Taylor (Jesse Carter). Deciding to leave the big mansion on Main Street, W. T. Carter called upon Briscoe to design a house for Number 14 but died before it was completed. His widow and, at various times, five generations of the family have lived there, including his daughter, Frankie Carter Randolph, Democratic national committeewoman, and his great-granddaughter, Patricia Carter Winkler (Mrs. Paul Winkler) and her family.

Birdsall Briscoe's design for the house of Etta Brady Garrow and her husband, J. W. Garrow, was published in the *Architectural Record* in 1915. Underwood Nazro, vice-president of Gulf Oil, built at Number 25 in 1916.

Those who built in Courtlandt Place were linked by many ties. John M. Dorrance, a cotton exporter, and his partner, Edwin L. Neville, built on adjoining lots. James Autry, who built at Number 5 in 1913, welcomed his Texas Company colleague Thomas J. Donoghue in 1916. Mr. Donoghue employed

Whitney Warren, the New York architect who had designed the Texas Company building at Rusk and San Jacinto. The house, which is exquisite in its architectural detail, was one of the first in Houston to have central heating. Young Dorothy Dunn never forgot that Mrs. Donoghue said "When we wake up in the morning, we are as warm as toast." As the adult Mrs. Tom Martin Davis, Dorothy Dunn said, "None of the rest of us were as warm as toast."

Open prairie and pasture stretched endlessly west from Courtlandt Place and Westmoreland. It was useful for squirrel hunting and for sons of the Courtlandt mansions to exercise the family riding horses. John Wiley Link bought 165 acres of this land and in 1910 laid it out as Houston's newest subdivision: Montrose. Downtown Houston's grid runs at an angle to the compass lines. Montrose Boulevard was drawn on a true north-south line and, from Westheimer to Main Street, had an esplanade with palm trees down the center. J. W. Link built the first mansion of many that would flank the boulevard. It was famous in town for its gold doorknobs. He later sold the big house at 3812 to oilman T. P. Lee.[7]

This was carriage trade. No tracks spoiled the elegance of the boulevard. Deed restrictions warded off commercial or business intrusion. Gradually the boulevard filled with mansions. Many of them were designed by Alfred C. Finn: for Henry H. Dickson, president of Dickson Car Wheel Company, at 3614 in 1917; for Walter W. Fondren, vice-president of the Humble Company, at 3410 Montrose in 1920. And when Chelsea Place opened off Montrose, Finn designed the big gates to mark its entrance.

Lovett, Montrose, and Yoakum boulevards, and Audubon Place were designed with esplanades and big lots for mansions. J. W. Link brought in seven train carloads of palm trees for the esplanades. But he never meant the section to be an exclusive domain of the big rich. Streets running between the boulevards offered lots as small as fifty by one hundred feet for seventeen hun-

dred dollars. This was still expensive land for the time, but suitable for middle-class, two-story houses and bungalows. From the start, Montrose School was one of the best elementary schools in Houston.

The Howard Hugheses built on Yoakum. An unusually beautiful woman, Allene Gano Hughes was born in Kentucky but reared in Dallas. Her father was a lawyer and her mother had graduated in the first class at Wellesley. Howard Hughes, Jr., lived in the Yoakum Boulevard house throughout his life in Houston.

Meanwhile, H. F. MacGregor, G. J. Palmer, and F. J. DeMerritt laid out Kenilworth Grove in a heavily wooded section along the newly graveled Caroline Boulevard. Edgewood, on the LaBranch car line, was a twelve-block addition between Hadley and Tuam, Chenevert and Chartres. Jesse H. Jones was president of the Edgewood Realty Company.

In 1907, Woodland Heights was one hundred acres of rich, sandy soil with soaring native oaks. A year later, it had a wide, imposing carriage entrance with a tiled roof, flanked by smaller roofed gates leading to the sidewalks. These were of "solid stone in the old Spanish mission style." Thirty-five houses had been built, costing from two thousand to fifty thousand dollars. The *Key* reminded that it was "only 15 minutes from the heart of the city."

South Houston was of the same vintage. The Western Land Corporation bought 1,375 acres nine miles south of Houston. It was on the path of the proposed interurban car to Galveston, but in its first year it already had four passenger trains a day stopping at its depot.

Port Houston, north of the bayou, was on the drawing boards to become a new Houston suburb. But the pull of the new Rice Institute and Museum of Fine Arts would prove too strong. Shadyside, Southhampton, and West University would grow up around what the *Houston Gargoyle* once called "Houston's Cradle of Culture."

Chapter Twenty-Six

Ima Hogg

IN MOVING his headquarters to Houston, Gov. James Hogg brought to the city his greatest gift—his children.

When his only daughter was born, Governor Hogg named her for the heroine of an epic poem written by his brother: Ima. When her grandfather heard, he charged into town to roar: "Jim! Do you *realize* what you have done to that girl?" It was too late. Ima Hogg's remarkable life had begun under the most burdensome name that could have been given an intelligent, attractive female.[1]

But as a very small child, she discovered music. She had absolute pitch and started playing the piano at three. Her father encouraged her. On the grand piano at the Varner-Hogg Plantation, there is a book of music he brought her from New Orleans with a table of contents written in his own hand.[2]

Ima Hogg's girlhood in Austin was not an easy one. After her mother's death when she was thirteen, Governor Hogg's sister came to take over the household. She was very much of the Victorian belief that children must be restrained, curtailed, instructed, improved, and above all, must not be allowed to think too much of themselves.

One day a little boy said, "Ima, that's a pretty dress you have on, and you look pretty in it." Aunt Fannie took Ima aside to say, "Ima, you are not pretty. You will never be pretty, and you must never let anyone tell you so." Ima Hogg was nearing eighty before she could throw off that old admonition and accept a compliment gracefully. But

her schoolgirl exuberance survived, and there were adventures.

When she was sixteen, she went with her father to Hawaii as part of the U.S. delegation to raise the Stars and Stripes over the islands. (Decades later she startled Hawaiian visitors to Houston by saying pleasantly, "I have met your queen.") On their way home, she and her father boarded a ship to go to Seattle. Suddenly the young girl burst into tears. She couldn't explain why, but she felt a great dread of this ship. Because the Hogg family felt and respected premonitions, Governor Hogg had the luggage off-loaded and changed their travel plans. The ship they had abandoned sank at sea with no survivors.[3]

She enrolled at the University of Texas at sixteen because her father thought her too young to study in New York. She was a slim girl with sunny hair. Virginia Bernhardt in her biography of Miss Hogg quotes a college friend, Gretchen Rochs Goldschmidt, who remembered seeing her ride across the capitol grounds: "What a picture of grace, skill, beauty and horsemanship! The black close-fitting riding-habit that only a woman of superb physique could carry off to perfection, the shining beaver with its fluttering veil . . . the gauntlets, the riding-crop, the long sweep of the robe over the feet; the erect . . . carriage in the side-saddle. . . . Ima Hogg, unapproachable as she appeared seen atop the gallant steed, was in reality a charming freshman. . . ."

While Miss Hogg was at the university, two French noblemen came to visit Governor Hogg in Austin. They escorted Ima and

Ima Hogg. *Courtesy Hogg Papers, Barker Texas History Center, University of Texas at Austin*

a friend to a ball. Ima's friend was very tall with a large bosom. Her escort was short with a very large beard. The catastrophe of the evening came when a brooch on the bosom became entangled in the beard—to Ima's lasting amusement.[4]

Her favorite subjects were German, Old English, and psychology. The two University of Texas years were, to her, a happy interim in which to have fun. She had so much fun that one professor refused to pass her. "You have not failed," he admitted, "but I want to repeat this course next year so that you will get more out of it." Ima smiled. She knew that next year she would be in New York, at work on the music that was the serious business of her life.

At eighteen, she entered the National Conservatory of Music. Antonin Dvořák was no longer its director and had returned to Bohemia. However, Miss Hogg said, "That wonderful black man who helped Dvořák with the *New World Symphony* was still there." This was Harry T. Burleigh, a gifted musician on the faculty, who sang to Dvořák the spirituals that he wove into the symphony.

Ima Hogg came home to tend her father in what they hoped was a temporary illness. After his death in 1906, she finished her studies in New York and came home to Houston for a few months. But now she was a grown woman of twenty-five and ready to study music in Europe.

Just as Houston had sent an entire bevy of young girls to school in Paris during the Civil War, it sent a surprising number of young musicians to major conservatories of this country and Europe during the early 1900s. As a small boy, Horace Clark, Jr., had begun his piano studies under Lucie Palmer Grunewald. At the New England Conservatory of Music in Boston, he became one of 4 honor students in a class of 104. In 1902, he went to Berlin to study composition and to perfect his technique. Joseph Moody Dawson studied violin at the University of Chicago, the Cincinnati Conservatory, and the American Conservatory of Music in Chicago. J. Will Jones, a black Houstonian, also went to the New England Conservatory and studied piano and organ in Boston. He ultimately became supervisor of music in the black schools of Houston.

Ima Hogg sailed from Galveston in 1907 and for the next two years studied under the masters of Vienna and Berlin. She and other young musicians—Wanda Toscanini, Leopold Stokowski and his bride, Olga Samaroff —reveled in the concerts, museums, and balls of Berlin. In those pre-war days, it was pleasant to see Kaiser Wilhelm riding in the park.

Olga Samaroff and Ima Hogg were born one month apart. Olga, as Lucy Hickenlooper in San Antonio, Ima Hogg in Mineola.[5] Both had been in music all their lives. Presumably they had been acquainted before their months together in the musical circles of Berlin and Vienna. However, taught and chaperoned by her Houston grandmother, Lucie Grunewald, Mme. Samaroff had started her European training in 1894 and by 1907 was well established as a concert pianist in Europe and America. She was better known throughout the cultural world than her new husband.[6] Handsome, magnetic, still speaking with the Oxford accent of his native England, Stokowski was the organist at St. Bartholomew's Church, New York.

"Olga Samaroff was a fine pianist, but a really great teacher," Miss Hogg once said of her friend. "She gave Stokowski his entree to the Philadelphia Symphony." In 1909, her musical studies in Europe at an end and now fluent in German, Miss Hogg came home to Houston to live. She seemed to have put the beaux and romances of her girlhood behind with a firm hand. Asked, at eighty-six, why she had never married, Miss

Hogg said: "When I was a girl, tuberculosis was thought to be hereditary. My mother died of tuberculosis, and I thought I should never have children. But, you know, it's just as well! I always liked a *handsome* man, and none of my beaux was any good! But I do regret the children."[7]

Will, Ima, and Mike Hogg lived in an apartment on Fannin. Will and Mike were partners in an oil and real estate firm. Sure that oil lay under the acres of Varner Plantation, Governor Hogg had willed that it not be sold for fifteen years after his death. "We were land poor," Miss Hogg said. She began to teach music, not only out of love but as a measure of self-support.

Often in her early years, Ima Hogg tried to throw off the onus of her name. She tried to blur the impact by signing "Imogene" to notes and photographs she gave to friends. But she never quite brought herself to take the necessary legal action to drop the name her father had given her. Instead, she lived a life so distinguished by elegance and philanthropy that she transformed the name.[8] One latter-day Houstonian observed: "I knew that at last I was a real Houstonian because Miss Ima Hogg's name no longer seemed odd to me."

Into the Twentieth Century

THOUGH THE ARRIVAL of the oil companies and their founders was more obvious, other men and women who would be important to the city moved into Houston in the first decade of the century. Lasting institutions were founded and built.

In 1900, Dr. Henry Barnstein left his native England to become the rabbi of Congregation Beth Israel at Crawford and Lamar. In 1905, Dr. Peter Gray Sears came to the Christ Church that his grandfather had founded. And in 1906, Dr. William States Jacobs was called to the First Presbyterian Church. Though different in background and temperament, all three had star quality. They moved swiftly into Houston's civic and cultural leadership.

The move from one of the world's oldest and most civilized cities to a sixty-eight-year-old town of fifty thousand must have been an abrupt change for Dr. Barnstein. Born in Dover, he earned his rabbinical diploma in London and a doctorate in philosophy from the University of Heidelberg. He had worked as a scholar and author with the British Museum. Because his liberal Reform views were out of step with the prevailing practice of Judaism in England, he answered the advertisement of Beth Israel, described as a Reform congregation. The cultured Englishman would change his name to Barnston during World War I.

Slender, of average height, Dr. Sears was the grandson of William Fairfax Gray and the son of a West Point graduate who had fought for the Confederacy and taught mathematics at the University of Mississippi. A graduate of the General Theological Seminary in New York. Dr. Sears accepted the Houston call in preference to offers from large Episcopal churches in New Orleans and Brooklyn. He was passionate in his support of good causes, and an eloquent speaker. His idealism and eloquence would, in the end, bring about a major break in the old church that the Gray family had founded.

Dr. Jacobs was a vast man of many parts and great charisma. The son of a South Carolina minister, he grew up in the orphanage run by his parents. He earned the first of his six degrees at nineteen and by the time he came to Houston was a star of the Chatauqua circuit. Poet, musician, and orator, he founded the Houston Knife and Fork Club, ran it as toastmaster with charm and brio, operated a soup kitchen for the indigent that fed many a hungry person, delivered baccalaureate sermons across the South, and developed a major Brahman cattle ranch.

From the start, church leaders of Houston reached easily across the barriers of faith. In 1904, as vice-president of the Beth Israel Congregation, J. N. Taub offered the use of the temple on Franklin Avenue to the First Church of Christ, Scientist, for Wednesday evening and Sunday services until the congregation could build a church. James D. Sherwood replied with "gratitude for this true expression of brotherly affection, in which the helping hand of the oldest religion on earth is extended to us in loving kindness."

Maurice Hirsch was still a small boy, but

already showing the exquisite southern courtesy for which he became famous. Congregation Beth Israel each year awarded a gold medal to the child who had made the greatest progress in the study of Hebrew. In 1905, Maurice tied for the medal with a little girl in his class. The *Minute Book* of the congregation shows that Maurice stepped aside and asked that the medal go to the lady.

An early supporter of the public library, Capt. J. D. Finnigan was a man of broad views in the rearing of daughters. He had flourished in Houston as leather merchant and investor. But in 1894, with his daughter's graduation from Wellesley and the sale of the old Rice house to Emma Richardson Cherry, he moved the family to New York. Annette Finnigan was young, attractive, and intelligent. She managed his New York office when he was away on business and became corresponding secretary of the New York City Equal Suffrage League. When the Finnigans came back to Houston in 1906, she continued handling his diverse business affairs and became president of the Hotel Brazos Company. When he died in 1909, he left his business in her hands. She ran it capably, but she had other interests. A woman of means, she was at the start of a lifetime of travel. She would become a major contributor of art to the Houston Museum of Fine Arts, the library, and the Natural History Museum.

Fresh from her New York experience, she was also an effective suffragist. The movement to give women the right to vote had begun in Texas in 1868 with the first Texas Reconstruction Convention—begun and ended. In 1903, while still in her twenties, Annette Finnigan and her two sisters, Elizabeth and Katherine, organized the first Houston Equal Suffrage Association. Fifty men and women attended the meeting and elected Finnigan president. Soon after, the Houston group called a state conference that was attended by some five hundred men and women. They founded the Texas Women's Rights Association, and Finnigan kept an apartment in Austin to lobby for the right

of women to vote. But woman's suffrage was not universally popular.

Pres. Grover Cleveland said, "Sensible and responsible women do not want to vote. The relative positions to be assumed by men and women in the working out of our civilization were assigned long ago by a higher intelligence than ours."

In Oklahoma in 1904, two Andersons and two Claytons founded the firm that would become the largest in the world with Houston as its headquarters. All four were from Jackson, Tennessee, and each brought a particular expertise to the partnership. Frank Anderson was in the Oklahoma Territory buying cotton for his uncle, who was a successful Fort Worth cottonman. Frank's brother-in-law Will Clayton was in New York in the cotton-export business. When the two young men agreed to go in business together, they included Frank's brother Monroe D. Anderson, a banker in Jackson, to handle the financing, and Will Clayton's brother Ben, who was experienced in shipping by rail and steamship.[1]

Thomas D. Anderson, son of Frank Anderson, tells the story: "By 1907, the company needed an outlet to the sea. M. D. Anderson moved from Jackson to Houston and established a financial office here because they borrowed against cotton that was stored in Houston warehouses awaiting shipment overseas. So he opened the first Anderson, Clayton office here, though he was never a cotton man in the old conventional sense." The quiet, thrifty bachelor with an impish sense of humor would one day give to Houston the M. D. Anderson Foundation that launched the Texas Medical Center.

Professor E. O. Smith, a leading black educator, organized the Negro Library and Lyceum Association in 1907.[2] It was housed in the Colored High School Building, and the City Council appropriated five hundred dollars annually for its upkeep. Helped by J. B. Bell, a wealthy grocer and real estate investor, the association raised fifteen hundred dollars to buy a lot on Frederick Street for a library building. Emmett J. Scott, who had left Houston to become an aide to Booker T. Washington, lent entree to Andrew Carnegie. In three years, with a Carnegie grant and a City Council appropriation of fifteen hundred dollars a year, the Colored Carnegie Library was completed.

The Houston YWCA opened a dining room and parlors for young women in 1907. The more advanced YMCA was completing a handsome building on Fannin at McKinney that would cost two hundred thousand dollars. In October when the cornerstone was laid, in what was still a Houston custom, a procession formed at the old hall and marched along Fannin to the site of the new. The building committee included W. A. Wilson, S. F. Carter, E. W. Taylor, Capt. James A. Baker, Jr., W. D. Cleveland, Sr., J. V. Dealy, and J. B. Bowles. Five stories high and designed to house one hundred and twenty-five men, the new YMCA had a lobby, reading room, gymnasium, bowling alleys, swimming pool, handball court, baths, and dressing rooms. Houston would see its first basketball games in this building.

The years that had brought so many outstanding newcomers to Houston also showed losses. Robert Scott Lovett, a partner of Baker, Botts, Baker & Lovett, lived with his wife and son in the big white mansion at Main and Gray.[3] Soon after his arrival in 1892, his firm became general counsel in Texas for the Southern Pacific Railway Company. Jesse Andrews, a young lawyer in the firm, remembered Lovett as one of the finest minds he had ever encountered. E. H. Harriman of New York apparently shared the opinion. He invited Lovett to New York as general counsel for the Southern Pacific and the Union Pacific Railroad companies. The Lovetts moved East in 1904, and five years later, when Harriman retired as president and chairman of the board of both companies, Lovett was his successor.

With Lovett's departure, Edwin B. Parker and Hiram M. Garwood moved up as partners.[4] In addition to Jesse Andrews, younger lawyers in the firm of Baker, Botts, Parker & Garwood were William Kimbrough, Clarence R. Wharton, and Thomas H. Botts.

From his first cub reporter days on the *Houston Post,* Will Hobby had been an outstanding newspaperman. As one of the youngest news editors in the country at twenty-five, he showed a knack for deploying squadrons of reporters to cover big stories swiftly and thoroughly. At twenty-six, Hobby became the *Post*'s managing editor.

Though Beaumont had got over the worst of its Spindletop growing pains, the *Beaumont Enterprise* was suffering from the sharp decline in the oil industry. In 1907, five Beaumont businessmen, determined to save the paper, invited Will Hobby to become editor, manager, half-owner, and, in time, full owner of the *Enterprise.* He accepted. The two hundred dollars a month they offered was more than the *Post* paid, but future ownership was the real lure.

With his lumber business flourishing, Samuel Fain Carter founded the Lumberman's National Bank in 1907. He was joined in the enterprise by Guy Morrison Bryan III of Galveston, a great-grandson of Moses Austin. A year later, Guy Bryan married Carter's daughter Florence.[5] Within four years the bank was planning Houston's tallest building. Early in 1907, the First National Bank board approved Pres. Alexander Porter Root's plan to give each clerk a month's salary "in appreciation for efficient service in 1906." Nobody foresaw that a nationwide financial panic lay just ahead. In the East banks began to fail, banks across the country grew shaky, the stock market slipped. But only one bank failed in Houston: the T. W. House and Company's private bank.[6]

Fred Lummis had not yet decided to study medicine when he and young E. L. Crain became friends at the Union Bank and Trust Company. Even younger than they, a black man named Barnes went to work for the bank. Perhaps forty years later, he came as a patient to Dr. E. L. Crain, Jr. "Did you ever wonder why I always come to you, Dr. Crain?" he once asked.

"Because you think I'm a good doctor, I hope!" Lillo Crain replied.

"No," said Barnes. "It's because your father and Dr. Lummis took such good care of me when I was a boy. My starting salary at the bank was three dollars and fifty cents a week. Every week, they made me put the fifty cents into a savings account. When I got a raise to five dollars, they held out a dollar for my savings account. Thanks to them and the nest egg they set up for me, I'm a millionaire now and I own four million worth of property on the other side of Dowling Street. That's why I come to Mr. Crain's son as my doctor."

The Baptist Hospital opened on September 1 in a two-story brick house at Smith and Lamar. Costing eighteen thousand dollars to build, it had eighteen beds and ten student nurses. It would grow on that site into the big Memorial Hospital with a record of generous charity care. St. Joseph's Infirmary, the *City Directory* said, "occupied an entire block of ground" at 1910 Crawford Street. Ward rooms were one dollar. Private rooms were two to three dollars a day. The Houston Infirmary Sanitarium on the corner of Washington and Tenth Street was operated by Dr. D. F. Stuart and Dr. S. C. Red. Rooms were one to five dollars "according to location."

By custom, funerals took place in the home. C. Ed Settegast, who ran a livery stable on Fannin Street, and John Kopf, a cabinetmaker who made caskets by hand as a sideline, had teamed up in 1901, as competition for Westheimer's. In 1907, they bought the old M. T. Jones mansion at 1209 Main Street, remodeled it, and offered the public something new—a funeral home.[7] The notion did not sit well with the more conservative Houstonians, but the death of a well-known ne'er-do-well changed things. He was headed for a pauper's grave when Settegast and Kopf took over. Because of the man's popularity, the simple services in their funeral parlor drew a large crowd. Apparently, many liked what they saw. Business picked up.

J. B. Earthman was from Fayette County, and tried blacksmithing, ranching, and transfer and storage before coming to Houston. In 1907 he and J. L. McCarty founded the Earthman-McCarty Company, Funeral Directors and Embalmers. As did other Houston undertakers, they respected the state law barring embalmers from using profane language in the presence of the deceased. On McCarty's death, it became a family business into the third generation. By 1912, Earthman's could charge $66.50 for a first-rate funeral. This was the start of what would become the nation's largest independent funeral home company.

The Magnolia Brewery, the Eureka Ice Company, and Henke Artesian Ice & Refrigerating Company all made ice from "the purest artesian water." Their wagons moved through every neighborhood. Icemen skillfully wielded icepicks to shape a twenty-five-, fifty-, or hundred-pound block for the customer and, using big, sharp ice tongs, carried it up to the house and swung it into the ice box. The ice business was fail-safe in the Houston that had only recently gained the comfort of electric fans.

Dairies by the dozen were scattered all around town. One of the newest was that of James B. Abercrombie, who had come from Richmond in 1906. It was a family business in which all his sons took part, from the milking of the Jersey cows to the delivery of the big cans of milk. Jim Abercrombie at fifteen drove the milk wagon, which was pulled by a horse misleadingly named Old Gracie. Old Gracie was a spirited young mare, part quarter-pony. There was a small, informal race track out from town in the land that would become Hermann Park. Smaller than his brother, Bob Abercrombie would saddle Old Gracie with a well-worn inner tube and enter the races—usually to win. This, as Patrick Nicholson writes in his biography, *Mr. Jim,* was the start of a lifelong interest in horse racing for the Abercrombies.

The Sakowitz Brothers, so well established in Galveston, reacted to the recurrence

Starting in 1904, the city government and city market shared this handsome building on Travis Street designed by George E. Dickey. When the council moved into the new City Hall on Bagby in 1939, a bus terminal took over the space. *Courtesy George Fuermann City of Houston Collection, Special Collections, University of Houston Libraries*

of hurricanes. While Tobe Sakowitz stayed in Galveston, Simon opened a men's clothing store in Houston. William L. Foley had his dry goods store on Travis. His nephews, James A. and Patrick C., opened their own Foley Brothers store at 505-7 Main Street.

By this time Jim Jamail had settled in to carve a niche for himself and his family in Houston. He had come from Lebanon in 1905 and opened a produce stand at Market Square. He soon gained a following among wise shoppers, who found that his fruits and vegetables were sure to be fresh and the best available.

Mary Cravens (Mrs. Rorick Cravens) recalls the Market Square of her childhood:

"They had sawdust on the floor and they had a place for meat and a place for vegetables and a place for fish. There used to be a strong smell of fish and of roasting coffee. Every night they would take the haunches of meat, put them on a hook, and raise them to the top of the City Market to get them away from rats. But the rats could go up the rope. That was a picture to remember. The Stude Bakery was across the street. It was a famous bakery where the men went at noon to drink coffee and eat bread and talk. And I remember that when I was a little girl, there was the 88's Saloon on Main Street, and we always had to walk on the opposite side of the street from it. Why I never knew."

Mrs. Eugene Pillot, whose husband had enjoyed so many trips to Europe in his last years, still lived in the family home at 1803 McKinney, guarded by the two iron dogs.[8] So did her son Teolin, who owned the city's best-known book, bookcase, and stationery store. Camille G. Pillot, who had polished off his education with three years of university in Paris, was a partner in Henke and Pillot groceries and vice-president of Henke Artesian Ice and Refrigeration Corporation. He and his wife lived in a sizable mansion at 1817 McKinney.

Elbert E. Adkins, who represented a chemical manufacturing company of Saratoga Springs, New York, lived at the Rice Hotel. So did Jesse Jones, who was now president of the South Texas Lumber Company and secretary of the M. T. Jones Lumber Company.

The Young Ladies Association of the First Presbyterian Church gave a farewell reception in honor of Dr. and Mrs. Allen C. Hutcheson. Newly married in 1908, they were leaving for China to represent the Southern Presbyterian Church as medical missionaries. The son of Congressman Joseph C. Hutcheson, he was a graduate of the Columbia University College of Physicians and Surgeons. Dr. Hutcheson was going to head the American hospital in Nanking, a city perhaps four times the size of Houston.

In 1906 or 1907, the Houston Golf Club on old San Felipe Road brought a team of touring English and Scots pros for an exhibition match on its nine-hole course. So many golfers came from out of town that they formed the Texas Golf Association then and there. As the number of golfers grew, so did the demand for a larger course. In June, 1908, a move began to find a bigger tract of land and to build a real country club. Members were warned that this would mean a big increase in the initiation fee (twenty-five dollars) and quarterly dues (four dollars and fifty cents).

Within a month the new club had filled the last of the five hundred charter memberships. They built their new clubhouse on 156 acres southeast of the intersection of Harrisburg Boulevard and the unpaved country road that became South Wayside Drive. They chose this site because the streetcars could bring caddies and children of members out to the club from downtown. The trip took twenty minutes by automobile.

The opening of the golf course, tennis courts, and clubhouse strengthened the assumption that Houston would continue to grow out in that direction. Col. Edward F. Simms bought 210 acres across from the club between Harrisburg and Lawndale. Colonel Simms was a graduate of Yale University with a law degree from the University of Virginia, but he made his fortune in the oil fields of Texas and Louisiana.

For his wife, Lillie Wier Simms, and their only daughter, Bessie (Mrs. Kenneth Franzheim), he built a mansion with a library, living room, dining room, and breakfast room on the first floor, a maid's room off the kitchen, a wine cellar and furnace in the basement, and seven bedrooms and five bathrooms on the upper two floors, as well as a big upstairs sleeping porch. He built gardens, stables, greenhouse, reflecting pools, lakes, and one of Houston's first swimming pools—a big one set some distance from the house. The estate required eight gardeners and five house servants to maintain. He called it Wayside.

In 1908, the February wedding of Marie Etta Brady and John Van Wanroy Garrow took place in the stately Greek-revival house known as Brady Place on Harrisburg Boulevard at Milby.[9] Calling it a brilliant social event, the *Daily Post* devoted columns to the flowers that filled every room, the gowns worn by the attendants, the wedding presents on display upstairs. The bride, daughter of the late Col. John T. Brady, was given away by her brother Sherman.

In 1908, the Rev. Horace Clark performed a double wedding for his granddaughters. Standing in the big bay window of the R. T. Flewellyns' house at 410 Austin Street, Nannie Clark Flewellyn married Dr. A. Philo Howard, and her sister Bessie married

Camille Pillot, who made a fortune in a variety of businesses, built this mansion at 1817 McKinney Avenue before 1900.

Thomas A. Helm. This was the house that John and Eugenia Andrews built in 1837 on coming to the Republic of Texas from Virginia. The marriage of Nannie Flewellyn to Philo Howard brought together two families that had settled Houston in its first two years.[10]

Not long after the double wedding, Mr. Clark read the vows to another granddaughter, Mamie Culpepper, who married Clark C. Wren. A native of Galveston, Clark Campbell Wren began studying law at fourteen, was admitted to the bar at nineteen, served eight months with the Third Texas Volunteer Guard in the war with Spain, and, before coming to Houston to practice law, enjoyed a brief fling at the professional stage. He explained to his enchanting fiancée that because he was just getting started in his law practice, she would be unable to have a maid right away.

"Then Clark," she said in a voice of fluting sweetness, "Mama needs me too. So we'll just wait." Without delay, the wedding took place in February, 1909; the young Mrs. Wren got her maid. Two years later, Mr. Wren became the youngest county judge Texas had ever had.

As usual, newspaper ads were tempting Houstonians to travel. "Ho! For an Ocean Voyage! Five Days on the Deep via Southern Pacific Steamships to New York. Two Days to Havana. Take the salt sea air."

The Houston Launch Club, founded in 1906, sailed out of the turning basin. It staged its first regattas in 1907 and 1908. The *City Directory* of 1910–11 devoted a section to "Marvelous Increase in Water Traffic". It said, "The tonnage carrying capacity has nearly doubled. The membership of the Houston Launch Club own over two hundred boats, mostly for pleasure." The boats were anywhere from 15 to 100 feet long. Camille Pillot's yacht, the *Augusta,* was 103 feet long. Its interiors of Honduras mahogany had a piano finish. Arthur Hamilton's yacht was the *Crescent*. Newspaper social notes reflect Sunday parties held aboard and weekend cruises.

Though most of the boats were for pleasure, Mayor H. Baldwin Rice bought an expensive yacht for one purpose: to promote the ship channel. Starting in 1909, he spent a large part of his personal fortune in that effort.

Houston was born as an inland port and continued to be a port that grew by the year. For much of the city's first century, most Houstonians lived in a circle around the business district that had its center at Texas and Main. They were closer to and more aware of the port than their late twentieth-century counterparts. They went to the port of Houston for business or pleasure, rather as air-age Houstonians go to the airports to take commercial flights or board private planes.

The big bandstand in the new Sam Houston Park attracted families on Sunday afternoon. In the summer of 1909, twenty-one thousand people attended thirty free band concerts. A gathering of four thousand was not uncommon. This was the chic thing to do. Almost thirty years after, an old Houstonian reminisced in the *Houston Post* of March 28, 1937: "On Sunday afternoons it was a favorite driving place of Houston's horse and buggy days. . . . I have witnessed in admiration the passing of shiny, new carriages of all types. One might note the English hack, the French barouche, the German landau, the low-aproned phaetons and carriages, or even the Irish dog-cart, the majority of them drawn by sleek-looking, high-prancing and thorough-bred horses."

Court House Square was cluttered with stones and building equipment. In 1907, the public had approved a five-hundred-thousand-dollar bond issue to build the long-needed new courthouse, and Albert Thomas Lucas won the contract to build it.[11] "When the dome of the new Harris county court house is in place," the *Houston Chronicle* reported in 1909, "its pinnacle will stand almost 100 feet above the highest point. . . . The plan calls for a tower 210 feet above the surface of the ground." When it opened on November 14, 1910, the *Post* reported that Harris County's courthouse was "one of the most beautiful . . . and most modern of its kind." The Harris County Humane Society was given permission to repair drinking troughs for the horses on the San Jacinto Street side.

At thirty-five, while doing business in cities across the country, Jesse Jones settled in to become a major and lifelong Houston builder. By 1908, he had three ten-story buildings going up—all topping the six-story Binz Building.[12] One was the Bristol Hotel. Modern, fireproof, it had two hundred rooms, a roof garden—the first in Texas—and a superb chef. Another swung him into the newspaper business: Marcellus E. Foster, owner of the struggling new *Houston Chronicle,* asked Jones to build a plant for the newspaper. He offered a half-interest in the paper as down payment. Foster got an excellent building, and Jones began a career that would make him publisher of the *Chronicle*.

His knack at financing buildings caught the eye of Bishop Seth Ward, who thought that such talent should be put to good use. Business had encroached upon the beautiful Shearn Church on Texas Avenue, and he wanted a new Methodist church at the south end of town. He asked young Jones to head the building and finance committee, to hire architects and contractors, to raise and borrow whatever money would be needed. Jesse Jones pointed out that he was a Baptist. With ecumenical breadth of mind, the bishop said that would not matter.

The new First Methodist Church was built at Main and Clay in a neighborhood of large Victorian houses, two or three to the block, and amid tree-shaded gardens surrounded by cast-iron fences. Jones finished the task in 1910. When he tried to return to the Baptist fold, the minister, the Rev. George Sexton, said firmly, "Not until the church is paid for." By the time the debt

As the new century began, Mayor Sam Brashier bought the Kellem-Noble land and house on the edge of town to create Sam Houston Park – the city's first. By 1910, when this picture was made, it had been landscaped into a Victorian delight with an old mill, a stream, a rustic bridge, and paths.

was cleared, St. Paul's Church was on the drawing boards and Bishop A. Frank Smith simply pre-empted his good friend, Jesse Jones, to head that building committee. Jesse Jones never managed to get back to the Baptist church.[13]

Automobiles had become so popular in 1909 that police had to ride motorcycles to enforce speed laws. Vast and jovial, Pres. William Howard Taft spoke to what the press called "ten acres of people" from a balcony of the Rice Hotel. On their own count, Houstonians estimated that their city had a population of 100,000. (They were unfazed a year later by the 1910 census estimate of 78,800. The *Chronicle* pointed to the city's 25,000 suburbanites.)

Fifty Houstonians who wanted to organize a Greek congregation met in Christ Church in February, 1910. A Greek Orthodox priest from New Orleans presided over the meeting, and among the leaders were James Cafcalas, Nick Xanthos, James Condos, and A. D. Polemanakos.[14]

The new Majestic Theater opened on the site of the old Shearn Methodist Church on Texas Avenue. Actors welcomed its modern dressing rooms and ample stage. A powerful rooftop fan pulled tired air up and out to change 250,000 cubic feet of air every

On the site of the old capitol, the Rice Hotel served as the reviewing stand for all gatherings and public events through World War II. In this George Beach photograph, made at the turn of the century, some latterday editor has airbrushed out the streetcar, telephone, and electric wires that crisscrossed the Main and Texas Avenue intersection. *Courtesy George Fuermann City of Houston Collection, Special Collections, University of Houston Libraries*

three minutes. Built of concrete and stone to ward off fire, it had a Pompeian entrance with marble walls, a ladies' waiting room "in the period of Louis the Magnificent," a marble staircase, a Flemish smoking room, and a children's playroom with nurse and toys. All this, of course, was expensive. Historian B. H. Carroll wrote at the time that the cost of three hundred thousand dollars "will doubtless prohibit its ever becoming a great revenue producer." It was a vaudeville house. It did produce revenue. It also became the birthplace of the Houston Symphony Orchestra.

Judge and Mrs. Edwin Parker moved out to Baldwin Street in 1910. Frank Lloyd Wright's design for the big house proved to be a forerunner of his prairie architecture with wide overhanging eaves, hip roof, spacious porches, and windows. George Lewis, the St. Louis park commissioner who then was more famous than Wright, landscaped the park in sweeping curves. Because it was shaded by eighty oak trees, the Parkers called their estate The Oaks. A distinguished-looking gentleman with a neat beard, Parker was not only counsel and officer in the Southern Pacific Railroad, Houston Lighting and Power, and Guardian Trust companies, but chairman of the Houston Park Board. He started a lifelong process of helping young men through college. Mrs. Parker, a musician of professional caliber, not only taught music, but helped set the rigorous standards of the Woman's Choral Club.

Mr. and Mrs. Clarence Wharton also used a Frank Lloyd Wright design for their house at 2204 Baldwin, but they did their own landscaping, with five informal gardens, one opening into another to create long vistas and expanses of lawn.

In 1909, 1910, and 1911, Houston had several stock companies. But vaudeville and movies were everywhere: between eight thousand and ten thousand Houstonians went to the movies every day. The *Chronicle* viewed with alarm the lack of an ordinance requiring "the separation of sexes in the motion picture shows." It recommended that policewomen patrol the dark aisles.

Again, Houston civic leaders were eager for the ship channel to be deepened. Congressman Tom Ball proposed that Houston form a navigation district that could issue bonds. This would enable him to go to Congress with a remarkable proposal: if Congress would go ahead with the plan to dig a deepwater channel from Houston to the sea, the city would pay half the cost. Never before had a city offered to share the cost to gain a major federal project. The unprecedented offer worked. Congress voted to spend $1.25 million to carve a twenty-five-foot channel and a bigger and deeper turning basin if the city would match the sum.

Houston approved the bonds almost unanimously, but when they were issued in 1911, the public did not rush to buy. The plan was in danger. Jesse Jones conferred with Mayor Rice, Tom Ball, William T. Carter, T. C. Dunn, and Camille G. Pillot. He offered to ask Houston banks to take the bonds in proportion to their capital and surplus. Many of the bank presidents had strongly argued for a deep-water canal. Jones made his plea, and in less than twenty-four hours, he could report that the bonds had

been sold. Every bank in the city had taken its share.

By 1910, the two Houston telegraph companies were handling 3.5 million messages a year, and Main Street was 2,313 feet long—more than twice the length of the original quarter-mile of paving stones. The Stowers Building at Congress and Caroline was the home for the Houston Labor Council and headquarters for a large number of locals.[15] The unions paraded every Labor Day.

In July, 1911, the Labor Council issued a report showing that Houston had 25,000 industrial workers. It said of the labor force: "Men, 15,000; women, 6,000; children, 15 years and under, 4,000. Organized: Men, 55 percent; women 2 percent. During the last ten years the hours of labor have been decreased all along the line from ten to eight. During the past ten years there has been an average increase in wages among the crafts of 25 percent."

"However," the report concluded, "during this same period, the . . . cost of living . . . has increased 40 percent. Thus it will be seen that the increased cost of living far exceeds the increase in pay secured."

Houston's health department employed a pathologist and a bacteriologist who checked the purity of milk, water, and foods and coped with transmissible diseases. In one year, the department treated 4,000 patients at the city dispensary, 550 at the hospital, and 36 at the pest camp. It vaccinated 2,000 school children for smallpox. It fumigated 783 rooms for tuberculosis, diphtheria, smallpox, scarlet fever, typhoid fever, and scabes. It fumigated two automobiles for scarlet fever and seven boxcars for smallpox.

Houston was now free of yellow fever. There had been no epidemic since the great plague of 1867. Diphtheria was a cruel killer of small children, and the health department treated tuberculosis as a highly contagious, transmissible disease. Yet then and for decades after, the idea lingered that tuberculosis was inherited.

In 1911, Houston claimed that no city was better equipped in hospitals and medical

Booker T. washington dinner party, Feb. 1911

When Booker T. Washington visited Houston in 1911, the black elite attended a dinner in his honor at the home of Dr. Benjamin J. Covington at 1220 Ennis. *Courtesy Houston Metropolitan Research Center, Houston Public Library*

care—"not barring even the famed Charity Hospital of New Orleans." The new Southern Pacific Hospital was on White Oak Bayou "far removed from the noise and bustle of the city," proud of its view of the stream and woods on one side, the Houston skyline on the other. It was steam heated, cleaned by vacuum cleaners, and lighted by electricity and gas. B. H. Carroll wrote that it had numerous bathrooms on each floor but only one or two bathtubs in the whole building, because "shower and needle baths" were preferable. The beds, he wrote, "are the ordinary hospital iron frames with absolutely luxurious mattresses and snow white linen. The chairs and tables are dark oak and rose wood."

The Northsworthy Hospital on San Jacinto at Rosalie offered ward beds, single rooms with or without a private bath, or two connecting rooms with or without a private bath.[16] The building was heated by hot water radiation.

Booker T. Washington came to Houston to speak in the City Auditorium in 1911. Charles Norvell Love, editor of the *Texas Freeman,* was in charge of arrangements, Mayor H. Baldwin Rice delivered the city's welcome to the distinguished founder of Tuskegee Institute, and Dr. Peter Gray Sears gave the opening prayer and benediction. Love listed as his backers Mayor Rice, W. D. Cleveland, and Mrs. Eugenia Flewellyn (Mrs. R. T. Flewellyn).

Houston was prospering. The flight to the suburbs continued and by the end of 1911, more than one hundred and fifty new real estate additions had been recorded at the courthouse. In the decade that ended in 1912, a contemporary historian wrote, Houstonians spent nine million dollars on "homes of all kinds from humble cottages to palatial mansions. Some residences have cost $50,000 to $75,000."

Throughout Houston, streetcar service was the best and surest way to get about town. The Houston Electric Company ran 191 streetcars on thirteen main lines. The Fannin Street car stopped at the southwest city limits marked by Eagle, turned across Main Street, and headed back to town on Travis. Anyone wanting to go to Bellaire had to transfer at Eagle to a little tram that took out across the vast, unsettled stretch between the city of Houston and the town of Bellaire. Of the two main long-distance lines, one went to Harrisburg, the other along Washington Avenue to the city of Houston Heights.

In September, 1911, the Houston-Galveston Interurban began to run. Its fifty miles of track had cost $2.5 million. Painted Pullman green, the cars carried fifty-four passengers and made eighteen round-trips a day. The electric trolleys made the trip in fifty-five minutes. No faster or easier way to travel between the two Gulf Coast cities has yet been found.

Automobiles, an Unnoticed Revolution

THE FIRST Houstonian to install a telephone back in 1878 must have wondered what to do with it. Whom could he call? And who else had a phone on which to call him? But Houstonians rushed to install telephones so swiftly that subscribers soon had an entire directory of numbers to choose from. The same spirit of venture marked the acceptance of the automobile in a year when there were no mechanics, garages, or service stations, when there were few paved streets, no paved highways.

In 1900, horse-drawn carriages, mule-drawn wagons, and electric streetcars were all anyone could need for transportation. Automobiles came into Houston as a sport, and an athletic and adventurous one at that. Nobody predicted that within twenty years, automobiles and horses would have traded places—the car to be driven for daily transportation and the horse to be ridden on fine mornings as exercise for Houston ladies and gentlemen. In 1902, the United States had twenty-five thousand passenger cars on the streets. Few foresaw that these would swell in number to provide a use for the oil gushing up out of the ground at Spindletop.

Houston's automobile age began quietly. In March, 1901, the Left Hand Fishing Club bought a car. Then, a Mrs. Adams acquired a steamer. By December 21, the *Houston Chronicle* could report: "Automobiles have come to Houston. . . . For more than a month now the agile, swift-moving steam machines have been dashing back and forth over the downtown streets." For Houston

and the automobile, it was apparently love at first sight.

George W. Hawkins is thought to have brought the first gasoline-powered car to town in 1901 or 1902. By the printing of the 1903 *City Directory,* he had set up the Hawkins Auto & Gas Engine Co. at 908 Texas. "Old Phone 1198, New Phone 232. We sell gasoline engines and irrigation plants. Also the famous Oldsmobile." That year, Mosehart & Keller shod horses and was in the business of repairing, painting, and trimming carriages at 1302-8 Franklin Street. The C. Jim Stewart & Stevenson listing referred to "blacksmiths and carriages, mfrs., horse shoers" at 1712 Congress Avenue, phone 1063."[1] Oil being advertised for sale was as likely to have come from cottonseed as from the ground. Oil dealers sold oil for lamps, oleomargarine, and lubricating.

Livery stables and blacksmith shops all over town stood ready to rescue the carriage or wagon with a broken axle or the horse that had lost a shoe. But what could those same stables and smithies do for the horseless carriage? Houstonians seemed not to worry.

Learning to drive was simple. The dealer told the buyer how to crank the engine, how to step on the throttle, how to steer, how to shift gears, and how to use the hand brake. After that, each driver took to the road.

In early 1903 C. L. Bering made the first cross-country trip from Houston to Rockport, carrying manilla rope for tows when needed. He was cheered all along his way and greeted by city officials at every town. Bering came home a confirmed motorist. Thereafter C. L. and Theo Bering, Jr., at 609-11 Main Street, sold Michelin tires and tubes, Weed's Tire Chains, and Mercedes Spark Plugs, along with their regular lines in hardware, crockery, and sporting goods.

On April 1 that year T. Brady became Houston's first driver to be ticketed. He was fined ten dollars and costs for "fast driving" down Main Street. He had exceeded the six-mph speed limit.

Banker James E. McAshan had one of the first cars in town. His grandson, S. M. Mc-Ashan, Jr., remembers it: "It was built like a great big soup bowl and had an open hood and a big copper water jacket around the cylinders. It only had two cylinders. It was a Reo. Water cooled. Made a big impression on a boy. Grandfather had the first license plate in Harris County."

In 1903 Henry Ford formed the Ford Motor Company with the aim of making cars to sell to the average man for $500. His first Model T cost $850. The Cadillac Model A of 1903 sold for $750. Cadillac, Olds, Packard, and Ford were the big four of the automobile industry.

By 1906, Houston had eighty automobiles, and the Houston Automobile Club members owned sixty-one of them. On June 21, 1909, the *Houston Chronicle* reported: "The first local party of automobilists to successfully make a trip from Houston to Galveston and return in a single day made the run on Sunday, leaving here at 6 o'clock in the morning . . . returning . . . about 9 o'clock in the evening."

This was no mean feat. Though shell or gravel may have been spread on some stretches, much of the road held the ruts left by wagons after the latest rain. There were no maps, no signposts. The automobilist set the odometer at zero and started out. Fifteen years later, the 1924 *Blue Book* gave these directions for the trip to Galveston:

0.0 HOUSTON, Main & Preston Sts. East on Preston St. Under RR 1.0, coming onto Harrisburg Blvd. Avoid left at filling sta. 6.6.

6.9 Left-hand road before RR; left. Thru DUMONT 11.1.2 Pass GENOA Sta. 14.8; Olcott Sta. 16.7.
22.5 WEBSTER, end of road. Left across RR and 1st right.
25.1 4-corner at church; right.
25.1 LEAGUE CITY, beyond RR. Left then right. . . .

And so on through Dickinson, La-Marque, and at last to Galveston at mile 51.9. But by the time the 1924 *Blue Book* was in print, sensible Houstonians were skimming to Galveston on the Interurban in fifty minutes. For the longer trip to Austin, the *Blue Book* directions listed some fourteen gates to private property that had to be opened and closed by the way. It is hard to know why, since stagecoaches had been making the trip for decades.

By 1910, the *Houston Automobile Register*, published by the club, gave the license numbers of 870 car owners. That motoring pioneer G. W. Hawkins, who lived at 111 Boulevard, Heights, now held license number 1 on his Maxwell. He had several Maxwells, presumably for rent or sale. His neighbors, John E. Patrick and D. D. Cooley, had Numbers 2 and 3 on their Maxwells. Houston's first automobile dealer seemed to have given up "the famous Oldsmobile" for the Maxwell, a car that Jack Benny would make even more famous.

By 1913 the *Houston Automobile Directory* listed 4,143 licensed automobile owners. In the four years from 1906 to 1910, automobiles grew more than ten times in number. And in the three years between 1910 and 1913, they multiplied by almost five. In an unnoticed takeover, cars were beginning to replace carriage horses in the stable at the back of the property. Saddle horses held out another two decades.

A horse fair was always a regular part of the annual No-Tsu-Oh Carnival. In 1910 the fair was held every night at the corner of Lamar and Main Street. Throngs gathered to admire and to buy. Advertisements touted five-gaited saddle horses, double harness to vehicles as well as single roadsters, trotters, hunters, and polo ponies. The emphasis here seems to be more on horses for pleasure and for sport than horses to use in business or hauling. But it is possible that only the far-sighted and dedicated motorists yet realized that a revolution was taking place. It was one that would change not only personal ways of getting about but the shape of cities and the economy of the nation.

Car dealers were ardent salesmen. The Imperial Motor Car Company at 1117-19 Prairie would sell a Pullman for anything from $1600 to $4500. G. W. Hawkins at Main and Walker offered a Maxwell coupe for $600, a touring car for $1,500. And Southern Motor Car Factory at Texas and Caroline offered to make a "Dixie" right there on the spot in any style or body for $1,875. For those desiring more sport, the 1913 *Houston Automobile Directory* advertised the "Pierce Vibrationless Motorcycle, 4 Cylinders: Power, Elegance, Simplicity, Economy, Speed, Cleanliness."

The 1913 *City Directory* lists dealerships for the Overland, Stutz, Ford, Maxwell, Packard, Buick, and Cadillac. Automobile liveries rented out cars as they once rented a horse and carriage. Westheimer Warehouse offered automobile storage. Mosehart & Keller and C. Jim Stewart & Stevenson had gone into automobile repair. Of the twenty-nine automobile agents and dealers in downtown Houston, at least thirteen were between 111 and 1711 Main Street. The city skyline might still be defined by steeples, but at street level it was dominated by automobile storefronts.

As early as 1910, both doctors and women dared to rely on the automobile. Dr. Philo Howard drove a Ford; Dr. Minnie Archer an Electric; Dr. W. R. Eckhardt an Oldsmobile; Mrs. T. J. Anderson a Winton; Dr. P. H. Scardino a Hupmobile. And though Sid Westheimer Co., Undertakers, still advertised that it had a silver-gray funeral car and sixteen matchless teams, along with "two score rubber tired vehicles," the big claim was that Westheimer had the only automobile hearse in Houston.

When the W. T. Carters still lived on Main Street, before their move to Court-

In 1908 William T. Carter moved his family into this Main Street mansion, which had a ballroom and stables.

landt Place, their first car was a Packard. Mary Carroll Kempner Reed (Mrs. Lawrence Reed) remembers her grandparents' car well. "They got someone from the Packard factory to be their chauffeur. His name was Jimmy. The speedometer was way over on the right corner and that was the prize place to sit, where you could watch the speedometer. They also had a car for grandmother. They had its roof raised a little bit not to interfere with her hats. Cars were pretty much made to order in those days."

The James L. Autrys were keen motorists. Judge Autry was known for the superb care he took of his 1910 Winton. Mrs. Autry drove an Electric. Judge Autry was a member of the Texas Automobile Association, the Automobile Club of Houston, and the San Antonio Automobile Club. One of his few unsuccessful investments was made in the Magnolia Motor Company. Several business firms owned more than one car. Levy Brothers at 311 Main had both a Packard and a Cadillac, and Abe Levy drove a Packard registered at home.

Vital statistics change with the times. The runaway horse was replaced by the automobile accident as a cause of death. Hyman Levy, the handsomest of the elegant Levy brothers, was one of Houston's first fatali-

Main Street, before World War I.

ties in an automobile accident when on his way to the Houston Country Club to play golf, and Sherman Brady, who owned the first really fast car, was killed when driving at high speed down the Galveston Road. In 1904, nine-year-old LaRue Sachs was killed when a motorized streetcar struck her. La-Rue Street off Washington Avenue was named for her.

Despite what seemed like a car in every garage, Houstonians continued to use the streetcar for routine trips. There was only one center of town, and a good streetcar line ran to it from every part of the city. Men rode the streetcar to the office to leave the family automobile with their wives; ladies often preferred the streetcar to finding a place to park when shopping on lower Main Street

at Foley's or lunching at Levy's. High school students well into the 1930s used the street-car, nimbly transferring from one line to an-other to go debating at another school, to go swimming, to see friends.

Whatever the make of car, however ex-pensive, it was open to the weather, wet or dusty, hot or cold. The day of the sedan with hard top and glass windows had not come. But the Sunday afternoon drive was as firmly on the social calendar as Sunday morning church. Regardless of weather, most of those privileged to have a car felt compelled to drive family and friends out across the coun-tryside every Sunday after dinner. In sum-mer, they wore dusters and goggles and gloves. The ladies wore scarves over their hats, partly to keep the hat in place against the stiff breeze coming in at thirty to forty miles per hour, partly to protect their hair from the dust stirred by every passing vehicle. In winter, on particularly cold or rainy days, the driver snapped isinglass curtains from the car's canvas roof to its body. Every car had a lap robe to provide warmth. On the coldest days, it was thought wise to start out with a hot brick at the feet.

The automobile crank fitted into a hole in front under the radiator. It took male strength to turn the crank often enough and fast enough for the engine to catch. It was harder in cold weather. Canny motorists covered up their car hoods with blankets or laprobes on cold nights in hopes of keeping the lubricants from congealing. On really cold mornings, some impatient motorists lit a charcoal heater under the radiator to warm it before trying the crank.

Ladies like Mrs. Albert Bath and Mrs. Will Clayton drove nice little electric cars because they started from the battery. The electrics steered with a stick, rather like the tiller of a boat, and had little vases inside in which fresh flowers could be put. Square, and with large glass windows on four sides, the electric somehow gave the impression of a mobile sun parlor.[2] Between runs, the electrics had to be plugged in to recharge their batteries. Mrs. Clayton did not like to drive very much, and when she saw another car coming, she would turn off into a side street until it went away.

On big wheels, automobiles rode high over the street. This was useful on roads with deep holes or ruts. The running board on each side under the doors had many uses. It served as a step for passengers to come aboard, rather as mounting blocks helped riders to mount their horses. When a picnic was planned, a big block of ice was tied on the running board. For short runs, children and young people sometimes hung on, standing on the running board. The running board survived through the 1920s but was stripped away by streamlining.

The work of paving Main Street with cobblestones had begun at the bayou in 1884–85. By 1910, the paving was 2,313 feet long—almost half a mile. For many years, Fannin Street was paved with wooden bricks of bois d'arc. After each of Houston's frequent rains, the wood would swell, popping out an occasional brick. In any block, a dozen or more bricks would lie about on the surface until street crews came along to chisel the errant brick down a bit and wedge it back in. When the big Percheron horses pulled heavy drays along Fannin, the clop-clop of their big hooves made a gentle, pleasant sound.

In the early years, no roads leading out into the countryside were paved.[3] Most had parallel ruts and unpredictable potholes. To small children, who viewed the drives with as much fear as pleasure, every road led to a detour. The detour was usually a primitive gash cut alongside the main road, often down a slope and through a ford across the creek. It was used while road repair was done or a bridge built. For some reason, detours seemed always to be muddy and slick. Getting stuck on the detour was a routine,

For the customary Sunday afternoon drive, Houstonians could motor out from town and cross the Brazos River on a one-car ferry. Unfortunately, skidding and getting stuck were almost as customary, as shown in this 1912 photograph. *Courtesy Mary Cullinan Cravens (Mrs. Rorick Cravens)*

to-be-expected part of the Sunday drive.

Julian Huxley, as a young biology professor at Rice Institute, bought a Model T Ford "costing about 100 pounds with petrol at 5 d a gallon!" As he wrote in his *Memories,* "It was a gallant little machine which I could drive across the prairies. In the winter vacation, I drove with a colleague in my new car to see Stark Young, professor of comparative literature at the State University at Austin, who had called on me in Oxford on hearing that I was coming to Texas. . . . This important route from Houston to Austin soon turned into a dirt road, so bad that at one swampy place I had to turn off into a field." He also got stuck.[4]

This was as late as 1915. Roads did not quickly improve. George Bruce recalled driving to Austin in the 1920s. "We went by Hempstead and had to cross the Brazos on a ferry that they pulled across. When we went to football games, we would start out awfully early that morning."

The automobile, which would ultimately remap cities and change every social custom, was already making itself felt—rather like the camel with his nose in the tent. In designing his own home on Heights Boulevard, George Hawkins was the first in Harris County to build a garage attached to his house. To gain access to it, he persuaded the Heights developers to push 10½ Street through to his driveway.[5] This is one of the few half-streets that reaches the Boulevard in that sector.

Supply rose to meet a new demand. The Gulf Filling Station at 1303 Main Street promised: "That Good Gulf Gasoline and Supreme Auto Oil will make your ride more pleasant." Automobile filling stations were now scattered up and down every street and avenue, many of them still doing part duty as livery stables or hardware stores.

Mark Edwin Andrews remembered best the Texas Lamp & Oil Company on Prairie, between Milam and Louisiana, across from Bering Cortes.[6] "They had a pump. You had a tank under the front seat, or at least the big Cadillac did. They used a funnel

about eighteen inches across, with a chamois stretched across it, to strain out the trash and water. They would build a fifty-five-gallon drum in your yard and keep it full if you were regular customers."

"The first car we had was a 1911 Cadillac," he said. "The top and the windshield were extras. It had gas headlights at the front (carbide), kerosene lamps at the dashboard, and at the tail a lamp. When darkness came, somebody had to light all those lamps. It had a big patent leather license plate that said '125 Houston' in brass. Mother and Father would put the car on the boat in Galveston and ship it to New York. After they had gone to the opera and seen the newest plays, we would tour New England wearing dusters and goggles. People would say "HOWston? Where is HOWston?"

His parents, Mr. and Mrs. Jesse Andrews, stayed at the old Waldorf on 34th Street and Fifth Avenue. "The car stayed at a livery stable somewhere around there. They brought it around one day and it had a flat tire. Father changed it right there in the street by the Waldorf. He had a mechanical pump on the engine that pumped the tire up."

All cars had frequent flats. Few had the luxury of a mechanical pump. Young men learned to patch the hole in an innertube, pump it back up to wheel shape, stuff it back into the heavy rubber casing, tuck it in all the way around with a long, canvas strip called a boot, and then, with a metal bar, prize the steel wheel back into the tire. Thereafter it needed a few more hard strokes on the pump to be sure it was properly inflated.

None of this daunted motoring enthusiasts. "In 1920," George Bruce recalled, "Mr. Herbert Godwin had two daughters—Ann and Elizabeth—and they used to bring friends home from Shipley or Bryn Mawr.[7] One girl from Baltimore had never been west of Baltimore and she wanted to see the *West.* So Mr. Godwin asked me to take them in his Hudson Super 6."

"We left Houston with the running

boards loaded. We took along canvas folding cots. We made San Marcos the first day on a trip to San Antonio and El Paso. We camped out every night. No tents. Mr. Godwin provided quail and rabbits. We had ice-boxes and stopped in every little town for more ice. The girls cooked. We had twenty-one flats and I changed every one of them. Along about the fifth or sixth flat, I found out why Mr. Godwin took me."

Chapter Twenty-Nine

Rice Institute

LAWSUITS BEHIND, finances in order, the trustees began the search for a man to head the future Rice Institute in January, 1907 – almost seven years after the death of its founder. They knew that they held a special trust. This would be Houston's first institution of higher education.

With serene confidence, they assumed that to get top-level nominees, they should begin at the top. They wrote twenty-five letters asking for nominations – including letters to former President Grover Cleveland and to the presidents of Cornell, Stanford, and Princeton.[1] Princeton's Woodrow Wilson nominated Edgar Odell Lovett, an astronomer of his own faculty.

In November, 1907, the board offered the presidency to Dr. Lovett. Pointing out that the school would be well endowed, Captain Baker wrote: "The trustees . . . will be disposed to give you a very free hand . . . they are broad minded and liberal and desire . . . to employ at all times the best talent that can be had anywhere. . . . The opportunity offered you is an unusual one. . . . Such an opportunity rarely comes to one so young in life."

At thirty-six, Edgar Odell Lovett was a remarkable scholar. Having completed a classical education in Greek, Latin, and classical literature, he went on to mathematics and astronomy. While both teaching and studying, he earned an A.B., a B.S., and an M.A. from Bethany College in West Virginia, another Master's and a Ph.D. from the University of Virginia. After studying mathematics in Leipzig and attending lectures in Rome and Christiana (Oslo), Norway, he came home with another Master's and another doctorate. All seven of his degrees had been earned by his mid-twenties, all with honors. He taught at Johns Hopkins and the University of Virginia and lectured at the University of Chicago. He turned down the presidency of Drake University to teach astronomy at Princeton. At twenty-nine, he was a full professor.[2]

The chance to create a new university aspiring to high quality must have been exciting. Dr. Lovett accepted the Rice Institute offer with a proviso: he must first have a year to visit the great universities of the world. He arrived in March, 1908, and employed F. Carrington Weems, a recent Princeton graduate, as his secretary. Next, a site and an architect had to be chosen.

With dreams of Oxford and Princeton dancing in their heads, the trustees thought briefly of a "down channel" campus so that the students could punt or scull on Buffalo Bayou. But they accepted Dr. Lovett's recommendation to buy a remote tract of three hundred acres southwest of Houston, more than a mile beyond the end of Main Street. Except for one cluster of trees, it was made up of open farmland and prairie with a creek known as Harris Gully cutting across its western section. Houstonians were dismayed. Why put this promising institution so far away that no streetcar went near it?

While the board dealt with ten different landowners to put together the tract, Dr. and Mrs. Lovett and Carrington Weems set forth to study the great universities of the

United States, Europe, and Japan.[3] This was a unique tour. Sailing in August, 1908, they traveled through Great Britain, Ireland, Scandinavia, Germany, Switzerland, Italy, France, Belgium, the Netherlands, Spain, Portugal, Greece, Austria-Hungary, and Poland. They went across Russia to Japan by the Trans-Siberian Express, and returned to Houston on May 7, 1909. En route, Dr. Lovett took part in scientific meetings. He read a paper at the Association for the Advancement of Science meeting in Dublin and to mathematicians of Stockholm and Uppsala at a dinner in Stockholm. This was the first scholarly paper presented from Rice Institute. He made friends of some of the great savants of the early twentieth century. Rice owed the high quality of its first faculty to that trip—to the friendships he made and the reputation he established.

Wherever he went, he told the story of the Rice Institute and asked advice of scholars, administrators, and statesmen. The only off-putting advice came from a Johns Hopkins University professor whom Dr. Lovett met in London. This gentleman, as Frederica Meiners wrote in her history of the institute, advised Dr. Lovett to hire Americans for his faculty, preferably Southerners, on grounds that it would be hard to attract anyone better to a local institute that was named for an individual. Besides, the learned professor said, America already had too many universities.

Dr. Lovett was determined that the Houston school should provide the best possible undergraduate and graduate studies leading to a Ph.D. So were his trustees. Banker James Everett McAshan also went abroad in 1908 to view European universities and reported: "My interviews with educators lead me to believe that the only way we can command patronage is to have men and apparatus that will challenge the appreciation of the earnest students of the world, who desire to achieve success, and not cater too much to those students who only go to college as a matter of good form."

Dr. Lovett used his trip to scout for faculty talent. "I always hoped to have one man from Balliol College Oxford and one from Trinity College Cambridge," he said.[4] "I got the Balliol man on that trip, Julian Huxley." Harold A. Wilson became the Trinity man on the first faculty.

This was an era of university building. Leland Stanford, the University of Chicago, and Rice Institute for the Advancement of Art, Literature and Science were all incorporated in 1891. Rice was delayed in opening by the litigation over Mrs. Rice's will and over Mr. Rice's murder.

The three-hundred-acre site was a clean drawing board, and Dr. Lovett had ten million dollars to use, one of the largest fortunes ever given to start a new institution. He had vision, a great deal of practical experience, and intellectual elegance. He also had a board that could appreciate his abilities and that would support his ideas. They agreed to operate out of income, leaving the principal untouched. This meant that they lacked the money to advance literature, science, and art simultaneously. They decided to advance art by seeking really fine architecture. Though the institute would provide a core of liberal education, it would start with an emphasis on science and then strengthen the humanities as it became possible.

For the architecture, Dr. Lovett recommended Ralph Adams Cram of Cram, Goodhue and Ferguson of Boston. To be sure that the scientific laboratories were the best available, he formed a committee of outstanding scientists to draft the specifications—men from Johns Hopkins, Princeton, Harvard, and the National Bureau of Standards.

Dr. Lovett also had a sense of occasion. The cornerstone for the administration building—later Lovett Hall—was laid on March 2, 1911, the seventy-fifth anniversary of Texas' independence from Mexico. The stone bears the inscription: *"Rather," said Democritus, "would I discover the cause of one fact than become King of the Persians."*

William Ward Watkin, an architectural graduate of the University of Pennsylvania,

Though the ornately carved Sallyport arched and soared, scholars had to walk through mud and rubble to take part in the opening ceremony of Rice Institute in 1912. No trees screened the new administration building from Main Street when John and Craig Cullinan came out for a drive. *Courtesy Mary Cullinan Cravens (Mrs. Rorick Cravens)*

moved to Houston to supervise building for Cram, Goodhue and Ferguson, and stayed on to found the department of architecture. Monolithic granite columns, cloistered passages, vaulted stone ceilings began to take shape. Houstonians liked to watch as Oswald J. Lassig, a German stonecutter, carved massive stones into the intricate capitals designed by the architects in Boston. On the site and in place, he carved squirrels, flowers, and arabesques.[5] He created portraits in stone of Leonardo da Vinci and Isaac Newton and impish caricatures of a worried junior and a happy little freshman. He carved owls in all sizes.

Long before the Rice opening, the *City Directory* of 1911 noted that it already had three buildings and landscaping valued at seven hundred thousand dollars. The editor concluded: "Non-sectarian and non-political, with 300 acres and an expected $10 million in endowment, Rice Institute has the means to live always."[6]

Construction turned the prairie into a muddy wasteland for almost two years, but the grand plan called for *allees* of live oaks planted in triple rows and extensive gardens. Edward Teas, founder of Teas Nursery in Houston, carried out the planting.[7] Seventy-seven young men and women enrolled in the first class. Ed Dupree was the first male, and Lillian Red, daughter of Dr. and Mrs. S. C. Red, was the first female in the first Rice class.

The formal opening of Rice Institute, held on October 10, 11, 12, and 13, 1912, was extraordinary. It would be hard to duplicate even in the era of supersonic jet travel. Out on a prairie still cluttered with the rubble of construction, great scholars of the United States, Britain, Europe, and Japan gathered in full, colorful regalia to welcome this new institute into the academic world.[8]

From Tokyo, Heidelburg, Edinburgh, and Paris, by steamship in a time when crossings took three weeks and more, by railroad trains of limited speed and comfort, they came. Each scholar must have taken the same trains as those described by Julian Huxley—Dr. Lovett's Balliol man. After visiting Yale, Harvard, and Johns Hopkins Medical School in Baltimore, as he wrote in his *Memories,* the young Englishman set out for "the long journey west and south to Houston."

In St. Louis he had time to walk through town to see the confluence of the Missouri and Mississippi—"even more impressive than my later sight of the Nile. From St. Louis, I went on by the Katy Flier, the star train of the M. K. and T. . . . The Flier, I found, 'flew' at an average of 34 m.p.h. This slow rate . . . was partly due to the poorness of the rails—it is hard to lay a perfect track across a thousand miles of sparsely populated prairie; but also to the delightful habit of mealstops. Instead of eating on the train, joggled from side to side, we would draw up at a station—I should say 'deepo'—scramble out, and be served excellent home-cooked food on big tables by motherly ladies in white aprons."

In Houston, Huxley was awed by the array of famous men who came for the opening. "There were nearly a hundred distinguished professors from American universities, and a galaxy of outstanding savants from Europe, including Borel, the French mathematician; Benedetto Croce, the Italian philosopher who looked more like a prosperous butcher than a savant; de Vries, the co-discoverer of Mendelism, from Holland, and Sir William Ramsay, the eminent British chemist and physicist, accompanied by his wife."

While here, the great scholars lectured, each in his own language. Sir William Ramsay, a Nobel laureate who had been knighted for his contributions in chemistry, spoke on the transmutation of matter. Hugo de Vries of the University of Amsterdam, spoke on the biological form of transmutation in heredity. Rafael Altamira Y Crevea, historian from the University of Oviedo, Spain, spoke on the history of human progress. Emile Borel of the University of Paris lectured on mathematics. Sir Henry Jones of Glasgow discussed philosophy. Vitor Volterra, a life senator of the kingdom of Italy, spoke on mathematics and the work of Henri Poincare. (Poincare had been invited, but had died after preparing his lectures for the Rice opening.)

Houston turned out to welcome these visitors at four days of breakfasts, luncheons, garden parties, concerts, and dinners. Mr. and Mrs. Jonas Shearn Rice gave a luncheon at the Thalian Club. Mr. and Mrs. Edwin Brewington Parker gave a garden party at five o'clock at The Oaks. The Kneisel Quartette of New York gave concerts at the Majestic Theater between these two repasts and again at night in the Faculty Chamber.

At half past nine on Saturday morning, the delegates and guests marched to the Sallyport for the formal outdoor dedication of Rice Institute. Henry Van Dyke of Princeton read *Texas, A Democratic Ode,* which he had written for the occasion. Texas Chief Justice Thomas Jefferson Brown spoke on education and the state. The Rt. Rev. Thomas F. Gailor, Episcopal bishop of Tennessee, spoke on education and the church. President Lovett spoke on William Marsh Rice and on the whole scope of the institute he envisioned.

Dr. and Mrs. Lovett gave a reception at the new Houston Country Club. Thereafter, the delegates went by special train to Gal-

Landscaping had begun when this picture was made from the main gate on Main at Sunset Boulevard in 1913, but the allees of live oaks had yet to be planted on the swampy site of Rice Institute. *Courtesy Woodson Research Center, Fondren Library, Rice University*

veston for a seafood supper and a night at the Hotel Galvez. Then by special train they came back to Houston for a religious service in the City Auditorium with a sermon by Dr. Charles Frederic Aked, pastor of the First Congregational Church of San Francisco. When it was all over, the seventy-seven students of the first Rice class went back to the classroom.

Julian Huxley went off to Germany for a year of further study in biology, as he had promised Dr. Lovett to do, before returning to found the department of biology.[9] In his two years in Houston, Huxley saw his first hummingbird and bought his first car, a Model T. He also discovered crayfish in the stream that ran across the campus. He and Dr. Radoslav Tsanoff, Rice philosopher, be-

came lifelong friends. At Joseph Cullinan's invitation, Huxley looked for birds like the vermillion flycatcher on strolls through the land that would become Shadyside.

Young bachelors of the faculty often gathered at tea time at the Crawford Street home of the Henry St. John Waggamans. The Waggamans had three charming daughters. Low-cut tea gowns were in fashion. One afternoon, an intellectual young gentleman was leaning over Miss Adele in absorbing conversation, when Huxley murmured to Miss Camille: "That's the most highbrow appreciation of a low-cut gown I ever saw."

But with the coming of World War I, Huxley went home to join up. And the Rice campus took on the discipline of an army camp.

Chapter Thirty

As the Twig Is Bent

By 1900, Houston's schools were over-burdened. The 273 teachers had 7,500 pupils to teach. The buildings were crowded, and the hurricane of September 8–9 damaged so many of them that classes could not begin on time. At the Fannin School, one of the city's best, children sat under umbrellas during heavy rains and holes were bored in the floor to let water drain out. At Taylor School, 63 children were jammed into one small classroom.

Although 1900 was a hard year for the public schools, it brought one great and lasting gift. Hoping to give children an appreciation of art, five women met at the home of Mrs. Robert S. Lovett on March 17, 1900, to found the Houston Public School Art League. Artist Emma Richardson Cherry, Mrs. Henry B. Fall, Mrs. George A. Volck, and Miss Gussie Howard elected Mrs. Lovett the league's first president, and Dr. Henry Barnstein and P. W. Horn vice-presidents.[1] When chartered by the state in 1913, it became the Houston Art League – the forerunner of the Museum of Fine Arts.

Going into debt to do so, the league hung framed copies of thirty-five famous paintings in each of twelve public schools. In a time when Houston had no museum and little public art in paint or marble, this was a way of letting children become familiar with classical works. The league bought a full-scale replica of the Venus de Milo for the high school. But there was a feeling in some circles that she was not sufficiently clad for daily association with young, impressionable students. Therefore, a group of twenty-four Houstonians, three civic clubs, and three corporations bought her from the league and gave her to the new Carnegie Library.[2]

Despite damage by hurricanes and the burdens of too many children for too few classrooms, Houston continued its decade-by-decade effort to create a good public school system. It was an uphill race against city growth. Between 1891 and 1908, the school population tripled. Teachers' salaries did not. The average in 1881 was forty-three dollars a month; in 1909 it was sixty-five. While the school board struggled to build for an inevitable future, the taxpayers carped about extravagance.

Rose Keeper was seven years old when she started to the Elysian Street School in 1902. In addition to the ABCs, it offered music and art and, as an elective, German. "Our principal was Mr. James B. Wolfe. He used to come on a horse and he would let some of us ride on it at lunch time. We used to carry lunch baskets to school. Mothers used to be very conscious of the looks of that lunch basket. It was usually a little wicker basket with a top and a handle, and a napkin peeking out the side.

"We had singing. We learned the scales and to read music. Miss Mamie Bastion was the art teacher. One of my teachers was Miss Nona Amerman, the daughter of Judge Amerman. At the end of the term, she had us all come to her house for an afternoon of entertainment. They lived on the banks of the bayou not too far from the MK&T Station. And she took us to the Market

At Professor Welch's academy the schoolhouse was simple, but the schooling was outstanding. Chris W. Welch opened his school in the big old house on Polk and Jackson in 1896. *Courtesy William Alexander Kirkland, an alumnus*

Square to witness the unveiling of the statue of Dick Dowling."

The overcrowding of public schools encouraged the growth of private ones. Professor Chris W. Welch had opened the Houston Academy in 1896 in a large house at Polk and Jackson. By 1900, he had sent graduates to Yale, Harvard, the University of Virginia, Washington and Lee, the University of the South, and the University of Texas. In 1906 he moved the school to a far larger house at Caroline and Hadley, where some ninety boys and girls were enrolled. Many of Houston's most distinguished citizens of the mid-twentieth century got their start under Professor Welch.[3]

Houston 1900, a Texas Blue Book, lists the Young Ladies' School operated at 1215 Main by three sisters: Miss Hargis, Miss Mary Hargis, and Miss Marcia Hargis.[4] One of the Hargis sisters married a Norwegian, left Houston, and ultimately became Henrik Ibsen's translator. The other two took five of their best pupils to Europe for a year and rented a large apartment in Paris. Like the Houston girls of the Civil War period, Edith Paine, Roene Masterson, Daphne Palmer,

Etta Brady, and Sally Sewell learned French, visited the great art museums of the day, and attended the theater. They made side trips to England, Italy, Germany, and the Bavarian Alps.[5]

With her two sisters, Miss Mary Waldo opened a school in 1904 in a house at Crawford and Lamar. The daughters of Jedediah Waldo, vice-president of the Missouri, Kansas and Texas Railroad, all three were college graduates. Miss Mary had had an additional ten years of study in New York, Cleveland, and Paris. She taught French and English, the Misses Virginia and Lula the other basic subjects. They soon moved to a larger house at Fannin and Lamar.

"After the first year, they decided to have only girls," Bill Kirkland said. "They made an exception for three boys, Allen Peden, Charlie Worley and me." The Waldo sisters had as early pupils Lois Cleveland, Marion Seward, Betsy Bailey, Madge Dow, Mary Allen, Kate Allen Weems, and Alice Bruce. Though Bill Kirkland ultimately married his little friend Lois Cleveland, he said, "Marion Holt Seward was . . . the glamour girl of our town. She had a donkey that would pull us on skates around the block on the sidewalk." Bill's grandfather, Alexander Root, soon got him out of the girls' school and into Professor Welch's academy so that he could learn the Latin and Greek that would be necessary for Princeton or Yale.

On September 1, 1900, the Basilian fathers opened St. Thomas High School in a frame building at Franklin and Caroline. A week later the hurricane damaged it severely. In 1903 the fathers bought a block bounded by Austin and LaBranch, Hadley and McIlhenny, and built the building that St. Thomas High School would occupy for a third of a century. The *City Directory* of 1903–1904 shows that the Incarnate Word Academy was a boarding and day school for girls, teaching "all branches of a Solid and Refined Education."

The Dominican sisters influenced education throughout the Gulf Coast. They staffed the Sacred Heart High School, which had been founded in 1897 when the parish was new. In 1905 it became the first Catholic school in Texas to be accredited by the Texas State Department of Education.

Meanwhile, a committee of Sacred Heart parishioners had been raising money for a select boarding and day school to be run by the Dominican sisters. Helped by John Henry Kirby and H. F. MacGregor, they put together two and a half acres out on the prairie southwest of town. The streetcar stopped two blocks short of the property and the only access was a footpath across a pasture where cows grazed. When streets were put through, the campus would be bounded by Truxillo and Cleburne avenues, San Jacinto and Fannin streets.

St. Agnes Academy opened in 1906 in the big, four-story building facing Fannin. Crepe myrtle trees and oleanders would grow up around it, and ivy would cover its walls. It would educate generations of Houston girls and was the first Catholic school to be affiliated with the University of Texas. But in the early years when it rained, day students had to walk through two blocks of mud. Many girls hooked a ride on the ice wagon. When

at last the streetcar line was extended out to Eagle, the nuns sent fresh, hot coffee to the conductor and motorman of the early morning run. In appreciation, the city allowed the sisters to ride the streetcar free of charge for years.

In 1904, Margaret Kinkaid opened a school for seven neighborhood children in her cottage on San Jacinto at Elgin. She never expected to keep them past the second or third grade and in 1906 took a two-year recess for the birth of her second son, William. By then, Houston had more children of school age than any other city in the state. In 1908, when Houston schools were even more crowded, Mrs. Kinkaid began again and, adding one grade at a time, went on to build another of the enduring private schools of Houston.

A German woman from Oyster Bay, New York, Jenny M. Eichler, had a school for preschool children in the parish house of Christ Church. It was known as Miss Eichler's University. She had three primary classes. One of them had as pupils Howard Hughes, Jr., Elizabeth Dillingham, Elizabeth Law, Alice Gray Sears, Dudley Sharp, Thomas William House, Ella Rice, Marion Spencer, Helen Wicks, Minnie Gates, Tommie Rice, Louise McClain, Lila Gates, and Dudley Colhoun.[6]

This small class of thirteen children produced some notable adults: Howard Hughes became an internationally known flyer, as well as an oil tool, aircraft, and motion picture executive, and one of the world's richest men. Ella Rice married Howard Hughes when they were both twenty. For years, during the depression, Elizabeth Dillingham wrote the radio soap opera *Stella Dallas*. When television came in, she was commissioned to write four television dramas a year for the Hallmark Theater. With the permission of E. M. Forster, she wrote a play based on *Where Angels Fear to Tread,* which ran for more than a year on the London stage. And Dudley Sharp became secretary of the air force in the Eisenhower administration.

Chaille Cage (Mrs. J. Lewis Thompson) had her first lessons in French from Miss

Miss Eichler's University, a pre–World War I kindergarten, produced Houstonians of international renown. *Left to right, first row:* Howard Hughes, Marian Spencer, Helen Wicks (Mrs. J. W. Link, Jr.), Elizabeth Dillingham (playwright Elizabeth Hart), Minnie Gates, and Tommie Rice. *Second row:* Louise MacClain (Mrs. John D. Adams), Lila Gates (Mrs. W. L. Redd), Miss Jenny Eichler, Alice Gray Sears (Mrs. W. Frank Akin), and Ella Rice (first Mrs. Howard Hughes, later Mrs. James O. Winston). *Third row:* Dudley Colhoun, Thomas William House, and Dudley Sharp. *Courtesy Christ Church Cathedral*

Eichler and so loved the language that she was one of five children who took French in first grade at Kinkaid. She majored in French at Dana Hall and Wellesley and as a young woman continued her studies at the Sorbonne.

The children took their exercise walking in the church cloister. They all grew up with vivid memories of the big Central Fire Station across the street on San Jacinto. It had a domed roof. Always there was the chance of hearing the fire alarm clang and seeing the horses charge off down the street pulling the hook and ladder wagon. With German firmness, Miss Eichler stressed the importance of *character* to her charges, but they loved her dearly. She vanished from

the Houston scene with the start of war with Germany.[7]

For private lessons in the arts, Houston was well endowed. It seemed always to have highly trained music teachers in every instrument. Anton Diehl, a versatile musician educated in his native Germany, opened the city's first all-round conservatory of music in 1905. Born in Wiesbaden, he had come to Houston in 1886. Though primarily a violinist, he became organist and choir master first at Christ Church and then at the Church of the Annunciation. He fought in the Spanish-American War but returned to Houston to conduct music groups, to found the Houston Quartette Society, and, in 1903, to marry Gabrielle Lavielle of Houston and France.[8] His conservatory faculty of fifteen taught harmony and theory as well as vocal and instrumental music, including the organ. Mrs. Diehl taught French.

She had come to Houston as a child with her older sister, Mrs. W. W. Willson, and her half-brother Georges Jouine. They spent their summers at Lavielle, the family home-place in France. Mr. Willson was head of the Gladys City Oil Company, which owned land at Spindletop, and was an early backer of Pattillo Higgins.

For lessons in drawing, painting, and sculpture, Emma Richardson Cherry was Houston's leading artist and art teacher. She had studied in New York and Paris and her work hung in the New York Academy of Design, the St. Louis Museum of Fine Arts, and the Chicago Art Institute. She not only taught her students how to draw and paint, but taught them art history and art appreciation as well.

Superintendent P. W. Horn, who took over the public school system in 1904, said plaintively, "The school board was accused of stupendous extravagance in erecting a high school building larger than the city would need in *a hundred years*. In fourteen years the building was not only full, but an annex had to be added." The annex gave the school one-third more space and left it still crowded. Superintendent Horn's system had innovations that educators from other towns came to see. Children were given annual eye and physical examinations. Boys had manual training classes; girls studied domestic science. Physical education stressed gymnastics as well as team sports. The common drinking cup was banished and drinking fountains installed.

Young Mrs. Presley Ewing was persuasive in her support of the superintendent's ideas. She organized the first Parent-Teacher Association and convinced the public that sanitary drinking fountains and adjustable desks were essential to classroom learning. Her sincerity made it hard for diehards to dismiss these improvements as mere frills. Horn wangled private contributions to maintain four kindergartens. Mothers' clubs in both black and white schools raised money and in 1909 alone spent $21,548 to add pianos, phonographs, and stereoptican equipment to the classrooms. The Art League provided classes in drawing and clay modeling as well as reproductions to hang on the walls.

Education for black children took a major stride forward under Horn. Between 1905 and 1910 he doubled the number of schools and introduced the vocational training that black leaders had been requesting for years. The response was rewarding. In 1910, 49.5 percent of the black children ages six to twenty were in school daily, compared with 54.3 percent of the whites. And in the ages six to fourteen, 74.4 percent of the black children went to school, compared with 72.7 percent of the native-born whites and 60.6 percent of the foreign-born.[9]

Superintendent Horn also had ideas that would sound like fresh new thoughts in the mid to late twentieth century. "In recent years," he said, "there has been a marked movement . . . in favor of the widest possible use of our school plants. . . . Schools are for the education not of the children alone, but of the community as a whole. . . ." In 1911, he started night classes where adults could continue elementary or vocational education, where young people who had to work by day could keep up in school by night. By 1915, Houston provided free textbooks to public school children.

Houston's superintendent was clearly a leader in modern education. But by their low pay, teachers were subsidizing the classrooms. The taxpayers were still not building an educational system that would make private schools unnecessary—or even make them less attractive.

All of Old Houston's children seemed to go to public schools at one time or another in the first two decades of the century—Fannin, Montrose, or Allen among them. As a school board member, A. S. Cleveland saw to it that his daughters went to Montrose. Also as a school board member, Rufus

Cage had his granddaughter Chaille go to Charlotte Allen School at Elgin and Chenevert for the third through six grades. "Then most of us went on to South End Junior High or Central High School downtown," Chaille Cage Thompson said, "until Central burned down."

Mary Carroll (Mrs. Lawrence Reed) said, "We had awfully good teachers at Fannin School. Professor Charles Jameson was principal. I saw my first airplane at Fannin. They let us out into the school yard to watch it go overhead."

Susan Clayton (Mrs. S. M. McAshan, Jr.) thought Montrose a delightful school.[10] "Each of us was given a plot of ground to grow vegetables for 'the war.' The principal was close to every pupil. He taught one or two classes in math and history. When it rained, the ditches along the edge of the road would fill. Boys would come to school in boats along the ditch. A great trick! There were fields all around, just fields." Mrs. McAshan particularly remembered the wonderful picnic dinner party given for Howard Hughes by his mother. "Every child in the school was invited."

When Susan was fourteen, she and her sister Ellen were sent East to Shipley. "Mother had to send us," she said, "because she had adopted two nieces, Louise and Sue Vaughn (whose mother had died), and six girls were just too much!" When Burdine and Louise went off to the National Cathedral School, two other nieces came down from Kentucky–Mary Louise and Dotty Wilson.[11] "Mother raised eight girls. She wrote them. Dressed them. Gave their parties and all their weddings."

Ellen Hamilton (Mrs. Edward Wilkerson) was the daughter of Edith Paine, who had had the lovely year in Paris with the Hargis class. The Hamiltons still lived in the big old Paine house with the ballroom on the top floor at 1505 McKinney. When Ellen had finished six grades at Kinkaid, her mother thought Central High would be much more convenient than South End

Junior High, but the principal did not think that Ellen could do the work. Her long-time teachers at Kinkaid put her through another semester of lessons in three weeks. She took the tests and entered–the smallest student in Central High.

The Prosso School prepared many young Houstonians for prep school in the east. In a house on Main Street at Rosalie, it was a small school but remarkable in its results. Both Dr. and Mrs. Richardson had Ph.D. degrees. His was from Harvard. They had a faculty of about ten teachers for thirty students.

"You had a one-on-one recitation every day in every subject," Mark Edwin Andrews recalls. "You got a grade every day in every subject, and a report card at the end of every week. The whole school was ranked from top to bottom. Mary Carroll always led the school. She was brilliant and beautiful. Walter Bradley and I were always at the bottom. He was Number 448, I was Number 450. They called on you by number: 'Number 450 . . .' and you'd get up and recite."

"Everybody had spelling every day in one big room. Martha Wicks, Helen Wicks, Ella Rice, Burnett Carson, John Dow, Andy Fondren, Doug Coward. . . . Altogether, it was a cram school, really, to get you into prep school." Although not all the young people were prepped at Prosso, large numbers went away for the high school years.

"The W. T. Carter boys were the first to go off to school, Harry, Aubrey, and Ching," Andrews reminisced. "No, the Hogg brothers went to Lawrenceville. At least Tom and Mike did. The Bakers went to Hill School in Pottsdown. Maurice McAshan and I went to Lawrenceville, Dudley Sharp went to Gilman in Baltimore, Tina Cleveland, Martha Scott, Joanna Nazro, Lucile McAshan, Chaille Cage–the girls went mostly to Baldwin or Shipley or Dana Hall."

"I had Latin and math at Prosso," Mary Carroll Reed said. "I was faced with Latin grammar before I had ever had any English grammar and poor Dad stayed a couple of days ahead to coach me. You could go outside to study, which was terribly nice. At Prosso I did every day's work every day. It must have been really annoying to the boys who didn't."

Soldiers sent to Camp Logan at the start of World War I brought five hundred school-age children with them. The new City Auditorium was put to use as a schoolhouse. Central High offered a course in wireless telegraphy, and ten thousand school children aided in Red Cross work.

Central High School burned down in March, 1919, and ten thousand dollars' worth of city-owned textbooks were destroyed. The students transferred to South End Junior High, where the 198 seniors graduated in May. South End had double shifts of classes until the new Central High School opened January 24, 1921.

Chapter Thirty-One

A Sweet Life

THE CEILING FAN was the great gift of electricity to Houston. There were no electric fans for the city's first sixty summers. Nonetheless, dinner was served at noon and supper in the early evening. The cocktail hour did not exist. Gentlemen came home for dinner at noon and usually took a nice nap before getting back to the office. In the homes of black Houstonians and white, the mosquito bar was important to both the postprandial nap and nighttime slumbers. Some Houstonians of the 1980s still had a clear childhood memory of the mosquito bar.

Reminiscing in 1984, Bill Kirkland said, "Hadley Franklin had a mosquito bar factory on the corner of Prairie and Travis. It was a profitable business then. Before the days of screens, we all slept under mosquito bars every night. They had a lightweight wood frame that pulled up to the ceiling in the daytime. And by a rope through pulleys, you just pulled it out and let it down. My grandfather [Alexander Root] would come home for lunch and sit down in the library and they would let the mosquito bar down. He'd take his nap and then go back to the bank."

The mosquito bar had long been a shield against the enemy. Half a century before, in her memoirs of the upper Gulf Coast, Lucie Campbell Lee wrote about the summer she and her sisters "stitched away" making the night dresses, chemises, petticoats, and corset covers for her sister's wedding trousseau. "I remember that the mosquitos were so bad that summer that the girls could only sew in comfort seated inside mosquito bars." Old-timers still used them in parts of Houston and along the Louisiana and Texas Gulf Coast through the 1930s.[1]

Unlike English children who grew up in India, Old Houstonians seem to have no youthful memories of being miserably hot in the summertime. Houstonians could dress for the heat—women and children in light cotton batiste, voile, or organdy, men in linen suits or Bombay seersucker, which was a combination of cotton and silk. And, starting with the twentieth century, the gentle lop-lop rhythm of the ceiling fans and the hum of the oscillating fans somehow soothed the spirit as they stirred the air.

In the Southern fashion, Houston children were very much a part of their parents' daily and social lives before and after World War I. The family usually spent evenings together. Grown-ups could entertain children with string games like cat's cradle and Jacob's ladder, or by making cocked hats and fans out of folded paper. While ladies of the family crocheted or did needlepoint, someone read aloud.

Pressley Ewing was a successful attorney who was a longtime president of the Z. Z. Club and at one point chief justice of the Texas supreme court. His wife Nell was so influential a civic leader that she was named to the Texas Women's Hall of Fame. But their daughter, Vesta Ewing Veatch, remembered a childhood of timeless family evenings in the big house at Fannin and Clay:

"There were no living rooms in those days. We had a parlor, where I was later to receive my 'company,' but the library was our living room. The walls were lined with bookcases—Dickens, Eliot, Bulwer Lytton, Scott, and Thackeray—and there was a shelf filled with volumes of poetry. Our home was halfway encircled by a verandah, and here we sat on summer evenings. It was here that my father inspired in me a love for poetry. . . . I can hear his melodious voice, even now, thrilling me with the drama and the beauty of *Locksley Hall,* from the slender green volume of Tennyson's poems."

Children went with mama to pay calls on elderly ladies. They were taken to the theater to see imported and stock company plays. As Malcolm Lovett recalled, they took part in the musicals, were costumed for the pageants, and danced for the entertainment of the king of the No-Tsu-Oh and his queen. (No-Tsu-Oh was a week-long festival held each November from 1899 to 1915.)

Mr. and Mrs. Monta Beach had an auditorium and ballroom on Main Street seating fifteen hundred, with "a new Steinway Orchestral Grand Piano" on its stage. The Beaches rented out their well-polished floors for dances and receptions, and though they themselves gave lessons in music and dance, they also let their hall for lessons given by imported teachers.

Miss Florence Settle came up from Galveston every Friday afternoon to give dancing lessons to the children, Malcolm Lovett remembered. "We would line up in two rows, girls facing boys, and when we had learned the steps in the row, then we would try them out dancing with a girl. In about 1911 or 1912, our parents decided that they wanted to learn to dance too. Capt. James A. Baker, Judge Edwin Parker, Dr. Joseph Mullen, and my father persuaded Miss Settle and her accompanist to stay in Houston on Friday nights. They would have dinner at various houses during the winter months and she would give them dancing lessons afterward. I remember spending the night

with Edwin Parker at the Oaks, or with Landes Knox, or Browne Baker, and we would sit on the stairs and watch."

Unsure of their mastery, the gentlemen were shy about dancing with anyone except their wives. Miss Settle responded to that by starting a Paul Jones: at the sound of her whistle, dancers had to change partners. From her lessons, Houston's famous Paul Jones dance club was born. Captain Baker was the first president. F. M. Law held the office several terms. The Paul Jones moved from private homes to the new Houston Country Club.

"In about 1914 or 1915," Malcolm Lovett continued, "Dr. Mullen bought a gold whistle at Tiffany's and from then on he used it to mark the change of partners." Descendants of the Paul Jones founders were still changing partners to the whistle seventy-five years later.

In Beaumont at the turn of the century, the J. Frank Keiths had an enormous swimming pool beside their big white house, as well as one indoors. Their daughter Olga entertained her friends there in the years before 1909, when she married Harry Wiess. But private swimming pools were still rare in Houston. The country club as yet had no pool. This did not keep boys from swimming.

"When the Houston Country Club moved out to Harrisburg," Bill Kirkland said, "Wayside was a road that hadn't been developed yet. Bob Mistrot and I used to walk to Preston, catch a streetcar, carrying our bags of lunch, and ride out to the club. We'd hunt golf balls. Just before we got out our lunch, we would go down by the No. 8 Green and go swimming in Brays Bayou and then eat our sandwiches. Then we'd take the streetcar back home."

In the summertime, many Houston children went swimming at the Heights Natatorium. It had a big, rectangular pool surrounded by locker and dressing rooms. It was tremendously popular in warm-weather Houston. With masculine freedom, boys like Maurice McAshan would catch the streetcar out to the Natatorium. "We had to transfer once or twice and it cost a nickel," S. M. McAshan, Jr., said. But girls had to be taken by an available mother.

The big houses of Courtlandt Place were home to many children of all ages—children of the Nazros, the Autrys, the Garrows, the Carrolls, the Carters, the Donaghues, the Dorrances. "Mary Carroll was my best friend," Tina Cleveland Sharp said of her childhood. She and her particular playmates were the "Eleven Little Lasses." "Before we went away for the summer, one mother or another would take us out to the Heights Natatorium to swim on Saturday mornings. Then we'd go to Levy's Tea Room for lunch. And then to a movie. In cooler weather, two or three mothers would take the eleven to spend the day at the Houston Country Club. There were swings and rings to play with. Then the gentlemen would come to play tennis, and I believe we stayed right on through supper.

"Courtlandt had the best skating and the best bicycling in town," Mrs. Sharp said. "Birthday parties were terribly important. I was eight when I had a little afternoon dance at home. All the children were adorably dressed, and Howard Hughes came with a bouquet and bowed."

Estelle Garrow (Mrs. Charles Perlitz) was younger than Tina and Mary, and easy prey for their games. She remembers the day they arrived at her door and announced "We have come to poison you." Because they were older, and therefore wonderful and admirable creatures, Estelle opened the door in pure delight. "I was so thrilled," she said.

The parents of the children in the big houses of Courtlandt were young and merry, too. "My mother had a marvelous little naughty streak in her," Mrs. Sharp recalled. "She was dainty, smaller than any of her daughters, a very Southern lady. She was terribly pretty and wore beautiful clothes. I remember she had one black and white dress made of tulle, with petals. My room was at the back of the house overlooking the rose

garden, and one night I was awakened by a great hilarity. I looked out. My mother and her young cousin Pat Houstoun were having a watermelon fight! And the next morning—mother and I shared a bath—I found hanging over the bath tub this lovely black and white tulle dress *dripping* watermelon juice!"

The Sess Clevelands spent their summers either in Maine or at a family place at Allegheny Springs, south of Roanoke. "The main house was on top of a hill," said Tina Sharp, "a nice one-story house. Every morning the ladies would sit on the big porch, knitting or crocheting, while someone read aloud. The house had a sitting room, card room and living room, and the big porch. The children would be off playing, first in a swimming hole, later in a pool. There were wonderful houses on the lawn, built of gnarled tree branches—a Spring house and a Summer house. We sometimes stayed in the old slave quarters. Each cottage was one room deep with a lovely breeze. No private baths. We traipsed on out back and over two or three doors. . . . When Daddy would have his vacation, we'd go on interesting trips like Niagara, or west to Estes Park. One summer we went out to the West Coast on a real sightseeing trip."

As among the English colonials, it was the custom to send women and children and the servants to the hills or the seashore for the summer months. Husbands and fathers came by train on weekends to the Hill Country near Hunt or to Bayridge.

"We were literally moving for the summer," Mark Edwin Andrews said.[2] "It took all day, starting early in the morning. We had three horses, a station wagon and a nice surrey. The station wagon had high wheels . . . I can't remember whether steel or rubber tires . . . pulled by one horse. We went through Harrisburg, Pasadena, on shell roads, then Deepwater, Deer Park, La Porte, Sylvan Beach. We had a little one-story house with three bedrooms, one bath, and a big front porch in front and back. Twelve houses faced the bay right on the bluff—

high. They had a pavilion, an octagonal building, at the head of the pier. The pier ran out into the bay three or four blocks, and at the end of it, the water was seven or eight feet deep at high tide and clear as a bell.

"Howard Hughes used to come down when he was a little boy. He liked the surrey, but not the station wagon. He'd say, 'Mrs. Andrews, are we going to take the surrey to meet Mr. Andrews?' He was fun, a very nice kid, and *smart!* And St. John Garwood used to come. He was great fun and had the longest legs of anybody I ever knew!"[3]

After the death of their parents, Bill, Mary Porter, and Laura Kirkland lived with their grandparents, the Alexander Roots at 1410 Clay.

"In the summertime," Laura Kirkland Bruce (Mrs. George S. Bruce) remembered, "Houston would pack up the whole family and servants and go to Bay Ridge – *why,* I don't know. They thought there was more breeze down there. But when the breeze was off the shore, it brought hordes of mosquitoes. Every house had a pier. And always the big discussions were who had the most *breeze*. The E. A. Peden house was out on a point. It had a verandah all the way around. Children sat around the table picking out crab meat. It seems to me that I spent all my time picking out crab meat. That's why I always buy crab meat already picked out now.

"Crabbing was a family affair. Edward Peden would take my sister and me gigging for flounder by flashlight. I never remember actually sticking one. It was all full of squeal and run and giggles in the dark. But crabbing was a family affair. Everybody would go out on the pier and drop down pieces of meat on a string. I was the most wonderful fleet of foot at putting the net under the crab."

Everybody knew everybody else at Bay Ridge. Sailboats and yachts moved from pier to pier or over to Red Bluff in a sociable way. And the informality of the life gave full rein to Houston's love of practical jokes. At the turn of the century, the Rev. Henry Aves and his wife kept a hospitable bay house open to large numbers of small boys and any adults who cared to take the cars down for the day. Apparently it amused Aves to see sedate ladies come to the shore in the full Victorian regalia of hats, gloves, long skirts, and petticoats. He would take them out for a boat ride. Well out from shore, and to the delight of the small boys, he would announce, "There's something wrong with this boat. You will all have to get out immediately and let me take a look." While his passengers stood in hip-deep water, he would turn the boat over, examine it carefully, right it, bail it out, and invite them back on board. Presumably, the ladies had to go back to town on the cars showing signs of their wade.

The idyll had its tragedies. On a pleasant August evening in 1908 a party of young people were sailing between Clear Lake and the bay, when Daphne Palmer fell overboard.

"She had several suitors on the boat," Bill Kirkland said, "and they all jumped overboard to save her – Ned Neville, Coke Burns, Fairfax Crow. And of course her brother, Edward Palmer." In great merriment they rescued their heroine, climbed back on board, and resumed their sail. Suddenly they realized that Edward Palmer was not with them. A recent graduate of Princeton, a popular young man, he had been at the start of a promising career at the First National Bank. His death saddened a city still small enough to be aware of such a loss. Years later, having married Ned Neville, Daphne Neville built Palmer Memorial Church for the brother who had drowned trying to save her.

In 1900, there were no weather reports to warn of approaching storms. When the hurricane struck on September 8, husbands in Houston had no way of getting to their families at the bay, no way of knowing whether they had survived. In the grim two days, when six thousand people were killed in Galveston, women and children in all the little houses along the bay faced the 110-mile-an-hour wind alone. Four-year-old David

Rice, who had been visiting his aunt, Mrs. S. K. McIlhenny, was lost in the winds and water.

In Houston, the hurricane felled trees, broke telephone and power lines, smashed windows and storefronts, flattened small houses. The roof of Temple Beth Israel on Franklin Avenue was blown off. However battered, Houston chartered the steamboat *Lawrence* to carry water and provisions down the flooded Buffalo Bayou to Galveston until the railroads could restore connections to the devastated island.[4]

Though less murderous, the 1915 storm was awesome. "You couldn't get much warning in those days," Ed Andrews said. "All I remember is that I never saw so much rain in my life. Waves up to the bluff. Thirty or forty feet of water. They would break and salt spray got all over the house. There wasn't much damage along on the land. The piers were all wiped out. But we were never under water."

Until electric lines reached Bayridge, Mr. Andrews said, the houses were lighted with kerosene lamps and had to depend on the gulf breeze for cooling. "When electricity came in, it would blink at 9:45 and the lights would go out at 10. We'd know to get the oil lamps going again.

"Schools of redfish and trout would come in. All about the same size. Miss Hattie Gribble, who was a teacher, and her niece married Jim Rockwell—she was wonderful. She used to round us up to go fishing. We'd go down to Morgan's Point. At Pizziola's, we'd get shrimp for bait. We had cane poles and straw hats. If the fish were biting, we'd catch a wheelbarrow full. It is the typical picture of a little boy going fishing.

"It was a sweet, simple life."

This is a recurrent phrase from many Houstonians who grew up in Houston in the first quarter of the century: "It was a sweet life."

This was in the era of annual church picnics, the big event of the year for all ages. The early ones were at the old fairgrounds at McGowan and Milam. It had a baseball

park and racetrack. Next came Merkel's Grove on Buffalo and German streets (later St. Charles and Canal) with big shade trees and a dance pavilion. Then Volkesfest Park opened up next to Merle Merkel's Grove. Congregation Beth Israel hired six streetcars for its picnics at Volkesfest Park, plus a large wagon to carry the baskets. The cars would leave Franklin and Jackson at eight in the morning and leave the picnic grounds at seven in the evening.

Smaller picnics were sometimes held on the bayou. The cotton barges of the Houston Direct Navigation Company often lay idle in the spring. Capt. John Atkinson would run a railing around his barge, stretch a tarpaulin over the top, and let young people go for an outing. John Dreaper remembered: "We got on at the foot of Main Street and were towed down to Clinton. There we'd have lunch and some of Frank Vance's ice cream, and run around a while, and then we'd be towed on down to the battleground. I remember the year Mr. Cleveland's warehouse burned, the water was awash with wholesale groceries washed down by the fire hose."

Starting in 1890, picnics were held at the new Magnolia Park. The Houston Belt and Magnolia Park Railway ran to it on what was known as the dummy line. It was also known by the irreverent as the "angel maker" because of its tendency to kill pedestrians. It started at San Jacinto and Commerce and had several open cars—like streetcars—back of a little locomotive. The Southern Pacific, which owned the dummy line, always rented a whole train for a picnic without asking how many would be aboard.

Finally came Sylvan Beach. Starting at nine in the morning, the train took the church picnickers down the old road to Galveston and then switched over to the Bayshore Line. "By that time," Bill Kirkland said, "all the boys would be hanging out of the steps. When we got to Sylvan Beach, we would all start running for the park to get a good table for the family. My family never attended, but I did. I'd go get a table for

Seventy-four years after the historic battle, the San Jacinto State Park opened with 327 acres on April 21, 1910, when Frank J. Schlueter made this picture. The grass had been trimmed, the lanes raked, the tree trunks whitewashed up to shoulder level. *Courtesy Bank of the Southwest/Frank J. Schlueter Collection, Houston Metropolitan Research Center, Houston Public Library*

somebody else so I'd be sure to have a base for food supplies. Then I'd help with their baskets.

"At that time the park had a lot of carnival features. A merry-go-round. A Ferris wheel. Little booths where you could get three balls for a nickel and throw at the dolls on the rack. If you got three dolls down, you'd get a quarter. So I'd pay for my whole afternoon's pleasure. Then there was always a baseball game. Finally they'd sound the whistle on the engine and we would traipse back up to the cars."[5]

For these outdoor parties of spring and summer, ladies wore hats and ankle-length dresses with the usual number of petticoats. Men wore suits, most of them dark. A few relaxed for the occasion by wearing soft, Byronic collars with flowing ties rather than the stiffer starched collar with four-in-hands.

Church picnics were lavish. Every family brought baskets filled with fried chicken, cold sliced ham, beaten biscuits, lace cookies, cakes, pies—the product of days in the kitchen. They spread tablecloths and provided plates and napkins. Bachelors browsed from table to hospitable table. A band played dance music. Because every church had so splendid a picnic, and in pure ecumenical spirit, small boys tended to be

In the No-Tsu-Oh Carnival's Flower Parade in 1911, king Edgar Odell Lovett and queen Annie Vive Carter were enthroned on giant petals. Gladys Ewing was the queen's maid of honor. Rorick Cravens, Burnett Carson, Ben Rice, and Malcolm Lovett were the pages. *Courtesy Edward Lillo Crain*

Presbyterians, Episcopalians, Catholics, Jews, Methodists, or Baptists—depending on which picnic was next on the summertime agenda.

Milton Baker, a black Houstonian, took a flying jenny to all the big picnics. Two powerful men turned the crank to make it fly and there were rings. If you grabbed a brass ring, you got a free ride. The jenny had straddle horses for the boys and carriage boxes for the girls. Baker lived on Fannin and Jefferson and was one of Houston's wealthiest citizens. Fred Vance, another wealthy black Houstonian, had an ice cream business and competed with Joseph Dawson for the claim of the best ice cream in town. He lived on Caroline and Pease behind his ice cream plant. Vance went to all the big picnics and sold ice cream biscuits for five cents, a dish of ice cream for ten cents.

He was one of the first to own ice cream freezers. Until then, John Dreaper said, "To make ice cream you put a bucket inside a washtub filled with ice and turned the bucket in the ice, back and forth with both hands. When the first freezers came out and they advertised 'WILL FREEZE ICE CREAM IN 20 MINUTES' . . . *amazing!*" said Dreaper. But to small Lois Cleveland, just old enough to get in on the last few such picnics, the lemonade made in the big black barrel with lemons and ice floating on top was the best lemonade ever made.

The era of such picnics ended with World

The last No-Tsu-Oh Carnival, in 1915, crowned Robert E. Paine king and Marion Holt Seward queen. Laura Winstead was maid of honor. Queen's pages were Estelle and Jane Garrow, and the turbaned genii were Wilmer Hunt and Gibbs Meador. The dream queen (*left*) was Imola Link. In doublet and hose, the princes were Dr. Andrew Casperson, Roy Watson, Malcolm Oliver, George Journeay, Brown Rice, Trafton Hathaway, Brook Leman, and Baldwin Rice. Queen's attendants were Fay Richards, Jewell Ayars, Aubrey Culberson, Oden McCarthy, Geraldine Dore, Dora Link, Mathilde Booth, and Lucretia Watson. Smiling at it all (*extreme right*), was Mrs. Robert E. Paine. *Courtesy Ellen Hamilton Pearson (Mrs. Edward Pearson)*

War I, when the government took over the railroads. Thereafter, each person had to buy a ticket at the rate of three cents per mile. This meant a dollar and a half for each man, woman, and child, or nine dollars for a family of six. Neither churches nor individuals could afford so much.

Each year as summer ended, Houston looked forward to the carnival in November. The carnival began in the mid-1880s as the Fruit, Flower, and Vegetable Festival, in an era when citrus fruit was being grown on the Gulf Coast. After a few years it faltered. The No-Tsu-Oh Association was chartered in 1899 for the purpose of crowning King Nottoc (cotton, spelled backwards) whose realm should be Tekram, in the broad domain of Saxet, and whose capital city should be No-Tsu-Oh (Houston, spelled backwards). Thus, the city was paying tribute to its chief market product, cotton.

The carnival was celebrated for six days, while bands played, floats covered with flowers paraded, tableaux held their magic moment for audience and camera, and at the grand ball, the king himself would crown his queen. In the carnival's last few years, the football game between the University of Texas and Texas A&M added to the excitement.

As with New Orleans' Mardi Gras, the carnival took months of planning, brought in tremendous numbers of tourists, elated the citizenry. The king was usually a well-known professional or businessman, the queen a debutante of the season. As a nephew of the city's founders, A. C. Allen was the first king in 1899, with Annie Quinlan his queen.[6]

In Houston's unending push to lure international shipping to the port, the 1909 carnival began with the arrival of King Nottoc XI aboard the Swedish steamer *Disa*. This was the first seagoing vessel to use the new Turning Basin. From there, the king (Capt. James A. Baker, Jr.) went by smaller vessel in a flotilla to the foot of Main Street, where the parade began.

As an example of the annual carnival splendor, Annie Vive Carter in 1911 wore a coronation gown of white brocade and duchess satin that was a replica of one worn by Queen Mary of England. It had a high collar of silver lace, was studded with imported rhinestones, and had a court train of American Beauty *velour de soie* trimmed with ermine. Jewels flashed at throat and wrists, and the crown on her dark hair was an exact replica of Queen Mary's. It was of gold encrusted with pearls and jewels and lined with crimson plush. King Edgar Odell Lovett—new president of the yet incomplete Rice Institute—was equally royal.

In 1912, the *Daily Post* reported "Thousands Cheer King Nottoc XIV." His majesty was Walter B. Sharp, whose queen was Garland Bonner. Judge William Masterson was crown prince, E. R. Spotts was regent. Fourteen days after his coronation, the greatly loved Walter Sharp was dead—possibly of a ruptured appendix. The whole city mourned.

Houston took No-Tsu-Oh seriously. After spending three months in the East on business, Jesse Jones headed home for the 1913 carnival. He missed his connection in Atlanta. Thirty minutes later, the tall Houstonian was on his way west in a private train, made up of one coach and an engine, which cost him $1,520. But he got to Houston in time for the coronation of R. C. Duff and Lottie Baldwin Rice, daughter of Mrs. Jo S. Rice.

In September, 1914, after three and a half years of construction, the Houston Ship Channel was nearing completion at twenty-five feet from Bolivar Roads to the Turning Basin.

In celebration, the 1914 carnival was named the No-Tsu-Oh Deep Water Jubilee. Two headlines dominated the *Daily Post* of November 8, 1914: "Russians on East Prussian Frontier," and in the same-size type, "All Readiness for Houston's Jubilee." King Nottoc had ceded his throne to the reverse-spelled King Retaw I (Eugene Arthur Hudson). The week ended with the coronation of his queen, Frankie Carter, daughter of Mr. and Mrs. William T. Carter.[7] The last carnival of Not-Su-Oh came in 1915 with Robert E. Paine as king and Marion Holt Seward his queen. World War I brought an end to the No-Tsu-Oh Carnivals, as it did to the big church picnics.

Living High

"HOUSTON—where seventeen railroads meet the sea." This graceful phrase was coined by Dr. William States Jacobs, pastor of the First Presbyterian Church. But by 1912, with the Interurban running to Galveston, Houston upped the count to eighteen. More than two hundred trains a day puffed and steamed into the new Union Station, designed by the architect of New York's Grand Central.

Houston felt in command of its destiny in 1912. By counting its suburbs, it could claim 109,594 people, making it the biggest city in Texas. The *City Directory* announced that "in cotton, lumber, rice and oil, Houston is preeminent"; the list should have included cattle. With Houston as their port, cotton farmers of Texas and the new state of Oklahoma funneled 2,464,167 bales through the city in 1910–11 and 3,257,174 bales in 1911–12. Forty-nine lumber companies were doing $40 million in business a year. Houston was the second largest primary market in the South. The pipelines from every major oil field of Texas and Oklahoma converged at Houston with several hundred additional miles of pipe being laid. The long-heralded Rice Institute was about to open. And Woodrow Wilson entered the White House with Houston's Col. Edwin Mandell House quietly at his side.[1]

All of this combined to quicken the flow between Houston and other ports of the world. Manchester, Liverpool, Hamburg, and Tokyo had their cotton factors in Houston. So did France.

The Houston Phonograph Company had a Main Street store and a Walker Avenue warehouse filled with Edisons and Victrolas, all with large trumpet-shaped horns. It kept a complete stock of Red Seal records. With panache, the company advertised records in twenty-nine foreign languages. It also had "phonographs specially built and in use, with instruction books and records to learn foreign languages. These are fast being adopted in public schools for class study." The study of modern foreign languages was at a peak in American high schools, but most students studied German, French, or Spanish. For Houston Phonograph to stock records in twenty-nine different languages suggests that Houston was still polyglot.

February, 1912, was bitterly cold. Houston firemen were answering four calls a day as people tried makeshift ways of adding warmth to home and workplace.[2] On February 21, the worst fire of Houston's history swept through the Northside, leveling forty-six blocks. Fifth Ward was a substantial neighborhood. Bernard Riesner, former city councilman and an iron and steel manufacturer, had a big brick house near the bayou on Young Street. The William J. Bissonnets lived on Maury. (The Bissonnets stressed the first syllable in their name.) Former Mayor John T. Brown had a family enclave on two blocks at the far end of Lyons Avenue. The Cornelius Nobles lived on Montgomery Road, which was later renamed North Main. The Joseph Stevensons lived on Nance and the C. Jim Stewarts on Dennis. Dr. S. H. Hillen, the Robert F. Nobles, and the Charles B. Murphys all lived on Maury.

Alfred C. Finn, the young architect who

Fire! The Mardi Gras parade of 1912 had ended and it was an icy February night when the worst fire in Houston's history swept through the Northside. *Courtesy George Fuermann City of Houston Collection, Special Collections, University of Houston Libraries*

would change the skyline of Houston in coming decades, lived on Odin.[3] So did John Lyons, proprietor of the Lyons House, a popular hostelry for men connected with the Southern Pacific Shops. Michael Lyons owned the grocery on Conti. Lyons Avenue was named after the family.

Many of the houses were large and handsomely furnished. St. Patrick's Catholic Church and school were on Maury and St. Mary's Episcopal Church close by. Children went to both to be with their friends and most of them attended Anson Jones School on Elysian. The vegetable wagon plied the neighborhood in the morning. In the afternoon a wagon came through selling hot waffles covered with powdered sugar.

Kathryn Noble, who later married John Wilcox and became president general of the United Daughters of the Confederacy, lived on Maury in her childhood. In 1985, she still had vivid memories of the nieghborhood and the night of February 21, 1912.[4] When school let out that afternoon, the sky was

dark and the wind cold. It was Mardi Gras, and all of Houston was preparing for the parade that evening. But as the wind rose, Kathryn's mother thought it wise to secure the window blinds with wire. At midnight, Kathryn's Uncle Bill came in from the parade. He was chilled through and said, "The wind is so strong you thought it could blow the costumes right off the people."

Customarily, the Southern Pacific shops blew the whistle every hour on the hour. But after the 1:00 a.m. toot, the whistle began to sound again without stopping. This meant an emergency. The Nobles went to the window and saw their world ablaze. The fire had started in an abandoned building. It was later thought that tramps had taken refuge there and had started a fire to ward off the intense cold.

Gale-force winds up to seventy-five miles an hour swept the flames from house to house. "We were only three blocks from where it started," Kathryn Wilcox said. While firemen played their hoses on the house, the Nobles dumped clothes in a sheet. The fourteen-year-old Kathryn looked regretfully at her mother's beautiful silver and china, and said a child's goodbye to them. It never occurred to anyone to take it along.

"My grandmother had just come back from Kentucky and had brought all her beautiful handmade coverlets. We had the family Bible that came over when the Nobles left England. I can see it now sitting there in the corner of the room. Because St. Patrick's Church was built of brick, everybody poured into the church to put their bundles inside, thinking they would be safe. The next morning not even the bricks were recognizable."

People fled block to block, only to see the flames gaining on them. As they ran, they were hit by big embers falling off houses or bouncing off trees, and they had to beat out the flames. Houstonians living south of the bayou were wakened by the red glow. Many set out to hunt relatives who lived on the north side. The reflection was seen as far away as Hitchcock. Fire engines from nearby towns came, alerted by the silent alarm of the reddened sky.

Without reason, the fire would skip a house. It circled Dr. John D. Duckett's house and torched the one next door. It is hard to imagine how the fire fighters conquered the blaze, because the wind continued to blow almost until dawn. The next morning, Ash Wednesday, there were no ashes to be seen. The wind had cleared them all away, leaving forty-six blocks in blackened rubble. "It looked as though somebody had swept it," Mrs. Wilcox said.

But not one person was killed.

"The next morning, Mrs. Stevenson—Mrs. Stewart's daughter—said, 'Now Kathryn, I think this is your bundle.' But it wasn't mine. And in the bottom was some twelve thousand dollars' worth of jewelry! Houston was so good to us. *Every*body offered to take somebody in. The churches opened shelters. The stores simply opened the doors and offered shoes and clothes. I had come

out wearing my outing nightgown. As I passed the old hall tree, I saw this hat of mine, a black velvet hat with the little blue plumes and all lined, and this plush coat. That's what I put on, and that's all I had. Nothing of mine was saved."

The Lyonses rebuilt Lyons House. The Southern Pacific shops and hospital escaped. But the Nobles and many others moved south of the bayou. The newly opened cottages at Sylvan Beach served as a way station throughout the summer enabling them to build or find new quarters over on Chenevert or Hamilton.

The Heights went unscathed. Dave and Bessie Kaplan went on with their plans to build a store catering to farm families coming into town from the nearby rural communities. It opened in 1913 on Yale at Twenty-Second Street. The sign over the porch said, "DKaplan Dry Goods, Groceries, Fresh Meats, Feed." Kaplan's-Ben Hur would celebrate its seventy-fifth anniversary on the same site, selling Baccarat crystal, Sheffield silver plate, Royal Copenhagen china, and Wedgwood plates with Beatrix Potter designs.

Charles H. Milby owned the new Milby Hotel, built in 1910.[5] He always lived in the big Milby house in Harrisburg, but he was becoming increasingly known in Houston because of his interest in county affairs. A man of genuine charm, he had led in the drive to build the new courthouse, and over the years he gave land, money, and time to help persuade Congress to deepen and improve Houston's ship channel.

Despite Houston's expanses of land, it had many more apartment buildings in 1912 than the average southern town. Architects saw tall buildings as one solution to Houston's summer heat. With inner courts to provide cross ventilation, they would catch the gulf breeze and be cooler than ground-level dwellings. The Rossonian on Fannin at McKinney and the Beaconsfield on Main at Pease were Houston's newest and finest. They stood in a residential section of mansions that occupied a half-block or a whole block each. The apartments were designed to be suitable neighbors to the mansions.

Costing half a million dollars, the seven-story Rossonian had a roof garden and seventy-four apartments with an ice plant in each. The eight-story Beaconsfield had only sixteen suites, two to a floor, but each had two screened balconies and six large rooms with fireplaces. It had parking for carriage or car, servants' quarters, and back stairs and elevators for deliveries. It was so substantially built that the sounds of Main Street did not intrude. The Beaconsfield was still a prestigious address in 1986.

The Savoy Flats, also with an ice-making plant in every apartment, was on Main at Pease. It had a big yard with swings and rings for children to play on. The McAshan Flats stood at Clay. They were among thirty excellent apartment buildings in the town of eighty thousand people.[6]

The Beaconsfield and the Savoy were home to a large number of corporate presidents and vice-presidents and their families, as well as widows of professional and businessmen. Some would later move out to Broadacres, to Shadyside, to Courtlandt or Avondale. But of the young couples who started out in the Beaconsfield, the Savoy Flats, or the Rossonian, at the Rice Hotel or later the Warwick, a surprising number stayed. They continued their apartment or hotel living as their children were born, grew up, and went off to college.

When the F. M. Laws moved to Houston from Beaumont in 1914, with their daughter Elizabeth and son Marion, they occupied half a floor at the Beaconsfield. Although Mr. Law became president of the First National Bank and president of the American Bankers Association, he lived out the remainder of his long life in the Beaconsfield—fifty-six years. Robert Welch, a quiet gentleman who was amassing a fortune in oil, real estate, and other investments moved into the Beaconsfield as one of its first residents and lived there until he died at the age of eighty-one in 1952.

Monroe D. Anderson, treasurer of An-derson, Clayton Cotton Corporation, moved into the Bender Hotel on his arrival in Houston and stayed there until the hotel was torn down. He lived so modestly that the chief bell captain of the hotel, who saw him off to work every morning, assumed that he was a floorwalker in one of the downtown stores—not the chief finance officer of one of the largest corporations in the world.

Despite the frugality for which he became famous, Anderson was charming and amusing, a delight to his small nephews. He was always a welcome dinner guest at the South Boulevard home of his sister-in-law, Mrs. Frank Anderson. He could enjoy his brothers' children, and when he went out on a date, he could take the flowers from Mrs. Anderson's dinner table as a present for the lady. He was a confirmed bachelor, with no apparent interest in marriage, but he enjoyed the company of charming widows. He had an immense enjoyment of automobiles.

In 1912, he bought a four-cylinder Cadillac. Then Cadillac came out with an eight-cylinder model. "Being a young bachelor he had to have the new car," his nephew Thomas Anderson said. "But in those days you didn't trade a car in. The dealers weren't prepared to handle used cars. So he kept them both. He would drive one car from the hotel to a garage that was about halfway to the Cotton Exchange Building, and park it, and then get in the other one and drive the rest of the way. The aggregate distance wasn't as much as a mile. He never in history walked from the Bender Hotel to the Cotton Exchange. In the afternoon, of course, he would reverse the process. . . . He loved to tease. He used to have dates with widows here in Houston, and one time he got a new car and he pretended to the lady that it would not go forward, only backward. He scared her to death by driving around the block three times in reverse."

In the early 1900s, the Hotel Brazos was a favorite place to dine. While the restaurants and bars along Main Street attracted men, the Brazos was outstanding for its quiet elegance and its French chef. A lady could safely stay there and dine alone in the hotel dining room. In warm weather, Houston couples or familes with small children liked to have dinner in the Brazos Court, a garden lighted by Japanese lanterns. An orchestra played every evening from six to nine o'clock. The Houston Country Club unashamedly hired away waiters trained at the Brazos. The food was so good, it was all so pleasant, that sixty and seventy years later, those who had dined in the Brazos Court remembered the charm of those summer evenings. The Brazos was so much a part of this small town, southern community that as a boy, Army Emmott made pocket money by shooting frogs in the bayou and selling them to the Brazos chef for their tender legs.

In 1912, the excellent G. F. Sauter's Restaurant on the corner of Travis and Preston also had a Ladies' Dining Parlor and the new Bender Hotel was fashionable for large dinner parties. The new First Methodist Church stood at 1320 Main. The new post office, which had cost half a million dollars, dominated its block on San Jacinto. The Sacred Heart Co-Cathedral at IIII Pierce was consecrated. Court Norton, Houston's leading tailor, incorporated the Barringer-Norton Company, the antecedent of Norton-Ditto.

Also in 1912, young Dr. James Greenwood built a sanitarium for the care of the mentally ill on six acres of land out on Old South Main Street Road. Born in Seguin, Dr. Greenwood had graduated from the University of Texas Medical School, studied pediatrics at Columbia University in New York, practiced medicine in Seguin, spent four years as physician in the Southwest Texas Insane Asylum, and taught medicine at the medical school in Galveston–all by the age of thirty-four.

He was a brilliant man. For instance, he patented a perpetual calendar based on the principle of differential years. While in Galveston and working with laboratory animals, he pioneered in research on blood transfusions. But he was best known for his compassion. The experience in the insane asylum convinced him that these were the patients

in greatest need and with the least offered to them. The Greenwoods lived on the sanitarium grounds. Their house was built in the southern plantation style with white columns two stories tall across the front. With twenty employees, and with Dr. Marvin Lee Graves and Dr. George Harrison Moody as associates, the sanitarium could care for thirty patients.

At thirty-seven, Jesse H. Jones was ready to make a major addition to Houston's downtown. In 1911–12, he invested $3.5 million to build a new Rice Hotel on the site of the old one, where the Capitol of the Republic had once stood. The eighteen-story hotel was designed with a lobby of white Italian marble. Its four restaurants ranged from a men's grill to a palm room and dining hall. It had a great banquet hall and a concert room. It had a kitchen on every floor for better room service. It had telephone booths, telegraph offices, and a carriage office, writing rooms, and a library. But it was the Rice Hotel roof that attracted Houstonians. At three hundred feet above Main Street, it promised cool breezes all summer. It had flowers, palms, ornamental lights, and an excellent orchestra. It was a delightful place for courtship and light romance.

The Lucas Construction Company built the new Rice Hotel. From England, James S. Lucas had brought his family to Houston by way of New Orleans and Galveston in the 1880s. He founded the company that built some of Houston's finest buildings, including the Cotton Exchange in 1884. On his death in 1888, Albert Thomas Lucas took over and expanded the business. To have bricks to his liking, he opened the Lucas Brick Yard near the bayou at Waugh Drive and the Houston Brick Yard down on the ship channel. In 1905, he paved the 2000 block of Milam with his own bricks and at 2017 built his home, a handsome stone house with slate roof and walls three bricks thick. He built the courthouse in 1910, the Rice Hotel in 1911, and the Humble Building in 1919–21.

Lacking air conditioning, Houstonians

made the most of their tall buildings to catch the gulf breeze in offices as well as at home. Founded by Samuel Fain Carter, the Lumbermen's National Bank had more than $3 million in deposits by the end of its first four years and became the Second National Bank. To house it, Carter planned to build Houston's tallest skyscraper. It was immediately nicknamed Carter's Folly because of its great height. Practical men insisted that bricks could not be stacked sixteen stories high.

With a steel frame structure, the Carter Building was faced with polished Texas granite, Bedford stone columns, terra cotta, and brick. It had handsome bronze doors, and the lobby was lined with Italian and Norwegian marble, as were all the fifteen office

In 1911, when under construction, this skyscraper was called Carter's Folly because practical men knew you could not safely stack bricks sixteen stories high. Samuel Fain Carter's bank on the ground floor was the first in Houston to be air-conditioned. *Postcard photograph*

floors. Every office had electric fans, base plugs, electric lights, illuminating gas, and wash basin. With an artesian well in the basement yielding three hundred thousand gallons a day, the building had icy water flowing from its fountains. It had a vacuum-cleaning system throughout. Four elevators sped from floor to floor at the rate of six hundred feet a minute.

The bank occupied the ground floor and was air-conditioned – the first air-conditioned bank in a city that would become the most thoroughly air-conditioned in the world after World War II.

Houstonians voted in 1912 to split the cost of paving streets between the property owners and the city. This spurred street improvement. In 1913 Texas Avenue was covered with wooden blocks that gave welcome relief from the dust and mud. Within three years, Houston had 196 miles of paving. But the system had a flaw: if the home owner did not wish to chip in, the section spanning his lot out to the middle of the street would go unpaved. Fifty years later, several old residential streets like McKinney Avenue had a hopscotch pattern, with a paved section on one side of the street but not the other, or in front of two houses but not the third.

The decade brought many weddings linking old families or old family to new: Rufus Cage, Jr., to Frances Sears; John Dreaper to Elizabeth Lemon; James House Bute to Clara Robinson; William Gray Sears to Bettie Bringhurst Gaines; William T. Carter, Jr., to Lillie Auguste Neuhaus; St. George L. Sioussat to Alma Cleveland Daily; William Stamps Farish to Libbie Randon Rice; Hugo Victor Neuhaus to Kate P. Rice; Edwin L. Neville to Daphne W. Palmer; W. Ernst Japhet to Edith Lawrence-Toombs; Louis Arthur Stevenson to Mary Louise Ayars; Ashley Newton Denton to Rosine R. Huston; William Hogue to Florence Marian Kent; John H. McClung to Dolores Pearl Guion, and Joseph W. Evans to Emily M. Scott.

In 1914, John H. Crooker was elected Harris County district attorney. Born in Alabama near Mobile, he was the youngest of the seven children his widowed mother had brought to Houston in 1893. They settled in Fifth Ward, notorious as the Bloody Fifth because so many fights went on. He was in seventh grade when his older brother ran off to mine for gold in the Klondike. Just entering his teens, John Crooker quit school to help support the family. He went to work for a justice of the peace, Judge M. McDonald, and became clerk of the court. At night he read law. In 1911, he passed the state bar. Judge McDonald promptly retired, asking that John Crooker be appointed to replace him. The district attorney's office was the next step in a career that would make him a founder of one of Houston's most prestigious law firms.

Chapter Thirty-Three

A Symphony, a Park, a Channel

FOR A CITY of scarcely more than one hundred thousand, Houston had a remarkable array of musicians, both amateur and professional, both teachers and performers. Many of them had studied in the best conservatories of the United States and Europe. But Houston still depended on imported symphony orchestras. Two Houston musicians were determined to do more: Ima Hogg and Julian Paul Blitz.

Ima Hogg had heard her first symphony concert at the age of eight in Madison Square Garden, when her father took her to hear an oratorio. At the University of Texas, she heard a *sinfonettia* from Mexico and was enthralled. In her mid-twenties she reveled in the rich orchestral fare of Berlin and Vienna. At thirty, an established music teacher, she set out to create a symphony orchestra in her adopted city.

After her return from Europe, as Hubert Roussel wrote in his history of the symphony, "she had been struck by the many good musical talents in Houston. The professional body was a large one . . . and there were amateur organizations that did work of exceptional standard." Miss Hogg found allies among members of the Women's Choral Club: Mrs. Edwin B. Parker, who was its president, and Mrs. H. M. Garwood, Mrs. William Abbey, Mrs. Gentry Waldo, and Mrs. Jules Hirsch.

Meanwhile, Julian Paul Blitz, a Belgian cellist of high calibre, had a similar idea. Sauter's Restaurant, at the corner of Preston Avenue and Travis Street, was one of Houston's finest. It was Viennese in atmo-sphere, it was elegant, and its chamber music ensemble played every day at luncheon and dinner. Blitz led a group that played music of Mozart, Beethoven, and Brahms as often as it played Strauss waltzes.

Blitz approached the women's committee with his ideas. He could recruit players if they could recruit supporters. Miss Hogg announced through the papers that a society was being formed to test Houston's readiness for forming an orchestra. A concert would be held to gauge public response.

In 1913, every restaurant with a claim to quality, every theater whether showing movies or live drama, and every host planning a reception or a ball had to have musicians to play. The 1913 season seemed to be unusually active so that instead of ending quietly during Lent, it went right on into the spring. The rich season included performances by Otis Skinner, Ethel Barrymore, Sarah Bernhardt, Lillian Russell, and Nazimova. "The town scurried about to theater affairs and gay parties," Roussel wrote. "The year itself was a hit."

Time was running out. With all his musicians busy performing, Blitz found it hard to get them together for rehearsals. Worse, summer was coming. Houston theaters usually closed for two months every summer because no attraction was strong enough to pull people into windowless theaters in July and August.[1]

But on the brink of summer closure, at five o'clock on the evening of June 21 in the handsome Majestic Theater on Texas Avenue, thirty-five musicians began to play under the baton of Julian Paul Blitz. B. J. Steinfeldt was concertmaster. Anton Diehl and Rosetta Hirsch were among the first violins. Blanche Foley, known for her lovely soprano voice, sang the "Divinites du Styx" from Gluck's *Alceste*. And the persuasive Dr. Henry Barnstein gave a little talk on the hopes and aims of the Houston Symphony Society.

The concert began at five because it had to be wedged in between the vaudeville's matinee and evening shows. Despite the heat of the day and the odd hour, the theater was nicely filled. The response was warm. Mrs. Willie Hutcheson, the *Houston Post* critic, concluded, "The concert . . . was a revelation to Houstonians, who, while realizing in a sort of offhand way that there is much musical talent in Houston, were yet unaware of the intensity of music study and the breadth of understanding and artistic conception of the majority of Houston musicians." Blitz's musicians were paid five dollars each.

Summertime was not the time to expect further effort from anyone. But in the cool days of October, Miss Hogg called the committee to a meeting at Mrs. Parker's home, The Oaks. They organized the Houston Symphony Association to establish an orchestra and sponsor regular concerts. Mrs. Parker was elected president and Miss Hogg vice-president. Other officers were Frantz Brogniez, H. F. MacGregor, Mrs. Z. F. Lillard, and Mrs. William Abbey. As conductor, Mr. Blitz was empowered to select his musicians.

The society's board included men who had often underwritten the cost of bringing opera, ballet, orchestras, and theatrical companies to Houston. And as Hubert Roussel pointed out, "This tradition of service has been carried on by their descendants, to the second and third generations."

The society signed up 138 guarantors who pledged a minimum of twenty-five dollars each to underwrite the 1913–14 season.[2] Suddenly the Houston Symphony Society was popular. Everybody seemed ready to join.

It opened its first season on December 19, 1913, before a capacity audience. It gave its second concert in March and closed out the season in assured success in May, 1914.

As early as 1911, Chamber of Commerce President Edward Peden had urged the city to plan its future growth. A year after Rice Institute opened, Mayor Ben Campbell saw that the institute was changing the face of Houston. Still with few trees, few buildings, and little landscaping, the institute was drawing Houstonians out to hear lectures and concerts and was stimulating new development out Main Street. Mayor Campbell commissioned Arthur Coleman Comey, a Harvard University landscape architect, to prepare a city plan for Houston.

Comey proposed a system of parks and parkways to ring the city. As park planners have done ever since, he saw Buffalo, White Oak, and Bray's bayous as natural sites for a green belt. He recommended a civic center, zoning to protect land value, and a planning commission to prepare and enforce an official plan. He called for Main Street to be maintained as a boulevard "for pleasure driving only" from Lamar to Bellaire Boulevard. And he wanted the city to create a large park across Main Street from Rice Institute. The city responded to his suggestions by bits and pieces, sometimes through private action, like that of George Hermann.

Hermann had always expected to give Houston parks, as well as the hospital on which he had set his heart. In May, 1914, five months before his death, he gave the city 278 wooded acres across from Rice to become Hermann Park, satisfying that portion of Comey's plan. This led Mayor Campbell to name a park board, including Hermann, Julian Settegast (his good friend and a Hermann estate trustee), and Edwin B. Parker. The board employed George Kessler, a St. Louis landscape architect who had designed park systems in Dallas and Baltimore, to lay out the new Hermann Park.

This was a balmy, gentle era, which seemed to stretch out invitingly into the future with no visible end. In early June,

Ima Hogg caught the Interurban for Galveston and boarded the *Bremen* for London. On June 23, Archduke Ferdinand was assassinated. In that summer and autumn of 1914, not many Houstonians thought that his death and the resulting rumpus in Europe would amount to much. Miss Hogg saw no reason to come home until autumn – by which time it was not easy to get a passage.

After eight years of study at three universities. Maurice Hirsch came home to open his law practice. At twenty-four, he may have been the best-educated lawyer in the state. He had graduated at sixteen from Houston High School as valedictorian and president of the senior class. In four years at the University of Virginia, he earned both a bachelor's and a master's degree and a Phi Beta Kappa key. He had a master's in law from the University of Texas and a doctorate of jurisprudence from Harvard, where he was case editor of the *Harvard Law Review*. But in 1914 he was coming home to stay. He was still soft-spoken and had retained all the courtesy of his southern upbringing. Though he would travel around the world twenty-six times over the next seventy years, he would build his career in Houston. His parents, Mr. and Mrs. Jules Hirsch, still lived in the house on Jackson Street where he was born. They strongly supported the new orchestra, and four decades on, their son would become president of the Houston Symphony Society.

In August, that once and future Houstonian William P. Hobby was elected lieutenant governor, to serve with James Ferguson as governor. Hobby was thirty-six years old, and because he needed to be in Austin only when the legislature was in session, he could continue his work as editor and owner of the *Beaumont Enterprise*. This was just as well. The lieutenant governor in 1914 received five dollars a day during a regular session, two dollars after the first ninety days.[3] Will Hobby would be reelected in 1916.

In the autumn of 1914, adult Houstonians enjoyed the *the dansant* (tea dance), newly imported from Paris. At five in the afternoon, they danced either in the candle-lit dining room of the new Rice Hotel or, in nice weather, in the roof garden eighteen stories above. On Saturdays, teenagers went to tea dances at the Art League, where for a dollar and a half they could dance all afternoon, proceeds benefiting the league. Parents found this a nice way to keep them occupied and to polish their dancing.

Motor buses were running on Main Street and three hundred jitneys were weaving in and out among private cars, trucks, mule-drawn drays, and horse-drawn ice, milk, and delivery wagons. As congestion grew, officers began to stand in the center of busy intersections to direct traffic. When Houston got its first traffic semaphore at Main and Texas, they still did – working the semaphore blades by hand. It was considered a great improvement. The air of downtown was thick with wires. Telephone and electric wires hung heavily overhead along sidewalks and crisscrossed intersections.

Throughout 1912, 1913, and 1914, men and dredges worked to carve the long-sought Houston Ship Channel out of the mud of Buffalo Bayou. The early visionaries had assumed that the deep-water channel would come to the foot of Main Street, bringing oceangoing liners to the city. Under the wise leadership of Representative Tom Ball, Houston compromised with Congress and settled for the Turning Basin to be created at Harrisburg. By that time, Harrisburg had become a part of Houston.

In 1912, the contractor had promised to complete the job in three and a half years. But the work was done by September, 1914, a year and three months ahead of schedule. Twenty-five feet deep, the channel led from Bolivar Roads to the Turning Basin. Houston was at last a genuine deep-water port.

The formal opening was impressive. To mark it, Pres. Woodrow Wilson interrupted a cabinet meeting in the White House to press a pearl-topped button that set off a cannon on the banks of the Turning Basin. But the problem now was to persuade shipping companies that their oceangoing vessels could safely navigate up channel to the Port of Houston.

On October 21, 1914, George Hermann died in a hospital in Baltimore. On October 27, Houston turned out for the biggest funeral in memory. He had been famous in the city for his frugality. Everybody in town knew that while his partners ate lunch in a restaurant, he stayed outside to eat a five-cent bag of peanuts. Everybody knew that he had lived in one room of the house he built, letting a friendly family occupy the rest in return for his meals. Everybody knew that he was still wearing as his best suit one that he had bought years before for a friend's wedding.

Yet, aware of his efforts to contribute to the city, Houston had come to respect him. The spectacular response to his death came even before the contents of his will were known. Houston schools and business and government offices were all closed by a public proclamation. Flags hung at half mast. The bell on top of City Hall tolled. The huge First Presbyterian choir sang. The funeral was held in the big, new City Auditorium. It was filled with all kinds of people coming to pay their last respects to this eccentric old gentleman who had never married "because wives are too expensive."

After a simple service, Dr. William States Jacobs read from the will to make public George Hermann's last gifts to Houston: land for Hermann Park; the site of the Hermann family home at Walker and Smith to become "a resting spot or breathing space" downtown and to be named Martha Hermann Square after his mother; and the bulk of his $5 million estate to establish a charity hospital.[4]

As Miss Ima Hogg was to say half a century later, Houston was lucky: The first people to become really rich were nice people, the kind who gave their money to enhance the city. William Marsh Rice gave his entire fortune to Houston to build a school. George Hermann gave his entire fortune to create parks and a charity hospital. They set an example that has been followed by wealthy Houstonians ever since.

Twilight of Peace

As WAR SPREAD across Europe in 1915, Houston was not yet ready to take sides. Throngs went to Grand Central Station to see the Liberty Bell on a freight car and hoped that Woodrow Wilson's recent election as president of the United States would "keep us out of war."

Houston had a growing sense of claim on President Wilson. Houstonian Edward Mandell House, his close political counsel in the presidential campaign, was now recognized as the chief adviser to the White House. He held no title, received no pay. Thomas W. Gregory of Austin (later of Houston) was attorney general.[1] As a more direct link, President Wilson's brother-in-law, Stockton Axson, who had left Princeton to head the Rice Institute English department, had become a star. His lectures, especially those on Shakespeare, were so popular that admirers in great numbers rode the trolley out from town to hear them.

Faithful to his campaign promise, President Wilson sent Colonel House as special emissary to Kaiser Wilhelm of Germany, hoping at best to avert a war that seemed imminent, or at least to get some personal evaluation of this powerful, eccentric monarch. (Long after in an interview published in *Liberty,* the kaiser said, "Colonel House almost prevented the World War."[2] Unfortunately, events moved more rapidly than the chancelleries of Europe.)

Always interested in the waterways, Mayor Ben Campbell hoped to create a bayou park system. His plan was advanced when, on April 30, 1915, the Stude family gave to the city 22.39 acres along White Oak Bayou at the foot of Taylor Street. The deed was signed by the six Stude children: Henry, Alphonse, Louis, Stokes, Emilie, and Henrietta. The *Houston Post* reported that the "natural park land, rolling, covered with beautiful grass and filled with native Texas trees," adjoined a seventeen-acre tract already in use as a park.

Houston now had its deep-water channel but could not attract deep-water ships. Major shipping companies were wary. As anyone could see on a map, Houston was not on the coast, and how could a ditch transform it into a deep-water port? What if a vessel made its way into the Turning Basin only to get stuck in the turn?

Houstonians who had invested their money and passion in creating the port now set out to lure ships into it. Colonel R. H. Baker and his son Burke Baker caught the attention of the Southern Steamship Company. In May, 1915, Burke Baker, who at twenty-eight was a trust officer of Bankers Trust Company, led a group to meet the steamship company's representative in Galveston.[3] They brought him up the channel on the *Zeeland,* the yacht Horace Baldwin Rice had bought to promote the port.

When the company did not promptly place Houston on its schedule, A. S. Cleveland and R. H. Spencer went to New York. They took with them a bond signed by one hundred citizens, promising to pay one thousand dollars each to the line if any losses were incurred in coming to Houston. All of this was typical of Houstonians' support of their city. The company waived the bond proposal and started service with the *Saltilla,* due to arrive from New York on August 19.

Mayor Campbell planned a "monster celebration" for the ship—declaring a holiday, digging barbecue pits two blocks long near the Turning Basin, arranging to feed ten thousand people. But on August 15 a storm slammed into the Texas coast, smashing not only the celebration but buoys and beacons along the channel. When Capt. Sinclair Taliaferro and Charles Crotty took a tug down the channel, they found that it had retained its depth. The *Saltilla* came in safely on August 22 and was the first of a line of Southern Steamship coastal vessels that plied the channel throughout World War I. They were from 281 to 300 feet long and drew up to 22 feet of water.

The 1915 hurricane was one of the most powerful in history. The barometer fell to 28.21 and winds reached eighty miles per hour. Three lives were lost and between $1 million and $2 million in property damage was done. In Houston the storm blew out windows and blew roofs off stores and houses. It ripped off the front wall and windows of Christ Church. Hotels and houses were filled with refugees from the bay shore. But this storm did not take the human toll of the 1900 hurricane.

The Herman Deterings had a bay house. As the water rose, they had to carry the children, one by one, to the train in order to flee the storm. They got home to 1417 McGowan only to find that an upstairs window had blown open, rain had poured in, and downstairs the soaked ceiling plaster had fallen in. They later found the bay house unscathed.

To John Fishback Grant in Galveston, the 1915 storm was one storm too many. He moved his wife, baby, and business to Houston. Mrs. Grant and their daughter Carolyn came up on the Interurban. Mr. Grant drove the family car, and it took him all day, from very early morning until dark. The car was an electric, and he had to stop to recharge the batteries in Dickinson. They

moved into the Rice Hotel and transferred their membership from Trinity Church, Galveston, to Christ Church.

As a gifted pianist, Mrs. Grant made a valued addition to Houston's musical circles. Homoiselle Davenport Randall had grown up in Galveston and had studied music in Berlin and New York City. In Houston, she was soon caught up in the new Houston Symphony Society. Listed on the program as Mrs. John F. Grant, she played Liszt's E-flat Piano Concerto for the final concert of the orchestra's 1916–17 season. She later served as chairman of the Women's Committee.

Scarcely noticed at the time, the city was gradually gaining able men from Huntsville. Out of their Huntsville friendships, they formed a network that would strengthen Houston. In 1905, John Campbell Williams left Huntsville, where he was the county judge, to practice law in Conroe.[4] The younger James Elkins was elected to replace him. Born in Huntsville and the son of a sheriff, Judge Elkins was a graduate of the Sam Houston Normal Institute. Although he was offered a whopping fifty dollars a month by the Houston Buffs to play professional baseball, he chose instead to earn a law degree at the University of Texas. He married Isabel Mitchell of Galveston in 1903 and opened a law office in his hometown.

As a beginning lawyer in Huntsville, he received one of his first cases from Col. John Wortham, the financial agent for the state penitentiary system.[5] The colonel had been secretary of state and a railroad commissioner under Gov. O. B. Colquitt. His small son, Gus, had been given a slingshot or some such tempting toy and managed to break a neighbor's window. She sued. Colonel Wortham asked Jim Elkins to take the case.

As Jim Elkins told it, he went to the angry woman and said gently, "I don't think you know this, but young Gus is just not quite *bright*. I don't believe you want to embarrass the family." Touched, the neighbor withdrew her suit and the Worthams repaired her window. (Judge Elkins liked to tell this tale to tease Gus Wortham, his life-long friend. Wortham had long since proved that he was very bright indeed, but not even he could prove that Judge Elkins had not used the ploy to get the case dismissed.)

After a period in Conroe, Judge Williams moved on to Houston, bought a house in Park Place and opened an office downtown. In 1915, Colonel Wortham moved to Houston and with his son Gus established the John L. Wortham and Son insurance business. Judge Williams bought the first house insurance policy Gus Wortham ever sold. In another two years, the Williamses and the Worthams would welcome the Elkins family to Houston.

By 1915, young S. M. McAshan had had five years of banking experience in Waco. Aware of his own grave illness, James E. McAshan, president of the South Texas Bank at Main and Franklin, called his son home to take over the bank. With his wife Aline, S. M. McAshan moved back to Houston to live on Lovett Boulevard, the new outermost section of town beyond Courtlandt Place.[6] Their three sons, Maurice, Jim, and Harris, found a neighborhood full of boys to play with.

Autumn of 1915 brought to Houston what it called the first all-woman's fair ever held. It began with a parade in which more than two thousand women marched. Its purpose was to further the interest of women in vocations and in home-making crafts. The *Chronicle* reported: "The first college women's banquet to be held in the South, and probably in the United States, was given . . . Saturday afternoon. Present were 275 women, representing 78 colleges, schools and universities in the United States and two abroad."

Despite this reminder of the existence of intellectual and educated women, the fair was largely focused on domestic interests. A year later, the Texas Women's Fair was marked by daily parades, one for school children, one for the Housewives League. At the exhibitions, the new milking machines drew the biggest crowds.

Although Angelina Pankhurst had led a group of Houston suffragists in a parade through the city in 1913, the 1915 fair went almost unnoticed as a sign that women were advancing. Historically, American women have surged toward goals in successive waves like this one–the wave that would carry them to suffrage.

As early as 1910, the *Atlantic Monthly* reported: "There . . . have always been stray women who have distinguished themselves in art, or politics, or religion, or science, but they were conspicious because they were strays. Achieving women are not very conspicuous now, simply because there are more of them. Indeed, the New Woman is almost ceasing to be new." The New Woman, however, could not vote.

As a railroad center, Houston had railroad hospitals that brought outstanding physicians to the city. Dr. R. W. Knox, who had his medical degree from the University of Virginia, came to Houston as chief surgeon of the Southern Pacific Railway and became widely known for his development of first aid methods. Dr. A. Philo Howard, who had come to Houston in 1907 as chief surgeon of the Frisco and Rock Island System, founded the Houston Clinic in 1916 with Dr. William Burton Thorning as his partner. The group soon had fifteen physicians representing every medical specialty.

Despite the war raging in Europe, life went on normally in Houston. Shopping downtown was leisurely, the stores gracious. Wide aisles separated the counters. The shoe and glove departments were always on the first floor. For a generation of ladies who called their party shoes "slippers," shoe salesmen measured the customer's foot to ensure a fit.

The glove counter had a row of stools. An attentive saleswoman wrapped a tape measure around the customer's knuckles while she sat with her elbow on the counter, her hand up. Next the saleswoman poked tapering wooden stretchers into each glove finger and sprinkled a little talcum powder inside. Finally she pulled the glove onto the customer's hand, smoothed the wrinkles down each finger, and stepped back to let madame decide if this particular suede or kid was what she wanted. Because no lady, young or old, could go to town or to church or to any social function without wearing gloves, this was an important decision. Ladies often used a favorite store as a meeting place, knowing that they were welcome to sit in the shoe department or at the glove counter until the friend arrived.

All the best stores had floor walkers, well-dressed courtly men who acted as hosts, helping iron out small difficulties, often escorting ladies to the carriage or car to carry their parcels. All the best stores provided charge accounts and free delivery of purchases to the house. In many stores, the business office was on an open mezzanine. The customer's five- or ten-dollar bill would go into a little basket. On a pulley, it would ride swiftly up to the balcony, making a jingle when it reached the top, and then sail back down bringing the customer's change and receipt.

Elevator operators in uniform guided the elevators on their slow upward climb, calling out the wares for sale on each floor: "Gents' furnishings. Ladies' ready-to-wear. Piece goods. Novelties."

Levy Brothers, expanding steadily, was known throughout the South as the first to take employees into the firm through stock shares. Foley Brothers, opened in 1900 by Pat and James Foley, was prospering. In 1916, Foley Brothers advertised a sale on women's stockings for nine cents a pair, women's shoes for $1.48 a pair and men's work shirts for forty-three cents apiece. In 1917 the brothers sold out to Robert I. Cohen of Galveston and his son George. The Mistrot-Munn Company, on its way to becoming a major department store, specialized in women's clothes. It advertised: "A thousand Tailored Hats, originally worth from $2.98 to $6.00, are on sale Friday and Saturday at $1.98."

Houston gained new talent and new institutions in 1916. The First Presbyterian Church, under the colorful leadership of Dr. William States Jacobs, acquired Ellison Van Hoose as choir director. Van Hoose had made his debut with the Metropolitan Opera Company and was the great Melba's leading tenor in opera and concert for five years. He had created the title role in Tchaikovsky's *Eugene Onegin* in New York in 1908, and he had sung for Queen Victoria at Buckingham Palace and Windsor Castle. The First Presbyterian Church became noted for its Sunday music and its annual performance of the *Messiah*.

The Rev. Clinton Quin, a young clergyman from Kentucky, succeeded the Rev. Charles Clingman at Trinity Church. Houston did not know that it was seeing the start of a remarkable career in joyous and entertaining civic service.

Houston was proud of Rice Institute and greatly interested in its growth. But few yet realized the force that it would exert in attracting newcomers to the city—Mr. and Mrs. Seth Irwin Morris of Madisonville among them. Carrie Holleman Morris was a graduate of Sam Houston Normal. In 1916 when she and her husband read in the papers that Rice was going to provide college education free of tuition, they decided that for the sake of their son's future, they should move to Houston.[7] When S. I. Morris, Jr., grew old enough, he did go to Rice; he later became its distinguished alumnus of 1981.

In 1916, Will Clayton brought his family

On one of their many trips to Egypt, the Claytons took along their two youngest daughters, Burdine and Julia, and a well-loved teacher, Lula Waldo, to tutor the girls. *Courtesy Ellen Clayton Garwood*

Birdsall Briscoe designed this house at 5300 Caroline for the William Lockhart Claytons in 1917,
with Mrs. Clayton as co-architect. The Claytons
bequeathed it to the city to become a branch library. *Photograph by Roger Powers*

to Houston from Oklahoma City as part of
the general move of Anderson, Clayton and
Company — soon to become the world's largest cotton company. "We moved to Houston," Clayton said, "because Houston was
the little end of the funnel that drained all
of Texas and the Oklahoma territory."

At thirty-six, tall, lean, handsome Will
Clayton was already well known in American and European cotton circles. He was
born in Tupelo, Mississippi, and reared in
Jackson, Tennessee. Over the protests of his
parents, he quit school after the seventh
grade and learned shorthand and typing as
his entree to business. On call at the local
hotel, he typed a speech for William Jen-
nings Bryan, who blamed the ills of the
South on high tariffs. From it, the boy
shaped a philosophy on international business that he held for the rest of his life.

At fourteen, Will Clayton was deputy
clerk of the chancery court of Madison
County, Tennessee. At sixteen, after a year
in St. Louis, he moved to New York City
to work for the American Cotton Company.
There he learned French by boarding in the
home of a French family and taking night
classes. At twenty-two, he was company
treasurer. At twenty-four, assistant general
manager of the company, he married his lifetime partner, the petite, vivacious Sue
Vaughn of Kentucky.[8]

When their first two daughters were quite
small, Clayton settled his family in Lucerne
for a summer by the lake. From there he
made trips to Bremen, Liverpool, and Milan, and opened an Anderson, Clayton office in Le Havre. On coming to Houston,
the Claytons began at once to build a
house for their growing family on a block

The young Museum of Fine Arts faced a sunken garden filling the large traffic circle on Main Street, designed by George E. Kessler as the entrance to Hermann Park. In 1928 Main Street still had an esplanade leading into town, and visible in the distance, the Niels Esperson Building dominated the downtown skyline. *Courtesy Houston Metropolitan Research Center, Houston Public Library*

of wooded land out on the newly opened Caroline Boulevard which had an esplanade down the center.[9]

Birdsall Briscoe was the architect who designed for them a red brick, Georgian house, with white columns flanking the front door, and with a tennis court and stables for two riding horses. As war loomed and Mr. Clayton was called often to Washington, Mrs. Clayton dealt with the builders and soon discovered that she had a flair for architecture, that she enjoyed building a house. This was the first of several she would oversee. Mrs. Clayton also plunged into the Art League campaign for a museum.

Although the war in Europe seemed remote to inland Americans, it was beginning to seem all too near to a port city where one white citizen in eight was foreign-born. Many Houstonians had relatives in England, France, or Germany. The German strain in Houston culture and society was especially strong.

The 1912 Comey Plan had called for Main Street to become a boulevard 120 feet wide as it led out of town, but it took an act of the Texas legislature to let the city condemn and cut that wide a swath.[10] Rather like a jigsaw puzzle, pieces came together in 1916 that would create a well-designed museum and park district near Rice Institute. Fortunately, most of the pieces were in the hands of George E. Kessler, landscape architect, with H. A. Kipp as engineer. Kessler, who had grown up in Dallas, was the park commissioner of St. Louis who had made

Joseph F. Cullinan's home, Shadyside, was the first house built in the enclave of the same name. After Cullinan's death, former Governor and Mrs. William P. Hobby bought it; it was razed in 1972 and the property given to Rice University by Mrs. Hobby. *Courtesy Mary Cullinan Cravens (Mrs. Rorick Cravens)*

his reputation planning Kansas City's park and boulevard system.

Kessler presented his design for Hermann Park in 1916, creating the Main Street traffic circle and sunken garden as its entrance.[11] By planting double rows of live oak trees from the 5600 to the 6400 block, he transformed the two-lane country road running by Rice Institute into the great boulevard envisioned by Comey. This enhanced both Rice and the park. Ultimately, Main Street was paved out to Bellaire Boulevard with four lanes and an esplanade for the "pleasure driving" that Comey foresaw.

Meanwhile, in February, 1916, Joseph Cullinan bought thirty-seven acres of land along the still unpaved South Main Street between the edge of town and Rice Institute. He, too, commissioned Kessler, who laid out the curving lanes of the subdivision that became Shadyside. This was something new in a city that had been tied to the grid pattern for all its eighty years of life. Kipp and Kessler worked together to bring the whole design of the park, Shadyside, and the Main Street boulevard into harmony.

No city in Texas had an art museum. With Dr. T. L. Blayney as president, the Houston Art League was ready to build one. The league knew that there was a triangle in the making where Main Street and Montrose Boulevard converged at what was to become Kessler's circle. The street completing the triangle on the north had yet to be drawn. The Art League had long had its eye on the tract, which was owned by George Hermann. He had once promised a third of it to the persuasive Mrs. Gentry Waldo for the league. Unfortunately, his promise never got as far as his will, which committed his money to a hospital. Bound by the terms of the will, the trustees offered to sell a third of the triangle at a reasonable price.

But Dr. Blayney and the site committee of B. B. Gilmer, Mrs. Waldo, and J. S. Cullinan knew that to have an adequate museum, they must try for the whole triangle. Mr. Cullinan negotiated a plan with J. J. Settegast, Jr., chairman of the Hermann board. In June, 1916, Mr. and Mrs. Cullinan anonymously gave the money to the Houston Art League to buy the triangle. The growing threat of war, however, delayed the start of building.

The Germans attacked at Verdun. The battle of Jutland raged. Like cities across the country, Houston grew increasingly war-conscious. Eleven thousand soldiers of the Second Division of the Regular Army had camped briefly on Houston's suburban prairie in the spring of 1914. At the Fourth of July celebration in 1915, the municipal song was sung to the tune of *Tipperary*. In June, 1916, Houston had a "preparedness parade" down Main Street. The federal building at Fannin and Franklin outfitted offices for U.S. Army, Navy, and Marine Corps recruiting. Port Houston was gorged with shipments of war materials to the Allies, and sentiment was rising against the kaiser.

The United States was still neutral. Cotton was still being shipped from Houston to both sides at good profit. But it was only a matter of time before the United States would enter the war. Germany had begun unrestricted submarine warfare. Overriding Congress, President Wilson armed U.S. merchant ships by executive order. Troops began to move through the city.

The Great War

THE WAR IN EUROPE shocked and distressed Houstonians of German background. Many still spoke German at home, subscribed to one of the city's several German-language newspapers, enjoyed all the cultural benefits of their heritage.

The Neuhaus family had become a part of Houston's fabric. Charles L. and W. Oscar Neuhaus were born near Schulenburg. Their parents were German born and German educated. Charley's wife Emilie had gone to boarding school in Germany. Their home on Courtlandt Place was filled with treasures brought over from Germany. Suddenly, for them and for all the Germans in Texas, the treasured heritage was being darkened by the kaiser's war.[1]

On Courtlandt Place, Jimmie Autry had a wireless. He told the neighborhood that should war be declared, he would shoot off a pistol, regardless of the hour. He heard the news and fired the pistol early on the morning of April 6.[2]

Tina Sharp said, "Everybody rushed out in their dressing gowns and negligees. I can see now my mother and Mrs. Neuhaus standing there where the hedge ended between the two houses, with tears pouring down their faces. Mrs. Neuhaus put her arms around my mother saying, 'Virginia, will you still love me?'"

In this momentous period, the *Houston Post* changed management. For twenty years the paper had been well run by the triumvirate of Rienzi Johnston, C. J. Palmer, and H. F. MacGregor, trustees of the estate of Jules Watson. Watson's son Roy, a graduate of Lawrenceville and Princeton, had spent those years in North Carolina, New York, and Chicago. He returned to his native Houston almost as a stranger in 1914. But he turned twenty-five in 1917, and on May 28, as his father had willed, he took over the flourishing paper. Handsome, blond, and idealistic, Roy Watson disapproved of most of the *Post*'s editorial and business policies. He and Colonel Johnston soon parted company, and the young owner swept out most of the senior editors. On principle, as a devout Christian Scientist, Watson banned all advertisements not only for patent medicines, but for wildcat oil stock, liquor, wine, beer, and yeast as well. Houston was too intent on the black headlines of war to notice.

Rice Institute immediately began to lose faculty and students to the services. President Wilson summoned his brother-in-law, Professor Axson, to become national secretary of the American Red Cross to serve in this country, France, and Italy. Twenty-five faculty members went to war. Lindsey Blayney, a German professor, fought in France and Macedonia. Professor of mathematics Griffith Evans worked on high-altitude bombing in France, England, and Italy. Julian Huxley served in military intelligence in the British army. Arthur Hughes entered the antisubmarine division of the British Admiralty. While on the National Research Council, Harold A. Wilson investigated antisubmarine devices both at the Naval Experimental Station in New London and at Rice.

The Rice class of 1917 had fifty-two graduates. Thirty-five of them left before commencement in June for training as officers at Camp Funston, Leon Springs, north of San Antonio. President Lovett went to the camp and conferred their degrees in a ceremony on the drill field. Of the Rice students who entered the service, eight would lose their lives.

Some Houstonians had anticipated the declaration of war. Palmer Hutcheson, son of Mayor Joseph C. Hutcheson, had graduated from Princeton in 1909 and the University of Texas law school in 1911. In 1916, he left his family and the family law firm to volunteer as a private in the 79th Field Artillery. After earning his commission, he went to France where he fought in the battle of St.-Mihiel and along the Meuse, Argonne, and Verdun Front.

Other Houstonians were quick to volunteer. Young Bill Kirkland left Princeton to join the navy as an aviation cadet. Walter Browne Baker left Princeton desperately hoping to get into the navy. Because he was extremely nearsighted, he memorized the standard eye chart and recited it when asked. The officer in charge passed him, but the pharmacist mate murmured: "The next time you take an eye test, try to look at the chart —not at the wall calendar."

In October Stephen Farish enlisted in the Army Air Corps, earned his commission in ground school and his wings at Kelly Field. Craig Cullinan, second of the Joseph Cullinans' five children, volunteered to the navy. Mike Hogg was commissioned lieutenant in the 360th Infantry, 90th Division, and went overseas. M. Tilford Jones joined the U.S. Army Signal Corps and learned to fly at Ellington Field.[3] Closing his music studio, Joseph Moody Dawson also entered the Signal Corps. During his wartime experience, Lieutenant Dawson invented a photographic device used in rifle practice that was ultimately adopted by the federal government.

Sons, as they were, of a Confederate major, the Weems boys all headed for service. F. Carrington Weems, who had his bachelors and masters degrees from Princeton, entered the army and became a lieutenant colonel on the general staff. At war's end, he was given the Distinguished Service Medal by his own government and made an officer of the Order of the Crown by the Italian government. Dr. Benjamin F. Weems, who had his A.B. and M.D. degrees from Johns Hopkins University, became a captain in the Army Medical Corps. Wharton E. Weems, who had a masters from the University of Virginia and a law degree from the University of Texas, became a captain in the Army Aviation Signal Corps.

Judge Clark Wren had served in the Spanish American War. Called back to duty as a lieutenant colonel, he went to France in the judge advocate general's department. At forty-two, J. Lewis Thompson, who had large lumber interests in East Texas, settled his affairs and recruited an entire company of volunteers from the mills and forests.[4] When the U.S. Army offered him a commission as major in a forestry regiment, he insisted that he had recruited *fighting* men. After training at Camp Bowie, Captain Thompson and his company went overseas.

Dr. Ernst William Bertner, a leading Houston surgeon, was the first of the many Houston physicians to enlist.[5] With a medical corps commission, he was assigned to the British Army and went overseas in June, 1917. Also in June, Dr. Fred Lummis left his practice to earn his commission and go to France with the Ninth Infantry. Dr. James A. Hill went to Washington as chief of the surgical division of Walter Reed Hospital. Dr. A. Philo Howard, president of the Houston Clinic, went overseas as a surgeon with the American Expeditionary Forces.

As they would again in 1941, women physicians took on extra duties during the war. Dr. Elva Wright had come to Houston in 1915 expecting to specialize in obstetrics. She had her medical degree from Northwestern and had done graduate work in Edinburgh, Vienna, Berlin, and London. But in Houston she discovered a high rate of tuberculosis. She founded the Houston

Anti-Tuberculosis League and served on the staff of the city-county tuberculosis hospital.

By June, 1917, 12,272 Houston men had enlisted with selective service. More would. Congregation Beth Israel placed tiny American flags at the seat of each member who had gone off to war. By August, forty-three small flags were flying.[6]

Some thirty-five hundred black Houstonians entered the segregated army, and when the Officers' Training School was opened to blacks at Des Moines, Iowa, twenty-six men from Harris County enrolled in the four-month course. The Des Moines graduation commissioned one captain, three first lieutenants, and seven second lieutenants—all black citizens of Harris County. All the Houstonians passed and were in line for commissions.[7] Carter W. Wesley, a graduate of Houston schools and Fisk University, was among the first black officers in the U.S. military.

Of black Houstonians in uniform, almost half went to France—some five hundred of them. Seven black Houstonians were awarded the Croix de Guerre, six were honored by Gen. John Pershing, and nine received the Distinguished Service Cross. One black Houstonian was credited with having captured a machine gun from the Germans after his comrades had been killed by sharpshooters and snipers.

Samuel C. Adams was one of the black Houstonians who served in France with the American Expeditionary Forces. His memories of Europe would later stir the interest of his young son. Dr. Samuel C. Adams, Jr., would become a foreign service officer, speaking French in Vietnam and, as the U.S. ambassador, in Francophone Niger.

Ever inventive, Howard Hughes had been developing a horizontal rotary drilling machine that could be used to plant mines under enemy trenches in long-range sapping operations. Both the English and French governments were interested in it, but with the U.S. declaration of war, Hughes offered the invention to his own government. Hughes Tool began to make Stokes mortars,

molds for dummy bombs, and parts for a device used in training airplane machine gunners.

In the early months of the war, life seemed curiously normal. In August, 1917, J. C. Hutcheson, Jr., was elected mayor with a vote of 4,270 to the 4,004 cast for J. J. Settegast, Jr. Doug Fairbanks was appearing at the Queen Theater and Bessie Love at the Zoe. The W. C. Munn Company advertised a sale: its usually $10 palm beach and panama white wash suits went for $5.25, and the company offered its $30 hand-tailored woolen suits for $19.50.

Expecting to stay in Houston only a few months, H. M. Duncan had come down from Kentucky in 1907 to visit his uncle, J. W. Neal, who was head of the Cheek-Neal Coffee Company of Houston, maker of Maxwell House coffee. Young Herschel took a temporary job. Discovering that he had an exceptional sense of taste and smell, he stayed on to start the Duncan Coffee Company. With the outbreak of war, he became a federal food coordinator to roast and distribute coffee. After the war his brother, Charles W. Duncan, joined the firm.[8]

William A. Vinson, a native South Carolinian, had grown up in Sherman, Texas, and had come to Houston in 1909 to start his law practice.[9] In 1917, on the urging of Will Hobby, Judge James A. Elkins came from Huntsville to join Vinson in forming a law firm. Elkins was thirty-eight, Vinson forty-three.[10] This was the start of a partnership that would have a strong influence on the growth and development of Houston.

Judge and Mrs. Elkins were staying at the Rice Hotel while they looked for a house. When the judge asked for Jesse Jones's advice on a suitable neighborhood, Jones responded, "Don't buy a house! You'll be tying up capital that you'll never get to use. Live here at the Rice as I do." The Elkins family settled into the Rice and lived there with their two boys until the Warwick Hotel was built. They never did buy a house. Neither did Jesse Jones.

Vinson was respected as a scholarly man

with a brilliant legal mind who preferred to concentrate on the law. Though Judge Elkins, too, was an able lawyer, he became the managing partner of Vinson & Elkins, a role that gave him a wider range of use for his talents. When District Attorney John R. Crooker left to join the army, Governor Hobby appointed Elkins to the post. James Elkins finished out the term and never again sought public or political life. But the experience propelled him into Houston's leadership. In the next decade, he would become one of Houston's most powerful men.

The Houston Red Cross chapter had been founded in 1916 with Jonas S. Rice as chairman. Now, as the war grew more brutal in Europe, civilians suddenly saw it as their way to serve their country. A corps of volunteers began to make bandages, knit sweaters and socks, and prepare bedside kits. When membership chairman Abe Levy announced that anyone could join by paying a dollar, Houston won the national award for having the highest percentage of its population in the Red Cross with 4,400 new members.

President Wilson had become acquainted with Jesse Jones through Stockton Axson. When the American Red Cross War Council planned to raise $100 million for its immediate war needs, Jones was asked to raise $150,000 in Houston. He raised twice his quota before being called to Washington for fulltime duty with the American Red Cross.

Black and white, Houstonians bought war bonds. School children could buy them at $1 down and $1 a week. Factory workers paid a day's wages each week or each month. Liberty Loan subscriptions had passed $2.5 million by June, 1917. Once again, Houston was answering the call to arms.

Nobody could foresee that Houston itself would soon undergo two deadly attacks from unexpected sources.

Chapter Thirty-Six

Mutiny

In July 1917, the War Department leased 2,019 acres in the forest three and a half miles west of town, and began to build Camp Logan – later the site of Memorial Park. On July 28, the 3rd Battalion, 24th Infantry, arrived from Columbus, New Mexico, with advance units of the Illinois National Guard due to come within a fortnight. Made up of black soldiers of the regular army, the 3rd Battalion was sent to guard construction. They set up a camp on ten acres of land the War Department leased between Logan and the city. Each day the soldiers went to Camp Logan for guard duty.

The 24th Infantry came to Houston with a fine record. After a long tour of duty in the Philippines, the regiment received a loving cup from the city of Manila in appreciation of the way the men had conducted themselves. Posted to San Francisco in 1915, the regiment's provost guards so impressed the chief of police that he offered several of them a place in his police force.

The black soldiers had never served in the South before. They were glad to find so large a black community, one that welcomed them warmly. Black ministers, schoolteachers, and social leaders often visited their camp – as did, of course, some less savory persons. But from the start, the soldiers were affronted by Houston's Jim Crow laws. Wearing the uniform in the service of their country, they resented water coolers marked "White" for the construction workmen and "Guard" for the black soldiers. They resented being called "boy" and treated like one. They

resented the word *Nigger.* They resented the often ugly heckling they got from white workmen at Camp Logan. They resented the attitude of streetcar conductors. All their resentments came to a focus on the Houston police.

Few black Houstonians, however distinguished, had reason to like or trust the city police in 1917, but they knew they could not win in a showdown. The infantrymen, who had been accepted as equals in their preceding tours of duty, felt free to express their anger to Houston police, matching curse for curse. The police reacted harshly to any move a soldier made. Altercations led to pushing and shoving. Some soldiers were roughed up at police hands. Within two weeks of their arrival, tensions were building on incident after incident.

In late afternoon of August 23, a rumor swept the guards' camp that one of their own had been killed by Houston police. By suppertime the rumor reached the guards on duty at Camp Logan.

The actual incident: Caught playing craps, two little boys ran away from the police. Chasing them, Officer Lee Sparks invaded the house of a woman who was doing her week's ironing. When she denied having seen the youngsters, he grew angry and slapped her. A private from the camp tried to intercede in her behalf and was arrested for interfering with an officer. When the unarmed Corp. Charles Baltimore of the camp's military police challenged the soldier's arrest, Sparks shot at him, hit him over the head with a pistol, and took him to jail.[1] The chief of police telephoned the Camp Logan officers to confer.

The soldiers' white commanding officer seemed not to comprehend the depth of their anger and, as word of the incident spread, failed to tell them that Corporal Baltimore had survived. By the time Baltimore got back to camp in a jitney–his face and head bearing the marks of the pistol butt–the mutinous soldiers were too fired up to back down.

Inflamed by the incident and ignoring their commanding officer, more than one hundred soldiers seized rifles and ammunition from the supply tent. Thereafter, the scene became kaleidoscopic. It took more than five thousand pages to record the testimony given by witnesses in the courts martial, and much of that testimony was contradictory.

It can be said that fifteen soldiers went down Washington Road toward the streetcar loop, expecting to join other mutineers on the march from Camp Logan. They fired into a jitney, killing the driver and wounding a passenger. They then returned to the guard camp.

By now, darkness had set in.

The larger group in the guard camp fired a frenzied volley of several thousand shots into the dark for some fifteen minutes, generally in the direction of Houston. In so doing they shot an army private in the abdomen. Remarkably, there were no other casualties.

Then, in a lull, the voice of Sgt. Vida Henry sounded–taking command. A soldier with eighteen years of impeccable military record, he told the men to take their canteens and plenty of ammunition, and to save one bullet for themselves. When some of his followers had second thoughts, he placed a rear guard with orders to shoot anyone who turned back. One member of that rear guard was Corporal Baltimore, who had been rumored slain.

Sergeant Henry formed the men into a column and at 8:50 P.M., with fixed bayonets, they marched toward town. They were out to get the mounted police who patrolled the San Felipe district, especially Police Officer Lee Sparks. Some wanted to shoot every white in sight. Some spoke of burning the town.

Night had fallen. Houstonians who were lucky enough to sense the danger took cover. But as the angry soldiers marched through the Brunner and San Felipe districts, they shot at people in cars and at anyone who walked out on the front porch to see what was happening. By twos and threes, Houston mounted police faced and fought a column of trained soldiers armed with the best rifle of the day–the Smithfield.

The marchers had gone about two miles, having killed or wounded men, women, and children at random, when on San Felipe Road, they faced an open car coming out from town to confront them.[2] Capt. J. W. Mattes of the Illinois National Guard was standing up in the car to order them to halt. They shot and killed him. Two others in the car with him were shot fatally.

This broke the mutiny. The anger drained away when they realized that they had killed an officer wearing the same uniform they wore. Sergeant Henry urged his men on to attack the police station, but the fire of mutiny could not be rekindled. After a long, unhappy parley, they turned to file back to camp. As though reviewing his troops, Sergeant Henry shook the hand of each of the soldiers until the last one had passed. Then he shot himself.

The shooting by black soldiers had lasted two hours. Twenty-six persons had been killed: fifteen white civilians, including four mounted police, two soldiers mistaken for policemen, and nine hapless bystanders, including a sixteen-year-old boy. Twelve other Houstonians were seriously injured and one of them, a policeman, later died. Four black soldiers died as a result of wounds that proved fatal: Sergeant Henry who shot himself, the soldier shot in the wild volley before the column left the camp, and a soldier accidentally shot during the march by a fellow trooper. Only one soldier was shot by Houston whites. He died from gangrene from a wound in the leg.

By a little after nine at night, as the news spread downtown, hundreds of white men broke into stores that dealt in guns and ammunition, seized weapons, and charged off in all directions. Some of them were hotheads out for foolhardy vengeance against the soldiers; some were terrified and hoping to protect themselves or their families. Many of them had never before held a gun in hand and were a much greater danger to themselves than to the soldiers.

Four prominent Houstonians tried to restrain them. Ed J. Hussion, owner of a printing company, Capt. C. C. Beavens, U.S. Attorney John E. Green, and Clarence Kendall, former county attorney, moved up and down Main Street urging the unruly mob to go home. The army acted to seal off Camp Logan from invasion and to seal soldiers in.

Brig. Gen. John A. Hulen of the Texas National Guard, a Houston railroad executive, set up headquarters in the Houston Post Building because of its telegraph office. After repeated tries, he managed to call Gov. Jim Ferguson out of a midnight conference in Austin. Governor Ferguson declared Houston under martial law at 12:30 A.M. with Hulen in command. During the night, a special train left San Antonio bringing an infantry battalion, while other trains brought companies of the Coast Guard and regular Army from Galveston.

But by midnight, Houston's leaders had united in a determination that no mob violence would be allowed, that no reprisals should be permitted. A committee of citizens, headed by National Guard Col. Jacob F. Wolters, a Houston attorney, drew up a list of five hundred leading men to be a *posse comitatus* to act under the sheriff's department.[3] By 3 A.M. the list was complete. The call to duty was issued on page one of the *Houston Post*. The *Post* has rarely had so

remarkable a front page as that of August 24, 1917.

"MARTIAL LAW DECLARED"

The banner headline was followed by a summary in inch-high letters "Negro soldiers . . . mutinied, slaying 13, wounding 19, officer of Illinois regiment slain, seven policemen are dead or wounded." The names of the dead, the dying, and the multiply-wounded were given in bold face.

The *Houston Post* became the official voice, the instrument of instruction, to all Houston. Using the *Post*'s front page that day:

○ **The general posted his order.** "All citizens will remain in their homes or usual places of business at once. No citizen not an officer will appear on the streets with arms. Parties will not assemble on the streets. Saloons will not be permitted to open. Places of business where arms and ammunition are sold, kept or stored, will remain closed. (Signed) Hulen." He warned that any incendiary oratory or any man not an officer bearing a gun, would be met with prompt arrest.

○ **Acting Mayor Dan Moody called upon** "every citizen of Houston, white and colored, to preserve the peace, to go quietly about their business and to rest assured that there is going to be a full inquiry and proper punishment for the crimes which have been committed."

○ **Sheriff Frank Hammond summoned his posse:** "The men named below, AND NO OTHERS, are asked to report at 7:30 this morning to Sheriff Hammon. NO ONE NOT NAMED ON THIS LIST IS WANTED."

Doctors, judges, engineers, store owners, bankers, and businessmen, such men as H. M. Garwood, W. D. Cleveland, and Judge William Masterson, were on list. By 7 A.M. more than four hundred had reported for duty. Colonel Wolters gave them their orders: "The purpose is not to go out after the Negro soldiers, but to police the city and maintain order—the law must be upheld by the citizens." They were divided into squads with a captain over each and deployed in thirty districts of Houston. For forty-eight hours, the citizens policed the city, doing the work of the disorganized police force and sheriff's department. Patrolling the streets with guns on their shoulders, they worked to calm anger and fears, to remind that law and order could best be served by the official forces of law and order.

The military was left to deal with the mutineers. Camp Logan spent all of August 24 gathering in soldiers—some of whom had mutinied, some of whom had spent the night in whatever safe haven they could find. One black soldier had taken refuge with a white family and returned to camp with a note from his host exonerating him from any part in the attack. It was signed by Mrs. J. W. Pratt, J. W. Pratt and C. A. Denny. Early in the morning of August 25, the entire battalion was moved back to Columbus, New Mexico. Columbus welcomed them.

Army investigators came to Houston to work on the case from every angle. Boards of officers were formed to interview every soldier at Columbus. The investigators filed charges against sixty-four men; sixty-three went on trial at Fort Sam Houston on November 1, 1917. The court consisted of three brigadier generals, seven colonels, and three lieutenant colonels; it consisted of five northerners, four southerners, and four westerners. Eight of the thirteen were graduates of West Point. Harris County District Attorney John H. Crooker, who had immediately begun his own investigation, was invited to assist the judge advocate general.[4]

This was the biggest murder trial in American history. But this was more than murder. In wartime, the soldiers had disobeyed their commanding officer and had used army rifles to kill civilians.

The testimony was confused, often conflicting.

The trial lasted four weeks. The presiding judge, Maj. Gen. John A. Hull, concluded that "nobody will ever know all that took place on that terrible night of August 23rd, 1917."[5] But more than half a century later, in a work of massive research, Robert Haynes pieced together most of what happened that night and in the courts martial that followed. In 1976 he published his findings in his book, *A Night of Violence.*

Forty-six men were given life sentences. Thirteen black soldiers were condemned to death. On the night of December 10, carpenters built scaffolds at Fort Sam Houston, one with six traps, one with seven. In the early hours of the next morning the condemned men were brought to the scaffolds. They were smartly uniformed and shaved. A black minister from San Antonio and two army chaplains were with them. They sat back to back in two rows of chairs. Quietly they hummed a mournful hum. By the light of a bonfire, the nooses were adjusted.

The colonel in charge gave the command: "Attention!" The thirteen men snapped to their feet and stood erect on the traps. At 7:17, the official hour of dawn in a still-dark sky, the colonel gave the signal with a downward sweep of his arms. The two levers were pulled simultaneously. By sunrise, the scaffold timber had been burned, the bodies buried, and a fence built around the grave plot.

Not until two hours later was the verdict made public. Black and white, the public was shocked by the suddenness and the secrecy of the executions, by the fact no time was given for appeal. White newspapers north and south pronounced the verdict just, but many questioned the ineptitude and negligence of the white officers involved. Black newspapers in varying degrees of anger focused on the police actions that had provoked the tragedy. C. N. Love, editor of *Houston Observer,* wrote of the mutiny, "The chances of it occurring would have been remote if a disciple of 'democracy' had not overstepped his bounds in dealing with a black soldier." Over the next few months, the verdict proved to be far more divisive than the crimes.

This was the first of three courts martial that would extend until March 26, 1918.

Transcripts of the testimony totaled more than five thousand pages, with almost three hundred witnesses.

Of the 118 men charged with mutiny, rioting, and murder, 110 were found guilty of at least one charge, 7 were acquitted. Though 29 were given the death sentence, only the original 13 were actually hanged. Many civic groups went to the White House to seek redress for the soldiers. President Wilson commuted the remaining death sentences. Presidents Harding and Coolidge ultimately ordered the release of those remaining in prison.

These points can be made:

1) The federal government should never have sent a black regiment to a Southern city in those Jim Crow days. The summer of 1917 was already tense with racial strife across the country. The East St. Louis riot was only the worst of five serious incidents. The Houston incident was different in that more whites than blacks were killed.

2) The Houston policeman was totally unjustified in beating a soldier. The soldiers could not be justified in mutiny. But this was a tragedy compounded of festering hurts, inflammatory rumor, and misunderstanding.

3) In terms of Houston's character: This was not a race riot in the usual sense of white and black fighting over shared turf. Houston has never had a major race riot in this sense. There was no rock throwing, no burning of buildings. No Houstonian joined the fray. In two evening hours of August 23, 1918, armed soldiers from out-of-state, marching under a sergeant's command, fought armed members of the Houston police department. Of the city's private citizens, neither Houston whites nor Houston blacks were involved.

4) The reaction of Houston's civic leaders was courageous and civilized. They took responsibility for their city. They defused an excited mob. They refused to let the violence spread through reprisals. They turned the military's problem over to the military. By the start of business hours, they had ensured the safety of Houston blacks.

But Houston was left scarred and shaken.[6]

Home Front

THE PROCLAMATION of martial law in Houston was Gov. Jim Ferguson's last important act in office. The same edition of the *Houston Post* that told of the mutiny carried a story on the legislature's decision to impeach the governor. A day later, the young, boyish face of Will Hobby appeared on the front page. Overnight he had become acting governor of Texas.

The political storm had been brewing in Austin for months. Governor Ferguson, who had little use for the University of Texas, came into office declaring that "too many people are going hog-wild over higher education." Will Hogg was chairman of the university regents and was committed with all his vigorous soul to his alma mater. Ferguson outraged the regents by demanding that six professors be fired because, he said, they were engaged in "an unholy spree of establishing an educational hierarchy." When the regents refused, the governor vetoed the university appropriations bill.

Will Hogg's term expired but he continued the fight from Houston, writing alumni, buying newspaper ads, charging the governor with putting "the putrid paw of politics on the state university." He was a formidable adversary.

At the height of this wrangle, Governor Ferguson was indicted by the Travis County Grand Jury on seven charges of misapplication of public funds, one charge of embezzlement, and one of diversion of a special fund. This shocked Houstonians and Texans everywhere. Impeachment proceedings began. On September 25, the Texas Senate removed Jim Ferguson from office, and Will Hobby, who had never expected to make politics a profession, took over the governor's chair—the youngest person ever to hold the office.

Work began on Ellington Field, a $1 million airfield for training army fliers. By November, 1917, thirty-three thousand soldiers were stationed at Camp Logan. Houstonians welcomed them, invited them to home-cooked meals, entertained them warmly. When a street dance was given for them in November, fourteen bands played along Main Street in the mile between Lamar and McGowen avenues, and seventy-five thousand people turned out for the party.

Edna W. Saunders, daughter of Mayor John D. Woolford, had majored in music and the arts at Stuart School in Washington and the Gardner School in New York before coming home in 1900 to make her debut.[1] In the war years, as an amateur at management, she staged free public concerts at the City Auditorium to which almost a hundred thousand people came.

Sugar and butter grew scarce. Tuesdays became meatless days at hotels and restaurants. And in December, the Red Cross sold kisses at the Bender Hotel for a dollar each. Military titles entered the marriage registry: Frankie Carter married Robert Decan Randolph, lieutenant, Naval Aviation Corps, Washington, D.C. Bonner Means married James Addison Baker, Jr., lieutenant, U.S. Army.[2]

Frankie Carter was a handsome, spirited young woman who throughout her life would attract affection and admiration, especially among the young. A golfer and horsewoman, she was part of a carefree society that managed to have fun even with a war on. Before going overseas, Mike Hogg had been one of her suitors. But one day during a yachting party, Deke Randolph fell overboard and Frankie promptly dived in after him. Mike Hogg gave up. He said to his friends: "I can see the handwriting on the wall."

Bonner Means and James Baker had met when she was fifteen at a dance at Beech's Auditorium. "All the high school dances were given there," Mrs. Baker said seventy-five years later. "I was walking with a partner down the center of the room and he [James Baker] was coming toward me with a partner. We had never seen each other before. He asked me for a dance on my program and he asked me how to spell my name. It was love at first sight. And we were engaged five and a half years. In those days, a man did not marry until he could support a wife. Then the war came and we were married right away."

Young Bonner Means gave up her studies at Rice Institute to marry. Commissioned a lieutenant at Leon Springs, James Baker went overseas, where he earned a citation for bravery. Fifteen years later, Mr. and Mrs. Baker would become the parents of James Addison Baker III, who would become secretary of the treasury in the Reagan administration and President George Bush's secretary of state.

Once war was declared, the inevitable gung-ho, all-out determination to serve the cause led to some absurdities. On the urging of faculty and students, Rice Institute was granted a Reserve Officers' Training Corps unit in 1916. All students, men and women, were members of the cadet corps. The War Department sent Maj. Joseph Frazier, U.S. Army (Ret.), to teach military science and tactics. Rice became a military camp. In the men's colleges, reveille sounded at 5:45 A.M.; rooms were inspected at 6:15; breakfast was served at 6:30; drill started at

7:30. Classes and labs came later in the day. Every cadet had to be in quarters (meaning his room) within twenty minutes after the close of dinner and stay there until 9:30. Taps sounded at 11:00 P.M. to call for lights out.

Though none of the women could live on campus, they too were put in uniform and drilled. They wore men's army hats and army nurses' shoes. Somewhat puzzled Camp Logan and Ellington Field soldiers found themselves saluting ROTC students from Rice when they met downtown.

Major Frazier, who might have succeeded, was transferred. His successor managed to march the men through a hedge on his first drill. Army red tape required the students to have permits and passes for almost every step they took on campus.

The novelty wore off. The students rebelled. By January, 1918, the campus had erupted. Protestors put the power plant out of commission, broke windows, and turned a fire hose on military officers. The Rice trustees had to grant that nothing in the Army General Order of September 20, 1916, had called for such a militarization of the campus. A peace was negotiated.

Though ROTC was carried to an extreme at Rice, students everywhere were plunged into military discipline. To the great amusement of her younger sisters in Houston, teenage Nina Cullinan marched and drilled with a broomstick over her shoulder at the exclusive Ogantz School.[3]

While Governor Hobby attended to state business, an embittered Jim Ferguson set out to reclaim the governor's chair. His campaign in the Democratic primary was based on invective and personal attacks on the small, quiet young man who had succeeded him. When the primary was over, Will Hobby had won by a vote of 461,749 to 217,012 for Ferguson. Hobby's total was the highest that had ever been cast for an opposed candidate for any office in Texas. In the autumn election, he received 148,982 votes to the Republican candidate's 26,713. He had now been elected governor in his own right, and the amendment he proposed to provide free textbooks to school children carried by a majority of more than two to one.

Finishing the Ferguson term had given Will Hobby time to set his own priorities. He quickly decided that if he was to accomplish what was best for the state, he must give no thought to the political impact of his actions. He would serve as governor—not as a perpetual candidate for the office of governor.[4] As a result, his administration was notable.

The Houston Equal Suffrage League, led by Annette Finnigan, and the Texas Women's Rights Association, had been campaigning for the right of women to vote since 1903. Hortense Ward, the first woman lawyer in Texas, gave the greater part of her time between 1913 and 1918 to the cause.[5] The British Parliament passed the first women's suffrage bill in 1916.

Governor Hobby believed that American women should have the right to vote. In February, 1918, to the dismay of his conservative supporters John Henry Kirby and Rienzi Johnston, and while running for re-election, the governor proposed an amendment that would enable Texas women to vote in party primaries. Whoever the Democratic Party nominated in the summer was always elected in the November elections. In a one-party state like Texas, to open the vote in the party primary would give women the vote where it counted. They would have their say even if not allowed to cast ballots in the elections that came after. Will Hogg and Joseph Cullinan favored the bill.

It passed the legislature with only one opposing vote. The *Houston Post* of March 27, 1918, announced that women would vote in the July primaries, but they had only seventeen days in which to register: June 26–July 11. Hortense Ward was the first woman in line on June 26. By July 11, 14,750 women had registered at the Harris County Courthouse. On July 27, for the first time, they voted in the Democratic primary. But Governor Hobby's amendment was rejected when submitted to the all-male electorate of Texas. On November 5, therefore, the *Post's* election coverage headlined: "Men of Houston Go To The Polls." Texas women had won one skirmish of the ballot box, but not yet their war for voting rights.

Many Texans were also jolted by the prohibition amendment to the U.S. Constitution. However, by the time two-thirds of the states had ratified it, Texas was more dry than wet by local option. Already 199 counties were dry, 43 others were dry for the most part, and only 10 counties in the state had no single dry precinct.[6]

In 1918, Houston annexed the city of Houston Heights and enjoyed the first snowstorm since 1895. Bellaire incorporated as a city. Mayor Joseph C. Hutcheson, Jr., resigned his office to accept appointment as federal district judge. After only sixteen months at Trinity Church, the thirty-five-year-old Clinton Quin was elected bishop coadjutor of the Diocese of Texas to help the Rt. Rev. George Kinsolving develop missions. Quin was the youngest Episcopal bishop in the United States. The eighty-seven-year-old presiding bishop of the Episcopal Church, Daniel Sylvester Tuttle, came down from New York for the consecration in Christ Church.

Houstonians were talking about President Wilson's Fourteen Points for Peace and the peace treaty signed between Germany and the new Bolshevik government of Russia. The war in France made strange names familiar—the Battle of the Somme, the Battle of Meuse-Argonne. Houstonians tried whale meat without taking to it as a staple. They embraced wheatless days, heatless days, and lightless nights—all in the service of their country. They planted war gardens, not a radical move in a time when cows were kept on McKinney and in Courtlandt Place and Shadyside. Ladies met for sewing bees where they tore up old sheets in long strips and rolled the strips for bandages to be shipped to field hospitals at the front.

Ellington Field was becoming one of the largest air bases in the country for flight training, with five thousand men and two hundred and fifty planes. Pilots and bombardiers trained at Ellington and there were also gunnery and radio schools. Kenneth Franzheim, an MIT graduate in architecture, was posted to Ellington for training in the Air Corps. He became a pilot and bomber, wrote a book on techniques and methods, and was made an instructor with the rank of captain. Bessie Simms was among the lovely young Houstonians who met and helped entertain the Ellington Field officers. She and Captain Franzheim were married after the war.[7]

By the early spring of 1918, more than one million American troops were in action on four sectors of the Western Front. Twenty Houstonians of the Twelfth Aerial Squadron from Ellington Field landed in England, and nine members of the city's health department were in the medical corps in France. The Thirty-Third Division at Camp Logan was shipped overseas in May.

Gus Wortham, leaving the insurance agency he had founded with his father, went overseas as commanding officer of the army's 800th Aerial Squadron in 1918. Calvin Garwood went overseas as a second lieutenant. Ben Taub started in 1917 as a captain in the First Texas Cavalry, but by 1918 was captain in the 132nd Field Artillery overseas. George Journeay shipped out to France as a captain in the field artillery that July. Capt. Mike Hogg, having fought through the St. Mihiel and Argonne offensives, was wounded in the autumn.

Donald Gregg of the Heights became the first Houstonian to be killed in action. He was followed by Marion Collier, Herbert D. Dunlavy, Edwin T. Hathaway, Henry R. Hill, Leroy B. Hinton, Herbert Scott Peddie, Edwin Riesner. . . . One by one the yellow envelopes arrived. Every Houston family with a man overseas learned to dread the arrival of a telegraph messenger.[8]

The *Houston Post* had reached a journalistic peak with its handling of the mutiny and was covering the war ably. But publisher Roy Watson's ban on liquor and patent-medicine advertising (in response to his

Christian Science beliefs) was taking its toll. To make clear his policy, he printed a reminder to readers every day in a front-page box like the one of July 27, 1918. It announced that the management had refused to publish 804 lines of "undesirable medical advertising" for the issue of July 26, and added: "During the forty-five days ending July 26th, 56,971 lines or approximately $3,987.00 worth of undesirable advertising was refused all for the purpose of making *The Houston Post* 'Your Kind of a Paper.'"

Aware that the paper was on a disaster course, Ross Sterling, president of the Humble Company, tried repeatedly to buy it. William Randolph Hearst offered Watson $1.15 million for it. Watson announced publicly: "The *Post* is not for sale, has never been for sale, and never will be for sale."

The lethal attack on the city, always a possibility in wartime, came from an unforeseen source: Spanish influenza. It reached Houston in September, 1918. Almost half the city's population was stricken and one hundred and eleven died. This flu left its victims too weak to move. Whole households were immobilized. For example, all the children and all the servants at the W. L. Clayton home were down with flu. Tiny, valiant Mrs. Clayton cooked and carried all the meals, all the medicines, all the bathing basins, all the bedpans for her four small daughters and four servants, while doing whatever else was essential in the big new house on Caroline.

Young David Bintliff lived in Woodland Heights with his parents. Influenza killed his mother, his father, and his brother, who had four children. Not yet twenty, David Bintliff took on the support of his brother's children. He worked for the Wells Fargo Express Company money department in the Union Depot on Texas Avenue. He would become a major developer, financier, and philanthropist some forty years on.

The epidemic waned in October. But it had killed an estimated twenty million people worldwide, more than half a million of them in the United States. This was almost ten times the number of Americans killed in action throughout the war of 1917–18. More than nine thousand Americans died on military posts in Texas, twice the number of Texans who were killed in war. Of Rice Institute's war fatalities, three were due to influenza in this country for each one who died of wounds overseas. Houston's death toll was comparatively light. But the eternal irony of war was there. John Cullinan survived warfare in France, but came back weakened by trench warfare. He died at home of the flu.[9]

At 4:15 on the morning of November 11, 1918, the *Houston Post* was on the streets, the newsboy cry of "EXTRA! EXTRA!" waking many who slept. The armistice had been signed. Automobile horns began to blow. Factory and locomotive whistles joined the joyous din, and the revelry began. The next day's *Post* told the story:

"At 6 o'clock the downtown streets were well filled, at 7 they were crowded, at 8 they were jammed, at 9 they were choked, and from then on it was one wriggling, squirming, squeezing mass of humanity, rudely awakened from sleep but joyously. . . ." Newspaper photographs show a solid pack of people on Main Street and Texas Avenue around the Rice Hotel.

Houston lost two hundred young men to the Great War that was to end all wars. Charles Hazen Patterson, wounded in the Meuse-Argonne offensive on the night of November 10, 1918, died of his wounds on December 10. For him, the armistice had come an hour too late.

In the Realms of Power

As IT ALWAYS seems to be, Washington was full of Houstonians throughout World War I. This was due not so much to promptings by Colonel House at the White House as by the prewar professional network of which Houston was a part.

Upon the declaration of war, Robert Lovett, New York railroad magnate and former Houstonian, was asked by President Wilson to organize the War Industries Board. He called on Judge Edwin Parker of Houston, who had succeeded him as a partner at Baker & Botts, to join the board as priorities commissioner. Will Clayton spent a year in wartime Washington as a member of the Cotton Distribution Committee of Bernard Baruch's War Industries Board. Through Dr. Stockton Axson, Jesse Jones came to President Wilson's attention and spent three years in Washington as director general of military relief in the American Red Cross.

Foremost among the Houstonians who were serving their government was Col. Edwin Mandell House. Through the closeness of their friendship, he acted as President Wilson's alter ego in a number of missions abroad before and during the war. Early on, and after House's meeting with the kaiser, the president sent him to confer with Clemenceau and Lloyd George. As the war neared an end, Colonel House won British and French acceptance of Wilson's Fourteen Points as the basis of the peace—a master stroke of diplomacy. After the armistice, Colonel House was one of the five American commissioners at the peace conference in France. He served as Wilson's second in command and took the president's place at the table in February and March when Mr. Wilson had to be in Washington.

With the peace treaty signed on June 28, 1919, Mr. Wilson sent House to the London conference to plan the operation of the mandates set up by the Treaty of Versailles. Soft-spoken, slender, courteous, with a gleam of humor, Edwin Mandell House won the trust of the world's most powerful leaders in 1918 and 1919. But in the fall of 1919, Colonel House returned to the United States so ill that he had to be carried from the ship on a stretcher. The president had been incapacitated by a stroke. The two men, so close for so long, never met again. Colonel House recovered his health. President Wilson did not.[1]

Charles Seymour in the *Handbook of Texas* wrote of House:

His conversation was fluent and stimulating, shot through with graceful humor. . . . He had an almost chemical quality in personal relations that stimulated the self-confidence of the person he worked with and fostered sympathy and trust. His kindness to younger men was unlimited, and he started many on the road to success.

The rule he laid down in politics was invariable: Do what's right. Through his relations with Wilson and his innumerable personal contacts, he influenced United States policy more than any other American not holding office.

Without cutting their ties to Houston, the Edwin Parkers were settling more and more into the nation's capital.[2] A founder of the Houston Symphony Orchestra before the war, Mrs. Parker became a member of the women's group that led to the founding of the National Symphony Orchestra some years later. Judge Parker became chairman of the United States Liquidation Commission and umpire for the Mixed Claims Commission between the United States and Germany. He was also commissioner of the Tripartite Claims Commission involving the United States, Austria, and Hungary.

These duties took him to Paris, where he was in charge of three billion dollars' worth of American property and was entrusted by the allied governments to handle the negotiations for settlement. Out of all this, he became internationally recognized. He was awarded the Distinguished Service Medal by his own country and was named an officer of the Legion of Honor by France. Belgium named him a Commandeur de l'Ordre de la Couronne and Poland named him a commander of the Order of Polonia Restituta.

The Parkers served Washington as they had Houston—she in music, he in education and foreign affairs. Their only child had been killed in a motorcycle accident in California years before. Judge Parker was a trustee of the Carnegie Endowment for International Peace and of George Washington University. He was in line for appointment to the United States Supreme Court when it was discovered that he had cancer. He was brought back to Houston for burial in Glenwood Cemetery beside his son.

In his will, Edwin Parker left one hundred thousand dollars to the national YWCA to establish the Katherine Parker Music Foundation. He left the bulk of his fortune to establish a graduate school in international affairs. He named Justice Harlan Fiske Stone and Secretary of State Henry Stimson to its board, with the idea that the school would be placed in Washington. Instead, the Parker School of International Comparative Law at Columbia University is the result of Houstonian Edwin B. Parker's lifelong interest in law and in foreign affairs.

Called to Washington in 1917, Jesse Jones turned his business affairs over to his associate, Fred I. Heyne, and took on wartime

Col. Edward Mandell House, shown here with President and Mrs. Woodrow Wilson, was President Wilson's most effective emissary before, during, and immediately after the first world war. *From the family collection of Colonel House's niece, Mary Elizabeth Caldwell Merrem*

duty.[3] President Wilson named Henry P. Davison, a senior member of J. P. Morgan and Company, chairman of the American Red Cross War Council. Jesse Jones joined him as director general of military relief and Davison's chief aide-de-camp. Used to organizing banks and building buildings, Mr. Jones brought order to the task. He set up fifty base hospitals and forty-five reconstruction hospitals. He formed a Bureau of Construction that built convalescent homes, recreation centers, warehouses, canteen depots, and canteen services. He dealt directly with the president and often traveled with him. He found that the best way to gain access to President Wilson was simply to show up at the White House.

After the armistice, Chairman Davison felt that the good will that the Red Cross had earned should not be lost. This was an opportune moment. Europeans had urged the creation of an international Red Cross ever since the Geneva Convention of 1882, but had thought only in terms of war. Clara Barton, founder of the American Red Cross, had urged an international organization to serve in *any* major disaster. Under her lead-

President Woodrow Wilson marched down Fifth Avenue on May 18, 1918, at the head of a Red Cross parade of some seventy thousand people. Jesse Jones and Joseph Tumulty (*from left*) marched with him. *Courtesy John T. Jones, Jr.*

ership, the American Red Cross had coped with such catastrophes as the San Francisco earthquake, the Johnstown flood, and the Galveston storm. Davison saw this as the moment for the Red Cross to become the worldwide agency for relief of human suffering.

After the Armistice, Davison and Jones sailed for Europe. They landed in England on the same day that President and Mrs. Wilson arrived from their triumphal visit to France. Eager for a quick decision on his idea, Davison sent Jones to see the president at Buckingham Palace.

As his taxi reached the palace gates, the high sheriff of London was leaving in a splendid carriage. As he would have done in Houston, Jesse Jones bowed. The sheriff bowed back. On this recognition, the guards at the gate waved Mr. Jones through. Once in the palace, he was told that the president and the king were out, but that he could wait. December is cold in London. To warm his toes, Jones took off his shoes and held his feet to the fire. A few minutes later, the president and the king walked in and Mr. Jones had to make his plea in stocking feet. But President Wilson agreed.

From London, Davison and Jones went on to Paris, Cannes, and Geneva. They met with representatives of France, Great Britain, Italy, and Japan to charter a League of Red

Cross Societies. And from their efforts, President Wilson included the idea of an international Red Cross in the Covenant of the League of Nations.

In September, 1917, E. A. Peden, president of the Peden Iron and Steel Company, was appointed federal food administrator for Texas by Herbert Hoover, the U.S. food administrator. At war's end, Mr. Peden went to Paris as Mr. Hoover's aide in the distribution of food to the people of devastated Europe. In 1919, he organized the large and successful European Child Relief of the American Relief Association.[4] He and Joseph Cullinan worked closely with Mr. Hoover in the effort to send food overseas. Whenever Mr. Hoover was in Houston, he was the Cullinans' house guest.

Despite the achievements of these Houstonians in national and international affairs, the city of Houston was seldom an item in the national news. As historian John Boles wrote, "Smaller in 1920 than Birmingham, Memphis, or Louisville, Houston did not really have an identifiable national image." Houston called itself the "Magnolia City," and considered itself Southern, as indeed it was in voice, social custom, and climate. But whenever a Houstonian gained national prominence, he was noted as a Texan and presumed to be a westerner.

At the war's end, from France and bases across this country, Houstonians were coming home. The 151 men of the 117th Supply Train were welcomed with "Rainbow Day." When the 359th Infantry returned, 6,000 Houstonians celebrated in a street dance. Returning in 1919 as head of the 132nd Field Artillery, Capt. Ben Taub was given a hero's welcome. In the joy of peace, Houston remembered the 200 of its young men who would not be coming home, and the many who had been wounded and maimed. A number of the war wounded convalesced at Camp Logan. Patriotism inspired the formation of the Gold Star Mothers—women whose sons had died for their country—and of the League of the Great War. Under command of Col. John S. Hoover, the league

became the first local post of the American Legion.

When a German U-boat was tied up in the channel for a week, thousands went to see it. And all Houston assumed that Ellington Field was going to become the center of the air age. "Plans to make Ellington . . . the greatest aviation field in the world were consummated Monday," the *Houston Post* announced. The greatest aviation field in the world was stillborn.

Congress proposed the nineteenth amendment to the U.S. Constitution on June 4, 1919. Having voted in the Texas primary in 1918, Houston women were eager to campaign for the amendment that would let them vote in national elections. Many of them attended the fiftieth convention of the National American Women's Suffrage Association in 1919, where Carrie Chapman Catt proposed the formation of the League of Women Voters to increase women's effectiveness in furthering good government.

The issue put the Texas legislature in a quandary. Congress was for it. The states of Illinois, Michigan, Wisconsin, Kansas, New York, and Ohio ratified it. But of the Texas men who had voted the legislators into office, a strong majority opposed granting women the right to vote.

Governor Hobby threw the entire weight of his office and his gentle, humorous persuasion behind what was called the Anthony amendment—after Susan B. Anthony. Without him, it is possible that Texas male voters would have balked. While Texans argued, Pennsylvania and Massachusetts voted to ratify. On June 28, 1919, Texas became the ninth state to ratify and, to Governor Hobby's deep satisfaction, the first Southern state to do so.

In August, 1920, the amendment became law. Houston women promptly founded their chapter of the League of Women Voters at the Rice Hotel with such leaders as Miss Florence Sterling, Mrs. Harris Masterson, Mrs. James Dore, Mrs. Neils Esperson, Miss Julia Ideson, and Mrs. Henry B. Fall.

Governor Hobby had already decided not to run for reelection in 1920. In slightly less than two full terms, his administration had given women the right to vote, doubled the per-capita spending on education at all levels, carried out judicial reforms, provided a budget system, doubled the number of highway miles, quadrupled the money spent on county roads, left the general revenue fund with the largest cash balance in history, and had more state money drawing interest than ever before. All this was done under the quiet leadership by which pleasant, charming, wise Will Hobby won the cooperation of the Texas Legislature.

Woodrow Wilson's great days were behind him. He was awarded the Nobel Prize for the peace treaty that established the principle of self-determination. All Europe was eager to join a League of Nations as a measure to end war. But Congress had swung into isolationism and rejected Woodrow Wilson's leadership. The League of Nations was formed without the United States. In 1921, Wilson left office crippled by a stroke and with a sense of failure.

This was a time when no pension was provided retired presidents. In the friendship that had grown up during the war, Jesse Jones saw that the President and Mrs. Wilson were in financial straits. He went to Cleveland Dodge, who had been Mr. Wilson's classmate at Princeton and lifelong friend. They knew they were dealing with a proud man, made sensitive by illness and defeat. With great care, therefore, they shaped a letter that said, in part, "We have created a trust which will provide an income to you, throughout the remainder of your life . . . and though we are prompted by our love and admiration of you, the trust is in fact intended as a slight material reward for your great service to the world. . . ." The trust gave the Wilsons an income of ten thousand dollars a year in quarterly installments.

Houston had felt a link with Woodrow Wilson since his days as a college president. It had often asked his help on city projects and had given him full support at the polls. It was fitting that a Houstonian should have been a part of the thoughtful plan to ease President Wilson's last year.

Chapter Thirty-Nine

Postwar

AFTER EVERY WAR, the prospect of peace acts as a powerful stimulant. With the war to end all wars won, Houston shared in a nationwide exhilaration. As though taken off a leash, Houstonians began to build the buildings they had been forced to table for the duration.

Will Hogg's business affairs had prospered, so that by the armistice, he was comfortably well-to-do. He began to collect antiques and paintings by Frederick Remington. With the discovery of a new and richer oil sand at Varner in 1919, he and the Hogg family began to amass a fortune. At forty-six, he knew how to spend it, both for his own enjoyment and for the benefit of humankind. He built an eight-story building at Louisiana and Preston, with offices for himself and his brother Mike in a penthouse surrounded by garden. He hung his Remingtons on its walls.[1] He kept an apartment in New York City. He took long, leisurely trips abroad with good companions.

Big, robust, confident, at times overpowering, he felt that the oil coming from the earth of Texas belonged to the people of Texas, not to the Hogg family. He thought the government should have held on to the treasures in the ground for the good of everyone.

Wealth enabled Will Hogg to exercise his passion for education. "In a well-ordered democracy," he once said, "no boy or girl with brains and character should be denied the opportunity of college training."[2] In 1919, the University of Texas advertised in all Texas newspapers that any ex-soldier qualified for admission would be given the money to attend. More than one hundred enrolled on Will Hogg's anonymous scholarships.

When he was president of the Ex-Students Association, his executive secretary John Lomax had a standing order: "When any student in the University of Texas gets into trouble, help him. As long as he is on the rolls of the university, he is my ward. If he needs money, lend it to him. If he is sick, get a doctor. If he gets thrown into jail, bail him out. If he dies and has no money or people, bury him. Don't wait to write or wire me; relieve the distress and then let me know at what cost."

But, Mr. Hogg added, "If you ever let anyone know where the money comes from, I'll never send you another blankety-blank cent."

It is impossible to measure how greatly these scholarships benefited society. Thanks to a Will Hogg grant, Tom Douglas Spies completed four years at Harvard Medical School. Fourteen years later, the American College of Physicians honored Dr. Spies "for outstanding contributions to the science of nutrition, and particularly for his studies in the nature and character of pellagra." Pellagra had been a drain on the southern economy, filling southern insane asylums with pitiful people who suffered delusions. Dr. Spies proved that pellagra was caused by a lack of niacin. With massive doses of Vitamin B complex, he restored pellagra victims to health and enabled them to work. This one scholarship resulted in ending an epidemic that had sapped the strength of the South.[3]

Will Hogg was a gentle giant, with a special gift for treating children as contemporaries. Small Mary Cullinan considered him her best friend. He and she were partners in the Catanimal Corporation, and of the many enchanting books he gave her, most had such an inscription as "To the president of the Catanimal Corporation from an ornery shareholder." All were signed "Bilog" –their private name for Will Hogg.

World War I had been costly to the Port of Houston. The Port not only lost shipping because of the German U-boats, but lost its dredges to war service. In aftermath, however, the port gained new impetus. "The war had proved the usefulness of the internal-combustion engine, thus creating a demand for petroleum," Marilyn Sibley wrote in her history of the port. This meant that oil would shape a new age in human history–though it came about so naturally that it never gained title as the Oil Age.

In 1918, most oil on the twenty-five-foot channel was shipped in barges. But oil tankers, considerably bigger and needing deeper water, were already in use. Though Houston was the largest spot cotton market in the world, the ship channel was not deep enough for cotton to be shipped efficiently. While the war still raged, Ross S. Sterling and Joseph Cullinan had pushed the Army Corps of Engineers to deepen the channel to thirty feet. The approval came through in 1919. Congress provided the money; the channel was deepened.

As Mr. Cullinan pointed out, a refinery needs deep water to the sea, abundant fresh water, large acreage, protection from floods and tropical storms. The Houston Ship Channel provided all these things as well as a nearby source of crude oil. Houston set out to make the channel attractive to refineries.

In the 1880s, Samuel E. Allen had built a white-pillared plantation house on the family ranch near the junction of Buffalo and Sims bayous. It had broad verandas, stables, and barns. When he died in 1913, he was one of the biggest taxpayers in Harris County and one of the largest landowners on the Gulf Coast. Rosa Allen, his widow, inherited his estate and made generous use of her inheritance.

To further the efforts to lure industry to the port, she sold the seven hundred acres of the Allen homeplace at less than the appraised value to bring the Sinclair Refining Company to the channel.[4]

Cotton firms promptly joined the oil refineries along the channel. Alexander Sprunt & Son, a cotton firm that had operated barges on the channel since the Civil War, built the Ship Channel Compress Company in 1922. A year later Anderson, Clayton's Houston Compress Company built the terminal known as Long Reach. This was the biggest private terminal on the channel. Anderson, Clayton had ridden the boom in American-grown cotton during 1914 and 1915. With Houston as its headquarters, it had opened an office in Le Havre in 1916 and immediately after the war established its presence in England and Germany. The company built large warehouses in Houston and later opened offices in Japan and China. In ten years, Anderson, Clayton and Company would become the world's greatest cotton factor.

The Port of Houston exported 275,879 bales of cotton in 1920, and 2,069,792 in 1930.

As oil wells grew in number, so did oil field services. Houston factories designed and made drilling equipment. Harry Cameron, a mechanical and architectural engineer from Indianapolis, had won a reputation at Spindletop, Goose Creek, and Humble as an inventive ironworker who could machine any tool a driller might need. Young Jim Abercrombie was a drilling contractor who frequently needed Cameron's skills. In 1920, when Jim Abercrombie was twenty-nine, he and Harry Cameron formed Cameron Iron Works with a capital of twenty-five thousand dollars.

S. E. J. Cox, a Houston oilman, established the first commercial airline to enter

Houston in 1919. His Southern Aircraft Company flew a Curtiss Jenny and two Curtiss Orioles. His pilot, Hal Block, made the first all-air trip from Houston to New York on June 20, 1921. His flying time was nineteen hours and forty-eight minutes.

In 1919, a few petroleum geologists began to meet for lunch at the Bender Hotel. In 1920 they elected D'Arcy Cashin their president. By 1923, when they chartered the Houston Geological Society, they had seventy-three members, including Alexander Deussen who was president of the American Association of Petroleum Geologists. With Wallace Pratt, Deussen invited the AAPG to hold its ninth annual meeting in Houston—the first of many. By 1950 this would be the largest local society in the world with eleven hundred geologists on the roster.

Though the era of medical specialization was well under way before World War I, most physicians were in general practice and most babies were delivered at home. After the war, Houston enjoyed not only the return of its well-known doctors from military duty but a vigorous infusion of new ones as well. The postwar period was marked by a trend toward specialization, by an effort to encourage hospital births, and by increasing talk of establishing a medical center in Houston.

Dr. Gavin Hamilton, a Canadian surgeon, had come to Houston in 1903. His graduate study in Vienna, Berlin, Edinburgh, and London had shown him the value of a teaching hospital associated with a university. He proposed linking Rice Institute to Hermann Hospital in a graduate teaching program that would form the nucleus of a medical center.

Dr. Alvis E. Greer, a graduate of Northwestern University medical school, was chief of staff of the Houston Tuberculosis Hospital. Though he had a large private practice, Dr. Greer could see the urgent needs of the community through his charity work at the tuberculosis hospital, the Houston

Municipal Hospital, and Baptist Hospital. Through the many medical organizations he served, he pushed the concept of Houston as a medical center for the Southwest.

Fairly new to Houston, Dr. Herman Johnson was a native of Vermont, who had a medical degree from the University of Buffalo. In 1920, after service in the Army Medical Corps with the British forces in France, he brought his family to Houston and specialized in obstetrics. Dr. Robert A. Johnston, who arrived in 1921, was also an obstetrician. A native of Alabama and descended from a long line of doctors, he had earned his medical degree from Johns Hopkins University and had served as assistant in gynecology at Columbia University Medical School.[5]

Dr. Ernst William (Bill) Bertner returned to Houston from overseas army duty by way of a year's graduate study at Johns Hopkins. As house surgeon of the Rice Hotel, he lived there with his wife. He was president of the staff of Houston Municipal Hospital and on the board of the Houston Academy of Medicine. Dr. Bertner had his heart set on establishing a medical center in Houston. But Houston would have to wait another quarter of a century for the medical center idea to become reality.

Harry Wiess, youngest of the Humble Company's vice-presidents, had moved his office to Houston during the war but usually went home to Beaumont every weekend. As a civil engineer, he was director of refining. His big task of 1919 and 1920 was to build the Baytown refinery.

The company chose a tract of twenty-one hundred acres on the ship channel to be near deep-water shipping. The boggy rice land was covered with a thicket of senna beans and surrounded by dense woods. The work went well as they drilled water wells, cleared trees, began to push power lines and a railroad from Goose Creek. Then the rains came—"for 100 straight days," according to men who worked there. Often the only access was on horseback, and the horses sank in the mud. With the rains came "clouds of flies and malaria-carrying mosquitoes, grasshoppers, office-invading snakes and bellicose Brahman bulls." It sounds worse than the Panama Canal ordeal. But in the end, the Baytown refinery became one of the largest in the world and would be important to the Allies in World War II.

In 1919, despite the epic struggle going on in Baytown, Harry Wiess commissioned William Ward Watkin to build a house at 2 Sunset Boulevard. Mr. Watkin saw this as an opportunity to relate the architecture of Shadyside to that of Rice Institute across the way and designed a Mediterranean villa. The Wiesses took possession in 1920, and their third daughter, Margaret, was born there. She was Dr. Herman Johnson's last planned home delivery.[6]

Black Houstonian Cliff Richardson and his family started another black newspaper, a weekly called *Houston Informer*. This paper would ultimately merge with the *Texas Freeman* to become one of the most powerful black voices in the Southwest.

In the hurricane season of 1919, fresh from the University of Texas, Miss Dewey Harris of Bastrop came to Houston to teach at Fannin School for sixty dollars a month. "You know nice ladies *only* taught school in those days," Dewey Harris Roussel recalled sixty-five years later. "My parents didn't want me to come because this storm was blowing in. Friends met me. They had a Ford with isinglass side curtains, but the side curtains did no good at all. Next morning going to school, the wooden blocks had buckled up out of the street and water was everywhere. My new, high-buttoned shoes were ruined!"

In her two terms as a fourth-grade teacher, Miss Harris taught Tina Cleveland (Mrs. Dudley Sharp), Jane Amerman (Mrs. Thomas Vanzant), and Bernard Sakowitz. "Bernard was the cutest little boy. He was always impeccably dressed in a suit with a flowing tie."

When spring came, the *Houston Post* offered her a summer job as a copy editor. She became the first woman in the United States to serve on the universal copy desk of a major metropolitan daily. Through her work she met and married the *Post* music critic, Hubert Roussel.[7]

With a master's degree from the University of Virginia and a law degree from the University of Texas, Wharton Weems entered the firm of Vinson & Elkins in 1919 and within two years was made a partner.[8] Vinson, Elkins, Sweeton & Weems was on its way to becoming one of the largest in the state.

R. C. Fulbright, a native Texan, had come to Houston in 1909 directly from the University of Chicago, where he had earned his J.D. degree. In 1919, he and John Crooker formed the law partnership of Fulbright & Crooker.

Herbert Godwin, who had brought his wife to Houston from Memphis in 1900, was one of the city's most successful cotton exporters. In 1919, he established the Godwin Foundation in Public Affairs at Rice Institute. The first three lecturers were former president William Howard Taft, British ambassador Sir Auckland Geddes, and Dr. Abbott Lawrence Lowell, president of Harvard. Within the next few years, Mr. Godwin would become a dynamic chairman of the Houston Park Board and vice-chairman of the Houston City Planning Commission.[9]

Houston had enjoyed baseball since before the Civil War. The Houston Base Ball Association was chartered in 1895 with a capital stock of three thousand dollars. John Henry Kirby was president, Si Packard vice-president, and Sam Taub secretary and treasurer. The Houston team won the Texas League pennant in 1913 for the fourth time. After the World War, as troops returned, amateur baseball flourished anew, with two thousand players in twenty leagues. Professional baseball was gaining ground. In 1920, John H. Crooker headed a syndicate that bought the Houston Baseball Club for sixty-five thousand dollars; Fred N. Ankenman was named business manager. In 1921, the Houston Buffaloes began to play at West End Park, with twenty-five thousand fans filling the grandstands. The Buffs won more than their share of games and league championships against Beaumont, Austin, and other teams. But their greatest days lay ahead.

In 1921, at Pierce Junction, Houstonian Hugh Roy Cullen drilled his first producing well. This launched a career that would be historic in the petroleum industry and in the annals of personal philanthropy. With his young wife Lillie, Cullen had started out in the cotton business in Oklahoma Territory. When he brought his family to Houston in 1911, he became a member of the Houston Cotton Exchange, expecting to continue in cotton and to deal in real estate. But the lively oil industry soon attracted him.

In 1918, he took a lease on one million acres in West Texas and drilled two wells in Crockett County and one in Edwards County. All three were dry holes. But with a stamina and courage that impressed oilmen, he turned to the forty acres he had leased at Pierce Junction and drilled again. The well produced, and he was on his way. The bulk of his production would result from the daring with which he drilled deeper and deeper wells, often in fields that had been abandoned. Within sixteen years he would be awarded a doctor of science degree from the University of Pittsburgh for his contribution to the understanding of oil structures in the United States.

In 1921, Oscar Holcombe was elected mayor of Houston, a city of forty square miles and one hundred and fifty thousand people. A comparatively unknown contractor from San Antonio, Holcombe would be elected mayor ten times in the next thirty years.

Despite $10 million in new construction, Houston had a severe housing shortage. Ten thousand newcomers could not find homes. Houston gained service on one of the country's eight transcontinental airlines, a route linking Savannah to San Diego. But unemployment was high, jobs hard to find.

The Ku Klux Klan reappeared in Houston in late 1920 and grew rapidly. In December, 1921, 2,051 Houston men were inducted in a ceremony "on the prairie a short distance south of Bellaire." The prospectus sounded conservative but not inflammatory: A member had to be a Protestant of Caucasian blood. He must believe in free public schools and swear to uphold all the laws of the United States, including the Eighteenth Amendment (Prohibition). Early on, the Klan claimed quite a few substantial citizens, but no lists are available. Many men, like Mayor Holcombe, attended one meeting and, disliking what they heard, never went again.

The Klan preached "100 percent Americanism," but it stirred racial and religious antagonisms alien to Old Houston's spirit. While some young men may have thought they were carrying on a romantic, post-Civil War tradition, it soon became evident that Klan leaders had an uglier and darker motive of intimidation.[10] White Houstonians began to worry about the safety of black friends and employees. Catholic and Jewish Houstonians were uncomfortable in their own city.

Newly called to the First Methodist Church, the Rev. A. Frank Smith found that he had the Klan's grand dragon in his congregation.[11] The young minister took a firm position: the Klansman could take his part as a church member, but all mention of the Klan must remain outside the church doors.

The oldest Jewish congregation in Texas, Beth Israel prepared to move from the first temple on Crawford to a new one on Austin and Holman. Buyers of the old site wanted immediate possession, and the new temple was not yet finished. Mr. Smith offered his friend, Dr. Henry Barnston, use of the First Methodist Church. Congregation Beth Israel held its services there for eighteen months.[12] Both Mr. Smith and Dr. Barnston were in serene defiance of Klan pressures.

As it did elsewhere in Texas, the Klan tried to restrict the social and moral behavior of nonmembers, to dominate by fear, and to influence city elections. It mailed hundreds of threatening letters to leading citizens. Klansmen abducted a white lawyer, cut off his hair, tarred and feathered his legs, told him to leave town, and left him on San Jacinto Street. A man due in court on charges of indecent exposure was abducted before his court appearance and brutalized. A black dentist was seized, taken to a deserted shack in Pearland, anesthetized, and castrated. The Klan news sheet bragged: "The Ku Klux Klan Is Here To Perform a Mission No Other Agency Can Reach." By 1922, the Klan had captured most of the county offices.

Houston leaders fought back. John Henry Kirby called on the Klan to disband and in a letter to the *Chronicle* charged that the Klan had violated constitutional guarantees of due process and trial by jury. He and Joseph Cullinan helped organize the American Anti-Klan Association. Threatened by mail and by phone, Cullinan took to keeping a gun close at hand. Both the *Post* and the *Chronicle* condemned the KKK. Judge Cornelius W. Robinson stated: "If we want tar and feathers for punishment, it is up to the people to write it into the laws."

John H. Crooker, former district attorney and officer in the judge advocate general's office, crusaded against the Klan in public speeches. One evening as he was leaving for a speech in Baytown, he received an anonymous telephone call: "Don't come down here tonight. If you do, you'll be sent home in a wooden box."

Said Judge Crooker: "Tell the carpenter to start building it. I am on my way." He went to Baytown, made the speech, and came home even more determined to fight the Klan.

The Klan did indeed gain influence for a while, but as its methods became more apparent, a backlash occurred. The Klan called upon Mayor Holcombe to fire three men in his administration because they were Catholics. He refused. When he ran for reelection in 1922, the Sam Houston Klan No. 1, claiming ten thousand members, set out to defeat him in what was the most out-

rageous campaign of Houston's history. They published their own newspaper to denounce the mayor as a drunkard and gambler. He was a member of the First Baptist Church in good standing, and neither drank nor smoked; to that time he had never gambled.

One week before the election, the Klan paper charged that Mayor Holcombe had been seen drinking and shooting craps at a big New Year's Day party. Holcombe challenged the Klan to prove it. He asked the Baptist Ministers' Association to hold a public hearing and try him on the charges. Of the thirteen ministers, nine were members of the Klan. The Klan produced two men who said that they had peeked over the transom of the room where the party was held and spied the mayor drinking eggnogg. Mayor Holcombe lined up six witnesses who were *in* the room of the infamous party and could attest that he had never been there. One of the six was the doorkeeper. As a result, the mayor was cleared, and all thirteen of the ministers offered to work for his reelection. He won with ease.

Such incidents as this stirred a growing anger. When a false rumor went around that a new Houston newspaper, the *Dispatch,* had Klan backing, advertisers shunned it. When the Klan endorsed her opponent, Miriam A. Ferguson was elected overwhelmingly—though few Houstonians wanted another Ferguson in the governor's chair. She subsequently lost office to Dan Moody, who was elected on his success as a district attorney prosecuting Klan leaders. It took a while to cleanse the air, but the ugly Klan chapter in Houston ended.

By 1922, the law firm of Clarence Fulbright and John H. Crooker was handling Anderson, Clayton's business and was growing so rapidly that it needed extra help. Temporarily they hired William Bates, a former district attorney in Nacogdoches. Bates started work on New Year's Day, 1923, and in four years was made a partner. John Freeman and John Crooker had both grown up in Fifth Ward—the "Bloody Fifth." Freeman earned a law degree at the University of Chicago in 1912 and joined the firm in 1924, after several years of private law practice. With Monroe D. Anderson as their chief client, and Dr. Ernst Bertner as their adviser, Colonel Bates and Freeman would become leaders in creating the Texas Medical Center.[13]

Jubal Richard Parton, born in Madisonville, had studied the humanities, law, and international law at the University of Texas from 1913 to 1917. After war years as a major in the Field Artillery, he came to Houston and at twenty-six was one of the founders of the Woodley Petroleum Company. At thirty-one, he was its president. This was the start of a career in the oil, pipeline, and sulphur industries that would equip him for service to his government in Washington during and after World War II.

With a degree in civil engineering from the University of Kansas, Warren S. Bellows came to Houston after the war, and by 1921 the W. S. Bellows Construction Corporation was well established. One of his first projects was the Auditorium Hotel. The company would go on to build the San Jacinto Monument, skyscrapers downtown, major buildings at the University of Texas and the University of Houston, and both the Alley Theatre and Wortham Center. Mr. Bellows would become one of the city's most effective civic leaders and the president of the Associated General Contractors of America.

From his arrival in 1897, Philip Battelstein was a successful Houston tailor. In the early 1920s, with his sons A. M., Harry, and Ben, he branched out to offer a complete line of men's ready-to-wear, including hats.

In December, 1922, the city received a present labeled "Do Not Open until Christmas." It was the acre and a quarter at Austin and Clay streets where the Root family home had stood. Mayor Holcombe accepted it from the children and grandchildren of Alexander Porter Root and Laura Shepherd Root, most of whom had grown up in the house. It was to be preserved as a public park.[14]

The Methodist Hospital was born in 1923 with the gift of Dr. Oscar L. Norsworthy. Born in Jasper, Dr. Norsworthy had graduated from Tulane, done graduate work in Vienna and Germany on the use of radium, and studied hospital methods in India, China, and Japan. He had moved to Houston in 1895. In 1908, he had built his own thirty-five-bed hospital and begun to specialize in radiology. In 1923, he was part of an American College of Surgeons group that went to South America to develop professional ties. On his return, he decided to give his hospital on Rosalie at San Jacinto to the Texas Methodist Conference and went to the Rev. A. Frank Smith to discuss it. Mr. Smith had in his congregation many business stalwarts—Judge James Elkins, Will Clayton, John T. Scott, W. W. Fondren, Jesse Jones, Fred Heyne, Raymond Elledge, Walter Goldston, and L. L. Nelms among them. Smith worked out the plan whereby the Methodist Conference would enlarge the building to provide one hundred and twenty-five additional beds. Dr. Norsworthy supervised completion of Houston's first Methodist Hospital. One day, as a part of the Texas Medical Center, Methodist Hospital would have 1,527 beds and be the largest private, nonprofit hospital in the United States.

Chapter Forty

Social Notes from the Twenties

WITH the world at peace, Americans plunged into a happy extravagance. They could travel freely. The seas were once again safe for the ocean liners. Trains began to run on time. Automobiles grew faster and cheaper. Dresses were inching up well above the ankle to express the new freedom women had tasted during the war. Hairdressers skilled in the art of the curling iron gave the new marcel wave to bobbed hair.[1]

Hats were still enormous. Ladies going to the theater matinee removed their hats when the house lights darkened. Gentlemen, as always, slid theirs into the wire cage attached under every theater seat for that purpose. Men still wore starched, detachable collars that had to be attached each morning with collar buttons. A leather case for collar buttons made a suitable Christmas present for a young lady to give a gentleman.

In 1920, though only eleven years old, the Houston Country Club was losing impetus. At the turn of the century, the town seemed to be growing eastward from Main and Texas. Most of Houston's finest residential sections were east of Fannin, along San Jacinto and Caroline, or along Texas, McKinney, Lamar, Dallas, and Clay. Park Place was a promising subdivision. The 210-acre estate of oilman Edward F. Simms on Wayside was one of the handsomest in Houston with its mansion, gardens, and swimming pool.

In 1909, with the opening of the club near Harrisburg and Wayside, it was assumed that handsome new neighborhoods would spring up around it and that the city's growth would continue eastward toward Harrisburg. None of this happened – probably because of the impact of Rice Institute, which opened in 1912.

The club golf course continued to flourish. Debutante balls were still held in the graceful, oval ballroom. But by 1920 many of the members had moved from the fine old sections near the business district out to Shadyside, Broadacres, or Montrose. Instead of moving toward the club they were moving away from it. The club was quietly dying.

As club president, Hugo Neuhaus – the "Baron" – persuaded the members to build a swimming pool. With his superb taste, he ordered one as elegant as a Roman bath. Harry Lindeburg designed a pillared loggia with green glazed woodwork. Pink sand for the plaster was brought from Spain. The water was cold. It revitalized the club. Children spent every summer day there, and adults gave evening parties in the loggia. In merry moments, young adults sometimes pushed well-dressed friends into the water.

Unfortunately, with his superb taste Baron Neuhaus also ran way over the pool budget. It was quite a while before the members realized that the lure of the swimming pool had prolonged the life of the club on that site for another thirty-five years.

Meanwhile, a more exclusive club was being formed. Every autumn, hundreds of thousands of ducks and geese arrived from Canada to winter on the Gulf Coast. In June, 1920, Houston's most exclusive private club was chartered—the Eagle Lake Rod and Gun Club. The members leased 1,475 acres of Eagle Lake. They bought three acres on shore for the clubhouse and moved in a frame building that had been a small-town hotel.

There was nothing glamorous about it. Houston had and has more posh clubs that cost more to join. But from the start, the Eagle Lake Rod and Gun Club has been the bastion of Old Houston. It gives its members a unique sense of privilege. It stirs unholy envy in those just close enough to know about the club but with no hope of entry.

Under its rules, a new man enters only upon the death of a member. His son has priority, but a second son has no hope of joining unless some other member's son waives his claim. For instance, Bill Carter could inherit the membership of W. T. Carter, Jr., but his younger brother Victor had to wait for an opening and then take his chances against other second sons. In his eighties, Camille Pillot insisted that younger Houstonians shook hands with him to feel his pulse in hopes that his membership would soon be open.

Fathers could, however, take their little boys along. In those flexible, easy-going days, a westbound train of the Southern Pacific Railroad would drop off a shooting party at Eagle Lake on Friday evenings, to be picked up again by the eastbound train on Sunday. James A. Baker III remembers from his boyhood the cold autumn weekends when his father took him duck hunting at Eagle Lake.

In the clubhouse, rooms flank the upstairs and downstairs corridors leading to a screened porch. White-painted iron beds have white bedspreads. The baths have clawfoot tubs and heaps of white terrycloth towels. The clubhouse has one new room. Because the members had nowhere to play cards or dominoes, Hugo Neuhaus, as president, built a common room with a big open fireplace. Again, his good taste carried him

over the budget. The members were rather vexed by the cost, but in cold, duck-hunting weather, they grew to appreciate the log fireplace.

Out of season, wives and children were allowed. Kate Neuhaus liked a room near the screened porch. Mrs. John T. Crotty and her daughter Betty (Mrs. Victor Carter) liked to take early morning walks. Spreading shade trees frame the view of the lake from the porch. With ceiling fans turning, it is a pleasant place to read or to watch the roseate spoonbills flying by. The staff provides old-fashioned, southern country meals for the hungry and brings lemonade and iced tea to the thirsty. But the Southern Pacific Railroad no longer stops for shooting parties.

Tall, handsome, and exceptionally well-dressed, Jesse Jones was an attractive escort for some of Houston's loveliest young women. Society took note when he was seen frequently at the symphony concerts with Laura Rice, elegant in her furs in the winter or carrying violets in the spring. She, however, married Richard Neff.

Then, at forty-six, Jesse Jones married Mary Gibbs Jones, formerly the wife of his cousin Will, in a ceremony at the residence of her son Tilford in December, 1920.[2] Until the Lamar Hotel was built, they had a suite at the Rice Hotel. Mr. Jones kept two Pierce-Arrow automobiles parked on Texas Avenue. In that way he always had one ready for a friend who might need it. Every day at noon, a Rice Hotel waiter brought luncheon to his office. His friend Will Hobby lunched with him there almost every week.

When their mother had died in Dallas, Mrs. Howard Hughes had become a mother to her two much younger sisters, Annette and Martha Gano. Between school and travel, the Gano girls came to feel more at home in Houston than in Dallas. Annette Gano, who had finished Wellesley in 1911 at the age of sixteen, went to France after the war to run a YWCA canteen. On her return to Houston she met Dr. Fred Lummis, who also had just come back from France. Several years later, they were married. Martha Gano was graduated from the University of Chicago in 1913. Her marriage to James P. (Pat) Houstoun completed the family move to Houston.[3] With the early death of Mrs. Howard Hughes, and with Mr. Hughes as often on the West Coast as in Houston, Dr. and Mrs. Lummis began to provide the home for the younger Howard Hughes that his peripatetic father could not provide.

After graduation from Rice Institute, Adelaide Lovett went to Paris to study at the Sorbonne. Her mother, Mrs. Edgar Odell Lovett, went with her. After earning her *diplome de la Sorbonne* in 1922, Adelaide came back to Houston and married W. Browne Baker, son of Capt. and Mrs. James A. Baker.

Rice Institute accepted women as students, but the dormitories were for men only. There were no reading rooms and the library in Lovett Hall was small. For the institute's first thirty-seven years, until Fondren Library was built in 1949, women had to sit in staircase windows or in unused classrooms to study. The Rev. Mr. Harris Masterson saw the need for a gathering place for students. When James Lockhart Autry died in 1920, his family wanted to give a memorial in his name. With their gift, Fr. Masterson built a community house for Rice students across Main Street from the campus. It was designed by Cram and Ferguson and William Ward Watkin to blend with the institute's Mediterranean architecture. Autry House opened in 1921.

Early in 1923, several young women felt they should do something worthwhile with their time. Up-to-date flappers, they wore their hair bobbed, their waistlines across the hips, their hems at mid-calf. But they had been bred in families that had always served the community and they expected to serve in their turn.

Fifteen women met in January, 1923, and founded the Blue Bird Circle, naming it after Maeterlink's bluebird of happiness. Mrs. Calvin Garwood was elected president. The other founders were Mrs. James R. Bailey, Mrs. John B. Bethany, Mrs. Vance Morton, Mrs. E. L. Crain, Mrs. P. F. Graves, Mrs. Norman Pillot, Mrs. A. Frank Smith, Mrs. Ralph Graves, Mrs. Roy Brand, Mrs. Perryman Moore, Mrs. J. Thad Scott, Mrs. James H. Park, Jr., Miss Carrie Scott, and Miss Annie Bess Moore.

The Blue Birds set out to raise money. They presented Jacques Abrams, who at age five was already recognized as a gifted artist. They gave bazaars. They gave all-day yachting parties aboard Camille Pillot's yacht. For a dollar and a half, you could cruise from the Houston Yacht Club at Harrisburg to the San Jacinto Battleground and there dine on barbecued chicken and salad sent from the Henke and Pillot store at Milam and Congress. Soon the Blue Birds were hemming cup towels. Their cup towels became famous in those pre-dishwasher days; restaurant owners bought them in large lots.

The circle was non-denominational and grew rapidly. Members volunteered at a day nursery for the children of working mothers. They helped to provide housing for single girls. But the Blue Birds were yet to find the cause to which they would give their best efforts.[4]

In 1920, the Houston zoo had an odd beginning. The U.S. government, thinning out the bison herds in national parks, gave Houston a bison. Named Earl, he was put in Sam Houston Park. The city bought a female companion but she was not long for this world of city life. The Camp Street Fishing Club donated a deer. Somebody bought a lion from a circus. The fear of hoof and mouth disease slowed the zoo's growth, but in January, 1925, it was moved to a thirty-four-acre site in Hermann Park. It had about four hundred mammals, three hundred birds, and one hundred reptiles and was named the Houston Zoological Gardens.

In 1924, twelve young Houstonians met in the house of Mrs. Luke C. Bradley to hear about the new national movement known as the Junior League. Its purpose was to en-

The *Augusta*, Camille Pillot's yacht, was 103 feet long, paneled with Honduras mahogany. *Cour-* *tesy George Fuermann City of Houston Collection, Special Collections, University of Houston Libraries*

able young women of education and privilege to learn how to serve the community wisely. It provided training for intelligent philanthropy. The Houston founders that day were Adelaide Lovett, Frankie Carter, Mary Porter Vandevoort, Lottie Rice, Elizabeth Godwin, Nora Cleveland, Ella Rice, Patty Lummis, Margaret Cullinan, Mary Cullinan, Rebecca Saunders, and Virgilia Chew.[5]

Enlisting thirty charter members, the Junior League decided to open a luncheon club downtown to raise money. Fathers, husbands, and beaux warned them they would never make a profit by serving only one meal a day. But the W. T. Carter Lumber Company owned the old Houston Lighting and Power Building on San Jacinto and Capital. W. T. Carter, Jr., let them use the basement. They donned aprons and became waitresses; the fathers and beaux who

had scoffed became part of their regular luncheon crowd. Society editors began to report on who was seen dining at the Junior League Luncheon Club.

Houston was enjoying the finest concert artists of the day, brought to town by Edna Saunders. After producing the free concerts of wartime, Mrs. Saunders turned to professional management in 1917. Backed by Houston civic leaders, she brought such artists as Rachmaninoff, Schumann-Heink, Jascha Heifetz, Tetrazini, Pavlova, Galli Curci, Fritz Kreisler, Chaliapin, and Mary Garden. Houston gave Caruso one of the largest audiences of his career. The city glowingly welcomed Ignace Jan Paderewski when he came back to play after a thirty-year absence.

Mrs. Saunders also imported the Chicago Grand Opera, the Scotti Grand Opera Company, the New York, Cincinnati, Minneapolis, and St. Louis orchestras. She achieved all this in the first four years of what was to be a long career as entrepreneur.

Well-to-do Houstonians—like the Jesse Andrewses and various branches of the Masterson family—often took the whole family to New York by train to enjoy a satisfying round of theater and opera. Before and after World War I, famous actors brought touring companies to Houston—Joe Jefferson, Otis Skinner, Maude Adams, Sothern, and Marlowe. But none of this quenched the local thirst for amateur theatricals. In every generation, proper Houstonians liked to act in their own shows. After the war, four amateur companies sprang up.

Founded by Mrs. March Culmore and Eugene Pillot, the Little Theatre got off to a false start in 1919. Mrs. Culmore had studied at the Academy of Dramatic Art in New York and at the University of Chicago's Department of Oration. In Houston, she staged historical pageants with casts of from three to eighteen hundred people. Pillot, grandson of the widely traveled Eugene Pillot, had studied at the New York School of Fine and Applied Arts, the University of Texas, Cornell, and Harvard, where he wrote his first plays. The *New Encyclopedia of Texas,* circa 1924, lists him as a talented playwright and Mrs. Culmore as drama teacher and owner of "one of the most palatial homes in Houston."[6] But by 1924,

their Little Theatre seemingly had vanished.

In 1919 and 1921, there was an active amateur theater movement, traced by Sue Dauphin in *Houston by Stages*. Jackson Purdy was a young actor with the Red Lantern Players who put on plays in the Heights. His family owned the lot and lumber yard at Yale and Fifth streets, enabling the Players to have their own theater. To float the Green Mask Players for a season, fifty Houstonians put up twenty-five dollars each. Season tickets sold for ten dollars; plays were staged at South End Junior High School. When the Rice Dramatic Club was formed in 1921, with Dr. J. W. Slaughter as producer, it dominated the amateur stage for the next several years. Reborn in 1925, the Little Theatre drew on the talent of all the earlier groups to achieve a long and successful run.[7]

Meanwhile, March Culmore, listed by the *New Encyclopedia* as a capitalist and vice-president of the Second National Bank, was a favorite of Houston youngsters. He had a bicycle shop on Main Street at Jefferson. So many of his clients recall that he fixed their bicycles without charge that it raises a question: Was the bicycle shop something he did for fun rather than for income? Ultimately he owned the entire block on Main Street and at his death willed $4 million to the Texas Medical Center. His bequest built a residency hall for interns and residents.

Chapter Forty-One

An Elegant Southern Town

IN THE FIRST YEARS after the war, Houston was the Magnolia City—a Southern town, smaller than Dallas, San Antonio, or Birmingham, Alabama. But it knew how to be elegant.

In 1920, planning a private golf club, Thomas H. Ball, Kenneth Womack, and William Stamps Farish went out into the country west of Montrose to buy 180 acres of wooded land and founded River Oaks Country Club Estates. Members would be allowed to buy lots south of the golf course. To design the clubhouse, they commissioned the young architect John Staub, who had come down from New York to supervise construction of the Womack and Farish houses in Shadyside. They paved the main street leading from Westheimer to the club and named it Ball Boulevard—later River Oaks Boulevard.

Will and Sue Clayton, while content with Caroline Boulevard as their home, saw this as an ideal country place. Mrs. Clayton's concern was for her four daughters and four nieces. By moving them to the country each summer, she could keep them safely out of automobiles during their vacations from school or camp. Mr. Clayton became a charter member of the club and bought a large lot.

Again calling on Birdsall Briscoe as architect, the Claytons started the first house in River Oaks. Resembling Mount Vernon, it faced the golf course. It was a country house with two big upstairs sleeping porches. Curving covered walkways led to a detached kitchen and a detached screened porch. It had a swimming pool and a tennis court.[1]

All this took stamina. Inwood Drive had not been cut through. Westheimer was paved only with oyster shells. The Claytons had to make their way across muddy terrain to check on progress. They were often out of town and once came home to find the chimneys in the wrong place. They had to be torn down, delaying completion.[2]

At that stage, River Oaks was meant to be no more than a club flanked by a few weekend homes. It was in no sense one of Houston's residential sections. *They* were all within three miles of Main Street and Texas Avenue. The Rice Hotel and the Beaconsfield Apartments were prestigious addresses. Some of Houston's nicest houses stood along Texas Avenue and McKinney. At about the time River Oaks was being laid out, Mrs. Arthur Hamilton was adding on to the big Hamilton house at McKinney and LaBranch. It already had a ballroom on the third floor, but she added a sun parlor, another bedroom and bath, and a set of back stairs and had a basement dug under the house for a furnace to provide its first central heat.

The mansions that flanked Main Street at Gray were in their prime. Christ Church, the First Presbyterian Church, and the First Methodist Church were all within an easy walk from home for many churchgoers. Some pioneers had taken a big leap when they moved out to Courtlandt Place or Montrose Boulevard. In fact, River Oaks was not very far from the downtown, but because no roads led to it, it seemed remote.

When River Oaks Country Club Estates opened, Will and Sue Clayton were the first to start building a house, their country place and summer ref-uge. Remodeled for year-round use, it became the home of Maurice and Susan Clayton McAshan. *Photograph by Roger Powers*

To most Houstonians, a move to River Oaks in 1922 would have been comparable to a 1975 move from River Oaks to the Woodlands.

Rice Institute served as a pivot, gathering around it a cluster of gracious residential neighborhoods. Hermann Park lay on its southeastern flank. The plan to build a Houston Museum of Fine Arts nearby enhanced the sense that this was, as the Houston *Gargoyle* called it, Houston's "cradle of culture."

New subdivisions and suburbs began to encircle Rice Institute. All of them were started by men who were successful in their professions and leaders in the community. They were the kind who gave developers a good name.

Though the Great War had delayed further building in Joseph Cullinan's thirty-seven-acre enclave, his house at Number 2 Remington Lane was completed by 1919.[3]

Designed by St. Louis architect James P. Jamieson, it was a mansion in the seventeenth-century English style. Surrounded by five acres of land, with a tennis court and stables, it was named Shadyside and gave its name to the entire enclave. Joseph Cullinan was a handsome, magnetic man. Mrs. Cullinan had great charm and was a gracious hostess. The big Shadyside attracted interesting visitors, ranging from Herbert Hoover, famous for his work with feeding wartorn Europe, to explorer Lincoln Steffeson. The children's favorite visitor was A. E., the Irish painter, poet, and member of the Irish Republican Army.

Cullinan had set aside Lot Q for his good friend Will Hogg, and Mr. Hogg went so far as to have Jamieson prepare preliminary drawings of a house for his brother Mike, his sister, and himself. He then went off to Europe on one of his prolonged tours without having confirmed his intention of buying. Cullinan therefore sold the lot to William Stamps Farish.[4] Farish, Hugo Neuhaus, and Kenneth E. Womack all turned to the famous architect of New York country houses, Harrie T. Lindeberg. And Lindeberg, in turn, persuaded his gifted young associate, John Staub, to come to Houston to take charge. With a master's degree in architecture from MIT, a Navy Cross for having been the first navy pilot to sink a U-boat, and an unusually charming wife, the personable John Staub was immediately taken into the innermost circles of Old Houston society.[5]

By 1921, the Cullinans' Shadyside had begun to acquire neighbors. The first of Lindeberg's Houston houses was designed for Hugo Neuhaus at 9 Remington Lane. It is an exceedingly handsome "cottage" with what was known as "the Lindeberg roof"—layers of closely-lapped, irregularly laid shingles that give the impression of thatch. While the house was being completed in 1923, the Neuhaus family put up in the guest rooms at the Houston Country Club—as other Houstonians did before and after.

"We had the run of the club," Hugo Neuhaus, Jr., recalled. "We had our meals in the dining room. When big parties were held, we ate on trays upstairs. My sister loved to write plays. We subjected the club members to our plays from time to time."

The Lykes Bros. Steamship Company had been founded in Galveston by the seven Lykes brothers and now had offices scattered from New Orleans to England and Germany. It ran ships to Cuba, Puerto Rico, Venezuela, and Central America. Because of the growing importance of the Houston Ship Channel, James McKay Lykes opened an office in Houston in 1923.[6] He brought his wife Genevieve up from Galveston to choose where they should live.

The great trees of Shadyside captivated the whole family. When they moved into Number 12 Remington Lane, Mrs. Lykes found a tub holding five dozen roses from the garden of Mrs. Hugo Neuhaus. The card

read, "From one mother of five to another." In her autobiography, Mrs. Lykes recalled that they found "a neighborhood lively with children, the Crottys, Wiesses, Cullinans, Heitmanns, Blaffers, Farishes, Womacks, and the Stude family."

Soon after the move, Frederica went off to Smith College and Buddy to school in Virginia. Vevie and Charlie were enrolled in Kinkaid. Small Dick went to Poe Elementary—"the new model public school." Their parents took up golf at Houston and River Oaks clubs. They joined the Paul Jones. Mrs. Lykes joined Assembly and served on the Museum of Fine Arts board. Jim Lykes joined the Eagle Lake Rod and Gun Club. The Lykeses had settled in to become a part of Old Houston, and the start of generations of Lykeses in the city.

The Lykes Bros. move brought business to the Port of Houston. The company bought the Daniel Ripley Steamship Company, which ran freighters to the North Atlantic, and the Tampa Interocean Steamship Company with service to the South Atlantic—Spain, Portugal, North Africa, and the Western Mediterranean. The Lykes family could offer their friends delightful cruises to countless ports of call in the easy days between world wars.

Shadyside, West University Place, Courtlandt Place, and Montrose, all begun before the war, spurred the postwar growth of other pleasant sections near the Museum of Fine Arts.[7] Former governor Ross Sterling developed Rossmoyne. Will, Ima, and Mike Hogg lived there until 1927, as did the Frank Sterlings until they built the great mansion on South Boulevard.

In 1920, architect J. W. Northrop, Jr., laid out West Eleventh Place, a narrow lane off the still unpaved County Road, soon renamed Bissonnet. He designed four of its seven houses. Starting in 1922, banker John T. Scott, with Mrs. James L. Autry and James Shelton, developed Waverly Court. Each of these cul-de-sacs ended in a small circle. Several of Scott's children built houses on Waverly; his son-in-law, James Ruskin

The old rectory of Christ Church Cathedral stood on the corner and the street was paved with wooden blocks when this picture was made in 1926. Of Houston's first churches, only this Episcopal church occupies the site it has held since the days of the Republic. *Courtesy Christ Church Cathedral*

Bailey, designed two of them. Waverly would receive its last addition in 1952 when Mr. and Mrs. S. I. Morris built the house at Number 2 designed by Wilson, Morris and Crain, architects.

Attorney John Crooker laid out the much larger circle of Shadowlawn off Bissonnet, building his own home on half of the two-acre island in the center, with Northrop as architect.[8] Shadowlawn grew at a leisurely pace over the next decades, but was consistently blessed with the work of outstanding architects: Harrie T. Lindeberg, John Staub, Maurice J. Sullivan, William Ward Watkin, H. A. Salisbury, and, after World War II, Howard Barnstone and Anderson Todd.

Johnny Crooker and his friends played sandlot baseball and basketball on the Museum of Fine Arts lawn.[9] "As I remember, Shadowlawn was paved with curbs and gutters," Crooker said. "Bissonnet was paved out two or three blocks to the west of us, and was still known officially as County Road or more familiarly as Poor Farm Road because it led to the county poor farm several miles west."

In the spring of 1923, attorney James A. Baker, Jr., announced the opening of Broadacres.[10] William Ward Watkin planned the thirty-four acre subdivision with twenty-five large lots, a park, and a tennis court. H. E. Kipp was engineering consultant. This was bald prairie. Young Ellen Hamilton (Mrs. Edward Wilkerson) often rode out from her home on McKinney to Montrose, where her mother's friend Peggy Dickson lived, and the two would take a pleasant canter across the unmarked plain.[11]

Baker had already built a house on Poor Farm Road that backed up to the prairie and assumed that he would move over into Broadacres as it grew. But the first home was too pleasant to leave. He and his son Jimmy often slept on the upstairs sleeping porch and could hear the lions roaring in the Hermann Park Zoo. As he grew into his teens, Jimmy Baker could bicycle to the River Oaks Country Club along Kirby Drive. "It was a shell road in those days," Secretary of State Baker recalled. His mother was still living in the gracious house sixty years later.

W. Browne Baker and his wife Adelaide built on Berthea. So did Adelaide's brother Malcolm Lovett and his wife Martha. Berthea was a cul-de-sac ending at the Broad-acres tennis court park. There Browne Baker, Jr., Lovett Baker, and their sister Graeme grew up, as did the Lovett children – Malcolm, Jr., Mary Hale, Eliza, and Edgar Odell Lovett II.

Looking across the flat prairie, Mrs. Palmer Hutcheson chose the lot on North Boulevard that had a single huisache tree growing on it. This huisache tree had always been used to tie up horses by young men riding out from town to shoot prairie chickens. Eleanor Hutcheson and Madeline Staub were friends, and the Hutchesons asked John Staub to design their house. This was the first house that Staub designed on his own in Houston. His work of the next forty years would lend elegance to Houston's loveliest neighborhoods, to its most exclusive country clubs, and to such public buildings as the first Junior League Building, Lamar High School, Reagan High School, Rice University's Fondren Library, and the University of Houston's M. D. Anderson Library.

Brian Brewster Gilmer and his wife Edna Daffan Gilmer employed William Ward Watkin. They postponed building so that he could travel to Spain to study Spanish architecture before designing their Mediterranean-style place with its tiled patio and enclosed garden. Alfred C. Finn, the architect for so many Montrose Boulevard mansions, designed the largest and most expensive house in Broadacres – Frank P. Sterling's.[12]

David Red and other architects designed houses in Broadacres. But Birdsall Briscoe, descended from the John Harris who founded Harrisburg, and John Staub, newcomer, divided most of Broadacres between them – as they did Shadyside and early River Oaks. Staub designed houses for Joseph A. Tennant, C. Milby Dow, William S. Cochran, and Rudolph C. Kuldell. Briscoe (sometimes as Briscoe & Dixon) designed houses for Edmond Pincoff, Jemison E. Lester, Robert W. Wier, William D. Cleveland, Walter H. Walne, Clarence Carter, and Mrs. Frank Anderson.

Frank Anderson, the first Anderson to enter the cotton business in Oklahoma territory, died in Oklahoma City of a ruptured appendix in 1924. After three years, Burdine Clayton Anderson saw that she had more family in Houston than in Oklahoma – her son Leland, her brothers Will and Ben Clayton, and her brother-in-law, M. D. Anderson. In 1928, she moved to Houston, bringing her two youngest sons, Tommy and Ben.

Tom Anderson went off to prep school in Virginia and then to Washington and Lee. But Ben settled into Broadacres where he found Walter Walne, Jr., Billy Cochran, Borden and Joe Tennant to play with and could bicycle to the new Sidney Lanier Junior High School.[13]

Burdine Anderson was quite as remarkable as her brothers. She, too, was born near Tupelo, Mississippi, and reared in Jackson, Tennessee. At fifteen she taught school. All her life she played the piano and organ for her own pleasure and in family chamber music. While living in Oklahoma City – the mother of six sons – she drove to Norman three days a week to study French and Italian.[14] She later translated books into Italian.

On arriving in Houston, Mrs. Anderson chose the wide-open space of South Boulevard for her home because she thought that it would be cooler in summer with no trees to block the gulf breeze. Designed by Birdsall Briscoe, the house she built remained one of Houston's most beautiful and gracious mansions. But the treelessness did not last.

The esplanades on North and South boulevards are fifty-three feet wide, each with a brick walkway down the center. Live oak trees were planted on both sides of the boulevards and in staggered double lines in the esplanades. As they grew to meet overhead, Broadacres became so attractive to birds that bird watchers stalked it regularly.

By this time, Hermann Park, started with George Hermann's 278 acres, had acquired another 111. Will Hogg bought the tract to tempt the University of Texas Medical

School to move up from Galveston. Failing, he let the city have it for the price he had paid.[15] The Miller Outdoor Theater, designed by William Ward Watkin and built on the bequest of Jesse Wright Miller, opened in 1923. The *Houston Press* called it "the first of its sort in Texas." Bridle paths throughout the park attracted Houstonians who rode or exercised their horses every morning.

Southampton Place, begun by E. H. Fleming in 1922, covered 160 acres and was defined by Rice Boulevard and Bissonnet. It banned apartments and duplexes and set a floor on building costs of from twelve thousand to fifteen thousand dollars on Rice Boulevard and eight thousand to ten thousand on Sunset. Houston promptly annexed it. Polly Pollard Marsters, who grew up in Southhampton in the 1930s, remembered that Greenbriar was not an all-weather road and that every spring, wildflowers covered the open fields lying between Greenbriar and the town of West University Place.

H. Birdsall Masterson developed the Cherokee Addition on Mandell and Cherokee between Bissonnet and Sunset. A part of the Obedience Smith survey and once a tree nursery, the addition was shaded by tall trees. Masterson had his own home on the corner of Mandell and Sunset and built a house a few doors down as a gift to the Episcopal Diocese for the use of Bishop and Mrs. Clinton Quin.

Across Mandell from the Mastersons, a Rice professor and his wife built a low, brownish red house that held Houston's interest for years. Austin Mardon was British, his wife American, and they had met at Oxford. From families of wealth, they had traveled extensively in Europe and Africa. They owned homes in England and the Canary Islands. They believed in simplicity and sunshine. Their house was built around a swimming pool. They dressed their small children in the simplest of cotton playsuits that looked to the proper Houstonians of the time like underwear. Except for those who

knew them, the Mardons were thought of as "those nudists."

"It was a biblical house in the Arab fashion," said Mrs. Larry W. Morris, their neighbor. "It had one big square room on top filled with books that was reached by an outside staircase. They had nine children under the age of twelve, and each child had a small room that opened toward the pool. The house had eighteen outside doors and none inside—just archways. The main room was twenty by forty feet. It was a wonderful house for parties. They made such wise use of their space. The house opened on the side and they had a tennis court in front. The garden was beautiful, with rose trees as high as your head. It all made so much more sense than the houses the rest of us were building."

Because so many new subdivisions in southwest Houston were being offered almost simultaneously in the booming 1920s, each one grew slowly, lot by lot, house by house, no two alike. The children in most of these sections went to Poe School, Lanier Junior High School, and, after 1935, Lamar High School. Some went to Kinkaid.

Meanwhile, E. L. Crain was busy surrounding Houston with new suburbs.[16] In October, 1923, the county auctioned off the County Poor Farm. Crain, who had already developed Cherryhurst, bought a large parcel of the treeless, marshy land south of Bellaire Boulevard.[17] He laid out a new subdivision named Southside Place, and offered houses to go on the lots. Although still engaged in banking, Crain enjoyed the real estate business.

E. L. Crain's Ready-Cut House Company was a successful forerunner of Levittown—an idea that would be hailed as new and original twenty-five years later. The catalogue showed pictures of the Colonial Bungalow, the English Bungalow, and the Spanish Bungalow. All the parts of a Crain house—windows, door frames, and cabinets—were made at the factory. Everything needed to complete the house, including the proper number of rolls of wallpaper, was delivered to the site. The building crew was optional. The Colonial Bungalow, an impressive two-story house with six white Greek Revival pillars across the front, sold for $9,000. The one-story Spanish bungalow for $7,750.

As he did in all his subdivisions, Crain first built a park with a large swimming pool and playground. He laid concrete sidewalks and graveled streets. On the recommendation of Edward Teas, Houston's leading nurseryman, he planted hundreds of Chinese tallows, as well as a fig tree and a Radiant Red rose bush behind each house. Deed restrictions not only called for brick, stucco, or stone for houses on Bellaire, Farbar, and Garnet, but provided that "no spirituous, vinous or malt liquors or medicated bitters capable of producing intoxication shall ever be sold, or offered for sale, on said premises."

Through his Ready-Cut House Company, Crain developed Pinehurst, Cherryhurst, Southside Place, and Garden Oaks —each with its park, each a planned community.

Neill T. Masterson was busy opening up the Rio Grande Valley for irrigated farming.[18] He ran excursion trains from Chicago through Kansas City to Houston and on to Harlingen to show farmers the valley's magnificent citrus orchards and endless fields of vegetables. A contemporary account read, "Even the far-famed delta of the Nile, the ultra rich section of tropical Mexico, India and Brazil, have no better soils than those found in . . . the Magic Valley of the lower Rio Grande."

As a little boy, Harris Masterson III got to go along on some of his father's excursions. He recalls that everything was done to make the trip special for the potential clients. " They'd have a barbecue down at the old MKT Station under the viaduct and then they'd take them on the train down to Brownsville. They'd take them across to Mexico at Matamoras for an evening." They even had a trained valet and masseur aboard, a man who had a diamond in his front tooth.

In the long history of the valley, Neill Masterson deserves credit as its enterpreneur. But high taxes on water, along with other problems, cost him his fortune. Retrenching, Mrs. Masterson was worried about the future of Clifton Lockhart, who had meant so much to the family for so long. Lockhart was the Mastersons' factotum. He was also young Harris's best friend. Harris had been best man at Lockhart's wedding.

Mrs. Masterson called Mrs. Jesse Jones and said, "Mary, I am going to do you the biggest favor of your life. I am going to let you have Clifton." (Clifton Lockhart finished his career with the Jesse Joneses at the Lamar Hotel, with one notable exception: When Harris Masterson and Carroll Sterling Cowan were to be married, Lockhart took the day off to drive them to Christ Church— despite the fact that Gen. George Marshall was that day the luncheon guest of Mr. and Mrs. Jones in their Lamar Hotel penthouse.)

The sleek fire horses that had so long delighted the city as they galloped to a blaze were retired by 1924, symbolizing the start of a new, swifter era. Houston was gaining impetus in what seemed to be an unending boom. It had mastered the art of growth by annexation.

The River Oaks Plan Matures

IN 1923, while out riding through the woods on the old Hanna homestead near the new River Oaks Country Club, Mike Hogg and Hugh Potter realized that this beautifully wooded land could be developed into a residential section. They took an option on two hundred acres.[1]

"Then Will Hogg blew in on one of his periodic visits," Hugh Potter recalled in a 1928 interview. Typically, Will Hogg thought in far bigger scale: "Why stop at two hundred acres? Why not buy out the country club? Make this thing something really big, something the city can be proud of?"

In early 1924, Hogg Brothers, Inc., began to buy all unreserved lots within the development and then to buy more to the east, south, and west. Because slums stood between the club and downtown Houston, land sold for as little as five hundred dollars an acre when they began. But as word of the grand plan leaked, prices soared to six thousand an acre. By May, 1924, they had acquired eleven hundred acres.

Will Hogg consulted Herbert Hare, who had studied landscape architecture and city planning at Harvard, and J. C. Nichols, who had built Kansas City's Country Club Plaza, the first big shopping center in the United States. The River Oaks master plan included esplanades planted with flowers (thirty-five thousand rose bushes), a fifteen-acre campus for River Oaks Elementary School, and two shopping centers, one at the end of River Oaks Boulevard and one on West Gray.

Shadyside had only large lots meant for mansions, but the River Oaks plan included large and small lots, and set a seven-thousand-dollar floor on building costs. It also called for the River Oaks Garden Apartments—128 apartments set in ten acres at Shepherd and West Gray. The River Oaks Will Hogg envisioned would be a model that would enhance city planning and city beauty. The concept was not unlike that of the Woodlands fifty years later.[2]

As a golf club, River Oaks had caught on quickly. But as a place to live, it seemed remote to most Houstonians. Though the Hogg brothers commissioned John Staub and Birdsall Briscoe to design a few speculative houses, all of which sold, most well-to-do Houstonians lived downtown or in the south end near Rice Institute. River Oaks was too country. It was too far from the downtown shops, restaurants, theaters, and churches. As for golf, they already had the Houston Country Club and the new Hermann Park golf course. The Glenbrook and Golfcrest clubs opened in 1924. At all five courses, women golfers teed off at hours when most men were at the office, store, or plant.

Will, Ima, and Mike Hogg, however, were committed to River Oaks. Because Will was involved in far-flung business enterprises and Mike was entering state politics, they left the building of the family house to their sister. Their fourteen-acre site had to be cleared of brambles and brush to reveal the towering old trees. Because Buffalo Bayou curves around two sides of the property, Miss Hogg named it Bayou Bend. She and John Staub worked together in designing the twenty-two-room mansion that was to be the Hogg family home. Between them, they invented a style of architecture they called Latin Colonial. The bachelor quarters for Will and Mike in the east wing had a kitchen, library, tap room, and small gymnasium. Sharing Ima Hogg's love for antique furniture, Staub shaped his colors and proportions to enhance her growing collection. And, of course, she had one grand piano downstairs, another in her own upstairs parlor. In 1926, Bayou Bend was finished and the gardens were beginning to take shape.

The first gardens were designed by Ellen Shipman of New York. Miss Hogg kept precise records of what seeds and plants were planted and how each fared. Ruth Landen succeeded Shipman. But it took the young landscape architect C. Pat Fleming to see that the gardens of Bayou Bend were too enclosed by thickets, that great avenues must be opened to give the gardens breezeways and free them of mosquitoes.[3] The partnership between Fleming and Ima Hogg created the vistas and sites for the sculptures she bought on her travels abroad. It led to the creation of the Diana Garden.

Characteristically, Will Hogg believed that the whole city could be beautiful. He bought the little red brick school house that had stood on Westheimer Road since 1910. Architects Birdsall Briscoe, John Staub, and J. W. Northrop painted the bricks white and remodeled it along lines of a New England town hall. The auditorium could seat three hundred people.

This was Will Hogg's Forum of Civics, chartered "for the betterment and beautification of the City of Houston and County of Harris, especially in respect to the present planning and future development of the City and County as interdependent communities. . . ." Houston's best citizens hurried to join. The executive board included A. C. Ford, Dr. Stockton Axson, James A.

Baker, Sr., Norman Atkinson, S. R. Bertron, Jr., and A. E. Amerman. However, Hogg's vision of a well-planned city was never realized.

Almost everyone, Hogg reasoned, could afford flower seeds, but there were no books to help gardeners cope with the Gulf Coast climate and soils. He persuaded Mrs. Cleveland Sewall and Mrs. Card G. Elliot to write a book and the Forum of Civics published the first *Garden Book for Houston*.

Not all Houstonians clung to city living. The John F. Grants had lived at the Savoy and at the Beaconsfield for almost ten years when they bought a lot in Shadyside and called upon Birdsall Briscoe to design a house. But while the house was still in the design stage, they decided to build it on their farm instead.[4]

The Grants' farm of fifty-two wooded acres was southwest of Houston, beyond Hermann Park. Main Street paving dwindled to gravel at Bellaire Boulevard, and Fannin stopped entirely at Eagle. But the Grants built the Briscoe house, dammed up a tributary of Bray's Bayou to make a swimming pool, laid out a tennis court, and acquired a horse for Carolyn, white Peking ducks, a goat, a cow, and a loon. Mr. Grant, who enjoyed animals, chose to use peacocks as guard dogs. He also enjoyed experimenting with plants. Captivated by the lavish color of the gardens in Charleston, South Carolina, he brought the first azaleas to Houston. It was he who introduced them to Miss Ima Hogg, who found that they flourished in the shade of Bayou Bend.

The Grants' house looked out on the virgin forest of Hermann Park.[5] As she approached her teens, Carolyn Grant had to be driven in to Kinkaid School from the country place. In 1987, Carolyn (Mrs. Ernest Bel Fay) gave to the Texas Medical Center the land on which the house stood to be the Grant/Fay Park. In the shadow of skyscrapers, the rolling lawn is an oasis of greenery across Holcombe Boulevard from the M. D. Anderson Hospital.[6]

Clare Knowles Fleming, wife of Lamar Fleming, Jr. *Courtesy Clare Fleming Sprunt (Mrs. Sam Sprunt)*

aware that it was preparing them for navy duty in a war that was never supposed to come. Carolyn Grant often had Alice Evans, Mildred Wood, and other friends out to her home in the forest, and Albert and Ernie came to play tennis and a swim.[7]

The Will Claytons welcomed the arrival from England of young Mr. and Mrs. Lamar Fleming, Jr., and their two small boys.[8] Sent to represent Anderson, Clayton in Europe in 1913 and serving as army liaison officer to the Italians during the war, Lamar Fleming had had nine years in Italy and two in England. Now almost grown up, Ellen and Susan Clayton remembered him as the eighteen-year-old "Uncle Lamar" who had taken them to Charlie Chaplin movies in Oklahoma City. Now Uncle Lamar spoke and wrote Italian fluently, French and German almost as well, and had a stunningly beautiful English wife.

Clare Knowles, born in Cheshire, met Lamar Fleming, born in Augusta, Georgia, when she was eighteen. Mr. Clayton and his young colleague were in England on business. "My mother's father did not usually invite businessmen to his home." Clare Fleming Sprunt said. "But because Mr. Clayton was so nice, he invited him to come and bring that young man along with him. For my mother, it was one of those first-sight things." After further meetings and many love letters, they were married at Hillbry Point, her home in Cheshire on February 7, 1920. She was not yet twenty, he eight years older.

Houston posed no fears to Clare Fleming. On their honeymoon in Spain, their car had stuck in the snow of the Pyrenees. They heard the howl of wolves and were rescued by hospitable Andorran smugglers. In Milan they had seen the rise of Mussolini. Rolling her baby out for an airing, Mrs. Fleming once found herself facing a startling array of Black Shirts. With Italian charm, they admired the baby and bowed her on her way. Though her family in England could take European dangers calmly, they viewed Houston with alarm. Her father wanted to

Albert and Ernest Fay were in their early teens when their father brought the family to Houston from New Orleans. They lived across the street from Mrs. Walter Sharp and her sons, Bedford and Dudley. The Fays had a sailboat, the *Sorceress,* which they kept at the Houston Yacht Club. With Dudley, they spent long hours in the sailboat, quite unsend her a mongoose to ward off the poisonous rattlesnakes, but was defeated by customs regulations.

In her first fifteen years in Houston, Clare Fleming entertained a stream of foreign visitors, as the far-flung network of Anderson, Clayton sent agents and executives to the company's world headquarters in Houston. They found the big house on Montrose Boulevard furnished in the Italian furniture brought from Milan and a hostess who dressed for dinner each evening.

A tomboy in childhood and a natural athlete who grew up on the golf course, Clare Fleming played bridge and golf in those carefree days before Hitler's *blitzkrieg*. She served her friends English high teas and taught her four small children to ride.[9] After the war that cost the life of her oldest son, she would become a dedicated volunteer in service to the patients at the Houston Tuberculosis, Jefferson Davis, and M. D. Anderson hospitals. Lamar Fleming would become president of Anderson, Clayton & Co., a major civic leader in the cause of educational opportunity, and a generous supporter of half the institutions in the early Texas Medical Center.

Early in the 1920s, the American holly tree was in danger. It was being cut every Christmas in such enormous quantities that it would soon be extinct. Joe Heiser was an accountant and auditor for the Texas Company. From Houston, he started a nationwide letter-writing drive to save the American holly. The campaign prompted laws to protect it, and the holly began a successful comeback. In 1923, Joe Heiser organized the Houston Outdoor Nature Club, the first environmental organization in Texas and the pattern by which many others would be formed.

To adorn ladies' hats, feather hunters had killed off the egret and had apparently driven the roseate spoonbill to extinction. In the 1920s, Joe Heiser discovered six spoonbills breeding on the remote little Vingt-et-une Island on the far side of Galveston Bay. The Outdoor Nature Club rallied forces. Joseph Cullinan, always concerned about birds, joined the fight. They recruited the National Association of Audubon Societies. By 1933, the International Association of Audubon Societies had added its efforts. After a decade of effort, Vingt-et-une Island became a bird sanctuary.

George Williams, Rice University professor emeritus, wrote: "Under protection . . . the Vingt-et-une spoonbills throve, and their descendants spread out to colonize the entire Galveston Bay area and upper Texas coast. Today . . . whenever I see one, a small voice inside me says, 'Thank you, Joe.'"

A Museum, a Park, and an Invitation

In 1923, Texas still had no art museum. But led by Mrs. Henry B. Fall, the Houston Art League had never faltered in its twenty-three-year effort to build one on its triangle of land at Main and Montrose.[1] While working to clear the site and pave sidewalks, the league continued to use the former home of Dr. William Eckhardt at 1806 Main for its exhibitions. In 1920, the members planted seventeen trees on the triangle. In 1922, they laid the cornerstone for the first unit of the proposed museum, and in 1923 they broke ground for construction. The league officers wielding the shovel were Mrs. Fall, Mrs. A. C. Ford, Mrs. A. S. Cleveland, Mrs. Luke D. Bradley, Mrs. J. W. Lockett, Mrs. F. W. Volck, and Mrs. W. S. Farish.

The first unit, built of Indiana limestone, was to be in classic design with Ionic columns. William Ward Watkin was the architect, with Ralph Cram of Boston as consultant. It would cost $140,000. Meanwhile, if the other two wings were to be built in an unbroken flow of construction, the time had come to raise a great deal of money.

In March, 1924, as the first unit neared completion, the businessmen on the board had a contract drawn up providing that a total of $200,000 or more "must be subscribed hereunder by solvent persons and corporations on or before the first day of June 1924 . . . to insure this foundation for the aesthetic unification of the people of our community." If the deadline were not met, all pledges would be nullified. The contract reserved the first fifteen spaces for subscriptions of $5,000 each. The league members formed teams and handed out lists of possible donors.

Mrs. Will Clayton offered to take the name of Will Hogg. "My husband contributed to one of Mr. Hogg's causes last week," she said, "and I am sure he will be willing to contribute to ours." She and Mrs. Joseph Mullen went to Hogg's office, taking the elevator up to the penthouse. When they found him at his desk, looking busy and a bit harassed, they quickly explained their mission.

"I won't give you a red cent!" said that gentleman forcefully.

Tiny and beautiful, Mrs. Clayton drew herself up to a formidable presence. "That, Mr. Hogg, is not the answer you received from my husband last week." She turned and swept out with Mrs. Mullen. They caught the still-open elevator while Hogg was trying to stammer his apology.

Will Hogg had a train to catch. Pressed for time, he had been thoughtless, but he instantly repented. It was not in his character to be rude to a lady. Hastily, before leaving town, he empowered his sister, Ima, to pledge a big donation and left her to repair the damage. Miss Hogg telephoned Mrs. Clayton and did her best, but got nowhere. Mrs. Mullen suggested that they might reconsider; Mrs. Clayton was adamant.

On reaching New York after the long, forty-hour train journey, Will Hogg telephoned Will Clayton. "Will," he said miserably, "I am devastated. I can't eat, I can't sleep, I don't know *what* got into me. I am catching the next train back home. Please

The first in Texas, the Houston Museum of Fine Arts opened on April 12, 1924. This photograph was made on opening day by Frank J. Schlueter.
Courtesy Archives Collection, Museum of Fine Arts

tell Mrs. Clayton that if she'll let me, I'll raise *all* the money for her." Mr. Clayton, the diplomat, asked Mrs. Clayton for her answer. She accepted graciously. And as a result, Will Hogg set out to raise all the money necessary to complete the Houston Museum of Fine Arts.

By April 5, the contract bore thirty-two signatures. On April 12, 1924, with James Chillman as director, the lovely little building facing the Main Street circle opened as the Houston Museum of Fine Arts—the first art museum in Texas. By November, many of the early signers had upped their gifts another $1,000–$2,500.

Newspapers of the day said that the first $90,000 for the new wings had been pledged anonymously by three men to guarantee the success of the fund drive and the building of the wings. Museum archives show that the unnamed donors were Mr. and Mrs. W. L. Clayton, Mr. and Mrs. Joseph Cullinan, and W. C. Hogg. Not only the museum but the Hogg-Clayton friendship was safe.

All kinds of Houstonians contributed. A former league member sent $39 from Chicago. An elderly widow living in a garage apartment sent $2. The Janowaski School gave $7. Several children gave $5 each—Mary Porter Kirkland, Laura Kirkland, Bedford Sharp, D. W. Cooley, and B. F. Carruth among them. Before 1925 ended, the museum treasurer, John T. Scott, could triumphantly report a total of $341,709.68.

As its president for eight lean years, Mrs.

Fall had held the league on course to its goal. Once, to pay bills for the sidewalk paving, she sent out a desperate plea for every member to go out and raise $237 immediately. Now the dream was reality. And as she said at the dedication, the museum was built by all Houston and now belonged to all Houston. It did not occur to anyone in the league that blacks should be admitted, or that the day would come when black Houstonians would be among the city's most admired artists.

The museum was fortunate in its first director. James Chillman was a professor of architecture and art history at Rice Institute. He had a gift for making art history interesting. Houstonians came to audit his lectures and he inspired numberless students to make history of art a college major and a life's work. He was building an informed patronage for the museum as well as its permanent collection.

With the museum realized, Miss Annette Finnigan could pursue her course of buying art for Houston. Now in her fifties, she lived in New York for reasons of health, but she had never lost her interest in Houston and its museum. She often traveled abroad and, in the leisurely custom of the day, ranged from London to Rome, to Athens and Cairo. Before each trip, she would consult James Chillman on what she might buy to fit into the growing collection. She had an educated eye and knew dependable dealers in the countries she visited so often.[2]

Annette Finnigan started the museum's permanent collections in the art of Egypt, Greece, Rome, and Byzantium and in the Indian and Persian textiles of the seventeenth to twentieth century. The famous Finnigan lace collection represents all major schools of lacemaking. By 1940, her gifts had formed more than half of the museum collection.

The museum was not, however, her only beneficiary. Finnigan gave to the Houston Public Library a collection of sixty-five rare books, including a Vulgate edition of the Bible once owned by William of Orange; a first Aldine edition of *Caesar's Commentaries,* printed in Venice in 1513; Terence's *Comedies,* published in Strasbourg in 1499; and a beautifully illuminated *Book of Hours.*

Her friend Julia Ideson said of her: "She was charming and intelligent. Her interest was always in world events and in world progress. She was always very forceful and mentally alert."

But Houstonians have never had to be rich to have influence or to improve their city. Good will, nice manners, a willingness to serve the community, have always been the criteria by which Old Houston judged newcomers as well as its own.

After a period as a convalescent center, Camp Logan was dismantled and the land was put up for sale. In July, 1923, Catharine Emmott had an idea. Why not preserve a small part of the big camp as a memorial to the soldiers who had died in service? English-born and a graduate of the London Conservatory of Music, Mrs. John Emmott was a respected music teacher. After her husband's death in 1914, she rented rooms in her big Washington Avenue house to wives of soldiers stationed at Logan. With them, she often played golf on the camp golf course and came to love the woodlands around it. At sixty-two, Mrs. Emmott began her crusade. She spent the summer taking the streetcar to City Hall, to the Chamber of Commerce, to club meetings, and to patriotic groups. Enthusiasm grew but progress was slow.[3]

In November, the Varner Realty Company, composed of Will and Mike Hogg and Henry Stude, bought 873 acres of the Logan land, planning a new suburb. But they were captured by Mrs. Emmott's idea. She had hoped for 100 acres, but Will Hogg always thought expansively. In April, 1924, although land prices were rising, his company offered to sell the property to the city at its original cost. He persuaded the Reineman Land Company to sell an adjoining 630 acres. Then he gave $50,000 toward payment of the debt. And after all those persuasive calls and visits from Mrs. Emmott, Mayor

The roof of the Museum of Fine Arts gave a sweeping view of the esplanade that ran from the sunken garden to Sam Houston's equestrian statue and beyond to the reflecting pool. Clipped hedges under the Texas star spelled Hermann Park. Hermann Hospital rose out of the natural woodland, and Rice Institute's Sallyport could be seen over the rooftops of Shadyside. In 1928 the double rows of live oaks planted on both sides of Main Street were still young. *Courtesy Houston Metropolitan Research Center, Houston Public Library*

Holcombe gave the park priority in his annual budgets.

Memorial Park was born with 1,503 acres of natural beauty.

World War I still seemed very close. In 1924, Will Hogg gave the Gold Star Mothers two hundred live oak trees to plant in memory of Harris County men who had died in service. Planted on Main Street or along the drive that curved around Hermann Park, each had a copper marker bearing the name of the man it honored.

At this point it is important to consider just how busy Will Hogg must have been in April of 1924. He was pouring his torrential energy into three channels at once: putting together land for a memorial park and helping the city raise money to pay for it; raising the entire sum needed by the Houston Museum of Fine Arts for its new wings; and at the same time putting together an entirely new tract of land that would become River Oaks—a task he finished in May, 1924.

The year was a busy one for most of Houston. In its first decade, the firm of Vinson & Elkins became one of the largest in Houston with a growing national reputation. When the towering Niels Esperson Building opened, the firm leased an entire floor. Despite this success, Judge James A. Elkins decided to branch out into banking. It seemed to the energetic judge that Hous-

For his party of May 2, 1925, Judge James A. Elkins invited the whole Vinson & Elkins firm to sail down the bayou for luncheon at the San Jacinto Inn. Not all are identified, but left to right by windows: *First,* Cameron Hightower, Fred Switzer, Mrs. Warren Dale, and small James A. Elkins, Jr. *Second,* Robert Keeland, Treva Leverton, George E. B. Peddy, and Warren Dale. *Third,* Robert A. Shepherd, Virginia Vinson, Mrs. William Vinson, Marie Fouts, Mrs. Robert Shepherd, Mrs. Clyde Sweeton, Mrs. Edna McDonald, and (standing) Julia Vinson. *Fourth,* William A. Vinson and Clyde Sweeton standing, Mrs. James A. Elkins (in profile), and Martha Vinson. *Fifth,* Judge Elkins (second from left, standing), Wharton Weems (to his right), William States Jacobs, Jr. (to his left), Sidney McClendon, Jr., Mrs. Wharton Weems, and Mrs. McClendon. *Sixth,* J. Willard Keeland and Edwin D. "Red" Adams. *Courtesy A. Frank Smith of Vinson & Elkins*

ton banks were Southern-gentleman-lazy about recruiting new depositors.

In 1924, with J. W. Keeland, a banker friend from the Huntsville days, he opened the Guaranty Trust Company on $110,000 capital and in eighty square feet of floor space. With characteristic vigor, he set a pace that made established bankers blink. He could refer law clients to his bank and could refer major depositors to his law firm.[4] He had an offfice in both and walked from one to the other. The Guaranty Trust soon outgrew its quarters. The day would come when it was Houston's biggest bank—First City.

From its earliest days, the city had tried to take care of its poor, chiefly through the churches and their women's societies. Most well-to-do families had private charities of their own. But in 1924, Houston had its first Community Chest campaign, with Burke Baker director.

At thirty-seven, Baker was president of several small oil companies, and within another year, he would go on to found the Seaboard Life Insurance Company.[5] Even in his university days, Burke Baker had shown a natural bent toward community service.

He had first moved into Houston's civic leadership in 1915, when he and his father successfully attracted steamships to the new turning basin. In the years ahead, he would serve the state and national YMCA, the Second Presbyterian Church, the Red Cross, and the boards of the Houston Museum of Fine Arts and Kinkaid School. He would give to the city the Burke Baker Planetarium and found the River Oaks tennis matches.

After decades of running the public schools, the city turned the task over to a new Houston Independent School District with an elected board. Dr. E. E. Oberholtzer arrived from Tulsa in May, 1924, to become superintendent. R. H. Fonville took over as president of the school board—giving to that often contentious body a few years of unwonted peace and harmony.

On bond money, Jefferson Davis Hospital was built, at Elder and Girard streets on land that had been given to Houston more than eighty years before by Augustus and John K. Allen. It opened December 2, 1924, as the city-county hospital for the indigent, staffed by volunteers from the Harris County Medical Society. The Houston Negro Hospital opened a few months later. This was the gift of J. S. Cullinan in memory of his son who had died after serving in World War I.

With Tom Tellepsen as contractor, the new Chemical Laboratory for Rice Institute was going up at a cost of $1 million. Born in Norway in 1888, Tellepsen had come to the United States with his parents in 1904. After working in New York City and the Panama Canal Zone, he went into the construction business in Houston in 1908.[6] He built the Miller Outdoor Theater in Hermann Park, and by the mid-twenties, his firm was one of the largest in the state. In the first half of 1923 it was at work on the new Masonic Temple Building and the Anderson, Clayton wharves that would be sixteen hundred feet long on the Ship Channel.

In the mid-1920s, the whole city seemed inspired to build. Margaret Hunter Kinkaid had started her little school for her neighbors' children in 1910, expecting to offer only kindergarten and the first few grades. But as the children grew older, the grades kept pace, as Susan Hillebrandt Santangelo wrote in her history of the school. After thirteen years, the old frame house on Elgin was outgrown.

One afternoon, Capt. James Baker, his daughter Alice Baker Jones, and R. Lee Blaffer called on Mrs. Kinkaid to offer their help on expansion. To their surprise she did not immediately agree. Rather she seemed ready to listen and negotiate. Throughout her years as the school's head, Mrs. Kinkaid had spent her summers at major universities to be better prepared as an educator. Wisely, she was reluctant to make a move that might lessen her control of the institution she had built.

This became clear when Blaffer, in a private meeting, offered to build a school for her and run it in a businesslike fashion. Mrs. Kinkaid replied that he could build it, if he liked, but that she would run any school associated with her name. They understood each other.

Kinkaid acquired its first board: R. L. Blaffer, Will Clayton, Burke Baker, Harry C.

Wiess, and E. L. Neville. Its mission was to find a site and build a plant big enough to include a junior high school.[7]

Meanwhile, Mrs. Kinkaid set out to inspect outstanding prep schools across the country. She found many of them "too dark." She wanted her school to let in plenty of light and air, and she wanted it painted in light, bright colors. She was a woman ahead of her time in many ways. The committee chose a site on Richmond at Graustark; William Ward Watkin designed the U-shaped building she requested. The new school opened in the fall of 1924.

The semitropical Houston climate encourages gardeners. The flowering season starts early and lingers into midwinter. Trees grow tall enough to shade a house in a decade. From its first years, Houston had commercial nurseries; early Houstonians grew flowers and planted trees. By 1900, mansions occupying a city block were surrounded by formal gardens and Victorian arbors. Houston Heights was known for its roses.

In 1924, seven young matrons founded the Garden Club of Houston. From this nucleus came an organization that would have a lasting influence on the city's private landscapes and public beauty. The founders were Mrs. Herbert Roberts, Mrs. Card Elliott, Mrs. Arthur Boice, Mrs. Robert Morris, Mrs. Harry Hilliard, Mrs. Charles Robertson, and Mrs. Curtis Walker. A year later, they took in forty additional members. All were serious in their work, analyzing soil, keeping careful records of their experiments with different elements and different plants, studying horticulture and floriculture, and always sharing knowledge and plants with neophytes across the city. Mrs. Roberts was the first president (1924–29) and Mrs. S. M. McAshan was the second president (1929–31). It is for her that the Aline McAshan Arboretum in Memorial Park is named.

When scarcely seven years old, the Garden Club of Houston committed itself to maintaining the gardens of the Museum of Fine Arts. To support this and other civic work, the club started the Fall Bulb Mart, which soon became famous in the Netherlands for the large quantities of Dutch bulbs it orders each year.

The *Houston Dispatch* was owned by Ross Sterling and had a healthy circulation. Sterling had resigned as president of the Humble Company and had sold his stock for $8 million. He was pouring money into the paper to make it Houston's finest. One day in 1923, Roy Watson invited Sterling to his handsome office in the Post Building at Texas and Travis and offered to sell the paper he had inherited at the price William Randolph Hearst had offered five years before—$1.25 million. Sterling wrote a check for the downpayment, agreed to pay off the rest in six months, and asked Will Hobby to take over the combined *Post-Dispatch* as a stockholder and director.[8] Ross Sterling's old friend Ray Dudley became general manager, and Charlie Maes managing editor.

In its first edition in August, 1924, the new *Post-Dispatch* proclaimed itself "an independent newspaper . . . supporting what it believes to be right . . . without regard to partisan politics." It proved its independence by supporting neither Mrs. Ferguson nor the Klan-sponsored candidate for governor, but the Republican candidate, University of Texas law professor Dr. George Butte. This was a startling move in a state that had been loyal to the Democratic Party since Reconstruction.[9]

Up to this point, the press was the medium serving the citizen's right to know what goes on in government and public affairs. Now that monopoly was being challenged. Radio was ready to go commercial. For several years, men and boys had fiddled with earphones and the uncertainties of crystal sets. In 1919, the Houston Radio Club was organized with young James L. Autry as president and J. W. Weatherford as secretary-treasurer. Most of the members made their own sets. At the age of ten, Edward Bourdon used his paper route money to buy his first tube for the joy of reaching KDKA in East Pittsburgh and WMC in

Memphis. Teen-aged Howard Hughes, Jr., had a whole room given over to all the best modern equipment and talked regularly with ham radio operators in this country and Latin America. Autry, Clifford Vick, and J. Grosse were among the first to hold radio licenses. Their success prompted the Houston Police Department to install a transmitter on the police station roof in the spring of 1922. In May, the *Houston Post* broadcast a Sunday concert from A. P. Daniel's radio plant at 2504 Bagby Street.

By 1924, William P. Hobby, president of the *Post-Dispatch,* saw the potential in the new medium. The paper took over the station that Will Horwitz had run for his theaters. The U.S. Department of Commerce Bureau of Navigation licensed the station as KPRC to broadcast "entertainment and like matter, also weather forecasts." The call letters stand for port, railroads, and cotton. The license was signed by Secretary of Commerce Herbert Hoover.

KPRC made its first broadcast on May 9, 1925. The station covered the World Series of 1925, when Pittsburgh won over Washington, and the Tunney-Dempsey rematch. Some twelve to fifteen thousand listened to the championship broadcast at the outdoor theater in Hermann Park. KPRC sent radio receivers to the state prisons and prison farms. G. E. "Eddie" Zimmerman, the station manager, suggested that in off hours, when not broadcasting, the station lend its transmitters for the police department to send robbery and theft reports to patrol cars.

The W. C. Munn Company was a major advertiser in both press and radio. Young Gladys James was Munn's assistant credit manager for seven years before marrying James Russell. "Munn's was Houston's only complete department store," she said. "Foley's was called a department store, but it and Levy's mostly had ladies' wear. Foley's had some children's clothes and other things. But the Munn Company occupied practically the whole block—Main Street to Travis to Texas to Capital. It had ladies' and men's complete clothing and shoes. Children's

William P. Hobby, 1920s. *Courtesy Houston Metropolitan Research Center, Houston Public Library*

clothes. A baby department, a jewelry department, a furniture department, any kind of house furnishings, rugs, draperies, pianos, Victrolas, automobile tires, a beauty shop, barber shop, shoe repair, a lunch room –

anything that you needed to live you could get at the W. C. Munn Company."[10]

While at Munn's, Gladys James had a few dates with Clark Gable, the young actor who was playing the second lead in plays put on by the Gene Lewis Stock Company at the Majestic Theatre.[11] She didn't find him much fun because his whole focus was on the play, on curtain time, on the theater. Lyn Tornabene's biography of Gable, *Long Live the King*, pronounced him still awkward in this period: "Simply opening a door or walking cross stage was a challenge to be overcome through repeated rehearsal."

Editor and Publisher, "The Oldest Publishers' and Advertisers' Journal in America," came out in June, 1924, with a massive, 276-page edition devoted to Houston. "On To Britain," it proclaimed. "Texas next – at Houston – in 1925." The Associated Advertising Clubs of the World were to hold their twentieth convention in England in July. This special issue supported Houston's bid for the 1925 convention. It carried full-page ads from the mayor, from Houston newspapers, department stores, industries, and business corporations, as well as from Dallas, Fort Worth, and Galveston. Mayor Holcombe filled two of the eleven-by-fourteen-inch pages with an article on Houston and Texas history, starting with French occupation in 1684.

An equal number of ads came from Britain. *Punch* and the *Daily Express* took a full page each; the *Times* took a centerfold. They were welcoming "American advertising men" to the world convention in London – though many delegates were women.

William S. Patton, president of the Advertising Association of Houston, led its large delegation.[12] One hundred and fifty Houstonians sailed from the Port of Houston on the French Line's *La Salle*.[13] Another fifty embarked from the East coast on seven other ships, including the *Republic* and the *Leviathan*. Whether they landed in Liverpool or Southampton, all were officially greeted. In London they heard the Prince of Wales open the session on July 14. They were entertained at a round of luncheons, dinners, balls, and side trips. They dined with Major and Lady Violet Astor at Hever Castle. They attended services in Westminster Abbey.

Then they gave their own banquet at the Hotel Cecil. With vintage wines served, the menu listed such tongue-in-cheek courses as *Delices de Sole Lone Star* and *Selle d'Agneau de Lait Rodeo*. The dessert was spelled out in plain English: "Honest-to-Goodness Texas Water Melon." They had brought along two hundred melons for the treat.

Perhaps it was the ice-cold melons, perhaps the promise of Southern barbecue and trips down the bayou: they triumphed. The Associated Advertisers of the World agreed to come to Houston for their 1925 meeting. Nobody made any reference to Houston's summer heat in pre-air-conditioning 1925.

New Library, New Hospital, and a Schism

THE CITY added twenty-five square miles in April, 1925. By then forty-two steamship lines were making Houston a port of call, and eighteen railroads met them at shipside.

This made it very simple for the members of the Associated Advertising Clubs of the World to gather in Houston in May for their twenty-first convention. Delegates came from Australia and New Zealand as well as Europe and the Americas. The *Editor and Publisher* of May 16, 1925, reported that "world peace and universal understanding" were keynotes of the convention. "The international air which marked the London program [in 1924] has, if anything, been intensified at Houston, with a strong Pan-American representation." The advertising manager of the *Times,* London, urged that "truth in advertising" be transformed from a slogan to a crusade.

In 1925, Enrico Cerracchio unveiled the great bronze statue of General Houston. Born in Naples, the sculptor had gained an artistic reputation in Pittsburgh before coming to Houston in 1914. Although he hoped to make Houston an art center, his lasting contribution continues to be the forty-foot-high equestrian statue that stands at the entrance of Hermann Park. It took him nine years to complete.

In 1925, Houston drama lovers and amateur actors officially chartered the Little Theatre. T. K. Dixon, Jr., was elected first president and Frederick Leon Webster named director. The board of trustees included W. B. Baker, W. L. Childs, Leslie B. Dufton, Stephen P. Farish, Mrs. R. D. Ran-

dolph, George V. Rotan, and Mrs. W. B. Sharp. They staged their first plays at the Scottish Rite Cathedral, but this cost them 40 percent of the proceeds. For the 1926–27 season they moved to Anita Street. British Consul Leslie Dufton lent the necessary English accent to drawing-room comedies and had a flair for character parts.

Then something happened that divided Old Houston society into two camps. In May, 1925, Will Hogg offered Christ Church $750,000 for its half block on Texas Avenue. It was a reasonable offer. All the other churches dating from the days of the Republic had sold their downtown property at great profit and moved to new sites a few blocks away. Mr. Hogg addressed his letter to Dr. Peter Gray Sears, whose grandfather had founded Christ Church March 16, 1839.

The vestry, after a brief discussion, turned the offer down. It decided, however, to put the proposition before the whole congregation with the proviso that not less than $1 million would be accepted. With an obvious lack of interest, the congregation tabled the issue until November. Dr. Sears departed on a three-month vacation, but he took with him a growing dream of what $1 million could do in mission work.

By November, the issue had become hot. Though the vestry would have taken a simple voice vote at a parish meeting, Dr. Gray insisted on a secret, written, tabulated and recorded ballot. The results, typed in triplicate, were deposited in the church archives: 170 votes for the sale, 423 against.

Dr. Sears could not accept the decision.

World peace was the theme of the Associated Advertising Clubs of the World meeting in Houston in May, 1925. Four thousand overseas guests were welcomed to Houston by Marcellus E. Foster, Mrs. Lou Holland, association president Lou Holland, Gov. Miriam A. Ferguson, former governor Jim Ferguson, Mrs. George S. Nalle, Col. George S. Nalle, Mayor Oscar Holcombe, former governor W. P. Hobby, local association president William S. Patton, and Robert H. Cornell. *Courtesy Kate Patton O'Neill (Mrs. Haylett O'Neill)*

He came back to it again and again, until, gradually, the issue stirred a city-wide controversy. Like Dr. William States Jacobs at First Presbyterian and Dr. Henry Barnston at Congregation Beth Israel, Peter Gray Sears was widely known throughout the city—a popular speaker before civic clubs, a cultural leader, a fund-raiser for many worthy causes. What he said was important to a far larger community than that of his church.

Houstonians who had never set foot in Christ Church grew heated in support of this beloved man of God, or equally heated at the thought of the city's first-born congregation giving up the site it had held since the days of the Texas Republic. Newspapers covered the controversy copiously; columnists and editors waxed eloquent. A proper Houstonian of another denomination had

a pamphlet printed urging that the historic church hold fast to its historic site.

Ingham Roberts, who favored the sale, proposed moving Christ Church brick by brick to Sam Houston Park. Writing in the *Chronicle,* he pointed out that the First Baptist Church had moved from Texas and Travis to Rusk and Fannin, to Fannin and Walker, to Main and Lamar. That the First Methodist Church had not only moved from its historic site but changed its name in the move. That the First Presbyterians had moved from their historic site at Capitol between Main and Travis to "their present beautiful building at Main and McKinney."

In a page-one editorial of several hundred words, the *Houston Chronicle* carefully straddled the issue.

Over the next several months, Dr. Sears

campaigned, urging his congregation to use the $1 million to pay off the debts of all Episcopal missions and to build another church somewhere else. (Ironically, Dr. Sears had never been offered $1 million. That was a figure the vestry had set as a minimum if selling were to be considered.)

Finally, unable to have his way and in a dramatic moment from the pulpit, Dr. Sears resigned. "Tears burst from the eyes of many in the great audience," the *Houston Post-Dispatch* reported. "Utter silence reigned for a moment, and then the concluding part of the service began. . . ."

But the controversy was over, leaving inevitable scars. Gradually Christ Church was drained of some of its most substantial members. Its losses fed the new Palmer Memorial Church. On the success of the Autry House across from Rice Institute, Mrs. Edwin Neville decided to build a student chapel in memory of her brother Edward who had drowned in a sailing accident long before. Daphne Neville had been one of the five Houston girls who spent a year in Europe with their teachers, the Misses Hargis. Perhaps it was from that memory that she asked architect William Ward Watkin to model the interior after the fifteenth-century Church of Santa Maria dei Miracoli in Venice. Within two years, Palmer Memorial became a parish church and Dr. Sears's last pulpit. Many families left Christ Church to join his new congregation.[1]

In 1925, Bob Smith moved to Houston.[2] Born in Greenville, Texas, Robert E. Smith was the son of a railroad man who had brought in some shallow wells near Bastrop. On graduation from Humble High School, Bob Smith worked for a succession of oil companies, sometimes as a roughneck, sometimes in the office. In 1922, in Tonkawa, Oklahoma, he bought two rigs for twenty-five thousand dollars and became a wildcatter. In Houston, at the age of thirty, he formed a partnership with Claud B. Hamill, son of the Curt Hamill who had helped drill the discovery well at Spindletop. Smith was at the start of a notable career in oil and real estate that would be best known for philanthropy and creation of the Astrodome.

The long-awaited Hermann Hospital opened in July, 1925—eleven years after George Hermann's death. As Houston's handsomest, it did not exactly fit its founder's plan of a charity hospital for the poor. With Alfred Finn of Houston as associate, Chicago architects designed the five-story building flanked by towered, seven-story bays. It had an elegantly tiled entry and lobby. It was built on Hermann land out beyond Hermann Park, with a natural woodland as its backdrop. The sixteenth-century Spanish style blended with the Mediterranean architecture of Rice Institute across Main Street. The *City Book of Houston* of 1925 said it cost $2 million. The WPA Writers' *Houston* says the hospital cost $1 million.

The manager, W. A. Childress, called it a wonder because it had "in the main one bed to the room (with no rooms having more than five beds), in contrast to the old hospitals which have 30 to 40 beds in each room or ward." It had five operating rooms, an electric kitchen, its own electric light plant, a twenty-ton ice plant, and every room was connected to the intercom. The head of the American Construction Association said, "There is no hospital like it in beauty and efficiency in the South."

All this had to be enclosed by a high fence to keep wolves of the surrounding woodland out of the hospital grounds.

Though built for three hundred beds, it opened with one hundred because, estate managers explained, the Hermann fortune consisted largely of open land and did not yield enough income to maintain more. All one hundred, they added, would be for charity patients.

Houstonians had never had a really handsome new hospital *given* to them before. A surprising number of candidates for free care showed up. In a *Chronicle* interview, Mr. Childress cited examples:

One well-dressed young woman wanted her aged mother to be admitted. "Can't you

The bronze statue of Sam Houston by Enrico Filberto Cerrachio stands at the entrance of Hermann Park, in the city named for the triumphant general. *Edward Bourdon photograph, courtesy of Mr. Bourdon*

afford to pay for her at some other hospital?" Childress asked. No, she couldn't. Asked for her mother's address, she gave one in a modest quarter of town. Asked for her own, she gave an address in an expensive downtown apartment house. Mother was not admitted.

A man wanted to be hospitalized for treatment of eye trouble. Childress asked if he didn't own a certain piece of property. The man said yes. "Then why can't you pay?" Childress asked. "Because I'm buying another piece of property and it takes all I can get to keep up with the payments." Childress added dryly that it reminded him of an item in a Northern newspaper: "The Rolls-Royce car of Mr. Jones McGillicuddy was stolen yesterday from in front of the county poor farm, where he was visiting his aged parents."

In explaining to the public what the new hospital could *not* do, Mr. Childress gave a picture of services the community provided in 1925: "The Hermann Hospital cannot be made into a poorhouse, an almshouse, a pest house or a home for the aged or infirm, or a branch of the insane asylum. The county provides a poor house; the city a pest house; the city and county an excellent hospital for the insane, as well as a general hospital for indigent or poor patients." This leaves the question of just what role there was for Mr.

Hermann's long-anticipated "charity" hospital to play.

In 1920, before the hospital had gone on the drawing boards, the farsighted trustees had gone to court seeking permission to have some rooms for paying patients to help support the charity wards. The success of this suit ultimately changed the nature and concept of the hospital. Starting with twenty-five private rooms, it had one hundred and twenty within fifteen years. On the court-approved principle, profit from the pay units helped maintain the charity wards. Houston had gained a modern general hospital.

Hermann served all Houston and enhanced the practice of medicine, but it did so in ways that George Hermann had not envisioned. From the start it had a school of nursing, and it became the first hospital in the vicinity to have regular internships and residency programs. Nonetheless, pay patients outnumbered charity patients.

Jefferson Davis, the joint city-county hospital staffed by volunteer physicians, took as many as it could of the sickest and most badly injured poor. Surgeons like Dr. Philo Howard regularly performed ten to fifteen operations a week on indigent patients. The hospital would soon be outgrown and succeeded by a new Jefferson Davis across the bayou.

Houston weather runs to extremes. The blizzard of December, 1924, covered the city in sleet. A northbound Santa Fe passenger train was derailed. Streetcars stalled, trees broke, and the roof of an airport hangar collapsed under the weight of the ice. In 1925, November rains fell for nine straight days, disrupting telephone and streetcar service, swelling the wood blocks of Fannin Street until they popped up like popcorn, making unpaved streets impassable, stopping all motor travel from the city. And in January, 1926, snow covered ground and rooftops.

Hoof and mouth disease threatened the big herds of cattle on Harris County ranches. The quarantine imposed was so strict that any dogs, cats, or livestock that walked through the disease zone were shot. Pilots were forbidden to land planes on the infected land. Inspectors brought in from California supervised slaughter of the stricken cattle.

Houston's Carnegie Library on the corner of Travis and McKinney was flourishing under the leadership of Julia Ideson. Ideson's career was remarkable from the start. She had become the city's first professional librarian in 1903. In 1911, she was elected president of the Texas Library Association. In 1913, she spent a year in Paris on a leave of absence. In 1916, she organized a library for the soldiers of Camp Logan before volunteering for overseas duty. In 1919, the American Library Association sent her to Brest to take over the Camp Pontenezeon library.

Back in Houston, she was recognized as a civic and intellectual leader. She sponsored debates and lectures on lively political issues that would have seemed both liberal and radical to some Houstonians in the more cautious times of the 1950s. Thanks to her influence, the city earmarked a percentage of its tax revenue for the library.

But the Carnegie Library which had loomed so large in 1904 was too small within fifteen years. As the city's population trebled between 1900 and 1920, patronage outgrew the number of books to be read and the space to keep them. Ideson told the press that conditions were "almost intolerable." By this time, Julia Ideson was widely recognized as an outstanding professional in the field. When she spoke, Houston listened. It took three years of prodding, but in 1922 the voters approved $200,000 in bonds for a new library.[3]

Ideson spent months visiting the big cities and big libraries of the country: New York, St. Louis, Chicago, Cleveland, Buffalo, Utica, Newark, Wilmington, and Providence. At the time, St. Louis was five times as big as Houston, Chicago twelve times as big.

The city, which had bought the library site from the First Presbyterian Church for

$7,880, sold it back to the church twenty-four years later for $100,000, with the building included. The proceeds built two library branches. Soon Ideson added four more and a bookmobile.

Mayor Oscar Holcombe agreed to use $92,000 from general funds to buy a site on McKinney Avenue. The handsome new Spanish Renaissance building opened on October 18, 1926. It would be further enhanced with murals by some of Houston's best-known artists—Emma Richardson Cherry, Grace Spalding John, and Ruth Uhler among them. William A. Vinson became president of the library board, a post he would hold with distinction until 1951.

In her career, Julia Ideson became president of the Southern Library Association and vice-president of the American Library Association. It was singularly appropriate for Houston to give her name to the library to which she had given so much.

As movies made in Hollywood grew longer and more lavish, as the cast of a few swelled into the cast of thousands, they required grander and grander theaters. The Metropolitan Theatre at 1016 Main Street had a domed interior in the Greco-Roman style and a large stage for vaudeville. Loew's State Theatre at 1022 Main was even more spectacular in the Egyptian style. Both were designed by Alfred C. Finn.

Using bond issues totaling $7 million in 1926, Houston opened new high schools: Albert Sidney Johnston, Stonewall Jackson, Jefferson Davis, Sidney Lanier, James S. Hogg, John H. Reagan, and Jack Yates. By this time, the Houston Public School system had a budget running past $2 million a year.

The school board employed a full-time architect, Harry D. Payne, who came from St. Louis. He was commissioned to design six schools in Houston, including the Edgar Allen Poe, River Oaks, and Woodrow Wilson schools. Over the next years, he would design fifty-four school buildings for the Houston Independent School District alone, including Cage, Chase, Field, Whar-

ton, and Forest Hills elementary schools, and the Phyllis Wheatley and Deer Park high schools.

"I was in my heyday then," Payne said as a man of ninety-four. "Some school board members didn't approve of hiring an architect. They couldn't understand why they had to pay architects a fee because all they do is draw a pretty picture."[4]

But as always, the growing city had more children to teach than it could quite house. However substantial the neighborhood, each new permanent building soon sprouted temporary one-story schoolrooms on the property. "The shack" became a familiar part of growing up in Houston.

While most of the nation depended on coal, coke, or smelly gas made from coal in 1926, Houston began to enjoy the benefits of natural gas. At a cost of $5 million, natural gas from Refugio County fields was piped in for domestic and industrial use. Even so, not many Houston houses or apartments built before World War II had central heat. With palm trees growing in neighborhoods throughout the city, Houstonians nursed the illusion that the Gulf Coast was subtropical—despite the bitter winter weather of December, 1924, November, 1925 and January, 1926.

Air conditioning was yet to come. Venetian blinds blocked the sun but let the breeze through. Sleeping porches were built to catch the gulf breeze. In mansion or cottage, ceiling fans, oscillating fans, and attic fans were the best hope for a cool night's sleep. Not many Houstonians could, as the entire Carter family did, sleep on top of a family skyscraper.

By the mid-1920s, six stories had been added to the sixteen-story Carter Building built by Samuel Fain Carter. It was a prestigious office building for leading architects, doctors, and lawyers. Members of the family spent the hottest of the summer nights sleeping on its roof twenty-two stories above the ground. Dr. E. L. Crain, Jr., Mr. Carter's grandson, remembers that beds were stored in a small building next to the elevator shaft.

"We would pull the beds out—my mother, my father and my brothers and I, and my cousins Florence and Carolyn Bryan —and we would sleep under the stars.[5] The next morning we would walk over to Grandmother's for breakfast." Mrs. Carter's house on Crawford had a huge yard where she kept chickens, pheasants, and a cow. Years later, she left her house to the Blue Bird Circle and her chickenyard to St. Joseph's Hospital.

Riding a Boom

LOOKING OUT the trolley windows as they rode home on the Interurban from Galveston, Houstonians of the mid-twenties marveled over the tall buildings they could see shooting up in the business district. The seventeen-story Medical Arts Building opened in 1926 was soon outdone by the twenty-two-story Petroleum Building with its Mayan motif and the Tejas Club on top. The Niels Esperson Building dominated the skyline briefly in 1927, but by 1929 the Gulf Building would pass it as the tallest building west of Chicago. A dozen more skyscrapers were on the drawing boards.

It was this buoyant, burgeoning city that attracted George and Herman Brown. In the preceding decade, Brown & Root of Austin had become known across the state as road builders. With Houston's surging population, the city was laying out so many new streets that the company decided to move its corporate headquarters to Houston in 1926, with George Brown in charge.

Herman and George Brown were born in Belton, Texas, in 1892 and 1898. Their great-grandfather was the first chief justice of the Supreme Court of the Republic of Texas. Their grandfather organized Lee County. Herman Brown started work as construction foreman for a road contractor. When his boss went out of business, he settled with Herman for nine months of back wages by giving him eighteen mules, four scrapers, a pair of plows, and six wagons—all mortgaged. At twenty-one, Herman Brown began to build roads and bridges. In 1917, he and Margarett

Root were married.[1] Her brother Dan Root became his partner in 1919.

George Brown had left Rice Institute in 1918 to enter the U.S. Marine Corps and in 1922 earned a degree in mining engineering at the Colorado School of Mines. He worked as a geologist for the Anaconda Company at Butte, Montana, until he was injured in a mine cave-in. As he convalesced in Belton, his brother and brother-in-law persuaded him to join their firm.

"I never thought I'd make any real money as an engineer," George Brown said long after. "What was important was the romance of engineering. Engineers were men who went to far places, who built things all over the world—as far away as China." That romance would come to him. Ultimately, Brown & Root Engineering Company would launch ships that traveled the world from the Port of Houston, would send its employees to every continent, and would put Houston on the threshold of outer space.

But in 1926, their chief concern was mud. With his brother-in-law Dan Root, Herman Brown was building roads and bridges all over Texas when George joined the partnership. A run of bad weather could tip a project from profit into loss. "We took two jobs in West Texas, where there was no rainfall, for every job we took in East and South Texas, where there was a lot of rainfall," George Brown said.

Their timing was good. The automobile demanded roads. Texas was out to build them. Congress had passed the Federal Road Act in 1916, and the state had formed the Texas Highway Commission in 1917. The move to Houston gave Brown & Root a chance at construction along the ship channel as well. It also brought to the city a young woman who would become a major art patron some twenty years on.

Alice Pratt, the daughter of Lillian Nelson and Minot Tully Pratt, was born in Siloam Springs, Arkansas, where her father, a Stanford graduate, was an engineer with the Santa Fe Railroad. After her father's death and her mother's remarriage, she went to Dallas to live with her mother's sister, Mrs. Leslie Waggener. Mr. Waggener, a banker and son of the first president of the University of Texas, collected paintings—American Impressionists and the Ash Can School, as well as the work of more famous artists like

Alice Pratt, one of the prettiest and most popular debutantes of her season in Dallas, married young George Brown, to the dismay of her aunt. *Courtesy Isabel Brown Wilson (Mrs. Wallace Wilson)*

John Singer Sargent, Albert Pinkham Ryder, and Edgar Degas.[2] At the Waggeners' the teen-aged Alice discovered the art that would give her lifelong joy. After graduation from Southwestern University in Georgetown, she made her debut in Dallas. But she was already in love with young George Brown, whom she had met in Georgetown.

Mrs. Waggener could not be enthusiastic about a suitor who always came to call for her beautiful niece in a construction truck. She was sure that George Brown had no promising future. To give the romance time to die a natural death, she sent Alice off to Europe for a sojourn of several months, much of which she spent in Paris, where she focused on the Louvre and other museums.[3] Next she had a few months in New York, plied by beaux, invited to Harvard and to West Point dances. Despite the good times, she wrote to George regularly; nothing weakened the tie between them. On Thanksgiving Day, 1925, they were married at the Waggeners' home.

The young couple lived first in a boarding house outside Houston, where George Brown was building a bridge. But within six years after their wedding, the unpromising George Brown was building for his wife and daughters a house on Inwood Drive in River Oaks. They would live there for the rest of their lives.

The *City Directory* of 1926 estimated Houston's population at 284,446, and Port Houston was ranked in the top eleven in foreign shipping tonnage. The Southern Pacific and the Missouri-Kansas-Texas Railroads built freight terminals along the channel, and the Morgan Line completed new docks and wharves at Clinton.

After his father's death in 1924, Gus Wortham carried on the insurance agency of John L. Wortham & Son. By 1926, he was doing so well that he decided to form a fire and casualty insurance company with $300,000 dollars in capital. Though he lacked $225,000 of that amount, he hoped to persuade three older friends to invest.

Judge James A. Elkins, J. W. Link, and Jesse Jones agreed to put in $75,000 each. As further help, Judge Elkins handled the legal work. When he had secured the charter in Austin, he telegraphed his younger friend: "The baby is born." Its way paved by the old Huntsville friendship, the American General Insurance Company opened in 1926. From its $300,000 start, it would grow into an insurance giant with $20.6 billion in assets and $112 billion in life insurance in force.

Jack C. Dionne's *Gulf Coast Lumberman*, the trade journal of the lumber industry, was gaining readers throughout the Middle West and Southwest. From Wisconsin, Jack Dionne had come to Houston by way of East Texas. A witty raconteur, he was a popular toastmaster and a successful fund raiser for the Community Chest. Because he published an equally successful West Coast journal, his daughters were as at home in Los Angeles and Hollywood as in Houston.[4]

Though America was basking in a prosperous peacetime, China was racked by civil war. The Nanking Incident forced Dr. Allen Hutcheson to give up his work of twenty years as head of the Nanking University Hospital. He cabled his brothers in Houston, "Everything gone . . . work, home destroyed." Houston felt this acutely. Dr. Hutcheson had gone to China as a Southern Presbyterian missionary. For years the First Presbyterian Church and Houstonians like the Clevelands, the Sewalls, E. A. Peden, and Daphne Palmer Neville had been sponsoring his work.

Mildred, Henrietta, and Allen Hutcheson, Jr., were born in China and learned Chinese before they learned English. Houston ways were strange to two young girls from China just entering college. "You see, missionaries didn't dance," Henrietta Hutcheson Schwartz recalled in amusement. "There was something in Shanghai that was really fairly wicked. They played Lancers. The girls walked in one direction and the boys in another. When the music stopped, you just touched the boy's hand. But a dance! Horrible!" She came home from every Rice

dance in tears. Dr. Hutcheson gave up and sent both girls to Wellesley.

After half a career as a doctor working to provide medical care and teaching to the Chinese, Dr. Hutcheson had a new way to make in his hometown. "The Houston doctors were wonderful to him," Mrs. Schwarz said. Dr. Hutcheson became the city health officer under Mayor Walter Monteith and for eight years was school physician for the Houston public schools. He also went into real estate and developed Kashmere Gardens on land left to the family by his father, J. C. Hutcheson.

It was time to annex again. Houston took in Harrisburg, Memorial Park, River Oaks, and Cottage Grove—all, until 1926, outside the city limits.

Ellington Field, once earmarked by Houston to become the national hub of the air age, was closed down and all its equipment auctioned off for $14,700. But in 1927, W. T. Carter, Jr., his sister Agnese Carter Nelms, and their brother-in-law, Dr. Judson Taylor, opened a 193-acre field on Telephone Road and called it the Houston Airport.[5] In February, 1928, a black-and-gold Pitcairn biplane landed with the city's first air mail. The outgoing mail carried a quart of buttermilk.

In the rush of city growth, scant attention was given to the birth in 1927 of two institutions that would someday loom large in Houston's cultural and economic life: the Houston Junior College and the Houston Negro Junior College. They would ultimately become the University of Houston and Texas Southern University.[6]

From the time of his arrival three years before as superintendent of schools, Dr. Oberholtzer had talked of a community college to be a part of the public school system. The Houston Junior College opened with 232 students. It was to offer practical education for working people, and college courses for those not qualified to enter a college or university. Wiley College of Marshall and Prairie View College had been offering extension classes for two years in Jack

Yates High School. Building on this, the black community founded the Houston Negro Junior College to train teachers. It received its first-class rating from the State Board of Education at the end of its second session.

Also that year, the Museum of Fine Arts opened the Museum Art School, giving it two floors in the east wing. Professional artists taught the classes.

Having outgrown the available space in the Houston Public Library, the Houston Museum and Scientific Society moved into its first building in the zoo in 1927. It would house the collections of two remarkable men. Born in England, H. P. Attwater had come to Texas in 1889 and dedicated himself to conservation of Texas birds. He founded the Texas chapter of the National Audubon Society, and the endangered Attwater Greater Prairie Chicken is named for him. His important collection was given to the museum in 1927 by Sigmund J. Westheimer, a leading Houstonian who from boyhood had shared Attwater's ideals.

Meanwhile, Major John E. T. Milsaps of the Salvation Army was a world traveler who collected rare books, curios, minerals, and shells, and items of historical and anthropological interest. As an anonymous donor, he started the library's rare book collection. He ultimately gave to the Museum of Natural Science a collection of 2,391 objects. At his request, the giver remained unnamed until after his death. The museum's collection would grow again with A. T. McDannald's gift of 10,000 North American Indian artifacts, but that collection would come to another and bigger museum building.

After a slow start, River Oaks was gaining houses but there was still a rawness to the landscape. To encourage study of gardening and gardening design, Mrs. Louis A. Stevenson and Mrs. E. Y. Cottingham, who were across-the-street neighbors, founded the River Oaks Garden Club on October 27, 1927.[7] The Stevensons and the Cottinghams had bought two of the first lots sold by Hugh Potter in the new neighborhood and were pleasant friends with Hugh and Tiel Potter.[8]

"We had our first meeting at the home of Mrs. Tex Bayless," Louise Stevenson said sixty years later. "We invited women whose River Oaks houses were either built or nearing completion."[9] Dues were a dollar a year. They closed out their first year in May with a show of their flowers on the River Oaks Country Club terrace. They had a bank balance of $8.44 which they spent on garden manuals for the members to study through the summer. Mrs. Stevenson was president for the club's first three years.

The club started planting the trees and shaping the gardens that created the enduring River Oaks landscape. It landscaped the grounds of the progressive new county school, the River Oaks School. In years to come, the club would sponsor the annual Azalea Trail to raise money for its civic projects and, when Bayou Bend became a museum, would maintain the Bayou Bend gardens and keep fresh flowers in every room.

Mike Hogg, at forty, decided to enter politics. In 1927, he ran successfully in the special election to fill the legislative seat left vacant by Norman Kittrell of Harris County. He championed "the little people" much as his father had before him. He opposed building pipelines to load oil tankers offshore because it would rob Houston's port of revenue, but also because they could pollute the Gulf waters. In 1928, he ran again and again won.

All this meant that he spent more time in his Austin home than in Houston. When he married Alice Nicholson Frazer of Dallas, he abandoned the bachelor quarters at Bayou Bend, and the couple moved into a house next door on Lazy Lane. Will Hogg spent the summer of 1928 in Europe and much of the winter on an extended trip through South America with his friend Irvin S. Cobb. Almost from the start, then, Bayou Bend became Ima Hogg's special preserve.

After fifty years of clanging and rattling over the steel rails, electric streetcars gave way to buses in 1927. With them went the Inter-urban to Galveston, marking the end of the fifty-five-minute run to friends or the beach. The Houston Electric Company gave the city the Interurban right-of-way on which to build a four-lane highway. It would be 1952 before it opened. For the next twenty-five years, Houstonians had to drive from downtown out Harrisburg and Broadway to the Galveston Highway, past the Japanese truck gardens to Webster and Dickinson to spend a day on the Gulf.

The short, pleasant trips provided by the steamboat and the Interurban had always made intercourse easy between Old Houston of all ages and born-on-the-island Galvestonians. There was a steady shuttling back and forth at any hour of any day, knitting the two social circles together. The friendships were close, casual, and neighborly. With the death of the Interurban, Houston and Galveston gradually lost that closeness, a loss compounded by gasoline rationing in the 1940s.

None of this was immediate. Galveston-born George S. Cohen and his wife Esther had moved to Houston with the family purchase of the Foley Brothers store in 1917 when Rice Institute was five years old. As a young couple in their thirties living on Kipling Street, they made friends with the youthful Rice faculty, particularly Dr. J. Willis Slaughter, a sociologist. The Cohens adopted Rice. In the 1920s they started a student loan fund governed by Rice professors. "It was a simple arrangement," Mrs. Cohen said. "Any student receiving a loan understood that he should repay it in order to make it possible for another youngster to receive a similar boost. We never had a student fail to repay."

Through their friends the Cohens could see that faculty members had no place on campus to meet informally. Seeking a way to honor his parents, George Cohen decided to give a faculty club building to Rice in honor of Robert and Agnes Cohen. He announced it to them on his mother's seven-tieth birthday, March 27, 1927. Some twenty-five Rice faculty members went to Galveston for the birthday celebration. Cohen House, designed by William Ward Watkin, opened eight months later on Thanksgiving Day.

In 1927, Mayor Oscar Holcombe named Will Hogg to chair a new City Planning Commission. Hogg embraced the task joyously. A. E. Amerman, W. E. Carroll, Hugh Potter, J. A. Embry, John F. Staub, and Dr. J. A. Kyle were members. They hired Hare & Hare of Kansas City, the firm that had shaped so much of Houston's landscape. They had the backing of the Park Commission Board.[10] With all this power, surely they could not fail.

The resulting plan, running to 136 pages, was thoroughly worked out and beautifully drawn. It considered problems of circulation, transit, transportation, waterways, aviation, and a major street plan. It considered a civic center, schools, and parks. It dealt with the platting of subdivisions. It was illustrated with photographs showing the errors and virtues of cities in Europe and America.

The final word came from Hare & Hare: "The people of Houston and their officials will have to decide whether they are building a great city or merely a great population." Despite the seemingly irresistible force of Will Hogg's enthusiasm, despite the array of citizens supporting the plan, Houston voted the plan down. Apparently, zoning was the hurdle that the voters could not clear.

Only the Civic Center made it to reality. A few years earlier, Hogg had paid $260,000 for land northwest of the business district. Surrounding Hermann Square, it lay between the bayou and the Houston Public Library. He thought it the logical place for a civic center to grow. Hare & Hare agreed. While unwilling to accept the whole plan, the Houston voters accepted the civic center proposal in 1927 by including it in a $6,975,000 bond issue. The city bought the tract. In the years to come, it would be occupied by the City Hall, the Jesse H. Jones

Hall for the Performing Arts, the Sam Houston Coliseum, the Albert Thomas Convention Center, and the Music Hall.

Will Hogg often bought up land that he thought the city *should* buy, with the aim of selling it at cost to the city when the need for it had been established. This was a ploy that would be used by such later citizens as Judge James Elkins and George and Herman Brown—always to Houston's benefit.

A Peaceable Kingdom

WHETHER in boom times or slack, Houston before and after World War I was a pleasant, safe place for the young. They could roam the city on skates, bicycle, streetcar, or horseback and were at home in many houses besides their own. Old Houstonians promptly called upon newcomers and brought them into the neighborhood circle. Everybody knew everybody else on the block. And there were no secrets, thanks to the network of children and servants who kept everyone posted on what everyone else was doing.

As her mother had before her, Ellen Hamilton Wilkerson was born and grew up in the big three-story house of her grandparents, the Robert Paines, at 1505 McKinney. Captain and Mrs. J. C. Hutcheson lived at 1417 with their children, Rosalie, Palmer, and Joe. At about the age of five, Ellen met her future husband in his cousin Joe's sandpile.[1]

"Between McKinney and Walker, LaBranch was a graveled street," Mrs. Wilkerson recalled. "We had ditches running between the yard and the street, with a bridge across from each front door, and a horse-hitching post. Right across McKinney from our house was an open pasture. This was useful for keeping the cow. We always had a cow. Everybody did. In the spring my nurse and I used to fish for crayfish in the ditches, but I never got any. She took them home."

Before her sister Edith was born, Mr. Hamilton sometimes took care of Ellen for an afternoon. "Dad had three tracks when

he baby-sat with me," Mrs. Wilkerson said. "One was to go to the Thalian Club to play cards. I remember sitting up at the bar with my legs straight out in front of me being fed Hershey bars by the bartender. Track two was to walk along McKinney to see Mr. Pillot. While I played with the dogs that stood guard at the Pillot house, he and Daddy talked yachts. He had the *Augusta* and we had the *Crescent*. The Yacht Club was at the turning basin, and we used to dive off the boats into the bayou to swim." The last track was to walk to Sam Houston Park to see the Little Brownie statue, the special favorite of all small Houstonians.

As children, Ellen and her friend Lynn Foster often rode their horses out Polk Avenue, which was graveled, and through the woods to the Houston Country Club. There they had a swim and a sandwich, and then rode home again. Lynn was the daughter of Dr. and Mrs. John Foster.

When the S. M. McAshans moved to Lovett Boulevard shortly before World War I, Maurice, Jim, and Harris found a neighborhood of boys to play with, including Curtis Quarles, Daphan Gilmer, and Joe Hutcheson. "There was a good place to swim in the bayou just above Shepherd Dam," Maurice McAshan recalled. "We used to go there on our bicycles. We all got poison ivy. Of course we all had chores to do, like tending the fires and exercising the horses. Those were riding horses—we had a car. My father used to ride every morning, sometimes with friends, sometimes with one of us. We would take the horses west, out past

Though the bayou and ship channel were always essential to Houston commerce, yachts and pleasure craft still plied the water in 1920 when Frank J. Schlueter made this picture. *Courtesy Bank of the Southwest/Frank J. Schlueter Collection, Houston Metropolitan Research Center, Houston Public Library*

Montrose, when we still had shell and gravel streets. But sometime in the 1920s, the city passed an ordinance against keeping horses in town, and they had to be kept in Judge Green's stables out Westheimer. He was counsel for the Gulf Company, but he had a stable and an exercise ring. Once the horses were moved out there, my father didn't ride so much any more."

After the 1919 fire that destroyed Houston High School, students were diverted for a year or more to South End Junior High. Allie May Autry (Mrs. Edward Kelley) was in the first graduation class of the rebuilt Central High School.

"Helen Wicks had a big car," she recalls. "We'd ride up and down Main Street and go to the Auditorium Grocery and get sandwiches and Hydrox cookies, and we would eat tamales out of a newspaper. We had a wonderful time. Nobody smoked, nobody drank, nobody did anything but what they were supposed to do. The only thing we pulled on our families was that we all wanted to put our hair up, and so we each went home and told that story that everybody else could put *hers* up so why couldn't I?"

Because Houston was crisscrossed by open ditches that served as storm sewers, fishing for crayfish was a citywide custom. Before World War I, Mr. and Mrs. Elliott Cage lived on Westmoreland and Garrett.[2] Their daughter, Chaille Cage Thompson, recalled: "The Southern Pacific Railroad track ran between Montrose and Garrett and it had great tall banks on each side. When we were five or six, our nurses used to take us fishing for crawfish in the ditch beside the track—my brother Elliott, Louise and Neill Masterson, and me." Mr. and Mrs. Cage were among the first to move out to Montrose Boulevard in 1920. "When we moved to Montrose and Alabama, there was nothing out there but the big Link house and one other."[3]

Not all parts of town were safe at night. David Bintliff lived in Woodland Heights and in 1921 was courting Alice James. "That was when the streetcars were charging an excessive fare—five cents—and our recreation on the weekend was to ride the streetcar all around to Eagle Avenue from the Houston Heights and back. When that fare went up to ten cents, I thought I'd die." Miss James lived with her parents in Houston Heights and the streetcar stopped running at eleven o'clock. "So I would have to walk back to Woodland Heights at night, and it was a scary walk through those woods. One night about half a dozen wolves jumped me, took out after me. Fortunately I had a stick in my hand and I hit one of them on the nose and turned him around, but if you don't think I was frightened! I ran like a scared rabbit. I was still shivering when I got home."

By this time David Bintliff worked at the bank for S. M. McAshan. "I was the flunky auditor. When he heard I was engaged to be married, he called me into his office and he gave me a big raise, I mean a whopper: A five dollar a month raise."[4]

Dorothy Dunn (Mrs. Tom Martin Davis) was the second of the five children of Bessie Parker and Dewitt Dunn. She was born in the house of her grandparents, Judge and Mrs. John W. Parker, on the corner of Elgin and Main.[5] "My grandmother came from Georgia," Mrs. Davis said. "She was a busy, busy woman. She and Mrs. Jesse Andrews never missed a Democratic precinct meeting or convention. They were always politicking, but she was interested in everything. There was a colored funeral home a few blocks away on McKinney, near San Jacinto, and she would go play the piano for colored funerals. It was the first time I had ever heard 'Glory, Glory Hallelujah' played at funerals."

Her sister Bessie was two years older. "The greatest thing that could happen to us," Mrs. Davis said, "was to go to Levy's Tea Room for lunch, and then to the old auditorium to see anybody who was playing. Then we'd go backstage and meet them. We had letters from Elsie Janis's mother for years after. We heard Fritz Chrysler, and Caruso, and Paderewski.

"Then we entered everything that came up. They had a diving contest, right on the stage of the Majestic Theater, and Bessie won it!" Dorothy Dunn went to St. Agnes Academy with her lifelong friends—Marie Lee, Dorothy Taylor, Lena Carroll, Carolyn Bryan, Estelle Garrow, and Mary Catherine Donoghue.

One summer, when the Dunn children were in their teens, the family rented the Will Claytons' country place on Inwood Drive for the summer because the Claytons were to be out of town. Whenever the Claytons did use the country house in the hot months, Mrs. Clayton always insisted that the whole family go to River Oaks Club every night for dinner. It was too hot, she said, to expect the Claytons' servants to cook.

Frankie Carter (Mrs. R. D. Randolph) was the Pied Piper to the young people around her, especially to her niece Mary Carroll (Mrs. Lawrence Reed). "She was marvelous to her nieces," Mrs. Reed said. "She used to take us out to the Natatorium, and then for a special treat on the way home, she would drive us around Glenwood Cemetery."

The Carters spent many weekend and vacation times in the big house at Camden, headquarters of the Carter Lumber Company in East Texas. "Frankie had horses up there and she helped us get started with riding. But she liked to play golf, so at the foot of the hill she had a little place leveled out and we were kept busy weeding—Maudie, Lena, and I, and then Gertrude and Dorothy Binz, and Bill and Victor Carter."[6]

Frankie's mother, Mrs. W. T. Carter, did not care for Camden and in 1923, after her husband's death, she bought a place at Lake George. "John Herbert, the black chauffeur, who was a terribly nice man, would take the car up," Mrs. Reed said. "When Frank started going to Lake George in the summer, she also started spending every day in Saratoga during the racing season. At one point, I think the *bank* became disturbed over so many checks that were coming in. She was awfully good about taking us over fairly often, to the races and even to Brooks (Saratoga's best club at the time).

"There was a very dapper gentleman named Charlie who was the bookie, and he would come around to our table at the clubhouse and scribble something on a little three-inch square of paper, because betting was illegal. And one afternoon Dinks (Dorothy Binz) and I were with Frank, and she said, 'Now, we'll really win us some money this afternoon. Just bet on the favorites and if you lose, double the bet.' Well, we got up to the fifth or sixth race not having won a race. I had lost a whole year's clothes allowance that afternoon. Dinks did too." Frankie made up the allowances they had lost and the memory remains golden: "She was just so much fun and just so good!"

The Neill Turner Mastersons still lived at the corner of Barnard and Day streets in 1914 when their youngest son, Harris, was born.[7] His grandmother, Mrs. Harris Masterson, lived at Burlington and West Alabama in the big yellow brick house with columns on two sides. Surrounded by Mastersons, Harris played the Westmoreland neighborhood, staying for dinner at whichever house offered the most promising fare. He went to Kinkaid with his lifelong friends—Carroll Sterling (Mrs. Harris Masterson), Ryland Howard, Ruth Farrar (Mrs. Clifton Iverson), and Marjorie Lee (Mrs. Andrew Kerr, Jr.) among them.

"Sister and brother always went to school in the pony cart. But they went to Professor Welch's and then to Prosso before going off to school. Sometimes I'd go in the pony cart. Usually Clifton took me. Kinkaid was on the corner of Elgin and San Jacinto in a big, two-story building with an extension built out back. There wasn't much playground. We played Red Rover, Red Rover, and hop-

scotch. We jumped rope—red hot pepper—and played baseball."

In 1920, the Neill Mastersons moved to Montrose, near the museum end of the boulevard. They had one of the city's few private swimming pools. "Montrose made it farther for me to make my daily rounds in Westmoreland, but I had a bicycle and I skated. Gradually I made friends with Tom Blake and Betsy Slaughter and Mary Frances Bowles who lived on West Eleventh. And then we went over to Shadyside to play with David Peden and Billy Farish. The Neuhauses and the Wiesses, John Blaffer, Kenny Womack—they were all there. And Burdine Clayton lived on Caroline and that was close in those days. We had horses. Mother rode every day. We had cows and horses on Montrose." Harris Masterson schoolhopped—Kinkaid to Montrose to Sidney Lanier and then, for six weeks, to San Jacinto High School.

I had a wonderful time. Miss Genevieve Johnson was the dean, and she had taught my mother in first, second, and third grades at Incarnate Word. She was quite a lady, very small, crippled—I think from polio—and everyone loved her.

She was in charge of the tennis team, and I immediately joined the tennis club. Eloise Steele was going to be Queen of the May, and Miss Genevieve would say, "Eloise can't find a place to park, and she has to go fit her May Queen costume. Will you drive her down to the Fashion?" So Eloise and I would have lunch at the Gables.[8]

Harris Masterson explored and enjoyed Houston to the fullest. "Houston had lots of theater." he said.

My Grandmother Johnston [Mrs. Rienzi Johnston] took me every year to Madame Schuman-Heink's "farewell concert" because she was grandmother's favorite. And there were the Victor Artists—as in Victor records—people like John McCormick. Sarah Bernhardt came twice to the old auditorium. Mrs. Saunders brought lots of things. Shows would come to Beach's Auditorium and the Scottish Rite Cathedral. One of the great events was Rudolph Valentino and Natasha Rambova. They came and danced the tango in City Auditorium.

I used to go to town every Saturday from the time I was about ten. Clifton would take me down and leave me at Sam Wilson's barber shop. It was a black barber shop and my barber was Goree Naylor. Then I'd walk about six blocks to the Zoe because they had a serial called *The Collegians* that I *had* to see, and the movie there. Then I'd go to the Rice Hotel Cafeteria for lunch, which cost me about fifty-five cents for roast beef, baked potato, and all that. Then I'd go either to the Queen or the Isis depending upon what was on. I made two movies every Saturday from the time I was about ten to fourteen.

I used to go home on the streetcar, or thumb a ride, or even walk. The corner of Main and Lamar, where Foley's is now, was the Jones Lumber Company, and next to that was Beach's Auditorium. On that corner all the Rice students stood to catch rides to school, and all the kids, too. We knew every third person that drove by anyway, so we could always catch a ride there. I think that the character of Houston is so *Southern*—accent, habit, everything—whereas Dallas and Fort Worth are completely different.

"The nice thing about Houston," George Bruce said, "was that you didn't have to be rich. I was never rich and got along just fine." He was voicing a sentiment regularly heard in the social circles of Old Houston. It applied to Old Houstonians who had lost their money as well as to charming young people just starting out.

Widowhood could abruptly deprive a woman of her livelihood. Chatelaine of a large and handsome home at middle age, she could be left on her husband's death with a large house that was expensive to maintain as her only asset. As gentlewomen did from Houston to Boston to London and back, many a widow of Old Houston took in boarders. Doing so made her no less a gentlewoman and no less welcomed in the best circles.

As the children born just before and after the war grew up into the jazz age, Houston treated them kindly. Mrs. Edward Wilkerson remembers driving about with her friend Rosalee Smith (Mrs. Thomas Maffitt). "Home from college, Rosalee and I used to

drive up and down Main Street, waving at our friends who were doing the same thing. Then we'd go to the Gables on Main for cokes. Then we would go to Coggans and play thousands of dollars' worth of records, and buy one of them for seventy-five cents!"

The Gables, which was the place to go in the twenties for Houston's young, was run by tall, redhaired Gaylord Johnson. He had started in the drugstore business at thirteen. The Gables, he advertised, was "the largest establishment of its kind here . . . with a full and complete line of drugs, sundries, toilet articles, school supplies, tobacco and cigars." But the big attraction was the soda fountain, where streams of teenagers met for a soda and light lunch.

The remarkable thing is that while Gaylord Johnson was running the most popular center for young people in town, he was continuing his studies at Rice Institute, earning one degree after another—A.B., M.A., and Ph.D. He also taught chemistry at Rice.

In the early 1920s, there was as much shuttling back and forth between Houston and Galveston as there had been in the 1840s and 1850s. The Interurban made the trip even easier than the steamboats had in their prime. The young people of Old Houston had close friends among the Galveston equivalent—those who claimed proudly to have been born on the island: "B.O.I."

Tina Cleveland's special friend was Cecile Kempner, the daughter of I. H. Kempner—head of one of "the three seignorial families controlling Galveston," in John Gunther's phrase. Down for a weekend, Tina was greeted pleasantly at Sunday morning breakfast by Kempner, but he soon had to leave to pick up his grandchildren. "I'm doing a reverse Bishop Sessums," he explained. The Rt. Rev. Davis Sessums, the Episcopal bishop who had baptized and would later later marry all daughters of Alexander Sessums Cleveland of Houston, had a child who married a Jew. The Jewish Mr. Kempner had one daughter who married an Episcopalian and another who married a Catholic, and it was he who was taking the children to Sunday school that morning.

In 1925, Allie May Autry (Mrs. Edward Kelley) was in the first group of nineteen debutantes presented by the new Allegro, formed to make just such presentations. The balls, teas, and luncheons were delightful, but the memorable party of that season was given at the Houston Country Club by the Cullinans in her honor. "It was a country dance," Mrs. Kelley said. "They even had a pig squealing contest, greased pigs! It was a dance to end all dances." Mary Cullinan Cravens recalls: "There was an old timey country circus in town. I went out there and got the side-show fronts to put around the walls. Everybody came in costume and we had a buggy they could have their picture taken in."

Miss Autry and several of her friends were having too much fun to marry just yet. So they banded together as the SOPHS—Still On Papa's Hands—for further merrymaking.[9] "We all went with the same group of boys and every other Friday night, we'd have a dance at one of our houses."

To the pleasure of his friends, Rorick Cravens had a Flying Jenny and often took Allie May Autry, Tina Cleveland, and Mary Cullinan up for spins. The air strip was in a bare, often muddy field out South Main where it crossed the road to Bellaire.[10] If Rory needed to land, there was always plenty of pasture and field around town. When his biplane needed water, he set it down, filled his leather flying helmet from the drainage ditch, and refreshed his steed. In 1929, Mary Cullinan and Rorick Cravens were married at St. Bartholemew's Church in New York. Because he was opening a Cravens Dargan office in California, they spent the next four years in San Francisco.

Though E. L. Crain had scattered new subdivisions all around town, he and his family lived on Lovett Boulevard. His sons Lillo and Carter were born at 1117.

"Henry Safford lived on Lovett," Dr.

E. L. Crain, Jr., said, "and Robert Houx, whose father was an architect on the Hermann Hospital. The Vinson children, Julia and Martha, were right across the street. We played ball, hide and seek, climbed trees. And every summer, we would rent a house at Bay Ridge. Then toward the end of summer, Grandmother would take us on a long trip in the old Packard." (The Hugh Roy Cullens, the Sess Clevelands, the William Pattons, and many other Houston families considered the long automobile trip out west or to New England and Canada the climax of summer vacations through the 1930s and until wartime gasoline rationing curtailed them.)

On Lovett, Henry Gates Safford, associated with the W. D. Cleveland Company, lived next door to Henry R. Safford, president of the Missouri Pacific Railroad. They were known as the cotton Saffords and the railroad Saffords.

The distance along Montrose Boulevard between Lovett Boulevard and the Warwick Hotel was not easily bridged by small children. Lillo Crain and Jim Elkins did not become close friends until they went off to camp in Colorado, Dr. Crain said. "Later we both went to Hill School at Pottstown. Walter Walne was there too—Ching and Maisie's brother—and Billy Cochran."

Judge and Mrs. James Elkins had lived most of their Houston years in the Rice Hotel. In the early stages of his law practice in Houston, the firm's major client was in the oil business in Mexia. Mr. Elkins had to spend several days a week in Mexia. He felt his family would be safer at the hotel.

"Not that there was a great deal of terrorism in Houston at the time." James Elkins, Jr., said in amusement. As small boys, Bill and Jim Elkins greatly enjoyed hotel life.

John Jones lived there and the Meadors.[11] So did Henry Taub and his brother John. And Alvin Romansky. There was a bowling alley in the basement and a natatorium. I'm sure it wasn't much of a pool, but in our day, thinking of it as we did, it was pretty snappy.

Also, you were sort of the little children, the darlings of the adults who lived there. They would always be doing something nice for us—taking us to a movie, or to the zoo.

There were an awful lot of nice newsboys on the corner of Texas and Main that you played with. Our best friends were the bellboys and the musicians who played on the Rice Roof. It was sort of one big family. One of the more colorful bellboys was Jakie Freedman.[12]

John T. Jones, Jr., remembers the Rice Hotel manager with sympathy. "I think that Barney Morton's primary duty was to keep Jim and me under control. On the Rice roof they had a big white cage full of canary birds. We decided to let them out to see if they could fly, and sure 'nuff—they *could*. They mostly flew away."

Mr. and Mrs. Elkins had good friends living at the Rice, including the Gus Worthams, the Taubs, Mrs. Neil Esperson, the John Freemans, and Dr. and Mrs. Ernst Bertner.

In 1926, the Plaza Hotel, designed by Joseph Finger, opened on Montrose. Dr. and Mrs. Edgar Odell Lovett moved in, and every day Dr. Lovett walked to his office at Rice Institute. On Sunday mornings he would often stop by Shadyside for Joseph Cullinan to join him on a constitutional. Small Betty Crotty, who lived on Remington, considered it a special treat when she was allowed to go too, skipping to keep up with their long legs.

The Warwick Hotel opened the same year. It was built by Don Hall, the contractor responsible for the Cotton Exchange Building, the Museum of Fine Arts, the Medical Arts, and the Houston Post-Dispatch buildings.[13] Two and a half miles from downtown, the Warwick had a large number of apartments with spacious living rooms, dining rooms, and bedrooms. The marble bathrooms were roomy. Though they had kitchens, the residents could also call on hotel room service. All rooms had double doors to the corridor—one solid, one louvered—to provide cross-ventilation on hot days.

When Jim Elkins was twelve or thirteen,

the Elkins family moved out to the Warwick. It was on the edge of the city with nothing but the Hermann Park woodland beyond. The boys could walk to Kinkaid and there was a whole neighborhood in which to play. "I guess my parents felt that growing boys would be better off 'in the country'—which the Warwick then was," Elkins said. "Jack Josey lived there and the Abercrombies.[14] We would go play baseball on the museum land where Cullinan Hall now stands, and Harry Masterson lived across Montrose Boulevard. Harry had a swimming pool. And then on Saturdays, my father would take me to the baseball game at South End Park—where the Cullen Center is now."

Hotel living also freed Mrs. Elkins for the charity work that was important to her. She was busy with the Red Cross and with the Blue Bird Circle. "Mrs. E. L. Crain was one of her very good friends, and Mrs. Michaux another. They liked the hands-on charitable enterprise. They rolled bandages themselves, they dyed the Blue Bird Easter eggs themselves. It was not one of those semicommercial operations."

Finishing at Kinkaid, Jim Elkins went to Sidney Lanier Junior High. The Elkins family chauffeur taught him to drive on North MacGregor, which was still unpaved. "There was no age limit and no licensing," he recalls. But after a period at San Jacinto High School, he was sent to the Hill School to prepare for Princeton. "I think they sent me because I had reached the point of wanting a car."

All this time, the Elkins family in the Warwick lived within waving distance of the Wiess family at Number 2 Sunset in Shadyside. Jim grew up acquainted with Caroline Wiess. But such is the chasm of a few years in childhood that he did not meet her sister, Margaret. Then, one day in 1940, he was in Pennsylvania Station, New York City, when he saw his friend Caroline and another girl on the escalator. There he met Margaret Wiess, whom he would marry. "The loveliest thing that ever happened to me."

The John T. Joneses, meanwhile, moved

to 3815 Montrose Boulevard and John Jr. went to Montrose School.[15] John walked to Montrose and bicycled to Lanier. There he met Walter Cronkite. "He was two years ahead of me," Jones said, "and absolutely crazy about journalism. He was editor of the *Purple Pup*. Mrs. Blanche Higginbotham was principal of Lanier and she was a *very* good principal."

Few schools were equipped to serve hot lunches. Mothers were more bothered by this lack than the children were. Carolyn Grant was looking a mite peaked one winter and, to her dismay, her mother sent their man to the school each day at noon. Mortified, Carolyn had to sit out in the car and eat her delicious lunch when she wanted to be having a sandwich with her friends. Nancy Spencer, however, was delighted when Col. Thomas Spencer bagged choice birds. Mrs. Spencer would send *their* man to school so that Nancy could dine off pheasants.

In the late 1920s and early 1930s, the Staitis added splendor to the lives of children living in Westmoreland. Mr. and Mrs. H. T. Staiti built the big house at 421 Westmoreland Avenue. Surrounded by spreading lawns, it had a gazebo and a covered arbor. Every Fourth of July, Mr. and Mrs. Staiti would give a party for everyone on the block.

"We looked forward to it all year," Frances Heyck said.[16] "They had magnificent fireworks displays and they gave sparklers to all the children. As I remember the neighborhood, there were Tommy McGowan, Fred Heynie, Jr., Hazel Goodman, Celeste Cohn, H. L. Simpson, and Jeanette Jackson."

Georgia Howard (Mrs. Henry Safford) remembers long afternoons of play in Westmoreland. "It was an utter heaven for children," she said. "When I was nine or ten, we lived on Burlington. The Burke Bakers lived there and the Frederick Parkers and Scott Field Bailey. There were lots of us. And on summer nights, we'd all gather in the Staitis' yard.[17] The Staitis would rent comic movies and set them up in their yard, and

on the Fourth of July they had all these wonderful fireworks with flags and George Washington's picture. And on just a regular summer night we'd play that game where you took chalk and drew arrows in the direction you were going—Fox and Hen?

"One person had the chalk. He'd have you count thirty to let him get away, and then you had to follow his chalk marks to catch him. It would be over fences and across garage roofs, and why we didn't kill ourselves I'll never know, but it was the most exciting thing in the whole world."

Georgia's parents, Dr. and Mrs. Philo Howard, moved to Audubon Place when she was eleven. "Mother was always organizing things for the church. The ladies would have benefit bridge games at the Rice Hotel —that whole ballroom full of bridge tables— and they'd sell tickets. They let my group dress up and trot around with a tray full of candy to sell to the players." A group that remained lifelong friends from childhood, it included Janet Houstoun (Mrs. Platt Walker Davis), Aubrey Randolph (Mrs. Parker Cushman), and Eveline Copley (Mrs. George Biehl).

"When I was about ten or eleven, on Saturdays we would take our allowance and get on the streetcar and go downtown to the movies. There were only three—the Metropolitan, Loew's, and the Majestic. Then we would go to Darcy's for lunch and come home on the streetcar." In high school, however, they went to the movies with dates. "You wore stockings and a hat and you went to the movies and then to the Gables and had a coke and then you came home."

Helen Drane, fair haired and the epitome of the protected Southern girl, was in her teens when she had a startling experience. One morning, her father suggested that she drive him to the office so that she and her friend could keep the car. The downtown stores had not yet opened, but after dropping him off, the two girls noticed a dress in a store window. They got out and were looking in the window when a policeman approached. "Young ladies," he said courteously. "I think you'd best go home until you are properly dressed." In the rush, they had not put on their stockings.

Like their mother, all the Drane girls were unusually lovely to look at. Like their father, all the Dranes were singularly talented in the arts. While in high school, Virginia Drane played the piano on KXYZ with Ted Nabors as her announcer. She played anything listeners requested by telephone. As Virginia Drane McCallon, she became one of the most respected fashion editors in the country.[18] Covering fashion openings in New York and Paris for the *Houston Post,* she did all her own sketches and photographic layouts.

Elizabeth Drane studied music with the intention of becoming a concert pianist. But after marriage and the birth of her daughter Jacqueline, she turned to painting. She ultimately became Wyatt Hedrick's architectural designer on buildings in Houston, Dallas–Fort Worth, and sites as far away as Iceland. Her work enhanced the Shamrock Hotel, Baylor University College of Medicine, the second Hermann Hospital, and schools throughout the Texas Gulf Coast.

Dr. Joe Drane became the first head of maxillo-facio reconstruction at M. D. Anderson Hospital. With his eye for color and form, he created prostheses that filled out the faces that had been changed by necessary surgery, and he established the department that would carry on the work. It was the first in the United States.

Decade by decade, Houston boys were expected to have a summer job as they reached high school and college age. In 1931, Tom Anderson, M. D. Anderson's nephew, worked for a month at the National Bank of Commerce as an assistant teller and made sixty dollars. "It was all mine," he said. "There wasn't any Social Security or withholding. I got the whole sixty dollars!" While in law school at Washington and Lee, he had a summer job with Fulbright, Crooker & Bates. "I helped the lawyers down there," he said. "I *suppose* it was help. I don't remember whether they paid me."

"My father said, 'You don't idle your summers away.'" James Elkins, Jr., remembered. "I started out as a runner in Vinson & Elkins, and then worked another summer at the National Bank of Commerce and another at American General."

The links are clear. Jesse Jones, who owned the bank, and Gus Wortham, head of American General, were longtime friends of Judge and Mrs. Elkins. Houston was crisscrossed by the network. The minister's son might work in the doctor's office. The banker's son would work for a law partnership, the lawyer's son would become a runner for a bank. Some of the more adventurous boys took on a summer of ranching, which was hard, hot work. Rotating, summer by summer, sons of the Old Houston network were familiar with most major business and professional firms in the city by the time they went off to college.

To a Wider World

OLD HOUSTON FAMILIES tended to float their children out across the world at prep-school or college age. Like those who sent their daughters to school in Paris for the Civil War years or to Paris for a year of schooling and travel at the turn of the century, Houstonians continued the custom in the 1920s and 1930s. Young Houstonians traveled abroad in summer holidays or – as Dudley Sharp did – by taking a year off from school.

After a stint at South End Junior High School and the Prosso School run by Dr. and Mrs. Richardson, he went off to Gilman School in Baltimore.[1] In lieu of his senior year, Mrs. Walter Sharp decided to take her son to Europe "for a practical education – seeing museums and things," Dudley Sharp remembered. She also arranged for an American Rhodes Scholar, Alan Valentine, to tutor Dudley at Oxford. There he discovered the joys of lacrosse and went down to London for his entrance examinations for Princeton.

"I was terribly happy at Princeton. It has a magnificent setting and it was stimulating. I am a slow learner and a slower reader. I had to put in an awful lot of hours there. We'd work really hard in the week and go to Philadelphia or New York on the weekend."

Though in the class of '27, Sharp actually graduated in 1928. In the interim year, he and his friend Arthur Foster made a round-the-world trip, starting on the West Coast. They traveled by train to Seattle, by steamship to Alaska, by the Skagway train to White Horse at the headwaters of the Yukon. "There were no real roads then," Sharp recalled, "and we had arranged for a Ford car to drive us to where we would take pack horses for a hunting trip back in the interior.

"The driver of the car turned out to be the White Horse banker's wife. She got us there in great shape after two days. You could almost duplicate this trip now on the Alaskan highway. It goes to many of the places we could reach only by pack horse." The two Princeton seniors had twenty-seven horses, a head guide, two Indian guides, and a Chinese cook to maintain them in the wilds for sixty days. When they returned to Vancouver, Mrs. Sharp came out from Houston to see them off on the long trip to the Orient.

They took a Canadian Pacific ship to Japan, where they met a friend from Princeton, Chugi Kabayama.[2] Kabayama, who was related to the imperial family, entertained them in Tokyo. As they were leaving to see other parts of Japan, he said, "Before you go to Manchuria, you should stop off for a visit with my uncle who lives on the way. He raises Arab horses and pheasants for the emperor. Just telegraph him which train to meet."

"This sounded marvelous to us," Dudley Sharp said. "So we sent the telegram, and when we got off the train, a Japanese gentleman met us in a buckboard. He had with him his wife, who was the most beautiful Japanese woman I have ever seen."

It was wild country. The gentleman said he hoped they would be comfortable because this was pretty much off the traveled paths. The young Americans said not to worry—they had just come from a hunting trip in the Yukon. The buckboard rounded a curve in the road. "There stretched a palace as far as you could see. It was an attractive old palace as well. The rooms were heated with fires under the stone floors. It had those deep baths with geisha girls to soap your back."

Before dinner their host offered them bourbon, a rare treat in the United States in 1927. "At dinner, one of us said how nice it was of Chugi to introduce us to his uncle."

Their host was surprised. "Oh! Do *you* know Chugi?"

Their good Princeton friend had forgotten to write his uncle to expect Dudley and Arthur. They were being entertained through the exquisite courtesy of a Japanese aristocrat who had had no idea who they were.

After a month in Peking they took a coastal ship for Shanghai to spend Christmas. It was a new British vessel, but Dudley felt a swelling in his neck. The boat put in at a small harbor, and a doctor came out and diagnosed the swelling as mumps. Dudley must take to his bunk. When Arthur came back to their stateroom from dinner, he said, "I don't know what makes this ship run. All the officers are drunk." Not long after, a shock ran through vessel. It had hit a reef. It began to sink.

"We had to get out the lifeboats," Sharp said. "The Chinese crew panicked. The boats they were in tumped over. The water had ice in it. Over a hundred people drowned. The coast guard picked us up the next morning. I must have looked pretty funny. I had wrapped a towel around my head to keep my mumps warm, and did have the sense to put on my overcoat. But I saved the most ridiculous things. I saved *all my neckties!* And we did spend Christmas in Shanghai."

They went on to French Indo-China for another hunting trip—big game in the jungle. Dudley came down with amoebic dysentery. "I had to be tied onto the horse to be taken back to Saigon. It was a French hospital, run by nuns. Wonderful people. They had discovered how to cure it only a year before. Until then, you just died. They gave me Epsom salts every night and castor oil every day for ten days. Then they began to give me arsenic. It was whatever the arsenic combination was that saved me." He had malaria at the same time, and spent a month in the hospital.

Apparently indestructible, Dudley Sharp got back to the jungle for a final week of hunting before it was time to start out for Indo-China by car.

In an era when Richard Halliburton would become famous for traveling *The Royal Road to Romance,* Arthur and Dudley went on to Angkor Wat, Calcutta, sightseeing across India, up the Persian Gulf on a ship, from Basra to Bagdad on one of the early British commercial flights, and in an open car across the desert to Damascus. The desert trip took forty-eight hours and they were told to bring pillows so they could sleep on the sand. They came home through Europe.

"Then I went back to Princeton for my senior year. I felt older and a little wiser," said Dudley Sharp. He returned to Houston in the fall of 1928 to go into the oil field equipment business with his brother Bedford Sharp.

The A. S. Clevelands, meanwhile, had taken their daughter Tina on a world cruise. "We left in December, 1926, and returned in the summer of 1927," Tina Cleveland Sharp said. "Mother and Daddy came on home at the end of the cruise. I met Lila and Mr. Godwin in Paris and we were there when Lindbergh landed.[3] It was the one great excitement of my early years."

"Mrs. E. A. Peden and her daughter Stella, and Elizabeth Law were there," she continued. "Mrs. Peden had a dinner party at that marvelous restaurant that Mike and Will had set up for Mike's batman." In the 1920s, all Houstonians going to Paris made a point of going to this one particular restaurant. It was owned and operated by a black man who had been Mike Hogg's sergeant during the war and who had received his start as a restaurateur from Hogg. Houstonians naturally wanted to boost the clientele.

Arthur Foster, who was on his way home from the round-the-world trip with Dudley Sharp, was at the dinner party but Dudley had lingered in Berlin. After all his years away at school, Dudley was scarcely more than a name to Tina. But the next time she and Arthur Foster met was when Foster arrived in Houston to be best man at the Cleveland-Sharp wedding.

Mary Carroll, Tina Cleveland's best friend on Courtlandt Place, had gone to Dana Hall in Wellesley, where she and Lib Masterson were roommates. "I don't know why, but it was taken for granted that we would go off to school at that age. I think they thought it was good for us to get away from home," Mary Carroll Reed said. When she was graduated after two years, she was sixteen and her parents thought her too young and naive to go to college. They therefore sent her to Europe with her sister Maudie, only slightly older.[4]

"Cora Bryan was our chaperone and she wasn't much older than Maudie," Mrs. Reed said. "After going to Baldwin, Maudie had attended the University of Texas, where she met John Bullington. We went to England, Scotland, and Paris. John was studying law at the Sorbonne, and we never got beyond Paris. We got an apartment and had a cook and a maid. Wasn't that *ridiculous!*" Unfortunately, the cook and maid had Sunday off. "So John would come and cook breakfast because neither Maudie nor I had an *inkling.*"

"Cora and I did a good bit of sightseeing and went to the shows at Patou and Chanel. I had arranged to have French lessons with an American but John canceled the American and signed me up with a French teacher. And he said, 'Enough of all these taxis. You must go by the Paris subway.'" So at sixteen,

Mary Carroll tootled around Paris on her own because her parents thought her too young to go off to college. Inasmuch as Paris was one of the safest cities in the world at the time, it was probably a sensible decision.

This was 1925, the first year of the Allegro presentation of debutantes, and Maudie was making her debut. In December, after six delightful months, the Carroll girls came home. And Maudie ultimately married John Bullington.[5]

By the scores, young Houstonians went off east to school. One reason for this was that Houston public schools did not offer eleventh and twelfth grades, and Kinkaid did not go past the ninth. Because A. S. Cleveland believed in public education, he sent his daughters to Houston schools as far as possible but sent them to boarding school for the college preparatory years.

Harry Wiess, knowing that money can vanish, believed that education was the most important thing he could give his daughters for their lifelong security. He also wanted to free them of provincialism. All three daughters started to Kinkaid. Each in turn was sent off to school. In 1931, after Kinkaid's two years of high school, Elizabeth Wiess went first to Farmington, then to Ethel Walker's in Simsbury, Connecticut. She was one of nine girls who went to Europe with four teachers for nine months—three in Paris, three in Rome, and three in London.

"Elizabeth had the finest mind and best education of any of us," her sister Margaret Elkins said. "She spoke several languages. She was extremely well read. When in France they studied French history and language and toured all of France. They were in Rome for Christmas. And of course they skied in Switzerland and had fun. Then the next year, her godmother, Mrs. Vernon Aderill, sent Elizabeth around the world."

Margaret, the youngest Wiess daughter, and her best friend, Wilhelmina Cullen, were in a class of five that included Lois Henderson, Ellis Colvin, and Charles Jackson. As Kinkaid added a grade, the class moved into it. But, Mrs. Elkins said, "I was long gone before twelfth grade." In 1940, over her protests, she was sent to Boston to Pine Manor, and there discovered opera, art history and skiing.

As it had in the nineteenth century, Princeton continued to draw students from Houston—Palmer Hutcheson in the early 1900s, Bill Kirkland, Harry Wiess, and Captain Baker's son Browne before the war, Dudley Sharp, Maurice McAshan, and Mark Edwin Andrews in the 1920s. Later in the 1930s would come James A. Elkins, Jr., Thad, Edward, and Palmer Hutcheson, Jr., B. W. Crain, and his cousin E. L. Crain, Jr. After Princeton, in 1939, Lillo Crain entered the University of Pennsylvania Medical School one hundred years after his great-grandfather had entered the Jefferson Medical School in Pennsylvania.

Ernest Bel Fay went to Harvard. Albert Bel Fay, Charles Dillingham, Billy and Victor Carter went to Yale, as did Hugo, Joe, Phil, and Harry Neuhaus. After World War II, Wallace Wilson, Pierre Schlumberger, Jr., and Peter Maffitt went to Yale, and James A. Baker III entered Princeton. The University of Virginia, Washington and Lee, and the University of the South at Sewanee drew many Houston boys.

Martha Wicks, after graduating from Baldwin School in Bryn Mawr in the late 1920s, went to Sarah Lawrence. "I didn't graduate," she said, "because I came home to marry Malcolm.[6] But Sarah Lawrence was wonderful. The Yale faculty would take classes. Nearly all my professors were from Yale."

Smith College always had a number of Houston girls among its students—Ellen Clayton, Margaret Cullinan, and Laura Rice in the early 1920s, followed by Mary Cullinan and Susan Clayton in the mid-1920s, by Harriet Bath, Nancy Spencer, and Mary Kingswell Smith in the 1930s, and in the 1950s by Isabel Brown, Louisa Stude, and Miriam Kass. Annette Finnigan was graduated from Wellesley in 1894. Chaille Cage went to Wellesley out of her admiration for Mrs. Fred Lummis, a Wellesley graduate. Francita Stuart went there in the early 1950s. Laura and Mary Porter Kirkland went to Bryn Mawr in the late twenties, Winnie Safford in the late thirties.

Carolyn Grant, after graduation from Madeira School, would have preferred Stanford in the 1930s and was accepted for admittance, but her father had his heart set on Vassar for his only daughter. In the late 1930s, Clare Fleming and June Heyer went to Vassar, where one of Clare's chums was Sissy Tarleton.[7] "We were ahead of our time," Clare Fleming Sprunt said. "We wore blue jeans to Vassar and Sissy wore a mink coat over hers."

Houston fathers putting a daughter on the Pullman car for the long trip east always scouted out the train to find some friend who might be asked to stand by the gentle creature in case of emergency. "In those times, Mr. Jones was *always* going to New York," Martha Lovett recalled. "We got to be quite good friends because whenever I was going to Bryn Mawr, Daddy would ask Mr. Jones to look after me."

Hugo Neuhaus, Jr., and his brother Joe were sent to a prep school in New Hampshire to learn the Latin they needed to enter St. Paul's in Concord. Graciously landscaped, the prep school was absurdly rigid in its rules governing play as well as study. Within hours after arriving, the Neuhaus boys planned their departure by taxi. "The Saturday we were going to leave," Hugo Neuhaus said, "Uncle Will Rice arrived in a huge limousine and took us away.[8] Aunt Laura Neff and Uncle Dick had a beautiful place in Franconia, so Uncle Will took us there."

Hugo Neuhaus, *père*, was one of a small group who had bought 1,250 acres in the Virginia hunt country. The central section of the plantation house dated from 1670. From there, Hugo and Joe entered the Stiverson School in Warrenton, Virginia. "We learned our Latin," Neuhaus said. "But we had only four days of school a week. On Saturdays we rode to the fox hounds and on Wednesdays to the drag hounds. We were only there one year but we loved it so that we didn't want to go home for Christmas."

Latin learned, they entered St. Paul's.

At St. Paul's you had two weeks at Christmas and two at Easter. Because we were from Texas, they gave us two extra days holiday travel. It actually took us four days to get home. We went from Concord to Boston, changed trains, and then came on to St. Louis in a through car. Many people were away at boarding school, and from St. Louis on down to Houston, the cars filled up with our friends. It was really exciting pulling into Houston station. Everybody's family would be there.

But travel was so simple in those days. I remember once getting to the Missouri Pacific Station just in time to make the train and I had forgotten my tennis racquet. So my father asked them to hold the train until he could send back home and get it.

Home was on Remington Lane, three miles out Main Street and three miles back. But they held the train.

All these young people felt they were from the South. Houstonians spoke with the soft voice of the Old South. Houston had its Confederate heritage. But whenever they went East, they were greeted as Westerners—to their annoyance.

"At Camp Nakanawa in North Carolina, most of the other girls were from Alabama or New Orleans," Frances Heyck recalled. "When I said I was from the South, too, they just turned me down. They insisted I was from the *West*."

Caroline Wiess (Mrs. Theodore Law) had the same experience. "We always said we were from the South," she remembered. "It used to burn us up because they would all refer to us as being way out West. The farthest west any of them had been was Buffalo, New York, and to them Palm Beach was the *South!*"

When people went off to school or on a prolonged trip, their family and friends gathered at the railroad station to see them off with flowers, candy, and books. If the travelers were going abroad by steamship, their well wishers not only came to see them off but came aboard for a party. Such parties were always well attended by those staying at home because during Prohibition, it was legal to serve the champagne on shipboard that would be illegal in a restaurant, club, or hotel on land.

There was no reason in the world to travel light. Red caps and porters came by the legion in every country. It was the heyday of the steamer trunk. The steamer trunk was essential for a month at summer camp or for two weeks in the hospital after childbirth. Once packed, it stood on end in stateroom or college dormitory room. On the left were drawers, and on the right hangers and a space to hang blouses, skirts, and dresses.

For a long trip to Europe, travelers took steamer trunks, suitcases, hatboxes, and, if expecting to be entertained formally, jewel cases. Matched luggage, of alligator or rawhide or suede, was initialed and very heavy. Movie stars, of course, traveled with a mountain of luggage. Their farewell parties were always photographed by the press for the edification of readers across the country, and they were usually pictured sitting on top of the mountain.

Surprise Party

TO ITS COMPLETE SURPRISE, Houston found itself gearing up for the Democratic National Convention of 1928. It did not have much time. The Democratic National Committee had met in Washington on January 12, 1928, to decide where to hold the June convention. Jesse Jones, as national finance director, was determined to wipe out the party's debt. He decided that if city bidding for the convention could be boosted high enough, the Democrats could start the campaign debt-free.

The bidding began at a subcommittee meeting held in his suite at the Mayflower Hotel. He had no thought that the Democrats might be willing to come so far south as Houston in the summer heat. Cleveland offered $100,000; Detroit, $125,000; and Chicago, $130,000. Suddenly, Mr. Jones's life-long enthusiasm for his hometown got the upper hand. He entered a bid to have the convention come to Houston and attached to it a personal check for $200,000. San Francisco, which had been biding its time, topped this with certified checks for $250,000.

As the proposals went to the full Democratic party committee, Jones thought further: the 1924 convention had been the first carried by radio. The 1928 convention would be heard on millions of radio sets. It would be covered copiously in newspapers with daily articles and featured in rotogravure sections. Big city newspapers would surely send their top political and social columnists. The wire services would certainly attend. Houston, he decided, could use the publicity.

The San Francisco delegate thought he held a winning card: "How many people did the gentleman from Texas say his convention hall would seat?" he asked.

"I said five thousand," Jones replied. "But if you give us the convention, we will build one to seat twenty-five thousand."

Houston got the convention. Jesse Jones called Mayor Holcombe to tell him that Houston was to be so honored, and that it now owed the Democratic National Committee two hundred thousand dollars in cash plus a new convention hall to seat twenty-five thousand.

Dazed but pleased, the city responded. Thousands came to greet Jones at the railroad station and a few days later six hundred gathered for a testimonial dinner. Dr. Stockton Axson, always eloquent, said, "Jesse H. Jones has passed all local boundaries; he is now a great national figure. I know that his principles are those of Woodrow Wilson, and, were Wilson alive today, I believe . . . he would favor Mr. Jones, of all men, to be President of the United States."

Other Texans promoted the idea. Jones did not. Although he may have fancied being a favorite-son nominee, he had never sought public office. Tall, distinguished-looking, always well dressed, recognized as a powerful man in business and politics, he nonetheless did not have the flair to be a successful campaigner. Although he wrote well, his voice was neither deep nor warm. He was not persuasive as a public speaker. He did not seek a serious nomination. But Dr. Axson's accolade tossed Gov. Dan Moody on the horns of a dilemma—one that must have cost him many sleepless nights between January and June. To nominate Jesse Jones would put the governor athwart that mighty force of nature—Will Hogg. Not to, after Dr. Axson's effusion, would be unthinkable.

By June, seventy-five thousand Houstonians had paid their poll tax, compared with fifty-two thousand two years earlier. Though the approaching convention heightened awareness of politics, these figures also reflected an already lively interest among Houstonians of all classes—especially among women. The February issue of the new *Houston Gargoyle* reported on a meeting of one hundred fifty Daughters of Jackson. The nonpartisan group had been formed to urge all women to register and pay the poll tax.

Florence Sterling, one of Houston's most admired women, explained the poll tax campaign, but the *Gargoyle* focused on young Oveta Culp, executive secretary. At twenty-three, Miss Culp was known across the state as parliamentarian of the Texas House of Representatives.[1] The *Gargoyle* gave more space to Culp's yellow ensemble and nice profile than to her plea that women vote, but, after listening, "we ceased to doubt Dan Moody's wisdom in seeking her advice and aid in the matter of handling . . . voters." The women present listened to what she said and signed up in force.

After the meeting, Mrs. Walter Sharp approached Culp. Tall, erect, Mrs. Sharp was as regal as Queen Mary of England and had a stimulating intellect.

"Miss Culp," she said, "Thank you for speaking up on the point. We must get to know one another." This was the beginning of a long, rewarding friendship. "Mrs. Sharp opened the world to many of us." Oveta Culp Hobby said long after. "She was interested in the mind and the thinking process. She organized a study group and saw to it that we learned about important national and international issues. For instance, she introduced us to such matters as the League of Nations report on the invasion of Manchuria, and on the meaning of the

Oveta Culp, well known throughout the state by the time she moved to Houston, is shown here in about 1920. *Courtesy H&C Communications*

German desire for *lebensraum*. She made us study hard. Every six months we started a new course. Mrs. Sharp was responsible for opening the eyes of people of my vintage to the great issues of the world."[2]

Mrs. Sharp's daughters-in-law were somewhat in awe of her. But Mary Cullinan Cravens had grown up playing with Mrs. Sharp's son Dudley, and at college age she had often traveled with Mrs. Sharp. "She was so beautifully dressed," Mrs. Cravens said. "She served wonderful food. Her house was carpeted in Oriental rugs and had the fragrance of sandalwood. She was glamorous!"

Houston was humming. Its new municipal airport had opened some months before in what the *Houston Post* called "the open-throttled roar of 113 airplanes, more land craft than had assembled on any American flying field in a concentration of army officers, commercial flyers and government representatives."

Though the convention hall was Houston's first order of business, it was only part of a building boom. Some $35 million worth of building had been contracted for. The old Allen warehouse near the junction of White Oak and Buffalo bayous was razed to make way for the Merchants and Manufacturers Building.[3] Jesse Jones's sixteen-story Lamar Hotel, designed by Alfred C. Finn, was under construction.

From the time of their marriage, Jesse and Mary Gibbs Jones had lived at the Rice Hotel in a large suite. But having captured the Democratic convention for Houston, Jones grew concerned about his approaching role as host to distinguished guests. As his newest hotel neared completion, he decided to add a floor on top for his own use. He telephoned John Staub and asked him "to design me a house up there." The resulting penthouse on the seventeenth floor, covering the entire top of the hotel, was one of Houston's most impressive homes. It provided views of the city from every bedroom, and from the gallery, the living and dining rooms, the palm court, and the terrace. Later Jones told Staub that he built it so that when Mrs. Woodrow Wilson came for the convention, she might be properly entertained.

At last, in 1928, John Henry Kirby opened his mansion at 2006 Smith. It had taken three years to build and every detail was luxurious.[4] Most Houstonians, however, had their eyes on two far larger projects. While downtown businessmen watched the coliseum go up, sports lovers were watching the new ball park being built on the east end of town. By this time, John Crooker had sold his majority interest in the baseball club to the St. Louis Cardinals, with Branch Rickey manager.

The Cardinals promised the Texas League a new stadium. The city closed off streets and provided free parking, but most of the fans would ride the Leeland Street trolley to the games. To start the 1928 season, Judge Kennesaw Mountain Landis opened the new Buffalo Stadium by throwing out the first ball before the twelve thousand cheering spectators. Jerome K. "Dizzy" Dean would soon become the Buffs' star player.

Between February and mid-June, the twenty-five-thousand-seat Sam Houston Coliseum was built and equipped with all the necessary telephone and telegraph lines. As conventioneers gathered, Houston's social and civic leaders welcomed them at the Hospitality House, a temporary building next to the coliseum. Houston weather lived up to its promise: every day was hot.

The *Houston Gargoyle* had come into being at the right moment. It was six months old when the convention opened on June 26. Patterned after the *New Yorker,* the weekly magazine had been started by Allen V. Peden, president, with John T. Scott, Jr., vice-president; Joe L. Fox was secretary-treasurer. Other directors (and backers) were Robert Neal, W. A. Kirkland, Mrs. Walter B. Sharp, and Roscoe E. Wright. The *Gargoyle* welcomed "the first National Democratic Convention held in the South since 1860."

Houston seemed to be expecting as many as one hundred thousand people–or more than one-third of its own population. "Houston streets and hotel lobbies are this week a motion picture of *Who's Who,*" the *Gargoyle* reported. It glimpsed "Virginia's governor, Harry Byrd, brother of Richard; Mary Roberts Rinehart, leaving the convention hall on her way to the Warwick; Nicholas T. Longworth waiting on the porch of the Houston Country Club for Alice Roosevelt Longworth to make a brisk, long-stepping appearance; Newton D. Baker, Woodrow Wilson's secretary of war, at the Lamar Hotel entrance; Jimmy Gerard, former ambassador, leaving the Rice; Gov. Albert C. Ritchie ringing for an elevator on the Rice roof; H. L. Mencken, smoking a normal-sized cigar; Graham McNamee in conversation with Oscar Underwood and John W. Davis near the Coliseum platform. . . ."[5]

This was heady stuff for young journalists–and the *Gargoyle* staff was very young.

In 1928, most Houstonians were Democrats. As Harris Masterson III said, "In the late part of the nineteenth century and the first part of the twentieth, we were all big Democrats. We were a Democratic area. The senators from the South and particularly a bunch from Texas were extremely powerful in the party."

Robert W. Wier, lumberman, directed first aid crews for casualties at Sam Houston Hall and Hospitality House. One each day, six Houston social leaders acted as hostess at the Hospitality House: Mrs. Henry B. Fall, Mrs. Walter B. Sharp, Mrs. Cleveland Sewall, Mrs. F. M. Law, Mrs. C. S. E. Holland, and Mrs. Lula Bryan Rambaud.

Every Houston club and restaurant was booked for one party or another. Mrs. Wilson, Mrs. Jesse Jones's house guest, was honored at a breakfast at the River Oaks Country Club by the four DAR chapters. She was honored again at a breakfast on the Rice Roof. Given by the local Democratic Club, it was open to anyone paying one and a half dollars. Will Rogers was the speaker. The Liberal Democrats gave a reception in honor of Mrs. Al Smith at the Houston Country Club, and Mr. and Mrs. Cordell Hull were honored at a reception on the lawn of the M. L. D. Martin home on Richmond Road.

Each day, the Sam Houston Hall was packed to the rafters, but the convention itself was without drama. Franklin D. Roosevelt, no longer on crutches but leaning on a cane and the arm of a companion, nominated Al Smith, as he had nominated him for govenor in the Happy Warrior speech four years before.

The moment had come for the leader of the Texas Democratic Party, Governor Moody, to nominate that giant of the party, Jesse Jones. Despite the outpouring of admiration for Jones, his support was not unanimous. Will Hogg opposed him vehemently. Each of these two titans were sure he knew best what was good for Houston. Inevitably they clashed. Jones also had a reputation for hard tactics in business that left a number of men feeling cut loose and angry.

Governor Moody knew that if he nominated Jones for president, Will Hogg and others would never forgive him. If he did not nominate Jones for president, he would be insulting the man who had brought the convention to Texas. When the hour came, Governor Moody sensibly took to his bed and was too ill to attend the nominating session. Rep. Tom Ball placed the name of Jesse Holman Jones in nomination. Jesse Jones received all the Texas votes and three from Alabama. Other favorite sons, like Cordell Hull, received home-state votes. Alfred E. Smith was chosen Democratic candidate for president on the first ballot.

Al Smith had been elected governor of New York four times. He was well liked and had achieved reforms. But with his tip-tilted derby and pronounced Brooklyn accent, he did not have universal appeal. He was also the first Catholic ever to run for the presidency—and this gave the demagogues their chance. They charged that if he were elected, the pope would come take over the White House. One particularly outrageous southern senator warned rural and small-town audiences that the pope would dig a tunnel under the Atlantic to get to Washington—an idea so novel that it seems a pity that Mr. Smith lost the election.

Herbert Hoover suited the mood of America. During the Great War he had led the American efforts to provide food and relief for Europe. As secretary of commerce under both Harding and Coolidge he had promoted the St. Lawrence Waterway and the Boulder Dam (later renamed the Hoover Dam). After the tainted administration of Warren Harding, the voters saw him as an honest, substantial man who could be trusted. He won easily. Withal, the Houston convention enabled Jesse Jones to pay all debts and convention expenses of the National Democratic Party and to turn one hundred and fifty thousand dollars in cash over to Herbert H. Lehman, his successor as finance director.[6]

In Good Times

IN 1928, the Model T Ford rolled away into automobile history. This was big news in the easy, cloudless days of what seemed to be unending prosperity and unending peace. On the Sunday after the Democratic Convention, the entire back page of the *Post-Dispatch* rotogravure section was given over to the announcement of the new Model A.

"The new Ford Roadster sells for $385, the Phaeton for $395, the Tudor Sedan for $495, the Sport's Coupe, with wide, substantial rumble seat, for $550, the Fordor Sedan for $625. . . ." The wide, substantial rumble seat would provide joy rides for two generations of carefree young Houstonians. New closed cars came with an electric windshield wiper. Open cars still required the driver to wag the windshield wiper back and forth by hand.

Skirts were not so short as the cartoons of John Held, Jr., implied. The middle-aged women photographed at the convention had hemlines at a discreet midcalf. The youthful model posing for the Ford ad wore a straight dress to just below the knee. The sporty young man with one foot up on the running board had on plus fours. By this time, the true flapper had bobbed her hair and plastered a spit curl on each cheek. Many rolled their stockings down below the knee and secured them by a double twist tucked in at the top. This roll defied gravity and offered provocative glimpses of the knee when the flapper danced the Charleston. Some of the more dashing women were beginning to smoke in public. The Spanish comb and a long cigarette holder marked the avant garde.

The New York speakeasy made a whole new range of cocktails popular. In Houston and most southern towns, the bootlegger made home deliveries. But the public drunkenness of the saloon days had ended. Most leaders in society obeyed the law. Tina Cleveland, for example, had never seen her father take a drink until they went to Europe where it was legal.

The *Gargoyle*'s fashion writer advised that "Everyone travels 'light' these days, that is with the minimum of necessary pieces in the lightest weight possible." The minimum included a leather toilet case, an ample suitcase to carry frocks and lingerie, another for wraps, shoes, riding boots, golf shoes, and accessories. All this was needed for a weekend in an era when a debutante could store the dress from her debut ball in a cigar box. Cigar boxes were made of cedar and served the purpose admirably.

With travel by trains and ocean liners, nobody went abroad for a week or two. It took longer than that simply to get there. Houstonians traveled around the world or spent a season abroad. In the summer of 1929, Agnese and Haywood Nelms took their three small children to spend two months in France.[1] They could leave them with a nurse in Deauville while they roamed around Normandy looking for things to enhance the house they were building in Sleepy Hollow. They came home in the fall in time for the twins to enter first grade at the new River Oaks School. Tiny Eva Margaret Davis was the first principal and Mrs. Nelms the first PTA president.

Will and Ima Hogg had both the time and the money to travel, occasionally together, usually with friends. With Bayou Bend at last built, furnished, and landscaped, Ima Hogg set out with her friend Eloise Chalmers for six months in Europe in May, 1929. She went to France, Sweden, and Denmark, and, with a group of Americans, to the Soviet Union. There she visited the Museum of Modern Art in Moscow and began to collect contemporary art with the purchase of a Paul Klee and two Picassos.

Before the year was out, she had also helped found a much-needed institution. Psychiatry and psychology were not the stuff of daily fare in 1929. But Miss Hogg had vivid memories of her own childhood. She remembered her mother's death and the pitiful unhappiness of her younger brother Tom. She realized that Houston had little to offer children who were unhappy or disturbed. She called together a group to found a Houston Child Guidance Center.[2]

As she had when she founded the symphony society, she began by establishing a strong board. Kenneth E. Womack was elected the first president; Mrs. R. E. Brooks, Jr., vice-president; Mrs. T. J. Caldwell, secretary; and Leopold Meyer treasurer. Gradually many of Houston's most distinguished social and civic leaders joined the board, while the founders continued to work unflaggingly to build the institution.

In the last days of postwar prosperity, Houston emerged as the leading industrial city in Texas, and moved up to sixth place among the nation's ports. The Houston Municipal Airport became home base for a fleet of crop dusters to attack the boll weevils plaguing the cotton plantations that surrounded the city. New buildings were shooting up on Main Street and along Texas Avenue. Most doctors and dentists had their offices downtown; the new Medical Arts Building on Walker filled quickly. Small buildings were tucked in amid the skyscrapers. Joseph Finger designed the charming little National Cash Register Company at 515 Caroline, and the new firm of Hedrick and

Gottlieb the stately Houston National Bank at 202 Main.

Sir Alfred C. Cossom of London designed the Petroleum Building at 1314 Texas Avenue, with Briscoe & Dixon and Maurice J. Sullivan as associate architects. The Tejas Club occupied the top floor. With its windows open on all four sides, it was wonderfully cool on summer evenings and had a splendid view of the city.

Every St. Patrick's Day, Joseph Cullinan flew his pirate's flag from the roof of the Petroleum Building. "The Jolly Roger," he said, "is intended as a warning to privilege and oppression, within or without the law—the latter including witch burners, fanatics, and the like, who fail to realize or ignore the fact that liberty is a right and not a privilege."

Dr. William States Jacobs, pastor of the First Presbyterian Church, had been a popular Chautauqua lecturer before coming to Houston at the age of thirty-five. He founded the Knife and Fork Club, with himself as president and toastmaster. Its purpose was to give enjoyable dinners in honor of famous visitors or outstanding Houstonians. He had a ranch near Webster where he pastured one of the largest herds of Brahman cattle in Texas. He was a man of great energy.

By the 1920s, Dr. Jacobs was caught up in the tide that was sweeping old downtown churches out to Houston's "cradle of culture." The Christ Church congregation had resisted the tide by a large vote of the congregation, only to watch many of its members transfer to the new Palmer Memorial Church. St. Paul's Methodist Church sold its property on McGowan and Milam to the Second Baptist Church for $153,750. The chimes, given by Mrs. M. T. Jones in memory of her husband, were not included. The new site on Main Street at Binz, part of the Hermann estate, cost $75,000, and the handsome American Gothic church designed by Alfred Finn cost another $750,000. The ten great bells, weighing from 250 to 3,000 pounds, were rehung 119 feet above the street in the new spire. During almost two years of construction, the congregation met in Temple Beth Israel.

As Dr. Peter Gray Sears had at Christ Church three years before, Dr. Jacobs envisioned selling the First Presbyterian Church downtown for $1.5 million or more and building a new one farther out. In 1928, the Presbyterians bought from the Hermann estate five acres of land near the Museum of Fine Arts and across Main Street from St. Paul's. They paid $5,000 in cash and secured a $245,000 note. But before they could build, the Great Depression hit. The downtown property proved hard to sell. The Hermann trustees took back two acres and reduced the note by $110,000. The Presbyterians decided to pay for the land before starting to build.

Even farther out on Main Street and outside the city, big houses were going up in the new Braeswood addition in 1929. A group of investors headed by George F. Howard had bought 456 acres at Main and Bellaire Boulevard from John Henry Kirby in 1927. The Braeswood Corporation called on Hare & Hare, Kansas City landscape architects, to work with Houston civil engineer William G. Farrington to prepare a master plan. It paved the stretch of Main between Bellaire and Brays Bayou and planted live oak trees along the esplanade. William P. Hobby bought the first house on Glenn Haven Boulevard in 1929.

In those last halcyon days of 1929, Allegro presented its largest crop of debutantes – nineteen of them. Tom Martin Davis, a recent law graduate of the University of Texas, had come to work for Baker & Botts. The firm always introduced its young men to Houston society and inevitably they turned up on the lists for debutante parties.

"There were garden parties in the summer time and many on the Rice Roof. That was before air conditioning. Men often wore white linen, but to any of the debutante parties, it was usually a tuxedo. I lived at 500 Westmoreland with a number of other young bachelors and I couldn't afford a car on my magnificent salary of $125 a month.

Edna Gilmer's fiance lived in Dallas, so I often escorted her. I'd walk out to the Gilmers' on North Boulevard, take her to the dance in her car, and at two in the morning, I'd take Edna back, park her car, and walk back to Westmoreland."

Few noticed the arrival in 1929 of Leon Jaworski, a precocious lawyer from Waco and the youngest person ever admitted to the Texas bar.[3] The son of an Austrian-immigrant mother and a Polish-immigrant father, he had grown up speaking German at home. His father was a minister who instilled in his son steadfast religious beliefs. Leon graduated from high school at fifteen and at nineteen had a law degree from Baylor University.

After two years in Houston, he would join the firm of Fulbright, Crooker, Freeman & Bates, and in 1935, before he was thirty, he would become the firm's youngest partner. Houston gradually realized that this gentle, soft-spoken young man was a star in the profession. But nobody could foresee that he would become internationally famous as chief U.S. prosecutor in the war crimes trials, or that he would lead the prosecution team that toppled an American president.

In 1929, the Junior League built its first building. Joseph Cullinan gave the league land on Stuart Avenue just outside the gates of Courtlandt Place. John Staub designed the Latin colonial building reminiscent of New Orleans with iron gates, copper roof, louvered blinds, patio, and gardens. It had shops on the ground floor to bring in income and a small stage in the big upstairs tea room for musicales and lectures.[4] In the new building, the Luncheon Club became more successful than ever, and the tea room was often rented at night for elementary and high school dances.

The residential sections between the Junior League building and Rice Institute were filling up. C. Milby Dow, the Laurence Bosworths, and the Rudolph Kuldells built on South Boulevard. Kuldell, a West Point graduate and a retired lieutenant colonel, was general manager of Hughes Tool Company. The Joseph Tennants and the Kemp Dargans built on North Boulevard. The George Copleys built in the center of Shadowlawn Circle, and the J. W. Parkers moved to Courtlandt. As the trees grew in Broadacres, the birds came. At Shadyside, Joseph Cullinan fed them every morning.

As a home place, River Oaks still seemed rather far from town for Old Houstonians wanting to be near their church and stores and theaters. But David Bintliff, as he was to do for decades, was thinking of future growth. Trapolina Road ran through a neighborhood of Italian truck farms west of the city. Bintliff bought property along the road between River Oaks and Post Oak Lane to start a new residential section.

"One Sunday," he said, "my wife and I were out there and I took an axe and chopped some briars down from the ravine that ran through my property. Alice was sitting in the car reading the morning paper. I was trying to pull these big vines out of a tree, when one of them broke off and I fell rolling down the ravine. My wife started laughing, and she said, 'I tell you what—when we build our home out here, let's call this Briar Hollow Lane.' And we did." That was the start of the many subdivisions Bintliff developed, and the start of a long list of Houston sections named Briar.

"My forte," he said, "has always been to buy up big tracts of land around a booming metropolitan center in this country and Central America." His 4,500-acre ranch west of Houston would be developed by Frank Sharp as Sharpstown.[5]

The flood that roared down Buffalo Bayou in May, 1929, damaged everything along its banks. The stock market crash of October was jolting, but few expected it to have lasting effects. And on December 25, snow and sleet gave Houston a white Christmas.

In the 1930 census, Houston had a population of 292,352. Apparently every man, woman, and child turned out on July 4, 1930, for balloon races at Bellaire Speedway

because the papers reported an attendance of "300,000 Houstonians." And in 1931, the Brazos Hotel, known for the cuisine and music of its Brazos Court, was razed to make way for the new Southern Pacific depot.

Col. Joseph Wood Evans, president of the Houston Chamber of Commerce, was elected chairman of the Harris County Houston Ship Channel and Navigation Commission in 1930, a post he would hold for the next fifteen years. Soon afterward he became a director of the U.S. Chamber of Commerce.

Houston has always been great on testimonial banquets. The Knife and Fork Club often played host. Governor-elect Ross Sterling was the honoree in December, 1930. The speakers traced his life—his birth on a farm near Anahuac, entry into the oil business in 1910, and founding of the Humble Oil Company. It was a life full of achievement for a man of fifty-five. Already he had been owner and publisher of the *Houston Post-Dispatch*, chairman of the Port Commission, chairman of the Hermann Hospital estate board, president of the YMCA, chairman of the Texas Highway Commission, trustee of Texas Christian University, president of Houston National Bank, and governor-elect of the state of Texas.

Ross Sterling's career in the oil business had lasted fifteen years—from 1910, when he bought two producing wells, to 1925, when he sold his Humble Company interests to devote more time to public service. He gave the YMCA of South Texas a wooded campsite on Galveston Bay in memory of his youngest son, Ross Shaw Sterling, Jr., and in 1929 bought one hundred acres of the old Sam Houston homesite at Huntsville to give to the state as a park. In all this, Governor Sterling held to the ideal of Old Houston: to treat personal wealth as a public trust.

The respected painter Frederic Browne taught at both Rice Institute and the Museum School. The Houston Museum of Fine Arts and the Museum School continued to stimulate local artists. Grace Spaulding John was one of the most dynamic in the late 1920s and 1930s. Mrs. John had studied at the Chicago Art Institute, the National Academy of Design, and the Art Students League in New York. On a Tiffany Foundation fellowship, she was one of eight young artists chosen to work at Louis Tiffany's home on Oyster Bay, Long Island. She was one of the first artists to set up a studio in Santa Fe and did some of her finest work there and in Mexico. The museum, however, could not provide display and sales space for local artists. Mrs. John therefore organized the first professional artists' gallery in Houston in the basement of the Beaconsfield. It opened on November 30, 1930.

The Savoy and Beaconsfield apartments were pleasant grounds, where friendships grew. In the early 1920s, the Thomas Spencers had lived in both at one time or another, as had the John H. Grants, the McDonald Meachams, the Henry Gates Saffords, and the William A. Vinsons. Nancy Spencer, Carolyn Grant, Lucille Meacham, and Martha Vinson played together. Gradually, some of the young couples moved out with their children into houses in the residential stretch from Courtlandt to River Oaks, but others—like the F. M. Laws—stayed for decades or for life.

Louise Spencer had always had an eye for antiques and colors. In 1929, she went into interior decoration, and with her husband's death in 1930, she invested her entire inheritance in the business. Born in Murfreesboro, Tennessee, speaking always with that elegant Southern accent, she took on the highly demanding career of buying antiques in New Orleans, New York, and London and having rich materials transformed into draperies and upholstery. She quickly emerged as one of Houston's leading interior decorators, whose work complemented the great houses designed by John Staub and Birdsall Briscoe.

Mrs. Spencer's most unusual client was Mrs. H. T. McClung, who lived her whole life submerged in purple. Everything she wore, everything she used, every wall, drapery, bedspread, and carpet in her house was in some shade of purple. When colored toilet tissue came into vogue, pale lavender rolls appeared in her bathrooms. She was a kind, thoughtful woman whose friends liked her, but she was sometimes identified as "Mrs. Purple McClung."

When Mrs. Spencer was ordering new draperies for the McClung house on Southmore, a New York dealer wrote in puzzlement: "Mrs. Spencer, what *are* you doing? A funeral home? We haven't had any call for purple damask in ten years."

The Rev. A. Frank Smith, beloved minister at the First Methodist Church, was elected bishop of the Methodist Episcopal Church, South, in 1930, and within three years became bishop in charge of the Texas Conference. From the first, he led in the movement to unite the Southern Methodists with the Methodist Episcopal Church. When that was achieved (in 1939), he was elected the first president of the combined Council of Bishops of the Methodist Church.

In September, 1930, Houston was shocked by the news from Baden-Baden, Germany, that Will Hogg had died. In the spring of the year, he had gone on one of his long jaunts to Europe. His sister Ima joined him there. A sudden gall bladder attack led to emergency surgery and he died on September 12. He was fifty-five. Ima Hogg accompanied the body home on the long, sad ocean journey. Funeral services were held in New York City and again in Houston. Among his pallbearers were Irvin S. Cobb, O. O. McIntyre, and Col. Edward Mandell House.

Houston had depended on Will Hogg for generosity and leadership and he had given it in full measure. Year after year, Houston had tried to thank him—to his horror. When the Museum of Fine Arts planned a reception in his honor, he left town. When the Rotary Club gave him an award for civic service, he wouldn't come; members had to corner him in his office and pin it on him. When Houstonians planned a surprise pre-

As the guest of Miss Ima Hogg at Bayou Bend, many a famous visitor has sipped a Bayou Bender on this terrace overlooking the Diana Garden. *Courtesy Museum of Fine Arts Archives*

sentation, he got wind of it and simply took to his bed, declaring himself much too sick to budge. But after his death, as Virginia Bernhard wrote, "there was no one around to prevent the tributes from being paid."

Writing in the *Houston Gargoyle,* Roscoe Wright called Will Hogg "this keen, contradictory, fiery, generous man . . . this tender tempest." The eulogies collected by Will's sister filled a large scrapbook.

Will Hogg had already given $1 million or more to the University of Texas and other educational enterprises, and yet another $2 million to Houston and various cultural institutions. No one knows how much he gave quietly in Houston, New York, and abroad. His will left the remaining $2 million or more

to the University of Texas with the provision that his family would decide how best to spend it.

As a child traveling with her father, Ima Hogg had visited schools, hospitals, and prisons. Governor Hogg understood that many of those in prison could have benefited by schools and hospitals. As a university student, Miss Hogg studied psychology under Dr. A. Caswell Ellis, who became her lifelong friend. And she herself had had periods of depression. All this prompted her to use her brother's money to establish the Hogg Foundation of Mental Health devoted to education and prevention.[6]

Ima Hogg was now the last member of the family at Bayou Bend. Gertrude Vaughn, who had become her personal maid and friend in 1919, was with her and continued to be for the rest of her life. Lucious Broadnax, who became her butler-chauffeur in the 1930s, was their guardian and strength by day. Mike and Alice Hogg lived next door. Three of the vast, strong Hogg men died in their mid-fifties—Governor Hogg, Will, and Mike. Tom died at sixty-two, Ima Hogg at ninety-three. None of the children of Gov. James Stephen Hogg had children. The line would die with Ima Hogg in 1975.

Chapter Fifty

The Great Depression

THE GREAT DEPRESSION closed the steel mills of Pittsburgh and Birmingham, throwing thousands out of work, leaving them unable to pay their doctors, landlords, or grocers. As automobile plants closed, Detroit could not pay its teachers, firemen, or police. Bank failures across the country stripped hundreds of thousands of men and women of life savings. Between twelve million and fifteen million industrial workers lost their jobs. Farm products sold so cheaply that millions of farmers lost their farms, while millions of city workers were losing their homes. Farmer and homeowner alike lacked the money for taxes and loan payments. Breadlines became common from New York to San Francisco. Thousands of homeless Americans drifted to the Gulf Coast in search of milder winters for outdoor camping.

Before it ended, the Great Depression was to have an even greater impact on the lives of all Americans than the Civil War. Houston could not escape.

Gradually, the depression pervaded Houston. In 1930, Mayor Walter Monteith named a committee to study the city's new problem of unemployment. An emergency relief office was opened. Unemployment continued to grow in 1931. Churches began quietly to help members who had lost their jobs and to broaden community services. Women of the First Presbyterian Church served seventy-five thousand meals in the winter of 1930 to men of all races and creeds. Women of other denominations came to help.

But not even the depression could dampen Houston enterprise. J. W. Sartwelle, operator of the Port City Stockyards and a cattleman known for his Brahmans, always sought ways to improve livestock and the Texas cattle market. He placed a newspaper ad to invite anyone interested in these goals to meet at the Texas State Hotel on January 30, 1931. Seven men showed up. They founded the Houston Fat Stock Show.[1] Sartwelle was president (a title he would hold for the next seventeen years); J. Howard West, Marcus Meyer, W. C. Munn, and Julian Weslow were all vice-presidents; W. S. Cochran was treasurer, and Haygood Ashburn, of the Chamber of Commerce, was secretary.

A year later they staged their first Fat Stock Show in the Democratic Convention Hall. It drew two thousand entries and lost twenty-eight hundred dollars. The founders made up the loss, and the show went on. Year by year, it grew, to become the largest livestock exhibition in the world, with more than twenty-five thousand entries from the United States, Canada, and Mexico. It would become a major institution in the city, in the cattle industry, and in the education of the young through generous scholarships. Houston was totally Southern in voice and ways. But the Fat Stock Show let Houstonians play cowboy once a year in a fashion that rewarded everyone.

Palmer Bradley, an authority on oil and gas law, was also an expert tennis player who won a number of tennis titles in Texas and New Mexico.[2] In 1931, he helped found the River Oaks Tennis Tournament—one that would gain international recognition.

In 1931, Dr. Jacobs resigned as pastor of the First Presbyterian Church. Dr. Charles King succeeded him. A Georgian, he was a graduate of the Union Theological Seminary in Richmond, Virginia, and had done graduate work at the University of Chicago. He had scarcely become acquainted with his deacons when, on September 10, 1932, the fine old church building on the corner of Main Street and McKinney was badly damaged by fire.

Dr. Henry Barnston and the Congregation Beth Israel promptly offered the use of their temple on Austin at Holman. Dr. King accepted and set out to rebuild. He had the backing of such elders as E. A. Peden, Thomas Watt Gregory, and David Hannah. Aware of the payments due on the five acres on South Main, Dr. King asked for a one-thousand-dollar cut in his salary. For the next twelve months, the Presbyterians met at Beth Israel while repairs were made. The new church would have to wait.

High school debaters became aware of a dynamic new force on the regional circuit. At sixteen, Johnny Crooker was on the San Jacinto High School debate team that competed against Sam Houston High. Sam Houston's coach was an unusually tall, gangly young Texan named Lyndon Johnson. At twenty-two, he was quite as persuasive as he would later be as senator.

Liking Johnny Crooker, Johnson paired him with L. E. Jones of the Sam Houston team and they set out to conquer the region. "He was the world's best salesman," attorney John H. Crooker, Jr., recalled. "He seemed able to understand other people's thoughts. He had leadership in spades. But he never demanded more of anyone than he was prepared to put in himself." In a later day, Pres. Lyndon Johnson would appoint John Crooker chairman of the Civil Aeronautics Board.

Will Hobby, whose wife had died in 1929, learned that young Oveta Culp had come to Houston to live. She was the parliamentarian of the Texas House and the daughter of his longtime friend, Ike Culp of Killeen.

Naturally, he looked her up. With her humor, lively intelligence, and interest in politics, he found that despite a great difference in their ages they had much in common. In February, 1931, they were married. For the next thirty-three years, they would work as a team in newspaper publishing, in radio and television management, and in service to their government.

Later in 1931, Mrs. Hobby was elected state president of the League of Women Voters. On her birthday, January 19, 1932, their son William Pettus Hobby, Jr., was born. Governor Hobby confessed to her: "I had no idea babies were so popular, or I would have put them in my platform." Jessica Hobby would arrive five years later, also on her mother's birthday.[3] Meanwhile, Oveta Hobby was her husband's partner in all they did, starting out as research editor of the *Post-Dispatch,* becoming literary editor and assistant editor in rapid order.

As the depression grew, Faith Home began to receive more children whose parents could no longer support them. As a board member, Ben Taub, a childless bachelor, gave new life and wider scope to this refuge for children.[4]

Ben Taub was a tall, handsome, courtly Southern gentleman. He had once been very much in love with a young woman who shared his feelings. Her Roman Catholic parents forbade the marriage, and Taub never married. He was, however, a popular figure and a favored escort in Old Houston society. Early in the depression he took a lead in helping the needy. He worked with the Social Service Bureau to bring families back together.[5] In 1931, he closed the nursery and placed Faith Home's babies and small children in foster families. At the same time, he began plans to buy new property on Shepherd Drive. Elected chairman of the board, he tackled the Harris County Commissioner's Court to pay for children they placed at the home and began scouting out the site for a summer camp at Spring, Texas, near Houston.

On Friday, October 25, 1931, two of Houston's seven banks were in crisis. The Houston National Bank, largely owned by Governor Sterling, and the Public National Bank and Trust Company, controlled by W. L. Moody III and Odie R. Seagraves, were on the brink of disaster. In any other city, by custom and by history, they would have failed.

At two o'clock Sunday afternoon, Jesse Jones called the heads of the other five banks to meet in his office on the thirty-third floor of the Gulf Building. He faced them with the fact that the two banks would fail by Monday morning unless something was done. Inevitably, the failures would destroy public confidence in all banks. The other five banks could count on a rush by their depositors to withdraw their money. Perhaps not one of the healthy five could stand a serious bank run.

Bill Kirkland, in his history of the First National Bank, *Old Bank – New Bank,* gives a dramatic account of that meeting. From time to time as the hours wore on, Jones had sandwiches and coffee brought in. Nobody left that room until five o'clock Monday morning. Some took short naps on the floor using folded coats as pillows. But all night long, the talk continued – each man analyzing the strength and weaknesses of his own bank, everyone planning and debating, suggesting and doubting.

"A second session began late Monday afternoon," Kirkland wrote, "and that, too, extended through until the following dawn. This session included a carefully selected number of professional men and business leaders. . . . It has been estimated that more than fifty men took part in these tense meetings of which no hint leaked out in those forty critical hours."

At first, some bankers flatly refused to lend a hand to the two weak members of the Houston clearing house. One president balked until Jesse Jones put a long distance call through to "a venerable chairman of the board," who was on vacation in New England. The board chairman converted his reluctant bank president. The session grew so tense that when one man threatened to jump from a window, another strode over to the window and opened it for him. He didn't jump.

By midnight, it was agreed that the two ailing banks could be saved only by the sale of one of them to strong ownership, and by cash contributions of $1.25 million for the rescue of the other.

First the bankers assessed the five banks in proportion to their deposits. Then Jones went to the phone again. The Houston Lighting and Power Company agreed to contribute one hundred thousand dollars, the Gas Company a hundred and fifty thousand. Jones called the president of Southwestern Bell Telephone Company in St. Louis, which owned the Houston Telephone Company. The phone company pledged fifty thousand. Anderson, Clayton Cotton Corporation gave twenty-five thousand.

The Joseph F. Meyer interests, long involved with Houston National Bank, bought control from Governor Sterling. The Public National Bank and Trust Company was merged into the National Bank of Commerce – Houston's smallest bank. It, in turn, received the $1.25 million amassed at the meeting as protection against the liabilities of the failing institution.

By dawn Tuesday, the job was done. The *Houston Post-Dispatch,* which had purposely delayed its first edition, carried news of the action that had saved Houston from a banking disaster.

But the First National Bank had taken on a two-hundred-thousand-dollar share in the refinancing plan and paid one hundred and fifty thousand cash as its part of the indemnity fund. This left it on thin ice. To protect First National, Martha Elizabeth Shepherd Roberts, the last surviving daughter of Houston's first banker, B. A. Shepherd; Mrs. E. L. Neville and Mrs. E. A. Peden, his granddaughters, with their husbands; John S. and W. S. Cochran, his grandsons; and other persons, though in lesser amounts, contributed stocks and lands to serve as collateral.

The result was that no bank in Houston failed during the Great Depression. Jesse Jones is due credit for bringing together the forces of rescue and implacably holding them on course until they agreed. But this unique operation also shows that the men and women who controlled Houston in 1931 were willing to be responsible for their city's welfare.

Meanwhile, Governor Sterling's financial reverses also cost him the *Post-Dispatch*. He had built a twenty-two-story building for the paper. Though former Gov. W. P. Hobby and R. L. Dudley were his chief associates in management, neither was a stockholder. Jesse Jones bought the *Post-Dispatch* in the name of J. E. Josey, board chairman of the National Standard Life Insurance Company and brother of Robert A. Josey, Jones's close personal friend. The paper once again became the *Houston Post,* with Josey as chairman of the board.

In those unsettled days, rumors could threaten the life of a bank that otherwise was quite stable. One such rumor jeopardized Judge James A. Elkins's bank. The Guaranty Trust Company, which he founded in 1924, had merged with the Gulf State Bank in 1928, to become the City National Bank.

It now shared a block on Main Street with the Kirby Theater. Talking movies were the novelty of the day. The public was swarming to theaters equipped with sound. While silent stars faded, the great actors of Broadway and London were the new stars of this controversial medium. When George Arliss starred in *Disraeli,* everybody was panting to see it. On the morning it opened at the Kirby, eager fans formed a line from the ticket office that soon stretched all the way around the block.

A line. A bank. A *run* on the bank? The frightening word swept through the streets. Was Judge Elkins's bank shaky? Jakie Freedman, Houston's beloved professional gambler, was one of the City National's biggest depositors—possibly its biggest. Arriving to make his usual morning deposit, Jakie saw the line, heard the rumor, and headed straight for Judge Elkins's open office door.

"Judge, are we in trouble?"

Judge Elkins was serene. "I don't think so, Jakie. But if you're worried about your money, feel free to draw it out."

Jakie put his hands to his head and rocked it gently back and forth. "I assumed," Judge Elkins said later, "that he was praying."

Jakie made up his mind: "Judge, if you go down, I go down. We'll start over together."

He walked out and, before the eyes of all in the lobby, made his deposit. Had Jakie Freedman withdrawn his money, perhaps over a hundred thousand dollars, it would not only have taxed the fund of available cash but could easily have started a run. The moviegoers went on into the Kirby Theater, unaware of their stellar role in what could have been a far bigger drama than *Disraeli.*

Chapter Fifty-One

Mr. Jones Goes to Washington Again

HOUSTON SURVIVED the depression without one bank failure. But the nation's banks had been in trouble for years and were failing by the hundreds all across the country. As the depression threatened the entire economic system, Jesse H. Jones was called to Washington for what became his greatest contribution to his government.

Pres. Herbert Hoover, grasping for ways to stem the destructive current of the depression, had proposed a Reconstruction Finance Corporation. It would place the powerful credit of the United States behind individual institutions. It was to lend money to banks, railroads, schools, businesses, agriculture, and other institutions in danger of failing. Hoover thought it would stop the plunge in prices of farm and industrial products. He assumed it would be needed only by smaller institutions. The big industries and big banks, he said, "are amply able to take care of themselves."

In January, 1932, with Houston's bank crisis behind him, Jesse Jones went off to spend two weeks in New York on business. Stopping by Washington on his way home, he called upon House Speaker John Nance Garner, with whom he was slightly acquainted. He also called on his old friend Carter Glass of Virginia, a member of the Senate committee then holding hearings on the president's RFC proposal. Both lawmakers were keenly interested in the plan and asked Jones to recommend capable men to serve on the bipartisan board.

Jones had always resented the Eastern seaboard's domination of banking. Now he was freshly disturbed by the number of defaults on foreign loans that the big New York banking houses had made in the 1920s. He therefore offered this advice: "If such a government agency is to be created, the directors should realize that most of the country lies west of the Hudson River, and none of it east of the Atlantic Ocean."

The president and Jesse Jones had known each other since the war when Hoover was food administrator and Jones was director of Red Cross military relief. On January 26, President Hoover sent to the Senate the list of those who would form the seven-man board of the enormous new government corporation. Jesse Jones was one of the seven.

Jesse Jones accepted, because in the two weeks in New York City, he had learned that conditions across the country were much worse than he had realized. He telephoned Mrs. Jones and said, "Pack your trunk and come on up. I am stuck with a steady, 365-day-a-year job."

This began Jesse Jones's second, longest, and most important service to his country. Mrs. Jones joined him, and for the next thirteen years they lived in Washington hotels, getting back to Houston sometimes for Christmas.

President Hoover's hope that the big institutions could take care of themselves proved short-lived. The first two applicants were the nation's biggest banking chain and the biggest railroad network in the country.

The RFC had an immediate impact. Before its creation, bank failures had amounted to $200 million a month. Thereafter, failures fell to $10 million a month. But in the lame-duck period of the Hoover administration, the country plunged more and more deep-ly into the Great Depression. About three weeks before Franklin Roosevelt's inaugura-tion, a banking panic began in Detroit and swept the country. Depositors rushed to withdraw, demanding cash or gold. On the March 4 inauguration day, many banks closed. Others limited the amount that could be withdrawn.

It was this crisis that prompted President Roosevelt to declare a bank moratorium on his first Monday morning in office. The banks remained closed until all could be ex-amined by Treasury officials. Those found to be sound reopened. The shaky ones were kept closed until they could be put on a sound basis. Those without sufficient funds did not reopen at all. Once a bank opened its doors again, its depositors had reason to feel that it could be trusted. The panic ended.

But banking reform was long overdue. Bank failure was common long before the 1929 stockmarket crash. Between 1921 and 1931, 9,277 banks closed in the United States —an average of three or more for each bank-ing day. Of these failures, 5,642 occurred be-fore Wall Street's Black Friday. President Hoover had called for sweeping bank reform in 1930. Senator Glass had been working on a reform bill since early 1931. It had been hung up in congressional committees ever since.

From the start, Jones saw that unless the federal government would guarantee the safety of deposits, there was no way the banks could regain public confidence. Be-coming chairman of the RFC under Presi-dent Roosevelt, he made federal deposit in-surance a priority. Vice-President Garner had been quietly pushing for deposit insurance

since his days as House Speaker. They found their greatest ally in Sen. Arthur Vanden-burg. When the bank reform bill was passed in June, 1933, Vandenburg's amendment es-tablished the Federal Deposit Insurance Cor-poration. Henceforth, the federal govern-ment would guarantee deposits for up to $2,500—enough to cover most accounts at the time.

Gradually the RFC was amended and im-proved by acts of Congress. Jesse Jones was adamant against any effort by Washington to control American business. At the same time, he saw to it that the RFC remained feasible and solvent. Jones said, "If the money is not likely to be paid in a generously allotted time, don't lend it. Make the loan if you can, but remember one of the great-est disservices you can do to a man is to lend him money he can't pay back."

In his years as chairman, the RFC lent more than $50 billion to restore the nation's economy. By so doing, it enabled the United States to prepare for the unforeseen global war that lay ahead.

Jesse Jones proved the ideal man to cope with the worst financial plight this country had ever faced. From his own experience in banking and building, in borrowing and lending, he saw clearly what each embar-rassed applicant needed. However, he was also firm in his requirements of manage-ment. Some found him a harsh task master. He sometimes acted swiftly and decisively in ways that, in 1986, might be challenged as arrogant if not unconstitutional. But it worked for the good of the country.

Many bankers, economists, and histori-ans have expressed the belief that, as much as any other public figure, Jesse Jones of Houston saved the private enterprise system in the United States. Certainly, he was a powerful force in that salvation.

Dark Days and Light

IN 1932, Franklin Delano Roosevelt defeated President Hoover by an electoral vote of 472 to 59 and by a popular majority of almost 7 million. Houstonians were overwhelming in their support of Roosevelt and of Texan John Nance Garner as his vice-president.

In the unsettling three days of the bank moratorium, Houston stores offered their own checks as "change." The utility companies extended discount periods; the streetcar company opened a credit department. Theaters accepted IOUs. Houston showed a certain gaiety in coping with this cashless society.

F. M. Law, president of the First National Bank, was often in Washington. He believed that the best chance for economic recovery was for business leaders to work with President Roosevelt. As president of the American Bankers Association, he helped revise the National Banking Act and draft the charter for the Federal Deposit Insurance Corporation.

The City of Houston was at low tide. In two terms as mayor, Walter Montieth had borne the onset of the depression. The city could not pay firemen or policemen, and the light company had turned off the streetlights. Oscar Holcombe, who had been mayor in the good days of 1921–29, was reelected in 1933.[1] Mayor Holcombe went to the banks. They agreed to help if he would cut costs, and they lent him money to pay the firemen and policemen. At his inauguration, he threw the switch that turned the streetlights back on. But to make the city solvent again he had to fire a fourth of its employees.

The depression was hard on individual Houstonians. The worst days came in 1932 and 1933. Some men went without work for a year or more. Churches opened soup kitchens, and among those in line were men and women who had never expected to need a free meal. The Esperson Building, the Houston Post-Dispatch Building, the Sam Houston Hotel, and the Warwick Hotel were sold at auction, and the Sterling Building, only two years old, changed hands. John Henry Kirby, proclaimed the city's outstanding lumberman and civic leader in 1900, was forced into bankruptcy.[2]

And yet. . . .

In the years of the Great Depression, Houston independent oilmen, like R. E. (Bob) Smith, Robert Welch, H. R. Cullen, James Abercrombie, and George Strake were amassing fortunes in the oil fields. George W. Strake was a comparative newcomer. A graduate of the Jesuit St. Louis University, he first came to Houston in 1924 after drilling successfully in Mexico. He married Susan Kehoe and took his bride to Havana, expecting to duplicate his Mexican strikes. Instead, dry holes and a dropping sugar market sent him back to Houston. But on December 31, 1931, Strake brought in his first well and on the strength of its flow sold half the acreage he had under lease to the Humble Oil Company for $4 million. This was the start of the Conroe oil field and of a personal fortune that the Strakes would share generously with Houston.[3]

Proper Houstonians were building handsome new houses. The Harry Hanszens, the Stephen P. Farishes, the J. Robert Neals, and the Wallace Pratts built on Lazy Lane. Mr. and Mrs. Hugh Roy Cullen built their house on Inwood Drive at River Oaks Boulevard. All were designed by John Staub.

Lillie Neuhaus Carter had been so pleased with the Carter Lodge that Staub had designed in 1929 that she encouraged the Cullens to commission him for their house. Hugh Roy and Lillie Cullen were already known for their generosity of spirit. They gave Staub carte blanche, asking only that they have space to entertain large groups of friends. The result, in Howard Barnstone's architectural judgment, was "a setting of unforced elegance and eminent livability." This house was begun and built in what other cities saw as the darkest days of the Great Depression.

Now in his early thirties, George Brown was doing so well that he was ready to build a permanent home for Alice and their three daughters, Nancy, Maconda, and Isabel.[4] They chose a lot in River Oaks next door to the Carrington Weems family. "The lot on Inwood cost something like nineteen hundred dollars," Isabel Brown Wilson said, "and I am sure the house cost less than twenty thousand." They moved into 3363 Inwood in 1932, and one by one, the three little girls started to River Oaks School.

The River Oaks Corporation advertised every week in the *Gargoyle*. It said that River Oaks was cooler than most parts of town because it was higher above sea level. It showed the floor plan of a fully landscaped, four-bedroom, two-bath house on Pelham Drive to sell for fifteen thousand dollars. And then in the spring of 1932, the corporation went so far as to offer a taste of River Oaks living: It had six new houses that it would lease for from six weeks to two months. Rents started at $95 a month.

Home from the glories of around-the-world travel and Princeton graduation, Dudley Sharp joined his brother Bedford in "a little company he'd started that made equipment for the drilling rig," Sharp said.

It was in the teeth of the depression. We rented a little machine shop. We were pretty primitive. It was down on Railroad Street just the other side of the tracks from Washington Avenue. It was a corrugated iron building with a dirt floor. We finally made enough money to put a concrete floor in it, and there was at least one summer there before we could afford to put in an attic fan. That corrugated iron building was really hot.

We made parts for slush pumps. I invented a better valve for a slush pump and a piston. We also made rotary slips. I found that J. P. Arnold, the dentist who worked on my teeth, had bought an interest in a patent on a slip. The slip holds the pipe when you're unscrewing it to put in another joint. I made a deal with Dr. Arnold to pay him a royalty if we could make the slip. They were made out of steel castings that we got from the Hughes Tool Company. They had a foundry. They were always very, very helpful to me. I don't know whether Howard told them to or not.

I'd take the back seat out of our Model A, four-door Ford and go out to the Hughes Tool Company and get the castings and put them in the back where the cushion had been taken out. Then I would bring them to the shop and we would machine them and I would inspect them and we would put them in boxes and I would put them back in the back seat of my car and take them to the express office. That was how we started our business. When finally we were able to afford a truck, it was a *pretty* big day!

Finally we did really very well with them. We had about 90 percent of the piston business in the world, and about half the valve business. And by that time we'd gotten out of our corrugated iron building.

This was the Mission Manufacturing Company. They got out of the corrugated iron building in 1933 when they asked John Staub to design the plant they built on Jensen Drive.

Just as war sometimes does, the depression heightened sentiments, stirred ingenuity and fellow feeling, prompted laughter and a kind of gaiety. But where it struck hard, it was brutal. Many Houstonians who were without work went without enough to eat. Honorable man and women were unable to pay their bills. Unemployed people fleeing the cold of northern winters came through Houston and on to the coast to camp under the shelter of trees near the shoreline.

The city's jobless registered at City Auditorium. By December 11, 1932, the local National Reemployment Office had assigned seventy-five hundred people to Civil Works Administration projects, but had another six thousand applicants on file. The Harris County Board of Welfare and Employment hired eight thousand men.

For anyone who had money there were bargains. The Southern Pacific Railroad ran three trains a day from Houston to New Orleans and a regular schedule of ships from New Orleans to New York. For $90.00, a Houstonian could travel to New York and back, receiving meals and berth while at sea. Children went for half fare. On fifteen-day round trips, the train ticket to Denver cost $29.95; to Dallas, Waco, or Fort Worth, $3.00; and to San Antonio, $2.75.

Houston sports fans were proud of handsome, likeable Edward Rotan II. Six feet three inches tall, he had starred as right guard on the Yale University football team, become intercollegiate heavyweight wrestling champion, president of the student council, and a member of the Torch honor society. The *Gargoyle* put its spotlight on him for all these honors and added, "Before coming home to enter the bond business, he will play on the all-star Eastern football team (Yale, Harvard, Princeton) in the summer Olympics." The Rotans were notable sportsmen. Ed Rotan's father, George, had won the Houston Invitational golf match six times between 1914 and 1926.[5]

Though Babe (Mildred) Didrikson grew up in Port Arthur and Beaumont, Houston was proprietary toward that unique athlete. In 1932, she singlehandedly won the team championship at the national Amateur Athletic Union women's track and field meet, defeating the whole Illinois girls' team thirty points to twenty-two. She went on to win two gold medals at the Olympic games, plac-ing first in the women's javelin throw and the eighty-meter hurdles.

The sports spectacle of 1932 in Houston was the arrival of the Louisiana State University football team to play Rice Institute. Sen. Huey Long considered LSU a part of the empire he ruled. LSU, he trumpeted, was going to beat Rice seventy-three to nothing. Three trains brought the Kingfish and, trailing in his wake, the Louisiana governor, the mayor of New Orleans, the 140- piece LSU band, hundreds of alumni, and one thousand LSU students, who came on a special three-dollar round-trip fare. Leaping from the train, Senator Long led the LSU band in a parade to the Rice Hotel. He was greeted —as he had expected—by Mayor Monteith, Rice President Edgar Odell Lovett, the mayors of Orange, Beaumont, and Galveston, and former governor W. P. Hobby. He was affronted that Sen. Tom Connally failed to show. Rice won the game by a slim two points (ten to eight) and Senator Long was so put out that he caught the first train to New Orleans—not waiting for his own.

After several years of study with voice teachers in New York, Daisy Elgin was engaged by Gigli to accompany him on his first tour of the South. In 1932, she was guest soloist with the Houston Symphony and could be heard every Sunday evening on the Frigidaire hour over KPRC.[6]

By 1932, Howard Hughes, Jr., had become a movie producer who was a favorite in Hollywood gossip columns. Exceptionally handsome, known to be one of the richest men in the country, he had spent unprecedented sums on *Hell's Angels. The Front Page* was a tremendous success. *Scarface* was banned by New York state censors and received frowns from the Hays Office.[7] Coolly, the young producer opened *Scarface* in New Orleans and announced that he would show it first in the forty states that had no censorship boards. Thereafter, he said, he would enter New York with a lawsuit against the officials who had banned it. Houston got an early showing on May 6, after the premier in New Orleans.

During the depression, the WPA kept artists employed beautifying public buildings. In her introduction to *Fresh Paint,* Susie Kalil wrote: "Eleven major murals (some of them privately funded) of more than fifty individual panels were completed in Houston's library, schools, department stores and office buildings." The Houston Public Library gained four panels by Emma Richardson Cherry, artist and art teacher, and murals by Ruth Uhler, the museum's curator of education. Angela McDonnell covered the library's lunettes with Spanish scenes. At Lanier Junior High School, Grace Spaulding John painted *The Pipe of Peace* for the main foyer. In this period, Edward M. "Buck" Schiwetz, Carden Bailey, Robert Joy, and Julian Rhodes Muench were exhibiting their works.

After two years at Ward Belmont in Nashville and a happy lifetime of painting at the Museum School, Eugenia Howard, daughter of Dr. and Mrs. Philo Howard, went to Europe to study painting in Florence and Munich. Gabrielle Soeurette Diehl, the daughter of Mr. and Mrs. Anton Diehl, was graduated from the New England Conservatory of Music and sailed for France to continue her studies at the Paris Conservatoire.[8]

By 1932, Houston emerged as the state's biggest city, surpassing Dallas and San Antonio. Houstonians gained air service to Atlanta. They voted overwhelmingly to repeal the Prohibition amendment and the Gulf Brewing Company spent $1 million to build a new plant to produce the first beer sold in Houston in fifteen years.

Oil had replaced cotton as the chief product of the Gulf Coast. Tomball was the center of new oil exploration. The bond issue of 1930 was still paying for seventeen road projects. Federal funds were paying for major improvements in the ship channel. Turning Basin Docks were being built. Houston received a generous share of federal help and put it to good use.

The Blue Eagle, symbol of the National Recovery Act, appeared in windows and on bulletin boards across town, meaning that the company would abide by NRA rules. The NRA gave non-union workers some of the protection on wages and hours that union workers had fought so hard to achieve. Until that time, a newspaper photographer, a company secretary, a store salesperson, or a janitor could be kept on the job for any number of hours per day and per week without overtime pay. During the depression, nobody who had a job dared quit, however hard the hours.

Houston's young people could go to Rice Institute free of charge, but throughout the rest of the country, hundreds of thousands of young men and women owed their chance at a college education to the National Youth Administration—a Roosevelt New Deal agency. A student could work for a dollar an hour in a great variety of jobs, usually on the college campus. A dollar was a good wage in a time when a hearty lunch could be bought for twenty-five cents, and when a boy's shirt cost thirty-nine cents.

And there were merrier things afoot six miles out on Humble Road. Epsom Downs, which cost $600,000 to build and landscape, opened on Thanksgiving Day, 1933, with twenty-seven thousand racing fans there. Parimutuel play for the winter meet totaled $2,929,801. Backers insisted that the races were pouring money into the Houston economy and providing jobs; detractors carped that it was more a matter of money changing hands.

The races paid off in other ways. On Charity Day six months after the opening, they brought in almost seven thousand dollars for the Bayshore Orphans Home and the Crippled Children's Fund. More than a thousand horses were stabled for the next autumn race meet. The track closed when the state legislature abolished parimutuel betting.

At the age of forty-six, Ben Clayton retired from Anderson, Clayton and the cotton business because he was plagued by a streptococcus infection in his digestive tract. (The infection continued for twenty years. With the arrival of penicillin, it was cured

Governor Franklin D. Roosevelt, Democratic nominee for the presidency, conferring with Colonel Edward M. House, wartime adviser of Woodrow Wilson and one of the early supporters of the Roosevelt presidential candidacy. The conference took place at Colonel House's summer home at Beverly Farms, Mass. Mr. Roosevelt termed the talk "just a chat."

In 1932 Gov. Franklin D. Roosevelt went to E. M. House's summer home at Beverly Farms, Massa- chusetts, for what he termed "just a chat." *Courtesy Mary Elizabeth Caldwell Merrem*

in eight days.) Nonetheless, he spent three hours a day in his office and acquired property and interests in Chicago, New York, and Los Angeles, as well as Houston.

Ben Clayton was an inventor. He invented a round-bale cotton press, among other things. He was interested in science, especially in the science of nutrition. In retiring, he established the Clayton Foundation with a gift of $10 million for research in sciences and the treatment of human ills. Over the next thirty years, he took special interest in the work of Dr. Roger Williams at the Biochemical Institute of the University of Texas.[9]

Though Edward Mandell House still thought of Houston as his home town, he lived in New York. Famous in this country and Europe as an elder statesman, he was asked by the press for his opinion on issues. He was a personal friend of the Roosevelts, invited often to the governor's mansion in Albany and later to the White House.

He had always been ahead of his time. In May, 1933, *Cosmopolitan* magazine carried an article headlined, "Women in Washington?" by Col. Edward Mandell House. It strongly urged the election of women to high office and listed women he thought suited to hold any office of government, including the United States presidency.

Mrs. John Wesley Graham, who had enlarged the First Methodist Church choir to a massive three hundred, organized the short-lived Houston Civic Opera.[10] For the World's Fair, she took fifteen hundred singers to Chicago. Special trains also carried several hundred opera lovers. On Texas Day,

August 23, 1933, the Houston company presented Verdi's *Aida* to an audience of fourteen thousand at Soldier's Field. (The colorful Mrs. Graham once said of her chief rival among voice teachers: "Her pupils sing like hell and she doesn't know it. My pupils sing like hell and I know it.")

For a number of years, the younger set had been aware of Roy Hofheinz.[11] When he graduated with honors from San Jacinto High School at fifteen, he was offered two scholarships to the University of Texas. But with his father's sudden death in a traffic accident, he turned down both and set out to support his mother. He sold aluminum pots door to door, booked musicians for dances all along the Gulf Coast, and worked as a radio disc jockey. As a skinny teenager, he was an entrepreneur of ingenuity and enormous energy. After a freshman year at Rice Institute, he transferred to night classes at Houston Junior College and the Houston Law School, becoming a lawyer at nineteen.

His classmate and sweetheart in high school and law school was Irene Cafcales, the daughter of a substantial Houston businessman. His daughter Dene Hofheinz Mann tells the story in her book, *You Be the Judge*.

When Mama went to apply for a job at a law firm after acquiring her law degree, she ran into Daddy in an elevator. They had broken up six months before and hadn't spoken to one another since. In the elevator he asked her to lunch.

Over a bacon, lettuce and tomato sandwich, he asked her to drive to Shreveport and get married. She accepted and off they went.

This was July, 1933. Both were twenty-one. The marriage would be one of rare closeness and devotion until Mrs. Hofheinz's death thirty-three years later.

In 1934, at the age of twenty-two, Roy Hofheinz was elected to the Texas House of Representatives. He was called "the boy orator from Buffalo Bayou." This was the start of a political and business career that would see him become county judge and mayor of Houston and would encompass radio, television, the Astrodome, and Ringling Bros., Barnum & Bailey Circus.

The Blue Birds, having served a variety of causes, came to a focus in 1934 when they built a little white cottage next to the Methodist Hospital on San Jacinto at Rosalie. The plan was sensible. The Arabia Temple Shrine financed surgery and medical care for crippled children, but a long hospital stay was expensive and not good for the child. The Blue Birds would operate a convalescent home for the Shrine's Crippled Children's Clinic, providing everything from beds and nurses to a teacher to help with school work.

Ice-skating rinks were a novelty in the South. The Polar Wave Ice Palace on Hutchins Street drew children by day and young couples by night. When it opened in the 1920s, a band played for the skaters, but by the mid-thirties, they skated to compelling waltzes chosen from a large record library. From his high school days, David Westheimer remembered the skaters as being "ultrasophisticated and very well-dressed." But for him, the high point came with the visit of Sally Rand, the fan dancer, who had been the most famous star of the Chicago world's fair. She skated with any boy who asked her. One of them was David Westheimer.

The depression led to Houston some newcomers who would stay. In 1932, the Shell Oil Company brought Ted Swigart over from California. This was the last stop for him after a career in Oklahoma, Washington, D.C., India, and Burma. His wife Erna joined the River Oaks Garden Club and the Blue Bird Circle. In 1934, C. Cabanne Smith, a mining engineer from Saint Louis, was transferred to town by the Houston Oil Company, of which George Hill was president. With his wife Lucy, Cab Smith was welcomed by Old Houston. McClellan Wallace of Chicago had to drop out of Princeton as family finances plummeted. "I thought if I was going to be poor, I might as well be *warm* poor," he said. In Houston he resumed and finished his studies. He also met and married Winifred Safford, newly graduated from Bryn Mawr. In the years ahead, all three of these men would become leaders in Houston's civic and cultural development.

Rather as Houston girls had waited out the Civil War in Paris, Mrs. Haywood Nelms decided to wait out the depression—for a year at least—in her beloved France. She leased the lovely Nelms house in Sleepy Hollow and took the children to Fontainebleau. She enrolled the twins, Nancy and Agnese, in a girls' school across the street from her hotel and entered Haywood, Jr., in Fontainebleau. This was probably the year that Agnese Carter Nelms took the *Cordon Bleu* course in cooking. Her exquisite French cuisine delighted her family and friends throughout her long life.

The depression continued to slow the growth of River Oaks. The corporation advertised in 1934, "The forbidding houses of so-called 'exclusive neighborhoods' find no counterparts . . . in River Oaks. For River Oaks makes no pretension to exclusiveness. It is a friendly neighborhood. And yet River Oaks attracts only the sort of people who make good neighbors. It is a neighborhood in which the people you like, like to live."

Southwestern Bell found it necessary to advertise the importance of phone service: "For only a few cents a day, you can have a telephone of your own. No more trips to the neighbors or the corner store." This is revealing in view of Houston's early embrace of the telephone.

River Oaks and Southwestern Bell combined could not provide enough advertising to save the *Gargoyle*. The depression killed it, costing Allen Peden the bulk of his fortune and throwing its talented staff out of work. Hubert Roussel, associate editor, went to the *Houston Press*.

To avoid firings, many companies cut salaries. Fifty years after the fact, Dewey Roussel, whose husband Hubert was one of Houston's most entertaining and distinguished journalists, could laugh at their mid-depression plight. "Hubert had gone to

When this picture was made, Agnese Carter was still a daughter in her father's home on Main Street but already a person of diverse interests. *Courtesy Patricia Carter Winkler*

work for the *Press* at thirty dollars a week. One week after he started, they gave a ten percent cut. So we had twenty-seven dollars a week to live on, and we were going to have this baby. We had rented a house on Plum Street, brand new, for fifty dollars, but paying the utilities, food and everything out of twenty-seven was . . . well! I had two or three publicity jobs, including one for the symphony. And the old lady we rented from would go to Weingarten's and bring us baskets of discarded fruit and second-day bread. We were glad to get it."

When the light company threatened to cut off the electricity, Roussel wrote back: "I'm going to pay you but you'll have to be patient. I'll tell you my system. When I get my bills, I put them in the trash basket, and when I get my paycheck, I reach in there and pull out two bills. If you don't quit harassing me, I'm not going to put you in the basket." In those pre-computer, more human days, it worked.

In early 1934, the Public Works Administration allotted $653,000 to Harris County for road work and sewers. In June, the Post Office Department began to build a new parcel post station. In July, the ship channel received more than a million dollars in federal funds for improvements. In September, the PWA approved Houston's application for a $1.2 million loan to build a new city hall.

In 1936 and 1937, another PWA loan helped build a new city-county Jefferson Davis Hospital on a ten-acre tract south of Buffalo Bayou. Houston put up $1 million and Harris County $500,000 for the $2,202,700 building, designed by Alfred C. Finn and Joseph Finger. Less than twenty years after, Jeff Davis would enter medical history and headlines around the world when Dr. Michael DeBakey of Baylor University College of Medicine there made the first successful repair of an aneurism of the aorta.

Throughout the depression years, construction stopped in most major industrial cities. Bank failures reduced individuals and companies to bankruptcy. Unscathed by bank failure, Houston not only had bond money and federal money to spend but local capital as well. The Rath Packing Company, the Sanitary Farms Dairies Creamery, the Mission Manufacturing Company, and Continental Can Company all built or expanded their plants.

Houston architects, engineers, technicians, and laborers were at work on even

bigger buildings. The nine-story Humble Building at Main Street and Polk had been the city's biggest office building when it opened in 1921. The company grew, and in the depths of the depression built the seventeen-story Humble Tower, designed by John F. Staub and Kenneth Franzheim. Costing $1 million, it opened in September, 1935.

After World War I, which he had spent at Ellington Field, Kenneth Franzheim had married Bessie Simms, daughter of Mr. and Mrs. Edward F. Simms of Houston. He started his architectural career in Chicago, moved to New York, and from there worked on several Houston buildings. From 1926 to 1929, he was an associate of Alfred C. Finn on the Gulf Building project. The depression hit New York City so hard that building stopped. Franzheim, therefore, bought the old Stephen Farish home on Crawford for an office and moved his headquarters to Houston. The Franzheims came to live in the Simms family mansion at 900 S. Wayside Drive.

Before it was over, the depression cost Colonel Simms all but forty of his more than two hundred acres, but the young Franzheims had all the joys of playing in the remaining expanse of gardens, lake, swimming pool, and bayou banks. "When we first came," Kenneth Franzheim, Jr., said, "Wayside Drive was still unpaved.[12] Though we were driven to Kinkaid every day to school, we were remote from the rest of town and had to make our own fun.

"It was a wonderful house for little kids to grow up in with a playroom in the basement and all sorts of cedar closets and box rooms where things were stored in the attic. It had an elevator from basement to attic. We had our dogs and could go across and play golf at the club. Harry Neuhaus and Steve Farish used to come to spend the night or for a weekend. It was too far for a one-hour visit."

Houston did not notice that an interesting romance was developing in New York City. After finishing at Kinkaid, George

Maria Prentiss Lucas Langham of Houston (*right*) married screen idol Clark Gable in the early 1930s. When her daughter George Anna Lucas married Dr. Thomas Burke in Houston in 1935, Gable came to Houston to give the bride away. *Courtesy Mrs. Thomas W. Burke*

Anna Lucas (Mrs. Thomas Burke) and her friend Nellie Green (Mrs. George Black) went off to school in Tarrytown, New York. George Anna's mother, the attractive widow of Alfred Thomas Lucas, was living temporarily in New York. One evening she took the girls to the theater where Clark Gable was playing, and they met him. This was the start of a romance. The two married in the early 1930s, and took George Anna and her brother to California to live. After learning shorthand and typing at the University of California at Los Angeles, George Anna Lucas acted as Clark Gable's secretary, answering fan notes and autographing pictures by the hundreds.

"They had a house in Beverly Hills and they had some wonderful times in California," Mrs. Burke said. "I think my mother was responsible for his learning certain graces. And oddly enough, he did not want to take the role of Rhett Butler. It was my mother who encouraged him to do so." But both Ria Gable and her children considered Houston home.

Back for the wedding of Lida Arnold to Herbert Edmundson, George Anna met Dr. Thomas Burke. Two months later, on March 16, 1935, they were married in the home of Dr. and Mrs. Charles Green on Institute Lane. Clark Gable came to Houston to give the bride away.

Before the crash, the city of Houston and the Southern Pacific Lines had agreed to build a new railroad station at 329 Franklin.[13] Despite the depression, streets were redrawn, the bayou banks shored up, new tracks laid. Designed by Wyatt Hedrick, the terminal was one of the handsomest in the country. The main waiting room had a ceiling that soared two stories above the marble and terrazzo floor. Massive pillars supported segmented arches of cream-colored marble. The woodwork was of black walnut. Murals showed Stephen F. Austin and the Baron de Bastrop in 1823, with a view of the Texas Capitol in the background, and Gen. Sam Houston entering the new town of Houston in 1837 with a background of the 1934 city and harbor. All this cost more than $4 million.

The Southern Pacific Station opened on September 1, 1934.[14] It was a gleaming, beautiful building that should have endured. No one foresaw the death of passenger trains. The station was razed twenty-seven years later to make way for a new post office.

Pump Priming

IN 1934, the Schlumberger Well Surveying Corporation became an American company and established its world headquarters in Houston, with an office in the Esperson Building. Henceforth the word *Schlumberger* would be a part of the oil field vocabulary. But it had taken twenty-three years of research and experiment to develop the process.

In 1912, Conrad Schlumberger, a professor of physics at the National School of Mines in Paris, had the idea that various kinds of earth—sand, shale, limestone—might react differently to electrical charges, and that by recording the differences, he could learn more about what lay hidden under the surface. After World War I, he was joined by his brother Marcel. They thought that electric logging could be used to find oil or minerals.

They were from a wealthy Alsatian family. Their father, Paul Schlumberger, agreed to finance the research necessary to develop the theory for use. Also an inventor, Conrad's son-in-law Henri Doll joined the team. On September 5, 1927, the Schlumbergers ran the first electric log down into an oil well, bringing up an accurate graph of the strata. They used a wooden winch operated by hand on a bicycle chain, Henri Doll said twenty years later. "That equipment was so encouraging that we have never stopped experimenting to this day."

The Humble Company gave the process a try in 1930, but the depression forced cancellation of the trial. In 1933, at the request of Shell Oil Company, Schlumberger sent crews to the Texas Gulf Coast. They were the vanguard of what would become a legion.

The Schlumberger log gave an accurate record of each stratum. For the first time, oil geologists could correlate the strata of one well with those of other wells nearby to gain a clear picture of where faults had occurred.

Although Houston could not foresee what the Schlumberger family would ultimately mean to the city's intellectual and cultural life, the oil industry had at last realized the value of electric logging. Schlumberger's only problem now was to hire and train enough technicians to fill the clamoring demand from oil companies. The company began to manufacture electric logging equipment in Houston for use throughout this country and abroad. French executives and engineers brought their families to live in Houston while they traveled the world from this new home. Eugene Leonarden, who had become Conrad Schlumberger's assistant after graduation from the Ecole Polytechnique, came to Houston as an early president of Schlumberger Well Surveying Corporation.

Conrad Schlumberger did not live to see the first profits from his twenty-five years of research, but he lived long enough to know that he had succeeded.[1] His nephew, Pierre Schlumberger, moved to Houston from France to succeed Leonarden as president of the company, and Henri Doll, while continuing research, became chairman of the board.

Schlumberger was an economic asset that

In 1938, with federal aid, Houston began construction on a new city hall, which looked across treetops to the soaring Gulf and Neils Esperson buildings. *Edward Bourdon photograph, courtesy of Mr. Bourdon*

any city sunk in the depression would have envied. But Houston was suffering less than most. Even in the middle of the depression, federal funds flowed into Houston. In early 1935, they built Houston Gardens, a housing project for 83 families on the north side. The Senate approved Port Houston's application for $3.4 million for deepening the channel to thirty-four feet. The state appropriated $250,000 to build the San Jacinto Memorial Shaft, and the Houston Centennial Subcommittee received a federal alloca-

tion of $400,000. Four Works Progress Administration projects employed 589 people. By 1935, the federal government had allotted $6.6 million in aid to Houston, and in 1935–36, the WPA alone worked on sixty-nine projects costing $2.2 million.

Houston in 1935 endorsed a $2.1 million bond issue for new schools. This, with added federal funds, built Mirabeau B. Lamar High School at Westheimer and River Oaks Boulevard, the Stephen F. Austin High School in the East End, the west wing of San Jacinto

High School, and three new elementary schools.

Rain began to fall in the first week of December, 1935. Buffalo Bayou swelled and overflowed its banks in the worst flood in the city's history. It did more than $1 million damage to property and threatened the municipal water supply. Six persons drowned. The flood waters rose and spread to stand hip deep in the drawing room and library of Bayou Bend. Boatmen rowed past the flooded first floors of downtown office buildings. A two-story building, undermined by water, collapsed into the bayou. National Guard troops patrolled the downtown.

Jobless men and women found manna from heaven in the flood. They fished from the bayou boxes and crates of food, clothing, furniture, and even electrical appliances that the flood waters had flushed out of warehouses along the banks. In the pure spirit of private enterprise, a few began to hawk their salvage from makeshift stands on the bayou bridges.

The bayou's rampage drove home the need for systematic flood control. The community sought help from the Army Corps of Engineers. Engineering plans began quickly. Elected county judge at the age of twenty-six, the youngest man ever to hold such an office in a major U.S. county, Roy Hofheinz led the move to establish a county flood control district. By 1940, Harris County and the federal government would agree to spend $40 million to build controls to divert future floods. This would result in the Barker and Addicks dams, completed between 1945 and 1948.

Ardent Democrats, Mrs. Jesse Andrews and Mrs. William Lockhart Clayton backed President Roosevelt. In Houston, as the elections of 1936 loomed, Susan Vaughan Clayton organized a women's division of the National Democratic Committee. It drew members from across the country.

Mr. and Mrs. Jesse Andrews owned homes in both Houston and Kansas City. Mr. Andrews had become managing part-ner of Baker & Botts, and chairman of the board of the Long Bell Lumber Company in Kansas City, the largest lumber company in the world. But the Andrewses were no less Houstonians. Mr. Andrews was a member of the first zoning committee in Houston and chairman of the Houston City Planning Commission for sixteen years.

Celeste Bujac Andrews was a Democratic force in both her home cities. "Mother was head of a Committee of 100 that was very opposed to any relaxing of the Prohibition amendment," her son Mark Edwin Andrews said. "She was *dry*. Each member of her committee had one hundred on a subcommittee, so Mother could produce ten thousand votes." Harry Truman of Missouri wisely sought the endorsement of Mrs. Andrews. She and Mrs. Clayton were alternate delegates to the Democratic Convention in Philadelphia.

Four years later Mrs. Clayton would again head the national Democratic women, with headquarters in Washington. Will Clayton and his small, pretty, dynamic wife differed over Franklin Roosevelt. She had a very personal feeling about her government. She saw in the WPA and NRA its way of helping the unfortunate with whom she had always sympathized. He thought many of the New Deal programs were stop-gaps. He disapproved of the plow-under farm policies. As John Chamberlain wrote in the May 19, 1947, *New York Times:* "Clayton argued that any artificial attempt to keep the price of U.S. cotton up, as the Hoover and Roosevelt administrations had done, would . . . result in increased acreage in Brazil, Russia and elsewhere. Thus . . . government intervention to save the U.S. cotton farmer . . . would only increase his troubles. Things turned out as Clayton had predicted."

Clayton supported Roosevelt in 1936 because of Cordell Hull's proposal for reciprocal trade agreements.

To hear President Roosevelt speak in Dallas, former Governor and Mrs. W. P. Hobby flew up for the day with Jesse Jones. On their way home, fire broke out in the

As chairman of the board of De Pelchin Faith Home in 1937, Ben Taub began to build five homelike cottages on the new property on Sandman Street. On opening day, September 15, 1938, he led the children on a tour of the new administration building. *Courtesy Henry J. N. Taub*

cockpit. The pilot, Ed Hefley, brought the plane down in a sharp descent from 7,000 feet to a crash landing. The copilot, Eugene Schacker, got the four passengers out, and despite heat that melted the door handles went back to pull Hefley to safety.

Oveta Hobby, the only woman on board, commandeered the car of a farm worker to take the badly burned copilot to the doctor in the nearest small town. When ambulance attendants delivered the crash victims to a Dallas hospital, she was so calm that it did not occur to anyone that she, too, had been aboard the plane. Schacker died from his burns.

As the Roosevelt years went on, companies across the country were awarded contracts to build public structures, like dams and bridges, that would benefit the local economy. Brown & Root had its share of what the Brown brothers called "pump-priming projects" on roads and port improvements. In 1936 the firm was awarded a joint contract with the McKenzie Construction Company to build the Marshall Ford Dam on the Colorado River near Austin—the largest construction contract in Texas. Brown & Root had never built a dam before, and this one required two million tons of concrete, and millions of tons of dirt fill. When completed, it would be twenty-seven stories high and a mile wide.

Thanks to oil money and rising benefits from the Port of Houston, well-managed stores in Houston found that their customers could still pay their bills. Sakowitz on the ground floor of the Gulf Building displayed the latest fashions. Though Mr. Simon and Mr. Tobe continued their interest in Sakowitz, the reins were shifting to the younger generation. After graduating from the University of Pennsylvania's Wharton School in 1929, Bernard Sakowitz had gone into retailing at Macy's in New York and then come home to the family business. By 1937, he was vice-president in charge of merchandising.[2]

After twenty-five years on the property given by Harriet Levy, the De Pelchin Faith Home had outgrown its quarters. As chairman of the board, Ben Taub wanted to shift from a single building to cottages that would be more homelike. He had $103,000 on hand. By applying for a WPA grant and adding city bond money, he built five cottages, a hospital, dining hall, and administration building on the new site on Sandman Street.

The new Faith Home opened in September, 1938.

The depression showed that poverty is hardest on those with the largest families. For years, Margaret Sanger had urged that poor people, especially those in cities, needed help in limiting family size. But in the 1930s, birth control was not a topic for polite conversation. Anyone who favored it was radical or bizarre or not very nice.

Houstonian Agnese Carter Nelms became caught up in the movement. As the daughter of W. T. Carter, the lumberman, she made her debut, enjoyed playing golf at the Houston Country Club, married Heywood Nelms, built a spacious house on Sleepy Hollow in River Oaks, traveled and lived abroad, spoke fluent French, and now had three young children. But Mrs. Nelms was also a person of rare intellect, enterprise, and compassion. Disturbed by a problem, she set out to solve it.

"All mothers have the right to decide for themsleves how many children they want," she said, "and all children have the right to be born under conditions which make for a strong, happy and useful citizen." But contraception takes knowledge and money. Those with money could limit their families. Those without money were bringing into the world more children than they could feed and clothe.

Agnese Nelms thought it a human injustice that poor women should be denied the right of choice that well-to-do women enjoyed. With her brother-in-law, Dr. Judson L. Taylor, she founded what became Planned Parenthood in Houston. In 1936, they opened the city's first Maternal Health Care Center in a cottage owned by the Binz family in Sam Houston Park. As persuasive social leaders, they gained the support of prominent Houstonians.[3] Patients were given physical examinations, instructions, and supplies. Donors supported the program, but if a woman could pay, she was charged fifty cents.

Despite the prestige of the board members, Planned Parenthood stirred opposition from the Roman Catholic churches and uneasiness in sedate bosoms. It drew support, however, from other churches and from more courageous individuals who could understand the need. When the Unitarian Church called for volunteers to help at the center. Mrs. Paul R. Mills and Miss Helen Steele, principal of Poe School, were the only two who volunteered. With Miss Eva Margaret Davis, principal of River Oaks School, Miss Steele set out to raise twenty-five thousand dollars.

Scoffers said that the poor would not come: so many came in the first three years that the Maternal Health Care Center outgrew its cottage. Dr. James DeWolfe, rector of Christ Church, offered the Green Foundation property at 1710 Capital Avenue for the clinic's use.

At the peak of the depression, some of the most highly skilled and highly educated men and women in the country were reduced to working for the WPA. The WPA provided not only manual labor on county roads but work for writers, artists, and architects. The Writers' Program of the WPA produced the valuable American Guide Series, a well-researched, well-written volume on each state, as well as one on Houston that was finished and published as World War II loomed. But by the end of the decade, most of those left on the WPA rolls were the least skilled.

It is clear that despite many individual cases of hardship, despite the acute need for free soup and bread, Houston as a city never felt the devastation of the Great Depression to the extent that most American cities did.

One Hundred Years Old

HOUSTON AND TEXAS were born with the battle of San Jacinto April 21, 1836. To celebrate the centennial, Houston began work on the San Jacinto Monument, which would be the tallest in the United States.

The battlefield park had been a long time in the making. It was 1853 before any move was made to mark the site and 1883 before the Texas legislature appropriated fifteen hundred dollars to buy ten acres. From time to time, the state bought more land until the San Jacinto State Park had 327 acres when it was dedicated in 1910. Daughters of the Republic of Texas spent twenty disappointing years trying to raise money for a towering monument.

The depression turned out to be the fairy godmother that granted their wish. As chairman of the Reconstruction Finance Corporation, Jesse Jones gave the plan personal and official support. The PWA and the WPA fitted the project into their building programs. Given this boost, state, county, and city officials, the Houston Chamber of Commerce, and the San Jacinto Battleground Association all pitched in.

The PWA granted $225,000. The federal centennial fund granted $385,000. The legislature appropriated $250,000. Patriotic groups gave $25,000. The terraces, reflection pool, and amphitheater brought additional appropriations. The fund reached $1.5 million before the centennial in 1936.

This largesse must be seen in its context. A popular song of the depressed times had a refrain: "Brother, can you spare a dime?"

It was a former architect-engineer making the plea.

Using a century-old plow, Jesse Jones and Sam Houston's son, Andrew Jackson Houston, broke ground for the shaft on March 27, 1936. In June, Franklin Roosevelt came to speak at the battleground. His invitation had been delivered to the White House by Moses Austin's great-great-granddaughter, Florence Carter Bryan.[1] Some 225,000 Houstonians welcomed FDR to Houston as conqueror of the Great Depression.[2]

Designed by Houston architect Alfred Finn, the monument was the Warren Bellows Construction Corporation's first major contract. The WPA reset old monuments, built roads, planted wild flowers, built bulkheads and piers along the bayou. The park acquired more land in 1938 for a total of 402 acres. Young landscape architect Pat Fleming was called upon to design park and gardens that would cost another $1.1 million. The tower was finished late in 1938.

The monument is 570 feet tall, with a 55-foot Texas star on top.[3] The eight carved panels at the base and William McVey's allegorical frieze trace the history of Texas from the arrival of the Europeans to the twentieth century. In the simplest words, carved in stone, the story of the Battle of San Jacinto is told. It is surrounded at the base by a museum of Texas history. Completed in 1939, the museum is administered by the San Jacinto Museum of History Association.

Houstonians had always used the battlefield for picnics and outings. Yacht Club parties sailed to it from the Turning Basin. Scout troops bivouacked and boys played baseball there. Amateur photographers went Kodaking there.

But the San Jacinto Monument brought the battlefield into its own. It reminds all who come of the significance of that short, swift, decisive battle. It is a monument to the ideal of freedom that drew men and women from all parts of the world to found a new nation, the Republic of Texas.

The park attracted 348,000 people in the first year after it opened. They came from every state, every Canadian province, every country in the Western Hemisphere, and twenty-five other countries. At the time, it was easy to get there: passenger trains arrived in Houston every half hour or so.

Centennial fever helped save the old City Cemetery. On West Dallas and next to the well-kept Jewish Cemetery, it held the grave of John Kirby Allen, one of the city's three founders. When the *Houston Press* reported on its dire state of neglect, the San Jacinto Centennial Association restored it and renamed it Founders' Memorial Park.

The Depression largely forgotten, Houston was resuming its normal boom. Parking meters appeared on downtown streets, rather to the annoyance of most Houstonians. They parked their cars slanted into the curb on Main Street and liked to sit and watch the crowds go by.

News boys hawked their papers in a wailing cry: "News paPER! News paPER! Houston *Post!*" When any big event occurred, the *Post, Chronicle,* and *Press* competed to see which could get its Extra out first. The cry of "EXTRA!" was loud and urgent, continuing "READ ALL ABOUT IT!" People rushed out of house and office to buy. One such Extra carried the tragic story of the kidnaping of Charles Lindbergh's baby. Not long after, another Extra carried heartbreak: "Lindbergh Baby Found Dead!"

Horse-drawn vegetable wagons made daily rounds, stopping at each house to sell carrots or lettuce or fresh tomatoes. In season, strawberry vendors hawked their wares, and year-round the hot tamale man did good business. The Good Humor wagon was a delightful innovation of the 1920s that sent children pellmell after the ringing bell to buy ice cream covered in hard chocolate on a stick for five cents.

The depression had sent prices tumbling. In 1936, a loaf of bread cost eight cents, a pound of butter forty cents, a gallon of gasoline ten cents. A boy's shirt cost thirty-nine cents, a genuine leather purse one dollar.

The average annual income was $1,713 and a new house cost, on average, $3,925.

The depression had also sent women's skirts plummeting from the knees almost to the ankles. In the mid-1930s, high school girls wore shirtwaist dresses and narrow skirts that stopped just above their neatly cuffed ankle socks. They wore fire-engine-red lipstick as soon as their mothers would let them. Evening in Paris perfume was considered sophisticated, and Evening in Paris bubble bath something new and even more sophisticated. Beauty parlors were opening. Beauty parlor operators became hair stylists. Finger waves and wave-setting lotion were new. Permanent waves were growing more natural. After all the centuries of gentle buffing to gain luster, women and girls suddenly painted their nails in various shades of pink and red.

Cosmetics had gone public.

Through the WPA, the depression in its last moments gave Houston a unique gift: Margo Jones. She came in 1936, as assistant director of the Houston Little Theatre under the Federal Theater Project. Born in Livingston, with a masters degree from Texas Women's University, Margo Jones had studied theater in California, Japan, China, India, France, and England. In mid-1936, she formed the Houston Community Players. The city recreation department paid her salary of seventy-five dollars a month and she was allowed use of the newly cleaned-up city incinerator building as a theater. (It was,

Houston noted, the same size as *La Petite Theatre* in New Orleans.)

Margo Jones was twenty-three. In the next six years, she would give Houston theater a reputation for vitality and would gain practical experience in theater-in-the-round. Her first play was *The Importance of Being Earnest*. Mary Alice Krahl, Mamie Hathaway, Irving Wadler, Rita Moise, Rowena John, Arthur Koch, Jr., Albert Horrocks, and Bill Koch were the nine members of the cast. Six of the nine chipped in a dollar to finance the production. Jackson Purdy was assistant director.[4]

Margo Jones staged Houston's first theater-in-the-round production in the air-conditioned bridge lounge of the Lamar Hotel. The audience sat on four sides of a square space. This new intimacy had an unexpected impact. In one scene Mary Alice Krahl was to ask Joe Finkelstein to bring her an ashtray from across the set. Carried away, a man on the front row picked up the nearest tray and handed it to her. By the time she left Houston, Margo Jones was recognized as a director and producer of outstanding gifts, and was being sought from West Coast to East.[5]

In the later 1930s, the Museum School drew Houstonians of all ages. Robert Joy, whose portraiture would capture Houston's leadership for decades, was an influential teacher. When Clare Fleming was about eleven years old, Lamar Fleming took her to the museum to enroll.

Clare Fleming Sprunt recalled:

The studio was where the Blaffer Gallery was later. Dad and I walked in. There was a wonderful skylight and it was a good studio. The nude model was posing and a lot of people were drawing. That day they were mostly adults. But before long, Gertrude Levy and St. John Garwood, and Rosalie Bosworth were in the class.[6] Neither Dad nor Mr. Joy nor I thought anything about the nude model. Later, children were banned from the adult classes and were not allowed to do life drawings.

When the model was not posing, we would run all around the room and see what was there. Houston had a small treasure trove. And I felt like I was at home with these things and

developed a feeling about art museums. If I were in a strange city and didn't know anyone, when I went to the art museum I felt right among friends.

Although M. D. Anderson enjoyed fishing and duck hunting, he never shared his brother-in-law's enthusiasm for exercise. While Will Clayton walked to the Cotton Exchange Building every morning from his house at 5300 Caroline, Anderson drove the short blocks from his hotel. Finding that he had high blood pressure, his doctor put him on a light diet of salads and fruits.

"Uncle Mon came regularly to dinner at our house," his nephew Thomas D. Anderson said, "and my mother always had his special diet prepared for him. Then, after eating the lettuce, tomatoes, and carrots, he would eat the meat, potatoes, and whatever the rest of us were having. He had his diet and a square meal on top!"

In a lifetime with Anderson, Clayton, M. D. Anderson knew most of the eight hundred employees by name. Notoriously thrifty and in an era free of federal income tax, Anderson amassed a fortune in the twenty years after 1916. In 1936, he established the foundation that would one day receive the bulk of that fortune and make possible, among other things, the Texas Medical Center. His friends and lawyers, Col. William Bates and John H. Freeman, were his co-trustees.

Tom Anderson said, "I think he should be remembered for kindness, a quiet sense of humor, generosity toward those in need, and an intense dislike of handouts to those who were able but unwilling to work and earn. He was certainly a man of integrity. Financial acumen—that was certainly there. In the family, he was lovable and a wonderful person. We were all crazy about him, my brothers and I."

At his death in 1939, after bequests to his family, he left more than $20 million for the M. D. Anderson Foundation. In his will, he asked that his money go "to the establishment, support and maintenance of hospitals, homes and institutes for the care of the sick, the young, the aged, the incompetent and the helpless among people. . . . To the promotion of health, science, education and advancement and diffusion of knowledge and understanding among the people." Like William Marsh Rice and George Hermann, the childless bachelor left to Houston his entire fortune.

The Rt. Rev. Clinton Quin, Episcopal bishop of Texas, was a merry gadfly who rounded up allies in a wide variety of good causes. He asked Episcopal church women to organize their efforts at Jefferson Davis Hospital to provide systematic help in offices and wards. Mrs. Richard Franklin, Mrs. Lamar Fleming, and Mrs. Joseph W. Evans were among the early leaders. By their uniforms, they became known as the Women in Yellow.

The Houston Junior College was outgrowing its quarters in San Jacinto High School. The Houston School Board had started it for Houston high school graduates, but it also drew young people who came to town to work. Guided by Dr. E. E. Oberholtzer, school superintendent, and Col. W. B. Bates, board chairman, the board voted in 1933 to expand the college into a four-year University of Houston. Palmer Hutcheson, as the board's attorney, carried the resolution to the Texas legislature to obtain the charter.

The new university's president and vice-president were outstanding. After earning his first two degrees at the University of Chicago, Dr. Obertholtzer studied for his Ph.D. at Columbia University during the presidency of Nicholas Murray Butler. Dr. Walter W. Kemmerer was a Phi Beta Kappa graduate of Lehigh, and at twenty-six had a doctorate from Columbia. A gifted teacher, he shaped the university's academic program. He later brought to the faculty a good friend from his Lehigh days, Dr. Charles Hiller. Dr. Hiller had studied at the University of Paris as part of his work toward a Harvard doctorate.

Born in mid-depression, the school had neither campus nor buildings. In May, 1935, the University of Houston held its first commencement at Miller Theater. Victor Alessandro, the distinguished head of public school music, conducted the Houston Independent School District band in the grand march from *Aida* as eighty seniors marched into the open-air theater.[7]

When a proposal to place the campus on 150 acres of Memorial Park stirred protest, Jules Settegast told his lawyer, John H. Freeman, that the Settegast estate might give 75 acres southeast of Buff Stadium. In the clubby way that Houston did things, Freeman told his partner Colonel Bates about Settegast's offer. They remembered that the Taub family owned 35 acres next to the Settegast land. The upshot was that Ben Taub and Jules Settegast gave the University of Houston the first 110 acres of its campus. Building had to begin by January 1, 1938, or the property would go to the city to become a park.

No street reached the wooded site. In early 1937, the city opened St. Bernard Street.[8] The depression agencies were still in place. The PWA approved an eighty-six-thousand-dollar grant. National Youth Administration workers, paid fifty cents an hour, began to clear the land.

Rosella Werlin's article in the *Houston Post* described Hare & Hare's landscape design. Despite its success in landscaping other Houston sections, Hare & Hare must have thought that Houston was on a parallel with Key West. In addition to platting quadrangles and placing various academic buildings, the design showed a bowling green and a swimming pool with a sand beach and a bath house.

Banker John T. Scott, Dr. Oberholtzer, and Dr. Kemmerer approached Hugh Roy Cullen. The idea of giving the children of working people a chance at education appealed to him. He agreed to head a $1 million fund campaign. They planned a big Houston Club dinner. With Col. Joseph Evans as toastmaster, the speakers' table presented a phalanx of Houston's economic and social power.

At the dinner, Cullen announced that he and his wife were giving to the university its first major building in memory of their son, Roy Gustav Cullen, who had been killed in the collapse of an oil rig. Cullen gave a glimpse of his own future course when he said: "Suppose that William Marsh Rice or George Hermann could live their lives over. Would they have waited . . . to do their great work of giving? Or would they have started giving . . . earlier . . . so that they could bask in the sunshine of their own creations?"

This was the start of a lifetime commitment to the University of Houston. Though Mr. and Mrs. Cullen had always responded generously to the needs of such civic institutions as the symphony, the Little Theatre, and the Community Chest, this marked the beginning of a philanthropy that would pour more than $22 million into the university by 1986 and that would spill over into other educational and cultural institutions of the city and state. Mr. Cullen had discovered a new joy in the life that had been so saddened by the tragic death of his only son.

Though still a gentle Southern town in atmosphere, with palm trees and magnolias growing across the city, Houston was growing. In 1937, the *Houston Post* reported that the city had 84,272 telephones, "more connections than any other city in the State or in the South." In 1938, the *Chronicle* gave the city the dubious title of "the champion parking meter city in the world," with 3,700 meters. And in 1938, Houston became the fourth largest port in the nation.

While the antebellum mansions of Galveston lingered on in fading grandeur, Houston ruthlessly razed great houses to make room for the growing business center. Several of the biggest Victorian houses at Main and Gray, however, including those built by the Levy family and the Robert Lovetts, survived encroachment through World War II.

St. Joseph, Baptist Memorial, Methodist, and St. Elizabeth hospitals were downtown, but Hermann Hospital was still surrounded by woods. A small road led to it

from Main Street. Dr. Jack Brannon, from Bastrop, newly graduated from Baylor Medical School in Dallas, came to Hermann as an intern.

"I was taught to be a gentleman and a doctor," Dr. Brannon said.

We lived in the hospital. We had our own private dining room, our private kitchen, our private cook. We had tablecloths and silver. We dressed for dinner.[9] We made ten dollars a month the first year and room and board and laundry. The second year we got twenty dollars.

Seventy percent of Hermann was charity; thirty percent was private. Our doctors had to teach interns and residents as well as care for their own private patients. The ones I remember, and that my vintage looked up to, were Dr. Judson Taylor who was chief of surgery, Dr. Billy Bertner, Dr. Allen McMurray, Dr. Charlie Green, Dr. Fred Lummis. We were taught the art of medicine. We went to the bedside with them to see their charity patients, then their private patients. Each of us watched carefully and we gained something. The private patients at that time were the ones who could afford hospitals; it was very expensive.[10] That helped introduce me to Houston. It made me want to stay in Houston.

No hospital was air-conditioned. "The operating room," Dr. Brannon said, "had big fans about three feet in diameter blowing all around, and as you operated some nurse was wiping the sweat off your brow. If a drop of sweat dropped into the abdomen they'd stop and pour ether on it to kill the bacteria. I remember when Dr. Judson Taylor came back from some eastern convention and he wanted to show all the other doctors what he had brought back. It was what the tennis players wear on their foreheads—a sponge. And from then on he kept them in the operating room and all the surgeons were given one to wear."

The doctors gave their services to the charity patients at Hermann. "I worked six months out of each year for twenty years in the charity clinics," Dr. Brannon said. "I would spend a half-day Wednesday seeing the patients and the other half-day on Saturday operating on the ones we'd seen on Wednesday." Towering Jack Brannon was the Rice Institute physician and a familiar figure on the bench at all Rice football games for decades. Mrs. Robert Lee Blaffer chose him for her personal physician. In later years, Dr. Brannon would be a founding force in the Seamen's Center at the Port of Houston.

Jefferson Davis Hospital on Buffalo Drive (later Allen Parkway) was the city-county charity hospital. Dr. Elizabeth Stripling (Crawford) found a very different kind of internship there in 1939 when she came up from the University of Texas Medical School in Galveston.[11]

"It was light on teaching but heavy on experience," she said. The internship did not fall into her lap. "My dad had been in the drug business in Nacogdoches since the turn of the century, and he said 'The Taubs have been sending me an order of tobacco every Monday morning since 1902. I ought to have some influence with him.' So I went to see Mr. Ben Taub at the Taub Tobacco Company. He was sitting up at a high desk and he had on a green eye shade and had those elastic bands around his shirt sleeves. Next I went to see Dr. J. E. Clark and Dr. M. J. Taylor and between the three of them I got in."

Dr. Crawford was the first woman intern at Jeff Davis. "They didn't give me a room, but they just flat didn't have any. So I didn't resent it. I bunked with the colored nurses and thanks to them I got hot lemonade in the winter and cold lemonade in the summer." Only Dr. W. S. Red was vehemently opposed to taking a woman as an intern. "But after I got in, he was the best friend I ever had." It was Dr. Red who finally managed to get quarters for the early women residents, including Dr. Carolyn Westphal, Dr. Betty Moody, and Dr. Helen Goldberg.

Dr. Crawford was to become one of Houston's most respected ophthalmologists, numbering among her patients Miss Ima Hogg, Jesse Jones, and George and Herman Brown.

Waddell's House Furnishing Company had long been one of Houston's finest furniture stores. Since the 1890s it had occupied a store on Prairie Avenue at Fannin. Before dawn on the morning of March 22, 1938, Waddell's caught fire. The flames spread swiftly. By dawn, twenty stores and buildings between Main and San Jacinto were ablaze. Wilson's Stationery Store, the YWCA Cafeteria, and Foley Bros. Dry Goods Company across the corner from Waddell's, were damaged by flames, smoke, or water. The fire was more costly than all the fires of the preceding year.

Christ Church was the worst hit. Firemen had always said that if Waddell's ever caught fire, the old church would go. When the walls fell in, they crushed the sanctuary and much of the parish house. But one firefighter, a Roman Catholic, was determined to save the rood screen if he could. While others fought other flames, he played his hose back and forth on the ornate wood carvings. Though most of the church lay blackened, the rood screen and pulpit could be and were restored, the memorial windows could be and were remade.

At seven in the morning, the church bell began to ring high in the smoke-filled air and Dr. James Pernette DeWolfe, the rector, began the daily service of Holy Communion at an improvised altar in the Sunday school.[12]

Houston rallied, Fred Heyne offered the old Majestic Theater. Dr. Charles L. King offered use of the First Presbyterian Church for Lenten services which were due to begin at noon. Dr. Henry Barnston and Mr. Ike Freed offered Temple Beth Israel for as many Sundays as might be needed.

By two o'clock in the afternoon, the work of clearing the rubble had begun. In six days of intense effort, the destruction was walled off and a temporary altar set up. Because the organ had been destroyed, musicians from the Houston Symphony Orchestra, under the direction of Ernst Hoffman, played for the first service of morning prayer on Sunday. Lenten services continued in the foreshortened church. Almost three thousand worshippers came to the Good Friday service. Throughout, rebuilding went on.

A Houston businessman telegraphed Dr. DeWolfe: "My sympathy and my pocket-book are yours." He was a Methodist. One of the first contributions toward rebuilding came from a young Jewish girl. And of course old members were inspired to new heights of giving. Once again, Houston was responding to need in the spirit that it had shown since its birth.

Six days after the big downtown fire, Houstonians faced another large newspaper headline: Col. Edward Mandell House had died at the age of seventy-nine in New York City. In Houston and Austin, flags were lowered to half-staff, tributes were paid, and his service to President Wilson and the nation was recalled. Private funeral services were held in New York. And then Edward Mandell House was brought home to Houston to the family plot in Glenwood Cemetery.

Houstonians began to get the feel of air conditioning—a technology that would transform life in the city. Early on, private railroad cars of the rich and famous had ways of fanning air over ice. The Second National Bank in the Carter Building was the city's first air-conditioned business office, but hotels and theaters soon invested in central cooling. The ten-story Ben Milam Hotel across from Union Station was the first in Houston to be completely air-conditioned. The York Ice Machinery Corporation installed a year-round system that controlled temperatures and humidity, and cleaned the air as well. It cost seventy-five thousand dollars.

As Christ Church was being rebuilt, John Mellinger and R. W. Horlock proposed that they add air conditioning. Horlock pointed out that if a hot-air furnace were used instead of steam radiators, the York company could devise a cooling system to blow air over ice into the church. He offered to give ten thousand pounds of ice every Sunday throughout all the summers ahead if the vestry would consent. Ready to celebrate its centennial on March 16, Houston's oldest

church became a pioneer in the new age of air conditioning.

But by default, Christ Church also let a piece of Houston's irreplaceable history get away. In 1843, when the yellow fever epidemic overcrowded the city graveyard, James West offered two acres of his land south of the bayou to be used as the Episcopal-Masonic Cemetery.[13] Some of Houston's first settlers were buried there—including Stephen Richardson, one of Austin's Old Three Hundred. Old stones marked the graves of the Key family. They were the children of Mrs. Priscilla Hadley Key, descendants of Francis Scott Key, and the grandchildren of Obedience Smith, who once owned all of southwestern Houston from Main Street west and south of Buffalo Bayou.

During the cholera outbreaks of 1846 and 1866 and the yellow fever epidemic of 1867, however, the graveyard took in late comers. With unpredictable numbers of deaths a day, plot ownership lost meaning and there was no time to provide proper gravestones. Old records were imprecise: "An English servt.," "A German Soldier," "Child," "Infant." Over the years, other cemeteries had come into use—Glenwood, Brookside, and Washington among them. Some of the most memorable first settlers had been ceremonially removed to Glenwood.

In the same month as the Christ Church fire, the city proclaimed the old Episcopal-Masonic Cemetery a public nuisance. Graves were unkempt, and shrubbery sprouted out through cracks in the vaults. There was apparently no move by anyone to save the historic site.[14] Busy rebuilding the church, the parish corporation simply bought lots at Brookside and moved the long dead to new ground. In the process, Henry W. Benchley, a former vestryman and grandfather of Robert Benchley, disappeared. Neither he nor his marker turned up at Brookside.[15]

Fire struck again shortly before Christmas in 1938. The Christmas tree that the Blue Birds had decorated for the children set the Little Hospital afire. Nobody was hurt and the Arabia Temple's young patients were shifted over to Methodist Hospital, but the cottage was in ruins.

Blue Birds Flora Root Cody, Sue Campbell Pillot, and Annie Vive Crain, turned to their husbands for help. As Dr. E. L. Crain, Jr., remembers it, "Dr. Claude C. Cody and Mr. Norman Pillot and Dad worked with the Blue Birds a lot on their projects, and so Mother and Mrs. Cody and Mrs Pillot asked them to rebuild the cottage at once. *Now!* It was Christmas Eve. The men had other things on their minds. They said no."

"And," said Dr. Crain, "none of them got any Christmas dinner." The cottage was quickly rebuilt.

The effort to find the cause and prevention of poliomyelitis grew in the late 1930s. The Harris County Chapter of the National Foundation for Infantile Paralysis, formed in 1934, gave an annual ball on President Roosevelt's birthday to raise money for research and care. From 1936 to 1946, I. B. McFarland was president of the chapter, to be succeeded by W. Stewart Boyle. In 1936, William S. Patton, vice-president of the South Texas Commercial Bank, began years of service as chapter treasurer. In 1937, N. J. Klein, a Houston ice cream manufacturer, gave Methodist Hospital its first iron lung.

Infantile paralysis had always had its victims, though comparatively few. Then, in the 1930s, poliomyelitis gained strength. The number of crippling cases grew, the number of deaths grew. It became epidemic. Though polio most often struck children, President Roosevelt's adult illness and lameness made it clear that nobody was safe. To parents, it began to seem that polio lurked all winter waiting to strike in the summertime. It appeared not every summer, not in every city, but the menace was growing. Each spring, the nation tensed for the arrival of an epidemic that had no known cause, but cruel and often deadly effects. Hospitals bought iron lungs, Research scientists everywhere were trying to find how polio was transmitted, why some were vulnerable to the virus, others not. Gradually, Houston settled into an annual summer dread.

Chapter Fifty-Five

As Segregation Grew

THOUGH A THIRD of Houston's population was black, black and white Houstonians lived oddly parallel lives. In the first years of freedom after the Civil War, black leaders welcomed the opportunity at last to create their own institutions. They built a self-sufficient and self-contained society. They had their own churches, own business operations, own restaurants, own stores and tailor shops, own clubs, own library, own holidays, and own charities.

In 1893, three black Houstonians, C. N. Love, Jack Tibbit, and Carter G. Woodson, founded the *Texas Freeman,* the city's first black newspaper and forerunner of the twentieth-century *Informer.* When the 1900 storm devastated Galveston, blacks organized a relief drive independent of the whites. They had black drill teams and black baseball clubs. They celebrated Juneteenth with parades to Emancipation Park and staged a carnival similar to that of No-Tsu-Oh.

But over the years, segregation gradually expanded. In earlier days, stagecoaches had not been segregated.[1] Neither were train cars. It was 1891 before Texas enacted a law requiring railroads to provide "separate, exclusive, equal accommodations for colored persons." The law divided the races, but the railroads never provided equal accommodations.

The *Houston Daily Post* promoted a "Happyhammer Club" for children who read the Sunday children's page. In 1898, though white and black children had always played together throughout the South, the paper began to limit membership to white children. By this time, white prisoners were in cells on one floor of the county jail, blacks on another. In 1903, despite protests from the streetcar company, the City Council ruled that streetcars must provide separate compartments for blacks and whites. In 1907, the City Council authorized segregation in hotels, restaurants, and theaters and, in 1922, a new city code segregated parks.

Though the City Council responded to pressures from those who feared black competition, other white Houston leaders balked. In 1909, R. S. Lovett, president of the Houston and Texas Central Railroad, received demands that black switchmen be fired and the jobs given to white workmen. He replied: "If the policy thus urged upon this company is to be the policy of the South toward the Negro, if he is to be allowed to do only such labor as no white man will do, and receive only such wages as no white man wants, what is to become of the Negroes? How are they to live? Food and clothes they must have. If not by labor, how are they to get the necessities of life? Hunger must and will be satisfied, prisons and chain-gangs notwithstanding."

In 1913, the city installed separate drinking fountains in front of City Hall, and the Union Station established divided waiting rooms. And it was as segregation grew that Annette Finnigan gave to the city the John Finnigan Park for Negroes on Lockwood Drive, naming it for her liberal-minded father.

Most white Houstonians assumed that segregation was as pleasing to blacks as to whites. Despite such inconveniences as that of bus and train segregation, some blacks seemed to agree. The *Red Book* of 1915, published by blacks and for blacks, gives a wide, pictorial view of black society. The editor wrote: "A worthy man in his race, whatever it is, loses that worthiness when he attempts to obliterate social and racial barriers imposed by a beneficent Jehovah. He must stay in his own to prove the worthiness of his life."

The *Red Book* pictures well-dressed men and women of calm dignity. Many of their two-story Victorian houses with wide verandahs stood on the same streets that were popular with white homeowners—Hadley, Chenevert, and Texas Avenue among them. Segregation was not as marked in 1915 as it would become by 1930. But as the city grew larger, the demarcation grew more evident. The predecessor to No-Tsu-Oh was an annual fruit and vegetable carnival in which both blacks and whites took part. When No-Tsu-Oh began, the blacks shifted to their De-Ro-Loc Carnival ruled by King La-Yol-E-Civ-Res.

Houston had the largest black population in Texas, and black Houstonians were proud of their achievements. They could point out that they were above the national average in literacy. In cities across the country, 18 percent of the blacks were illiterate, in Houston only 16 percent. Up to the start of high school, black children had a better attendance record at school than whites, and a much better record than the city's foreign-born whites. Although Washington, D.C., had "an Afro-American population of 95,000," the *Red Book* noted, Houston had almost twice as many black homeowners as did the nation's capital.

Black Houstonians, like whites, traveled widely. Dr. Frederick Lights, pastor of Antioch Baptist Church, attended the World Baptist Congress in 1905 and then toured France and Britain. Five years later he went to the World Foreign Mission Congress in Edinburgh and from there toured France, Belgium, and Germany. But . . .

However successful they might become in business or the professions, however well educated, the black Houstonians were called by their first names by all whites. They received little courtesy from Houston police and often had to depend on their network of white friends to get fair treatment. The worst treatment of blacks, as of any minority, usually came from those who feared the competition and, unfortunately, from the police.

Nonetheless, those who considered themselves "nice people" of both races shared lifelong courtesy and friendships that traversed the color line. They attended each other's weddings and funerals. They stood by each other in time of trouble.

Samuel C. Adams had served overseas during World War I and was a well-paid boilermaker in the Southern Pacific shops until the massive lay-offs of the depression cost him his job. He went to work for W. D. Cleveland on South Boulevard. "He was chauffeur, yardman, butler, and friend," his son Dr. Samuel C. Adams, Jr., said. "I can remember how close the feelings were. Though it was my daddy who worked there, all of us were involved with the Clevelands in some way. We used always to go there on Christmas Day. That is where I got my first bicycle. The house backed up to Bissonnet. We always went in that way." A graduate of Prairie View and Houston College for Negroes, Mrs. Adams was a teacher for thirty years.

Dr. Adams, who would become one of the State Department's most decorated foreign service officers, grew up in the heavily wooded Fourth Ward. In its quite shade, he had no sense of being a part of the city only a mile away. "I remember shooting turtles in Buffalo Bayou," Dr. Adams said. "It was a neighborhood of people from the farms. Many of my neighbors had just come to Houston from East Texas and Louisiana. I grew up knowing the myths and legends and attitudes of farm people. Many of them spoke only French." The Louisiana French of the Fourth Ward attuned young Sam

Adams's ear to the language he would use in French Indo-China and North Africa.

"There was a whole etiquette that one had in relationships with whites," Ambassador Adams said in 1986.

As I grew up, it never occurred to me that they were human beings, that they had problems, that they got sick or their children caused them worry. And the only instances of harassment that I knew . . . it was happening to other persons rather than to me.

My parents were strivers. All three children went to Gregory Institute and were deeply schooled in what one needed to do. I was taking piano lessons, violin and trombone lessons and going to the Y. I had a *Chronicle* paper route that I worked up until I had 1,050 subscribers and a whole team of little boys delivering for me. My parents exercised a remarkable kind of discipline. But it never occurred to me that there would ever be anyone but whites in the banks or stores. Only one Negro I knew was a railway clerk. The only Negro that I ever heard referred to as other than John or Bill was Dr. Lanier [R. O'Hare Lanier, former U.S. minister to Liberia and the first president of Texas Southern University].

But one thing I know: even with all my education, and whatever honors have come to me, my father could walk down to the offices here in Houston and get more respect than I can get now. When my father wanted to buy the house on Wichita, he didn't just go in the FHA office as S. C. Adams. Mr. Cleveland's lawyer had already called down there.

There was a network. So it wasn't just Sam Adams coming in.

At sixteen, the younger Sam Adams graduated from Booker T. Washington High School at the top of his class and won a one-year scholarship to Fisk University. Slim, not yet fully grown, he went off to Nashville. "Mr. Cleveland gave me several of his suits and Mother had them cut down to fit me. They were all black. I'll never forget the first time I had money of my own to buy a suit that wasn't black."

Midway through his first year, the ambitious young Houstonian realized that he would need help to return for the second year. He wrote thirty letters to famous people. One answered. Henry Ford wrote that he could come work every summer in the Dearborn plant and return to school each fall. The Henry Ford Trade School took the young men to art museums and symphony concerts as well as teaching them the skills of automobile manufacture.

As a result, Samuel C. Adams, Jr., graduated from Fisk, earned his masters, and then went on to get his doctorate in sociology at the University of Chicago. He would become one of Houston's outstanding contributions to the foreign service, first in Vietnam and Cambodia, later as U.S. ambassador to Niger, and ultimately as chief of the African department of the Agency for International Development.

But between graduate school and the foreign service lay four grim years. When World War II began, the young black Houstonian with Ford Trade School training and a good start on his doctoral degree, was reduced to carrying tools and bringing in cokes for the white workers at the Norfolk Navy Yard. The white union would not let him turn a screwdriver. He quit to volunteer as an aviation cadet. Only at Tuskegee and Maxwell Field, Alabama, could a black cadet get flight training. Cadet Adams was sent to San Antonio.

The Aviation Cadet Center there, so pleasant for white airmen, was dismal for black enlisted men. They had no chapel, no PX, no recreational facilities. "Most of them were in transportation or mess squadrons. Most were barely literate," Dr. Adams said. Finding a white chaplain who was incensed at these conditions, he became the chaplain's assistant and organist to try to improve conditions. In 1946, given the Meritorious Service Award, he returned to the freer world of graduate school at the University of Chicago.

Chapter Fifty-Six

Polo, Anyone?

FROM HOUSTON'S earliest days, horses were important to young and old. Long after the automobile garage replaced the stables in the back yard, well-to-do Houstonians kept saddle horses for a morning ride, ponies for the children, gaited horses for exhibition riding, and polo ponies for the sport. But by the mid-1920s they could no longer keep them stabled at home. They had to send them to Almeda Stables near Hermann Park or out Westheimer to Green Pastures or Tall Timbers.[1]

At the corner of Westheimer and South Post Oak, the Houston Riding and Polo Club had riding rings, jumps, and a tiny clubhouse, and it stabled members' horses.[2] The club's annual horse show was covered by the *Gargoyle* in its heyday. It reported on the fifteen hundred spectators gathered for the exhibition riding, on the blue ribbons awarded, and on the rounds of luncheons at River Oaks Club and other parties stemming from the horse show.

In the late 1920s, the horse was the main reason for the spread of country places along North Post Oak Lane between Westheimer and the unpaved Memorial Drive that ran through Memorial Park and beyond it to the west. Just as the Will Claytons had pioneered in the untracked forest of River Oaks Country Club Estates to build a weekend retreat from their home on Caroline Boulevard so, only three years later, did other couples—many of whom lived on Courtlandt or Montrose or in Shadyside—begin to build weekend places in the woodlands west of Memorial Park.

Polo players and horse breeders, the Farishes called their country place Huisache.[3]

In 1926, Frankie Randolph and her husband Deke commissioned John Staub to build a stable on what became South Post Oak Lane. They laid out bridle trails and jumps. The Randolphs were a handsome couple, memorable on horseback. Deke Randolph rode his gaited horses with the grace and ease of an aristocrat. Given light hands and a beautiful seat, he stirred the admiration of successive generations of horse-loving children.

In 1929, Mrs. Randolph's brother, William T. Carter, Jr., and his wife Lillie Neuhaus went much farther out the country road to what became West Friar Tuck Lane and bought some hundred acres of woodland. Hare & Hare, the Kansas City landscape architects, dammed up a tributary of Buffalo Bayou to make a lake, and John Staub designed a lodge with a massive log fireplace, wide plank floors, and weathered oak framing timbers.[4] The Carters, who lived at Number 18 Courtlandt, used to motor out to their country place for a weekend or a fortnight or longer.

Both Mrs. Howard Hughes and Mrs. Harry Wiess loved horses and, in the early 1920s, they rode almost every morning. By 1930, the Wiesses had three daughters, each with a pony. Every morning when Elizabeth, Caroline, and Margaret came down for breakfast before going to school, they would find their mother in riding habit. Olga Keith Wiess had a beloved three-gaited gelding named Star, which she stabled at Tall Tim-

Olga Keith Wiess rode every morning. Star, her three-gaited gelding, was her favorite mount. *From*   *the Wiess family collection*

bers until the Wiesses bought a large piece of property between Buffalo Bayou and Memorial on North Post Oak Lane.

"Mother really just wanted a stable for Star," her daughter Margaret Elkins said. "Daddy was the engineer, Mother drew the plans, and Mr. Staub proportioned it and chose the building materials." The result was The Stables on North Post Oak Lane.

Mrs. Wiess acquired a five-gaited mare. Mr. Wiess laid out five miles of bridle paths and supplied his daughters with hunters and jumpers. Up until World War II, the Stables housed a dozen horses tended by skilled grooms. Elizabeth and Caroline enjoyed the jumps. Margaret privately preferred to play baseball and ride her bicycle.

The Stables gradually grew into a gracious country house set in woodland. "First they built a tennis court because Daddy was an avid tennis fan," Mrs. Elkins said. "The swimming pool came later when we had all learned to swim. At one time or another, all of us have lived there for a while. When Daddy was having the Sunset Boulevard house air conditioned, the whole family moved out to the Stables."

(Years later, after astronaut Frank Borman had returned from his historic space flight around the moon, he and his wife Susan, close friends with James and Margaret Elkins, spent a few days in the solitude of the Stables.)

As additional weekend places were built on both sides of Buffalo Bayou along Post Oak Road, newspapers began to refer to "the

The Wiess family's Stables in the forest west of   Memorial Park. *From the Wiess family collection*

millionaires' country estate section." Which, of course, it was. None of them expected to *live* out in those remote woodlands.

By the mid-1930s, Memorial Park surpassed Hermann Park in bridle trails. "My mother took me for my first riding lessons at Tall Timbers stable," Clare Fleming Sprunt said.

San Felipe Road had some sort of hard surface on it, but wasn't exactly paved, and it ran right out into the country. We forded the bayou near the River Oaks Country Club golf course, down near the railway trestle, and went into Memorial Park to ride.

Josephine Abercrombie rode gaited horses and it was a much more professional endeavor. But my sister Mary and I, and Virginia Jago, Lila Gordon, Floy Saville, Adrienne Meek, and Rosalie Bosworth rode the bridle trails. My sister Mary and I later got into the hunter/jumper class because we had a quarter-horse that did not look like or move like a hunter,

and could jump very high. He was an atypical quarterhorse. He looked more like a mule.

Josephine Abercrombie began to ride at four and at six showed her own pony, Lomita. Perhaps remembering the days when his brother Bob raced Old Gracie on the track in Hermann Park, Jim Abercrombie encouraged his daughter, and she became one of Houston's leading young riders. Not yet in her teens, she won the title of Champion Child Rider at the All American Show in Fort Worth.

In 1938, hunting land for a stables for Josephine, Jim Abercrombie went farther south and paid eighteen thousand dollars for one hundred acres on Post Oak Road in the fringe of Bellaire. It would become the site of the Pin Oak Horse Shows, a major source of money for Texas Children's Hospital.

Whereas River Oaks Estates had centered around golf and tennis, these country places were first and foremost for horses, riding and polo – though tennis was a close second.

In the 1930s, the Post Oak lanes had not yet been paralleled by a freeway and the woodlands had not been sliced by San Felipe, Woodway, and Memorial drives. The best way for these friends to get from one country place to another or from the Houston Polo Club to the Carters' or the Wiesses' was by horseback. When the weather was nice on the weekend, they would ride out to one country house or another for lunch, and perhaps for tennis and a swim, before riding back again. It was wonderfully pleasant.

By 1938, these gatherings prompted the idea of a new club to adjoin Memorial Park and be devoted to polo, swimming, and tennis – the Bayou Club.[5] The charter of July 25, 1939, was signed by Robert D. Farish, Stephen P. Farish, W. St. John Garwood, S. M. McAshan, Jr., Hugo Neuhaus, R. D. Randolph, and Harry C. Wiess. Three weeks later, the membership elected Stephen Farish president, St. John Garwood vice-

president, Maurice McAshan treasurer, and J. Virgil Scott secretary.

John Staub, Stephen Farish, and Baron Neuhaus explored the woodland west of Memorial Park on horseback until they found a suitable site for the club. The land they chose was owned by the University of Texas, and Mike Hogg helped them acquire it. Staub designed the gracious clubhouse in the style of southern Louisiana plantation houses of the eighteenth century. The main lounge was on the second floor, cooled by breezes coming through screened porches. Exterior stairs led down to the terrace and swimming pool. The grill room and locker rooms were at ground level. The clubhouse opened in 1940.

Houston's loveliest country club building, it was a labor of love for John Staub and one of his finest works. From the first the Bayou Club was Houston's quietest, most elegant, and most prestigious country club. As River Oaks membership fees soared into the thousands after World War II, the Bayou Club's stayed comparatively low. But it was and continues to be almost impossible to get in except by inheritance.

For They Were Young

LIFE, sweet and free for Houston children between two world wars, was notably pleasant for the young singles and young marrieds of Old Houston society. The social circle encompassed Dallas, Austin, San Antonio, and Galveston with the young unmarrieds taking the train from one to another for the biggest parties.

In 1935, Helen Sharp came over from Austin to go to Genevieve Lykes's costume ball. "I saw her across a crowded room," Tom Anderson said half a century later.[1]

Everyone agreed that the debut parties of Elizabeth and Caroline Wiess, one in 1935 and the other in 1939, were the most beautiful Houston had yet seen. Pavilions covered the back lawn at Number 2 Sunset, white for Elizabeth's party, pink for Caroline's. A school friend from Farmington days, Mary Wood of Chicago came down for Elizabeth's party and met Billy Farish.[2] Though Camilla Davis had lived her life in Dallas, her first visit to Houston was for Caroline Wiess's debut. "It was all in pale pink and they had a fine band. I was put with John Blaffer."[3]

All three of these meetings led to marriage.

Daughter of the Wirt Davises of Dallas, Camilla had graduated from Wellesley at nineteen and wanted to go to law school. Her quite remarkable mother, who had been a reporter on the Dallas *Times Herald* and owned one of the few bookstores in Dallas at the time, wanted Camilla to make a debut and marry. Camilla agreed to a debut only if Elsa Maxwell would stage it. She did, and

Life came to the party.[4] As couples arrived at the Baker Hotel in formal evening dress, they were separated and sent off to rooms filled with costumes and masks. They returned to a ballroom filled by masked unknowns. It was exciting. The Conga line snaked happily all the way through the Baker Hotel lobby and through the Adolphus Hotel and back.

In Dallas for a friend's debut party at Idlewild, Caroline Wiess was dancing when Bill Francis cut in on her partner. She was engaged to someone else at the time, but— "Something turned over."[5] That was it for both of them, though they would not marry until after World War II.

Big houses in the city seemed often to have a small house somewhere on the grounds. It might be used for guests, or given to newlyweds until they could find a place of their own. Early in the century, S. M. McAshan, Jr., was born in his great-grandfather's guest house at Main and Clay. When Hugo Neuhaus married Kate Rice, they lived in a house on Jonas Rice's property between Caroline and LaBranch until after the birth of Katherine, Hugo, Jr., and Joe. When Kate's sister Lottie married Stephen Farish, her father built them a little house in his garden.[6]

The guest house on Mrs. Walter Sharp's property at Fannin and Eagle was used by a succession of newlyweds. After a year in business, and confident of the future, Dudley Sharp married Tina Cleveland on January 8, 1929. They lived in a little house. "It had originally been a gardener's or care-

This picture of the Wiess family was made in happy times before World War II. *Left to right:* Caroline (Mrs. Theodore Law), Elizabeth (Mrs. Lloyd Hilton Smith), and Margaret (Mrs. James A. Elkins, Jr.), with their parents, Harry and Olga Keith Wiess. *From the Wiess family collection*

taker's house when the Sauters owned it," Mr. Sharp said. "After Fannin was put in, it was moved across the street and fixed up for my brother Bedford when he married Patty Lummis. There was a lake out there."

Then along came the Great Depression.

"Everybody was in the same boat," Sharp said.

We couldn't travel and we had to find our fun around here. My brother built a tennis court. We would have tournaments. Everybody would come and bring their own food and booze. We would provide the ice and the seltzer water and the tennis court. We would have a great time. I remember George Bruce was *quite* a tennis player. And so was Malcolm Lovett.

We'd go to Galveston. We built a little beach house on East Beach below the sea wall. Just two bedrooms and a bath, but a nice place to go when it was hot. And of course we had parties in each other's homes. It was pretty simple. It was a very good life.

Tina Sharp was also committed to the Little Theatre. The beautiful, young Mrs. Sharp was elected president of the Little Theatre board in 1932. Fifty years later she would be elected president of the Alley Theatre board.

The Shadyside Tennis Club had an impromptu beginning at the Cullinans' tennis court. As Bill Kirkland wrote years later, "Born with the Depression in the early '30s —maybe born *of* the Depression, for golfers had begun to learn that tennis was more

economical in time as well as in money—
the Shadyside Tennis Club had no constitution and by-laws, no dues, no membership
committee. It was just a group of congenial
tennis players, all of equal status—well, except for certain self-appointed officials."

Joseph Cullinan had built the court for
his children. "It pleased him that friendly
professional and businessmen would gather
at his tennis court on Saturday afternoons
and Sunday mornings. Players gathered
without appointment or prior notice. . . .
New members were men invited informally
for a game or two who, if congenial, slipped
into regular step."[7] As the numbers grew,
Jack Wray began to line up the matches, arranging doubles when necessary to give everyone a chance to play.[8] They had long days
on Saturdays, but everybody had to be home
in time for one o'clock dinner on Sundays.

In the late 1930s, Winthrop Rockefeller
came to Houston for a year's experience in
the oil business. Young, nice-looking, and
friendly, he merged easily into the set of
young Houstonians, going to the bay or
playing tennis with such particular friends
as Billy Farish and Bob Wood. At the end
of his stay, his parents, Mr. and Mrs. John
D. Rockefeller, Jr., came down and he gave
a party at the Tejas Club to introduce to
them his new friends before saying goodbye.

It was a hot summer night. High up on
the Petroleum Building, the Tejas Club was
usually cool with its windows open on all
four sides. His friends arrived, the girls in
charming frocks with white gloves, the men
in white linen. They found all the windows
closed because Mrs. Rockefeller feared the
draft.

Not long after her marriage to former
governor William P. Hobby, Oveta Hobby
was out for her morning ride on the Hermann Park bridle trail. A man cantered past,
then reined in and lifted his hat. "May we
ride together?" he asked. "I am an old friend
of your husband's. My name is Jakie Freedman." When the young Mrs. Hobby got
home she delivered Mr. Freedman's greet-
ings to her husband.

"Yes," said Governor Hobby. "He *is* a
very old friend. He used to be a bellhop at
the Rice Hotel, and when I first ran for
governor, he organized the Bellhops for
Hobby. When Jakie's your friend, he's your
friend."

By the 1930s, Jakie Freedman's was the
place for the young to go in the spirit of
adventure. He and Mrs. Freedman had a big
Southern-colonial mansion fourteen miles
from downtown on a lonely gravel road beyond the end of Main Street.

This was a very handsome, very expensive, and very illegal gambling casino. It was
also very exclusive. Surrounded by high
fences and with guards at the gate, Jakie
Freedman allowed no one to enter his place
who lacked good manners or whom he considered a risk. He was not open every evening, and he preferred to keep the numbers
down to about forty.

"The ones who get inside can afford it,"
Freedman explained to newsman George
Fuermann. "A man comes to the gate and
gives his name. If he is somebody I want to
invite inside, he is allowed in the gate and
I meet him on the porch myself. If not, he's
told, 'Mr. Freeman isn't at home tonight.'
I don't want to hurt anybody."

The young people of Old Houston were
made welcome, allowed to gamble just
enough for excitement—and no more. Mr.
Freedman remembered James A. Elkins, Jr.,
from their days at the Rice Hotel, when one
was a popular bellhop and the other a small
boy. By this time, Jakie Freedman was one
of the largest depositors at Judge Elkins's
bank. "When Margaret and I were dating,"
Jim Elkins said, "we thought we were daring and dashing to go to Jakie Freedman's.
We didn't know that whenever we showed
up, Jakie called our parents to ask if it was
all right for us to be there."

"My father never went to Jakie's," Margaret Wiess Elkins said, "because it was illegal. As the president of the Humble Company he did not think it appropriate for him
to be there. Daddy loved horses and betting
on horses, but he would go to Kentucky or

Florida where it *was* legal. But he knew we would come to no harm with Jakie."

"Jakie's was off bounds because gambling was illegal," Caroline Wiess Law said, "but my father was secretly so grateful to Jakie for looking after us. Even though we tried not to let him know we'd gone (we'd sneak in at all hours and tiptoe up the stairs), he always had ways of knowing where we were." Partly, of course, because Jakie told him.

"Jakie would take care of all those little wet-behind-the-ears boys and girls who would come in with ten or fifteen dollars at the most in their pockets," Mrs. Law said. "He would let them lose that and never, ever cash a check. Instead, he'd say 'Go down to the kitchen and have some scrambled eggs.' If I tried to cash a one-dollar check, Jakie would say 'Caroline, go dress up the front room, listen to the music. Don't clutter up the dice table!' We just adored Jakie."

But Jakie Freedman, a gentleman at heart, had a double standard. Though he looked after the young, he let the chips fall where they might with his regular customers, and the chips started at five dollars each. One night, George Bruce said, a well-to-do Houstonian was down some two hundred thousand dollars. He invited Jakie to settle for twenty cents on the dollar.

"No," said Jakie serenely. "I'm a businessman just as you are."

George and Laura Kirkland Bruce, Dorothy and Tom Martin Davis, the Gus Worthams, and the Sam Taubs often went to Jakie's. "One evening, the gambling was in full swing," Dorothy Davis recalled. "When the alarm sounded it meant a ranger raid. In a flash, every gambling table became a pool table and while some men played pool, most of us gathered around the piano to sing, and Virgilia Chew began to dance!"

There was never any link between Jakie Freedman's Domain Privee [*sic*] and the Maceo operations in Galveston. Each respected the other's turf. Sam Maceo's Balinese Room, far out on a pier from Galveston, lured Houstonians down with superb cuisine. The huge menus carried such items

as "Oysters sur Flaming Sword" and "Soup du Jour en Cup." An elaborately served dinner cost half what it would cost in a Houston restaurant. The Maceos made their money on the gamblers in the back room. The big name bands played there, and Alice Faye married Phil Harris at the Maceos. But during one crackdown, Sam Maceo was arrested. Someone asked Jakie Freedman: "How do you think Sam will come out?"

Jakie replied soberly: "He'll get out all right. But it's ruined him social."

The well-to-do young married set of the late 1930s lived a graceful life. They had all the joys of sailing, polo, and travel and the freedom made possible by good help in the home. A couple with young children might have a cook, a nurse, and a butler-chauffeur. When inviting friends to come to dinner, a hostess aged twenty-three or twenty-four would often say: "We're dressing." This meant dinner gowns for the ladies and dinner jackets, black tie, and black patent shoes for the gentlemen.[9]

Homoiselle Haden had graduated from Rice Institute when she and Albert Bel Fay were married in 1935. They spent their first year in New Haven, while Albert earned his B.S. in geology and a commission as ensign in the U.S. Naval Reserve. A year later, Homoiselle's cousin Carolyn Homoiselle Grant and Ernest Bel Fay were married at St. Bartholomew's, New York.

"We had to marry there because of the Newport/Bermuda Race," Carolyn Fay explained in reasonable tones. "Albert had had this boat designed and built—a beautiful boat, forty-four feet long, the *Starlight*. We married between my graduation from Vassar and Ernie's from Harvard, and it was a lovely wedding in the chapel, an exquisite place."

Back home in Houston after the Bermuda race, the newlyweds resumed their sailing in Galveston Bay. "At the time," Carolyn Fay said, "the Houston Yacht Club was more for power boats than for sail. The Fay brothers decided we needed to form a small sailing club." Five friends got together: Al and Ernie, Bill Farish, Boy Streetman (William McIver), and Dudley Sharp. They found a nice piece of property they could buy from Kenneth Womack. S. I. Morris and Robert Clemens designed the clubhouse. The Texas Corinthian Yacht Club opened at Kemah on Labor Day, 1938.

Soon after their marriage in 1936, Ernest and Carolyn Fay were at John and Wandy Winterbothams' wedding in Galveston. "We were sitting at a little table out in the garden with Tina and Dudley, who were building a house on North Post Oak Lane. Dudley said, 'If I buy the farm next to my house will you take a piece of it and come live next door to us?' We said 'Sure.' He went to the phone and bought the farm."

The Fays had been looking at lots in River Oaks with John Staub as counsel, but with his blessing, they changed sites and in October, 1938, moved to 105 North Post Oak Lane near the Sharps. A year later, Albert and Homoiselle Fay joined them at Number 99. At the same time, John Staub was completing the Houston Riding and Polo Club house at South Post Oak Road at Westheimer.

The cycle was repeating: River Oaks had started out as a country place for tennis and golf, only to become a very elegant residential neighborhood. The first young couples to buy property along Post Oak and Memorial Drive built stables and polo grounds for weekend and holiday use. By 1938, North Post Oak Lane was becoming an elegant enclave of suburban living. Within four decades, the polo club on South Post Oak had given way to a new city known as the Galleria. The gracious houses and shaded lawns of South Post Oak would vanish under the high-rising Houstonian Hotel and conference center that would provide Pres. George Bush with a *pied a terre* in Houston.

The Howard Hughes Houston Knew

HOWARD HUGHES'S LIFE began and ended in Houston, tracing a meteoric course between the beginning and the end. He was born on Christmas Eve, 1904. His father was one of the two founders of the Sharp-Hughes Tool Company. His mother, Allene, was one of the beautiful Gano sisters of Dallas. He went to kindergarten at Miss Eichler's University in the parish house of Christ Church.

Howard was often late, to the distress of Miss Eichler, who had the German appreciation of promptness and discipline. On his tardy mornings, she would tell the other children that they must not play with Howard until he could learn to be on time. Two small rebels ignored the dictum—Ella Rice, a beautiful child at the age of five, and Elizabeth Dillingham, tiny, witty, and popular. They staunchly flanked Howard as the class took walks up and down the cloisters for their midmorning exercise. And Howard went through life with a complete lack of interest in being prompt.

Tall, dark-haired, handsome, Howard was an intelligent and creative child. He went to Montrose School and to South Central Junior High. Early on he was absorbed in radios, cars, and all the inventions of his boyhood. Dudley Sharp, Mark Edwin Andrews, and Mary Cullinan, his chief playmates, were all aware of a particularly bright mind in their midst. They usually played in the Sharps' big yard on Main at Eagle.

"We used to play at Dudley's," Mary Cullinan Cravens said. "Dudley and Howard were both inventors and they had a work-shop. It had all kinds of chemical things, not toys but the real thing. They had a great big high swing, and we would swing high and make bets on who could go the farthest if they jumped out. The rest of us did it for fun. But Howard was trying to work out the curve of where you'd land—the trajectory. At that age! Ten or twelve! Even I was impressed as a little girl. Playing any game, he always had some theory. And he wanted to know the mathematics of everything."

Ed Andrews remembers Howard's invention of a self-propelled bicycle. "It was early days for the self-starter," he said. "Dodge cars had a very unusual one with a twenty-four-volt starter and a twenty-four-volt battery. It became a generator when the car speeded up and was very powerful. Howard put a drive wheel on his bicycle—a little wheel with a groove in it—on the front handlebars so that the little wheel would turn on the tire of the front wheel of the bicycle. He put the battery on the rack at the back and a wire to the starter and a wire to the handlebars with a switch. When you closed it, ZWOOSH! He charged us a nickel a ride. We rode up and down Main Street for one nickel. One block. A nickel was a lot of money then. But Howard was good-looking and fun and nice and smart."

The Stutz Bearcat was a powerful and splendid sports car. It could travel ninety miles per hour given a clear stretch of road on which to do it. One day when Howard was fourteen, he rode the streetcar downtown to the Stutz dealer's to see a new Bearcat that had come in. After looking it over, he said to the man, "I would like to have this. Would you please send it out to my house?"

The dealer was nonplussed. He knew that Howard was too young to drive, but the tall dark-haired boy was quite serious. The man called Howard Hughes, Sr., at the Hughes Tool Company to ask approval.

"Did Howard say what he wanted to do with it?" Mr. Hughes asked.

"Yes sir. He said he wanted to tear it down."

"Very well," said Mr. Hughes. "Send it on out."

Mr. Hughes was something of a night owl, and often on his way home from his plant he would stop by the *Houston Post* to pick up Will Hobby after he had put the morning paper to bed. On that particular night, amused by the incident, Hughes told Governor Hobby about it.

Marion Law, a contemporary, also knew about the odd purchase. He said that Howard did indeed take the powerful motorcar apart and put it back together, making a minor improvement that Stutz later adopted.

The story gains poignance in light of the fact that Marion Law wanted a Stutz Bearcat more than anything in the world. As his twenty-first birthday approached, he was brought down from the University of Texas to the Baptist Hospital in Houston for an appendectomy. The physicians planned to operate at dawn on Halloween morning—Marion's birthday.

Mr. and Mrs. F. M. Law came to the hospital the night before. "Now Marion," said his father, "tomorrow you will come of age." It occurred to Marion that if he were ever to get a Bearcat this was the propitious moment: He was turning twenty-one, he was going under the knife, he was the only son. And his father was clearly leading up to a speech of presentation. With each deliberate phrase, Marion's hopes rose.

"We shall be here tomorrow morning, but of course by then you will be under sedation. We thought you might like to

Howard Hughes, Jr., shown here at age twelve, was a brilliant child with a gift for invention. *Photograph © Houston Post*

know tonight what your birthday present will be. We have decided to give you . . ."

Marion held his breath.

"We have decided to give you a paid-up life insurance policy."

Said Marion faintly. "Who's the beneficiary?"

In all fairness, Mr. Law, who would soon become president of the American Bankers Association, had given his son what he himself would have appreciated most at the age of twenty-one.

The Hugheses lived on Yoakum, an easy bicycle run from the Sharps' house on Main. "Howard was interested in radio and telegraphy," Dudley Sharp said, "and he had the darndest radio station set up in their house on Yoakum you ever saw. He got very skilled at the dot-dash system of the Morse Code and talked to people all over the world.

There is not any doubt in my mind that Howard was a genius. We played together a great deal as children. Whatever he did, he did well. When he took up golf, he became a two-handicapped golfer at the old Houston Country Club. When he took up aviation, he became a champion cross-country flier. When he decided to go around the world by plane, he set a record."

Sharp remembers Howard's mother as "a lovely, lovely woman with great poise and great charm. She was a Gano." Susan Clayton McAshan recalled the wonderful birthday parties Mrs. Hughes gave for her little boy and all the children in his class at Montrose School. Young Mrs. Hughes died when Howard was sixteen.

Boys who did not know him well thought of him as the snooty son of a rich man. One of these was young Elliot Cage. The Cages lived on Montrose at Alabama, and when Mrs. Hughes died, Mrs. Cage insisted that her son go pay a proper condolence call on his schoolmate. Reluctantly, Elliot went. Hours later, he had not come back. On his return, he was in an exalted state, having spent the entire afternoon with Howard in Howard's superb radio workshop and studio.

Having made friends, the two boys often played golf together at the Houston Country Club. One morning Howard was so late in arriving that Elliot started a game with the chef's son, leaving Howard to catch the streetcar back home again.

Always a restless spirit, Howard Hughes, Sr., went often to Hollywood to visit his brother Rupert, who was a writer, director, and producer of films. Although it required two or three flatcars, he often shipped his cruiser, the *Rollerbit,* by express out to California, where he enjoyed entertaining movie stars.

Because he was spending most of his time on the West Coast, Hughes turned his son and his house on Yoakum over to his wife's young sister Annette.[1] Mr. and Mrs. Hughes had become Annette's parents when her own mother died. After Annette's marriage to Dr.

Fred Lummis, the Lummises became young Howard's family. They loved the boy, but he was not an easy responsibility. He could never be persuaded to carry a house key. Whenever he got in late, he took a brick, broke the pane on a French door, and went in and up to bed. The next day the glazier had to be called to repair the pane, only to have it broken again—and again.

Rather casually, young Howard went to Rice Institute, still inclined to keep his own hours. "It was a constant problem of discipline," his cousin Fred Lummis said. "In those days they *did* expect you to come to class on a fairly regular basis." Miss Alice Dean, one of the institute's most gifted teachers, had to fail Howard in math.

If to be an introvert is to hold yourself to your own inner standards, then Howard Hughes was an introvert throughout his life. He did what he wished to do, what he expected of himself. Nonetheless, for years after, he considered the Lummises and the house on Yoakum as home.

As a young man, Howard Hughes, Jr., kept up with his family and boyhood friends and looked upon Houston as home. *Photograph © Houston Post*

When he was twenty, his father died suddenly of a heart attack during a business conference at the Hughes plant. After his legal disabilities were removed, young Howard Hughes inherited a major manufacturing plant and one of the greatest fortunes ever amassed in the oil industry. He was president and sole owner of the Hughes Tool Company. Sensibly, he left in place the managers his father had installed: Frank Andrews, vice-president; Col. R. C. Kuldell, general manager; C. S. Johnson, secretary-treasurer; and H. W. Fletcher, chief engineer.

This does not mean that he took no interest in the enterprise. Steam-powered automobiles no longer prowled the streets of Houston. They had been good cars, but after one or two exploded, they lost out to the gasoline engines. At twenty, Howard Hughes set out to have his company develop a new steamer.

"It was rather like a Stutz Bearcat," Dudley Sharp recalled. "A real sports car. The fanciest. But it had one peculiarity. When parked after a run, it would sit quietly while pressure built up–or something–and all of a sudden backfire. Howard liked to leave it parked downtown on Main Street. A crowd would collect to stare because it was something to see. Then suddenly, it would go BOOM! That was Howard's great practical joke."

Not yet twenty-one, Howard Hughes married Ella Rice, whom he had known since their kindergarten days at Miss Eichler's. Ella was the daughter of the David Rices, who lived on McKinney.[2] An unusually handsome young couple, they were married in her sister Libbie's garden at Number 10 Remington Lane. This was the newly completed mansion of Libbie and William Stamps Farish. The wedding was the first big social event in the house.

Dudley Sharp was in the wedding. "We all had on white linen suits because it was pretty hot at that time of year." The marriage was short-lived.

"Howard was just not the kind of person who would ever take care of a wife," Sharp said. "He was always off doing something and he ran these peculiar hours. He didn't sleep much. He would have his business meetings in a car somewhere at 2:00 A.M. and he might disappear for a day or two without Ella's knowing where he was." The marriage ended in divorce.[3]

Howard Hughes was a brilliant man. He was tall and handsome. He had inherited a business that cleared $60 million a year after taxes at a time when $60 million had the buying power of $600 million by 1986 dollars. Before long, he was off to Hollywood to experiment with film making, to apply his genius to aviation, and ultimately to create the Spruce Goose.[4]

"He was impatient with learning things in the ordinary way," Dr. Lummis said. "He wanted to know what he needed to know and didn't want to waste time. I think his genius lay in the ability to identify the people he needed to do what he wanted done. Some who worked with him on the Spruce Goose said that in exchanging information, he was terribly quick to learn, and never domineering or superior. And in his thirties, at least, he had a magnanimous vision of what he would do with all this money."

In July, 1938, Howard Hughes commanded the world's spotlight by flying around the world in ninety-one hours, eight minutes, and ten seconds–a world record. He landed at dusk on July 14 and was met at Floyd Bennett Field in Brooklyn by Mayor Fiorello La Guardia and Grover Whalen, president of the New York World's Fair of 1939. The event was covered by what the *New York Times* called "the most elaborate radio set-up ever assembled." More than three hundred and fifty radio stations were hooked up to carry the WABC broadcast from "at least seven microphones." This all required "more than five automobile loads of apparatus . . . taken to the field by the Columbia system." Surely that pleased the longtime radio buff.

Hughes and his crew had circled the world in a special Lockheed that was a monoplane with two rudders. They refueled at Paris, Moscow, Siberia, Alaska, and Minneapolis. On July 15, New York gave them one of the biggest parades of its history. Characteristically, Howard Hughes insisted that his two navigators, his radio man, and his mechanic, along with their wives, be included in the parade, as well as the seventeen technicians who fed him data during the flight. To the *Times,* he belittled his part and said it was a group effort.

New York was enchanted. Here was a handsome hero who bore his honors modestly. Almost two million New Yorkers cheered from the streets and windows. Next day, the street department swept up eighteen hundred tons of tickertape and shredded telephone books—even more than had greeted Charles Lindbergh on his triumphal return.

The parade was late in starting because it had to wait for Howard Hughes to shave.

Then he came home to Houston for the first time in three years. At his request, there were no escort planes to bring him in, and only the thirty-five hundred employees of Hughes Tool and Gulf Brewing Company were allowed inside the airport fence. Lt. Gov. Walter Woodul, Mayor R. H. Fonville, and Col. W. B. Pyron, chairman of the Chamber of Commerce Aviation Committee, were there. Houston welcomed Howard Hughes by rechristening the airport in his honor.[5] KPRC and KTRH broadcast the arrival to one hundred stations in this country and Canada and, by shortwave, to Europe.

A quarter of a million Houstonians lined the parade route from the airport to the Rice Hotel, where a banquet was waiting for Howard Hughes. There, Gov. James Allred commissioned him a Texas colonel and appointed him the Texas commissioner to the New York World's Fair and Golden Gate Exposition of 1939.

Clearly, Howard Hughes was at this mo-

ment a national hero. In November, he was awarded the Collier Trophy for "the greatest achievement in aviation in America, the value of which has thoroughly been demonstrated by actual use during the preceding year." Pres. Franklin Roosevelt made the presentation.[6]

His old friends liked him, loved him. But his odd loneliness was already beginning to appear. "He did not often come back to Houston," Dudley Sharp said, "and when he did, it might be one o'clock in the morning." With her husband, Rorick Cravens, Mary Cullinan would see Howard when they went to California—at first. But gradually he seemed to withdraw from the friendship.

"We lost touch," Sharp said. "But he had developed some peculiarities that I caught the trail of later." As secretary of the air force in the Eisenhower administration, Sharp went out one day to visit the Lockheed Aircraft Company in California. He saw a four-engine Constellation parked right across the taxiway of the main runway.

It was Howard's. One of the Gosses, who ran Lockheed, told me that Howard would not let them move that plane. Of course he bought so many airplanes from them that they respected his wishes. They had to build a new taxiway around it.

They told me that every couple of weeks, about two in the morning, he would come out, climb up in the plane, turn on all the engines, get them all up to speed, and then turn them all off again. Then he would drive away in the dark. That plane stayed there a couple of years. I later learned that he had several— I *think* eight—DC-6s, a big four-engine transport, stashed around the United States at different airports with a full crew ready to fly all the time. And he never flew any of them. The crew would fly them a certain number of hours to keep in shape, but he never used any of them.

But this was all after I knew him. He had gone out into a different world. A world of his own.

Faraway Wars

FOR A BRIEF HOUR on the evening of October 30, 1938, many Houstonians forgot all family, business, and earthly problems. These dwindled in the scare that Martians were at that moment landing in New Jersey to attack Earth. The next morning, Americans woke up feeling a little foolish. Orson Welles's radio drama, *War of the Worlds,* had stampeded many a sane person into quite silly behavior. But as war clouds darkened in Europe and Asia, Americans were perhaps more vulnerable to scares—and to foolishness. Ivy League students swallowed goldfish and founded the Veterans of Future Wars.

This was wry humor. In the mid-1930s, almost continuous warfare in Asia and Hitler's brazen military exercises in Europe disturbed the peace. From one troubled spot or another in China, missionaries began to come home to Houston, telling of tragedies they had seen. The Spanish Civil War was debated hotly in American college and university classrooms. Few Americans could quite take Hitler seriously. He *looked* so absurd. His wild rantings against Jews could not, surely, sway intelligent Germans. But gradually, Jewish refugees from Hitler's Germany began to arrive in Houston, telling grim stories of life in their homeland. In March, 1938, Hitler's tanks rolled into Austria.

In September, 1938, French Premier Edouard Daladier and British Prime Minister Neville Chamberlain met Hitler in Munich and signed treaties of peace that ceded him Czechoslovakia's Sudetenlands. They were pilloried for appeasement. In fact, there may

have been nothing else they could do. Though Britain's factories were revving up, they were not yet in full production. And Daladier, though strengthening the French defense, could not throw France alone against Hitler's overwhelming armies.

The United States was no mightier. As German Field Marshall Hermann Goering built the most powerful air force the world had seen, the United States was still flying on the Liberty motors of World War I. In 1938, Congress granted huge sums of money to modernize the navy and army, but factories had to be built before production could begin. In 1939, the United States declared its neutrality. After twenty years of peace, the United States was powerless.

By 1939, William P. Hobby—still called Governor after his terms in Austin—had managed the *Houston Post* for fifteen years, first during the ownership of Ross Sterling, then of Jesse Jones. Oveta Hobby was assistant editor and known for her informative articles on international affairs. The *Post* had struggled to survive during the worst days of the depression. In 1939, Will and Oveta Hobby decided to buy the paper and the printing plant in a red brick building on the corner of Polk Avenue and Dowling.

Jesse Jones considered Will Hobby one of his best friends. It was assumed in Houston that Jones had given the Hobbys a very generous deal because he thought it wrong for both major newspapers to be under one ownership. In fact, Jesse Jones made the same stiff business provisions in selling the *Post* to his friends that he would have made to anyone else. After a courteous interval, the Hobbys refinanced the loan through Fred Florence at Wirt Davis's Republic of Texas Bank in Dallas. The Jesse Jones–Will Hobby friendship never faltered.

The U.S.S. *Houston* docked at the Port of Houston on April 8, 1939, for its first visit in five years. The city felt a fresh surge of pride in the cruiser that was its namesake.

For those who could ignore the ominous signs of war, 1939 was a particularly nice year. Girls and women discovered the word "nylon." Nylon stockings were as sheer as silk, stronger than silk, and, miraculously, they dried overnight on the towel rack. The hemline of dresses began to climb back toward the kneecap.

Then there were the movies. Hollywood produced some four hundred motion pictures, including *Wuthering Heights, The Wizard of Oz, Ninotchka, Mr. Smith Goes to Washington, Goodbye Mr. Chips,* and *Gone with the Wind*. The whole country wondered whether the Hays Office would permit Clark Gable to utter Rhett Butler's famous last line: "I don't give a damn."[1] Houstonians had to take in three films a week to keep up. And with each of the superb films, they saw newsreels. The face of Franklin Roosevelt became as familiar to every Houstonian as that of his closest relative.

At about this time, Denton Cooley changed course. His father, Dr. Ralph C. Cooley, was a successful dentist and an inventor whose dental products sold well. "The most enduring of these was Copalite," Denton Cooley said, "a varnish to treat the cavity before the filling is put in. It is still used and manufactured as a family business. Because Dad was a dentist, I thought I would be one."

After finishing Lanier Junior High and San Jacinto High School, Denton Cooley entered pre-dentistry at the University of Texas at seventeen. He had several courses in common with the pre-med students and made straight A's. He played varsity basketball. At six feet four, he was topped by only one other player, who was six feet five.

One weekend he went to San Antonio, where a friend was interning at the Robert Green Hospital. It was Saturday night in the emergency room, and there were so many people there who had been cut up in fights or hurt in accidents that the intern said, "Denton, don't you want to sew up a few lacerations?"

"That did it," Dr. Cooley said. "I switched to pre-med." In June, 1941, with war looming, he registered for an accelerated medical course at the University's Medical School in Galveston, transferring in the fall to Johns Hopkins University.

The St. Anne's Catholic parish had first built a parish house in 1929 on the property on Westheimer Road at Shepherd Drive. Designed by Maurice Sullivan, the complex had grown by stages for a decade and by 1939 the big St. Anne's Church and bell tower were nearing completion. Farther out Westheimer, a group of Episcopalians founded the Church of St. John the Divine. They began to build a modest frame church set back among the trees on River Oaks Boulevard.

And by 1939, the small Junior League Health Center downtown was seeing fifty-three hundred children a year. Volunteer doctors checked their vision and hearing. The clinic gave routine immunizations, free dental care to some fifteen hundred children a year, and speech training. This clinic was the seed from which the Junior League Outpatient Clinic of Texas Children's Hospital would grow.

For thirty-four years, Mrs. Walter B. Sharp, her sons, and their families had enjoyed the gracious place on Main Street that she and her husband had bought on first coming to Houston. But Main Street was becoming commercial. Because of its trees, lovely gardens, and lake she tried to give the property to the city as a park. On being turned down, she sold it to Sears Roebuck, which promptly cut down every tree and built a two-story building and vast concrete parking lot. When completed, however, Sears did offer Houston the newest thing in department stores: an escalator.

After passing Dallas in population in 1932, Houston consolidated its claim as the biggest city in Texas in 1939: it led not only in population but in the number of dwelling units, building permits, bank deposits, new and total automobile registrations, electric meters, gas meters, and telephone connections, in school enrollment, newspaper circulation, and square miles within the city limits. Surpassing New Orleans, Houston became the foremost port in the South. It was now the third largest seaport in the nation, topped in tonnage only by New York and Philadelphia.

Built with the help of depression-born federal funds and designed by Joseph Finger, Houston's new City Hall opened in 1939. A series of paved terraces led down to the reflecting pool and garden of Hermann Square, which George Hermann had bequeathed to the city in 1914.

After years of planning, Ripley House opened in 1940. Daniel Ripley had been a veteran steamship operator and Port of Houston board member. It was through his influence that the first ship sailed directly to Europe from Houston with a load of cotton. When he died in 1921, he left $1 million to establish the Daniel and Edith Ripley trust fund "for the betterment of the community." Designed by Birdsall Briscoe and Maurice Sullivan, Ripley House was Houston's largest community center. It provided a wide variety of services with a gymnasium, an auditorium seating three hundred and fifty, a branch library, nursery school rooms, woodworking and sewing rooms, and medical examining rooms.

In 1940, Hugh Roy Cullen gave two hundred and fifty thousand dollars' worth of stock to the Houston Ship Channel Navigation District to enlarge the channel.

Houston was on the brink of a new, greater surge of growth stimulated by war. After signing with the Soviet Union another of his worthless peace treaties, Hitler invaded Poland on September 1, 1939, and took the country in twenty-eight days. The Soviet Union, presumably safe under a peace pact

In 1939 the changed city skyline featured the new ten-story City Hall, designed by Joseph Finger. Its facades were finished with Cordova shell limestone and its interiors with marble, nickel, and decorative plaster. The carved heads of Texas wildcats flanked the big clocks on all four sides of the tower. *Edward Bourdon photograph, courtesy of Mr. Bourdon*

with Hitler, invaded Finland. The heroic Finnish resistance against its giant neighbor roused admiration throughout what was left of the free world. Houstonians thrilled to the strains of the *Warsaw Concerto* and *Finlandia* at symphony concerts and on the radio. Harry Wiess headed a fund drive for Finnish relief and Howard Hughes, Jr., offered to guarantee its success.

In 1940, Germany invaded Denmark and Norway on April 9, and the Netherlands, Belgium, and Luxembourg on May 10. The Nazi tanks rolled through Luxembourg in a day and through the Netherlands and Belgium as though on a field exercise. The Belgian surrender May 28 left British and French troops stranded at Dunkirk on the coast of France. There the tiny Royal Air Force held off the German bombers while 300,000 men waded out to British rescue vessels—rowboats, motor boats, sail boats, fishing boats, houseboats. That gallant rescue stirred Houston as nothing else had in the battles going on around the world.

With the fall of France, Nazi forces occupied all of Western Europe. Britain stood alone. Vowing to be in London by August, Hitler set out to bomb the British into surrender. The Battle of Britain began. Flying the Spitfire fighter planes, the Royal Air Force denied the Luftwaffe its victory. This bought time for the United States.

President Roosevelt was rebuilding the nation's forces as rapidly as he was allowed to do. Many congressmen were from districts that had no great interest in the fate of England and France. But like a vast ship, the United States was slowly, slowly turning around to face a ruthless enemy.

In 1940, the War Department reopened Ellington Field as a major army air base. Congress voted some $7 million to build barracks for 240 officers and 4,020 enlisted men, as well as two hundred and fifty units for civilian employees. The new Houston Municipal Airport terminal, designed by Joseph Finger, opened just in time to receive the wartime surge of passenger traffic.[2] *Architectural Record* cited it as one of the best modern airport terminals in the country.

In 1940, while still building the Marshall Ford Dam, Brown & Root of Houston was commissioned to build a large naval air station at Corpus Christi. This was another joint venture in which the Warren Bellows Construction Company of Houston had a share.

The United States was still neutral throughout 1940 and for most of 1941. But as National Guard officers, J. Lewis Thompson, Newton Wray, Clark Wren, and Gaynor Jones were called to active duty with the 36th Division Field Artillery at Brownwood, as were the younger Raymond Cook and Ryland Howard.

Raymond Cook, a graduate of Rice Institute and the University of Texas law school, believed that war was coming. In 1940, he left the law firm of Andrews, Kurth to volunteer to the National Guard. The guard was so ill equipped that the new recruits had to drill with broomsticks over their shoulders. When sent to the 36th Division in Brownwood, Private Cook had to teach his instructor how to use the slide rule to work out the trajectory of an artillery shell. He and Ryland Howard were sent to Officers' Candidate School at Fort Sill, Oklahoma, for commissioning.

C. Cabanné Smith had graduated from the Missouri School of Mines with a reserve commission in the Army Corps of Engineers but had not been to camp in four years. By early 1940, he was sure that war was inevitable. At thirty-six, working in an essential industry (the Houston Oil Company), and with a wife and two children, he was unlikely to be drafted. But with his wife Lucy's understanding, he plunged into reserve classes to restore his army standing. In the summer of 1941, he reported for duty to Col. Dwight Eisenhower, acting chief of staff of the Third Army in San Antonio. With the Third Army under General Patton, Capt. Cab Smith would cross Europe from the Normandy Beach, through the Battle of the Bulge, the Siegfried Line, and across the Rhine to Germany.

Hitler's invasion of Yugoslavia and Greece in April, 1941, convinced John H. Crooker, Jr., that war was imminent, and he volunteered. His commission in the naval reserve came through on December 6, 1941—the morning before the Pearl Harbor attack. He was assigned to intelligence in the Eighth Naval District and ultimately went to New Guinea and the Philippines.

Brothers-in-law Marvin Greenwood and Ben Anderson were building airplanes. A Rice Institute graduate, Marvin had a masters degree in aeronautical engineering from

Cal Tech. Ben, a University of Texas graduate in geology, had completed a concentrated course at Curtiss-Wright Technical Institute in California. In 1939 and 1940, they ran a small airplane factory in Ben and Mary Anderson's garage on Piping Rock Lane in River Oaks. It was a convenient place to work.

With the fall of France, the plane making that had seemed interesting and pleasant became tremendously important. Taking their nine-month-old baby, Ben and Mary Anderson and her brother Marvin Greenwood drove two cars twenty-four hundred miles to Seattle in three days. There the two Houston men went to work for Boeing.

Within six months, Greenwood was made assistant chief of preliminary design for the Boeing company. He was not yet thirty years old. Before the war ended and they all came home to Houston, Greenwood would become involved in the design of Boeing's first jet bomber—the B-47. And in 1986, Ben Anderson would give to the Fondren Library at Rice University his collection dedicated to the history of flying—some thirty-eight hundred rare books, pamphlets, bound periodicals, albums, scrapbooks, photographs, and model airplanes.[3]

Campaigning for a third term in 1940, President Roosevelt asked Jesse Jones to become secretary of commerce and continue as federal loan administrator. By this time, the Joneses had lived in Washington for eight years, and Jones had never cashed a salary check. Jones joined the cabinet.

With most of Europe occupied by Hitler's armies, the Latin American countries had lost their markets. To cope with the problem, Will Clayton went to Washington that summer as deputy to Nelson Rockefeller, who was coordinator of inter-American affairs. Lamar Fleming, Jr., succeeded Clayton as president of Anderson, Clayton.

In a lifetime spent in international business, with his global knowledge and his special expertise in Latin America's politics and economy, Will Clayton was the recognized authority in this field. Even so, seeing what the loss of European markets meant to Latin America sharpened his understanding of the interdependence of nations—a seed of the Marshall Plan. In October, 1940, he became deputy federal loan administrator and vice-president of the Export-Import Bank. He was also put in charge of buying strategic materials essential for American defense. The United States' stockpiling of these materials supplied the solution to the problem of Latin America's lost markets.

The women's division of the National Democratic Party had headquarters in Washington. As its founder, Sue Clayton was making speeches urging a third term for President Roosevelt. The Claytons settled into Washington again, not to leave for seven years.

In November, Franklin Roosevelt was re-elected to an unprecedented third term. On January 2, 1941, Oscar Holcombe, after seven terms as mayor, was succeeded by C. A. (Neal) Pickett.

And in January, 1941, the old Christ Church acquired its youngest rector, John Elbridge Hines. A native of South Carolina, he was a Phi Beta Kappa graduate of the University of the South and of the Virginia Theological Seminary. Looking even younger than his thirty years, the big, handsome Hines was eloquent, and his lovely young wife was charming. Sunday morning attendance soared. Having come from an old, downtown parish in Augusta, Georgia, John Hines believed that the historic half-block on Texas Avenue should serve all of downtown Houston. He was soon caught up in raising money for the Houston Symphony and the YWCA. Swiftly in the years ahead, he would become bishop of the Episcopal Diocese of Texas and ultimately presiding bishop of that denomination in the United States.

Chapter Sixty

Oveta Culp Hobby and an Army of Women

NEWSPAPER headlines competed with news-reels in the motion picture theaters to bring the war in Europe to Houston eyes. The *March of Time* documentaries showed stark battle scenes. The transatlantic broadcasts from London were somber. The voice of Edward R. Murrow became familiar as, each evening, he said: "This is London." The German *blitzkrieg*, Dunkirk, the fall of France, the Battle of Britain. . . . Each day Europe's war swept closer.

American reaction was sharply divergent. Most Americans hoped the Allies would win but without American help. Across this majority, isolationists on the one side squared off against interventionists on the other.

In the South, with its strong heritage from the British Isles, a growing number of Americans felt that this was America's war. But to many Midwesterners, FDR's Lend Lease to Britain meant that he was a traitor to his country. Colonel McCormick's Chicago newspaper urged the idea of "America First." Sen. Robert Taft commented dryly that President Roosevelt apparently confused America's defense with Britain's defense. On the West Coast, the fall of France and bombing of Britain were viewed with marked detachment. The war was so far away.

September 14, 1940, Congress reluctantly approved the first peacetime draft in the nation's history. It was to be in effect for only one year. On October 16 of that year, 77,177 young men of Harris County received their notices to come register for the draft. Few Houstonians of draft age had ever seen a man

in uniform except in Armistice Day parades. Suddenly, sons and brothers were being sent off to boot camp and officers' training schools. Some viewed it as a lark. Their parents were less happy. All of a sudden, the War Department began to receive thousands of letters – up to ten thousand a day – asking questions. If there's no war on, why take my son away from home? Why can't Billy come home for his birthday? Are you sure that he is being fed properly? Other letters were from women wanting to know how they could serve their country.

In the hot June of 1941, Oveta Culp Hobby was in Washington on KPRC business with the Federal Communications Commission when she received a telephone call at her hotel from Gen. David Searles. He asked her to come to the War Department to organize a section on women's activities. She refused, explaining that she had a husband, two small children, and a full-time job with the *Houston Post*.

The general poured out the trouble he was having in communicating with women and girls across the country. He asked if she would take a sampling of the letters home with her, study them, and draft the kind of answers that should be sent, and, further, would she draw up for the War Department an organizational chart on ways women could serve. A short time after, from Houston, Mrs. Hobby sent a variety of sample letters and the chart and plan General Searles had requested. Her task was done – she thought.

One Sunday she was called from the family dinner table by a long distance call from General Searles. Would she, he asked, come to Washington long enough to set the plan in operation, and then come back for three or four days a month to supervise it? Again she refused. In the summer of 1941, travel from Houston to Washington by train or plane was tedious. To spend three days there would cost her seven from home and office.

But when she returned to the dinner table and told her husband about the call, Governor Hobby laid down his knife and fork: "You shouldn't have made him have to ask you a second time," he said gently. "Any thoughtful person knows that we are *in* this war, and that every one of us is going to have to do whatever we are called upon to do." Mrs. Hobby went back to the telephone and called General Searles.

In July, 1941, Washington newspapers showed pictures of a very young woman over captions that read: "To Interpret Army for Women," and "Mrs. William P. Hobby, executive vice president of *The Houston Post*, becomes woman's editor of the army's bureau of public relations." Oveta Hobby was thirty-six years old.

"For every one of the 1,500,000 men in the Army today," she said in an early interview, "there are four or five women—mothers, wives, sisters, sweethearts—who are closely and personally interested." Throughout the summer and autumn, she was head of the Women's Interest Section, War Department Bureau of Public Relations.

President Roosevelt's effort to prepare the nation for war was bruisingly controversial. Feeling was intense on both sides. America Firsters, Colonel McCormick's newspapers, many Midwest and West Coast leaders, continued to fight every appropriation proposed to Congress. On the other hand, the League of Women Voters, in one of its rare political moves, urged the repeal of the neutrality act.

The draft had run its year and was about to expire in August, 1941. If it were allowed to end, most of those thousands upon thousands of young men would be coming home again. The isolationists were in full voice:

John L. Lewis, the United Mine Workers leader who hated Roosevelt, said the draft was the equivalent of a dictatorship. Sen. Burton K. Wheeler of Montana called the military build-up "mad hysteria."

A young Texas congressman named Lyndon Johnson was on the House Armed Services Committee. He and Speaker Sam Rayburn feared that the vote might go against the draft. They asked Secretary of State Cordell Hull to send Congress a special, urgent message. Hull wrote a message so moving that it brought tears to some congressional eyes. Speaker Rayburn read the letter to Congress and immediately, before the tears could dry, called for the vote.

The motion to cancel the draft was defeated by one vote, 203 to 202. Japan's attack on Pearl Harbor was only four months away.

Gen. George Marshall saw in Oveta Hobby the person he needed to plan this nation's first army of women in uniform. At his request, she studied the women's armies of Britain and France and prepared a plan by which the United States could avoid the early mistakes made by those two countries, all of which had to be corrected later.

The job done, she started home in early December, expecting to have Christmas and New Year's in Houston. It was a Sunday. On the way, she stopped in Chicago to address the American Farm Federation Convention on the subject of women's role in the not-yet-begun war. As she stepped off the plane, reporters met her with the news of the attack on Pearl Harbor. In the inspired speech she made that day, General Marshall liked to say, "Oveta Hobby made the nation's first declaration of war."

The Japanese raid on Pearl Harbor had a wonderfully clarifying effect' on the mind of the nation. Japan had left the United States with no alternative. At last, the War Department was on the roll, doing what had to be done, and Oveta Hobby was part of the team.

Secretary of War Henry Stimson and General Marshall now asked that she find what jobs women could do in regular army procedures with the least special training. Next General Marshall sent her to Capitol Hill to testify in the hearings on the proposed women's army and the many ways women could release men for frontline duty. He asked her to give him the names of women who might command this new army.

General Marshall read the list she submitted, turned it face down on his desk, and said, "I'd rather you took the job." Mrs. Hobby said she could not. Her husband said she could. Caught between these two men whom she respected most in the world—patriots both—Oveta Culp Hobby became the first director of the Women's Army Auxiliary Corps. She was thirty-seven. She was in the vanguard of the legion of Houstonians who would rush to serve their country.

The first months were hard, often exasperating, sometimes amusing, sometimes heartbreaking. The new director had to travel constantly on the trains of the day, speaking to large groups of Americans about the new and radical proposal to induct volunteer women into army service.

Though the U.S. Army had always had a nursing corps, though Army nurses wore uniforms, that—somehow—did not count. To take young women and turn them into uniformed troops was quite another thing. The public reaction ranged wildly from total disapproval to enthusiasm. The American press, still largely male, had never thought to ask a commanding general what color shorts and skivvy shirts his troops wore. But reporters asked Director Hobby if WAAC underwear would be khaki-colored.

So far, of course, there were no uniforms to upset anybody. The new director had the only WAAC uniform in existance. She traveled with an electric fan and an iron. Each night she washed the khaki uniform and hung it in front of the fan to dry, and every morning she ironed it to wear to the day's public appearances.

It was not attractive. To make the WAAC uniform appealing to young American women, the director had called on top couturiers to design dresses, skirts, hats, and bags. The results would have been chic. But the Army Quartermaster's Corps vetoed the leather belt—waste of leather; it vetoed the pleat in the skirt—waste of cloth. The resulting WAAC uniform was designed by the Army Quartermaster's Corps and looked it. But the women who wore it learned to be proud of it for the achievements it represented. Because a woman in uniform must have her hands free for drilling and saluting, the WACs and WAVES introduced a new style soon adopted by civilian women—the purse carried on a strap over the shoulder.

Ignoring the carefully drawn proposal that would have saved America from repeating Britain's early mistakes, Congress refused to make the women's corps an integral part of the Army. The corps, therefore, was an auxiliary. This put the women in a kind of War Department limbo. On the first pay day, the quirk in military thinking posed a real problem. The comptroller general's office decreed that it could not pay the women doctors of the WAAC because the comptroller was authorized only to pay "persons serving as doctors in the military service and women are not persons." Secretary of War Henry Stimson had to make a rush trip to Capitol Hill for a special act of Congress to enable Director Hobby to pay her physicians.

If Director Hobby sent a request to the Army Engineers for plans for barracks to house WAAC contingents, Army Engineers replied that they worked only for the Army, the WAAC was *not* the Army, therefore. . . . Director Hobby and her staff had to draw their own barracks plans. In the first months, Director Hobby often worked all day and all night, went home for a shower, and returned for another day at the office. Throughout the war, the director of the nation's first women's army was never assigned a car for official use. In a time when almost any army sergeant was master and king of his own jeep, she had always to call for a car when and if one were available in the pool.

Gradually the corps took shape, completed the first training, acquired the uniforms, was ready to report for the duty that these women had offered their country. Commanding officers, who in a lifetime of Army experience were quite used to Army nurses, were thrown into a flap at the thought of women soldiers. Informed that a detachment of WAACs was being assigned to his post, one commandant moved quickly to segregate them from his men. He housed them in the farthermost barracks on the post and had a high fence built around it. He published a schedule whereby Waacs could go to the post movie two nights a week, while the men—presumably taking their wives or dates with them—would go on the other five nights of the week.

Less important and more amusing was the invitation Colonel Hobby received from the Army-Navy Club. Written under obvious duress and strong emotion, the letter invited her, as an officer in the U.S. Army, to make use of the club facilities. But would she mind, the club official added, coming in by the back door? Any shavetail lieutenant in the Army could use the front door —but not the commanding officer of two hundred thousand soldiers in this new woman's army.

Gradually the Army and civilian America grew accustomed to privates, corporals, and lieutenants in skirts, and by the time the WAAC became the Women's Army Corps, a true part of the Army, World War II was demanding the best from everyone.

The Wacs proved themselves quickly and well. Army charts began to show that one Wac could do the work of two men in certain tasks—from secretarial work to PBX operation to kitchen patrol to parachute folding. All volunteers, all there because they wanted to serve their country, all selected through careful screening, the average Wac was a more eager and dedicated soldier than anyone had thought possible. Each woman knew her work was important because it released a man for combat.

When the WAAC was organized, Congress had cautiously agreed that perhaps the women could do 54 Army jobs. Before Colonel Hobby was satisfied, they filled 239 different jobs and did almost every kind of work open to noncombatants. To inspect her troops, Colonel Hobby had to fly in military planes to every theater of war.

By the time Gen. Dwight Eisenhower was in England preparing for D-Day, his call was constant: "Send me more Wacs." By 1944, WAC headquarters had requests from commanding generals around the world for six hundred thousand women—three times the total authorized strength of the corps.

Colonel Hobby kept her sense of humor throughout, but those who knew her best felt that she gained an even deeper understanding and sympathy for humanity in general and women in particular. Though she always insisted that she had "never had to fight for anything," though she never carried the shoulder chip of militant feminism, she developed in the Army an abiding awareness of the barriers many women have to surmount.

Colonel Hobby's dark hair acquired a frosting of silver during war. The twelve- and fifteen-hour days robbed her—temporarily—of her youthful look. By July, 1945, Oveta Culp Hobby was exhausted and ill. Throughout, Will Hobby had done all he could to ease the strain. He and the children telephoned every day. During a national telephone strike, a Houston telephone supervisor received his daily and familiar call to Washington.

"Now Governor," she said, "is this call really necessary?"

"Course 'tis," said Will Hobby firmly. "Got to talk to Oveta." The call always went through.

But the long days, the problems, the tensions stacked up. Colonel Hobby knew that she had completed the work she had been asked to do. When she requested permission to resign, she was asked to take her final physical examination at the Pentagon because it would be less noticeable. "If you go to Bethesda," Pentagon officials explained,

The first WAAC Training Center at Fort Des Moines, Iowa, was bitterly cold on Valentine's Day, 1943, when WAAC Director Oveta Culp Hobby reviewed her troops with first lady Eleanor Roosevelt. *Official Signal Corps photograph*

"we'll be bombarded by people wanting your job for somebody."

Drooping with fatigue, Colonel Hobby walked the long corridor from the driveway ramp to the Pentagon dispensary, not sure she would get there. She emerged with a card certifying that she was fit for overseas duty. On her release, Governor was waiting for her with a stretcher. He took her to the train and directly from Washington to Doctors' Hospital in New York for rest and treatment. But the long task was completed.

Colonel Hobby received the Distinguished Service Medal for outstanding service. The citation said, in part, "Without guidance or precedents in the United States military history to assist her, Colonel Hobby established sound initial policies, planned and supervised the selection of officers and the preparation of regulations. The soundness of basic plans and policies . . . is evidenced by the outstanding success of the Women's Army Corps. . . . Her contribution to the war effort of the nation has been of important significance."

On January 19, she was forty years old and at the beginning of a civilian career that would also be of important significance to her country. She would return to publishing and would pioneer in television. She would serve on the U.S. delegation to the U.N. Conference on Freedom of Information and the Press in Geneva in 1948. As a member of President Eisenhower's cabinet, she would be the first secretary of the new Department of Health, Education and Welfare. She would be the first woman to be president of the Southern Newspaper Association, and in that role she would prompt American publishers to enter the new age of computer technology. Her second forty years would be quite as outstanding as her first.

Infamous Day

HOUSTONIANS READ good news in the Sunday morning papers of December 7, 1941. "Works of Masters of Many Ages to Make City Great Art Center," the *Houston Chronicle* reported in an article from New York City. Mr. and Mrs. Percy S. Straus were bequeathing their art collection to the Houston Museum of Fine Arts. This was, the *Chronicle* reported, "one of the most extraordinary and complete in its field of any of the private collections . . . in the United States."

Mr. and Mrs. Straus had chosen Houston partly because their son, Percy S. Straus, Jr., was a Houston resident and partly because they believed in encouraging regional art centers across the country.[1] Mr. Straus expressed hope that Houston would become the art center of the Southwest.

It was a magnificent collection, a magnificent gift. But by midafternoon of Sunday, December 7, the radio newscasts had wiped out all thoughts of anything but Japan's attack on Pearl Harbor.[2]

Southerners had been preparing for this day. The Battle of Britain had stirred Southern patriotism. College boys were taking civilian pilot training courses. Young men from Alabama, Mississippi, and Georgia were off to Canada to join the Royal Canadian Air Force in hopes of being sent to England. The Southern Baptist Convention meeting in Birmingham resolved that there are "some things worth fighting for and worth dying for." Bundles for Britain were flourishing in Houston.

The white South was still largely homogeneous. Most white Southerners traced their ancestry to England, Scotland, Wales, or Ireland. But there was another reason for the patriotic surge, one often voiced in 1940 and 1941: The South is the only part of the country that has known defeat, that has experienced occupation. Houston was still a very Southern city in attitude as well as in voice and manners.

Will Clayton, Jesse Jones, Oveta Hobby, and Robert Lovett were already in Washington as part of President Roosevelt's effort to prepare for war. Once again Houstonians were being drawn to the center of power and sent out across the world in its exercise.

The attack on Pearl Harbor sent young men and boys tumbling into the recruiting offices. In Houston, more remarkably, middle-aged men—thirty-five to forty-five years old—were quick to leave successful business and professional careers to volunteer. Most had wives and children; few would have been drafted. It would mean a smaller income and bigger expenses. But they used all the ploys and pulled all the strings of the old-friend network to wangle themselves into uniform and, once in, to get overseas.

The armed services, however, were not always quick to accept them. Those who had served in World War I had the best chance. Big, handsome, gentle Bill Kirkland had been a naval aviation cadet twenty-three years before. The day after Pearl Harbor, he walked out of the First National Bank where he was a vice-president and over to the navy recruiting office in the post office on San Jacinto.

The young recruiting officer looked at him in puzzlement. "Can you type?" No. "Can you wigwag?" No.

"I don't know what to do with you. Why don't you go down the hall to see the man who is recruiting officers?"

Ultimately, the determined Mr. Kirkland went to New Orleans to volunteer. He was commissioned lieutenant commander and assigned to the Office of Naval Officer Procurement of the Eighth Naval District. There he relieved an Annapolis graduate for sea duty. He began to receive urgent visits from his Houston friends who saw in him their entree to the Navy. And he started agitating to get himself from behind the desk and off to sea. Meanwhile, his wife Lois and their daughters, Barbara and Virginia, joined him in New Orleans.[3]

The news of Pearl Harbor roused other Houstonians. "About 4 o'clock Sunday afternoon," S. M. McAshan, Jr., said, "we all got together and said let's go to New Orleans tomorrow and see if we can't get in. Monday morning about six of us caught the train to volunteer to the navy."

All these men were in splendid physical condition. All were swimmers, golfers, tennis players, and sailors. Most were exceptionally tall. But, as McAshan said, "We were about thirty-nine or forty years old, some older. St. John Garwood, Dudley Sharp, Jack Wray. . . . They weren't ready for us. The navy turned us all down—at first. They said they had plenty of men younger than we but they might be able to use us in some civilian capacity."

Although he was forty-six, St. John Garwood fared best because he had been a cavalry lieutenant in the Texas National Guard in 1918–23.[4] Leaving his substantial law practice, he gained a commission as lieutenant commander in naval intelligence and went to Chile for three years. The Chilean government awarded him the Orden al Merito

This wartime photograph of Bill Kirkland was made in New Orleans. *Courtesy Barbara Kirkland Chiles (Mrs. Clay Chiles)*

Chile before he left for final duty at the Pentagon.

S. M. McAshan, Jr., was vice-president of Anderson, Clayton Cotton Corporation. Three weeks after Pearl Harbor, he received a call to come to Washington. They asked him to go to Turkey to buy chrome ore.

I told them that I don't speak French very well, that all my career has been spent in Latin America and I speak two languages there [Spanish and Portuguese] and they might like to look at my record before sending me to Turkey.

I went home again. Three days later they assigned me to Brazil. On January 2, 1942, I went back to Washington. They said get all your clothes packed because you're going to be in Brazil a long time. We're turning you over to Col. Lucius Clay, head of the Army Service Forces. You won't be in uniform because Brazil is not at war. Clay will tell you what to do.

The McAshans shipped their car on the last freighter from the Port of Houston to Rio de Janeiro, and Susan Clayton McAshan flew down with her husband. Brazil was on strict gasoline rationing, so they put a charcoal burner on the car. Maurice McAshan set up an office and started preemptive buying. "We bought manganese, iron ore, mica, quartz for radios, all kinds of leather, all kinds of strategic materials that Brazil could provide for our war effort. We bought to keep the Nazis from getting it." They built railroads to the port from the various iron ore, manganese, and quartz mines.

"I spent all the three and a half years frantically shipping those materials. Most of the ore went to England because they were worse off than we were. Shipping was the toughest thing—getting ground transportation to the port, getting cargo on ships, getting the ships together for our navy to convoy back up to the states because the German submarines were working the South Atlantic."

One day Admiral Ingram called McAshan down to his flagship docked in Rio. The navy, he said, had just sunk an entire convoy of German ships loaded with rubber. "The whole South Atlantic off the point of Natal," he said, "is afloat in bales of rubber."

"The result was that they skimmed forty thousand tons of rubber off the surface of the ocean," McAshan said. "We got much more rubber off the sea than we got out of

rubber development in the Amazon in the whole war."

Meanwhile, Susan McAshan studied Portuguese every day and, with her husband, became a part of Rio de Janeiro society. Their car with the charcoal burner never went anywhere without a full load of passengers—whether to the office or to the golf course.

One day the British ambassador paid a formal, diplomatic call on Mr. McAshan. The conversation was in diplomatic third person: His Majesty's government would like to suggest. . . . It is the hope of His Majesty's government that the United States would consider. . . . In essence, Britain was asking for America's share of the manganese.

Proper Houstonian Maurice McAshan, Princeton graduate, thought it over and then delivered the reply for his president: "Well, we ain't gonna do it."

"We *couldn't*," McAshan said forty years later. "The agreement was clear that out of all these ores, we were to get almost all the manganese."

Andrew Jackson Wray and Rorick Cravens, both sons-in-law of Joseph Cullinan, had spent many a happy and perhaps hazardous hour in Cravens' Flying Jennie. When Jack Wray was snubbed by the navy, he joined his brother-in-law in volunteering to the Army Air Force. Leaving Cravens Dargan to civilian hands, they went off to Miami for officers' training. Because Cravens could play the bugle, he wangled his way out of marching. Miami Beach was full of airmen. RAF cadets marched in parade as they sang "I've got sixpence, jolly, jolly sixpence." Clark Gable was in officer training. Chaplains held church services out under the trees.

Newly commissioned, Lieutenant Wray and Lieutenant Cravens were ordered to San Antonio. When Rorick Cravens was assigned to Randolph Field, his wife Mary and children joined him.[5] Jack Wray was stationed at the San Antonio Aviation Center. His wife Margaret and daughter Lucie came over for weekends and holidays. At times San Antonio was a wartime extension of the Shady-

Mark Edwin Andrews, who spent the war devising incentives to prompt companies to save the government's money. *Courtesy Mark Edwin Andrews*

side neighborhood. Major Wray soon discovered young Sgt. Maj. John Howard. On office duty by day, Sergeant Howard was perfectly willing to babysit with small Lucie in the evenings.

Mark Edwin Andrews was thirty-eight on October 17, 1941. He was a lawyer, an industrialist, and a successful independent oilman. On December 8, he went to the post office to apply for a navy commission and was turned down for lack of twenty-twenty vision. Next day, he went to San Antonio to see a friend who was a colonel screening candidates for officer training. There he passed the physical and came home to wait for his commission as a captain in the army.

It took Dudley Sharp almost six months to wangle his way into the navy but once he did, it was with a bounce. "There was a vice admiral around here who knew that I had spent a lot of time operating a cruising sailboat. He felt I could go straight into subchaser training in Miami without going through boot camp. I later regretted that because I had to study hard on my own to learn the Morse code and signal flags I needed to know."

Dudley Sharp was co-owner and manager of Mission Manufacturing Company, making products important to the war effort. He had a wife and children. At thirty-six he was unlikely ever to be drafted. But his worry was that he might not get sea duty.

Wars have a way of starting up more slowly than eager patriots can quite understand. But while waiting, life can go on.

Not yet called to duty, Ed Andrews and Dudley Sharp, who had been roommates at Princeton, decided to go to their fifteenth reunion in June. They stopped in New Orleans to let Sharp take his navy physical. By this time Bill Kirkland was in charge of naval officer procurement in the Eighth Naval District. Andrews thought, "Why not make another try for the navy?" Commander Kirkland agreed.

This time, while undressing for the examination, Andrews noticed the eye chart and remembered that the doctor had said, "Read the line that has the smallest letters you can read."

"I got up close enough while undressing to read the twenty-twenty line," Andrews said. "The letters were O C D L F N T C O C, and I made up a little rhyme: Ohenry Certainly Did Love Fine Native Tunes C O C. I passed.

Next, the two Houstonians stopped in Washington, partly to see their friend Browne Baker in the Navy Department, and partly hoping to expedite their commissions. Browne Baker, vice-president and trust officer of the Guardian Trust Bank, had never lost his youthful love for the navy.[6] On a call from Secretary of the Navy James Forrestal, he had come to Washington in May, 1942, to head up the contract negotiation section. Secretary Forrestal instructed Baker to build a team of men he knew well, who were sufficiently well off that they could afford to live in Washington on the salaries offered, and who were good traders. Working directly under Forrestal, they were to negotiate Navy contracts for services and supplies. When Andrews and Sharp reached Browne Baker's office, he said: "Where have you been? I've been hunting for you for two days. I have jobs for both of you."

Dudley Sharp declined. He was going to sea. Mark Edwin Andrews was interested. In the long conference of that morning, a navy captain said to Ed Andrews: "You will be one of a very small group of men who will be responsible for spending vast sums

Browne Baker, called by navy secretary James Forrestal to form a team of men he knew to be good traders. *Courtesy W. Browne Baker, Jr.*

of money—literally millions, even billions of dollars before this war is over."

Andrews accepted the job. But the Princeton reunion with its late-night partying almost queered the deal. Returning to Washington on Monday after the reunion, Andrews was dismayed to learn that he had to take yet *another* physical. What if they used a different eye chart? The same chart and the same Ohenry rhyme got him safely through. Then to his complete astonishment, the doctor said he had failed because his pulse rate was too fast.

In all his years of prep school and college football, tall, strapping Ed Andrews had never been anything but robustly healthy. He persuaded the doctor to give him an hour or so before trying again.

"I don't think it will go down in an hour," the doctor said. "But you just knock on my door when you feel ready and we'll see."

Andrews headed for the nearby Washington Hotel to call his father's friend, a prominent lawyer and one of Washington's three city commissioners. "Mr. Spaulding had just had a heart attack, and I knew he would know the best heart specialist in Washington." Spaulding did indeed. The doctor sent his nurse to meet Andrews at the Union Drug Store across the street. She gave the pharmacist a prescription for a drug to slow the heart beat, and Andrews took it. As the beat slowed, Ed Andrews hurried back, knocked on the doctor's door, had his pulse taken, and passed. The next day he was sworn into the navy, not to leave it until 1946. (There were a ticklish few days when it looked as though he might get an army commission as well, but the navy handled the matter.)

As he had wanted to do, Dudley Sharp went immediately to sea in command of a subchaser, out of Key West and into Gulf and Atlantic waters. Submarines were prowling the Gulf and the subchaser was assigned to the convoys on the Galveston, New Orleans, Key West, and Guantanamo run.

"It was 110 feet long and made of wood," Dudley Sharp said.

We had no radar, no underwater sound equipment. I had to use my own binoculars and my own forty-five automatic pistol. And we had World War I mountain guns with which we were supposed to combat the submarines. We had a depth charge on the stern end and if we had pushed it overboard, it would have blown us up. If a sub had come along, we couldn't have been of *any* help at all to the ships we were convoying.

Then I was assigned to a destroyer escort that would take underwater demolition crews to go ashore in boats, blow up mines and clear the way for landing troops. It was being built at a shipyard outside Boston for service in the Pacific. Tina came up and we had a nice time for a couple of months.

Later in the war, Dudley Sharp would hitchhike home from the Pacific with Bill Kirkland on the badly damaged U.S.S. *Houston*. One of the phenomena of that far-flung war was that friends and acquaintances bumped into each other in some of the most remote corners of the world or by a seemingly impossible coincidence. The Houstonians overseas became familiar with the phenomenon.

When Nazi submarines prowled the gulf, Dudley Sharp went to sea as commander of a sub chaser that was 110 feet long and made of wood. *Courtesy Tina Cleveland Sharp*

Talbot Wilson and S. I. Morris had an architectural partnership when Wilson was drafted under the first peacetime draft.[7] "So Talbot went off to war," Morris said, "which was nothing but going to camp. Then the war started and we both went. He was an army engineer in field artillery and I was a navy engineer in ordnance. We both wound up in China for about two years and actually met out there one time." Commander Morris was awarded the U.S. Legion of Merit and the Order of the Cloud and Banner from China.

A partner of Fulbright & Crooker, Leon Jaworski thought of himself as being late to volunteer to service. As he wrote in his memoirs, it took him three months to make the decision. "I was thirty-six, with three children in grade school. As I watched friends and younger associates don their uniforms, I grew more and more restive. . . . I believed seriously in the debt I owed this country, which had embraced my parents as immigrants from Europe. . . . My father came to this country because he felt the freedoms he cherished were being threatened in his native Poland and in all of Europe."[8]

As Jaworski realized, it was his wife Jeanette "who would have to manage . . . on my army pay and whatever savings we had." He also felt an obligation to his firm. In April he asked the Harris County courts to set as many of his cases as could be handled. For two months, he was in court every day until he cleared his case load. That done, he volunteered in June, 1942. He had his physical at Ellington Field, was commissioned a captain, bought his uniform at Battelstein's—and *then* was told to hold up. The army had noticed that his blood pressure and heartbeat were borderline.

His own physician, aware of Jaworski's normal good health, believed that the condition came from the pressure of the two concentrated months in court. He gave Jaworski pills to slow the beat.

Back for a new test, Jaworski took a pill, and just as the medical corpsman snapped the cuff around his arm, an air raid alert sounded. "We all had to evacuate the building, run a distance, then flatten ourselves on the ground. When we returned, despite the medication, my blood pressure was high and the technician was concerned."

Surreptitiously, Leon Jaworski popped another pill and, again waiting his turn, almost went to sleep on the examining table. This time it was the lowness of his blood pressure that startled the corpsman. Really baffled by all this, the army tested Leon Jaworski again the next morning and the next evening. At last, he passed. He was commissioned captain in the Judge Advocate General's Corps.

Once his commanding officer heard on the military grapevine that the new man on base was an outstanding trial lawyer, Captain Jaworski was kept busy trying cases for the Eighth Service Command. In December, 1943, he was assigned to the top-secret trials of German POWs who had murdered fellow prisoners because they had been less than fanatical in their Nazism. In one case at Camp Chaffee, Arkansas, a young German soldier, age twenty-one, volunteered for work not required by the Geneva Convention but for which he was paid, because he wanted to send more money home to his bride. For this, fellow POWs beat him to death.

"To allow those who committed violent acts to go unpunished would have been equivalent to licensing the Nazi subgovernments that operated in every camp," Jaworski wrote. "We had an obligation to uphold the rights of those prisoners then under our protection." The experience helped prepare him for the war crimes trials in the American zone of occupation.

At first, the Nazis upheld Geneva conventions in treatment of captives. But as they saw the end coming in the summer of 1944, Nazi police were officially instructed not to interfere with civilians who attacked prisoners of war. With the German surrender, Colonel Jaworski became chief of the War Crimes Trials Section with headquarters in Germany. His first case was one of the worst: Six Americans airmen, being marched by their guards through the streets of Russelheim, were set upon by civilians, beaten brutally to death, and buried in a mass grave.

The evidence was gathered painstakingly.

The defendants had three interpreters, German as well as American. They had the best defense lawyers, German civilian as well as American military. The trial was conducted not only to seek justice, but to demonstrate to a people indoctrinated in Nazism how the courts of justice work in a free society.

Colonel Jaworski also prosecuted doctors and nurses who had committed mass murder of Jews at a Nazi hospital. He was present when the army opened up the Dachau concentration camp to the world's horrified view. He developed the case to prosecute forty men and women charged with murder of prisoners at Dachau.

The exact number killed or starved to death at Dachau will never be known. They were of all ages. The American forces rushed in with emergency medical care and food. Between May 2 and June 6, 1945, ten thousand emaciated prisoners were treated, but in that month, one hundred died each day from dysentery, starvation, and typhus. It was very hard for Leon Jaworski to keep faith with his minister father's precept never to hate another human being.

Though asked to stay on for the approaching Nuremberg trials, he had more than enough points to obtain his discharge. He was awarded the Legion of Merit for "exploring entirely new fields in the realm of international law." The citation said that "he played a vital part in the development of the Dachau Concentration Camp case. Colonel Jaworski's legal brilliance, determination, and exceptional devotion to duty reflect the highest credit upon him and the armed forces of the United States."

Maurice Hirsch was fifty-one. Shortly after Pearl Harbor, he was called to Washington by Secretary of War Henry Stimson to join the Army Renegotiation Board. In 1944, Hirsch was commissioned a colonel and entered the judge advocate general's department. Soon after, he was transferred to the general staff corps. He finished the war as a brigadier general with the Distinguished Service Medal and a wife. Secretary of War Patterson was best man at General Hirsch's wedding to Winifred Busby in the chapel at Fort Myer, Virginia.

From early 1942 through 1943, Bill Kirkland sat at his desk as executive officer in charge of naval officer procurement in New Orleans, helping one friend after another go to sea. But at last he managed to draw sea duty. The new U.S.S. *Houston* was just coming into Norfolk from her shakedown cruise. However tall, erect, and fit, Lieutenant Kirkland was forty-six years old. When he went aboard, the young officer in charge said incredulously, "You're reporting for *duty?*" But the ship had acquired an outstanding addition. He worked up to being officer of the deck, issuing orders and maintaining the ship's speed in the convoy. The captain was also wise enough to give him an office. There he wrote the letters telling parents of a son's death, or counseled young sailors feeling far from home.

Then one day, just as he was coming in from four hours watch on the bridge, a Japanese plane torpedoed the *Houston*, breaking her keel. The next morning as they were being towed by the *Boston*, the Japanese dropped a torpedo in the stern. Of its 1,200 crewmen, the *Houston* put 1,000 overboard in life jackets to be picked up by other ships. Bill Kirkland was one of the 198 who stayed with the damaged ship on the slow, limping voyage home to drydock. At Hawaii, they picked up Lt. Dudley Sharp, who had been ordered to New York. Kirkland ended the war where he had begun, at his desk in New Orleans.

Jubal Richard Parton, who had been a major in field artillery in World War I, was forty-six and president of the Woodley Petroleum Company. After the attack on Pearl Harbor, he took a leave of absence from Woodley and went to Washington to join the staff of the Petroleum Administration for War.[9] He became chief of staff of the U.S. Delegation on the German Reparations Commission at Potsdam and Moscow in 1945.

Michel Halbouty, who had his own geological consulting firm, had held a reserve commission since graduation from Texas A&M in 1931 and promptly returned to active duty. After fourteen months as an instructor in military tactics at Fort Benning, he was sent to Washington as chief of petroleum production in the planning division of the army-navy petroleum board under the joint chiefs of staff.

Leaving Baker & Botts, Dillon Anderson joined the army, rising from major to colonel while dealing with the British over Lend Lease. His first flight from Washington to Cairo took him three weeks, going down the coast of South America with frequent fuel stops. But he managed to call his friend Calvin Garwood while in Algiers, and once in Cairo, he and his friend Harris McAshan were billetted together for several weeks. McAshan, a Houston banker, was handling reverse Lend Lease transactions. Before it was over, Colonel Anderson worked in every capital of North Africa and the Middle East. He met Churchill, Roosevelt, Chiang Kai-Shek, and King Farouk. But Dillon Anderson saw the high cost of world war. "We are infinitely poorer by the men we lost and the irreplaceable nature of resources which we dedicated to the destruction," he wrote later. "We shall never know how many Lincolns, Wilsons, Jeffersons, or Franklins lie in foreign graves in their youth or beneath alien seas."

Chapter Sixty-Two

A Crowded World

BEFORE Pearl Harbor, Houston enjoyed the luxury of space. In restaurants, tables were spaced widely apart so that each was an island for private conversation. White tablecloths and napkins were universal. Even fairly simple places had a head waiter who seated customers. String ensembles softly played semiclassical music at luncheon and at dinner.

The Houston voice reflected the Southern pace of the city. At restaurants, when a guest ordered milk with his lunch, the waitress would inquire, "Sweet milk or buttermilk?" Looking forward to a party, one Houston couple might offer another a ride: "We'll carry you all to the Abercrombies' this evening."[1] And in planning a day, a Houstonian might decide to go to town. When? "Directly." Actually, this was pronounced "dreckly" and it meant after awhile.

Motion picture theaters had ushers, who escorted each newcomer to a seat, lighting the way with a flashlight. All elevators had an elevator operator at the controls. Department stores had wide aisles between the counters and a sales person behind every counter. Escalators, fairly rare before Pearl Harbor, moved so slowly that even the most timorous could step aboard safely. Barber shops, which offered shaves as well as haircuts, also had a section set aside as a shoe shine parlor.

Passenger cars on trains had widely spaced seats and rarely were all seats filled. Pullman-car porters provided paper bags for ladies' hats to be stored and carried long whisk brooms to dust the soot off departing gentlemen.[2]

Suddenly, with war, the world became crowded. As its men went off to service, every city seemed to bulge with newcomers, yet offices had fewer persons to do the same amount of work. The pace quickened. Hours lengthened. And where did all the people come from? No city changed more dramatically than the nation's capital, and Houston accounted for a share of the change.

In 1939, Washington was a gentle Southern town. By early 1941, the army alone had grown from 7,000 civilian employees to 41,000. Three hundred architects and 13,000 workmen were needed to build the Pentagon, and when finished, though it held 40,000 War Department men and women, it was already too small. The same kind of expansion was going on in the Navy Department, at the new National Airport, in the innumerable bureaus of government. In the last months before Pearl Harbor, Washington grew at the rate of 50,000 a year. And all these people had to have a place to live.

In late spring of 1942, Browne Baker and Mark Edwin Andrews were joined in the negotiating section by more Houston friends: Leland Anderson, thirty-eight, financial vice-president of Anderson Clayton; Lt. I. H. Kempner, Jr., thirty-eight, vice-president of Sugarland Industries, the largest refiner of sugar in the country; and his brother Lt. Harris Kempner, forty, of Galveston,

During the spring tennis matches at the Stables in the 1930s and early 1940s, buffet lunch and backgammon made pleasant diversions between sets. Here, Tina Sharp is scoring a point. Clockwise from her are Ed Salrin, Connie Stewart in the background, Ginny Rotan and Olga Wiess standing, Lloyd H. Smith, Anne McLean, and John Louden. *From the Wiess family collection*

vice-president of I. H. Kempner and Company. All were good traders.

One of Leland Anderson's first assignments was to cope with three of the country's biggest steel companies, which were under indictment for price fixing. Company executives seated themselves before his desk and asked him what they should do.

"If I were you," Anderson said mildly, "I'd go home and work out a fair estimate of cost and submit a bid based on the estimate." When the bids came back in, all were far lower than the original price. One was down by almost half.

To this nucleus of Gulf Coast men, Secretary Forrestal and Baker gradually added a variety of businessmen from other parts of the country. But each one was known well by someone already on the team. Roughly twenty men did the work of the navy's contract negotiation section, devising contracts that would encourage a company to find ways to save money; buying billions of dollars of ships, planes, and equipment; negotiating every contract with integrity and ingenuity; and in the end, saving this country many millions of dollars. By the war's end, the Browne Baker group had spent 10 percent of all the money spent by the United States for that war.[3]

On orders of Secretary Forrestal, Ed Andrews received rapid out-of-line promotions to the rank of captain and was awarded the Legion of Merit.[4] Both Browne Baker and Leland Anderson were awarded the Department of the Navy's Distinguished Civilian

Leland Anderson, tagged by Browne Baker for the team of navy traders. *Photograph © Houston Post*

Service medal by Secretary Forrestal. This is the highest honor the navy can give to a civilian.

In the camaraderie of wartime, those lucky enough to have a living room sofa were generous about offering it to a friend who was house-hunting. In the spring of 1942, before Adelaide Baker, Marguerite Andrews, and Essemena Anderson had joined them, Leland Anderson and Ed Andrews shared a garret room in Browne Baker's house. They

insisted ever after that Browne Baker made them wash all the dishes.[5]

It was in June, 1942, that Mary Kempner joined her husband, Herb.[6] "The night I arrived," Mary Kempner Reed said, "Browne Baker had us to dinner. He had a place in Georgetown and he was doing the cooking. It was so hot that Browne sat with his refrigerator door open to cool off."

The Kempners rented a house in Falls Church, Virginia, found for them by a family friend. Fortunately they had left their sons for the summer with Mary's mother, Mrs. James Judson Carroll, at 16 Courtlandt Place. The sewer system in their Falls Church neighborhood collapsed. They could break their lease but had one week to find another place.

They moved into a house on Sixteenth Street owned by a manufacturer of office furniture. "There was an office desk in every single room in the house," Mary Reed said. "We had to have them stored to get enough space. Harris Kempner, coming up from Galveston, stayed with us for the summer. In the fall the boys came up. Denny went to the Friends' School and Jim to nursery school." In two years the Kempners made three moves.

All Washington worked a full six-day week throughout the war and these were usually ten- and twelve-hour days. Getting food, even with the necessary ration stamps, was harder in Washington than in Houston. "Sometimes it took three changes of bus to get a chicken," Mrs. Reed recalled. Herb Kempner caught scarlet fever. Going to see him every day, his wife had to take a three-way combination of streetcar and bus to get to the Bethesda Naval Hospital and back.

"But we were young and we had fun," Mrs. Reed said. "Several of us got together and rented a tennis court for Sunday mornings. When my mother came up to visit, we invited Mr. and Mrs. Jones and Mr. and Mrs. Clayton to dinner.[7] One evening when the Kempners were in town, Oveta came. She was too busy for us to see much of her."

It was late summer before Adelaide Baker took the train to Washington, and in the continuing innocence of the times, it was quite safe for Browne Baker, Jr., sixteen, and Lovett Baker, eleven, to drive from Houston to Georgetown in the family station wagon. Browne was about to enter Exeter and Lovett to go to school in Washington.

Because the Leland Andersons had three children under the age of six, one a brand new baby, the family did not join Mr. Anderson until September. They lucked onto a nice house in Kensington, Maryland. It had oil heat and was right on the bus line. Civilian navy employees got no break on rationed gasoline. Anderson drove a carpool, picking up one captain and three lieutenants at seven every morning and bringing them back after six every evening. But in times of acute gasoline shortage, he and they took the bus.

As the war in Europe neared an end, Houstonians were still coming to Washington. After a year and a half in the Pacific, Lt. Ernest Fay was sent to Washington and put in charge of the personnel desk at the Navy Bureau of Personnel. Wheeler Nazro, who had captained a destroyer escort, was ordered to Washington and joined the contract negotiation section headed by Browne Baker.

After reaching the West Coast on the *Houston,* Lt. Dudley Sharp was ordered to Silver Spring, Maryland. There he was administrative manager of the Applied Physics Laboratory run by Johns Hopkins University. "I was never allowed to tell anyone where I was working," Sharp said.

The main project, a very important one, was to develop the proximity fuse. It was designed to shoot down attacking aircraft. In the conventional fuse shot out of a gun, you had to guess how long it would take to get to the plane and set a time: Guess, set fuse, hope it will work. The proximity fuse was triggered by the proximity of the attacking aircraft. It had a tremendous success against the Japanese and turned the sea war around. I was in Washington for the last year of the war.

The atomic bomb was a surprise. We knew something secret was on. But the Germans and the Japanese were working on a bomb too. *Some*body was going to get it. It ended the war and we came home to Post Oak Lane.

Tina Sharp joined her husband in Washington; they had to move five times during their brief Washington stay, each time because the owner was returning from overseas and wanted his house back. On their last move, they took over the house being left by the Kempners, who were going home. The Sharps celebrated VJ Day in Washington with Carolyn and Ernie Fay. The movement and uprootings of war had ended in one more shared experience in a lifelong friendship.

They Also Served

THE LOSS of the cruiser *Houston* three months after the attack on Pearl Harbor jolted the city. In the Battle of Java in March, the *Houston* helped knock out two heavy Japanese cruisers. Then, a day later, she sailed through the Sunda Strait bound for Java and was never heard from again.

The *Houston Post* led a campaign to raise money for a new cruiser and to recruit one thousand volunteers to replace the men lost.[1] By May 31, 1942, the volunteers were ready. On Memorial Day, one thousand young men gathered downtown on Main Street in front of the Loew's and Metropolitan theaters to be sworn into the navy by Rear Adm. William A. Glassford. Another quarter of a million people were there to cheer. Edward A. Bourdon, a photographer who spent his career photographing Houston in all its moods and activities, hung out over the street from a theater marquee to take his picture of the volunteers. This was the picture used by *Life* magazine a few days later.

After the ceremony, the thousand marched to Union Station, where five trains waited to take them to the San Diego training base. Another six hundred men had signed up too late to be a part of the memorial group. A brass plaque commemorating the mass swearing-in was set into the sidewalk on Main Street. In December, Secretary of the Navy Frank Knox came to accept a certificate for the $85 million in war-bonds Houstonians had bought to build a new *Houston*.

War bond sales were a major homefront enterprise. Movie stars were in demand to lure crowds into the Music Hall or City Auditorium. When Jane and Titi Blaffer were working on a war bond sale, their father spoke to Howard Hughes, Jr., in Hollywood. Their friend Howard sent his plane over to Houston filled with rising Hollywood stars: James Stewart, Mischa Auer, Tyrone Power, Henry Fonda, Nancy Kelly, and Olivia de Havilland among them. Before the rally, the stars were made welcome at the Blaffer home in Shadyside. There they were surprised to see that their hostess preferred to light her home by candlelight. (Though bathrooms and kitchen were given the benefit of electric lights, Mrs. Robert Lee Blaffer liked the glow shed by scores of candles in candelabra and chandeliers through the rest of her house.)

Houstonians were zealous in their Red Cross work, scrap iron drives, victory gardens. Civil defense volunteers learned first aid. Galveston was blacked out, as was every seacoast city. Gradually Houstonians began to nurse aging automobiles and to be grateful for recapped tires.

Growing numbers of soldiers were leaving wives and children to cope alone. The Harris County Red Cross Chapter expanded to help as many as two hundred families a day. And as Americans were captured, the chapter traced prisoners of war through the International Red Cross.

"In 1941, ninety percent of all dressings used by the U.S. armed forces were made by Red Cross volunteers," Helen Seymour wrote in her Red Cross history. "Commer-

When the USS *Houston* was lost in early 1942, Houston pledged the money and the men for a new cruiser. On May 31, 1942, one thousand volunteers gathered on Main Street to be sworn in by Rear Adm. William A. Glassford. Edward Bourdon hung out over the Kirby Theater marquee to take this picture. *Edward Bourdon photograph, courtesy of Mr. Bourdon*

In Houston for a giant war bond sale planned by Jane and Titi Blaffer, popular movie stars gathered in the Shadyside home of Mrs. Robert Lee Blaffer. *Left to right, standing:* James Stewart, Mischa Auer, Jane Blaffer (Mrs. Kenneth Dale Owen), Tyrone Power, Richard Green, Titi Blaffer (Princess von Furstenberg), and Noah Dietrich, chief executive officer of Hughes Tool Company. *Seated:* Mrs. Henry Fonda, Olivia de Havilland, Nancy Kelly, and Henry Fonda. *Edward Bourdon photograph, courtesy of Mr. Bourdon*

cially manufactured dressings, plentiful in peacetime, met only about one-tenth of the need." In Houston, Mrs. John Marr was chairman and Mrs. Thomas W. Gregory vice-chairman of the Red Cross. Young women and old met to tear, roll, and package bandages just as their mothers had in World War I.

Another Red Cross group sat at sewing machines in a parish room at Palmer Memorial Church making pajamas, Laura Kirkland Bruce (Mrs. George S. Bruce) recalls. While the others sewed, Mrs. Hugh Roy Cullen volunteered to do the sweeping to keep the floor free of pins, scraps, and thread.

Katherine Dionne (Mrs. Newton Wray), who was on the chapter board, went to England to set up a large Red Cross club at a heavy bomber base outside London. "I was constantly running into friends from Houston," she said long after. "Sometimes I would go to London to meet Harris Masterson and Joe Hutcheson—they were in intelligence. At one point in 1944, everyone had to sign and turn in their five-pound notes. When Joe Ingraham was checking signatures, he noticed my name and looked me up." She opened another club in Germany before coming home in 1947.

The Red Cross Motor Corps, Mrs. Seymour wrote, "was for neither the frail of body nor the timid of spirit. Volunteers had to be able to change their own tires, pick up stretchers, service their own cars, and administer first aid." Each corps member supplied her own car and bought her own uniform. The captain appointed in 1941 was Texas women's golf champion Kay Pearson. Harriet Bath, Leota Smith, and Mary C. Logan were later captains.

The United Service Organization chapter, founded by Dewey Roussel, was pronounced by many visiting servicemen to be the finest in the country. Churches welcomed men and women in uniform and turned church parlors and parish houses into writing rooms and coffee bars. Countless numbers of servicemen and women were taken home for Sunday dinner or potluck supper. Marion Law, Jr., who owned the Houston Book Store on Main Street, installed comfortable chairs and kept his doors open and the coffee hot until long after dark every day and weekend.

Houston's women served the war effort in a variety of ways. Although she was married and had small children, Mrs. Tom Martin Davis added nurse's aide work to her Junior League duties. "They were awful days," she said frankly. "Jan Peterkin and Eloise Nazro and I worked at the old Baptist Hospital and at St. Joseph's. It nearly killed me. I learned then that I could never be a nurse. But I did it."

Every city had a secret airplane tracking center. Except for the few hundred who worked there, noboby knew that it existed. In a circle around Houston, volunteer civilian plane spotters stood on duty in around-the-clock shifts. Every plane that entered the circle was reported to the center. There, standing around a large table, young women in earphones used colored pencils to mark the path and progress across the big map. Each of these tracings had to be completed in seconds. At the same time the message went to the fighter command regional office, where army, navy, and Civil Aeronautics Authority men were on constant alert. If

none of them could identify the plane and account for its flight, it would be taken as an enemy raider and interceptors would be sent up to defend the city.

Margaret Wiess did both hospital work and plane tracking. "I worked through the Red Cross," Margaret Wiess Elkins explained. "You went to three different hospitals in the first three weeks, with Jeff Davis required. Then there was the old Methodist down on Rosalie and the original Hermann. I worked as a nurse's aide from nine to twelve every day, and then did other things in the afternoon. And Mary Farish, bless her heart, was probably the greatest nurse's aide that ever lived.[2] We used to see her sailing out her front door at dawn every morning. Glory Morris was head of the USO and our job there was to find lodgings for the wives and children of men who had been sent to Ellington Field."[3]

Three afternoons a week, Margaret Wiess went to the information center in the Houston Club Building to track airplanes. "I loved it," she said.

It was a type of glamour. Not everybody could do it and it was the first time I had ever been fingerprinted. You felt like you were really doing something.

But I had this funny feeling that because I hated nurse's aide I was giving more to my country through the nurse's aide. I really couldn't stand it. All the smells, the bedpans. I never got used to them. So that was my war effort.

Jim Elkins had been turned down for the services because of his vision, and he worked tremendously hard for the Red Cross. That is really where I got to know him.

Ellington Field was burgeoning with soldiers and airmen. Reopened in 1940, it became an advanced training center for bomber pilots. The mighty B-17 Flying Fortresses roared over Houston. At an Ellington Field dance in 1944, Margaret and Wilhelmina Cullen met two air force captains. In 1945, Margaret married Capt. Douglas Marshall and Wilhelmina married Capt. Corbin J. Robertson, Jr.

In 1943, Ellington graduated the first class

of Jacqueline Cochran's WASPs. "The idea was," Marjorie Sanford Thompson (Mrs. Braxton Thompson) said, "for women to ferry planes from the factory to the port of embarkation, to release men for overseas duty. But when three of the new B-26 bombers had crashed in a month, killing the crew, the air corps had to do something to raise morale.

"Eighteen of us agreed to fly the B-26s as a morale booster. Before we signed on," she recalled, "we had to make out our wills. The air corps dentist made an impression of our teeth for future identification. I willed my billfold to my parents. Braxton Thompson was my squadron commander." They were married five days before he went overseas, and Sandy Thompson wound up towing B-24 bombers out over the Gulf of Mexico as targets for navy gunnery practice – eight runs a day.

After graduation from Smith and her Houston debut, Nancy Spencer started her acting career at the Pasadena Playhouse in California. But with war, she came home to Houston prepared to be a Rosie the Riveter. She worked the night shift in a factory making binoculars for the navy. Invited to join a USO company to entertain troops in the Pacific, she gladly went. They got to Iwo Jima and toured the Pacific for six months in *Blithe Spirit*. She played Elvira.

"This was right after VJ Day," she said. "It was always outdoor theater. You'd look up and see the twinkling lights of the cigarettes of Japanese snipers who had come out of their caves to watch the show. One time we played on an aircraft carrier off Saipan. On the flight elevator. As you crossed the stage, you'd be running up, as the ship tilted, and then you'd turn around and go running down the stage. It was an experience and a half."

One night at a Seabees party, a large man loomed up in front of her and asked for her telephone number.

"Here on Guam?"

"No," he said. "at home. My mother lives in Houston and I have a ham radio friend.

I can ask my mother to telephone your mother and tell her you are all right." It brought unrehearsed tears to her eyes.[4]

Houston could see the tragic cost of war. From Europe and the Pacific, wounded men were being brought back to army hospitals in every state.

Ralph (Andy) Anderson, a beloved sports writer and columnist for the *Houston Press,* started out selling war bonds.[5] He soon plunged into a wholehearted effort to help the wounded and maimed young men. He invented attachments for sports gear to enable them to play the games they had always played. As an ardent outdoorsman, a hunter and fisherman, he arranged ways for them to enjoy the outdoors. He promoted wild game dinners to be served at the several veterans hospitals in South Texas. He visited 172 other veterans' hospitals in the country as a volunteer-at-large, entertaining and leading the wounded back to sports they could enjoy. Through him, a park for handicapped veterans was established on the east shore of Lake Houston.

The war scattered Houstonians of all ages around the globe. With so many friends away, a gang of congenial people formed simply to have fun. "All ages came together," Margaret Elkins said. "Bill Goldston, for instance, was much older than Jim and ended up being one of his best friends. George Black, Billy and Kathleen Goldston, Tommy and George Anna Burke – I remember once we were playing poker and there was a fourteen-year gap on each side of me. Of course, Wilhelmina Cullen and I were always together."

It was basically from this group that Houston Holidays stemmed. No records were kept but Jim Elkins, Margaret Wiess, and Caroline Wiess, whose fiance was at SHAFE Headquarters in Paris, were among the leaders.

The McCloskey General Hospital in Temple, Texas, was filled with young men who were permanently disabled. Some were paraplegics, paralyzed by shrapnel in the spine. Some had lost one leg or two, or one arm.

Houston Holidays was formed to ease their way back into civilian life. "The concept was to bring wounded soldiers who were about to be dismissed from the orthopedic hospital to Houston for a holiday," Caroline Wiess Law said. "We were trained by the doctors at Temple to know what to do if someone fell or needed help. We brought down a few at a time—six or eight. We lined up private swimming pools. We took them to the symphony, to pop concerts. We had casual dinner parties in private homes. All this was to let them get back into civilian life before they went home. They were quite wonderful."

"Nellie and George Black, Saralee Tooke and Jack Tooke, Marjorie and Lincoln Frost, Tommy Thompson—all helped," Mrs. Law said. "Marjorie was head of the Business and Professional Women's Club and knew all sorts of attractive, capable young women. Tommy Thompson was an amusing oilman who played the ukelele."

"Marjorie Frost was especially helpful," Margaret Elkins said. "With her publicity, we got donations. We could take the men to restaurants for dinner. The USO would get dates. We always tried to have a picnic or a barbecue and always had a choice of homes. People would hear about Houston Holidays and just offer."

Houston Holidays made a lasting contribution to Houston: the Pin Oak Horse Show, which helped make Texas Children's Hospital possible. In 1945, Houston Holidays asked Jim Abercrombie if they could stage a benefit horse show at Pin Oak Stables. Yes, he said, but only if he were allowed to pay all the expenses and turn the gross receipts over to Houston Holidays. They had their horse show and that was the start. In 1946, the first of the annual Pin Oak Horse Shows was held. As it grew, Abercrombie and his friend Leopold Meyer used it to gain impetus for planning, building, and financing the future Texas Children's Hospital.

Even with a War On

GASOLINE was rationed. Tires were rationed. Sugar was rationed. Nylon disappeared from the stores and went into parachutes.[1] A *New Yorker* cartoon showed two world-weary young blondes meeting over a martini. The caption: "Oh you know. It was the old, old story. He plied her with presents—butter, sugar, nylons. . . ."

Houston built few houses and fewer buildings during World War II. But ideas and effort were still unrationed. In the war years, the city gained a medical center, Rice Institute gained an oil field, and black Houstonians gained—at last—the right to vote in political primaries.

Houston doctors had been talking about a medical center for decades. At last, in the 1940s, the M. D. Anderson Foundation provided the impetus and the money to create the Texas Medical Center in Houston.

The Anderson trustees—John H. Freeman, Col. William Bates, and Horace Wilkins—had been looking for the best way to spend the large amount of money left in their trust by Monroe D. Anderson. Sometimes they met on Brentwood Drive under the ceiling fan on Colonel Bates's back porch to consult with Dr. Homer Rainey, University of Texas president, and Dr. John Spies, head of the university's medical branch in Galveston. Sometimes they went to the top floor of the Rice Hotel to confer with Dr. William Ernst Bertner, long-time proponent of a medical center.

In June, 1941, when the Texas legislature voted to spend five hundred thousand dollars to build a cancer hospital, Anderson trustees saw their way. They offered to match the state's money and provide twenty acres on an appropriate site for a teaching hospital in Houston to be run by the University of Texas.

The appropriate site would be the land that Will Hogg had always hoped would be used by the University of Texas for a medical school. In December, 1943, the Anderson trustees paid the city a hundred thousand dollars for the 134-acre tract that had been added to Hermann Park.[2] Meanwhile, Baylor University wanted to move the medical school it had operated in Dallas for forty years. Baylor trustees approached the Anderson Foundation. The foundation agreed to give Baylor a site, $1 million for a building, and another $1 million over the next ten years for medical research. The Houston Chamber of Commerce raised another half a million dollars for the medical school, and Baylor accepted.

As dean, Dr. Fred Elliott had revitalized the Texas Dental College and persuaded the Texas legislature to make it a part of the University of Texas. The Anderson trustees earmarked a dental school site next to that of the cancer hospital. The first components of a medical center were rapidly coming together under the influence of the M. D. Anderson trustees. But they realized that the medical center would need its own governing body. In 1945, they set up the nonprofit Texas Medical Center, Inc., with Dr. Bertner as its first president; Mr. Freeman, vice-president; Dr. Elliott, secretary; and James Anderson, treasurer.[3]

Shown here in its early days, the Ezekiel W. Cullen Building overlooked a large reflecting pool. *Courtesy Special Collections, University of Houston Libraries*

Baylor wanted to move the medical college to Houston as soon as the spring term ended. Baylor trustees Earl Hankamer and Ray Dudley found temporary quarters in the old Sears Roebuck warehouse on Buffalo Bayou, and classes began in July, 1943. Mr. and Mrs. H. R. Cullen gave Baylor eight hundred thousand dollars for a building. Kenneth Bentsen was called upon as architect. The Baylor University College of Medicine's Cullen Building was to be the first building completed in the Texas Medical Center after the war. (With the arrival at Baylor of Dr. Michael DeBakey and at Anderson Hospital of Dr. R. Lee Clark, the Texas Medical Center would begin immediately to gain worldwide recognition.)

All this was phenomenal. Across the country, church denominations, philanthropists, and cities have built hospitals. But here, a diverse group of Houstonians, depending on private philanthropy, set out to build from scratch an entire medical center dedicated to research, teaching, and patient care. The idea would attract private money from many other Houstonians, millions of dollars from Hugh Roy Cullen, and millions more from the M. D. Anderson Foundation.

This was before the days of the Hill-Burton Hospital Act (which would play a part in postwar building) and before the days of massive federal research grants. Of course, everyone expected such a medical center to provide employment and stimulate the economy. But perhaps no one involved in

1943 foresaw that the Texas Medical Center would become the world's largest, renowned for its medical breakthroughs. When that day came, of the $1.5 billion given to the medical center, more than a fourth would have come from Houston donors and foundations.[4]

The summer concerts in the Miller Outdoor Theater began by public demand.[5] The idea was proposed in a letter that Hubert Roussel, the *Houston Post* music critic, ran in his column. It prompted a flood of letters clamoring for an outdoor concert. Conductor Ernst Hoffman thought that he could put on a concert with forty performers for six hundred dollars. But could they pass the hat? What if nobody came? At that point, N. D. Naman, a financier and music lover, gave a thousand dollars anonymously for a trial concert.

By seven o'clock on a hot August evening all roads leading into Hermann Park were choked. Fifteen thousand people came to hear the first concert. When the hat was passed, the audience gave more than enough in quarters and dimes to cover the costs. A second concert could go on. By 1941, the summer season had grown to six concerts. The Public Music Association was chartered, with Oveta Culp Hobby as president. Roy Demme was treasurer, and Mr. Naman's son Bernard served on the board. In 1943 the Houston Symphony Society made the summer season a permanent part of the orchestra schedule.

The most remarkable performance was given in 1942, as Roussel wrote in his history of the orchestra, when Tchaikovsky's *1812 Overture* was to be played. "In place of the cannon shot called for in the score, it was decided to use rockets that could be tossed by a mechanical sling and would explode 150 feet in the air. Nobody thought to announce this. As a result, the audience took it to be an air raid, and there was a spectacular rush. . . ."

Walter Walne had been an able symphony society president for five years, but he feared that the war would cost the symphony both musicians and patrons. Thinking it best to suspend concerts until after the war, he resigned as president. The society turned to Hugh Roy Cullen. He had never been on the board, but his wife was a staunch board member and Mrs. Ernst Hoffman's close friend.[6] In the words of Roussel, "Roy Cullen adopted the orchestra as simply as though it had been another acreage lease." Cullen agreed to serve for the duration of the war and no longer.

And for the duration Roy Cullen managed the orchestra as an instrument to serve the war effort as well as the cause of music. He set a taxing pace. Once he even combined the orchestra with a wrestling match to sell war bonds. He and Ernst Hoffman became a team. Whenever money was a problem, Cullen wrote a check. Though the old City Auditorium could seat four thousand, men and women in uniform swelled audiences to overflowing.

Rice Institute was gaining a new generation of friends. George Brown believed that every young American capable of higher learning should be able to go to college – at public expense where necessary. This gave him a natural feel for the tuition-free Rice Institute, his early alma mater. Harry Wiess had never gone to Rice. He felt that his first obligation was to the Massachusetts Institute of Technology because it had provided the experts to help build the great Baytown refinery. His second was to Princeton, which had educated him. But by 1941, he saw Rice as a way for him to give something back to the community and committed himself to the institute's future.

In 1942, as judge of the probate court, Roy Hofheinz learned that almost half of the Rincon oil field was going to be sold. The property was part of the large but debt-ridden W. R. Davis estate that was up for probate. Heavy tax liabilities made the property too expensive for private investors, but not for a tax-exempt body. Roy Hofheinz had spent his freshman year at Rice, and it occurred to him that if there were some way in which Rice Institute could buy the field,

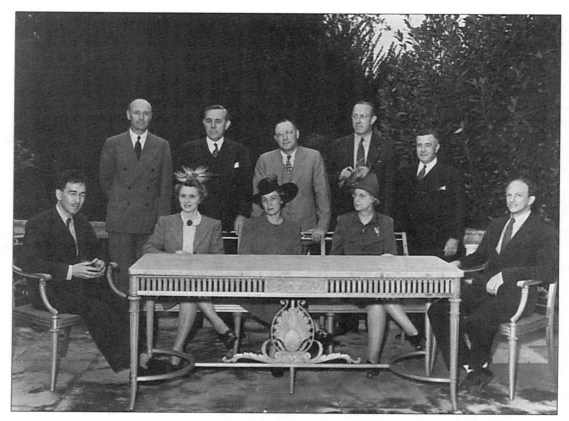

A wartime meeting of the Houston Symphony Society Board held on the terrace of the Hugh Roy Cullens' home. *Left to right, seated:* Ernst Hoffman, conductor; Mrs. Paul Ledbetter; Mrs. Ray Dudley; Mrs. Cullen; and Isaac Arnold. *Standing:* Ted Swigart; Mr. Cullen; Leopold L. Meyer; and Harry Bourne, orchestra manager and contrabass player, and Joe Henkel. *Courtesy Houston Metropolitan Research Center, Houston Public Library*

the school's endowment would be greatly enlarged.

George Brown welcomed the idea and took the proposal to the Rice trustees. "They didn't want any part of it," he recalled. "They felt the whole thing was a gamble, and Rice didn't have any business with an oil field."

With Harry Wiess as an ally, George Brown changed tactics. He and his brother Herman each offered to give $50,000 toward the earnest money. Mr. and Mrs. Wiess, Mr. and Mrs. Stephen P. Farish, and Mr. and Mrs. H. R. Cullen gave $25,000 each. Mr. and Mrs. W. S. Farish gave $15,000, and Harry Hanszen $10,000. The M. D. Anderson Foundation contributed $300,000. With half the $1 million purchase price in hand, they persuaded the conservative Rice board to put up the other half. In the next forty years, the investment would add more than $60 million to the Rice endowment.

Won over, the trustees elected George Brown to the board in January, 1943, less than a month after the Rincon deal was completed. He would become the first Rice alumnus to be elected chairman, and would lead the university into unprecedented growth in both its endowment and its plant.

In 1942, Schlumberger, the pioneer oil

well surveying company, brought to Houston a young French couple who, in the next forty years, would heighten the city's appreciation of art and dramatically enhance Houston's reputation as a cultural center.

The war was still new to Americans, but Jean and Dominique de Menil, both in their early thirties, had already had their share of adventures. Jean de Menil was a *saboteur*. Once the vice-president of a Paris bank, he had joined the Schlumberger company and could travel across Europe on his business credentials as a Schlumberger executive. But his covert assignment for the French Resistance was to sabotage as many oil shipments from Romania to Nazi Germany as he could. Meanwhile, Dominique de Menil, the daughter of the inventor of the Schlumberger process, went to the family home place in unoccupied France to give birth to George, their third child.

In 1941, Jean de Menil became president of Schlumberger Overseas and Schlumberger Surenco.[7] In 1942, after a year in Venezuela, the de Menils moved to Houston to stay. They found a pleasant, two-story house on Chevy Chase with a small screened porch for summers without air conditioning and a big side yard where their small children could play.

Despite the wartime shortage of staff, the Museum of Fine Arts was being kept alive by its director, James Chillman, Rice professor of fine arts, and Ruth Uhler, museum curator of education. When Will Hogg died in 1930, his collection of the works of Frederick Remington was one of the largest in the country. They hung in the penthouse office that he shared with his brother Mike. After Mike's death from cancer, Ima Hogg gave the collection of fifty-three oils, ten watercolors, and the bronze *Bronco Buster* to the Museum of Fine Arts.

Miss Hogg had grown up in politics, and she took a lively interest in local issues and world affairs. In 1943, she ran for a seat on the Houston School Board because she thought it wrong for public education to be left entirely in male hands. Both Dr. Ray Daily, an ophthalmologist, and Miss Hogg ran against male candidates. Both won. Both were excellent board members.[8]

Still nudged by her concern for unhappy and disturbed children, Miss Hogg persuaded the board to start a visiting teacher program. Specially trained teachers took schooling to the homes of disturbed children who could not fit into classroom routines. Ima Hogg worked to reform the teachers' salary scale and to equalize pay for all teachers—elementary and high school, blacks and whites, men and women. She helped develop a painting-to-music program in the art classes and saw to it that the high schools, then segregated by race, provided art lessons for both blacks and whites. From her position on the Women's Committee of the Houston Symphony Society, she promoted concerts for children. These student matinees, a permanent part of the symphony season almost fifty years later, have introduced thousands upon thousands of Houston children to classical music. Some school board members considered Ima Hogg a flaming liberal and did not look kindly on so much do-gooding.

Winnie Safford Wallace, Betty Crotty Carter, and Mary Wood Farish took on the task of selling the concert idea to the schools.[9] Betty Carter said, "We had to call on every single school principal, high school and grammar school, public and private, black and white to get them to accept. It was interesting. When the buses brought children in to the matinees, we were agreeably surprised at how well it went." Despite her several successes, Miss Hogg found school board politics and divisions disheartening. Having accomplished much, she did not run again.

As doctors went off to war, Houston acquired a new generation of doctors who were women. Dr. Paul Ledbetter invited Dr. Mary Ann McKinney, who was a resident at Chicago Lying-In Hospital, to join his practice. Originally from Nacogdoches, she had graduated from Tulane University Medical School and interned in British missionary hospitals in India, where she coped with the full surgical and medical range. Dr. McKinney was a tall, slender young woman with short, dark curly hair and a feminine elegance of dress. She also was an exquisite surgeon with a flair for diagnosis, but she would make her mark in obstetrics.

Dr. Laura Bickel was born in Pennsylvania. The daughter of a physician, she earned her medical degree at the University of Wisconsin and had a residency at the Chicago Children's Hospital. Dr. David Greer, one of Houston's best-loved pediatricians, brought her to Houston. A natural athlete, tall Dr. Bickel skied, swam, and sailed and had the chic of well-tailored tweeds.

When she opened her own practice in the Holden house on Oakdale, she furnished it with fairytale maps on the examining room walls.[10] She had not only toys in her inviting parlor but an old typewriter upon which a toddler could bang. During polio epidemics, she rocked the child whose mother was barred from the hospital room. She was among the first physicians to suspect the connection between German measles and birth defects. She became an associate professor of pediatrics at Baylor College of Medicine. In the years ahead, many of her patients would refuse to graduate from her care.

Dr. Goldie Ham took over Dr. Maurice Menier's obstetrical practice when he went in the service. She had short, crisp hair and an inevitable cigarette, and she had a great competence. Her patients loved and trusted her.

Fred Lazarus, Jr., head of the Federated department store chain, came to Houston to visit his son Ralph, who was stationed at Ellington Field. At loose ends by day, he explored the city and discovered there was no department store. Sears was far out on South Main. The downtown stores sold only clothing and gifts. The great Munn Store that once sold everything from baby bootees to automobile tires was long gone.

George Cohen was president and principal owner of Foley's at Main and Preston. His brother-in-law Leopold Meyer was vice-president and, with four other Meyer brothers, a minority share holder. Each of four Meyers managed a department, ran his own advertising, and controlled his own display window, rather like separate fiefdoms.

Though the major banks were on lower Main Street nearby, the neighborhood was shabby. The best clothing stores—like Sakowitz, the Fashion, Levy's, and Battelstein's—were farther uptown near the Gulf Building. With the thought of building a new and bigger store after the war, George Cohen had taken an option on the First Presbyterian Church property at Main and McKinney. He offered Foley's and its option to Fred Lazarus.

In 1944, Federated agreed to buy. The new Foley's began in the old Foley's building, with Max Levine as manager.[11] Unfortunately, the Meyer brothers, who knew what Houstonians would buy, promptly retired. "The man we brought in to manage the basement store was from Minneapolis," Max Levine recalled. "He went to New York to buy clothes for his fall season. When the goods came in, we found he had bought a thousand dozen sets of flannelette underwear! For Houston!"

The change gave George Cohen and Leopold Meyer more time for war bond sales and other civic measures. Foley's Overseas Canteen shipped thousands of packages across the world to Houstonians overseas. The new owners were surprised, however, to find that in Houston—as in much of the South—the best customers expected to pay their bills only once or twice a year. To the gratitude of merchants throughout the city, the new management introduced the thirty-day account.

Foley's bold new plans for postwar building attracted national attention. Picking up George Cohen's option, Federated paid the First Presbyterian Church $1.5 million for the half-block of McKinney between Main and Travis.

Foley's bought the property in June, promising the congregation the use of their church until building materials should come back on the civilian market. Eight months later, Foley's sold the property to Woolworth's for well over $3 million. *Life* magazine and the news wire services told America that Woolworth's had paid two thousand dollars per front inch on Houston's Main Street. Moving farther south, Foley's bought the entire block on Main between Lamar and Dallas and leased another block across Travis for a parking garage. *Houston* magazine pronounced all this "the largest transaction of its kind in the city's history. The new store will be the first new, complete department store to be built in the country since 1929."

The Presbyterians called on architect Maurice Sullivan, and both Foley's and Woolworth's called on architect Kenneth Franzheim to stand by to design handsome new buildings as soon as possible after the war.

World War II brought to the black citizens of Texas a voting right that they had been seeking through the courts for decades. Texas was a one-party state. Whoever won a nomination in the Democratic primaries ran with no real opposition in the election. Nomination equaled election. Any black citizen who had paid a poll tax could vote in the general elections, but by then the race was over.

The Texas legislature made repeated efforts to keep black citizens from having a voice in state politics. In 1923, it acted to bar any black from taking part in the Democratic primaries. In 1927, the Supreme Court ruled the White Primary Law unconstitutional because it infringed upon the "equal protection of the laws" clause of the Fourteenth Amendment. The legislature then enacted a new statute declaring that "every political party in this state . . . shall have the power to prescribe the qualifications of its own members and shall in its own way determine who shall be qualified to vote . . . in such political party." The Supreme Court sent the second White Primary Law after the first.

Again, the state government was trying to violate the equal protection of the laws clause.

Giving up on legislation, party leaders turned to the Democratic party convention. On May 24, 1932, the convention voted to limit party membership to white citizens. In 1935, the Supreme Court granted that blacks could be excluded from the primary because a Democratic party convention – not a state government agency – had barred them. As non-members they could not vote in the primary. The Democratic Party was, under this ruling, a private club authorized to choose its own members.

Five years later, in 1940, Dr. Lonnie Smith, a well-known black dentist, filed suit against S. E. Allwright, election judge of the forty-eighth precinct of Harris County in Houston's Fifth Ward. Dr. Smith charged that he was denied a ballot in the Democratic primaries solely on the grounds of his race – which of course was perfectly true.

Born in Yoakum, Dr. Smith was a graduate of Prairie View A&M College with a dental degree from Meharrey Medical College in Nashville. After his marriage to Janie Dunn and four years of practice in Galveston, he moved to Houston. The Smiths lived on Lyons Avenue, and Dr. Smith's dental office was at 409 Milam. Dr. Smith was a director of the Houston chapter of the National Association for the Advancement of Colored People, a member of the Houston Citizens Chamber of Commerce, and active in the YMCA, the Boy Scouts, and Community Chest campaigns. He was patently qualified to be a voting citizen.

In April, 1944, in an eight-to-one decision, the Supreme Court reversed the 1935 ruling that a political party was a private club: "The party takes its character as a state agency from the duties imposed upon it by state statutes; the duties do not become matters of private law because they are performed by a political party."

The ruling came in time for black Houstonians who had paid their poll tax to vote in the July 24 primaries.[12] Although a number of politicians across the South orated against the decision, most white Houstonians accepted it with calm. On July 25, 1944, the *Houston Post* reported that of the 5,000 blacks holding poll tax receipts, 2,618 voted —more than half. Of the 158,000 registered whites, a third had voted. Clearly, the deci- sion had provoked no angered rush to the polls by white Houstonians. On Dr. Smith's death in 1971, the Texas House and the Texas Senate each passed resolutions of tribute to this "dedicated and distinguished citizen." Houston named a public library in his memory.

Chapter Sixty-Five

Plowshare to Sword

ALMOST every city in the country claimed importantly that "we are third down on Hitler's list to be bombed." Because of its shipyards and oil refineries, and because of the realistic fear of attack by submarine from the coast, Houston's claim was perhaps more valid than many. Indeed, the federal government was at first slow to award contracts to a city so near the coast, but Congressman Albert Thomas and the Houston Chamber of Commerce put an end to that.

Far more than many other American cities, Houston was in the vanguard of war production. In July, 1940, the Houston Shipbuilding Corporation had laid the first keels of thirty-seven Liberty Ships ordered by the U.S. Maritime Commission. It took 254 days to launch the first one. In the sudden buildup, most of the shipbuilders were new to the job. But soon they cut the time down to 53 days from keel to launch. The yard took on new workers. It had six thousand employees in March, 1942, and almost twenty thousand by July. They worked forty-eight to fifty-six hours a week.

Industries geared up. In 1940, the fourteen refineries along the ship channel had provided 11 percent of the nation's gasoline production. Working around the clock for four months at the Deer Park plant, Shell Oil turned out the country's first barrel of toluene in December. It then expanded to produce from two to ten million gallons a year. This petroleum product is used to make explosives. The War Department gave Humble Oil and Refining Company a $12 million contract to make toluene. The company would also make more than one billion gallons of aviation fuel during World War II. Houston was at the start of a soaring new career in petrochemicals. By 1945, investments in petrochemicals would amount to $600 million.

Hughes Tool Company spent more than $3.7 million to expand its plants and hired fifteen hundred new workers to make bomber parts. Reed Roller Bit produced airplane parts. The McEvoy Company made machine gun tripods. Early in 1941, Sheffield Steel Company began to build a steel plant. Cameron Iron Works made depth charges for antisubmarine warfare.

Hitler's *blitzkrieg* into Poland in 1939 had convinced Jim Abercrombie that war with Germany was inevitable, and he retooled Cameron Iron Works for war industry. It made roller turner attachments for turret lathes so well that Commander A. D. Blackledge of navy ordnance turned to Cameron to make the new, untested K-gun (a depth charge projector) and the arbors that the K-guns fire. With Herbert Allen and Ed Lorehn in charge, the company would make 14,826 of the K-guns between 1941 and 1945.

Oscar Holcombe, having stepped down as mayor, turned the Oscar Holcombe Construction Company into making hutments for the army, houses for the navy, and precut structures for shipment overseas.[1]

Anderson, Clayton was in a joint venture with Brown & Root to make eight-inch shells. On lathes supplied by the army, the Anderson, Clayton machine shop turned out shells, packed each in a separate wooden box, air freighted them to New York, and shipped them by fast ship to Le Havre. By 1944, they were going to General Patton's army in the Battle of the Bulge.

By 1944, the Eastern Seaboard desperately needed natural gas as fuel for home and factory. The Tennessee Gas Transmission Company of Houston (which would become Tenneco in 1966) was formed and within eleven months had completed and was operating a 1,265-mile gas pipeline to West Virginia.

Schlumberger organized the nonprofit Electro-Mechanical Research, Inc., for the United States Army and gave the army engineers the first prototype of a vehicular-mounted mine detector. As the war went on, the company developed mine detection equipment for the army, navy, and air force and designed a detector that recovered the 240-ton treasure of gold and silver that the

George and Herman Brown, whose shipyards won them a Navy E for excellence every year of the war. *Courtesy Isabel Brown Wilson (Mrs. Wallace S. Wilson)*

Bank of the Philippines had shoved over the cliff into the ocean at Corregidor.

Roger Hanquet, Schlumberger's general manager in Houston, was trained by the OSS to parachute into France before D-day to organize the French resistance forces. He was made an American citizen the night before his jump, and a second lieutenant the next day—both by overseas radio. He earned the Distinguished Service Cross for his months of work with the French underground.

Most contractors of the 1940s laid off construction workers whenever a project was finished, letting them find work elsewhere. Their only security lay in their labor union. Herman Brown kept his employees on the payroll. Most of the men at Brown & Root worked for the company on an annual contract, and the company ran an open shop. As a result, the Browns could take on a new project quickly.

Brown & Root had got into shipbuilding before the attack on Pearl Harbor. "The first contract was to build four pursuit crafts," George Brown recalled in an interview with Paul Bolton. Another Houston firm had held the contract for a year without producing even one. "Although we had never built a ship, we . . . had some good electrical engineers and mechanics and craftsmen from the Marshall Ford days. We took it on a lump sum price and had no idea whether it was high enough to make a profit or not."

The Browns formed the Brown Shipbuilding Company and invested $2 million in the Greens Bayou plant. By early 1941 they were building ships. The big test for George and Herman Brown came in 1942 when, on twenty-four hours' notice, they accepted a lump sum contract to deliver a specified number of much bigger ships at a specific price by a specific date.

Though materials were hard to get and workers scarce, Brown Shipbuilding amassed a force of twenty-five thousand men. Destroyer escorts and landing craft began to move down the ship channel on schedule.

Many of the shipyard workers came from the farms and small towns of East Texas and Louisiana and had never spent time in a big city. Brown Shipbuilding published a weekly journal of shipyard news—who had married, whose baby had been born, who had gone on a vacation, who had bought a house. The journal tied the twenty-five thousand families into a community within the far larger city of Houston. As John Boles, editor of the *Journal of Southern History* points out, the war years in Houston changed their lives. Though many would gladly return to the farms and small towns, it would be with different interests and aims. Others would stay on to make new careers in the city.

Until 1943, natural gas had little value. Companies removed the hydrocarbons and then pumped the dry gas into the ground for storage, or burned it off in flares. The silvery gold flames high in the air were a beautiful sight in the night on the oil field— and a horrendous waste. The Browns used natural gas to power the shipyard.

In 1944 and 1945, the Rice Hotel looked like an extension of the Navy Department with so many naval officers waiting for a landing craft or subchaser to be launched. Great Lakes shipbuilders complained that too many contracts were going to Gulf Coast shipyards. Secretary of the Navy Forrestal sent Leland Anderson of the negotiating section and a navy inspector to report on Brown & Root. Anderson's report was one page long. It said, in effect: Brown & Root has built the most ships at the least cost with the highest quality and in the best time of any shipyard under contract to the navy. The naval inspector's report was two inches thick and said same thing.

Before the war was over, George Brown said, Brown & Root's contracts with the navy totaled something in the neighborhood of a billion dollars. "We built 354 combat ships. Once we launched eight ships in one afternoon and had Speaker Rayburn and Secretary Frank Knox there to watch." Each war year while in the shipbuilding business Brown & Root won the Navy E for excellence, and at war's end, the Pacific Ocean was dotted with Houston-built ships.

By the war's end, Brown & Root was one of the biggest construction firms in the world. After the war, the Browns took on the cost-plus project of rebuilding U.S. bases on Guam. This was only the start of an even bigger future, ranging from NATO bases across western Europe to NASA's Manned Spacecraft Center in Houston.

Chapter Sixty-Six

V-Mail

HEADLINES and newsreels told the big story of World War II. Houston saw the war through the letters of its men and women in uniform. Houstonians learned to make the most of wispy sheets of folded paper called V-Mail. In them, those at home would sense adventure, danger, discomfort, humor, heroism, and tragedy.

Ernest Bel Fay was called to duty before Pearl Harbor because he had graduated from Harvard with a reserve commission as ensign. In 1938 Albert and Ernest Fay had started their own shipyard to build sailboats and in early 1941 had begun making boats for war. Ordered to the China Sea in the comparative peace of mid-1941, Ernest Fay asked for and got a deferment.

The *Houston Post* of January 25, 1942, reported the launching of a PC-501 by the Seabrook Yacht Corporation, "the first fighting craft completed on the Texas Gulf Coast since war with the Axis began." The little ship had a torpedo and could sink a battleship. The Fays were also making crash boats. But with the attack on Pearl Harbor, Ernie Fay was called up.

"All his friends gave him a wonderful farewell party at the Yacht Club," Carolyn Fay said. "Here was Ernie, the first to go, and his sailing friends wanted to give him the finest kind of send-off. They even gave him an official *sword!* An absolutely beautiful sword and scabbard. We were all weeping and carrying on. And then he got his orders the next day: Report to *Galveston!* They put him in charge of a *yacht.* They put some guns on it and he was in command of the yacht patrol out of Galveston. So we all moved to Galveston for a while."

This let-down did not last long. Soon Ernie Fay was commanding a subchaser in the gulf, then a destroyer escort in the Pacific. There he won the Legion of Merit because his ship, unaided, sank a Japanese submarine. Adm. Chester Nimitz awarded him the medal in the Pacific; the citation was signed by President Roosevelt.

Albert Bel Fay, who had earned his commission as ensign at Yale, spent three years on active duty, starting as commanding officer of a subchaser and ending the war as lieutenant senior grade on the U.S.S. *Yokes* at Okinawa.[1]

John T. Jones, Jr., was at the University of Texas when he was called to active duty as a cavalry officer in late 1940. He would serve fifty-eight months, rising from lieutenant to captain, moving from Fort Knox to Northern Ireland and England, then Algeria and Tunisia. On Valentine's Day, 1943, he was captured by the Germans in Tunisia.

"They flew us to Italy for fourteen days' quarantine to be sure we had no noxious diseases. Then they steamed all our clothing and washed us off and put us in trains to Germany. I went to Offlag 9a-z. Then in June they sent us by rail to Poland." Meanwhile the Red Cross had telegraphed Mr. and Mrs. Jones in Houston that their son was safe. His sweetheart, Winifred Small, was in Europe with the Red Cross, but to write to John, she had to send her letters to her mother in Austin, where her mother put them in a different envelope and sent them to John in prison camp.

"The Germans had all their Allied prisoners segregated by country and by rank. If you were an officer, you were not allowed to work. We spent most of our time plotting ways to get out. But where do you go from Central Poland? One man got all the way into Hungary before they picked him up." They were moved to a larger camp near Potsdam, where they were liberated by the Russians.

"They scared the hell out of us . . . taking our names and fingerprints. We were to be sent to Odessa on the Black Sea. So most of us escaped. I was in the same camp with Amon Carter, Jr., a guy I'd known at the university. In all the coming and going, Amon and I and a couple of other people from Texas got out and to American forces across the Elbe River with an old armored car. I think the first thing they gave us was the comic page from the *New York Tribune*."

Within months after the attack on Pearl Harbor, American transport pilots were shuttling across the Atlantic to ferry bombers to England. Boys barely through high school, who had never been out of the county before, were flying the Atlantic.

A third-generation Houstonian, David Westheimer was twenty-four and a Rice Institute graduate when he entered the air force. Within a year he was a first lieutenant stationed in North Africa. On December 19, 1942, the *Houston Post* announced that its former reporter, David Westheimer, was missing in action.

"David was shot down in a raid over Naples," his older brother Milton said. "He was a navigator on a B-24 based in Palestine. I was at my mother's house for dinner when the wire came that he was missing. The War Department said that the plane was seen to hit the water and break in two and there were some survivors. They could see them struggle in the water. Then a few weeks later, we got a call from a ham operator in South

America who had heard an amateur broadcast from Italy that the Italians had picked up the survivors. David's name was on the list."

David Westheimer spent two years in prison camp, first in Italy, then in Germany. "They allowed the family to send a package every two months, and it was strictly defined in size," David's brother said. Mrs. Westheimer could cram so much in the small package that the Red Cross sent her on a lecture tour to help other parents of prisoners.

David Westheimer returned home thin and ill. However, in years after, he not only used the experience to write *Von Ryan's Express*, which became a best selling novel and motion picture, but when called, went back to the air force in another war.[2]

The Bone Pile had been bachelor quarters for a succession of young men, including Lloyd Smith, Charlie Snead, Jake Hershey, Bill Motter, Ted Cooper, and McClelland Wallace. The attack on Pearl Harbor ended its story. An alumnus of the Bone Pile, Mac Wallace volunteered to the army early in 1942. Lieutenant Wallace spent most of the war in India and Burma laying a pipeline in the Himalayas. "It was to supply plane fuel for the Flying Tigers and motor fuel for trucks," he said. "We completed it about the time the war was over."

Finishing medical school in 1943, Edward Lillo Crain, Jr., interned briefly at Roosevelt Hospital, New York, before entering the U.S. Naval Reserve. At twenty-six, the slim doctor was attached to a Marine battalion of assault troops in the Pacific. In a short, brilliant military career, he earned the Navy Cross, the Silver Star, the Purple Heart, the Asiatic-Pacific Campaign Medal, two bronze service stars indicating participation in two major battles, and the World War II Victory Medal.

The Silver Star was awarded ". . . for conspicuous gallantry and intrepidity in actions as battalion surgeon of the Marine Infantry on Pelelieu Island. . . . Lieutenant Crain heroically attended the wounded while under heavy, concentrated enemy fire. . . . He was painfully wounded in the hand . . . but with great fortitude continuously worked throughout the day and night while under enemy artillery, mortar, and machine gun fire, giving aid and relief to the wounded . . . and conducting them to safety. After sixty hours of work under fire, despite his painful wound, he refused to leave his post until ordered to do so by his battalion commander. . . ."

The Japanese dug in to hold their Pacific islands. The Marine battalions invaded island after island in some of the most costly battles of the war. Lieutenant Crain was in the landing on Okinawa. On May 9, 1945, he saw that because of fierce fighting in a valley, the wounded were lying uncared for. His citation says, "Withering machine gun and mortar fire made it impossible for stretcher bearers to reach the wounded men . . . but he, with utter disregard for his own personal safety, went into the valley and administered medical aid. Moving from man to man through deadly machine gun crossfire . . . his untiring and skillful aid saved the lives of at least ten of the more critically wounded. Despite intensified fire . . . from enemy-held caves surrounding three sides of the valley, Lieutenant Crain cared for all the men, staying with them for over five hours until an amphibian tractor could be sent to evacuate the wounded." He was awarded the Navy Star—the highest honor the navy can give for extraordinary heroism in action. In his published resume, Dr. Crain makes no reference to World War II service.[3]

Finishing his architectural studies at Harvard, Hugo Neuhaus, Jr., turned in his final thesis on the Friday before the Sunday of the Pearl Harbor raid. On the Monday after, he volunteered to the Army Air Corps in Cambridge before heading home. By February, 1942, he was at Randolph Field, San Antonio. He was training to be a bomber pilot when he flunked the high altitude test. "The lack of oxygen incapacitated me. I couldn't pretend I was all right. So they washed me out of flight training."

He went to New Guinea as administrative officer of a bomber group. All his friends were in England or Europe, buying lovely and fascinating things, and he was in New Guinea. So he sent a signed, blank check to a friend in London and said, "Buy me something as a souvenir of the war." He had in mind a little something from Bond Street perhaps.

The friend discovered a set of flat silver, among the first ever made, so rare that it should have been in a museum. Glowingly, reverently, the friend described the purchase in the letter to Hugo. A young bachelor, with no plans for marriage at the time, Hugo Neuhaus was dismayed. Father, too, wrote to inquire with a degree of sternness if Hugo were aware that some person in London had cashed a check for $1,800 made out in an unknown handwriting but with Hugo's signature.[4] The silver, heavily insured, never arrived. The war ended. Hugo Neuhaus came home. The insurance company paid for the missing treasure. Neuhaus was blithe: he'd never wanted flat silver anyway.

In 1946, he opened an architecture office in Houston. He was an unusually handsome man—slender, with dark hair, dark eyes, and a singular sweetness and grace. In January, 1947, he and Mary Wood Farish were married.[5] And then one day, his father called to say that a very heavy wooden crate had arrived from England. It was the silver. When Hugo Neuhaus went to the insurance company to refund the payment, he was turned down. The company had already written off the loss.

Two days after the Pearl Harbor news, Tom Anderson reached New Orleans to volunteer. Navy intelligence was expanding and his application was quickly accepted. Meanwhile, Ernest Muller, the Anderson, Clayton Cotton Corporation's longtime executive in Paris, had been closing down European operations. At last he cabled the Houston office that he had collected most of the outstanding debts, had delivered the money to Switzerland, and was sailing for the United States.

Navy intelligence received word that a ship bound for New Orleans had a German spy aboard. Lieutenant Anderson was dispatched to the dock to investigate. He boarded the ship and gave a happy welcome: "Uncle *Ernest!*" The supposed German spy was the Swiss-born Mr. Muller whom all the Claytons and Andersons had known since childhood. After sea duty in the Atlantic, Lieutenant Commander Anderson left the service, four years to the day from his swearing in.

John H. Freeman, Jr., who was majoring in architecture, left Yale in 1943 to enter the Army Air Force. He was sent to the Bronx campus of New York University to study meteorology. "At the time," he said, "only five or six universities offered a degree in meteorology; N.Y.U. was considered the poorest in the field. Most of the cadets in the program were math and physics or engineering majors, and I graduated in June, 1944, at the bottom or next to the bottom of the class." He was posted to Ellington Field.

Then the air force decided to give a proficiency examination to all its meteorologists in the United States and Hawaii. When the results came in, an unbelieving Second Lieutenant Freeman was told that he had made the second highest score in the country. "In March, 1945, they said I was urgently needed in Manila," Freeman said. "From San Francisco to Manila took us forty-nine days. When I left, Roosevelt was president and we had wars going in Europe and Japan. When I landed, Truman was president and the war in Europe had ended. The whole world had changed."

In Manila he was told that he was to supervise the meteorology that the air force would need for the invasion of Japan. "And," said Mr. Freeman, "I didn't know any more than I had known when I graduated at the bottom of my class in the least-demanding meteorology school. Fortunately, the man on the job had been an insurance statistician, was good at geophysics, and knew what he was doing. He couldn't express himself very well. I at least knew enough meteorology to tell what he was trying to say and could say it for him. We made an effective team." They were never put to the test.

Back in Houston, the day came when John H. Freeman, Jr., met Dr. John C. Freeman, Jr. Comparing notes, they found that both had grown up in Montrose, sometimes living within a few blocks of each other. Both had been in air force meteorology during the war.

By this time, Dr. Freeman was a professor on the University of St. Thomas faculty with a growing reputation in the field of storm research. He had entered the air force with a Rice degree in math and physics and a masters in meteorology from Cal Tech. In the air force he had been weather officer in the Caribbean, in New Guinea, and—because of his obvious competence—at the Master Analysis Center in Washington. After the war, he earned his doctorate in meteorology at the University of Chicago. The only blot on his distinguished resume was a grade in the low seventies on the air force proficiency examination given to every meteorologist in the country in 1945.

In a military force that was supposed to depend entirely on serial numbers, John H. Freeman had been given John C. Freeman's test score.[6] Fortunately, the dropping of the A-bomb made an invasion of Japan unnecessary.

In Memoriam

ON APRIL 12, 1945, Franklin Delano Roosevelt died in Warm Springs, Georgia. As commander in chief he had lifted this nation out of inertia and isolationism. He had led the Allied forces against a global fascism that threatened world freedom. Now he was gone. Twenty-five days later, Nazi Germany surrendered unconditionally.

President Truman, Joseph Stalin, and Winston Churchill met in Potsdam to discuss the coming invasion of Japan. Two Houstonians were there: Will Clayton, assistant secretary of state, and Maj. Jubal E. Parton, chief of the U.S. delegation on reparations. They were present when the report came that the atomic bomb had exceeded all expectations in destructive power.

Civilians had been on the front lines of this war from the start. Nazi bombers had dropped tons of TNT on London, had flattened Coventry, had reduced Stalingrad to rubble. Allied bombers had smashed city after city in Germany. Italian planes had strafed refugees walking along country roads in France. But this was a new and more powerful weapon. On behalf of the allies, President Truman issued two warnings to Japan without effect. On August 5, a lonely plane dropped the atomic bomb on Hiroshima. Japan did not yield. On August 9, the second bomb smashed Nagasaki. On August 10, Japan sued for peace. The war that Japan had forced upon the United States was over.

The A-bombs destroyed two cities and killed thousands. By ending the war, they saved the lives of all those Japanese civilians who would have been in the path of Allied invasion and saved uncountable American and Allied lives in the invasion forces. V-J Day had come. Houston churches filled with people, prayerfully grateful.

Houston had learned the cruel cost of war early on. William Stamps Farish, Jr., was a superb horseman and polo player, but he entered the Army Air Corps as a flyer. When he was stationed in San Antonio, his wife Mary and small son Will joined him. With the roar of planes and formation flying, army air shows were inspiring. In 1943, flying in a San Antonio rally to sell war bonds, Billy Farish crashed and was killed. His wife and four-year-old son were in the stands watching.

Ray Lofton Dudley, Jr., born in Houston in 1919, grew up in the lovely house and garden the Dudleys called Oak Shadows.[1] Graduating from Princeton in 1941, he entered the navy as an ensign and returned to the Princeton Chapel to marry June Wooden.[2] Transferred to the Naval Air Station at Jacksonville, Florida, he finished Officers' Gunner School with high honors and applied for lighter-than-air duty. During the required physical examination, he was found to have cancer of the throat. He died in the Naval Hospital on November 20, 1943. He was twenty-four.

Bayard Turner Gross Dudley, the Dudleys' second son, was known by those who loved him as Bogie. He was blessed with "the wild joy of living." Born in 1922, he went to Houston schools, Choate, and Rice Institute. He was a cadet in the ROTC. He took civilian pilot training and loved flying. With the Japanese attack on Pearl Harbor, he volunteered to the air force.

In the months of his flight training – Fort Worth, San Angelo, Ellington Field – he met Carolyn Dodson. They were married in San Angelo in August, 1943. Two months later he captained a Flying Fortress across the Atlantic to England. In packing to go, he saved room for his beloved Victrola. After one bombing mission, he wrote: "How wonderful it is to be sitting in front of a fire, listening to Beethoven, after sweating it out with flak and Jerries for hours."

His letters to his wife were filled with plans for their future. As a married man and captain of his own Flying Fortress, Lieutenant Dudley had found maturity. He wrote that his roommate was asleep: "The poor kid is tuckered out. He's only twenty." Bogie was twenty-one.

In his first seven missions over Germany, Lieutenant Dudley had to bring two bombers limping back to base too badly shot up to fly again. On December 19, 1943, he received the long-delayed word of his brother's death and wrote home: "I always thought I'd teach Ray and Bill how to fly.[3] Now Ray is the one who'll be checking me out on a new set of wings. I hope it won't be soon . . . but nobody could be a better teacher than Ray."

On his eighth mission, on December 31, 1943, eight Nazi fighters attacked his ship. Badly damaged, with two engines aflame, and while he fought the controls to give his crew time to jump, the big bomber turned in a slow, lazy spiral downward. At fourteen thousand feet, it exploded. With four of his crewmen, Bayard Dudley is buried in the little village of Lesperon, south of Bordeaux.

Ryland Howard, son of Dr. and Mrs. A. Philo Howard, had gone into the Field Artillery before Pearl Harbor. While stationed in West Texas, he married Edith Anson in San Angelo and they had a son, also named Ryland. Lieutenant Howard transferred to the air force and by 1944 was stationed in England. After D-Day, he was flying a reconnaissance plane over enemy lines near the French coast when he was shot down over St.-Lo. It was July 4, 1944. He was barely thirty.

Jimmy Anderson, the oldest son of Mr. and Mrs. James Anderson, was at Texas A&M University when World War II began. He volunteered to the air force and by 1944 he was based in North Africa, flying a P-47 in missions over Italy. His squadron was skip-bombing in the Italian hills when one bomb failed to release. He flew back over the sea to bail out and was seen floating safely on a life raft. But a sudden Mediterranean squall blew up. His body was washed ashore. Born in 1921, he died November 19, 1944. He was twenty-three.

Lamar Fleming III, known as Billy and the oldest son of Mr. and Mrs. Lamar Fleming, was studying aeronautical engineering at Massachusetts Institute of Technology during the Battle of Britain. Already a flier, he very much wanted to leave school and join the Royal Canadian Air Force but was delayed by the need for minor surgery. After Pearl Harbor, he volunteered to the U.S. Air Force. He had hoped to be a fighter pilot, but he was assigned to fly a B-26, the Martin Marauder – a fast, stubby plane with short wings, twin engines, and fast takeoff. It was a tactical bomber used to hit military objectives. During the Battle of the Bulge, the winter weather was so bad that the airmen could not provide the needed air cover. When it cleared, they flew mission after mission. The situation was desperate.

On one mission, as they flew at low level, antiaircraft fire took its toll on the whole squadron. Perhaps his plane had flown too far, perhaps the fuel tanks had been damaged. Billy Fleming got his Marauder almost back to base when he saw that he could not make it. He ordered all aboard to bail out, which they did, but he apparently realized that there had been no response from McNulty, the tail gunner. Fleming tried to bring the crippled plane down, crashed, and was killed on December 27, 1944. He was twenty-three. The next day, the German drive was stopped.

Hubert Roussel, Jr., slender as his father, had grown up on Brompton in West University, going to Poe, Lanier, and Lamar. He was a happy and determined athlete. He founded and trained the Roussel Runts, a forerunner of Little League in his West University neighborhood. "He was given that complete love of nature that makes the storm as acceptable as the sunshine," his father wrote. He left Texas A&M to volunteer to the air force. As an aerial gunner, he flew on one of the earliest B-29 bombers in the Pacific. In letters home he wrote, "It is good to look down on the earth from a great height. It seems then so peaceful and orderly." In December, 1944, his plane was shot down over Saipan. He would have been twenty-one years old on January 10, 1945.

Dick Mayo Lykes had grown up on Remington Lane, going to Poe School and Lanier, singing in the choir at Palmer Memorial Church. Dicko left Washington and Lee to enter the navy. He went to the Pacific where, on April 14, 1945, his ship came under air attack. Ensign Lykes was in command of the twenty-two men in the rear gun battery when a Japanese plane that they had shot down fell on their ship—slicing away the stern and all on it. He was twenty-one.

Mr. and Mrs. Ray Dudley lost two sons within forty-one days. Privately, for a few close friends, they published two small books: the first, *In Memoriam, Ray Lofton Dudley, Jr.* and the second, merely *Bogie*. Of the second, composed largely of letters from Bayard and about him, Frederica Dudley wrote: "I could feel only bewilderment and despair. How was it possible to portray the joyous, gallant, clear-thinking, completely dedicated young lad as he really was? . . . He knew so clearly why and for what he went forth to offer and, if need be, to give his life. It is because I feel that he is so typical of so many 'young knights in shining armor' that

I have endeavored in the selection of letters to show him just as he was: filled with the joy of living, highly confident that he would come back, but with an almost religious zeal about his flying and doing the job well. The gradual evolution of the adventure loving lad into the calm, dignified man dedicated to the task of restoring to mankind peace, freedom and the right to happiness is here; the facing of death, unafraid; the ultimate triumph of the human spirit."

On what would have been his son's twenty-first birthday, Hubert Roussel wrote in the *Houston Post* of the challenge of his son's life and death.

He went to his death for what he loved, doing the hard duty he chose for himself, as thousands of other typical American boys have done in this battle for decency.[4]

In a sense they were all my boys; in a sense my own boy belonged as much to every family in this country as he did to me. I have wept for the others as I have wept for him, but we can not repay them in tears. We can only resolve, with all the fury and fire in our souls . . . to win the victory for which they died, and having won it, to secure the peace in which they truly believed—a peace that will actually make the world better and safer, and not merely a training ground for another generation of youth to be slaughtered at the whim of warmakers.

The voice of the dead in this struggle is the most terrible command ever given the races of man. . . . Let it ring in the ears of politicians and statesmen, and let us see that they never escape it.

Billy . . . Ray . . . Bogie . . . Ryland . . . Jimmy . . . Lamar . . . Hubert . . . Dicko . . . the few typical of the many. They had their counterparts throughout the nation. Between December 7, 1941, and December 31, 1946, 407,316 Americans in uniform were killed.[5] Houston suffered heavy losses in the generation that would have given it leaders well up to its sesquicentennial year.

Will Clayton and the Marshall Plan

IN JUNE, 1946, Congress voted to create a new post in government: undersecretary of state for economic affairs. It was created for Will Clayton. This was in simple recognition of what he had been doing for some time. The work he did would lead directly to the Marshall Plan and, beyond, to the birth of the European Common Market.

William Lockhart Clayton was everything that a diplomat should be. Charming, with a beautiful speaking voice, with white hair and black brows, he was remarkably handsome. At six foot four inches, he had the lean, graceful walk of a Gary Cooper. More, he had the Southern courtesy of his upbringing. It was not punctilious courtesy. It was a natural expression of his gentle concern about the comfort and welfare of others. No person walking with him could ever go through a door *after* him. When any woman entered the room, he stood in an easy courtesy to be sure that she had a chair. In rare occasions when he grew angry during a negotiation, he became more and more polite, icily polite.[1] A master of the English language in speech and writing, a man of broad education, he had the gift for explaining complex issues in logical simplicity. His humor was quiet. His twinkle contagious. When it was time to put work aside, he knew how to enjoy good company. His staff always started out by loving him and grew quickly to respect him to a degree bordering on hero worship.

Will Clayton had been outstanding all his life. Each year he built anew upon his cumulative experiences and comprehensive reading. A State Department official noticed that in congressional hearings, Clayton always recalled every point made by earlier witnesses and replied aptly to each. As a statesman, he regularly used the shorthand he had learned for his first job in Jackson, Tennessee. In overseas conferences, he used the French he had taught himself as a twenty-year-old cottonman in New York City. And from all his years in international business, he remembered the productive land and factories of pre-war Europe. He could see what war had done to that productivity.

From the days of Cordell Hull, whose belief in free trade he shared, Will Clayton had worked closely with every successive secretary of state – Edward Stettinius, James Byrnes, and George Marshall. In 1944, Stettinius named him assistant secretary of state for economic affairs. Clayton was chairman of the economics section of the U.S. delegation at Chapultepec in February, 1945, and at Potsdam in July. And starting in 1945, he was chief of the U.S. delegation at the various council sessions of UNRRA.[2] When France was liberated in mid-1945, he went to Paris to meet with Jean Monnet and arrange to ship food to France.

Britain needed help in rebuilding just as urgently as it had needed help in war. Shortly after V-J Day, Clayton went to London to negotiate a loan to Britain and returned to Washington to convince Congress that the United States should lend $3.75 billion. In July, 1946, Congress approved the British Loan; President Truman signed the bill.

As undersecretary of state, Clayton

Will Clayton, 1940s.

It was soon apparent that the Soviet Union saw opportunity in the ruins. What the Bolshevik revolution had done for Communism in Russia, the destruction of war and weather might very well do for the spread of Communism in Western Europe. Individually and together, State Department officials tried to plan what could be done to restore Europe as a continent governed by law and able to raise the food and manufacture the goods it needed.

As a man who had been in international business for more than forty years and president of the world's largest cotton company, Will Clayton saw the corporate destruction of Europe as no general or ambassador was likely to do. Further, he knew that unless Europe could be restored, the United States would be at a loss for markets. Without the European buying power, the United States would soon slump into an even worse depression than that of the 1930s.

In the winter that blighted European farmlands, Will Clayton saw that the United States must make a bigger, more comprehensive effort. He brought economist Norman Ness over from the Export-Import Bank to head the financial and development policy division.[3] "In February," Ness said, "I asked my section heads to name the five countries . . . that were in the most desperate straits. But the figure came out nine. We couldn't name *only* five. Nine countries— France, Italy, Austria, Belgium, Holland, Germany, Britain, Greece and Luxembourg —were all in desperate straits."

Meanwhile, Will Clayton had made his own observations. On March 5, 1947, flying to Tucson, Arizona, he drafted a historic memorandum: "The reins of world leadership are fast slipping from Britain's competent but now very weak hands. These reins will be picked up either by the United States or by Russia. If by Russia, there will almost certainly be war in the next decade or so, with the odds against us. . . . The United States must take world leadership, and quickly, to avert world disaster.

"In every country . . . Russia is boring

roamed Europe and the Americas on the business of his government. Wherever he went, he saw more clearly the wreckage of a once prosperous continent. All who traveled Western Europe in the first months after the German surrender were horrified by the damage. The United States responded with big loans to Britain, France, Greece, and Turkey. UNRRA delivered food and other essentials. Americans sent a flow of food parcels across the Atlantic to friends, relatives, and strangers. Then came the terrible winter of 1946–47, when seeds froze in the ground and blizzards blocked shipments. This was followed by a long summer drought.

from within. This is a new technique. . . . We must cope with it, and quickly, or face the greatest peril of our history. . . . Nations whose integrity and independence are vital to our interests and to our security are on the very brink and may be pushed over at any time. . . ."

Meeting with foreign ministers on postwar treatment of Germany and Austria, Secretary Marshall realized that the Russians were stalling. With delay, Moscow could gain time for hunger to grow in Europe. General Marshall warned America that Europe was in danger. "Disintegrating forces are becoming evident. The patient is sinking while the doctors deliberate."

In late March, Mr. and Mrs. Clayton sailed on the *Queen Elizabeth* for London. Mr. Clayton was due in Geneva by April 11 to head the U.S. delegation to the multinational negotiations that would result in the General Agreement on Tariffs and Trades (GATT). In Geneva, he heard distressing accounts of food shortages. Conditions were worsening.

Ivan White, first secretary and economic counsel of the U.S. Embassy in Paris, saw Clayton in Geneva and listened to his thoughts on what needed to be done. White said that it "was closely paralleled later in General Marshall's talk. It was apparent to Ambassador Caffery and me that Will Clayton's thinking and planning really pioneered the Marshall Plan." In late April, Secretary Marshall called George F. Kennan, a specialist in Soviet affairs, to head a group of men to plan European recovery, all of whom had read Clayton's first long memorandum.

The Claytons flew home on May 18. They were in the air twenty-four hours. After six weeks in Europe, Will Clayton was even more deeply concerned. Nine countries were on the verge of collapse. Revolution and chaos would be next. On the long Atlantic flight, he wrote a more urgent memorandum. In strong, simple language, he made his points: Without prompt and massive aid from the United States, Europe would collapse, jeopardizing the future peace and

security of the world. Europe's economic collapse would have immediate, disastrous effects upon the American economy.

He brushed aside Bernard Baruch's proposal for a commission to study Europe's need and America's assets. "Our resources and our productive capacity are ample to provide all the help necessary." The president and secretary of state, Clayton wrote, must "make a strong spiritual appeal to the American people to sacrifice a little themselves, to draw in their own belts just a little, in order to save Europe from starvation and chaos . . . and at the same time to preserve for ourselves and our children the glorious heritage of a free America."

Will Clayton estimated that Europe needed six or seven billion dollars in goods every year for three years, chiefly in coal, food, and shipping services. This three-year grant, he said, should be based on a European economic federation worked out by the European nations under leadership of Britain, France, and Italy. "Europe cannot recover from this war and again become independent if her economy continues to be divided into many small, watertight compartments as it is today."

On May 27, he sent his memorandum to Dean Acheson, with a request to see Secretary Marshall. His personal report was even more compelling. He could speak of whole families living in caves near shattered Naples, of babies born in the caves. He spoke of peasants unwilling to raise farm crops for the cities because there was nothing to buy with the proceeds. He told of factories lacking fuel to make the buttons or thread or shoes the peasant wanted to buy. He spoke of "the millions of persons slain, the cities destroyed, the shipping sunk, the railways and bridges broken, the machinery worn or obsolete, the fields long starved for fertilizer."

Dean Acheson later recalled the intensity and detail with which Clayton described what he had seen. "Not only Acheson but others in the department testify to the vividness and impressiveness of Clayton's recitals during those days, to the sense of urgency he imparted for taking immediate action," Joseph M. Jones wrote in *The Fifteen Weeks*. "He was probably one of the most direct and important influences in the 'triggering' of the Secretary's speech at Harvard."

General Marshall accepted Harvard's invitation to speak on June 6 and used the occasion to deliver the Truman administration's answer to the new global crisis. This was the historic Marshall Plan speech.[4] The speech was quiet. Using much of the language of the Clayton memorandum, Secretary Marshall described the conditions that threatened the stability of the European continent and of the world. The United States would help Europe, he said, if the European nations could agree on a plan and work together to rebuild.

As Clayton wrote later, "In the simplest terms, it is a proposal that America . . . enable these people to continue to eat and work until they can stand on their own feet." But it was also a challenge. "This is the business of the Europeans," Secretary Marshall said. "The initiative, I think, must come from Europe. The role of this country should consist of friendly aid in the drafting of a European program and of later support of such a program so far as it may be practical for us to do so."

The Harvard address might have gone almost unnoticed. But Undersecretary Acheson had alerted the chief London correspondents in Washington to telephone the whole speech immediately to London, getting it there days ahead of the diplomatic pouch from the embassy. "The response to Marshall's speech was immediate, electrifying the free world," President Truman wrote in his memoirs. Britain's Foreign Minister Ernest Bevin and French Foreign Minister Georges Bidault cabled Secretary Marshall that they would take the initiative he had suggested.

Secretary Marshall sent Will Clayton to Paris to make the U.S. position quite clear on two points: 1) The recipients of Marshall Plan must not only organize themselves into a committee of cooperation, but must agree

to continue that cooperation after the aid should end. 2) This committee should work out the measure and mechanics of the aid and present a plan to the United States.

George Kennan's policy planning staff had made an important contribution: That the United States must not be the instrument to divide Europe. Therefore, Secretary Marshall made the offer to all European countries – the Soviet Union included. "Our policy," he said, "is directed not against any country or doctrine, but against hunger, poverty, desperation and chaos." Poland and Czechoslovakia cabled Washington their wish to be included in the Marshall Plan.

Promptly, Bevin and Bidault invited Soviet Foreign Minister Molotov to meet with them in Paris. But Moscow had no wish to see the European nations coming together in peace as they had in war. Molotov, therefore, rejected the requirement of European cooperation. He withdrew, taking the reluctant satellites with him. Moscow began a propaganda campaign to picture the Marshall Plan as a dastardly American trick. Europe was then and there divided – but not by any American move.

With the Russians out, Britain and France called a meeting of sixteen nations of Western Europe in Paris in July. They were Austria, Belgium, Britain, Denmark, Eire, France, Greece, Iceland, Italy, Luxembourg, the Netherlands, Norway, Portugal, Sweden, Switzerland, and Turkey. Their delegates formed the Committee on European Economic Cooperation – CEEC – to draw up an economic program for themselves and West Germany. Sir Oliver Franks was chairman. Thus was launched what Winston Churchill called "the most unsordid act in history."

Many men in the State Department worked on the plan for European recovery. President Truman was the first to give it Secretary Marshall's name. Will Clayton never claimed the Marshall Plan as his own. He thought of it as his government's answer to the threat of world chaos.

But those closest to the scene again and again make it clear that his were the idea, the driving force, and the practical application.

"It was Will Clayton's audacity of imagination," Norman Ness said in retrospect. "August, 1947. World crisis. If there was to be leadership it had to come from us and we were fortunate to have a man in the White House who could take it. For us there was consolation in knowing Clayton was over us, and there must have been for him in knowing Truman was over him."

Emilio Collado, who at the time was the U.S. director of the International Bank, said: "Clayton was superior to other economists in that inside his head he had a clear, simple notion of where he ought to go. It was like a brightly lit-up lane inside him. He could make compromises, for he was a reasonable man and a man of the world, but, having made the compromise, he did not take off from that point on the next problem. On the next problem, he came back to his fundamental concept again. Since he retired from the government, there has never been another person like him."

After the 1950s, Americans grew accustomed to an endless flow of foreign aid to other countries. But in June, 1947, this was startling new language. No country had ever done what the United States proposed to do. The *London Observer* said, "In the whole history of the world, no continent has ever offered to save another from economic catastrophe."

The dry summer sent Europe's economy further on its downward spiral. France had the lowest wheat yield since the days of Napoleon. Paris was gray. It had had no new coat of paint in eight years. Doors still bore bullet holes from the Nazi occupation. But there was hope in the air. Paris was buoyant. As the delegates of sixteen nations met in the Grand Palais, Will Clayton was at the center of the negotiations. He, U.S. Ambassador Lewis D. Douglas, and Ambassador Jefferson Caffery were the "friendly aid in

the drafting" that Secretary Marshall had offered. One by one, each nation had to put the common good ahead of national interests, had to sign the treaties that would make the vast plan work. By summer's end, Europe had met the Marshall Plan challenge.

In a partisan and competitive city like Washington, nobody is revered by everybody. Will Clayton had his share of opponents and snipers. During the summer and fall of 1947, Will Clayton and the European recovery plan had opposition. The remarkable thing is how little.

In December President Truman proposed adoption of the Marshall Plan to Congress. It was understood, he said, that European recovery could be achieved within four years at a cost of some $17 billion. To restore decent living standards in Europe would cost 5 percent of what the United States had spent in the war against the Axis, or 3 percent of our total national income in the four-year period. "The estimates of the experts," President Truman said, "showed that it was well within the capacity of the American people to undertake."

Throughout the talks in Paris, and with congressional approval, Clayton held the delegates to two main goals: To reduce international trade barriers and to make the kind of concerted effort Europe had not made in modern times. Lowered tariffs and a cooperative economy would be the start toward the European Economic Community, the European Common Market. Toward a restored and united Europe.

Michael Hoffman wrote in the *New York Times Magazine* of September 21, 1947:

For nearly five months . . . the United States has been represented in Europe by William Lockhart Clayton. . . . He has been the dominating figure in the international tariff discussions. In Paris . . . his has been the voice of America at the sixteen nation conference on the Marshall Plan. . . . Because of his white hair, his bronzed profile, his height towering above the average European, he is a marked man wherever he goes.

Having turned his knowledge of economic

forces with spectacular success to his own advantage, it is small wonder that Clayton has more confidence than most men in his ability to exploit these forces for the greater good of mankind. . . . He is probably the only man who ever created a $75 million business and lived to hear himself denounced as an impractical dreamer. . . . The ideas behind the plan are Clayton's. Up to now Clayton *is* the Marshall Plan.

Will Clayton in 1947 was better known across Europe than in the United States. Many Europeans saw him as the man who brought salvation. In this period, several nations—Britain and Denmark among them—managed to adopt an economic system of socialism without giving up their political system of democracy. Having voted in socialism, they could, if they chose, vote it out again. But the Soviet brand of Communism, wherever it spread, put the people under the iron clamp of totalitarian government—Poland, Hungary, Czechoslovakia, and East Germany.

As chief architect of the Marshall Plan, Will Clayton did as much as any one person could do to save Western Europeans from succumbing to Soviet Communism, to save them for the free world. President Truman and Sec. George Marshall who held the ultimate responsibility, the Foreign Service officers in the European capitals, the State Department staff, and the generous American spirit—all combined to bring about the miracle of European recovery. But it was Will Clayton who saw the damage, understood what it meant, knew what had to be done, outlined the solution, and made others see what he saw. Rarely has this country had a statesman who so completely filled the role destiny had assigned him.

Chapter Sixty-Nine

Suite 8-F

EIGHT-F. Suite 8-F of the Lamar Hotel. To longtime Houstonians, the number and letter conjure up legends of power plays, fabulous deals secured by a shake of the hand, political choices made by friendly consensus. The legends are never sinister. Somehow, the happy band that frequented 8-F were the most trusted leaders in town. Basically they met to have a good time. Everyone assumed—with accuracy—that when they proposed and planned, Houston's best interests would be served.

From 8-F would come plans for a quail shoot in West Texas or the annual trip to the Kentucky Derby. But also from 8-F came the decision on which candidates they would back, a multimillion-dollar deal on a pipeline, the purchase of land for a future airport to be sold back to the city at cost when the time came, and ultimately, the placement of NASA's Manned Spacecraft Center.

Eight-F was the Browns' suite. Though Brown & Root's main office was in Houston, Herman Brown continued to live in Austin until 1948. He would come down for a few days in the middle of the week and then go back to Austin for the weekend. The Browns rented Suite 8-F to give Herman a place to stay. The whole family used it.

"There was one year when Mike and I were little that we spent quite a bit of time in 8-F," Louisa Stude Sarofim said. "Aunt Maggie had to be in Houston for treatment of her pulmonary difficulties and Mike and I had the Lamar Hotel to romp in. We were like Eloise at the Plaza."[1]

Frank Oltorf, who was for years Brown & Root's representative in Washington, tells the story of 8-F:

It had two bedrooms and Margarett and Alice furnished it. One of the nice things about it was that it was so simply furnished. Antiques, but nothing showy, nothing flashy. It was a very warm, unostentatious apartment.

Herman loved having friends and cronies. He liked to know what people were thinking and keep his ear to the ground. Brown & Root closed every day at 5:15 and various friends would come up to 8-F for a social hour. His man Ralph Fox would fix drinks. They would laugh and have a good time. It was a social thing. But of course it became a center for making plans for politics and business things, like organizing Texas Eastern.

Eight-F was the home of many an important out-of-town guest. If they were negotiating with Standard Oil of California and if its president came, they would put him up in 8-F. Lyndon Johnson often stayed there.

Eight-F was quite a different thing from 7-F. Seven-F was Gus Wortham's Lamar Hotel suite where he, Jesse Jones, and Col. Joe Evans played bridge every Wednesday and Saturday.

"Between Judge Elkins, Gus Wortham, Jim Abercrombie, Jesse Jones, Jim West, Will Clayton, Oscar Holcombe, Roy Cullen, Governor Hobby, and the Browns," Posh Oltorf said, "they ran the politics of Houston in the 1930s and 40s."[2]

By the 1930s, Judge James A. Elkins was a quiet power in Houston. One of his admirers once said, "Judge doesn't practice law, he practices influence." In this case, the word influence meant force of ideas, of will, of persuasion to get the best things done in the most efficient way. If he or anyone else came up with a good idea, Judge Elkins was inclined to reach for the phone and get the thing attended to before the day was out.

His friend Naurice Cummings said: "He could always give you all the time you needed. If you asked for something, he attended to it immediately. He had a knack for getting people to do things. And to do it *today*. One time the National Supply Company [Cummings's company] wanted to build a steel plant on the ship channel, and I went to Judge Elkins. He got on the phone and in thirty minutes had located property owned by Tilford Jones that was exactly what we wanted." This was typical. Years later and with similar speed, Judge Elkins brought W. Albert Lee and Gov. and Mrs. W. P. Hobby together for the sale of Lee's television station to the Hobbys' KPRC.

Though Oscar Holcombe had won his first election on his own, the crew of 8-F liked his performance as mayor and backed him in a number of later elections. Though they did not always agree on a candidate, all of them supported Sam Rayburn, most of them supported John Nance Garner. While they were unanimous in support of Franklin Roosevelt against Herbert Hoover, the group split on that colorful and controversial leader as he headed for a third term. George Brown supported FDR to the end.

From his days as a congressman, Lyndon Johnson was a welcomed visitor and, from those visits, usually received generous backing. Eight-F believed, with reason, that LBJ had been rooked out of the Senate seat by Pappy O'Daniel forces in the election of 1941.

In his biography of Jim Abercrombie, Dr. Patrick Nicholson tells of a gathering in 8-F in honor of Beauford Jester, the Democratic nominee for governor. LBJ was there. The grapevine had it that W. Lee O'Daniel would not run again for the Senate, and Herman Brown asked Mr. Jim what he thought of LBJ's making a second try. LBJ sometimes lamented the fact that he was often called a "tool of the oil industry" outside of Texas and "a wild-eyed liberal" when he sought campaign funds in some quarters of his own

state. The 8-F endorsement would help him, both in votes and in contributions.

Johnson ran for the Senate with full 8-F backing. "One of his best fund-raising sessions was held on the top floor of the Kentucky Hotel in Louisville, as the group gathered for their traditional weekend at the Kentucky Derby," Dr. Nicholson wrote.

Judge Elkins was famous for putting a bet on every starter. He had just come out ahead after severe losses in the traditional crap game. When Jet Pilot won, Judge Elkins was so pleased that he gave all his winnings to Herman Brown for the LBJ war chest and promised a substantial contribution as well. Everyone else followed suit. Congressman Johnson became Senator Johnson in the famous eighty-seven-vote win over Coke Stevenson.

"Every year 8-F went to the Kentucky Derby," Posh Oltorf said, "Jim Abercrombie, Judge Elkins, Jesse Jones, Gus Wortham, Jakie Freedman, George and Herman Brown, Milo Abercrombie, Naurice Cummings, William Smith. They would stay two or three days, and LBJ and Senator Russell and maybe one or two other senators would fly over and join them."

Posh Oltorf and Lyndon Johnson were frequently asked about the Brown brothers —brothers so close, both white-haired, both so courteous in the old Southern fashion. "They were remarkable men," Oltorf said. "They had a complete devotion to each other, and their lives were so interwoven it is hard to tell where one started and the other began. The Brown partnership agreement was the most amazing thing I ever saw. Everything they owned, they owned together, fifty-fifty—except their homes and personal possessions like their wives' jewelry. If Herman bought a share of stock in his name, George would automatically own half of it. If George bought a farm, it would be half Herman's. I asked Herman about it."

Herman Brown explained to Oltorf: "Brown & Root takes up so much time. If George were out doing something else, I might feel he's spending more time doing things for himself than for us, and if I were out, he might feel the same way. This way, always, anything we do is being done for both of us."

"That was the whole spirit of the thing," Oltorf said.

Now, there was never any doubt that the final decision was left to Herman. George was the younger brother. Herman had founded the firm, and George had a tremendous respect for him. I always felt that George was the idea man. He could come up with ten very unusual ideas and Herman would shoot eight of them down as being ridiculous. He would then jump on the other ones and *off* the two would go. George had this tremendous imagination and would come up with tremendous ideas. Herman was very practical.

George was very much at home in New York and Washington and with the presidents of the large corporations. Herman preferred the Austin and Houston business community. But he could charm anyone. Both of them could. George was more diplomatic. Herman could be tough.

One day Herman Brown showed Posh Oltorf a letter from an old man who wrote: "Dear Mr. Brown: I am not sure you will remember me, but back when you were building roads near Rogers, I had a feed store and I sold you feed on credit to feed your mules. I am in a low state of income, ill, and I am in a rest home. But I think about the old days and I hope this letter finds you well and prosperous."

"I imagine he hopes I'm more prosperous than well," said Herman Brown with a grin. "But I remember the old man, just as though it were yesterday."

Not until after Herman Brown's death did Oltorf hear the end of the story: Herbert Frensley, the Browns' friend and treasurer of the company at the time, was also shown the letter that day.[3] Brown said, "Herbert, find out where this old man is and send him two hundred dollars a month for the rest of his life."

"That," said Posh Oltorf, "was typical of Herman."

"They were all like that," he said, continuing his commentary on the 8-F cast of char-

acters. "The thing that interests me so is the way they *believed* in philanthropy. They not only believed in philanthropy, but if you didn't contribute to the cultural life of Houston, you were a poor citizen. They would call on anybody within their organization and assign them to work. All of them supported worthwhile causes for the arts, but when it came to the arts, Gus Wortham liked to get on the phone and raise money himself. He believed as strongly as any man I ever knew in the cultural promotion of Houston. He wanted to hear the symphony play. He'd go to the ballet and knew something about it. He was just one of the most elegant gentlemen I ever knew. . . . Governor Hobby had the driest wit of any of them. So much of Governor can't be captured in a book, because he talked with his eyes and his little throw-away lines. He was such a delightful man."

All the 8-F men who were so intent on Houston's welfare were comparative newcomers. From the days of the Republic, in every generation, the newcomers have come in, blended with Old Houston, gained tradition, and lent vitality for new growth.

In 1946, with the war over, the War Assets Administration declared the Big Inch and the Little Big Inch pipelines surplus and put them up for sealed-bid auction. The two lines had been built by the government in 1942 to carry oil to the East Coast and had cost $160 million.

The story goes that in Suite 8-F one afternoon, the usual group of friends had gathered. Among them were Judge Elkins, Charles Francis, and Wharton Weems—all from the Vinson, Elkins & Weems law firm —as well as Gus Wortham, Jim Abercrombie, and the Browns.

Judge Elkins said, "George, why don't you buy the pipe lines and put gas through them?"

Brown later said, "We had the background of the pipeline and the ambition to be in the gas business. We did a lot of research on it." The Browns asked the engineers at their Greens Bayou plant to see if it would be cheaper to convert these pipelines to gas or to lay new ones. The engineers favored using the existing lines.

The group moved accordingly. The Browns founded Texas Eastern Transmission Company with Charles Francis of Vinson, Elkins & Weems handling the legalities. The chums of 8-F became stockholders, as did others. When the time came, Francis carried a sealed bid for $143,127,000 to Washington. It was by far the highest bid, and the Brown brothers were now in the oil and gas business.[4] A month later, Texas Eastern announced its plans to spend $40 million to add compressors and other equipment that would triple the flow of gas through the lines to 425 million cubic feet a day.

All this stemmed from a pleasant agreement in 8-F. This was not the last or the biggest of their constructive plottings.

Chapter Seventy

A Fairy Story

ON A Friday afternoon in 1945, nobody noticed that a small Houstonian went out to the municipal airport, boarded a plane, and flew off into a new life. Louisa Stude was seven. Ever since the birth of her brother, her mother had been quite ill. In the pressures of wartime, her father, Micajah Stude, had found it increasingly difficult to cope. At one time in her early childhood, Louisa Stude Sarofim remembers being in an orphanage in the big house on the Baker Estate.[1] "It was a wonderful house for small children, and the park with the big oak trees was a lovely place to play." Apparently this refuge closed, and she was staying with her father's friends, the Dewitt Gordons, when she began to receive letters from Mrs. Herman Brown of Austin.[2]

Margarett Brown invited Louisa to come to Austin for a visit. Louisa accepted. On the flight, Louisa said to her new friend, "I have a brother who lives in Austin." Mike was four. She had no memory of having seen him. From a very early age, Mike had been in the care of the Seton sisters. The next day Mrs. Brown went to the nuns to ask for Mike. For the first time, Louisa and Mike could be together.

"Sunday was fried chicken day and I remember Uncle Herman pounding on the table and talking politics. He bought me a watch and a funny little camera." Before the visit ended, Mrs. Brown asked Louisa if she and Mike would like to come live with her and Mr. Brown. Louisa said she would like that. And thus was formed the family that the Browns had always wanted and never

before had. Micajah Stude, however, continued to be a warm part of his children's lives.

Margarett Root was born in Taylor and went to Southwestern in Georgetown, where she met Herman Brown. "He was cooking behind a counter," Mrs. Sarofim said. "Next he went to make vegetable soup for the mule team. That's how he got into construction. When they were married, she transferred to the University of Texas. But she loved her independence. She never wore her wedding ring."

Unfortunately, from an early age, Mrs. Brown was plagued by bronchial problems. "Before we came along, they had some wonderful times. She had done the Andes in defiance of the altitude, though she had to have some special medication to do it. Then they went to Europe, because of Uncle Herman's German heritage. Though I think she entered art through history and reading, Munich perhaps stimulated her interest. Of course, Aunt Alice (Mrs. George Brown) had a great eye for beauty and for art. Later Aunt Alice became her best friend in Houston. But Aunt Maggie's life was more intellectual. She read constantly."

Alice Brown's daughter Isabel was in school at St. Mary's Hall in San Antonio. "Aunt Maggie loved for her to come to Austin and would read out loud to her while she ate green plums. There was a special bond between them. Aunt Maggie was forty-seven when she took us, I believe, and never well from that very first Friday on the plane. In Austin she had a tilted bed with oxygen handy. But she loved fashion. Dressmaking began at once. I remember my first dress was of black taffeta with a beautiful lace collar, and I had lots of dresses with smocking."

After taking on the two small children, Margarett Brown became a tremendously stimulating figure in their lives. "We spent the first summer in Cuernavaca. I had to learn my multiplication tables. Lawrence and Nettie Favrot were there and their children spoke only Spanish. But Aunt Maggie thought we should see America first, so the next summer we went to Santa Fe and the summer after to Wyoming."

When the Browns bought Fort Clark, Louisa and Mike could have all their friends out to visit. Louisa Sarofim said:

She was very strong in self-discipline. She got up every morning and took care of that mob of teenagers. But we learned to make beds *well* and to shell peas. She seemed to have great height in my respect and awe and amazement at this phenomenal person.

She was indomitable. Every morning of our lives, she got up to be at the breakfast table with Mike and me and to say goodbye to us when we went to school.[3] She was an older mother. She tried to do all possible in exercise and diet to stay healthy and young. She had

beauty of a sort. She had *looks*. She had a wonderfully perverse sense of humor that not all of my friends enjoyed. But she was a stimulation to all the group growing up when I did.[4] She had a great belief in education. We had Spanish lessons and piano lessons. She was interested in pictures and books and discipline. We always had fun, but it was always there.

She was rather like Edith Sitwell. At Aunt Maggie's dinner table there was no small talk. The discussion was about real issues. She didn't have the breath to waste on small talk.

They had an incredible variety of friends, diverse friends. Uncle Herman for all his growl and bearlike reputation had sweetness and kindness. He was the softer one of the two. They made a wonderful pair.

At last, the Herman Browns moved with their children to Houston. They bought the house at 3335 Inwood, partly because it was an interesting John Staub house and partly because it was next door to George and Alice Brown—their best friends. These four founded the Brown Foundation, which has poured and continues to pour millions of dollars a year into enhancing the cultural, scientific, and intellectual climate of Houston. Their children carry on the Brown family traditions of philanthropy.

Still Unknown

As 1946 began, the world felt like dawn. The war was over. Rebuilding could begin. The United Nations gave fresh hope that humankind could find a way to keep this precious peace.

Once more, the United States had emerged from global war unscarred by bombs or battles. Nonetheless, after sixteen years of depression and war, American cities bore the look of neglect. Houston was run down: streets were pockmarked with potholes, buses were old and undependable.

Though there were neighborhood shopping centers, Houston had only one business and commercial district, and it was downtown.[1] So were the First Presbyterian Church, the First Christian Church, and the First Baptist Church. From the First Methodist Church out to the Warwick Hotel was called "the fabulous five miles." This referred to a few popular restaurants and a few nice little dress and antique shops. It was neither fabulous nor was it five miles long, but it had charm.

The Pillot house with its two iron dogs still stood on McKinney Avenue with a Pillot in residence. Between San Jacinto and Dowling, McKinney still had the hopscotch pattern where pavement extended to the middle of the street before one house, but not before the house next door or across the street because the homeowner some forty years before had decided not to pave.

There were no one-way streets, nor was there the need for any. Fannin Street dwindled into a lane and stopped at the entrance to Hermann Hospital. Montrose and Heights boulevards were shaded by trees in the esplanades and were flanked by well-kept old mansions. The big Levy and Lovett mansions stood on the corner of Main and Gray. The Beaconsfield Apartments remained a prestigious address.

Houston had begun the war with 384,510 people. In 1946, 478,000 people were trying to squeeze into a city that lay within the prewar boundaries or in what would become known as the Loop. Many were lifelong Houstonians simply trying to come home from war service around the world. For newcomers, finding a place to live in Houston in 1946 was hard. As the Beaumont crowd had in 1904, the Tulsa oil crowd arrived in the last years of the war and first years after. They brought with them accents and customs of the West. Oil companies were gladly taking on geologists as they left the services or the university.

A fresh influx of attractive, highly educated young singles and couples came to Houston from the northeast. Most, as newcomers always have, found Houston better than they expected.[2] As a worldwide enterprise, Anderson, Clayton brought to Houston a new generation of young men.[3] Among them were Jean Daladier, son of former Prime Minister Edouard Daladier of France; two German princes, Richard and Valdemar Hesse; and David Challinor, originally of New York City and newly out of the navy. Young bachelors got together to rent houses for bachelor quarters.

Newcomers found a small, friendly, Southern town. Strangers on an elevator or passing on a sidewalk were likely to nod to each other or say "Good morning." Any woman stranded at the roadside by a flat tire could depend on help from the next man who drove by. Compared with that of New York or Chicago, Houston traffic was quiet. In many cities, a split second was defined as "the time between the green light and the first honk of the horn behind you." Houston drivers rarely honked. But on the first day after gas rationing ended, everybody was astonished at how many cars were on the streets. Once again, Houston had acquired the luxury of a rush hour.

Americans were still driving prewar cars. Wartime shortages lingered while factories were retooled for civilian production. Linen and silk were slowly returning to the shelves. Nylon was emerging in cloth for dresses as well in knit for stockings and slips. Simple staples like sugar, coffee, and toilet tissue were often so scarce that markets might set a limit of one to a customer. Newlyweds setting up housekeeping had to wait weeks for the arrival at the store of a new refrigerator or to find a sofa made of good materials. But every morning the milkman delivered milk and butter to the kitchen door. The laundryman brought in clean clothes and picked up the next batch to be cleaned.

New telephones were still hard to get. As always, it depended on knowing the right person. One lawyer had no luck when he tried to wangle a phone for his new office through a phone company executive. But his secretary obtained one within a few days because she had a friend who was a telephone lineman.

Price controls kept rents at depression levels. A one-bedroom apartment with a living room, dining room, dressing room, and bath, equipped with an attic fan and a floor furnace, rented for $48.40 a month. But because so few houses and apartments had been built between 1930 and 1946, it was hard to find anything to rent. Hotels had a three-day limit on a guest's stay. Every garage apartment in Houston could have been rented three times over.

One day, Mrs. Theodore Heyck had a caller at her home on West Alabama. A nice-looking woman explained: "I rent the apartment back of you and my window looks out at the wall of your garage. Do you you mind if I paint it?" Mrs. Heyck gave her permission. After the caller moved away the Heycks discovered that she had painted a landscape on the garage to provide a view.

The city had two universities: Rice Institute and the University of Houston. Texas Southern University had not yet grown from the Houston College for Negroes.

Still privately supported, the University of Houston had almost twelve thousand students. Tuition was high, but many of the students were former servicemen and women coming to school on the G.I. bill. Veterans with families lived in trailers and shacks near the campus. The university had only four permanent buildings.[4] Classes spilled over into old houses around town.

In the thirty-four years since its opening, Rice Institute campus had gained the grace of arching live oaks and deep shade. In keeping with its policy, it had scarcely more than a thousand students, five or six boys for each girl. Tuition was free. It had four classroom buildings, the Cohen House, and the old power house campanile of 1912—"one of the most beautiful smokestacks ever built."[5] But the Rice Library was in a small room in Lovett Hall. The stadium consisted of a football field with two facing ranks of wooden seats. Although three residential halls provided quarters for male students, the institute had no dormitories for females.

Houston skies were clear, clean, and sparkling. Europeans compared them to the Greek skies so admired by British poets and sun-hungry Scandinavians. In all the warm days from spring to late autumn, garden and patio parties were popular. Because Texas was in a prolonged drought, mosquitoes were forgotten. Rettig's and D'Arcy's were the favorite ice cream parlors for a treat after a symphony concert in the Music Hall. Every summer, the outdoor watermelon parlor on South Main Street out past Sears

Nina Cullinan and Adelaide Lovett Baker at the Stables, 1940s. *From the Wiess family collection*

gave respite from unair-conditioned homes.

The Museum of Fine Arts had a small but excellent collection in the lovely little building built in the 1920s. Houston had an active Little Theater, three splendid motion picture theaters, and a number of pleasant neighborhood houses. The Houston Symphony Orchestra ranked comfortably with that of New Orleans, Dallas, or Atlanta. The elegant restaurants that had pleased discriminating palates from the turn of the century to the Great Depression had given way to a few good steak houses like Hebert's, a few good seafood restaurants like Kelly's. When Madeline Pollard opened Mad Tony's with French cuisine on Montrose Boulevard, it made quite a splash.

In 1946, the city was vibrant with things about to happen: Downtown Houston was dotted with excavations where new buildings would go. Tall cranes marked the skyline that was dominated by the Gulf Building. Houstonians quipped that if you left your car on a parking lot overnight, you might return to find it sixteen stories up on a new building. Oveta Culp Hobby made her classic comment: "I think I'll like Houston if they ever get it finished."

For five years, Ellen Clayton Garwood (Mrs. St. John Garwood) had nursed the idea that Houston needed a new college preparatory school with high standards. The earlier ones, like Professor Welch's Academy and the Prosso School, had died with their founders. Many of Old Houston's children were going off to school in other states, including the Garwoods' sons, St. John and Will. With Richard Neff, Jr., they were at the Arizona Desert School in Tucson. A Phi Beta Kappa graduate of Smith, Mrs. Garwood had discussed her idea of a new school with Alan Chidsey, her sons' headmaster. Now, back home after the war, they were ready to found one.

With Mr. Chidsey in town, they called a meeting at the Claytons' house on Caroline in late December, 1945.[6] The Rev. Thomas Sumners, James O. Winston, Jr., R. E. Smith, and Mr. and Mrs. Merrick Phelps formed a sponsoring committee. They invited Alva Carlton, Mrs. William Stamps Farish, Mrs. W. S. Farish, Jr., Ardon Judd, and Lewis N. White to join them. January 13, 1946, Jim Winston was elected chairman, Ellen Garwood elected secretary, and Alan Chidsey appointed headmaster. St. John's School was born.

It grew instantly; on February 2, Mrs. Farish announced that she would give the school its first building as a memorial to her son, W. S. Farish, Jr., who had been killed during the war. Mr. and Mrs. Hugh Roy Cullen gave the school five and a half acres on Westheimer adjacent to the little Church of St. John the Divine. On February 5, the chairman was authorized to ask for bids on the plans drawn by Hiram A. Salisbury and to form a contract with the church to govern the use of facilities they had in common. Enrollment opened March 15, and by March 18, more than one hundred and fifty applications had been received. In five days, the future student body had outgrown the future buildings.

The Cullens had always given money away, starting at $5.00 to the Salvation Army when they had very little cash on hand. As Roy Cullen's daring oil exploration began to pay in 1933, they gave $7,500 to the Houston Symphony Orchestra. The more they gave the more they seemed to enjoy it. In 1945 they gave $100,000 for the Houston College for Negroes. At about the same time, Mr. and Mrs. Cullen gave $1 million to each of four hospitals—Hermann, Memorial Baptist downtown on Lamar, Methodist on Rosalie at San Jacinto, and Saint Joseph on La-Branch and Crawford.

Promptly, the Rt. Rev. Clinton Quin, bishop of the Episcopal Diocese of Texas, went to his good friend: "Mr. Cullen," he said, "the Episcopalians are planning to build a hospital as soon as we can get the money." With equal promptness, Cullen handed over the fifth $1 million check. This started the

drive that ended in St. Luke's Episcopal Hospital almost a decade later.

In the next few years, Memorial Hospital used the gift to build a nurses' home on land given by Mrs. J. W. Neal. That cost so much that the Cullens later gave another $1 million to equip the building. St. Joseph simply went on expanding, gaining additional gifts from the Cullens in the process. Hermann used its $1 million to start the first of the new Hermann Hospitals.[7] It would face toward the forest of the soon-to-come Texas Medical Center. In 1946, both the school and the hospitals lay in the future.

The Navy Hospital stood far out on the plain at Holcombe Boulevard and Almeda Road.[8] The original Hermann Hospital still backed up to a forest. The Texas Medical Center—being referred to as the "$100 million medical center"—was on the drawing boards. The drawings showed driveways winding through a woodland with an occasional building here or there.

Houston was, in 1946, the same Southern town that it had been throughout its history. For five years, Houstonians in the War Department, in the Navy Department, in the State Department, and on the Cabinet had wielded world influence. Many of them were famous in Paris and Geneva—as Houstonians Edward Mandell House and Edwin Parker had been in 1919. They had spent billions of the nation's dollars to fight the war and to restore order amid chaos. They were known, trusted, and depended upon by two successive presidents of the United States. They had changed lives around the world. They had improved the quality of life for uncountable millions of the earth's people. Now they were coming home, to be citizens of Houston again.

They were the most recent in the unending line of Houstonians serving their government at the highest levels: Sam Houston, Albert Sidney Johnston, James Reilly, Col. Edward Mandell House, Judge Edwin Parker, Thomas W. Gregory, Jesse Jones, Browne Baker, Mark Edwin Andrews, Leland Anderson, Jubal Parton, Robert Lovett, Oveta Culp Hobby, Dudley Sharp, Will Clayton. . . .

But the city that sent them into the halls of power had never yet come to the attention of the country or of the world they served. The nation's press seemed to have no awareness of the city of Houston.[9] References to it were rare. A Martian searching for the name in the newspapers and news magazines would have found more about Atlanta, New Orleans, Dallas, or Birmingham. In simple fact, the Houston of 1946 received less attention from the world at large than had the Houston of Sam Houston and the Battle of San Jacinto.

Houston was poised on the launching pad to world fame—heart surgery, the Astrodome, NASA, the moon landing: "Houston, the eagle has landed." But in 1946, Houston was the nation's unknown city.

Appendix: Civic and Social Leaders

MAYORS OF HOUSTON (From *Mayor's Book,* Texas Room, Houston Public Library)

James S. Holman, 1837; Francis Moore, Jr., 1838; George W. Lively, 1839; Charles Bigelow, 1840; James D. Andrews, 1841–42; Francis Moore, Jr., 1843; Horace Baldwin, 1844; W. W. Swain, 1845; James Bailey, 1846; B. P. Buckner, 1847–48; Francis Moore, Jr., 1849–52; Nathan Fuller, 1853–54; James H. Stevens, 1855–56; Cornelius Ennis, 1857; Alexander McGowan, 1858; William H. King, 1859; Thomas W. Whitmarsh, 1860; William J. Hutchins, 1861; Thomas W. House, 1862; William Anders, 1863–65; Horace D. Taylor, 1866; Alexander McGowan, 1867; Joseph R. Morris, 1868–69; T. H. Scanlan, 1870–73; James T. D. Wilson, 1874; I. C. Lord, 1875–76; James T. D. Wilson, 1877–78; Andrew J. Burke, 1879; William R. Baker, 1880–85; Daniel C. Smith, 1886–89; Henry Scherffius, 1890–91; John T. Browne, 1892–96; H. Baldwin Rice, 1896–98; Samuel H. Brashear, 1898–1900; John D. Woolford, 1900–1902; O. T. Holt, 1902–1904; Andrew L. Jackson, 1904–1905; H. Baldwin Rice, 1905–13; Ben Campbell, 1913–17; J. J. Pastoriza, 1917; J. C. Hutcheson, Jr., 1917–18; A. Earl Amerman, 1918–21; Oscar F. Holcombe, 1921–29; Walter E. Monteith, 1929–33; Oscar F. Holcombe, 1933–37; R. H. Fonville, 1937–39; Oscar F. Holcombe, 1939–41; Neal Cornelius Pickett, 1941–43; Otis Massey, 1943–47; Oscar F. Holcombe, 1947–53; Roy M. Hofheinz, 1953–55; Oscar F. Holcombe, 1955–57; Lewis W. Cutrer, 1958–64; Louie Welch, 1964–74; Fred Hofheinz 1974–78; Jim McConn, 1978–82; Kathy Whitmire, 1982–

MUSEUM OF FINE ARTS

Presidents of the Board (In March, 1978, the title changed from president to chairman of the board.): John T. Scott, 1924–28; A. C. Ford, 1928–30; Herbert Godwin, 1930–32; William D. Cleveland, Jr., 1932–34; John F. Dickson, 1934–36; George A. Hill, Jr., 1936–39; J. Virgil Scott, 1939–41; Ray Dudley, 1941–43; John P. Bullington, 1943–46; John Wiley Link, Jr., 1946–47; John Hamman, Jr., 1947–50; Thomas D. Anderson, 1950–53; Francis G. Coates, 1953–58; Theodore E. Swigart, 1958–60; S. I. Morris, Jr., 1960–63; Edward Rotan, 1963–67; S. I. Morris, Jr., 1967–68; Edward Rotan, 1968–69; Alexander McLanahan, 1969–75; Harris Masterson III, 1975–79; Isaac Arnold, Jr., 1979–

First board of trustees, 1923: Dr. Joseph Mullen, Dr. Henry Barnston, John T. Scott, B. B. Gilmer, W. S. Hunt, Kate Scanlan, H. H. Dickson, Abe M. Levy, John F. Dickson, A. C. Ford, Will Clayton, and Mayor Oscar F. Holcombe

First directors: Mrs. Kenneth Womack, Mrs. W. S. Hunt, Mrs. John F. Grant, Mrs. Will Clayton, Mrs. H. H. Lummis, Mrs. Joseph Mullen, Mrs. R. W. Knox, Mrs. Thornwell Fay, Mrs. A. W. Paddock, Mrs. J. W. Parker, Mrs. James A. Baker, Mrs. Edgar O. Lovett, Mrs. H. M. Garwood, Mrs. James Cravens, Miss Ima Hogg, Miss Lennie Latham, and Miss Augusta Jones

Houston Symphony Orchestra

Conductors: Julian Paul Blitz, 1913–16; Paul Berge, 1916–18; Frank St. Leger, 1933–35; Ernst Hoffman, 1937–47; Efrem Kurtz, 1948–54; Ferenc Fricsay, 1954; Sir Thomas Beecham, 1954–55; Leopold Stokowski, 1955–61; Sir John Barbirolli, 1961–67; André Previn, 1967–69; Lawrence Foster, 1971–78; Sergiu Commisiona, 1980–88; Christopher Eschenbach, 1988–

Presidents of the Houston Symphony Society: Mrs. Edwin R. Parker, 1913–17; Miss Ima Hogg, 1917–21; Mrs. H. M. Garwood, 1921–31; Dr. Joseph R. Mullen, 1931–34; Mr. Joseph Smith, 1934–36; Mr. Walter H. Walne, 1936–42; Mr. Hugh Roy Cullen, 1942–45; Miss Ima Hogg, 1946–56; Gen. Maurice Hirsch, 1956–70; Dr. Charles F. Jones, 1970–75; Mr. Fayez Sarofim, 1975–78; Mr. John T. Cater, 1980–82; Mrs. Edward W. Kelley, Jr., 1982–84; Mr. John D. Platt, 1984–87; Mr. E. C. Vandergrift, Jr., 1988–89; Mr. J. Hugh Roff, Jr., 1989–

Chairman of the Board (The office of chairman of the board existed for eight years.): Mr. Gus S. Wortham, 1946–48; Mr. F. M. Law, 1948–50; Mr. Warren S. Bellows, 1950–53; Mr. Harmon Whittington, 1953–54

Presidents of the Houston Symphony League: Miss Ima Hogg, Mrs. John F. Grant, Mrs. J. R. Parten, Mrs. Andrew E. Rutter, Mrs. Aubrey L. Carter, Mrs. Stuart Sherar, Mrs. Julian Burrows, Mrs. Hazel Ledbetter, Mrs. Albert P. Jones, Mrs. Ben A. Calhoun, Mrs. James Griffith Lawhon, Mrs. Olaf LaCour Olsen, Mrs. Ralph Ellis Gunn, Mrs. Leon Jaworski, Mrs. Garrett R. Tucker, Jr., Mrs. M. T. Launius, Jr., Mrs. Thompson McClery, Mrs. Theodore W. Cooper, Mrs. Allen H. Carruth, Mrs. David Hannah, Jr., Mrs. Albert T. Kister, Mrs. Edward W. Kelley, Jr., Mrs. John W. Herndon, Mrs. Charles Franzen, Mrs. Harold R. DeMoss, Jr., Mrs. Edward H. Soderstrom, Ms. Lilly K. Pryor, Ms. Marilou Bonner.

Eagle Lake Rod and Gun Club

The first members, as listed on February 9, 1921; Dr. N. N. Allen, Benj. Andrews, James A. Baker, James A. Baker, Jr., C. W. Barker, S. R. Bertron, Jr., John S. Bonner, J. Stuart Boyles, C. B. Brett, W. T. Carter, Jr., C. L. Carter, Ennis Cargill, L. A. Carlton, J. J. Carroll, J. H. Chew, Wm. D. Cleveland, Jr., H. M. Crosswell, John F. Dickson, Raymond Dickson, John K. Dorrance, F. B. Duncan, DeWitt C. Dunn, W. S. Farish, A. C. Ford, J. A. Giraud, Herbert Godwin, Mike Hogg, James P. Houstoun, Howard Hughes, W. S. Hunt, Palmer Hutcheson, E. G. Maclay, Tovell Marston, A. L. Nelms, Jr., Haywood Nelms, E. L. Neville, Hugo V. Neuhaus, D. D. Orr, R. C. Patterson, E. A. Peden, C. G. Pillot, J. H. Pittman, H. M. Potter, Ed Prather, F. C. Proctor, Dave Rice, George V. Rotan, John T. Scott, W. A. Sherman, E. R. Spotts, J. L. Storey, S. Taliaferro, J. Lewis Thompson, E. E. Townes, O. S. Van DeMark, C. R. Westmoreland, W. H. Walne, H. C. Wiess, and R. A. Welsh

Houston Geological Society Presidents

D'Arcy Cashin, 1920; John R. Suman, 1923–24; Dilworth S. Hager, 1925; Donald C. Barton, 1926; Frank W. DeWolf, 1927; Paul Weaver, 1928; George Sawtelle, 1929; J. Brian Eby, 1930; A. G. Wolf, 1931; John M. Vetter, 1932; Marcus A. Hanna, 1933; Wayne F. Bowman, 1934; Merle C. Israelsky, 1935; Phil F. Martyn, 1936; John C. Miller, 1937; Perry Olcott, 1938; W. C. Thompson, 1939; G. S. Buchanan, 1940; Carleton D. Speed, Jr., 1941; Donald M. Davis, 1942; Leslie Bowling, 1943; William B. Milton, Jr., 1944; Olin G. Bell, 1945; Shapleigh G. Gray, 1946; Charles H. Sample, 1947

The Advertising Association of Houston

The Advertising Association of Houston Committee that went to London in 1924 to invite the Associated Advertising Clubs of the World to Houston: William Patton, chairman; George Cohen of Foley's, vice-chairman; and George B. Forristall, Gus Mistrot, H. A. McCelvey, R. H. Cornell, Harry C. Howard, Ray Dudley, Paul L.

Wakefield, Guy Harris, John Payne, and Dale C. Rogers. The delegation included Vernon A. Corrigan, Miss Anne Corrigan, Miss Ima Hogg, Mrs. E. A. Peden, Mrs. John Wesley Graham, Mrs. William Patton and her daughters Kate and Mayola Frances, J. W. Neal of the Chamber of Commerce, Robert G. Cohen, John Buckley, R. M. Farrar of the Harbor Board, J. M. West, Tobias Sakowitz, Sam Rouse, John Dyer, J. M. Rockwell, and Carle Aderman.

Notes

Chapter One. BORN OF REVOLUTION

1. Six generations of his descendants would live in Houston. Moses Austin's daughter Emily married James Bryan and had five children. After his death she married James Franklin Perry and had six children. In the sense of the FFVs (First Families of Virginia), they were among the first families of Houston. In the 1980s, James Perry Bryan, Jr., Stephen Carter Cook, and Paul Gervais Bell, Jr., represented the sixth generation, their children the seventh.

2. The empresario contracted to recruit colonists and establish a colony within twelve years. The cattleman was entitled to a *sitio* or a square league—about 4,428 acres. The stock farmer would get both a *labor* (177 acres) and a *sitio*. For his work, the empresario received three haciendas (five *sitios*) and two *labores* for each two hundred families he brought in. The colonist had to occupy and cultivate his land within two years or lose it. All colonists must adhere to the Roman Catholic faith. Stephen F. Austin charged his colonists twelve and a half cents an acre to cover surveying and maintaining peace with the Indians. (Some colonists thought this too much.)

3. Ezekiel Thomas's great-great-grandson was Robert Cummins Stuart IV. His daughter Francita married Philip Koelsch. Rosalee Allen Smith Maffitt (Mrs. Thomas S. Maffitt) was Ezekiel Thomas's great-great-granddaughter. Her son Peter married Holly Herring. The Koelsch children, Robert and Frances, and the Maffitt children, Edward, Rosalee, and Allison, are seventh-generation Houstonians.

4. Rebecca Jane's husband, Samuel W. Allen, later combined the Thomas League with holdings south of the bayou to build a cattle empire.

5. His daughter Mary Jane married Andrew Briscoe. Dorothy Knox Howe Houghton (Mrs. Thomas Woodward Houghton) is their great-great-great-granddaughter. The Houghton children are seventh-generation Houstonians.

6. General de Zavala, a scholar and statesman, formerly Mexico's ambassador to France, became vice-president in the interim government. He died November 15, 1836, at his plantation across Buffalo Bayou from the San Jacinto battlefield.

7. Sherman's daughter Lennie married Col. John T. Brady, and their daughter Lucy married attorney Wilmer Sperry Hunt. The Hunt children were Wilmer Brady and twin daughters, Lucy and Lennie. Wilmer Brady Hunt married Eugenia Howard, a descendant of Georges Capron. They had four children: Robin McCorquodale, a novelist; Dr. Wilmer Grainger Hunt, an environmentalist; Nancy Lou Hunt Kiesling, and Sperry Hunt. General Sherman's daughter Caroline married J. M. O. Menard and had six children. Belle Sherman married Judge William E. Kendall of Richmond and had six sons; Lucy Kate Sherman married Louis W. Craig and had three sons, Leonard, Doddridge, and William Kendall Craig. By 1986, the family had entered its sixth generation in Houston.

8. Colonel Gray started another of the first families. Gray Avenue is named for his son, Peter Gray, lawyer, judge, and a founder of the latter-day firm of Baker & Botts. His daughter, Susan Alice Gray, married Claudius W. Sears. The Sears's son, W. G. Sears, became a Houston attorney, as did his son, George D. Sears. Colonel Gray's grandson Peter Gray Sears was the rector of Christ Church from 1905 to 1926. Mr. Sears's daughter, Alice Gray, married Frank Akins.

9. It would take him a year. He missed the Battle of San Jacinto, the national election, the first meeting of Congress in Columbia, and the city of Houston's birth.

10. On the orders of his surgeon Alexander Ewing, General Houston was taken at once to New Orleans for treatment. The trip took seven days, and Houston seemed near death on his arrival. The crowds that met the little ship were so stunned by his tragic appearance that the band and cheering fell silent. A schoolgirl began to cry. She was Margaret Lea, who one day would transform his life.

Chapter Two. THE CAPITAL

1. The dinner may have taken place in Frost Town, as the Allens lived there briefly before moving to Houston. Hugo Neuhaus, Jr., Houston architect, philanthropist and great-great-nephew of Charlotte Allen, told this story.

2. Austin colonists from New York, three Bordens fought at San Jacinto, including John P. Borden. It was he who founded the Borden family of Houston. Alexandra Madeline Tennant, daughter of the James Browder Tennants, is a sixth generation Houstonian.

3. During Sam Houston's slow recovery from his wound, Burnet and Lamar did all they could to oust him as a national leader. Burnet even dismissed Dr. Alexander Ewing from the army for having accompanied his half-dead patient to New Orleans for treatment. But Houston received 5,119 votes, Ashbel Smith 743, and Stephen Austin 587.

4. Galveston Island was the beach where sailing vessels could land people and cargo. On April 7, 1836, Colonel Gray wrote in his diary, "The island is forty miles long—only three trees on it. No habitation."

5. Instead, the Allens built the Capitol at their own expense and retained title to it.

6. Francis Richard Lubbock, *Six Decades in Texas; or, Memoirs of Francis Richard Lubbock, Governor of Texas in War Time, 1861–63,* ed. C. W. Raines.

7. Now the intersection of Hyde Park and Commonwealth.

Chapter Four. FIESTA

1. The original street names are still in place except for Homer Street, renamed in honor of Stephen F. Austin, who had died at forty-two, and Milton Street, which became LaBranch in honor of the first U.S. minister to the Republic.

2. Francis Lubbock, who was at the ball, and Adele Looscan, who drew on the memories of her mother, Mary Jane Harris, wrote almost identical accounts of the evening. Lubbock's was published in his *Six Decades in Texas.* Hers, signed "Texan," appeared in *Ladies Magazine* and the *Houston Post.* Houston's Looscan Library is named for her.

3. The daughter of John R. and Jane Birdsall Harris, Mary Jane left school in New York state in 1836 to join her brother DeWitt in Harrisburg. John Birdsall was Jane Harris's cousin. Crawford Street was named for Joseph Tucker Crawford.

4. The contrast between well-dressed people and their rough houses continued for some time. Dr. Andrew Forest Muir referred to "the hovel" in which Sam Houston lived. Audubon's description validates the term.

5. The uniform was given to the San Jacinto Museum.

6. In Houston's heartbreak over his divorce, he drank so heavily that his protective Indian friends renamed him "Big Drunk." After he married Margaret Lea, he became a teetotaler.

7. Jacob Cruger, a New Yorker, was seventeen, but he had been Houston's postmaster and assistant secretary of the Texas Senate. He was business manager of the *Telegraph* for fourteen years. He and Moore also owned the *Morning Star.*

Chapter Five. MODERN CITY

1. This was the modern style of Queen Victoria's girlhood.

2. After the capital moved to Austin, the buildings reverted to the Allens.

3. Mrs. Andrews's daughter by her first husband, Bettie Tighlman, married John T. Dickinson, who came to Houston from Scotland in 1839. They were Eugenia Howard Hunt's great-grandparents.

4. Andrew Briscoe, of the Old Three Hundred, and Mary Jane Harris, whose father founded Harrisburg, started one of Houston's first families. Their grandson, Birdsall Parmenas Briscoe, became a leading Houston architect in the twentieth century. Adele, who married Maj. Michael Looscan, was a founder and early president of the Texas Historical Association. Jessie married Milton Grosvenor Howe, a graduate of Dartmouth and a captain in the Confederacy.

5. Sadie Gwinn Allen Blackburn (Mrs. Edward A. Blackburn, Jr.), elected president of the Garden Clubs of America in 1989, is a fifth-generation descendant of Harvey Allen.

6. This was before the days of the hand-cranked ice cream freezer. The ice was cut in

blocks during New England winters and brought by sailing vessel to the Gulf Coast and by steamboat up the bayou. House had a hand in almost every major project to benefit Houston. His son, Edwin Mandell House, became world famous as Woodrow Wilson's adviser.

7. Dentists, surgeon-dentists, and barbers all seemed ready to cup and bleed anyone in need of this medical treatment.

8. Long Row was a row of one-story stores, replicated on the original site at 1100 Bagby by the Harris County Heritage Society.

9. Twentieth-century Houston owes its biggest trees to the nurserymen and gardeners of the 1830s.

Chapter Six. MAGNET

1. Mrs. Gray omitted the name of her daughter Evelina, who was in the party. Margaret Stone is presumably her sister.

2. In 1946, Houston was growing so rapidly that a newcomer compared it to a precocious child. She was enchanted to discover through Mrs. Gray's diary that the Houston of 1946 was reflecting its 1839 character.

3. John Birdsall was a cousin of Jane Birdsall Harris, whose husband founded Harrisburg. He married Mary Jane Allen, sister of Augustus and John Allen.

4. "His sister's" was the house at Main and Prairie that the Andrew Briscoes bought in 1837 and later sold to John Birdsall.

5. For the next one hundred and fifty years, newcomers would make the same remark, "Better than I expected."

6. Bee County was named for Bernard Bee. From South Carolina, he had studied law and served on the staff of his brother-in-law, Governor James Hamilton. He came to Texas after falling out with the governor over the nullification dispute of 1832. As Lamar's secretary of state, he went to Mexico on an unsuccessful mission to gain recognition of Texas independence. As the Republic's minister to the United States, he spent much of his time in Washington from 1838 to 1841.

7. Dr. Ashbel Smith went to London as charge d'affaires in 1842 and lived at 103 Jermyn Street. George Terrell and James Hamilton also served there.

Chapter Seven. LIVELY CITY – 1839

1. At the time of his death, he was chairman of the board of regents of the University of Texas.

2. Ezekiel Cullen had settled in San Augustine in 1835. He pushed his bill through the Texas Congress between January 4 and January 26, 1839, but resigned when appointed district judge by President Lamar. Pres. Zachary Taylor sent Judge Cullen to Nicaragua to study the possibility of digging a canal from the Atlantic to the Pacific. He was a purser in the U.S. Navy in the 1850s, but returned to Texas in 1871. The Ezekiel W. Cullen Building at the University of Houston was built by his grandson, Hugh Roy Cullen, and Mrs. Cullen.

3. Hugo Neuhaus, Jr., Joseph, Philip, James Harrison, and Katherine Neuhaus (Mrs. Townsend Munson) are descendants of Horace Baldwin.

4. Captain Latham's daughter Justina married William Cleveland. Tina Cleveland Sharp (Mrs. Dudley Sharp) and Lois Cleveland Kirkland (Mrs. W. A. Kirkland) were among Captain Latham's great-granddaughters. Virginia Kirkland Innis, Barbara Kirkland Chiles, and Dudley Sharp, Jr., were among his great-great-grandchildren. Their children form the sixth generation in Houston.

5. Gail Borden, Jr., who had a year and a half of formal schooling, was brilliantly inventive. On a sailing vessel from England, he saw children sickened by impure milk and began to seek a method of preservation. In 1856, he patented his process and organized the company to market Borden's Eagle Brand Condensed Milk. He established a meat-packing plant at Borden, Texas, and a sawmill and cooperware factory at Bastrop. After the Civil War he built a freedmen's school and a white children's school, organized a black day school and a black Sunday school, helped build five churches, and partially supported many poorly paid teachers, ministers, and students. He died in Borden in 1874 and was shipped by private car to New York for burial.

6. The original presses were fished out of the bayou and put back in use by someone else.

7. The Franklin Debating Society was an ancestor of the Houston Lyceum, forerunner of the Houston Public Library.

Chapter Eight. MELTING POT

1. President Houston freed the Mexican prisoners.

2. When Mirabeau B. Lamar succeeded Houston as president, Indian fortunes plummeted under Lamar's harsh policies.

3. Dresel had ten good years, enjoying

Houston, New Orleans, and much of Texas. But at thirty, he died of yellow fever.

4. Houston was to be the capital until 1840. Elected president in 1838, Mirabeau B. Lamar encouraged a prompt selection of a new site. By late 1839, Congress had held its last session in the Capitol on Main Street. New immigrants were quartered there by the Allens, who owned it.

5. Though several Texas blacks owned, bought, and sold slaves, the most notable was William Goyens, a free black from North Carolina, who settled in Nacogdoches. He ran a boarding house and was a blacksmith, gunsmith, wagon manufacturer, freight hauler, mill owner, and land speculator. In 1832, he married a white woman from Georgia. He was an associate of such prominent Texans as Thomas Rusk and Sam Houston. When he died in 1856, he was one of the state's richest men and owned more than twelve thousand acres of land.

6. As folklore editor of the Federal Writers Project in 1938 and 1939, Botkin interviewed scores of former slaves.

Chapter Nine. A FOREIGN MISSION FIELD

1. At the age of forty-two, Austin died of pneumonia in Columbia shortly after being appointed secretary of state.

2. Shearn Methodist Church, one of the loveliest ever built in Houston, stood for a few years on that site.

3. He was no relation to Augustus and John Allen.

4. Augustus and John had four brothers: Samuel L., George, Henry R., and Harvey H. Allen.

5. He soon became first bishop of the Diocese of Galveston.

6. St. Vincent's measured twenty-five by fifty and had twenty pews. Cast in 1843, the 218-pound bell hanging in its steeple was described by the *Morning Star* as "the best piece of workmanship of the kind ever completed in the Republic."

Chapter Eleven. UP FROM DEPRESSION

1. In contrast, Sam Houston's Indian policy cost $350,000 in five years.

2. The Houstons lived in Huntsville. Their daughter Margaret married Weston L. Williams from Mississippi. Widowed, she moved to Houston in the late 1880s and lived at 1208 Calhoun. Their son Royston Williams married Stella

Root, who grew up on Root Square. The Williamses' son Franklin married Annie McKeever, and the Franklin Williamses' daughter Charlotte married James A. Darby. The Darbys' grandchildren are the great-great-great-great-grandchildren of Sam Houston, all living in his namesake city in 1986.

Chapter Twelve. AMERICANS AGAIN

1. Table diaper is a nineteenth-century British term for table napkin.

2. The Shepherd family has run to six generations in Houston, giving Shepherd Drive and the Shepherd School of Music their names. Among the sixth-generation descendants are the children of Virginia Kirkland Innis, Barbara Kirkland Chiles, and George S. Bruce III. Stephen Pond, the great-great-great-grandson of B. A. Shepherd, married Catherine Barada, the great-great-great-granddaughter of Gen. Sidney Sherman.

3. The city bought the Kellum-Noble House and property in 1899 to create Houston's first park. By 1954, the house had been neglected for decades. To secure its preservation, Marie Lee Phelps (Mrs. Sam McAshan), Faith Bybee (Mrs. Charles Bybee), and Harvin Moore, restoration architect, founded the Harris County Heritage Society. The society has added other significant old houses to Sam Houston Park.

4. Though many couples simply separated, as the Allens did, divorce was not rare. A town of four thousand, Houston recorded ten divorces between December, 1840, and April, 1845.

5. The Rice house now stands in Sam Houston Park.

6. In the much older Huntsville, Alabama, there were wealthy women who prided themselves on having never been out of the county.

7. Frances Blake married Robert Cummins Stuart, Jr. Francita Stuart Koelsch (Mrs. Phillip Koelsch) is her great-great-granddaughter.

8. Mary Elizabeth Caldwell Merrem (Mrs. W. E. Merrem) is the great-granddaughter of Thomas W. House. Her grandson, Dr. Rolfe Williams, and his daughter, Cameron Parker Williams, represent the sixth and seventh generations of the House family in Houston

Chapter Thirteen. ANTEBELLUM

1. Amusingly, modern encyclopedias refer to Perry's "great show of force" in Tokyo harbor. Leaving the navy in 1856, Gray returned to Hous-

ton and became state engineer. The letters excerpted here are in the family archives of Ellen Robbins Red (Mrs. David Red), Horace Taylor's great-granddaughter.

2. Cattle brought by the Spanish and the Austin colonists multiplied until by 1860 Texas herds were estimated to run from three to four million head. As trains radiated out from Houston, cattle could be shipped and Houston profited.

3. He was no relation to the Allens who founded Houston.

4. The Allen Ranch included the latterday Allendale, South Houston, Freeway Manor, Garden Villas, Hobby Airport, Glenbrook Valley, and Meadowbrook.

5. Members of the Hunt, Perlitz, and McCorquodale families are fifth-generation descendants of this marriage. Brady Island is a remnant of Brady's large estate.

6. Six generations of McAshans have lived in Houston. They came to La Grange from Virginia as Austin colonizers. S. M. McAshan, who came to Houston as a young man, married Mattie R. Eanes in 1855. Their children were James Everett, Samuel Ernest, Annie, and Virginia. James Everett McAshan became president of South Texas National Bank. His children were Mary B., Samuel Maurice, Hoke S., Hildreth, J. E. Jr., and Burton McAshan. Samuel Maurice McAshan's sons were S. M. McAshan, Jr., who became president of the Anderson, Clayton Cotton Corporation; James E. McAshan, a lawyer with Baker & Botts, and Harris McAshan, banker. S. Ernest McAshan's children were Annie and Sam, the father of Sam McAshan, Jr.

7. The Raphael children were Joseph, Rebecca, Emanuel, Moses, Sarah, and Julia. Emanuel played a part in the founding of Rice Institute.

8. Richard W. Dowling was born in Tuam, Galway County, Ireland, in 1838. Because of the potato famine, the family came to New Orleans. When his parents died of yellow fever, Dick and other children joined relatives in Houston. In 1857, he married Elizabeth Anne Odlum. Tuam Street was named for his birthplace, Dowling Street for him.

Chapter Fourteen. WAR

1. Gravestones of the 1860s in the old Jewish Cemetery are marked "Dutchy of Rosen," "Alsace," "Bavaria," "Native of France," and "Born in Russia."

2. Dr. Ashbel Smith had served as a combat officer in the Mexican War. As colonel he commanded Confederate forces on the Matagorda Peninsula.

3. After the war, Emma Seelye's book, *The Nurse and Spy,* sold 175,000 copies. She gave the royalties to hospitals. In 1884, she attended a reunion of the regiment. She is buried in the G.A.R. burial lot in Washington Cemetery.

4. Kennedy built this two-story, brick building in 1848. In the 1960s Dr. and Mrs. Charles Kennedy Bruhl restored it, and it reopened as La Carafe. Dr. Bruhl is Kennedy's great-grandson.

5. Shapley Prince Ross, father of the two Rosses, was U.S. agent of the Brazos Indian Reservation near Waco in the 1850s. Sul Ross attended Baylor University. In 1859, when he was twenty-one years old, he captained the frontier ranger company that attacked a Comanche village and found the long lost Cynthia Ann Parker.

6. Peter Ross married Laura Harrison. Their daughter married Jonas Shearn Rice, whose children were Laura Rice Neff, Kate Rice Neuhaus, and Lottie Rice Farrish. Hugo Neuhaus, Jr., Joseph Rice, Philip R., Harry, and Katherine Neuhaus are great-grandchildren of Peter Ross.

7. F. W. Heitmann opened a hardware store at 113 Main Street in 1881, where it stayed for eighty-nine years. After his death, his son Fritz became president, and his daughter, Mrs. Edward Lorenzen, vice-president. In 1941, his grandson Fred Heitmann entered the firm.

Chapter Fifteen. LES BELLES PARISIENNES DE HOUSTON

1. Palmer Memorial Church was named for Will Palmer's son, Edward, drowned in Galveston Bay.

2. The letters are from the family papers of Virginia Kirkland Innis, Justina's great-granddaughter. Tina Cleveland Sharp, Lois Cleveland Kirkland, and Nora Cleveland Fuller were Justina's granddaughters.

3. Laura was B. A. Shepherd's daughter and the grandmother of Laura Kirkland Bruce (Mrs. George S. Bruce, Jr.).

4. Van Alstyne, Texas, was named for Mrs. Van Alstyne.

5. Captain Lathem was fortunate in that the Empress Eugenie was considered conservative in her dress by fashionable Parisians. She led no young girl to want the most extreme of the crinoline styles with their expensive yardage.

Chapter Sixteen. DEFEAT

1. Though they spelled their names differently, General Granger was the younger brother of Charles Grainger, who lived on Texas Avenue. In uniform, the general came to call. When the maid opened the door, she screamed: "Run! The Yankees have come to get us all!"

2. Born in 1861, E. N. Gray graduated from the Jefferson Medical College in Philadelphia in 1893 and practiced medicine for fifty-seven years on the staff of Memorial, Hermann, St. Joseph's, and Jefferson Davis hospitals.

3. Rosalie was the niece of Mayor Horace Taylor.

4. Major Weems and Maria Nash Carrington of Virginia were married in 1876. They had four children: Fontaine Carrington, Benjamin Francis, Wharton Ewell, and Kate Allen Weems.

5. Captured at Gettysburg, Barziza spent a year in a federal hospital and prison. After escaping, he used the underground network that took fugitive Confederates to Canada and, by way of Bermuda, back to the South on a blockade runner.

6. It is for him that Elgin Street is named. Old Houstonians pronounce the street name with a hard *g*.

7. Some sixty years later, Lamar High School was built on the school site. Of the Westheimer boys who joined their uncle, Sid started the livery stable and transfer business and later the Westheimer Undertaking Company; Sigmund J. founded the Westheimer Transfer and Storage Company; David owned a drug store; and Max had an insurance business. Adolf Westheimer, who inherited the transfer and storage business, fought in the Spanish-American War. He was the father of Mark Westheimer, attorney, and of the author David Westheimer.

8. She resigned the post in 1872, possibly because of her marriage to Lord Stewart and a subsequent, if brief, life in Britain.

9. Dr. Roberts was essential because as an avowed Unionist, he could swear to the integrity of the other directors, all known to be Confederates.

10. Davis had sided with the Union, had spent most of the war fighting Confederate forces along the Rio Grande, and accepted the Texas surrender in Galveston. He campaigned for all ex-Confederates to be disfranchised and for the state to be divided. His personal unpopularity was so great that any official he appointed became immediately suspect.

11. Bethel Coopwood was the grandfather of David Coopwood Bintliff, the Houston financier and land developer.

12. Samuel W. Allen was the great-great-grandfather of Francita Stuart Koelsch (Mrs. Philip Koelsch), Peter Maffitt, and Charles Milby, among others.

13. Dick Dowling has no living descendants. His sister's great-great-grandchildren include Anna Caraway Ivins, Jim Caraway, Ben Dowling Caraway, Joseph B. Collerain, Mary C. Alford, Janet C. Gilmore, and Joan C. Horak.

14. Hugh Rice was the great-grandfather of Hugh Rice Kelly, Houston attorney.

Chapter Seventeen. RECOVERY

1. The 1868 population would be hard to estimate. Wartime refugees were going back to Galveston, plantation people were moving into town, troops were quartered in the city.

2. William Hines Kirkland married Laura Shepherd, daughter of B. A. Shepherd. Their children were William A. Kirkland, Laura (Mrs. George S. Bruce Jr.), and Mary Porter (Mrs. Arthur Vandervoort). Thomas Gilbert Masterson, grandfather of James and Archibald, had moved to Brazoria County in 1832. His wife, Christiana Roane, was granddaughter of a U.S. Supreme Court justice. She often read law to her sons and grandsons. Half a dozen of them became judges.

3. William, Odin, and Clarence Kendall became leading Houstonians.

4. Houstonians delighted in processions. They liked to carry silken banners and march to band music on any occasion from church picnics to dedications, from graduations to funerals.

5. Cleveland, Texas, was named for him.

6. At their peak, hoop skirts measured fifteen to eighteen feet around, posing a problem in carriages, parlors, and church pews. On the street, they got entangled in carriage wheels and acted like sails on a schooner in high wind.

7. Dr. T. J. Heard of Galveston was the first president. Dr. R. T. Flewellen of Houston was elected the second president, Dr. D. R. Wallace of Waco the third, and Dr. D. F. Stuart of Houston the fourth.

8. Colonel Brady was one of the first Houston lawyers to appear before the U.S. Supreme Court after the war. He and his first wife had two children: Lucy Sherman who married Wilmer Sperry Hunt, and Sidney Sherman Brady. After his first wife's death, the colonel married Estelle Jenkins, daughter of Judge George P.

Jenkins and Henriette Davis Jenkins. Their daughter Etta B. Brady married J. W. Garrow.

Chapter Eighteen. PROSPEROUS PEACE

1. As a town of thirty thousand, Houston had thirty bars. Its temperance societies had three hundred members.

2. The boat gave its name to Clinton.

3. Judge Baker's son, Capt. James A. Baker, became famous during the New York trials of William Marsh Rice's murderers; his grandson developed Broad Acres and his great-grandson became U.S. secretary of state.

4. Later it was renamed the Sweeney & Combes Opera House.

5. Tuberculosis was still considered hereditary rather than contagious. It was glamorized in novels and operas. In Louisa May Alcott's *Jo's Boys,* Jo gives a dose of cough syrup to a boy suspected of having tuberculosis, and then hands the spoon to her own small son to lick.

6. William Marsh Rice's brother Frederick married Charlotte Baldwin Randon. Her daughter Libbie Randon became the oldest sister of the Rice children: Jones Shearn Rice, William Marsh Rice, Jr., Baldwin, David, Minerva, Fred, Lillian, Benjamin, George, and Nettie.

7. Jack Yates High School was named for the minister.

8. Henry Lummis was the son of Dr. Hiram Holt Lummis and the father of Dr. Frederick Rice Lummis and of Patty Hogg Rice Lummis, who married Walter Bedford Sharp.

9. The Bujacs' daughter married Jesse Andrews and became a leader in the Democratic Party. Their grandson, Mark Edwin Andrews, was assistant secretary of the navy in 1947–49. Marguerite McClellan and Mark Edwin Andrews, Jr., are their grandchildren.

10. Musician, teacher, and nurse, Keziah Payne DePelchin must have been brilliant. But credit is also due to her stepmother who taught her all she knew, even how to play the piano on a cardboard keyboard.

11. Dr. Smith was president of the regents when he died at eighty-one on January 21, 1886, at Evergreen Plantation on Galveston Bay. He is buried in the State Cemetery at Austin.

Chapter Nineteen. ON WITH THE NEW

1. Nicholas Linzza installed the arc light on a pole at Main and Preston. Once as he sat on an insulated stool trimming a carbon electrode, the town marshal walked by and slapped him on the back. Both were knocked to the ground by the shock. Thereafter Linzza noticed that people stepped off the sidewalk when they saw him coming.

2. Stores stayed open in the evening. Clerks received no overtime pay.

3. Rienzi Melville Johnston married Mary Elizabeth Parsons. Their children were Hallie, Harry, and Libbie Mary. Libbie married Neill Masterson. Their children were Neill T., Jr., Elizabeth, and Harris III. Harry Johnston became managing editor of the *Post.* Hallie Johnston Russell wrote a popular column. Harry M. Johnston, Jr., was city editor of the paper in the 1950s before becoming chief of the Atlanta bureau of *Time.* The colonel's granddaughter, Mary Elizabeth Johnston, was a *Post* reporter before joining the editorial board of *Fortune.*

4. MacGregor Park is named for H. F. MacGregor.

5. Before her death in 1919, she was named to the Texas Women's Hall of Fame for her civic leadership.

6. In 1893, Sid Westheimer turned this business over to his brother, Sigmund, and opened the Westheimer Funeral Home. He owned much land in Houston, had a six-hundred-acre stock farm in Harris County, and became one of the county's largest taxpayers.

7. In her book *Victorian and Edwardian Fashion,* Alison Gernsheim tells the story: "Not unreasonably, a Turkish lady whose curiosity got the better of her manners asked the British Ambassador's wife in Constantinople: 'Are *all* the ladies of your country deformed like you?'"

8. Sess Cleveland was named for Davis Sessums, Episcopal bishop of Louisiana. Bishop Sessums came to Houston to perform the wedding ceremony of each of his namesake's daughters at Christ Church: Nora Cleveland to Charles Fuller of New York, Lois Cleveland to William A. Kirkland, Tina Cleveland to Dudley Sharp.

9. Herman Detering married Helena Stuer. Their children were Alma, Elsie, Herman, Carl, and Lenore.

10. After thirty-six years with the James Bute Company, Mr. Welch resigned as secretary-treasurer in 1927 but stayed on the board of directors. He had long since become tremendously rich on oil, sulphur, banking, and real estate.

Chapter Twenty. FIN DE SIECLE

1. Quality Hill was a neighborhood of large houses along the bayou near the intersec-

tion of Franklin and LaBranch.

2. The law firm of Baker, Botts, Baker & Lovett, of course, was prospering as chief counsel for several of these out-of-state corporations, especially the railroads.

3. In 1911, the timber rights brought four million dollars.

4. He married Carrie Banks of Galveston. The Carters' children were Clara, Florence, S. F. Carter, Jr., and Annie Vive.

5. In 1900, Mr. Heyck married Frances Giraud, daughter of Richard A. Giraud. He was active in the Chamber of Commerce, the Turnverein, the Houston Club, and the Houston Country Club.

6. Grace Oveta Hobby, daughter of Paul and Janet Hobby, and Will, Carter, and John Beckworth, sons of John and Laura Beckworth, are the fifth generation of the Hobby family living in Houston.

7. Dr. Cooley married Louise Goldborough Thomas in Baltimore and they had five daughters, Mary, Louise, Susan, Florence, and Helen. He founded the Texas Heart Institute.

8. Seven years later, the church sold the Travis Street half for $7,780 as a site for the first Carnegie Library.

9. In 1959 the house was moved to Sam Houston Park.

10. This was the greatest snow storm in Houston history, though not the coldest. Galveston Bay froze over.

11. Charlotte Allen was buried in Glenwood Cemetery. John H. Allen was buried in Founders Memorial Park, Houston. Augustus Chapman Allen, cut off from the city by the Civil War, was buried in Brooklyn, New York.

12. The daughter of the Harrisburg founder, Mrs. Briscoe was now in her late seventies. She died in Houston in 1903.

13. Lynch Davidson married Katie Calvert in June, 1897. They had three daughters: Mrs. John K. Dorrance and Mrs. Naurice Cummings of Houston, and Mrs. Benjamin Hines of New York City.

Chapter Twenty-One. Houston's Builders

1. Willie Hutcheson was a woman of independent spirit. Divorced, she resumed her maiden name, took up a newspaper career, and smoked cigars.

2. The Stokowskis' daughter, Sonya Maria Thorbecke, and granddaughter, Christine Thorbecke Shane, became Houstonians.

3. Hally Bryan (Mrs. Emmett Perry) was the granddaughter of Stephen F. Austin's sister. Her nieces—Carolyn Bryan (Mrs. Frederick R. Thompson), Florence Bryan (Mrs. Raymond Cook), and Hally Bryan Clements (Mrs. Thurman Clements)—are great-great-granddaughters of Moses Austin.

4. The German, by Webster's definition, was "a dance consisting of capriciously involved figures intermingled with waltzes, etc. A cotillion. A social party at which the German is danced."

5. Jonas Rice, a graduate of the Texas Military Institute in Austin, married Mary J. Ross, Peter F. Ross's daughter. He was chief of staff for Gov. Sullivan Ross, was named to the San Jacinto Battleground Commission by Gov. T. M. Campbell, and was named superintendent of the Texas National Penal System by Gov. Joseph Sayers.

Chapter Twenty-Two. Good Old Days

1. When Ralph Rupley moved with his parents from Victoria to Houston, one of his after-school jobs was lighting street lamps downtown. He became a successful furrier.

2. In 1907, the Central Christian Church moved to the big brick building on Main after seventeen years in the Victorian-Gothic church at Capitol and Caroline.

3. The big houses, so like the nineteenth-century mansions still standing in Galveston, gave way to the growing business district in the 1930s and 1940s. But Agnese Carter Nelms used the ballroom floor of the Carters' Main Street mansion when building the Heywood Nelms home on Sleepy Hollow in River Oaks, later purchased by Mrs. Thomas Pew.

4. After John Brady's death, the torch had been carried on by William D. Cleveland, Horace Baldwin Rice, William M. Read, H. W. Garrow, Charles H. Milby, Thomas W. House, Jr., Ed Sewall, and Eber Worthington Cave.

5. In 1898, he married Melange Binz, daughter of Jacob Binz, the skyscraper builder. Their son was B. J. Settegast.

6. Jesse Jones was born in Tennessee. When he was nine his father sold the farm to enter his brother's lumber business in Texas.

7. After her husband's death, Mrs. Jones, her daughters, and her nephew moved to the Capitol Hotel. Though she later moved them all into a baronial mansion at 2908 Main Street, Jesse Jones kept his taste for hotel living ever after.

8. The German pronunciation of Neuhaus

suffered a sea change. The Carl Ludwig branch pronounces it Newhouse, and the W. Oscar pronounces it Niehouse, but they share Ludwig as progenitor.

9. The house had been built in 1847 by Nathaniel Kellum.

10. Lewis Randolph Bryan married Mattie Shepherd. Their children were Lewis Randolph Bryan, Jr., and Mary Shepherd Bryan. Mary married Paul Gervais Bell. Their son, Paul Gervais Bell, Jr., married Sue Ledbetter, daughter of Dr. and Mrs. Paul Ledbetter, and their children are seventh-generation descendants of Moses Austin.

11. John and Stella Bonner Means were South Carolinians. His great-uncle was governor when Fort Sumter was fired upon. Bonner Means attended Central High School, Sweetbriar Academy, and Rice Institute.

12. Though he continued to manage his aunt's lumber company for five years, Jones also went into business for himself. His biographer, Bascomb Timmons, wrote that thanks to Jones and J. M. Rockwell, Mrs. Jones's one-million dollar inheritance grew to three million. M. T. Jones also willed valuable land on Buffalo Bayou to his son Will.

13. Mrs. Keeper was the mother of Sam Keeper.

14. Customarily, the washerwoman brought her children to keep the fire burning and haul water. The employer provided noonday dinner and enough take-home for supper.

15. Mrs. Donaldson was the mother of Sarah Emmott (Mrs. Army Emmott).

Chapter Twenty-Three. MURDER

1. *William Marsh Rice and His Institute* was written by Sylvia Stallings Morris, who served as editor of the papers and research notes of Dr. Andrew Forest Muir, Rice historian. Much of this story of murder is drawn from her book.

2. While married to Arthur Hearn, Elizabeth Bates Hearn lived at the Plaza Hotel. The *New York Times* of November 28, 1912, described her wedding to Ambassador da Gama in "the new town house of Mr. and Mrs. Elbert H. Gary at 856 Fifth Avenue." Mayor Gaynor performed the civil service and the Rev. Dr. Percy Stickney Grant, rector of the Church of the Ascension, the religious ceremony. Among the twenty guests present were her sons, Arthur and Morris Volck. When Elizabeth da Gama died in Paris, the *London Times* of April 26, 1937, announced a requiem mass at the Church of the Assumption, Warwick Street, "for the repose of the soul of Mme. Elizabeth da Gama, widow of Domicio da Gama, the late Brazilian ambassador." The *New York Times* of May 10, 1937, reported her death in Paris, noting her membership in the Colony Club and the Daughters of the American Revolution, and the services held in the Abbey Mausoleum at Arlington National Cemetery. The life begun in Huntsville, Texas, had taken her to three continents and into the highest social circles of the major capitals of the world.

3. Just what Patrick had to do with either Volck case is not clear. Harris County Court House records show the names of other lawyers in both the divorce and the countersuit. But in an interview published in New York newspapers during his trial, Patrick claimed to have represented the husband in his divorce suit, then the wife in her suit for community property. It may not be true; Patrick was a creative liar.

Chapter Twenty-Four. OIL

1. James Autry's grandfather, Micajah Autry, died fighting Santa Anna; his father was Speaker of the House of the Mississippi legislature. Born in 1859, James L. Autry attended the University of the South at Sewanee but at seventeen moved to Corsicana. There he claimed land granted by the Republic of Texas to his grandfather's heirs. At twenty, he was licensed to practice law, and at twenty-four was a judge in Navarro County. In 1896 he married Allie Kinsloe in Corsicana. They had two children, Allie May Autry, who married Edward Watson Kelley, and James Lockhart Autry, Jr. The Kelleys had two children, Allie Autry and Edward Watson Kelley, known as Mike. Mike Kelley was named to the federal reserve board in Washington in 1987.

2. William Campbell and his wife Sarah settled in Lampasas. Their daughter, Sadie, married Robert Lee Blaffer. The Blaffers had four children, John, Jane, Cecile (Titi), and Joyce, all born in Houston.

3. Both were in the last decade of their lives. James S. Hogg died on March 2, 1906. William Campbell died on April 6 of blood poisoning from a puncture wound he received at Hogg's funeral. He was forty-seven. His widow became the first woman stockholder in the Texas Company.

4. This was not his first meeting with royalty. He had met the reigning Hawaiian queen in 1898 as a member of the U.S. delegation welcoming annexation of the islands.

5. From Bradford, Pennsylvania, Thomas Donoghue married Mary Sullivan. Their son Francis was born in Bradford, their son Gerald in Beaumont, and their daughter Mary Catherine in Houston. Mary Catherine married Edwin Rice Brown of Deer Park and Houston. Of the Texas-based members of the first board, Donoghue was the only one still with the Texas Company after 1913.

6. A roughneck is a driller's helper. For the ambitious, roughnecking led up the oilfield ladder.

7. The market boat carried produce to Galveston and brought back stock for sale. At twenty-three, Ross Sterling married Maude Abbe Gage. At twenty-five he went into the produce commission business at Galveston but lost it in the 1900 storm. Opening a store at Sour Lake, he got caught up in the oil business.

8. William Wiess was the son of Simon Wiess, who had come to Beaumont from Poland in 1839 after years of shipping in Turkey, New England, the West Indies, and Louisiana.

9. Howard R. Hughes and Allene Gano of Dallas were married in 1903. His brother, Rupert Hughes, became an author, playwright, and film director in Hollywood.

10. In 1897, Walter Sharp married Estelle Boughton of Dallas. They had three children, Walter Bedford Sharp, Kathleen, and Dudley Crawford Sharp, who became secretary of the air force in the Eisenhower administration.

11. In 1903 John T. Crotty married Regina Padden of West Virginia. They had three children, John William, Frank Bernard, and Elizabeth Jane. Elizabeth married Victor Neuhaus Carter.

12. H. T. Staiti married Odelia Reisner of Victoria in 1901. The Staiti house on Westmoreland was moved to Sam Houston Park by the Harris County Heritage Society in 1988.

13. The Robert Welch Foundation has benefited the M. D. Anderson Hospital in Houston, Texas A&M University, Prairie View A&M, the University of Houston, and Texas Southern University, all in the state system, as well as Baylor and Rice universities.

14. At sixteen in 1872, Niels Esperson landed in New York with five dollars and a train ticket to San Francisco. He spent fourteen days crossing the country. While working for a Danish cattleman, he taught himself English from Webster's dictionary. He studied geology under California's state geologist and prospected for gold in California and Colorado and for oil in Oklahoma and

Kansas. In Houston, his interests included oil, rice, manufacture, real estate, and the ship channel. He was one of the founders of Great Southern Life Insurance Company.

15. In 1909, Thomas A. Spencer married Louise Chesnutt of Murfreesboro, Tennessee. They had one child, Nancy (Mrs. James T. Heyl).

16. The field was named for the town of Humble, which had been named for Pleasant Humble, a justice of the peace. It gave a deceptively modest name to a powerful corporation.

17. Several hundred persons signed a tribute that said, in part: "By his death we are brought to an even greater realization of his high attainments, his stainless honor, his strength and power and courage and resourcefulness for conquering difficulties; his gentleness and consideration for all his fellow workers; his genial and never-failing spirit of charity towards all men."

18. Harry Wiess did not move his family to Houston until 1919. His wife was the former Olga Keith of Beaumont. They had three daughters, Elizabeth, Caroline, and Margaret—Mrs. Lloyd H. Smith, Mrs. Theodore Law, and Mrs. James Elkins, Jr.

Chapter Twenty-Five. THE BEAUMONT CROWD

1. Old Houstonians made the same wistful plaint in 1946 about the influx from Tulsa, West Texas and the East. The 1908 version comes from *Key to the City of Houston.*

2. To the annoyance of old Houstonians, old San Felipe Road was renamed West Dallas.

3. The Sharp property became the site of a Sears store.

4. Ella Cochrum was born in 1880 in Kentucky and brought by her parents to Corsicana. When she was fifteen, her father died and she left school to help her mother with five brothers and a baby sister. She met Walter Fondren when he was drilling a well near her home. They were married on Valentine's Day, 1903. Their three children were Sue (Mrs. W. B. Trammell), Walter, Jr., who married Mary Doris Ledwidge, and Catherine (Mrs. Milton Underwood).

5. The Neuhaus children, all born at Hackberry Plantation, were Hugo Victor Ludwig Neuhaus in 1882, Ilse (Mrs. Joseph H. Richardson) in 1887, and Erna (Mrs. Morton Crawford King) in 1891.

6. The children of William T. and Maude Holley Carter, all born at Camden, were Lena (Mrs. James J. Carroll), Jesse (Mrs. Judson Taylor), William T. Carter, Jr. (who married Lillie

Neuhaus), Agnese (Mrs. Haywood Nelms), Aubrey (who married Marjorie Leachman), and Frankie (Mrs. R. D. Randolph). The W. T. Carter family is unrelated to the Samuel Fain Carters.

7. The Link-Lee house became the administration building of the University of St. Thomas.

Chapter Twenty-Six. IMA HOGG

1. The myth that Ima had a sister named Ura still lingers. Many life-long Texans believe it to be true. In the 1960s, it appeared in a "Dear Abby" column. In the 1970s, an elderly woman visiting the Bayou Bend museum insisted that she had gone to grammar school in Houston with "poor little Ura." But Gov. James Hogg had only one daughter–Ima.

2. Drawings that she made as a child show that Ima Hogg also had artistic talent. In adulthood this was evident in her eye for art and antiques.

3. Miss Hogg often recalled this experience. Probably the last time she told it was to her friend, Mrs. Braxton Thompson, the day before leaving for London, where she died.

4. In 1962, Miss Hogg told this story to the Princesse de Croy who was visiting Bayou Bend from Paris. She was the daughter of the Frenchman who had escorted Ima to the ball.

5. Leopold Stokowski, too, was born in 1882.

6. Their granddaughter, Christine Thorbecke George (Mrs. Shane George), became a Houstonian of the 1980s. Stokowski became conductor of the Houston Symphony Orchestra in 1955.

7. Miss Hogg gave this explanation to her friend Barbara K. Dillingham.

8. Ima Hogg was the leading force in founding the Houston Symphony Orchestra. She founded the Houston Child Guidance Center. She restored and gave to the University of Texas the Winedale Inn property as a center for ethnic studies. She gave to the state of Texas the Varner-Hogg Plantation as a park. She gave Bayou Bend, her home and collection of early American furniture and art, to the Houston Museum of Fine Arts. And given disposition of her brother Will's estate, she established the Hogg Foundation for Mental Health.

Chapter Twenty-Seven. INTO THE TWENTIETH CENTURY

1. Mrs. Frank Anderson was Will Clayton's sister.

2. The E. O. Smith Middle School is named for the educator. Born in Alabama, he attended Birmingham schools and graduated from Fisk University.

3. This son, Robert A. Lovett, was assistant secretary of war during World War II and served as undersecretary to Gen. George Marshall in both state and defense departments. In April, 1948, while General Marshall was out of the country, Lovett was acting secretary of state. From 1951 to 1953, he was secretary of defense.

4. Hiram Garwood, born in Bastrop and graduate of the University of the South, practiced law, served in the Texas Legislature, and was a Bastrop County judge before moving to Houston in 1902. Judge and Mrs. Garwood had three children: Louise, Calvin B., and W. St. John Garwood.

5. The Bryans had four children: Guy Morrison, Carolyn Laura, Florence Carter, and Hally Ballinger Bryan II.

6. Woodrow Wilson appointed T. W. House, Jr., postmaster of Houston.

7. Mrs. M. T. Jones and her daughters had moved out of this house to the Capitol Hotel on the death of her husband. They later moved to the still bigger house at 2908.

8. The Heritage Society moved the house and its guard dogs to Sam Houston Park in 1965.

9. The Brady mansion was moved around the corner to 3801 Wilmer in the 1920s. It became a sandwich shop.

10. The Howards had four children, Eugenia, Ryland, Georgia, and Philo Howard, Jr.

11. Mr. Lucas was the father of George Anna (Mrs. Thomas Walker Burke).

12. Alfred C. Finn was the architect on most of the fifty skyscrapers Mr. Jones built in the next fifty years.

13. Mr. Jones's funeral was held at St. Paul's Church.

14. James Cafcalas was the maternal grandfather of Houston Mayor Fred Hofheinz.

15. Among the unions were the Bookbinders; the Brewery Workers; the Carriage and Wagonworkers; the Icemen's Protective Union; the Carriage, Cab and Delivery Wagon Drivers' Union; the Theatrical Mechanical Association; the International Alliance of Theatrical Stage Employees; the Journeyman Tailors; the Painters and Decorators; the Shirt Waist and Laundry Workers' International; the Soda Water Workers' Union, and the Stenographers' and Typewriters' Association.

16. The hospital was ahead of its time. Not all hospitals built in the 1950s had private baths.

Chapter Twenty-Eight. AUTOMOBILES, AN UN-NOTICED REVOLUTION

1. Mr. Stewart was the great-grandfather of Garth Bates, Stewart Bates, and Molly Bates (Mrs. James Maynard).

2. With the invention of the self-starter, a woman could start her own car. This ended the electric runabout.

3. In 1912, Houston bragged that three hundred miles of shell road led out of the city. Shells, crisp and clean when first laid down, turned to mush under rain and traffic.

4. Stark Young later became a drama critic in New York City.

5. From the papers of Randy Pace of 1435 Heights Boulevard.

6. Mark Edwin Andrews, Houston lawyer and industrialist, was assistant secretary of the navy 1947–49.

7. The Godwin daughters became Mrs. Charles McLean and Mrs. DeWitt Gordon.

Chapter Twenty-Nine. RICE INSTITUTE

1. Woodrow Wilson had been a Princeton classmate of William Marsh Rice II in 1879. Younger men, like Palmer Hutcheson, remembered Wilson as a professor. Harry Wiess studied mathematics under Dr. Lovett.

2. Edgar Odell Lovett was born in Shreve, Ohio, in 1871. In 1897 he married Mary Ellen Hale of Mayfield, Kentucky. They had three children, Adelaide, Malcolm, and Laurence.

3. Rice paid two hundred and fifty thousand dollars for 190 acres, but Charles F. Weber held on to his eight-acre farm. The board finally paid him seven thousand dollars an acre.

4. Edgar Odell Lovett interview in his office in 1947.

5. James C. Morehead, Jr., gives a delightful account of the construction in his *Walking Tour of Rice University.*

6. This notion may have delayed efforts by Rice trustees to gain endowment.

7. Edward Teas moved the Teas Nursery from Carthage, Missouri, to Bellaire in 1907. He planted the Montrose, Yoakum, Lovett, and Audubon esplanades. He landscaped the grounds for Robert L. Blaffer, H. M. Garwood, Harry C. Wiess, Joseph B. Cullinan, John T. Crotty, W. D. Cleveland, and B. F. Bonner.

8. The program of the opening was a folio bound in suede, with architectural drawings in color of the future campus. It gave a biographical sketch of the savants, including Sir Henry Jones, fellow of the British Academy; Privy Councillor Baron Dairoku Kikuchi, former president of the universities of Tokyo and Kyoto; John William Mackail, professor of poetry at Oxford; Privy Councillor Wilhelm Ostwald of Germany, Nobel Laureate in chemistry in 1909; and Carl Stormer, member of the Norway Academy of Science.

9. Huxley, who would gain worldwide fame, was proud of his post at this raw young university. He referred in his memoirs to "this exciting job in the U.S.A."

Chapter Thirty. AS THE TWIG IS BENT

1. Mrs. C. R. Cummings was the second president, Dr. Margaret Holland the third, and Mrs. George Heyer the fourth.

2. When the Carnegie Library closed, the peripatetic Venus moved to the new Houston Public Library. As durable as her prototype, she was still standing in the Julia Ideson Building eighty-six years after her arrival in Houston.

3. One picture of the Welch school includes Mary Porter Kirkland, Mayola Frances Patton, Adelaide Lovett, Grace Leavell, Michael Mellinger, John S. Mellinger, Allen V. Peden, Doris Japhet, McIver Streetman, H. Malcolm Lovett, Benjamin B. Rice, Jr., William States Jacobs, Jr., Charles Neuhaus, Robert Dabney, J. Victor Neuhaus, Nell Streetman, Tilford Jones, Claxton Parks, George P. Macatea, Jr., Edgar Block, William A. Kirkland, Walter Bedford Sharp, Sterling Adair, Ralph Neuhaus, Dudley Niday, Eugene Meador, Carl Dudley, Richard M. Taliaferro, Edward D. Peden, Lee Cottingham, Jesse Dudley, Wilbourn Campbell, Fred M. Golding, John Cullinan, Carter Grinstead, Norman Pillot, John Thad Scott, Jr., Henry Cortes, Emil Japhet, Margaret Scott, and Elizabeth Taliaferro (pronounced Tolliver).

4. "Miss Hargis" was the first-born daughter and by the custom of the day had no need to use her first name in social listings and calling cards. Ima Hogg, for example, had cards engraved simply "Miss Hogg." This Blue Book listing, therefore, was the correct usage.

5. Edith Paine married Arthur Hamilton. Roene Masterson married Elliott Cage, Daphne Palmer married Edwin Neville. Etta Brady married John W. Garrow. Sallie Sewall married George Horton.

6. Howard Hughes, Jr., was often late to

school and Miss Eichler reprimanded him for being tardy. But this twig could not be bent. In their teens, Chaille Cage, Joanna Nazro, and other girls found Howard incurably late for dates.

7. In the 1980s, Mrs. Malcolm Lovett was told that during World War I, in fear of anti-German sentiment, Miss Eichler remained hidden in a Houston home throughout 1917 and 1918, unbeknownst to friends or neighbors.

8. The Diehls had four daughters: Zelie Marie, a pianist; Gabrielle, a violinist; and Elizabeth and Antoinette, who taught French. Gabrielle married Wilson Portevent Fraser. Their daughter, Gabrielle (Babette) Fraser married David Warren, and the Frasers' grandson, Robert Wilson Fraser Warren, is a fourth-generation Houstonian. Zelie married Leland Valentine Dolan; their sons are Leland A. and George D. Dolan

9. Many white children under the age of twelve were working ten-hour days in laundries and stores. If a parent died, the oldest daughter often quit school to help her mother, the oldest son to take a job.

10. The High School for the Performing and Visual Arts was built on the Montrose site.

11. Louise married Ben Reed Barbee; Sue married Court Norton; and Dotty Wilson married Henry L. Wrightman, Jr.

Chapter Thirty-One. A Sweet Life

1. Lucie Campbell Lee was the great-great-aunt of Mary Martha Wren Boyd, Clark C. Wren, Jr., Nancy Wren Harris, and Dr. Robert Wren.

2. Mark Edwin Andrews, a Houston lawyer and industrialist, was assistant secretary of the navy in 1948 and 1949.

3. St. John Garwood became a justice of the Texas supreme court. He married Ellen Clayton and they had two sons, W. St. John Garwood, Jr., and William Lockhart Garwood, both lawyers. After two years on the Texas high court, 1979–80, Will Garwood became a judge in the Fifth Circuit Court of Appeals.

4. Galveston refugees flooded Houston for weeks. Houston newspapers each day listed survivors who had reached the mainland.

5. After graduation from Princeton, Bill Kirkland turned down a contract to play pro baseball. He later helped bring national league baseball to Houston.

6. Succeeding kings were John Henry Kirby, 1900; Dennis Call, 1901; Jesse Jones, 1902; B. F. Bonner, 1903; Presley K. Ewing, 1904; Jo S. Rice, 1905; C. K. Dunlap, 1906; H. M. Garwood, 1907;

James D. Dawson, 1908; James A. Baker, 1909; W. T. Carter, 1910; Edgar Odell Lovett, 1911; Walter B. Sharp, 1912; R. C. Duff, 1913; Eugene A. Hudson, 1914; Robert E. Paine, 1915.

By year, the queens and the men they later married were: 1899, Annie Quinlan, E. T. Randle; 1900, Julia Mae Morse, W. D. Cleveland, Jr.; 1901, Augusta Goodhue, Eugene Solari of New Orleans; 1902, Claire Robinson, James H. Bute; 1903, Bessie Kirby, James S. Stewart; 1904, Florence Carter, Guy Bryan; 1905, Sallie Sewall, George Horton; 1906, Gertrude Paine, David Daly; 1907, Alice Baker, Murray Jones; 1908, Mamie Stuart Shearn, Ed Forbes; 1909, Lillian Neuhaus, W. T. Carter, Jr.; 1910, Laura Rice, Richard Neff; 1911, Annie Vive Carter, Edward Lillo Crain; 1912, Garland Bonner, George Howard; 1913, Lottie Baldwin Rice, Stephen Farish; 1914, Frankie Carter, R. D. Randolph; 1915, Marion Holt Seward, Robert S. (Cotchy) Neal.

7. Later Mrs. R. D. Randolph, liberal Democratic Party leader in Texas.

Chapter Thirty-Two. Living High

1. In the fall of 1912, House moved from Austin to 115 East 53rd Street, New York City. Mr. Wilson went there so often that it became known as America's No. 10 Downing Street.

2. Most Houston houses lacked central heat until World War II. Some prewar houses had individual steam radiators with gas jets that were lighted by a match. Others had gas-fired space heaters. Floor furnaces appeared in the 1930s.

3. At seventeen, Alfred Finn came to Houston to work for the Southern Pacific Railroad. He took a correspondence course in architecture and became an apprentice draftsman for Sanguinet and Staats, a Fort Worth architectural firm. In 1913, Finn's first commission was the M. E. Foster Building at 715-19 Main Street. He designed the San Jacinto Monument, the Music Hall and Coliseum, the Gulf Building, and many other buildings for Jesse Jones.

4. Mrs. Wilcox was elected president general in 1945, the youngest in UDC history. She was entertained by Mrs. Harry Truman and her daughter Margaret in Independence and in the White House, and by Margaret Mitchell in Atlanta.

5. William P. Milby was a member of the Texas Congress 1842–44. He was from Delaware, his wife from Maryland. Their son Charles was born in Indianola, came to Harrisburg in 1872, married Maggie Tod of Galveston in 1879, and

went into the coal business with Andrew Dow.

6. Including new suburbs like Westmoreland and Courtlandt, Greater Houston claimed a hundred thousand.

Chapter Thirty-Three. A SYMPHONY, A PARK, A CHANNEL

1. Churches sent their ministers off on long summer vacations.

2. This was at a time when twenty-five dollars could buy a winter overcoat or a tailored suit.

3. In 1915, Will Hobby married Willie Cooper, daughter of former Congressman Samuel Bronson Cooper. She died in 1929.

4. In Houston lore, George Hermann meant for the Martha Hermann Square to be a safe haven against arrest for cattlemen coming into town to get drunk on Saturday nights.

Chapter Thirty-Four. TWILIGHT OF PEACE

1. Thomas Watt Gregory was an 1885 law graduate of the University of Texas. His children were Houstonians Jane Gregory Heyer Marechal (Mrs. Greer Marechal) and Thomas W. Gregory, Jr.

2. For this magazine article, George Sylvester Viereck interviewed Kaiser Wilhelm in exile in the Netherlands.

3. Burke Baker was born in Waco in 1887. After graduation from the University of Texas and study at Harvard, he married Bennie Brown of Cleburne in 1911. The Burke Baker Planetarium was his gift to Houston.

4. The Williams children were John C. Williams, Jr., Margaret, Anne, Dorothy, and Willoughby. Willoughby Williams ultimately held a position in American General.

5. Wortham and his wife Fannie had three children: Fanetta (Mrs. James A. Hill); Gus, who married Lyndall Finley; and Katherine, known as Cad, who married Robert Davis. The two Davis daughters were Fannie and author June Davis.

6. Mrs. McAshan, the former Aline Harris, was a founding member of the Pi Beta Phi chapter at the University of Texas and twice president of the Garden Club of Houston.

7. S. I. Morris, Jr., married Suzanne Kibler of Columbus, Ohio. They had five children, Peter, Maria, David, Laura, and John. Mr. Morris was a major supporter of the Museum of Fine Arts, as well as of Rice. Of the many buildings his firm of Wilson, Morris, Crain and Anderson

designed, the best known is the Astrodome. Mrs. Morris became a leader in the Garden Club of Houston and a national fundraiser for Wellesley, her alma mater.

8. Sue Vaughn brought to the marriage the gift of fun and enjoyment. Taking on a man's responsibilities while still in his teens, Will Clayton was hardworking to a fault. In his Houston years, he gained the easy humor and charm that endeared him to colleagues and to world leaders.

9. Four daughters and four of their cousins grew up in the house. Ellen, an author, married W. St. John Garwood; Susan, a philanthropist, married S. M. McAshan, Jr.; Burdine, a poet, married Jack Johnson; and Julia, a lawyer, married Dr. Ben Baker of Johns Hopkins University.

10. Jules Settegast, chairman of the Chamber of Commerce Good Roads Committee, urged that all Houston streets be 120 feet wide to take care of future traffic. Unfortunately, his advice was not followed.

11. Fannin had not yet gone past Eagle.

Chapter Thirty-Five. THE GREAT WAR

1. Anti-German feeling prompted absurdities. In 1917, zealots called for a ban on German music, "despite the fact that London audiences were . . . calmly enjoying *Tristan and Isolde* during an air raid," Olga Samaroff Stokowski wrote in her autobiography. But she had known Colonel House all her life. When the Woodrow Wilsons visited the Houses near Boston, she and Mark Twain's daughter Clara, each married to an orchestra conductor, "laid the matter before the President and Colonel House." They left with "an official verdict that it was not necessary to extend current warfare to composers long since dead nor to deprive our audiences of musical masterpieces that belong to the world."

2. James L. Autry III died only five years later. Graduated with honors from Rice Institute, he had become vice-president of the American Petroleum Company. His mother gave the city the property occupied by the Houston Center for the Mentally Retarded. A park at Shepherd Drive and Allen Parkway commemorates the gift.

3. M. Tilford Jones, the grandson of the millionaire lumberman M. T. Jones, married Audrey Taylor in 1917. Their daughter, Audrey Louise Jones, married John A. Beck during World War II.

4. Thompson had two sons. Lewis, a Princeton graduate, married Chaille Cage; Ben,

a University of Virginia graduate, married Frederika Lykes.

5. Dr. Bertner was a graduate of the University of Texas Medical School in Galveston. While a resident in New York City, he was the anesthetist for an operation on Jesse Jones. Jones brought him to Houston.

6. From a congregation that numbered fewer than 280.

7. Ilena B. Benda wrote about the achievements of black Houstonians in her book, *Our Community War Service Memorial, Houston and Harris County, Lest We Forget*, 1919. Unfortunately, she did not give the names of those honored.

8. Charles W. Duncan, Jr., would become president of Duncan Foods, Houston; chairman of Coca Cola, Europe; a deputy secretary in the defense department; and President Carter's secretary of energy.

9. W. A. Vinson married Ethel Turner in Sherman in 1900. They had three children: Virginia (Mrs. J. Griffith Lawhon); Julia (Mrs. Charles William Dabney, Jr.), and Martha (Mrs. Dean Emerson).

10. Judge and Mrs. Elkins had two sons: William S. and James A. Elkins, Jr.

Chapter Thirty-Six. MUTINY

1. Houston police often shot at the ground near the feet of persons being questioned.

2. This sector became West Dallas.

3. Among those on the list were Hugo Neuhaus, Clarence Kendall, Harry Attwell, W. S. Cochran, Maurice McAshan, Denton Cooley, Maurice Hirsch, Jules Settegast, Jr., Oscar Holcombe, H. B. Washburn, Henry Stude, Pat Foley, Norman Kittrell, Jr., Charlie Bering, March Culmore, Capt. Sinclair Talliaferro, Judge A. E. Amerman, Joe DeGeorge, Arthur Binz, J. W. Link, R. A. Kendrick, M. R. Waddell, W. S. Lubbock, R. W. Dundas, H. C. Mosehart, Harvey Cullinan, W. S. H. Minchen, T. J. Donoghue, G. L. Noble, Sam Green, R. F. Greenwood, Henry Hamblen, Charles Shearn, Jr., Kenneth Krahl, J. C. Hutcheson, Jr., J. R. Marmion, Ira McFarland, W. C. Munn, E. A. Peden, D. E. Peden, Ed Black, R. M. Fonville, H. Baldwin Rice, W. S. Hunt, Arthur Dunn, R. W. Wier, F. C. Clements, Dan Japhet, Gus Japhet, Hugh Potter, D. W. Michaux, George A. Hill, Jr., John H. Freeman, B. A. Riesner, Jr., F. F. Arnim, F. Fatjo, E. C. Guion, and Louis Roos.

4. Judge Crooker had seen Captain Mattes

shot while standing in the open car trying to quell the mutiny.

5. Between May 15 and June 12, 1928, the *Gargoyle* carried a series of five articles on the mutiny, written by a former army major. In his research, he came to have a sympathy for Sergeant Henry. Henry had been distressed by the East St. Louis riot where white mobs ravaged a black neighborhood, killing thirty-nine people. Apparently, in the last hours of his life, he thought Houston was going to be another East St. Louis.

6. This tragedy inspired the formation of a Houston chapter of the National Association for the Advancement of Colored People.

Chapter Thirty-Seven. HOME FRONT

1. Mrs. Saunders grew up in a tree-shaded house at Texas and Fannin. In 1917, backed by Edwin B. Parker, she brought in Anna Pavlova and the Boston Symphony Orchestra. The evening cleared only fourteen dollars, but she had found the career that would enrich Houston until her death in 1963.

2. Among the many wartime weddings: Lelia Tudor Torrey to Fitzhugh Carter Pannill, Mary Augusta Fraley to Ralph Clarkson Cooley, Marian Holt Seward to James Robert Neal, Erna Neuhaus to Morton Crawford King, Stella Root to James Royston Williams, Mathilde Booth to Wharton Weems, Lottie Kathleen Blakeley to Browne Botts Rice, Audrey Thompson to Martin Tilford Jones.

3. Nina Cullinan gave the Cullinan Hall to the Museum of Fine Arts in memory of her parents.

4. His son, Bill Hobby, would make the same decision as lieutenant governor in 1987.

5. After her divorce, Hortense Malsch brought her three daughters from Edna to Houston Heights. She married Judge W. H. Ward and passed the state bar examinations in 1910. Her daughter Marguerite married Judge John H. Crooker. Her grandson, John H. Crooker, Jr., has a silver loving cup inscribed: "Hortense Ward: A remembrance for faithful service to Texas women from the Houston Equal Suffrage Association, March 21, 1913–March 21, 1918."

6. Prohibition was prompted by the growing excesses. Saloons made streets unsafe. Opening in the morning, they sent a steady flow of drunken men reeling out, often to sicken or to pass out on the sidewalks. "Father, dear Father,

come home with me now," was not considered funny in 1915.

Prohibition let a generation of Americans grow up who never saw a drunk. Mark H. Moore, professor of criminal justice at Harvard, points out that cirrhosis death rates for men dropped from 29.5 per 100,000 in 1911 to 10.7 in 1929. Hospital admissions for alcoholic psychosis were cut in half between 1919 and 1928. Homicide rates that climbed sharply between 1900 and 1910 leveled off in Prohibition's fourteen years.

7. Of the Franzheims' children, Lillie Wier and Elizabeth were born in Chicago and Kenneth Franzheim, Jr., was born in New York City. They grew up at Wayside, the Simms family place.

8. Dunlavy Street was named for Herbert Dunlavy, Waugh Drive for Tom T. Waugh, and Jensen Drive for Lawrence Jensen. Until the 1950s, a street linking Elgin to Westheimer bore the name of Hathaway. Edwin Riesner, a graduate of Texas A&M University, went to France in February, 1918. Promoted to captain on June 12, 1918, he was killed in action at Chateau-Thiery June 14. His body lies in the National Cemetery of France. Young Street, where the family lived, was renamed Riesner Street. Poor Farm Road was renamed for George Hermann Bissonnet but usage has changed the pronunciation from *Biss*onnet to Bisso*net*.

9. Mr. and Mrs. Joseph Cullinan gave the Houston Negro Hospital as a memorial to their son, John.

Chapter Thirty-Eight. IN THE REALMS OF POWER

1. There had been rifts between Wilson and House during the Versailles conference, but no real quarrel. Wilson's stroke left him a sometimes fretful man. When Colonel House called at the White House, he was told the president was too sick to see anyone. House never referred to the break and continued to be an influence in world affairs.

2. The Parkers sold their estate, The Oaks, to Capt. James Baker. He willed it to Rice Institute. Known as the Old Baker Estate, it was an orphanage in the early 1940s and a temporary site of the M. D. Anderson Hospital in the 1950s. Architect Lavone Dickinsheets Andrews adapted the house for hospital use. It no longer stands.

3. Son of a German-born Confederate officer, Fred Heyne was born in Houston in 1878. By 1917, he was Jones's close friend and an officer in most of the Jones enterprises, including the

Bankers Mortgage Company, National Bank of Commerce, and Jones Lumber Company. He married Hallie Brookshire; they had one son, Charles. After her death, he married Mayne E. Green; they had a son, Frederick J. Heyne, Jr.

4. Peden headed the committee that raised eight hundred thousand dollars to build a new YWCA. After the death of his wife Ione, he married Cora Root. They had four children, Allen, Edward, Ione, and Stella.

Chapter Thirty-Nine. POSTWAR

1. Will Hogg ultimately had one of the largest Remington collections in the country.

2. Years later, George Brown, as chairman of the Rice University board, expressed the same belief.

3. Tom Spies was the brother of Dr. John Spies, at one time head of the University of Texas medical school in Galveston.

4. Mrs. Allen used stones, timbers, and paneling of the old home to build a seaside house on Bay Shore. In 1921, she offered use of the beach house to the Episcopal Diocese of Texas. It became the first Camp Allen, providing summer camping for boys and girls and an adult retreat.

5. Dr. Johnston married Marie Louise Hogg.

6. In the late 1940s, Dr. Herman Johnson helped shape the department of obstetrics and gynecology at Baylor University College of Medicine. Margaret Wiess, who married James A. Elkins, Jr., believes that her son James III was Dr. Johnson's last delivery.

7. The Roussels had three children, Stephanie (Mrs. William Claud Milburn), Hubert de Tavanne Roussel, Jr. (killed in World War II), and Peter Harris Roussel, who became a White House spokesman in the Reagan administration.

8. Wharton Weems and Mathilda Booth were married in 1918. They had three children, Elizabeth Virginia, Benjamin F., and F. Carrington Weems.

9. Mr. Godwin was variously vice-president of the Houston Philosophical Society, president of the Green Mask Players, a director of the Museum of Fine Arts, and a Christ Church vestryman. Born on a plantation near Memphis, Herbert Godwin finished Emory College in Atlanta at nineteen. He taught Latin at Bolton College near Memphis. He and Lila Humphreys were married in 1896. They had four children: Elizabeth (Mrs. DeWitt Gordon), Ann (Mrs. Charles

I. McLean), Lila (Mrs. Thomas W. Moore), and Virginia. The DeWitt Gordons had two daughters, Lila and Jean.

10. In the Rice *Campanile* of 1922 a picture of masked, white-robed figures is headed "The Ku Klux Klan of Rice Institute," with a subhead "The Year The Owls Were So Bad."

11. Great-grandson of an Austin colonist, A. Frank Smith was born in Elgin, grew up in Corsicana, graduated from Southwestern University, and went to Vanderbilt Theological Seminary. In 1923, he received the D.D. degree from Southwestern. In 1915, he founded what became the Highland Park Methodist Church, Dallas. He married Bess Patience Crutchfield of Blossom, Texas.

12. Temple Beth Israel later offered its haven to St. Paul's Methodist Church and to the First Presbyterian Church.

13. John H. Freeman and Edna Stewart, who had met at Central High School, were married in 1912. While studying Texas law, he worked for the Stewart Title Company. After serving overseas in World War I, he practiced law with Sterling Meyer and Mayor Ben Campbell.

William Bates, who led his law school class at the University of Texas and was twice wounded in France, returned to Nacogdoches. He married Mary Estill Dorsey in 1919. He was elected district attorney, but his fight against the Ku Klux Klan cost him reelection. He moved to Houston to practice civil law.

14. The park fell into disuse. Sixty-five years later, through the Park People, Root Square was relandscaped and on June 18, 1987, rededicated with two of the original donors present—William A. Kirkland and Laura Kirkland Bruce.

Chapter Forty. SOCIAL NOTES FROM THE TWENTIES

1. Ladies wore "invisible hairnets" made of human hair matching their own. This gave an oddly rigid look, as though the coiffure had been varnished. In the 1950s, women got the same effect with a lacquer spray. (Hence the commercial name of Spraynet.)

2. Among weddings of the 1920s were those of Rosalie Hutcheson to Laurence S. Bosworth, Lois Cleveland to William A. Kirkland, Huberta Nunn to Hiram M. Garwood, Josephine Dawson to Lobel Alva Carlton, Jane Throckmorton to Presley K. Ewing, Cad Carter Wortham to Robert C. Davis, Hildegarde Storey to George Baldwin Journeay of Liverpool, Helen Wicks to John Wiley Link, Jr.

3. The Lummises had four children: Allene (Mrs. Paul S. Russell); Anne (Mrs. George F. Neff); William, who married Frances Bradley; and Dr. Frederick R. Lummis, Jr., who married Marilyn Graves. The Houstouns also had four children: Janet (Mrs. Platt Walker Davis, Jr.); Sara (Mrs. John H. Lindsey); James P. Houstoun, Jr., who married Evelyn Nicholson; and William Gano Houstoun, who married Marian Fleming. All eight are first cousins of Howard Hughes, Jr.

4. In 1949, the Blue Bird Circle Children's Clinic became the first in the South for research and treatment in epilepsy.

5. Later Mrs. Browne Baker, Mrs. R. D. Randolph, Mrs. A. S. Vandervoort, Jr., Mrs. C. P. Greenough Fuller, Mrs. Stephen Farish, Mrs. DeWitt M. Gordon, Jr., Mrs. James Winston, Mrs. Bedford Sharp, Mrs. Andrew Jackson Ray, Mrs. James Rorick Cravens, Mrs. Sanders Miller, and Miss Chew.

6. The *Encyclopedia* says that Mrs. Culmore led the Texas Federation of Women's Clubs in the campaign for the Good Roads Bill by the Texas legislature, adding: "She has the distinction of being the only woman ever to attempt this work." Then hurrying to reassure: "Lillian Culmore is . . . a lover of home, is domestically inclined in every way and is in fact a woman's woman."

7. Ima Hogg, Dr. Stockton Acton, Lottie Rice (Mrs. Stephen Farish), Caroline Levy, Mr. and Mrs. John Clark Tilden, J. T. Rather, Jr., Blanche Higgenbotham, Dewey Roussel, and Julia Ideson were all part of this shifting scene.

Chapter Forty-One. AN ELEGANT SOUTHERN TOWN

1. The Clayton house was later remodeled for year-round use.

2. Though the Claytons' was the first house started, the Joseph Chews' house at 3335 Inwood was the first completed. Designed by John Staub, it was bought by Mr. and Mrs. Herman Brown in the 1940s.

3. Gov. and Mrs. William P. Hobby bought Shadyside in the 1940s. It was razed in 1972, and Mrs. Hobby gave the land to Rice University.

4. The sale of Lot Q in Will Hogg's absence may not have prompted him to create his own residential section, but the larger Hogg property made possible the Bayou Bend Museum.

5. Born in Knoxville, Tennessee, John Staub

served in the Naval Reserve Flying Corps in World War I and in the navy in World War II. In 1919 he married Madeline Delabarre of Conway, Massachusetts, a graduate of Parsons School of Design in New York. They had three children, Dr. John Delabarre Staub, who married Alice Michaux York; Nancy, who married William Wareing, and Caroline, who married Charles Callery.

6. James Lykes was from Tampa, the son of Dr. H. T. Lykes. Mrs. Lykes was from Tallahassee, the daughter of Justice Charles Breckinridge Parkhill. They married in 1906.

7. A. D. Foreman first sold lots in West University Place in 1917. It was incorporated in 1925.

8. John Crooker had already developed subdivisions east of Almeda. He was a founder of Fulbright, Crooker. This became Fulbright, Crooker, Freeman, & Bates, one of the largest law firms in the country, and, by 1986, it was Fulbright & Jaworski.

9. The gang included Henry and Ebbe Holden, Charles Westmoreland, Bernard Lorino, Walter Myer, and Lawrence and Leroy Towles. With a B.A. from Rice Institute and a law degree from the University of Texas, John Crooker, Jr., joined his father's law firm of Fulbright & Crooker.

10. The 1896 *Blue Book* lists Captain Baker as Jas. A. Baker, Jr., his father as Judge Jas. A. Baker, and his son as Jimmie. On his father's death, Captain Baker dropped the "Jr." and Jimmie acquired it. Thus, the fourth James A. Baker is listed as III. All have been attorneys. All but the fourth entered the firm of Baker & Botts.

11. When Dr. and Mrs. Wilkerson moved to South Boulevard, her father said that he had shot prairie chickens in what became her garden.

12. Mr. Sterling's widow, Isla Carroll Sterling Turner, gave the house to the Museum of Fine Arts, which sold it to Gus and Lyndall Wortham. They bequeathed it to the University of Houston as the president's residence.

13. At Lanier he made friends with Walter Cronkite, Frances Heyck, Elizabeth Nelms, Virginia Davis, Ralph Michels, and Billy Eckhardt.

14. The Anderson sons were James E., Frank, W. Leland, Robert, Thomas Dunaway, and Benjamin Moore Anderson. James became personnel director of Anderson, Clayton in Houston, and Leland its financial vice-president. Thomas D. Anderson became an attorney and Ben Anderson an airplane manufacturer.

15. Will Hogg held reversionary rights over how the land of both Memorial and Hermann parks should be used. The rights carried over to his estate.

16. Born in Longview, E. L. Crain attended Southwestern University and moved to Houston in 1903. In 1915, he married Annie Vive Carter. They had three children: Edward Lillo, Jr., Carter F., and Richard Crain.

17. The Southside Place land had been held briefly by the firm of Haden and Austin. Auden Street was named by combining Austin and Haden. Edloe was named for Edward Lillo Crain.

18. Born in Brazoria County, a graduate of Washington and Lee University, Neill T. Masterson came to Houston in 1904. He married Libby Johnston, daughter of the Rienzi Johnstons. They had three children, Neill T., Jr., who married Madora Foster, Elizabeth (Mrs. Franklin F. Devine), and Harris III, who married Carroll Sterling Cowan.

Chapter Forty-Two. THE RIVER OAKS PLAN MATURES

1. Mike Hogg owned a hunting lodge nearby that he called Tall Timbers. Hugh Potter became president of the River Oaks Corporation. Howard Barnstone's book, *The Architecture of John Staub,* gives the best account of the development.

2. One writer implied that Will Hogg promoted Memorial Park to increase the value of his River Oaks land. This is unlikely. Between his purchase of the parkland and his sale to the city, its market value had soared *because* of the River Oaks plan. That he sold at his original cost is evidence that he was prompted more by civic interest than personal gain.

3. C. Pat Fleming, who attended the University of Texas, worked on the first campus landscaping. He studied architecture and gardens in Europe. He landscaped the San Jacinto Monument grounds. He designed gardens for Mr. and Mrs. James A. Elkins, Jr., Pierre Schlumberger, Alice Reynolds Pratt, and R. Thomas McDermott. His design for the Prudential Life Insurance Company received the American Association of Nurserymen award in 1955.

4. The Grants sold the Shadyside lot at 4 Longfellow Lane to John T. Crotty. The Crottys sold the property to Mr. and Mrs. Rorick Cravens.

5. In city directories of the early 1940s, Hermann Park was credited with 545 acres and "scenic drives, tennis courts, an 18-hole golf course and

clubhouse, bridle paths, picnic areas and play-grounds, zoological gardens containing more than 1,000 specimens and a museum of natural history." But the Hogg tract held only the bridle paths.

6. Thomas Church designed the Grant/Fay Park. The tiles that roof the gazebo were blown off Trinity Church, Galveston, during the 1915 hurricane – the church where John Fishback Grant and Homoiselle Davenport Randall were married, where their daughter Carolyn was baptized.

7. Later Mrs. Fletcher Pratt and Mrs. Paul Sherwood. Carolyn married Ernest Bel Fay; her cousin Homoiselle Haden married Albert Bel Fay.

8. At twenty, Lamar Fleming, Jr., represented Anderson, Clayton in Bremen, Paris, and Vienna. Two years later he was head of the Milan-Genoa office. The Lamar Fleming Middle School on Octavia and Lamar Fleming Avenue in the medical center were named for him.

9. Lamar Fleming III was born in Italy, Douglas in England. Clare and Mary were born in Houston, to their great pride. Once, an English cousin visiting from his home in Africa said: "In my yard we have lions and hartebeests." Clare replied impressively: "In our yard we have *hens*."

Chapter Forty-Three. A MUSEUM, A PARK, AND AN INVITATION

1. A graduate of Baylor Female College, Mrs. Fall came to Houston in 1905. As president of the Texas Federation of Women's Clubs (1913–15), she helped pass the state's compulsory education law and helped build the State School for Girls at Gainesville. She gained tax-exempt status for the Houston Museum of Fine Arts. As president for fourteen years of the women's auxiliary to the Baptist Hospital, she led in building its free ward. Traveling through Europe, she sent articles to the Houston newspapers.

2. Finnigan made some twenty-five or thirty trips abroad. At her death in 1940, she left her private collection to the museum.

3. Born in 1862 near London, Catharine Mary Elizabeth Taylor sailed for America in 1887 to marry her childhood sweetheart, John H. Emmott. After twenty-five days at sea, the ship reached Galveston, and they were married at Trinity Church, with the ship's captain giving the bride away. Army Emmott was her youngest child.

4. Judge Elkins was president, Mr. Keeland general manager, and E. P. Greenwood and Wharton Weems vice-presidents. William A. Vinson was on the board. Contemporaries say that Judge Elkins ran the bank.

5. When this company merged with the American General Life Insurance Company in 1945, Baker became president and later chairman of the board. The Bakers had four children: Burke Baker, Jr., Rennie, Anne (Mrs. Rutherford R. Cravens II), and Cary.

6. In Houston, Tellepson married Larson Ingeborg. They had three children, Howard, Hortense, and Lorraine.

7. Blaffer led the fund drive, aided by the board and W. S. Farish, Kenneth E. Womack, and J. W. Evans. Mrs. E. L. Neville led a women's committee: Mrs. W. L. Clayton, Mrs. Alice Baker Jones, Mrs. J. J. Carroll, Mrs. W. T. Carter, and Mrs. E. R. Spotts.

8. When Will Hobby returned to the *Beaumont Enterprise* in 1921, the city had a new paper. He bought it but in 1922 he handed the reins to Jim Mapes and moved back to Houston.

9. Even though Henry MacGregor was a trustee of the *Post,* when he ran for Congress as a Republican in 1904, the paper supported his Democratic opponent.

10. With the passing of the Munn Company, Houston had no complete department store until after World War II.

11. This was the third theater of the name. Karl Hoblitzelle, a force in the theater business, had three successive Majestics, each grander than the one before. The first Majestic was renamed the Queen in 1910; the second became the Palace in 1923 when edged out by the third.

12. He was also vice-president of the South Texas Commercial National Bank. Born in Danville, Virginia, Patton became a leader in the Community Chest, the county chapter of the National Foundation for Infantile Paralysis, the Foreign Trade and Foreign Policy Association, and the Harris County Historical Society.

13. The French liner was chartered by K. A. Corrigan, Will Clayton, E. A. Petlen, Ross Sterling, John Henry Kirby, A. E. Kiesling, M. E. Foster, George Cohen, Jesse Jones, and Russell Jacobe. It became the first trans-Atlantic passenger steamer to run on regular schedule from the Port.

Patton's committee included George Cohen of Foley's, vice-chairman; and George B. Forristall, Gus Mistrot, H. A. McCelvey, R. H. Cornell, Harry C. Howard, Ray Dudley, Paul L. Wakefield, Guy Harris, John Payne, and Dale C. Rogers. Among those who joined the delegation were Vernon A. Corrigan, Anne Corrigan, Ima Hogg, Mrs. E. A. Peden, Mrs. John Wesley Graham, Mrs. William Patton and her daughters Kate and Mayola Frances, J. W. Neal of the Chamber of Commerce, Robert G. Cohen, John Buckley, R. M. Farrar of the Harbor Board, J. M. West, Tobias Sakowitz, Sam Rouse, John Dyer, J. M. Rockwell, and Carle Aderman.

Chapter Forty-Four. NEW LIBRARY, NEW HOSPITAL, AND A SCHISM

1. Margaret Wiess Elkins said, "It was because they were all such good friends–the Nevilles, the Hoggs, the Bosworths, Hutchesons, and Carters. Dr. Sears had come out to our house and baptized all three of us. So my family went along."

2. R. E. Smith married Vivian Leatherberry. After World War II, she became an outstanding philanthropist, as president of the Blue Bird Circle and as a major contributor to medical research.

3. The Rev. Harris Masterson, Jr., Rice chaplain and unflagging leader for civic improvement, chaired the building committee. It included the library board president Henry Dickson, William Vinson, Elizabeth Fitzsimmons Ring, R. H. Byers, and the Rev. E. P. West. They commissioned Cram & Ferguson of Boston to design the building. Watkin & Glover of Houston were associates; W. A. Dowdy was the city architect.

4. Payne retired at the age of seventy-five. Twenty years later, when Phil Ewald and Larry Burns of Kendall/Heaton Associates were asked to design a major addition to Poe School, they consulted Mr. Payne.

5. The two cousins became Mrs. Raymond Cook and Mrs. Frederick R. Thompson.

Chapter Forty-Five. RIDING A BOOM

1. Brown College at Rice University is named for Margarett Root Brown.

2. Dr. Leslie Waggener was ad interim president until 1896.

3. After Mrs. Brown's death in 1984, her daughter Isabel Wilson found boxes filled with color pictures and postcards saved from the mu-

seum trips that schooled Mrs. Brown in art. All three of her daughters, Nancy, Maconda, and Isabel, were born in Houston.

4. The three Dionne daughters were Dorothy (Mrs. Edward Babcock), Katherine (Mrs. Newton Wray), and her twin Betty Ann (Mrs. Jack Brannon). Dr. and Mrs. Brannon had two children, Gay and Jack Brannon, Jr.

5. Sold to the city, it became the Houston Municipal Airport then, after enlargement, the International Airport and ultimately the Hobby Airport.

6. The Houston Colored Junior College of 1927 became Houston College for Negroes in 1934-35, Texas State University for Negroes in 1947, and Texas Southern University in 1951.

7. In 1906, attorney Lee Clarence Ayars brought his wife Beulah and his daughters, Louise and Orissa, to Houston from Columbus, Texas. Louise studied painting at the Newcomb College art school for two years before coming home to make her debut. She married Louis A. Stevenson. They had three children, Orissa, Louis A. Stevenson, Jr., and Anne. Orissa married Robert Eckhardt, Anne married Patrick Nicholson, and Louis married Babette Millian of Paris.

Judge and Mrs. James V. Meek moved to Houston from Columbus with their daughters, Rosalie, Mildred, and Henrietta. Henrietta married Erwin Y. Cottingham, founder of the Houston Stamp and Stencil Company. This company made bronze plaques for the San Jacinto Monument and for historic trees in Texas, among other things. The Cottinghams had three children: Katherine (Mrs. Julian LaRoche), Erwin Cottingham, Jr., who married Katherine Sanguily, and Elizabeth (Mrs. E. K. Sanders).

8. Tiel Way is named for Mrs. Potter, whose name was actually Lucille.

9. The garden club's charter members were Mrs. H. K. Arnold, Mrs. A. C. Bayless, Mrs. W. T. Campbell, Mrs. O. J. Cadwallader, Mrs. Joseph Chew, Mrs. E. Y. Cottingham, Mrs. Ray Dudley, Mrs. H. B. Finch, Mrs. John Foster, Mrs. Calvin Garwood, Mrs. John Green, Mrs. Ardon Judd, Mrs. Herbert Kipp, Mrs. Charles Koenig, Mrs. Sidney Long, Mrs. Sam Merrill, Mrs. T. M. Norsworthy, Mrs. Charles Oliver, Mrs. David Picton, Mrs. George Sears, Mrs. Cleveland Sewall, Mrs. John Staub, and Mrs. Louis Stevenson.

10. E. R. Spotts was chairman of the Park Commission, which included E. L. Crain, John

F. Dickson, W. D. Cleveland, James Anderson, Paul B. Timpson, M. E. Tracy, J. C. McVea, Robert L. Cole, J. W. Slaughter, Mrs. E. C. Murray, Herbert Godwin, and J. S. Pyeatt.

Chapter Forty-Six. A PEACABLE KINGDOM

1. Ellen was the daughter of Edith Paine and Arthur Louis Hamilton. Her grandparents had come to Houston shortly after the Civil War. She married Dr. Edward Wilkerson. They had four children: John Hamilton, Martha Neale, Edith Brooke, and Ted Wilkerson.

2. Chaille Cage Thompson was the daughter of Roene Masterson and Elliott Cage. Her great-grandfather, Rufus K. Cage, came to Houston from Tennessee in the 1860s. His son Rufus married Ella Reed, and their son Rufus Cage, Jr., married Frances Sears. Chaille Cage married J. Lewis Thompson, Jr., and they had one son, J. Lewis Thompson III.

3. J. W. Link spent sixty thousand dollars on the mansion, which he sold to oilman T. P. Lee for ninety thousand. It became the first building of the University of St. Thomas.

4. David Bintliff and Alice James were married on January 23, 1923. They had two daughters, Beverly (Mrs. Daniel C. Arnold) and Marjorie Ann (Mrs. Raleigh W. Johnson, Jr.).

5. In 1926, Judge and Mrs. Parker built a home at Number 2, Courtlandt Place.

6. Maudie Carroll married John Bullington; Lena Carroll married Dillon Anderson.

7. Harris Masterson III is a descendant of Thomas Gilbert and Christina Roene Masterson, who came to Brazoria County from Tennessee in 1832, and of Jesse Alexander Harrison Cleveland, who came to Brazoria from Virginia in 1833. Masterson's son Harris (first of the name) married Sallie Stewart Turner. Their children were Harris Masterson, Jr., who married Elizabeth Simpkins; Roene, who married Elliott Cage; and Neill, who married Libbie Mary Johnston, daughter of Rienzi Johnston.

8. Eloise Steele was one of the generation's beauties, noted for her sweetness and lovely speaking voice. She married Leslie Coleman and, after his death, James Walsh. The Fashion, one of Houston's finest women's clothing stores, was owned by Ben Wolfman.

9. The SOPHS were Allie May Autry, Ella Rice, Chaille Cage, Margaret Lester, Helen Wicks, Lucille Lister, Martha Scott, and Lucile McAshan.

10. The Shamrock Hotel was the first structure on the field.

11. Elliot, Eugene, and Gibbs Meador were the sons of N. E. Meador, who was the president of the Rice Hotel, a vice-president of the National Bank of Commerce, and a director of the *Houston Chronicle*.

12. Later the owner of a popular gambling establishment.

13. Born in Florence, Don Hall earned a degree in mechanical engineering at Cornell University in 1908. In 1915 he married Virginia Dorrance. They had three children, John, Betty (Mrs. Ben Sewell), and Don Hall, Jr. The Halls lived at Number 4 Courtlandt Place.

14. With their baby daughter Josephine, James and Lillie Abercrombie moved to the Warwick in 1927 after two years in Colombia.

15. In his kindergarten class were Harry Jewett, Malcolm Monroe, Moise Levy, Ed Brooks, Raymond Pearson, Jr., and Mark Liverman, "the son of our kindest teacher."

16. Mr. and Mrs. Theodore F. Heyck lived at 240 West Alabama. They had four children: Theodore R. Heyck, an electrical engineer; Joseph Giraud Heyck, a Rice football star; Anne, who married Dr. Thomas Cronin; and Frances Heyck, first executive secretary of the Junior League Outpatient Clinic and later community relations director of the Texas Children's Hospital.

17. The Staiti house was moved to Sam Houston Park in 1988.

18. Virginia Drane married Homer McCallon, city manager of Loew's Theaters, and Elizabeth Drane married Brig. Gen. Stuart Haynesworth.

Chapter Forty-Seven. TO A WIDER WORLD

1. Dudley Sharp was a naval officer in World War II and became President Eisenhower's secretary of the air force. He used to ride his bicycle or skate to South End. "We were big on skating in those days."

2. During World War II, Mr. Kabayama and his family were kept under house arrest in the Imperial Palace grounds because they were suspected of being too fond of Americans. After the war, he became Dudley Sharp's Mission Manufacturing Company representative in Japan.

3. This was Herbert Godwin, multifaceted civic leader.

4. Apparently, this was Carter family custom. In about 1910, Frankie and Agnese Carter

were sent abroad by their father, W. T. Carter, Jr., thereby beginning Agnese Carter Nelms's life-long fascination with France.

5. After the death of her husband, Maudie Carter Bullington became an archeologist whose digs restored many pre-Columbian artifacts to the government of Mexico.

6. Martha Wicks and Malcolm Lovett were married at Christ Church June 4, 1929. The son of Dr. and Mrs. Edgar Odell Lovett, Malcolm Lovett was an attorney with Baker & Botts.

7. Later Sissy Farenthold, candidate for governor of Texas.

8. William Marsh Rice, Jr.

Chapter Forty-Eight. SURPRISE PARTY

1. Born in 1905, the daughter of Rep. Ike Culp of Killeen, Oveta Culp as a child often attended legislative sessions with her father. In 1926, before she had reached voting age, she was named parliamentarian of the Texas House.

2. Mrs. Walter Sharp was married in 1897, widowed thirteen years later. Independently wealthy from the sale of her interest in the Sharp-Hughes Tool Company to Howard Hughes, she became an outstanding civic leader. She endowed a lecture series at Rice Institute, helped finance the *Houston Gargoyle,* and helped women gain educational and political opportunities.

3. In 1974, the restored M&M Building became the downtown campus of the University of Houston.

4. It later served as the Red Cross chapter headquarters.

5. A handsome polar explorer, author, and lecturer, Adm. Richard Evelyn Byrd was more famous than his brother.

6. Lehman became governor and U.S. Senator from New York.

Chapter Forty-Nine. IN GOOD TIMES

1. The Nelms children were Haywood, Jr., and twins Agnese and Nancy.

2. The Houston Child Guidance Center, 3214 Austin, is the result of that first meeting.

3. Leon Jaworski married Jeannette Adams, also a Baylor University graduate, who played the organ at his father's church. They had three children, Joanie, Claire, and Joseph.

4. It later became Brennan's Restaurant.

5. Frank Sharp was no relation to the family of Dudley Sharp.

6. The Hogg Foundation opened in 1940

with Dr. Robert L. Sutherland as first director and president.

Chapter Fifty. THE GREAT DEPRESSION

1. Later the Houston Livestock Show and Rodeo.

2. Born in Grayson County, Bradley earned his B.A. from the University of Texas before the war, his law degree after. He moved to Houston in 1920 to join the law firm that became Andrews, Kurth, Campbell & Jones. He married Genevra Harris.

3. William P. Hobby, Jr., newspaper and television executive, became lieutenant governor of Texas. He married Diana Poteat Stallings, and they had four children: Laura, Paul, Andrew, and Kate. Jessica Hobby became a magazine publisher and married Henry Edward Catto, Jr., of San Antonio, later ambassador to the Court of St. James. They had four children: Heather, John, Will, and Elizabeth or Isa.

4. The Taub family tradition for philanthropy in Houston has been carried on by his nephews, Henry J. N. Taub and Col. John Ben Taub, and in the next generation by H. Ben, Marcy, and J. N. Taub II.

5. Later the Family Service Bureau.

Chapter Fifty-Two. DARK DAYS AND LIGHT

1. Born in Mobile, Alabama, Oscar Holcombe grew up in San Antonio and in 1912 married Mary Grey Miller. Their daughter Elisabeth married H. Markley Crosswell, Jr. They had two children, Holcombe and H. Markley Crosswell III.

2. Carl Leatherwood wrote in the *Houston Post* of May 4, 1986, "Of the 14 million acres of virgin pine timber standing in East Texas at the turn of the century, less than 1 million acres remained in 1932. . . . As forest resources and lumber prices dwindled, workers started going hungry."

3. Four times a papal knight, George W. Strake was awarded the Grand Cross of the Order of St. Sylvester by Pope Pius XII. Mr. and Mrs. Strake gave a twenty-seven-hundred acre camp to the Boy Scouts. The Strake family built a building for the University of St. Thomas, gave St. Joseph's Hospital $5 million, and microfilmed the entire Vatican library for St. Louis University.

4. Nancy Brown Negley Wellin of San Antonio, Mrs. Ralph O'Connor, and Mrs. Wallace Wilson of Houston.

5. Ed Rotan married Virginia Douglas.

6. The *Gargoyle* said that she could endow even the theme song "Sweetheart of Sigma Chi" "with a measure of warmth, beauty, and intelligence."

7. The Hays Office was the film industry's creation to cut out anything that censors might be expected to censor.

8. Gabrielle Diehl (Mrs. Wilson Poitevent Fraser) became a supporter of the Houston Symphony, Houston Grand Opera, Houston Ballet, Museum of Fine Arts, and Bayou Bend Museum.

9. The Texas Medical Center became a major beneficiary of Ben Clayton's foundation.

10. A native of Illinois, Mrs. Graham studied music in Boston, New York, Paris, Nice, Milan, and Berlin. In 1909, she married John Graham, president of a hat company, and began teaching voice. She studied further in Latin America, China, and Japan and was noted for her large collection of diamonds, including four stones weighing twenty carats.

11. Mayor Fred Hofheinz said, "I am a potpourri of Americana—Louisiana French, German, pioneer American, Greek." The first Hofheinz came as a Lutheran missionary from Germany to San Antonio in the 1880s. His son Fritz was a railroad man in Beaumont and married a Louisiana Cajun. Their son Roy was born in Beaumont in 1912. When railroading hit hard times, Fritz Hofheinz moved the family to Houston.

Greek-born James Cafcalas was a restaurant and theater owner and a founder of the Greek Orthodox Church in Houston. He married a daughter of the Van Zandt family from Tennessee. Their daughter, Irene, was born in 1912.

The Roy Hofheinzes had three children. Roy, Jr., was the first Rice undergraduate to receive a Rhodes scholarship. After two years at Oxford, he was graduated with honors from Harvard and earned a doctorate in modern Chinese history. He commands nine languages. Fred Hofheinz majored in economics at the University of Texas and earned his Ph.D. and his law degree in the same year.

12. Kenneth Franzheim, Jr., became ambassador to New Zealand and Tasmania after World War II.

13. This was the site of Henke's Wagon Yard, which had opened at 807 Congress in 1872. As farmers came into town to sell their cotton, men were posted to direct them to Henke's, where they could camp and buy supplies. Slums moved in. The site became notorious as Vinegar Hill, with Tin Can Alley as its main street. In 1887, the Houston and Texas Central Depot was built there.

14. The honored guests were descendants of Sidney Sherman, who built the railroad that became the Southern Pacific Lines: his daughter Mrs. Lucy Sherman Craig and his grandchildren, Mrs. F. E. Russell, W. E. Kendall, O. M. Kendall, and W. K. Craig.

Chapter Fifty-Three. PUMP PRIMING

1. Dominique Schlumberger de Menil (Mrs. John de Menil) is the daughter of Conrad, and granddaughter of Paul Schlumberger. As she said at the opening of the Menil Collection, her grandfather made the gift of the museum to Houston possible by his willingness to finance the visionary research proposed by his son Conrad. Pierre Schlumberger was the son of Marcel.

2. Bernard Sakowitz married Ann Baum, a Rice Institute graduate from San Antonio. Their son Robert Sakowitz would take over the stores in the third generation.

3. Among early members of the board were Mrs. Will Clayton, Mrs. David Picton, Mrs. W. Aubrey Smith, Mrs. Raymond H. Goodrich, Robert Dabney, Mrs. Orville W. Rote, Mrs. S. M. McAshan, Jr., Dr. Henry Barnston, Mrs. George Heyer, Dr. Paul W. Quillian, Mrs. Virgil Scott, Mrs. John Bullington, Miss Rosalie Farish, Mrs. John Suman, Mrs. Lamar Fleming, the Rev. J. Elmer Ferguson, B. B. Gilmer, Frank Sterling, and Ewing Werlein.

Chapter Fifty-Four. ONE HUNDRED YEARS OLD

1. The daughter of Mr. and Mrs. Guy Morrison Bryan, Florence Carter Bryan married Raymond A. Cook. They had four children: Florence, Frank, Lawrence, and Stephen. Stephen married Allyson Priest, and their children, Stephen and Elizabeth, are seventh-generation Houstonians.

2. A surprising number of American presidents have visited Houston: Grant, Harrison, McKinley, Theodore Roosevelt, Taft, Harding, and Hoover. Franklin Roosevelt was the first Democrat to come. Presidents Eisenhower, Kennedy, Nixon, and Johnson came after World War II.

3. The Washington Monument is 555 feet high, the Eiffel Tower 984.

4. Rita Moise became co-owner with her

husband, Charles Cobler, of Cobler's Bookstore in the Village. Miss Krahl became a leading voice and speech coach.

5. Margo Jones was co-director of the first production of *The Glass Menagerie* in 1944. She staged Maxwell Anderson's *Joan of Lorraine* with Ingrid Bergman.

6. This was W. St. John Garwood, Jr. Gertrude Levy married Howard Barnstone, and Rosalie Bosworth married James G. Ulmer, Jr.

7. Victor Alessandro, Jr., became the conductor of the San Antonio Symphony.

8. It became Cullen Boulevard.

9. Presumably this was a coat and tie, not a dinner jacket.

10. Health or medical insurance was uncommon.

11. Dr. Stripling and Jack Crawford were married in 1941. At sixteen, Elizabeth Stripling was inspired to become a doctor by a Tulane University medical student who taught her biology one summer—Mary Ann McKinney. Also from Nacogdoches, Dr. McKinney became a Houston internist and gynecologist.

12. In 1940, Dr. DeWolfe became dean of the Cathedral of St. John the Divine in New York and later bishop of Long Island.

13. The city opened a graveyard in 1836. Death was not the great leveler: the city reserved sections for respectable citizens and carefully segregated "criminals, persons of infamous character, such as commit suicide, and such as are killed or come to their death from a wound received in a duel." The cemetery was crowded. The *Morning Star* of August 5, 1841, said "The grave yard at Houston contained five years after its opening 6,000 souls." After 1840, other graveyards were opened by Masons, Episcopalians, Jews, and Germans.

14. Cleared of graves, it became a parking lot.

15. The tendency may have been hereditary. In his biography of Robert Benchley, Nathaniel Benchley tells that when he and his mother took Benchley's ashes to be scattered in Nantucket, they found the urn empty. They thought father had played his last joke.

Chapter Fifty-Five. As SEGREGATION GREW

1. In 1835, in the diary of his trip from Virginia to Texas, William Fairfax Gray referred to two black passengers who were on their way to see friends.

Chapter Fifty-Six. POLO, ANYONE?

1. All this was English saddle. After World War II, newer Houstonians took up trail riding using western saddle, prompted by the growing Houston Livestock Show.

2. In 1986, A Weingarten's grocery store stood on the site, catercornered across from Neiman Marcus.

3. The three Farish brothers were born in Mississippi: William Stamps Farish in 1881, Stephen Power Farish in 1891, and Robert Farish in 1894. All were oil company presidents: W. S. Farish of the Humble Oil and Refining Company; Stephen of the Navarro Oil Company and Reed Roller Bit, and Robert of the Farlyn Oil Company.

4. Howard Barnstone's book, *The Architecture of John Staub*, gives a beautifully illustrated account of the Post Oak-Memorial development, as it does of the earlier River Oaks. The Forest Club leased the Carter Lodge from 1945 to 1949. After World War II, Victor and Betty Carter reclaimed it. The Carter estate became the Sherwood Forest subdivision.

5. In this same year, the Houston Riding and Polo Club commissioned John Staub to design a new clubhouse. It was built, but demolished when the club gave way to city growth.

Chapter Fifty-Seven. FOR THEY WERE YOUNG

1. Helen Sharp was the daughter of Texas Supreme Court Justice and Mrs. John H. Sharp. In 1938, she and Thomas Dunaway Anderson were married in Austin. They had three children: John S. Anderson, a Houston attorney, and Helen (Mrs. John Shaw) and Lucile Clayton (Mrs. Richard H. Streeter), both of Washington, D.C. Mrs. Anderson served on the boards of the National Cathedral in Washington and the Garden Club of America and became the first vice-regent from west of the Mississippi to become regent of the Mount Vernon Ladies' Association.

2. The daughter of Gen. Robert Wood, chairman of the board of Sears, Roebuck, Mary Wood married William Stamps Farish, Jr. They had one son, Will Farish.

3. John and Camilla Blaffer had five children: Camilla (Coco), Catherine (Trinka), Sarah, Joan, and Lee.

4. A frequent feature in *Life* magazine of the period was a section entitled "Life Goes to a Party."

5. Caroline Wiess and Bill Francis were mar-

ried at Christ Church in May, 1946. After his death in Washington, while serving in the Eisenhower administration, she married Theodore Law.

6. This was a large Rice family compound. Jonas Rice and his brother Will "shared everything," Hugo Neuhaus, Jr., said. They had the street closed between their two properties.

7. Among members between 1930 and 1946 were W. Browne Baker, Robert W. Collins, Rorick Cravens, Craig Cullinan, Maj. Leslie Dufton, Gaylord Fauntleroy, W. St. John Garwood, De-Witt Gordon, Arthur Jago, William A. Kirkland, John H. London, Malcolm Lovett, Harry McCormick, Harold M. McCullough, Hugo Neuhaus, J. E. Neuhaus, D. D. Peden, Merrick Phelps, Bedford Sharp, Dudley Sharp, Lloyd H. Smith, Joe Tennant, Harry Washburn, Harry C. Wiess, James O. Winston, Andrew Jackson Wray, and Newton Wray.

8. Jack Wray married Margaret Cullinan and they lived at Number 3 Remington Lane. Their daughter Lucie married Anderson Todd. The Todds had two children, Emily and David, both Princeton graduates.

9. Their parents usually changed for dinner when having dinner guests, and many of them, like Mrs. Lamar Fleming, even when no guests were expected.

Chapter Fifty-Eight. THE HOWARD HUGHES HOUSTON KNEW

1. Mr. Hughes, Sr., kept a *pied a terre* at the Beaconsfield.

2. David Rice, son of Frederick Allyn, married Mattie L. Botts. Their daughters were Ella and Libbie Rice. Jonas, David's older brother, married Mary J. Ross, the daughter of Col. Peter Ross. Their daughters were Laura, who married Richard Neff; Kate, who married Hugo Neuhaus; and Lottie, who married Stephen Farish.

3. Ella Rice Hughes later married James Overton Winston, Jr. They had three children: James O. Winston III, David Rice Winston, and Elizabeth Rice Winston.

4. Before World War II, the Defense Plant Corporation commissioned Hughes and Henry J. Kaiser to create a large airliner requiring no materials needed for war. Using laminated birch wood, Hughes built a plane with eight propeller-driven engines. When it finally flew in 1946, it had lost its importance.

5. The honor did not stick: it was discovered

that under state law an airport cannot be named for a living person.

6. Given each year by *Collier's Weekly,* the award was made under the auspices of the National Aeronautics Association.

Chapter Fifty-Nine. FARAWAY WARS

1. The Hays Office was Hollywood's in-house censor. Until the last scene of *Gone with the Wind,* no Hollywood film had allowed the worst villain to utter one cuss word.

2. Born in Austria in 1888, Finger had come to the United States in 1906, to Houston in 1912.

3. This is the Benjamin Moore Anderson Historical Aeronautical Collection in the Woodson Research Center. Ben Anderson was named for his uncle, a founder of Anderson, Clayton.

Chapter Sixty-One. INFAMOUS DAY

1. Percy Straus, Jr., who became Percy Selden, was a world traveler and big game hunter. His wife Marjorie Selden became a leading environmentalist, working for bayou preservation and hike and bike trails.

2. Oddly, Americans were indignant at Japan for not declaring war before striking.

3. William Kirkland served in the navy in two world wars, served on the Houston School Board and the City Council, and was president of the First National Bank. He was president of the Texas Bankers Association in 1947-48 and at various times was president of the Philosophical Society of Texas, senior warden of Christ Church, secretary of the Ripley Foundation, treasurer of the Texas Medical Center. He backed professional baseball in Houston and helped underwrite the Houston Gargoyle. He was the epitome of Old Houston dedicated to the public good.

4. Garwood became a Texas Supreme Court justice.

5. Nancy Cravens, Rorick Cravens, Jr., and Patsy Cravens.

6. Browne Baker was the son of Capt. James A. Baker.

7. They later founded Wilson, Morris, Crain and Anderson, one of the largest architectural firms in the country.

8. The Rev. Joseph Jaworski was an evangelical Lutheran who spoke several languages. In Waco he preached his sermons in German—a language that proved useful to his son.

9. J. R. Parton had studied international law

at the University of Texas. He was chairman of the university board of regents from 1935 to 1941. In 1950–51, as consultant to the secretary of the interior, he organized the Petroleum Administration for Defense. He returned as consultant to Secretary of the Interior Stewart L. Udall in 1961.

Chapter Sixty-Two. A CROWDED WORLD

1. As elsewhere in the South, "you all" always implies two or more people. To ask "How have you all been?" covers the entire family of the person being addressed.

2. Trains left windows open to catch the soot-filled breeze. Under the burden of troop movements, every operable engine was attached to every train car still able to roll.

3. After the war, when Herbert Kempner had returned to the Sugarland Industries, his wife asked him if the Washington experience had made any change in him. "Well," he said, "one of my men told me he had made a terribly expensive mistake. I asked how much, and he said $10,000. And I said 'Oh that's not much!'"

4. He returned to Washington as assistant secretary of the navy, 1947–49.

5. When they succeeded to the room, Browne and Lovett Baker counted ninety-six steps from street to garret.

6. I. H. Kempner, Jr., died in 1953. Some years later, Mary Carroll Kempner married Lawrence Reed.

7. Mr. and Mrs. Jesse Jones, Mr. and Mrs. Will Clayton, Col. Oveta Culp Hobby.

Chapter Sixty-Three. THEY ALSO SERVED

1. In fact, only one of the thousand was assigned to the new *Houston*. But Bill Kirkland, a fourth-generation Houstonian, was aboard when she was torpedoed and helped bring her home.

2. Widowed by Billy Farish's death in a plane crash, Mary Wood Farish lived with her son Will in the Farish family home until her marriage in 1947 to Hugo Neuhaus, Jr.

3. Glory Huckins Morris, a Smith graduate, became a leader in Houston museum circles after the war.

4. In August, 1946, Nancy Spencer married Dr. James Heyl at Christ Church. They had four children, Peter, John, Hilary, and Timothy.

5. This was the father of Ralph Anderson, the architect, a partner in Wilson, Morris, Anderson and Crain, designers of the Astrodome and of the Houston Post Building.

Chapter Sixty-Four. EVEN WITH A WAR ON

1. Neiman Marcus Stocking Club members received first chance at nylons as they came in. Many women painted their bare legs with stocking-colored pancake makeup and drew a stripe down the back to resemble a seam. Grant's and Woolworth's had experts who could mend a run. Rayon stockings were abominable.

2. The sale of the park land was approved on December 14, 1943, with 741 votes cast in a citywide referendum.

3. James Anderson was the nephew of M. D. Anderson.

4. This estimate was made by Dr. Richard E. Wainerdi, Texas Medical Center president, in June, 1989.

5. Jesse Wright Miller, an early Houston cotton merchant, bequeathed to the city the money that built the theater.

6. Mr. Cullen enjoyed music and played the piano by ear.

7. When the de Menils became naturalized American citizens, Mr. de Menil dropped his title of baron and changed his name from Jean to John. Their children Christophe, Adelaide, and George were French-born. Francois and Philippa were born in Houston after the war.

8. Dr. Daily was reelected many times and was an active influence on the growth of the University of Houston.

9. Mrs. McClelland Wallace, Mrs. Victor Carter, and Mrs. William S. Farish, Jr. (later Mrs. Hugo Neuhaus, Jr.).

10. This had been the home of Mr. and Mrs. Henry M. Holden, the parents of Henry M. Holden, Jr., and Ebbe Holden.

11. Max Levine was manager of the first Foley's built by Federated. He supported causes ranging from the Houston Symphony Society to the Houston Council on Alcoholism,

12. Meant to discourage blacks, the poll tax kept citizens of all races from voting during the depression. In states where it was cumulative, Americans who lost their jobs or had salary cuts could not pay the sum of several years' back tax and were, in effect, disfranchised.

Chapter Sixty-Five. PLOWSHARE TO SWORD

1. He returned to office in 1947.

Chapter Sixty-Six. V-MAIL

1. In 1976, Albert Fay became ambassador to Trinidad and Tobago.

2. A captain in the Air Force in 1950, David Westheimer retired as lieutenant colonel and was awarded the Air Medal and the Distinguished Flying Cross. Westheimer Road was named for his great-uncle, M. L. Westheimer.

3. After residencies in New York and Boston hospitals, Dr. Crain opened his practice in the newly built Hermann Professional Building. He married Betty Adams. They had six children: Marjorie, Joan, Liza, Danny, Gene, and Annie Vive.

4. In 1946 this would buy two automobiles.

5. Mary Wood Farish was the widow of William S. Farish, Jr., the first cousin of Hugo Neuhaus, Jr. Her son, Will Farish III, became a leading race horse breeder. Queen Elizabeth II often visited his Kentucky breeding farm. It was at his Palm Beach home that President-elect George Bush spent his first days of rest after the 1988 campaign.

6. Three times in later years, the bank they both used gave Dr. Freeman's deposits to Mr. Freeman's account. Once at the University of St. Thomas, John H. Freeman's daughter Connie was given the A-mark earned on an exam by John C. Freeman's daughter. This play may have acts yet unwritten.

Chapter Sixty-Seven. IN MEMORIAM

1. Mr. and Mrs. Ray Dudley were owners and publishers of Gulf Publishing Company.

2. Before his death, the Dudleys had a daughter, Fredrica.

3. William Gross Dudley, Bogie's younger brother, took to the air as a navigator. A Rice graduate, he earned a masters in chemistry at the University of Texas and made his career at Gulf Publishing Company. He and his wife Margaret had five children, Lucinda, Katherine Elizabeth, Bayard Turner Gross, Robert Douglas, and William G. Dudley, Jr.

4. The Roussels' other children were Stephanie (Mrs. William Claude Milburn) and Peter, born after his brother's death. Peter Roussel was a spokesman for the Reagan White House.

5. This was Europe's second generation to be ravaged in twenty-five years. Great Britain lost 400,000, the Soviet Union 3,000,000, the Free French 167,000, Poland up to 10,000,000. Germany lost 3,250,000, Italy 200,000, Japan 1,500,000.

Chapter Sixty-Eight. WILL CLAYTON AND THE MARSHALL PLAN

1. In Houston, Clayton's courtesy was an established simile. Of Steve Farish, the *Gargoyle* once said: "Like Will Clayton . . . he seems to have preserved . . . princely courtesy."

2. United Nations Relief and Rehabilitation Administration.

3. Preparing a biography of her father, Ellen Clayton Garwood interviewed foreign service officers who had worked closely with him. The quotations of officials used here are from her interviews, each initialed by the interviewee.

4. Because Kennan had headed the policy planning division for four weeks and written its report, some assumed that he "masterminded" the Marshall Plan. Many State Department officials rebut the theory. Norman Ness said: "Kennan told us, before Secretary Marshall's talk, he would go somewhere in the country and he was going to write a memo. This was . . . after the issue had been posed by Will Clayton."

Ivan White said that "the study which Kennan's shop had prepared . . . was good on outlining the importance of Western Europe to the United States . . . but pretty fuzzy as compared to Will Clayton's thinking on how to go about seeing that Western Europe *did* survive."

Chapter Sixty-Nine. SUITE 8-F

1. Mr. and Mrs. Herman Brown adopted Louisa and Mike Stude when she was seven and he four. Born in Houston, they were the children of Micajah Stokes Stude and Lucy Binyon Stude.

2. Neither Governor Hobby nor Will Clayton came often to 8-F, but they were no less a part of the leadership. Frank Oltorf was never a lobbyist. He was not in Washington to push legislation. His assignment was to make friends with civil servants in government departments. If a stack of applications was waiting to be processed, Posh Oltorf would bring the Browns' proposal to the attention of the friend in charge and ask if it might be given an early chance for consideration—to be accepted or rejected on its merits.

3. Frensley later became president of Brown & Root.

4. The Texas Eastern Transmission Company was incorporated in Delaware with George R. Brown as chairman of the board, E. Holley Poe of New York as president, Charles I. Francis of

Houston as vice-president, and Herman Brown as a director.

Chapter Seventy. A Fairy Story

1. The house built by the Edwin Parkers, bought by Capt. James A. Baker, and finally the first headquarters for M. D. Anderson Hospital.

2. "I think Ed Clark, the lawyer, had something to do with it," Mrs. Sarofim said. "Aunt Maggie was very fond of the Clarks."

3. At six and seven, Louisa Stude went to Montrose and Saint Agnes Academy. Returning with the Browns, she began at Kinkaid and then, in eighth grade, went to St. John's.

4. Jessica Hobby, Nancy and Fairfax Crow, and Patsy Cravens among them.

Chapter Seventy-One. Still Unknown

1. They were in the Heights and West University Village, at the Montrose-Westheimer intersection, and in such far-flung places as Bellaire and Southside Place. Before the day of supermarkets, each had a big grocery store (Weingarten's, Henke and Pillot or Minimax), a drug store (Mading's), and a neighborhood movie. Only West University Village had a Rice Food Market, opened by William Levy in 1937.

2. As Millie Gray had said on arriving in 1839.

3. In later years, Jean Daladier saved Paris from tasteless modernization by restoring seventeenth-century buildings for new use on the Qaui de la Tournelles and in the Marais. After graduate study at Yale, David Challinor became director of the office of international activities of the Smithsonian Institution, Washington.

4. The Roy Gustave Cullen Building and the Science Building opened in 1938, the Recreation Building and the Industrial Building in 1942.

5. In the words of James C. Morehead, Jr., professor of architecture.

6. The Garwoods lived at 5300 Caroline, while her parents, the Will Claytons, were abroad for Marshall Plan talks.

7. The Corbin J. and Wilhelmina Robertson Pavilion.

8. The Navy Hospital 1944–46, Veterans Hospital thereafter.

9. Foley's new store brought a unique burst of national publicity because it was the nation's first big new department store in seventeen years and was designed by Kenneth Franzheim on a completely new concept. In contrast, the smaller and younger city of Dallas was regularly featured as Big D. It was decades before the *New York Times* included Houston on its list of cities for weather report and forecast.

Bibliography

BOOKS AND ARTICLES

Agatha, Sister M. *The History of Houston Heights from Its Foundation in 1891 to Its Annexation in 1918*. Houston, Tex.: Premier Printing Co., 1956.

Anchorage Foundation. *Houston's Cradle of Culture and Environments: Three Architectural Walking Tours of the Museum Area*. Introduction by Stephen Fox. Houston, Tex.: Rice Design Alliance, 1985.

Audubon, Lucy Bakewell, ed. *The Life of John James Audubon, the American Naturalist*. New York: G. P. Putnam's Sons, 1875.

Bacon-Foster, Corra. *Houston, 1900*. Houston, Tex.: C. B. Foster, 1900. (Texas Blue Books.)

Baker, James A. *The Patrick Case: Transcript of Stenographic Notes of a Talk made by Captain James A. Baker, a Number of Years Ago at a Firm Meeting, the Name of the Firm Then Being Baker, Botts, Parker and Garwood, and Now, Baker, Botts, Andrews and Shepherd, August 6, 1954*. [Houston, Tex.], 1954.

Baker, Botts, Andrews and Wharton. *Baker, Botts in World War II*. Houston, Tex.: North River Press, 1947.

Barnstone, Howard. *The Architecture of John F. Staub, Houston and the South*. In cooperation with the Museum of Fine Arts, Houston. Austin: University of Texas Press, 1979.

———. *The Galveston That Was*. New York: Macmillan; Houston, Tex.: Museum of Fine Arts, 1966.

Barziza, Decimus et Ultimus. *The Adventures of a Prisoner of War, 1863–1864*. Edited by R. Henderson Shuffler. 1865. Reprint, Austin, Tex.: University of Texas Press, 1964.

Bate, W. N. *General Sidney Sherman, Texas Soldier, Statesman and Builder*. Waco, Tex.: Texian Press, 1974.

Beard, Norman, ed. *Municipal Book of the City of Houston, 1922*. Houston, Tex., 1923?

Bel Geddes, Joan. *Small World: A History of Baby Care from the Stone Age to the Spock Age*. New York: Macmillan, 1964.

Bernhard, Virginia. *Ima Hogg, the Governor's Daughter*. Austin, Tex.: Texas Monthly Press, 1984.

Blandin, Isabella Margaret Elizabeth. *History of Shearn Church 1837–1907*. Published for the Benefit of Shearn Auxiliary of Woman's Home Mission Society, Houston, Tex.: [J. V. Dealy Company, Printers], 1908.

Boles, John B. "As Others See Us: Travelers to Houston, 1836–1984." *Heritage*, Fall, 1986.

Botkin, B. A., ed. *Lay My Burden Down: A Folk History of Slavery*. Chicago, Ill.: University of Chicago Press, 1945.

Brown, John Henry. *Indian Wars and Pioneers in Texas*. Austin, Tex.: L. E. Daniel, [189–?]

Bryant, Ira Babington. *The Development of the Houston Negro Schools*. Houston, Tex.: Informer Publishing Company, 1935.

Carroll, B. H., Jr., ed. *Standard History of Houston, Texas, from a Study of the Original Source*. Knoxville, Tenn.: H. W. Crew and Co., 1912.

Chasins, Abram. *Leopold Stokowski, a Profile*. New York: Hawthorn Books, 1979.

Chesnut, Mary Boykin Miller. *A Diary from Dixie*. Edited by Ben Ames Williams. Boston, Mass.: Houghton Mifflin Co., 1949.

Clark, James A., with Weldon Hart. *The Tactful Texan: A Biography of Governor Will Hobby*. New York: Random House, 1958.

Clark, Joseph L. *A History of Texas, Land of Promise*. Boston, Mass.: D. C. Heath and Co., 1939.

Clayton, Will. *Selected Papers of Will Clayton*. Edited by Frederick J. Dobney. Baltimore, Md.: Johns Hopkins University Press, 1971.

Cohen, Anne Nathan. *The Centenary History, Congregation Beth Israel of Houston, Texas, 1854–1954*. [Houston, Tex.], 1954.

Cotner, Robert C. *James Stephen Hogg, a Biography*. Austin, Tex.: University of Texas Press, 1959.

Daniel, Oliver. *Stokowski, a Counterpoint View*. New York: Dodd, Mead and Co., 1982.

Dauphin, Sue. *Houston by Stages: A History of Theatre in Houston*. Burnet, Tex.: Eakin Press, 1981.

Davis, Ellis A., and Edwin H. Grobe, eds. *The New Encyclopedia of Texas*. 2 vols. Dallas: Texas Development Bureau, 1926.

Debray, X. B. *A Sketch of the History of Debray's (28th) Regiment of Texas Cavalry*. Austin, Tex.: Eugene von Boeckmann, 1884.

Domenech, Emmanuel Henri Dieudonne. *Missionary Adventures in Texas and Mexico, 1846–1852*. London: Longman, Brown, Green, Longmans, and Roberts, 1858.

Dresel, Gustav. *Gustav Dresel's Houston Journal: Adventures in North America and Texas, 1837–1841*. Translated and edited by Max Freund. Austin, Tex.: University of Texas Press, 1954.

Edwin B. Parker: A Memorial by His Professional Associates. Houston, Tex.: Rice University, Woodson Research Center, n.d.

Fehrenbach, T. R. *Lone Star: A History of Texas and the Texans*. New York: American Legacy Press, 1983.

Fox, Stephen. "Braeswood, an Architectural Tour," *Cité*, Winter, 1986.

Frantz, Joe Bertram. *Gail Borden: Dairyman to a Nation*. Norman: University of Oklahoma Press, 1951.

Franzheim, Kenneth. *Drawings and Models of Some of the Recent Work of Kenneth Franzheim: Together with Sketches of a Few Proposed Buildings*. Houston, Tex.: Privately printed, n.d.

Fuermann, George. *Houston, Land of the Big Rich*. New York: Doubleday, 1951.

———. *Houston Recalled: Six Miniatures*. Houston, Tex.: Baxter and Korge, 1968.

Garden Club of America. *Annual Meeting, Houston, 1939*. Houston, Tex., 1939.

Garwood, Ellen Clayton. "Will Clayton, a Short Biography." *Texas Quarterly* 1, no. 2, supp. (Winter, 1958).

Gouverneur, Marian. *As I Remember: Recollections of American Society during the Nineteenth Century*. New York: D. Appleton and Co., 1911.

Gray, Millie. *Diary of Millie Gray, 1832–1840, Recording Her Family Life Before, During and After Col. Wm. F. Gray's Journey to Texas in 1835, and The Small Journal, Giving Particulars of All That Occurred During the Family's Voyage to Texas in 1838*. Published for the Rosenberg Library Press, Galveston, Tex. Houston: Fletcher Young Publishing Company, 1967.

Gray, William Fairfax. *From Virginia to Texas, 1835: Diary of Col. Wm. Fairfax Gray, Giving Details of His Journey to Texas and Return in 1835–1836, and Second Journey to Texas in 1837*. 1909. Reprint, Houston, Tex.: Fletcher Young Publishing Co., 1965.

Greene, Casey. "Guardians against Change: The Ku Klux Klan in Houston and Harris County, 1920–1925," *Houston Review* 10, no. 1.

Gunther, John. *Taken at the Flood; The Story of Albert D. Lasker*. New York: Harper & Row, [1960].

Hacket, Sheila, *Dominican Women in Texas: From Ohio to Galveston and Beyond*. Published for Sacred Heart Convent. Houston, Tex.: D. Armstrong Company, 1986.

Harris, Dilue Rose. "Life in Early Texas, the Reminiscences of Mrs. Dilue Harris." *Quarterly of the Texas State Historical Association* 4 (July, 1900; April, 1901): 85–127; 155–89.

Hatch, Orin Walker. *Lyceum to Library: A Chapter in the Cultural History of Houston*. Houston: Texas Gulf Coast Historical Association, 1965.

Haynes, Robert V. *A Night of Violence: The Houston Riot of 1917*. Baton Rouge: Louisiana State University Press, 1976.

"Hermann Hospital, the University Hospital, Texas Medical Center." *Horizons,* Summer, 1980.

History of Texas Together With a Biographical History of the Cities of Houston and Galveston. Chicago, Ill.: Lewis Publishing Co., 1895.

History of the Churches of Houston and Directory of the First Baptist Church 1897. Houston, Tex., 1897[?].

Hitchcock, H. Wiley, and Stanley Sadie, eds. *The New Grove Dictionary of Music*. New York: Grove's Dictionaries of Music 1986.

Holley, Mary Austin. "The Texas Diary, 1835–38." Introduction and notes by J. P. Bryan. *Texas Quarterly* 8, no. 2 (Summer, 1965).

Holman, David, and Billie Persons. *Buckskin and Homespun: Frontier Texas Clothing, 1820–1870*. Austin: Wind River Press, 1979.

Houghton, Walter R., James K. Beck, James A. Woodburn, Horace R. Hoffman, A. B. Philputt, A. E. David, and Mrs. W. R. Houghton. *Rules of Etiquette and Home Culture; or,*

What To Do and How To Do It. Chicago, Ill.: Rand McNally & Co., 1882.

Houston Blue Book 1896: A Society Directory, 1896. Houston, Tex.: J. R. Wheat, 1896.

Houston City Directory for 1866. W. A. Leonard, comp. Houston, Tex.: Gray, Strickland & Co., 1866.

Houston City Directory, 1884–85. Houston, Tex.: Morrison and Fourmy Directory Co., 1885[?].

Houston Foundation. *Patriotism at Home: Report of the Houston Foundation.* Houston, Tex., 1917.

Houston Gargoyle. Edited by Alan Peden. Issues for 1928, 1929, and 1930. Houston, Tex.: Mayfair Publishing Co., 1928–30.

Houston Chronicle, October 11, 1985, "Texas Business Hall of Fame for 1985."

Houston Post, January 29, 1986, "Architect Built School to Endure," interview with Mr. Payne.

Houston Review; History and Culture of the Gulf Coast. Vols. 1–8 (1979–86).

Hunter, Helen, Denise Nosal, and Mary Gillette, eds. *Houston Women from Suffrage to City Hall.* Houston, Tex.: League of Women Voters of Houston Education Fund, 1987.

Ikin, Arthur. *Texas: Its History, Topography, Agriculture, Commerce, and General Statistics.* Reprint, Waco, Tex.: Texian Press, 1964.

In Memoriam: "Bogie," Bayard Turner Gross Dudley, January 17, 1922–December 31, 1943. [Houston, Tex.], 1944[?].

In Memoriam: Ray Lofton Dudley, Jr., August 6, 1919–November 20, 1943. [Houston, Tex.], 1944[?].

Iscoe, Louise Kosches. *Ima Hogg, First Lady of Texas: Reminiscences and Recollections of Family and Friends.* [Austin, Tex.]: Hogg Foundation for Mental Health, [1976].

James, Marquis. *The Raven: A Biography of Sam Houston.* New York: Blue Ribbon Books, 1929.

———. *The Texaco Story: The First Fifty Years, 1902–1952.* Houston, Tex.: Conde Nast, 1953.

Jaworski, Leon. *After Fifteen Years.* Houston, Tex.: Gulf Publishing Co., 1961.

———. *Confession and Avoidance, a Memoir.* With Mickey Herskowitz. Garden City, N.Y.: Anchor Press, Doubleday, 1979.

Johnston, Marguerite. *A Happy Worldly Abode: Christ Church Cathedral, 1839–1964.* Houston, Tex.: Cathedral Press, 1965.

Jones, Joseph M. *The Fifteen Weeks.* New York: Viking Press, 1955.

Kalil, Susie, and Barbara Rose. *Fresh Paint: The Houston School.* Houston, Tex.: Texas Monthly Press, 1985.

Kelly, Hugh Rice. "Peter Gray." *Houston Lawyer,* January, 1976.

Kemp, Louis Wiltz. *The Signers of the Texas Declaration of Independence.* Houston, Tex.: Anson Jones Press, 1944.

The Key to the City of Houston, 1, no. 1, December, 1908.

King, Edward. *The Great South.* Edited by W. Magruder Drake and Robert R. Jones. Baton Rouge: Louisiana State University Press, 1972.

———, and J. Wells Champney. *Texas: 1874.* Houston, Tex.: Cordovan Press, [1974].

Kirkland, William A. *Old Bank-New Bank: The First National Bank, Houston, 1866–1956.* Houston, Tex.: Pacesetter Press, Gulf Publishing Co., 1975.

Larson, Henrietta Melia, and Kenneth Wiggins Porter. *History of Humble Oil and Refining Company: A Study in Industrial Growth.* New York: Harper, 1959.

Lomax, John A. "Will Hogg, Texan: An Atlantic Portrait," *Atlantic Monthly,* May, 1940.

The Lone Star State: History of Texas, Together with a Biographical History of the Cities of Houston and Galveston. Chicago, Ill.: Lewis Publishing Co., 1895.

Lubbock, Francis Richard. *Six Decades in Texas; or, Memoirs of Francis Richard Lubbock, Governor of Texas in War Time, 1861–63.* Edited by C. W. Raines. Austin, Tex.: B. C. Jones and Co., 1900.

Lykes, Genevieve Parkhill. *Gift of Heritage.* Houston, Tex.: 1969.

McCalla, William Latta. *Adventures in Texas, Chiefly in the Spring and Summer of 1840; With a Discussion of Comparative Character, Political, Religious and Moral; Accompanied by an Appendix, Containing an Humble Attempt to Aid in Establishing and Conducting Literary and Ecclesiastical Institutions.* Philadelphia, Penn.: Privately printed, 1841.

McCants, J. T. *Some Information Concerning the Rice Institute.* 1955. Reprint, Houston, Tex., 1971.

McComb, David G. *Houston: A History.* 1st ed., rev. Austin: University of Texas Press, 1981.

Macon, N. Don. *Clark and the Anderson: A Personal Profile.* Houston: Texas Medical Center, 1976.

———. *Mr. John H. Freeman and Friends: A Story*

of the Texas Medical Center and How It Began. Houston: Texas Medical Center, 1973.

———. *South from Flower Mountain; A Conversation With William B. Bates.* Houston: Texas Medical Center, 1975.

Mann, Dene Hofheinz. *You Be the Judge.* Houston, Tex., Press of Premier, 1965.

Matthews, Harold J. *Candle by Night: The Story of the Life and Times of Kezia Payne De Pelchin, Texas Pioneer, Teacher, Social Worker and Nurse.* Boston, Mass.: Bruce Humphries, 1942.

Meiners, Fredericka. *A History of Rice University: the Institute Years, 1907–1963.* 1st ed. Houston, Tex.: Rice University Studies, 1982.

Meyer, Leopold L. *The Days of My Years.* Houston, Tex.: Universal Printers, 1975.

Morehead, James C. *A Walking Tour of Rice University.* Houston, Tex.: Rice University Studies, 1984.

Morris, Sylvia Stallings, ed. *William Marsh Rice and His Institute; A Biographical Study.* Edited from the papers and research notes of Andrew Forest Muir. Houston, Tex.: Rice University Studies, 1972.

Muir, Andrew Forest, ed. *Texas in 1837: An Anonymous, Contemporary Narrative.* Austin: University of Texas Press, 1958.

———. "William Fairfax Gray, Founder of Christ Church Cathedral, Houston." *Historical Magazine of the Protestant Episcopal Church* (December, 1959).

Municipal Book, City of Houston, Period Ending December 31, 1928. Houston, Tex.: 1929[?].

Nicholson, Patrick J. *Houston Country Club Seventy-Fifth Anniversary, 1908–1983.* Houston: Houston Country Club, 1984[?].

———. *In Time: An Anecdotal History of the First Fifty Years of the University of Houston.* Houston: Pacesetter Press, Gulf Publishing Co., 1977.

———. *Mr. Jim: The Biography of James Smither Abercrombie.* Houston: Gulf Publishing Co., 1983.

Oberholtzer, Edison Ellsworth. *The Growth and Development of the University of Houston, a Summation, March, 1927–May, 1950.* Houston: University of Houston, 1950.

Olson, Bruce A. "The Houston Light Guard: A Study of Houston's Post-Reconstruction Militia and Its Membership 1878–1903," *Houston Review* 7, no. 3 (1985).

Olmsted, Frederick Law. *Journey through Texas; or, A Saddle-Trip on the Southwestern Frontier.* New York: Dix, Edwards & Co., 1857.

"On to Britain: Texas Next–at Houston–1925." *Editor and Publisher,* June 21, 1924.

One Hundred Years in Houston: Compiled and Composed for the Observation of the Centennial Celebration of Cochran's Insurance Agency, a David C. Bintliff Interest. Houston: Times Printing Co., 1956[?].

Pearson, Edmund. *Five Murders with a Final Note on the Borden Case.* Garden City, N.Y. Doubleday, Doran & Co., 1928.

Pen and Sunlight Sketches of Greater Houston: The Most Progressive Metropolis in the South. Houston, 1911.

The Progressive [Houston] 1 (October, 1909).

Red, Ellen Robbins. *Early Days on the Bayou, 1838–1890: The Life and Letters of Horace Dickinson Taylor, Houston, Texas.* Waco, Tex.: Texian Press, 1986.

Red, S. C., ed. *A Brief History of the First Presbyterian Church, Houston, Texas, 1839–1939.* Houston: Wilson Stationery and Printing, 1939.

The Red Book of Houston: A Compendium of Social, Professional, Religious, Educational and Industrial Interests of Houston's Colored Population. Sotex Publishing Company, 1914.

Reid, Mary. "Fashions of the Republic," *Southwestern Historical Quarterly* 14, no. 8 (1942).

"Rice Records in War Service, 1917–18". *Rice Institute Pamphlet* 6, supp. (1919).

Rice University Review, Fall/Winter 1968.

Rice University Studies. Vols. 1–67 (Apr., 1915 Spring, 1981). Title varies: *Rice Institute Pamphlet* 1–47 (1915–61).

Richardson, Norval. *Colonel House, the Texas Years, 1858–1912.* Abilene, Tex.: Hardin-Simmons University Book Store, [1912?].

Riddle, Don, comp. *River Oaks: A Pictorial Presentation of Houston's Residential Park.* Houston, Tex., 1929.

Roemer, Frederick. *Texas: With particular Reference to German Immigration and the Physical Appearance of the Country.* Translated by Oswald Mueller. San Antonio: Standard Printing Co., 1935.

Roussel, Hubert. *The Houston Symphony Orchestra, 1913–1971.* Austin: University of Texas Press, 1972.

Santangelo, Susan Hillebrandt. *Kinkaid and Houston: 75 Years.* Houston: Gulf Printing Co., 1981.

Selle, Ralph Abraham. *J. S. Cullinan and the Birds of Shadyside.* Houston: Outdoor Nature Club, 1937.

Shadowlawn, an Architectural Tour. Houston: Rice Design Alliance, 1983.

Sibley, Marilyn McAdams. *The Port of Houston, a History.* Austin, University of Texas Press, 1968.

———. *Travelers in Texas 1761–1860.* Austin: University of Texas Press, 1967.

The Social Directory of Houston. Volumes for 1955, 1965, 1982, 1983, 1986. Houston: Mount Vernon Publisher.

Southside Place, U.S.A. Houston, Tex., 1976.

The Standard Blue Book of Texas, Who's Who? N.p., n.d.

Stokowski, Olga Samaroff. *An American Musician's Story.* New York: W. W. Norton, 1939.

Strode, Hudson. *Jefferson Davis, A Biography.* 2 vols. New York: Harcourt, Brace and World, 1964.

Strom, Steven. "Cotton and Profits across the Border, William Marsh Rice in Mexico, 1863–1865." *Houston Review* 8, no. 2 (1986).

"A Study of Texians in 1890." *Harper's Magazine* 1890.

Timmons, Bascom N. *Jesse H. Jones, The Man and the Statesman.* New York: Henry Holt and Co., 1956.

Tornabene, Lyn. *Long Live the King: A Biography of Clark Gable.* New York: Putnam, 1976.

Treadwell, Mattie E. *The Women's Army Corps.* United States Army in World War II: Special Studies. Washington, D.C.: Office of the Chief of Military History, Dept. of the Army, 1954.

Truman, Harry S. *Memoirs.* Vol. 1: *Year of Decisions.* Garden City, N.Y., Doubleday, 1955.

Verniaud, Marshall. *Southampton: A Mini-History of the First 50 Years.* Houston: Tex.: Southampton Civic Club, 1975.

Von der Mehden, Fred R., ed. *The Ethnic Groups of Houston.* Houston, Tex.: Rice University Studies, 1984.

Webb, Walter Prescott, and H. Bailey Carroll, eds. *The Handbook of Texas.* Supplement edited by Eldon Stephen Branda. 3 vols. Austin: Texas State Historical Association, 1952–76.

Weis, Gretchen E., "The Man: Of a Singular Mold," *Horizons,* Summer, 1980.

Wharton, Clarence. *The Republic of Texas: A Brief History of Texas from the First American Colonies in 1821 to Annexation in 1846.* Houston, Tex.: C. C. Young Printing Co., 1922.

Wilson, Michael Edward. *Alfred C. Finn, Builder of Houston, a Catalogue of Drawings of the Firm in the Houston Public Library, Houston Metropolitan Research Center.* Houston: Houston Public Library, 1983.

Works Projects Administration. Writers' Program in Texas. *Houston, A History and Guide.* Houston: Anson Jones Press, 1942.

Young, S. O. *A Thumb Nail History of the City of Houston, Texas: From Its Founding in 1836 to the Year 1912.* Houston: Press of Rein & Sons, 1912.

———. *True Stories of Old Houston and Houstonians: Historical and Personal Sketches.* Galveston: Oscar Springer, 1913.

MANUSCRIPTS (Unless otherwise noted, manuscripts are in possession of the author.)

Adriance, Lois B. "Descendants of Moses Austin, 1793–1983."

Andrews, Mark Edwin. "My Navy Experiences, 1942–1949."

Bolton, George. Interview of George Brown, April 6, 1968. Courtesy of Mrs. Wallace Wilson.

Clark, Ellen McCallister, and Thomas D. Anderson. "Mount Vernon: The Texas Connection."

Feagin, Joe R. "The State in the 'Free Enterprise' City: The Case of Houston." Department of Sociology, University of Texas, Austin.

Gillett, Charles. Diary of the Rev. Charles Gillett, First Rector of Christ Church, Houston. From the Papers of Andrew Forest Muir, Woodson Research Center, Fondren Library, Rice University.

Gray, William Fairfax III. "The Unpublished Letters and Journal of William Fairfax Gray III." Richmond, Va., 1936. From the Family Papers of Ellen Robinson Red.

LaRoche, Katherine Cottingham. "The History of the River Oaks Garden Club, 1927–1977." Courtesy of Mrs. William B. Cassin.

Lee, Lucie Campbell. "Samples." Memoirs from the Campbell family papers, courtesy of Nancy Wren Harris, great-grandniece of Mrs. Lee.

Levine, Max. "A Venture in Retailing, Federated's 'Foley's of Houston." Oral Business History Project, College of Business Administration Foundation, University of Texas at Austin, October, 1969.

Muir, Andrew Forest. "William Marsh Rice, His Life and Death." In the Woodson Research Center, Rice University Library.

Seymour, Helen. "History of the Houston Area Red Cross, 1916–1980."

Widener, Ralph W., Jr. Untitled manuscript in the Clayton Library Center for Genealogical Research, Houston, Texas.

Index

Houston, The Unknown City, 1836–1946 was composed into type on a Compugraphic digital phototypesetter in ten point Galliard with two points of spacing between the lines. Galliard was also selected for display. The book was designed by Jim Billingsley, typeset by Metricomp, Inc., printed offset by Thomson-Shore, Inc., and bound by John H. Dekker & Sons, Inc. The paper on which this book is printed carries acid-free characteristics for an effective life of at least three hundred years.

Texas A&M University Press : College Station